THE LATE
KING'S GOODS

Collections, Possessions and Patronage of Charles I
in the Light of the Commonwealth Sale Inventories

Edited by
Arthur MacGregor

Alistair McAlpine
in association with
Oxford University Press

London and Oxford
1989

Alistair McAlpine, 33 Cork Street,
London W1X 1HB
in association with
Oxford University Press, Walton Street,
Oxford OX2 6DP
New York, Toronto, Delhi, Bombay, Calcutta,
Madras, Karachi, Petaling Jaya, Singapore,
Hong Kong, Tokyo, Nairobi, Dar es Salaam,
Cape Town, Melbourne, Auckland, and
associated companies in Berlin and Ibadan.

British Library Cataloguing in Publication Data
The late king's goods: collections, possessions
and patronage of Charles I in the light of the
commonwealth sale inventories.
1. Patronage. Great Britain, history
I. MacGregor, Arthur, 1941-
700'. 79

ISBN 0-19-920171-4

Designed by Gordon House
Typeset by the Printed Word
Litho origination by Magnet Litho
Printed in Great Britain by The Hillingdon Press,
Uxbridge, Middlesex.

THE LATE
KING'S GOODS

A true Inventory of severall Pictures nowe in
y Custody of M.r Henry Browne &c. viewed and
apprised y.e 8.o September 1649.

Pictures w.ch Came from Wimbleton, as foll.

	li: s: d:
Imprimis 3 Landshapes at	02: 10: 00:
6 Enamelled peeces 3 of them being in Ovalls at	12: 00: 00:
2 little sea peeces of porsellis in Ovalls at	02: 00: 00:
1 little greene Landshape 6 inches long at	02: 00: 00:
1 little peece of a Mary & y Child 3 inches long at	02: 10: 00:
1 peece of Mary w.th flowers 6 inches Long at	00: 10: 00:
1 peece of y King of ffrance uppon Marble	00: 10: 00
1 peece of a Child Carrying a Crosse at	00: 10: 00:
1 round peece w.th spanish grapes at	02: 10: 00:
2 peeces of greene Landshapes 9 inches long at	03: 00: 00:
1 peece of a S.t on Marbell 6 inches long at	00: 10: 00:
1 peece of Mary in y Cloudes on Marble at	00: 10: 00:
One peece of Christ on y Crosse at	02: 00: 00:
One peece of y King of ffrance w.th Marie y Child	00: 10: 00:
One peece of Christ w.th a garland at	00: 10: 00:
One little peece of winter at	02: 10: 00:
One peece of drawing w.th apen on parchm.t at	00: 02: 06:
One peece a hermitt on Marble at	00: 10: 00
One peece of Christ praying in y garden at	00: 10: 00:
One peece of Naturall stoone at	00: 10: 00:

33 02 06:

Contents

Acknowledgements

The task of compiling this volume would have been quite impossible without access to the standard text of *The Inventories and Valuations of the King's Goods 1649-1651,* published by Sir Oliver Millar in the Forty-Third Volume of the Walpole Society (1970-1972). The cooperation of Sir Oliver and of the Editor and Council of the Walpole Society in agreeing to the extensive use made of their text in the present volume is gratefully acknowledged.

List of Illustrations

Abbreviations and Conventions

Acts and Ordinances   *Acts and Ordinances of the Interregnum 1642-1660* (eds. C.H. Firth and R.S. Rait) (London, 1911)

BL   British Library, London

Bod. Lib.   Bodleian Library, Oxford

CSP   *Calendar of State Papers*

Commons Journals   *Journals of the House of Commons*

DNB   *Dictionary of National Biography*

Inventories   O. Millar (ed.), *The Inventories and Valuations of the King's Goods 1649-1651* (Walpole Society 43) (London, 1972). Catalogue entries in the *Inventories* are cited in the present volume in the form of marginal notes giving page and entry numbers thus: 65 [94].

King's Works   *The History of the King's Works* (London). The period 1485-1660 is treated in two volumes: III and IV. The essays referred to here are by Howard M. Colvin and Sir John Summerson: 'The Royal Castles' (III, pp.225-333) and 'The King's Houses' (IV, pp. 1-364).

Lord Journals   *Journals of the House of Lords*

OED   *Oxford English Dictionary*

PRO   Public Record Office, London

Van der Doort's Catalogue   O. Millar (ed.), *Abraham van der Doort's Catalogue of the Collections of Charles I* (Walpole Society 37) (London, 1960).

SP   State Papers

VCH   *The Victoria History of the Counties of England*

Vertue, *Note Books*   George Vertue, *Note Books* I-VI, Walpole Society [I] 18 (1929-30), [II] 20 (1931-2), [III] 22 (1933-4), [IV] 24 (1935-6), [V] 26 (1937-8), [index] 29 (1940-42), [VI] 30 (1951-2).

All dates cited in the text are given according to the Gregorian ('New Style') calendar, in which the new year begins on 1 January.

Denmark House.   During the earlier part of the seventeenth century Somerset House was commonly referred to as Denmark House, in honour of Anne of Denmark to whom it was granted by James I (see p. 23). Both forms appear in the *Inventories*. Throughout this volume Denmark House has been adopted as the standard form of reference.

James I.   In the interests of brevity, James VI of Scotland and I of England is referred to simply as James I.

Somerset House.   See Denmark House, above.

1   The King's Goods and the Commonwealth Sale. Materials and Context

Arthur MacGregor

The Act for Sale of the King's Goods

Marginal numerals refer to page and entry numbers in the *Inventories* (see p. 11)

Whereas the Goods and Personal Estate heretofore belonging to the late King Charl[e]s, and to his Wife and eldest Son, have been, and are justly forfeited by them, for their several Delinquencies; And though the same be of considerable value, yet in regard many parcels thereof are dispersed in several hands and places, they may for want of a certain accompt, probably be spoiled or imbezled, or made away without advantage to the State, if due care be not had, and some speedy course taken to prevent the same: The Commons of England assembled in Parliament, taking the premises into their serious consideration, have thought fit and resolved, That the said Goods and Personal Estate, heretofore belonging to the persons abovenamed, and to every or any of them, shall be inventoried and apprized, and shall also be sold, except such parcels thereof as shall be found necessary to be reserved for the uses of State.[1]

The preamble to the 'Act for sale of the goods and personal estate of the late King, Queen and Prince', passed by Parliament on 4 July 1649, sets the scene for the lengthy appraisal of works of art, tableware, regalia, clothing and other belongings of the royal family which forms the basis of the following analyses. In the course of the seven years since Charles I had taken flight from London, Parliament had alternately protected and desecrated, husbanded and squandered individual elements of the royal estate.[2] Now, with the King five months dead and his family fled abroad or under control of the state, a line was to be drawn under these events, a final reckoning was to be compiled, and the assets of the crown were to be liquidated.[3]

The need for action was clear enough: not only were there debts accrued by the late King to be cleared, but the government was chronically short of money to pay its own servants in the civil and military service; with the monarchy abolished, the trappings of kingship had been rendered obsolete; the whiff of papism that lingered in the tapestried galleries and painted chapels of the royal houses offended puritan sensibilities; and the vast wealth represented by the contents of the royal palaces–now redundant or turned over to the accommodation of administrators, soldiers, or privileged individuals–stood in constant danger of spoliation. Nothing less than a controlled displenishment of the royal house and household was now demanded.

The task of quantifying and evaluating the physical assets of the monarchy was one which Parliament, with the aid of its professional administration and with executors appointed specifically for the purpose, was able to put in hand fairly readily, as described below. None the less, it was not to be achieved overnight, nor without difficulties.

Two years after publication of the first Act (during which time many of the goods had already been sold) an additional Act was passed which sought to qualify the terms of reference of the first.[4] In particular, the 'goods and personal estate' of the title of the first Act were 'deemed and taken to extend only unto all Jewels, Plate, Furs, Hangings, Statues, Medals, Pictures, Wardrobe-stuff, and all other Household-stuff and Utensils whatsoever, and to all Libraries (the Library of James's Houses, with all Medals, Rings, Globes and Mathematical Instruments in the said Library only excepted)'. Contrary to public expectation, the second Act, by narrowing the range of assets earmarked for settlement of the King's debts, worked gravely to the disadvantage of his creditors, a potential £100,000-worth of estate being excluded in this way.[5] At the same time, goods belonging to all the King's children, in addition to those of Prince Charles as previously specified, were now brought within the compass of the Act, but these in no way compensated for the new limitations.

13   The King's Goods and the Commonwealth Sale

The Trustees, Contractors, and Treasurers

The first concern of the Act was for the appointment of a board of Trustees, 'for the enquiring out, inventorying, apprizing and securing of the said Goods and Personal Estate'. Those appointed were named as John Humphreys, apparently a tailor of Westminster; George Withers (or Wither), a well-known poet, pamphleteer and political activist of Westminster; Anthony Mildmay, formerly a groom of the Privy Chamber to Charles I but no friend to the King; Ralph Grafton, a draper and upholsterer in the parish of St. Michael's, Cornhill; Michael Lampier (or Lampriere), a prominent figure in the Parliamentary party in Jersey, resident in London since 1643; John Belchamp (otherwise Jan van Belcamp), formerly Keeper of the King's Pictures; Philip Cartwright (or Carteret) of Jersey; Henry Creech, a skinner of London; John Foach (or Foche), a haberdasher of London; and Edward Winslow, governor of the Plymouth Colony, resident in London since 1646.[6]

The Trustees were authorized to visit 'any and every house or place whatsoever, where any of the said goods, or any part of the said Personal Estate doth lie', in order to make 'a true and perfect Inventory . . . and to make a just and equal apprizement of the same . . . according to the true value thereof, as they in their judgements and consciences shall think the same may be sold for.' They were to be responsible for the security of the goods and for preventing 'any spoil or imbezlement thereof'. In the case of goods which lay too distant to be appraised where they lay, the Trustees were empowered to have them removed to some more convenient place. In pursuance of their task, the Trustees were given authority to summon such persons as might have personal knowledge of the royal properties or of the whereabouts of goods; such witnesses could be examined under oath and could be committed to prison if they proved recalcitrant. Anyone found to have 'concealed, imbezled, purloyned or made away' with goods was to be assessed by the Trustees for the value of the missing items and reported by them to the Barons of the Exchequer, who were to exact the same amount from the offender.

The Trustees were also charged with gathering information concerning debts incurred by the King, Queen and Price of Wales, and to assess the sums due to creditors from the proceeds of the sale. Their conclusions concerning the validity of each case were to be conveyed to Parliament, along with an assessment of the claimants as to 'whether their condition be necessitous so that they cannot bear the want of their said debts';[7] the personal soundness of the creditor, and the degree of his commitment to the Parliamentary cause, were also to be gauged.

To assist them in the execution of their duties the Trustees were empowered to appoint a clerk-register 'and such other Agents or Officers as they shall think fit'. On 16 January 1651, for example, the Council ordered that a letter be written to the Trustees 'to recommend S[r] Baltazar Gerbiere unto them to be considered by them as farre as by their Instruccons they may, the Councel lookeing upon him as a person whose endeavours are for the service of this Commonwealth'.[8] The post of clerk-register was occupied (not without some incident) by Thomas Beauchamp.[9]

From the proceeds of the sales the Trustees were to be allowed seven pence in the pound 'for their own and their Agents and Officers pains and charges', to include all charges except messenger services and the cost of keeping in custody those witnesses exhibiting reluctance to cooperate.

Under the Act of 1649 a number of individuals designated 'Commissioners and Contractors' were charged with the task of carrying out the sale of the goods according to the valuations assigned them by the Trustees. This team included Daniel Norman, merchant of the Isle of Jersey; John Hales, merchant of London; Clement Kynnersley, formerly an officer of the Removing Wardrobe and later to become Wardrobe Keeper to the Protector; and John Price, Henry Parre and William Allen, 'gentlemen and citizens' of London.

The Contractors were enjoined to sell all goods 'according to their best skill and judgement', at or above the values assigned them by the Trustees. Receipts from the sale, along with appropriate accounts and details of purchasers were to be rendered up periodically to the Trustees and Treasurers for the sale, the latter named in the Act as Humphrey Jones and John Hunt, both citizens of London. The Treasurers were allowed two pence in the pound from monies received to meet their expenses. Under the terms of the additional Act, they were also authorized to make payments to creditors.

Invested with such extensive powers and responsibilities, it was perhaps inevitable that the officers appointed for the sale should find themselves embroiled in controversy. 'The prosecution of discoveries', according to a contemporary pamphlet,[10] 'occasioned many reproaches, scandals, clamors, disobligations, and vexations upon the said Trustees'. A number of the aggrieved parties evidently held parliamentary office and were, it was said, instrumental in forming a House of Commons committee with powers 'to examine the business touching the Charge of Corruption against Mr Beauchampt, Clerk to the Trustees for the sale of the late King's Goods' and also 'to examine the Abuses and Misdemeanors of any Trustees, Contractors, or other Officers . . . in taking any Bribes, Rewards, or Fees, not allowed unto them'.[11] On the evidence of the (somewhat partisan) document already mentioned, it would seem that certain of the promoters (named in the State Papers as Oldisworth and Thomas)[12] had contrived to have themselves elected to the committee and used their privilege further to abuse the Trustees: 'Who can expect justice', asks its anonymous author, 'where the offendor is the Judge?' A degree of sympathy may be accorded to the view that 'the said Trustees have had the worst imployment that ever honest men had . . . having to do between men in Authority, who had not only power but occasion themselves to the use of the goods.' In any case, none of the charges seems to have been upheld and no formal admonition issued from the committee.

The Inventories

A prime duty of the Trustees was the compilation of 'a true and perfect Inventory' of the goods, wherever they might lie, 'expressing in the said Inventory or Inventories, the several sums or values at which the several parcels shall be apprized'. From each master inventory three duplicates were to be produced, giving details of where and in whose custody the goods were to be found. Retaining the original in the care of the Clerk-Register, the Trustees were to send one duplicate to the Council of State, one to the Contractors and one to the Treasurers appointed to receive the proceeds of the sale.

Brief details of all the surviving inventories are given by Sir Oliver Millar in the introduction to his published version – a composite, necessarily, on account of the incomplete nature of the extant copies.[13] Although they follow a standardized format (Frontispiece), the inventories vary widely in the quality and degree of detail they provide. None the less, they constitute, as Sir Oliver has observed, 'a record, unsurpassed in this country, of the accumulated possessions of a royal family and provide the principal single source for our knowledge of the appearance of the royal houses in the early Stuart period'.[14]

Mention may also be made of several copies compiled at various times after the sale, whether for official purposes or out of antiquarian interest, as mentioned by the same author.[15] It was the acquisition of one of these by Lord McAlpine that prompted publication of the present volume.[16]

The majority of the dated inventories were completed between June and October 1649; the brief list of goods at Woodstock manor house is dated 23 October 1650, while a few items which had found their way into other hands before being delivered to the Trustees were inventoried only in November 1651. Thirty-four of the fifty-seven separate lists indexed by Millar[17] are undated. Most of the goods were viewed *in situ* but some (from Greenwich, Whitehall, Wimbledon and other sources) had already reached Denmark House (see below) before appraisal, while others had been granted on loan to furnish apartments provided by the state to privileged individuals. One small but curiously disparate group, comprised largely of religious vestments, sacramental vessels and petticoats belonging to the Queen, was 'stopped being at Sea in the Port of Topisham'.

The Reserved Goods

In the Act of 4 July 1949 provision was made for 'such particulars' as the Council of State should think fit to be 'reserved for the uses of the State', their total value not to exceed £10,000. The additional Act of 17 July 1651 doubled the amount which might be reserved, and the final figure reached was more than five times the original sum at £53,000.[18] The procedure for earmarking these goods was for the Council, within fourteen days of receipt of any inventory from the Trustees, to make its selection from the goods listed and to inform the Contractors of its choice; the Contractors were 'thereupon to forbear any sale of such particulars until further Order from Parliament'. The proposals having been considered by Parliament, the council would then issue the Contractors with a warrant (for those items approved for reservation) or a permit for continuation of the sale (for those disallowed).

Certain failures in the conduct of the sale ensued from this procedure. On more than one occasion the Council had to urge the Trustees to complete their surveys at Whitehall and Hampton Court so that a selection could be made for addition to the reserved goods,[19] and on 10 May 1650 the Trustees were admonished for selling 'diverse necessary things' from Greenwich, despite the fact that the house, along with its fixtures and fittings, had meanwhile been reserved for the use of the State.[20]

Furthermore, the several increases in the value of the goods reserved worked against the interests of the creditors, the already inadequate income generated by the sale being further reduced by these exclusions so that the prospect of settlement of the King's debts receded even further.[21]

The Sale

On 20 July 1649 provision was made by the Council of State for rooms in Denmark House to be put at the disposal of the Trustees; the great hall was fitted out for display of the goods some weeks later.[22] It has been suggested that, apart from the items from Hampton Court, all the goods inventoried were sold at Denmark House,[23] but it seems doubtful that this is altogether true (see pp. 38, 42-3). The process of dispersal began in October 1649 and was largely completed by the end of 1651; some groups of items, however, were not disposed of until the summer of 1653. How much material was exposed for sale at any one time is unclear: in the Act the Trustees are charged with 'causing publique notice to be given by the space of one week beforehand or more, of the time and place when and where they intend to begin to set to sale any part or parcel of the premises', so that goods from different houses (or of a differing nature) may have been sold at different times. Amongst the complaints later brought against the Trustees was one that they had 'broken their trust' by failing to give due notice of sales and by disposing of goods unjustly.[24]

The appointees had been authorized by the Act to enter into contracts with prospective customers and on reaching agreement were to 'cause an Entry to be made in a Book, to be kept by their Clerk-Register for that purpose, and to such entry the Buyers to subscribe their names respectively, which Entry and Subscription shall make the bargain obliging on both parts'.

Sales were further formalized by the issue of receipts to buyers (Fig. 1), confirming purchases to be 'their own proper Goods and Chattels for ever', while formal notification of each sale was forwarded to the Treasurers. All transactions were at first in cash, according to the prices fixed by the Trustees, or higher. By May 1650 a disappointing £35,271-worth of goods had been sold, in addition to £8,563 raised from plate melted down: general impoverishment due to the effects of the Civil War, and a widespread reluctance among the affluent to profit from the King's death (which some saw as martyrdom), have been cited as restraining factors.[25]

In accordance with their commission, the Trustees submitted to Parliament the names, arranged in two separate lists, of those citizens with the most pressing claims against the Crown estate. The neediest cases, amounting to 120 individuals, were contained in the first list of 'Creditors, Servants, Widdows and Orphans'.[26] With approval from the Commons (granted 14 March 1650), a total of £12,800 was dispensed to creditors named here: those to whom small sums were owing were paid in full, while those owed larger amounts received only part of their dues in cash, the remainder in some cases being made up in kind with unsold goods, according to the Trustees' valuations. In the registers, however, such items are recorded as being 'sold' to the individual concerned.

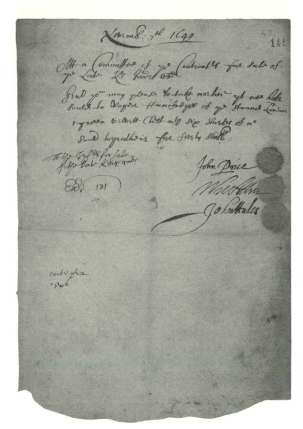

Figure 1 *Receipt* issued by the Trustees to Roger Humfreys, acknowledging sale of a chest and six shirts formerly belonging to Henry VIII. Public Record Office (SP29/447). Crown copyright: reproduced with permission of the Controller of Her Majesty's Stationery Office.

Figure 2 *Proforma instruction* to the Treasurers of the Sale from the Trustees, to pay George Pollard, a creditor on the 'second list', the sum of £12. 7s. 10d. Public Record Office (SP 28/285). Crown copyright: reproduced with permission of the Controller of Her Majesty's Stationery Office.

A longer second list, comprising some 970 of the King's less necessitous creditors, gained parliamentary approval on 22 July 1651.[27] A greater proportion of those named here were prepared (or were persuaded) to accept goods in lieu of cash, although some received their dues in money (Fig 2). Numbers of them banded together to form syndicates, each headed by an individual empowered to deal on behalf of the others to a maximum sum of £5,000.[28] Working in liaison with the creditors, the Contractors apportioned unsold goods into a number of 'dividends', which were drawn in lots by the syndicates; responsibility for sharing out the goods amongst the individual members, or of liquidating them for cash, was a matter for the members of the syndicates. A total of some £77,500-worth of goods was disposed of in this way, accounting for a greater proportion than the cash sales in the grand total eventually realized.[29] A further £10,000 or more remained outstanding to necessitous creditors—chiefly minor court officials—on the second list, while over 400 creditors not classified as needy were yet owed about £90,000.[30] When, however, in January 1654 the Trustees petitioned the Protector for permission to settle more of these debts, agreement was withheld and the sale was wound up.[31]

Something of a market evidently developed in unredeemed certificates, to judge from the activities of a certain 'Mr Jackson of the Sequestration Office who . . . bought at a low scale many warrants of the creditors'.[32]

A catalogue of the names of purchasers and the sums involved, extracted from the Contractors' registers, gives the total value of the goods as £184,717. 5s. 3d., those unsold being valued at £4,499. 7s. 2¾d.[33] An account of the expenses claimed by the Trustees and Contractors is preserved in the Public Record Office.[34]

With so many reluctant recipients of the King's goods, it is not surprising that many of them quickly found their way into new hands.[35] In the case of collectors' items such as the better quality paintings, many can be traced to new foreign owners, notably Philip IV of Spain, Cardinal Mazarin, the Archduke Leopold Wilhelm (then governor of the Austrian Netherlands) and the wealthy German banker Everard Jabach (who later sold them on to Louis XIV of France). The whereabouts of some of them can still be traced today (see Chapter 5), although many of the less distinguished works disappeared without trace. One fortunate exception was the large number of lesser quality paintings which entered the Reynst collection in Amsterdam, to be bought later by the States of Holland and returned to Charles II at the Restoration in the form of the 'Dutch Gift'. Others to the number of seven or eight hundred were reclaimed by the Crown from new owners within the British jurisdiction at this time, some freely given but many forcibly repossessed.[36]

The Royal Household

In attempting to digest the mass of material registered in the inventories, it should be understood that while some of it relates specifically to the 'King, Queen and Prince'–their robes, regalia and personal collections–a larger proportion, including much of the domestic equipment, furnishings and plate, played a wider role in the maintenance of the vast extended family of courtiers, officials and servants that constituted the royal household.

The household ramified extensively in several dimensions. Socially, it was widely diversified, from the select group of aristocratic companions and advisers who attended directly upon the king, through the middle-ranking career administrators to the army of grooms, laundresses and scullions on whose labours the smooth operation of the household ultimately depended. It was also dispersed geographically, some elements being stationed permanently in the houses described below and others following their immediate masters as they progressed from place to place. Estimates of the total numbers involved vary, as indeed the size of the household itself varied from year to year and from reign to reign.[37] A total of 1,800 members has been suggested for the time of Charles I, of whom one half might have been on duty at any one time.[38]

Two principal divisions were recognized in the Stuart period: the household above stairs, generally called the Chamber, and that below stairs, usually called *the* Household. The duties of the Chamber were concerned primarily with the formal aspects of court life, while the Household maintained the supply of essential goods and services: 'what the Household was responsible for providing, the Chamber saw consumed with due pomp and elegance'.[39]

The 500 or so functionaries of the Household below stairs have been conveniently reviewed elsewhere.[40] Controlled by the Lord Steward and the Board of Greencloth, they procured, prepared and delivered to the dining hall the vast quantities of food and drink consumed at court on a daily basis. The laundry, woodyard and chandlery also fell within the scope of the Household (see also Chapter 12, below).

Under the rule of the Lord Chamberlain, the Chamber was subdivided into a number of departments varying in importance and prestige.[41] Those closest to the sovereign himself were the Bedchamber and the Privy Chamber, as discussed further below. Amongst the other offices of particular significance in the present context were the Removing Wardrobe (which included ten clerks or keepers of standing wardrobes); the Robes, with a staff of nine; the Jewels, with seven officers; and the Works, with a permanent staff of about twenty, supported by varying amounts of hired labour. A further 250 miscellaneous offices included physicians and chaplains, limners, a clock-keeper and instrument maker, a perfumer and numerous musicians. There were also four officers of bears, bulls and mastiffs, fifteen harriers, thirty-one falconers and thirty-five huntsmen.

Outside the Household and the Chamber, the Stables formed the largest unit, with 186 grooms and farriers and higher officials, all under the powerful figure of the Master of the Horse.

In addition to those owing direct allegiance to the King during Charles's reign, some 400 courtiers and servants of all levels were attached specifically to the households of Henrietta Maria (about 180 persons), Prince Charles (a further 144) and the other royal children.

A large number of these household members were accommodated within the royal houses. Some of the more senior qualified for maintenance in the form of diet (involving, sometimes, considerable quantities of food and drink) while others might receive 'bouge' or 'bouche of court', in the form of bread and ale, firewood and candles (see pp. 373, 379). To the considerable burden of supporting itself and its royal masters, the household had the added responsibility of accommodating and maintaining the hordes of noblemen, foreign princes, ambassadors and others who had business of court, as well as *their* households in turn.

By the early seventeenth century the medieval practice of maintaining the court in a state of almost permanent mobility was much abated, although custom and periodic outbreaks of pestilence continued to prompt intermittent removals of the court from one house to another.[42] James in particular was never greatly at ease when weighed down with the panoply of court life and spent a large part of each year progressing from house to house, often accompanied only by a small detachment from the household,[43] in order to decimate the game reserves of each property in turn. Charles observed the rather more formal traditions of the annual progress, at least until 1637. In both instances, however, these tours were normally limited to the few royal properties easily accessible from London, as described below. Not only did the short distances involved minimize the problems of removing the household and all its attendant baggage from place to place, but the maintenance of several of these establishments as 'houses of access', each with a standing complement of furnishings and equipment, further eased the well-established routine (see p. 21).

Although varying in detail from place to place, the arrangement of the royal apartments in each of these houses reflected the highly formalized organization of the Chamber. The principal accommodation was normally divided between the king's side and the queen's side, which mirrored each other in their essentials. Much of the king's public business (including dining in public) was carried out in the Presence Chamber. Under James, a measure of the informality and ease of access which had been a feature of the Scottish court was allowed to permeate the Presence Chamber, but a more formal – almost austere – regime was enforced after Charles's accession: the presence of all those to whom the privilege of dining at table in the Presence had been extended was now demanded as a duty; the gentlemen ushers were to see, however, that no-one pressed too close upon the King and, in particular, that none but peers, bishops and privy councillors should tread on the carpet surrounding his table.[44]

Beyond the Presence lay the Privy Chamber, accessible only to noblemen and councillors sworn of that Chamber, and beyond that again lay the Withdrawing Chamber, the Bedchamber and the other privy lodgings, all the exclusive domain of the king himself and the select few engaged in his personal body service. Here the Groom of the Stool held sway, performing all 'offices and services of honour' to the king's person. The establishment of the Privy Chamber and the Bedchamber with their respective staffs in this form was something of an innovation, wrought by James I on the arrangements which had operated since their codification in the Eltham Ordinances of 1526: there it had been the gentlemen of the Privy Chamber rather than the Bedchamber who had rendered body service to the king.[45]

In the larger palaces there was space in plenty for the various departments and their eponymous staffs to be accommodated according to design, but frequently it was found necessary to compromise according to the facilities available: the Lord Chamberlain and his staff might be allowed forty rooms to themselves at Whitehall[46] but elsewhere it was found necessary at times even to combine the Presence and Privy Chambers (in which case strict rules were enforced governing the regulation of the chamber according to whichever function was being fulfilled at the time).[47] At smaller establishments the gentlemen attending the king had to make shift where they could[48] while the lower orders were everywhere lodged above the domestic offices in which they toiled.

The Royal Houses

With few exceptions, the major properties occupied by the early Stuarts were a direct legacy from their Tudor forebears. The reigns of Charles and James were unmarked by radical building programmes, and, although important elements were added to certain of the existing palaces at this time, the overall trend was one of decline. From a maximum of fifty major properties held by the Crown under Henry VIII, the numbers dwindled to a dozen by the outbreak of the Civil War.[49]

The great castles, which had formed necessary and tangible expressions of

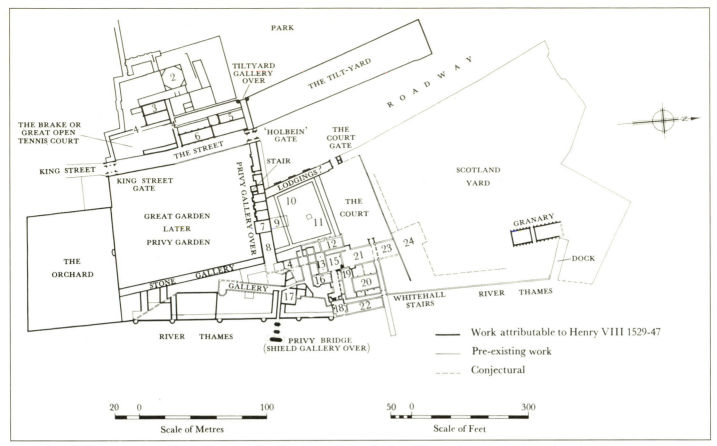

Figure 3 *Whitehall Palace:* plan of the buildings attributable to Henry VIII and Edward VI. 1 cockpit lodgings?; 2 cockpit; 3 small tennis court; 4 bowling alley?; 5 small open tennis court; 6 great close tennis court; 7 King's bedchamber over?; 8 King's withdrawing chamber over; 9 Council chamber over; 10 privy garden, later preaching place; 11 pulpit; 12 great wine cellar; 13 King's presence chamber over; 14 King's privy chamber over; 15 court; 16 Queen's presence chamber over; 17 Queen's bedchamber over; 18 privy kitchen; 19 ante-chapel; 21 great hall; 22 master cook; 23 pantry and buttery; 24 great kitchen. Reproduced by courtesy of English Heritage.

Figure 4 *Whitehall Palace from the Thames.* Etching by Wenzel Hollar. Reproduced by permission of the Trustees of the British Museum.

royal power in the Middle Ages, diminished in importance under the Tudors in favour of more commodious residences built with convenience rather than impregnability as their principal requirement. A number of castles, however, remained in the royal domain under the early Stuarts: Carisbrooke on the Isle of Wight, which was to figure poignantly in the latter days of Charles I; Ludlow in Shropshire, given over to the uses of the Council in the Marches; Kenilworth in Warwickshire, leased from 1624 to the Carey family; Windsor, a favourite resort of both James and Charles; and the Tower of London itself, still an impressive stronghold, providing depots and offices for departments of the royal household but no longer used as a residence.

Of the legacy of great houses bequeathed by Henry VIII, only seven palaces continued to be maintained for their original purposes up to the time of the Civil War: Greenwich, Hampton Court, Nonsuch, Oatlands, Richmond, St. James's and Whitehall.[50] Four notable acquisitions had been made in the intervening period: Somerset House (later Denmark House), which came to the Crown with the fall of the Lord Protector in 1551; Theobalds, acquired from Sir Robert Cecil in 1607; Holdenby in Northamptonshire, conveyed to James I in 1608; and the manor of Wimbledon, bought for Henrietta Maria in 1639 by Charles I. Two somewhat decayed manor houses should also be mentioned here: Bewdley in Worcestershire and Woodstock in Oxfordshire.

In addition to these, three hunting lodges acquired by James I were to play a disproportionately significant role in the life of the court during his reign, addicted as he was to the hunt: these were Royston, Newmarket, and, from its acquisition in 1609 until its sale some time between 1618 and 1630, Thetford.[51]

These were the properties to which the Trustees for sale of the Kings Goods turned their attentions in 1649. The following accounts may serve to set in context the contents which form the subject of the main text.

Whitehall Palace

The origins of the royal palace of Whitehall lay in York Place, London residence of the archbishops of York. Under Thomas Wolsey, who held the See of York from 1514, York Place was extensively rebuilt and enlarged before being surrendered to Henry VIII in 1529. Thereafter Whitehall was attached to the 'Kynges Paleis att Westmynster, buylded and edified there before the tyme of mynde'[52] and became known alternatively as the new palace of Westminster, replacing the fire-damaged old palace as the principal residence of the monarch.[53]

The disposition of Whitehall was markedly diffuse and lacking in formal symmetry (Figs. 3-4).[54] Among its most noteworthy characteristics were the lengthy galleries that knitted together its disparate elements and, in some instances, provided opportunities for display of paintings, sculpture and tapestries: the Privy and Stone Galleries were the most important, followed by the Matted, Shield and Bear Galleries. Effectively bisected by the public highway from Charing Cross to Westminster, the unity of the complex was maintained by carrying the Privy Gallery across the road at first floor level by means of the Holbein Gate, one of two gatehouses set athwart the thoroughfare. These gateways represented the most striking visual foci of the palace, which otherwise presented an unremarkable perimeter to public view.[55]

Internally, however, Whitehall was appointed in a manner that fully acknowledged its royal status. It has been observed that 'it was indeed the tapestries and other furnishings that did most to transform the complex of interconnecting chambers and galleries into a display of royal opulence that owed more to the painter, the gilder, the carver and the embroiderer than it did to formal architectural design'.[56]

By the time of James's accession the palace was in a state of some dilapidation and in need of additional kitchens and butteries. Henry VIII's cock-pit was converted into a theatre at this time. Following the destruction by fire in 1619 of the latest in a series of somewhat makeshift banqueting houses, James commissioned a new and splendid replacement: built to a design by Inigo Jones, construction was completed within three years at a cost of £14,940 4s. 1d. The banqueting house itself was the only element ever built in a wonderfully ambitious plan prepared by Jones which, had it been achieved, would have replaced the piecemeal arrangement of Whitehall with one of the most splendid and formal palaces in Europe. Jones's designs[57] give a vivid insight into the character of the palaces that the Stuarts might have occupied had they not been permanently short of cash.

Cromwell later chose Whitehall as his principal residence, lodging in the first instance in apartments near the cock-pit before moving into more appropriate – not to say regal – accommodation in the spring of 1654, as reported in the *Weekly Intelligencer*:

The Privy Lodgings for his Highness the Lord Protector in *Whitehall*, are now in a readiness, as also the Lodgings for his Lady Protectoress; and likewise the privy Kitchin, and other Kitchins, Butteries, and Offices, and it is conceived the whole Family will be settled there before *Easter*.[58]

Since May 1649 the Council of State had also been installed at Whitehall.

20-1 [1-16], 54 [1-6], 68-72 [1-61]
130-35 [1-120], 155 [60, 66], 298-321 [1-353]
327-407 [1-1124]

Apart from paintings (from within the Privy Lodgings), statues (to the number of over a hundred)[59] and clocks and plate (in the Whitehall jewel house), the large majority of items inventoried there are hangings and tapestries (many of them already loaned out to furnish state-granted apartments), with carpets, beds and bedding, other furnishings (mostly chairs and stools) and curtains following in that order.

Whitehall reverted to the Crown at the Restoration, but disastrous fires in 1691 and 1698 robbed the palace of all its principal buildings, save for the Banqueting Hall: built as the ceremonial centre of the palace, the most sombre spectacle it had staged was the execution on 30 January 1649 of the monarch whose estate forms the subject of this volume.

St. James's Palace

The royal palace of St. James's (Fig. 5) took its name from the 'spittle for mayden lepers' dedicated to St. James the Less which had occupied the site a little to the west of Westminster and Whitehall throughout the Middle Ages. In 1531 the

Figure 5 *St. James's Palace, the Park, and Westminster Hall*. Detail from an etching by R. Sawyer after a drawing by Wenzel Hollar, 1660. Reproduced by permission of the Trustees of the British Museum.

hospital was conveyed by its trustees to Henry VIII, who founded there 'a goodly Mannor, annexing thereunto a Parke, closed about with a wall, of bricke now called S. *Iames* Parke serving indifferently to the saide Mannor, and to the Mannor or Pallace of Whitehall'.[60]

James I allocated St. James's to Henry, Prince of Wales, and until the Prince's premature death in 1612 much of the expenditure there reflected Henry's athletic and aesthetic predelictions. To the tennis court inherited from Henry VIII, bow butts were added in the park and a miniature artillery range was formed in the orchard; in 1607-9 a riding-house was built and in 1609-10 a library was fitted out, its first accessions being books from the library of John, Lord Lumley, acquired by the King. One of the galleries at St. James's was newly wainscotted at this time to receive Prince Henry's growing collection of paintings.[61]

Following Henry's death, St. James's was granted to Charles. Radical improvements were prompted by his projected marriage to the Spanish Infanta, notably the building of a chapel for celebration of the Catholic rite. In the event it was another Catholic queen, Henrietta Maria, who was to worship there after her marriage to Charles in 1625. A further innovation came in 1629-30 with the building of a sculpture gallery in the gardens to a design of Inigo Jones, to house the newly acquired collection of the Duke of Mantua.[62]

On 11 September 1645 the Commons resolved that the King's younger children should be lodged at St. James's[63] and on 19 January 1649 they were joined by their father, now in military custody. Soldiers filled the palace's ancillary buildings; the tennis court and the riding house became billets for the infantry.

When the Trustees began their work there, they found the goods dominated by over 550 paintings and more than 300 pieces of sculpture; hangings (over 100), carpets, beds and bedding account for most of the rest. Also of interest are the models of fortifications, ordnance and soldiers recorded in the armoury – relics, perhaps, of the youthful Prince Henry.

Following the Restoration, St. James's reverted to its role as one of the secondary royal palaces, until the destruction of Whitehall in 1698 displaced the household and led to its official relocation, forming itself anew as the Court of St. James.

139-57 [1-256, 1-99]
256-74 [1-291], 298-321 [1-353]

Denmark House (Somerset House)

Founded by Lord Protector Somerset in 1549, Somerset House remained unfinished when, in 1552, the Duke lost his head and his estates were declared forfeit to the Crown. In the partition that followed, the mansion was granted to the Princess Elizabeth, who lodged there from time to time until her accession; thereafter, her court was transferred to Whitehall.

Certain features of Somerset's mansion were truly innovatory in the English context: in particular, the principal frontage, facing the Strand, has been described as 'the first front in England consciously composed with classical elements' (Fig. 6).[64] The remainder of the house was disposed around two courts, a large one adjacent to the Strand frontage and a smaller one towards the Thames.

Early in the reign of James I, Somerset House was assigned to the Queen, although Anne of Denmark is thought not to have made full use of the property until extensive rebuilding which she instigated in 1609 had been completed, operations which were to cost some £34,000.[65] The great (upper) court of the Protector's scheme was almost completely rebuilt at this time; the lower court was also altered and two major galleries were added (Fig. 7). By the spring of 1617 the Queen was installed in her palace in time to entertain the King to an extravagant celebration on Shrove Tuesday, on which occasion he caused the name to be changed in her honour to Denmark House.[66]

Within two years the house was to serve for the lying in state of Anne's body, brought from Hampton Court where she died on 2 March 1619 and not interred until 13 May. In that year Denmark House was granted to Charles, although his principal residence remained at St. James's. On Charles's marriage, Denmark House was added to Henrietta Maria's jointure. Some years later the Catholic chapel (originally set up in one of the existing rooms) was rebuilt anew for the Queen's purposes on the site of the former tennis courts.

Figure 6 *Somerset House (later Denmark House):* built by Edward Seymour, Duke of Somerset, as Protector of the Realm (1547-52). The Strand frontage is shown here, recorded shortly before 1776. Drawing by William Moss, Hope Collection, Ashmolean Museum, Oxford.

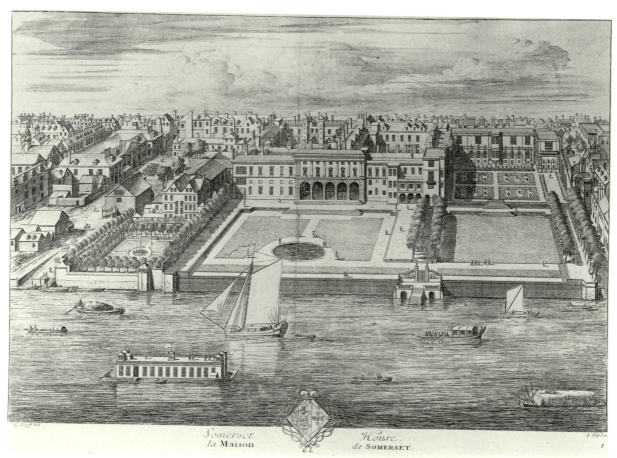

Figure 7 *Somerset House (later Denmark House):* view from the Thames, including improvements wrought under Anne of Denmark between 1609 and 1619 and under Henrietta Maria in 1661-2. After a drawing by Leonard Knyff. Greater London Record Office (Maps and Prints).

Along with St. James's and Whitehall, the galleries and terraces of Denmark House received a share of the statues from the Gonzaga collection acquired by Charles in the early 1630s: thirteen sculptures were eventually inventoried in the gardens. Fewer than fifty of the paintings listed at Denmark House are said to have originated there, although a further thirty-four appraised in the chapel were presumably in their original positions; the fact that so many of these were of a religious or overtly Catholic nature (such as the portrait of 'A pope in w^t sattine'), suggests that iconoclastic activity must have been very limited, despite official sanction by Parliament in 1643.[67]

Denmark House was among the premises granted to the Earl of Northumberland to house the royal children placed in his care,[68] although he seems to have made no use of it; instead it served a number of functions including the display of the mortal remains of Oliver Cromwell in 1658. Most importantly in the present context, a number of rooms (including the great hall) were turned over to the Trustees and Contractors for sale of the King's Goods: here the bulk of the items were displayed and the contracts of sale exchanged. At the end of the sale the Trustees were replaced by the military when Denmark House, like so many of its neighbours, became a barracks.[69]

Greenwich Palace

From the reign of Edward I the manor of Greenwich formed part of the royal demesne until, under Henry VI, it was granted to Thomas Beaufort, Duke of Exeter, after whose death it passed to Humphrey, Duke of Gloucester. Humphrey obtained leave to 'embattle the manor of Greenwich, build with stone, enclose and make a ditch and erect a tower within' but on his premature death it once more reverted to the Crown and was further developed to form the palace known as 'Pleazaunce' or Placentia. Under Henry VII further improvements were made and for the remainder of the Tudor period Greenwich formed one of the principal royal palaces. Henry VIII and Elizabeth were both born there.[70]

The siting of the palace (Fig. 8), on the tideway below London, had much to recommend it, the Thames providing a means of easy communication with the other royal properties lying upstream. (Not inappropriately, a 'Barge. Cloth. of redd vellv^t embroidrd all over wth y^e Armes. of England' was among the items sold from Greenwich in 1649). The main entrance faced the river, access being gained via a massive gatehouse to the principal courtyard; flanking courtyards

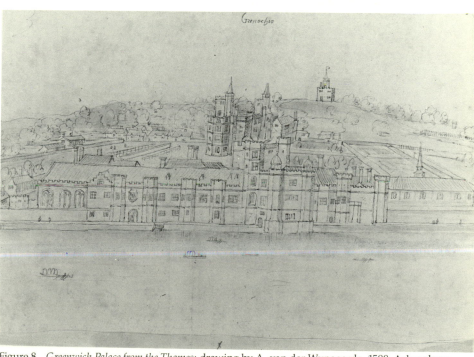

Figure 8   *Greenwich Palace from the Thames*: drawing by A. van der Wyngaerde, 1588. Ashmolean Museum, Oxford.

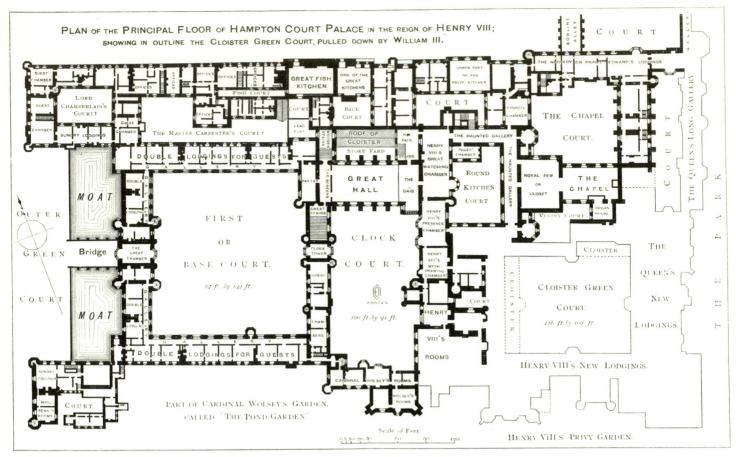

Figure 9 *Hampton Court*: plan of the principal floor during the Stuart period. From E. Law, *History of Hampton Court*.

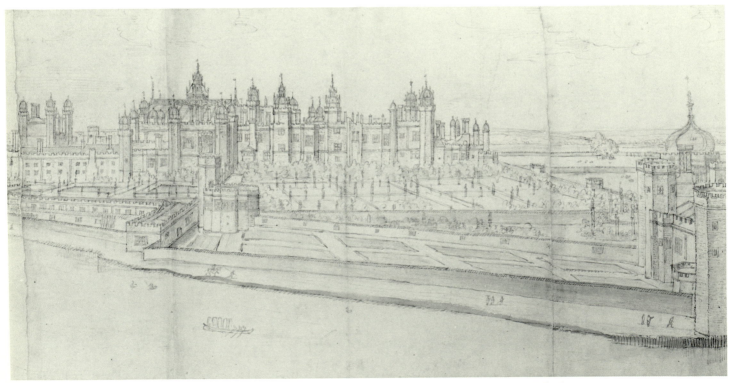

Figure 10 *Hampton Court Palace from the south*: drawing by A. van den Wyngaerde, 1558. Ashmolean Museum, Oxford.

26   Arthur MacGregor

adjoined on either side. Apart from the 'grete Armery house', where the manufacture of English armour was to be placed on an entirely new footing, Henry's other major innovations were mostly of a sporting or recreational nature.

Under Elizabeth, improvements were of a more domestic complexion, including new kitchens, scullery, bakehouse and coal house; she also installed new fountains, one of them an elaborate construction with 'two greate cestornes'.

James I rebuilt the garden front of the palace, enclosed the park (which Henry VIII had enlarged) with a brick wall and constructed there a 'snow conserve'.

In 1613 Greenwich was added to the Queen's jointure and within three years work had begun at her instigation on a new venture, described as 'some curious devise of Inigo Jones' and with an estimated cost of over £4,000: this was to be the 'House of Delight', now known as the Queen's House, built to span the public road that separated the palace gardens from the park.[71] Following the death of Queen Anne in 1619, Greenwich palace was granted to Prince Charles, retained by him after his accession and settled on Henrietta Maria in 1629.

55-6 [1-32], 62-8 [34-144]
137-50 [1-9, 1-256], 216 [23], 248-9 [1-25]
384 [803-9]

In 1652 Parliament resolved that palace, contents and estate should all be sold off, though no buyer was found for the palace and interest among the items inventoried is largely limited to the 130 or more paintings and some thirty-six pieces of sculpture. By 1652 John Evelyn found the Queen's House had been 'given by the Rebells to *Bolstrood Whittlock* one of their unhappy Counsellors',[72] while the palace, uncared for throughout the Civil War, sank to the status of prison for hordes of Dutch seamen and the kitchens were let to a contractor who supplied biscuits to the army. Inevitably, the toll on the fabric was appalling, so much so that at the Restoration there was little choice but to demolish it and build anew. Only the Queen's House survived this indignity and was indeed enlarged for Henrietta Maria in 1662.

Hampton Court Palace

On Midsummer Day 1514, Cardinal Wolsey obtained from the Knights Hospitallers a 99-year lease of the manor of Hampton Court in Middlesex (Figs. 9-10), with leave to alter and rebuild it. Interpreting the terms of his lease in the widest manner, Wolsey spent the next ten years in transforming the modest house into a palace of such outstanding beauty that it attracted the covetous eye of Henry VIII: by 1529 the Cardinal had been induced, no doubt with the heaviest of hearts, to exchange his earthly paradise for the King's palace at Richmond.[73]

The principal improvements wrought by Henry included the construction of some twenty domestic offices to boost the capacity of the kitchens, an indoor bowling alley and a tennis court. He also transformed Wolsey's great hall with customary extravagance and impatience. With an eye to improving the hunting there, he annexed an extensive tract of land to form Hampton Court Chase, for 'nourishment, generation and feeding beasts of venery and fowls of warren'; this was to become the focus of an enlarged tract of hunting ground, embracing several adjacent manors to form the Honour of Hampton Court.

Henry's successors were all regular visitors to Hampton Court. Edward VI was born there. Elizabeth's introduction to the palace was as Mary's captive, but following her accession it became a favourite residence. To beautify it further, Elizabeth authorized utilization of a quantity of white marble to build fountains at Hampton Court.

James I often visited in the early years of his reign, hunting in the spring, returning in the autumn and (as Elizabeth had done) for Christmas. Prince Henry was lodged at Hampton Court with his household for a time, and Queen Anne died there in 1619. Little expenditure took place under James, although a pest house was constructed, removed at some distance, 'for the Receipte of infected persons which were sent from his Ma^tes House of Hampton Courte that it might be free from infeccon of the contagion against his Ma^tes coming thither.'[74] An ice house or 'conserve of snow' was also built in 1625-6.

A major improvement under Charles I was the cutting of a new watercourse (variously termed the King's, Queen's, Cardinal's or Longford River) in 1639, to supplement Wolsey's piped supply with water drawn from the River Colne. Hampton Court was Charles's first refuge when he fled from London in 1642, and later became his prison during two months of house arrest in 1647, before his ill-fated dash to Carisbrooke.

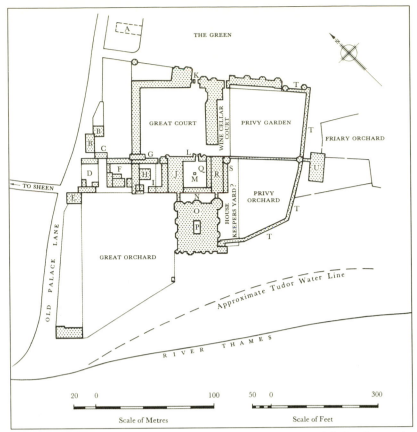

Figure 11 *Richmond Palace*: diagrammatic plan based on Wyngaerde's drawings and on documentary evidence. A position of bakehouse?; B offices of plummery and clerk of works?; C position of watergate?; D woodyard lodgings and house of office; E cistern house; F poultry house, scalding house, aumery room and ale buttery; G pantry and larders; H kitchen; I flesh and fish larders, and pastry; J hall; K outer gate; L middle gate building; M fountain court; N passage building; O royal lodgings; P paved court; Q King's closet; R chapel; S Queen's closet; T galleries; U friary church. Reproduced by courtesy of English Heritage.

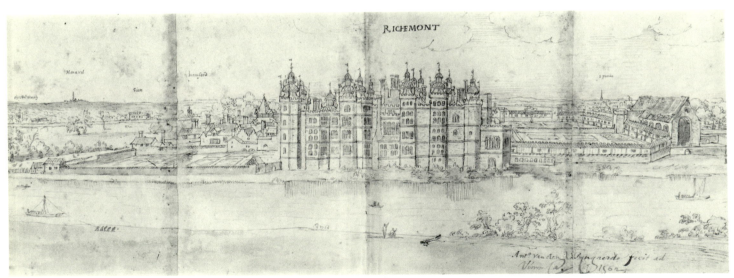

Figure 12 *Richmond Palace from the Thames*: drawing by A. van den Wyngaerde, 1562. Ashmolean Museum, Oxford.

First signs of threat to the fabric had manifested themselves in 1645 when, following the Parliamentary victory at Naseby and the seizure of Hampton Court as state property, Sir Robert Hadow ordered the destruction of 'popish and superstitious pictures' and other fittings in the chapel. None the less, a considerable sprinkling of such paintings survived among nearly 350 inventoried at Hampton Court in 1649. Over 250 hangings, many of them sumptuously woven, as well as large numbers of richly embroidered cushions and other furnishings add to an impression of luxurious appointment, while a few musical instruments and hounds' collars survived as tokens of the recreation of a century of monarchs.

Initial plans to sell off Hampton Court were replaced by a resolution that it should be kept 'for the public use of the Commonwealth'. Cromwell installed himself there for five years, savouring the pleasures of the palace with as much enthusiasm as any monarch, hunting in the park and even reviving some elements of court ceremonial at table in the great hall. Cromwell's son Richard harboured ambitions of inheriting the palace but was thwarted by Parliament, with the result that it survived intact to be returned to Charles II at the Restoration.

Richmond Palace

The character of the royal palace at Richmond (formerly Sheen) in Surrey was largely determined by the major reconstruction completed at a cost of over £20,000 by Henry VII in 1501, when the king decreed that henceforth 'it shuld be namyd his manoyr of Rychemount'. Henry VIII showed little sentimental attachment to the place: he felt no compunction in exchanging the right of use with Wolsey in return for access to Hampton Court in the late 1520s, but after Wolsey's fall in 1530 it reverted to the crown. Elizabeth died there, as her grandfather Henry VII had done.[75]

Richmond was granted by James I to Prince Henry in 1610, the year of his investiture as Prince of Wales. Under the influence of the innovative prince, plans were introduced to transform the gardens with an elaborate water system incorporating fountains and grottoes, all designed by Salomon de Caus, but they perished with Henry's premature death in 1612. Henceforth Richmond was held by Charles and was settled by him on Henrietta Maria in 1626.

Some impression of the character and disposition of the palace can be gained from a panoramic view by Wyngaerde and from the Parliamentary survey of 1649 (Figs. 11-12).[76] The constituent buildings were in a variety of media, their rambling layout reduced to some order by grouping them around a series of courtyards, varying in size according to importance. Principal among these was a court bounded on the Thames frontage by a three-storey freestone block, 'leaded and battayled' and with fourteen turrets which 'very much adorne and set forth the fabrick of the whole structure'. The royal apartments lay within this block, the privy and presence chambers occupying most of the twelve rooms on the first floor. Access to the upper floors was gained by means of a lofty stair turret, the 'canted tower', which formed 'A cheife ornament unto the whole fabrick'.

In an adjacent courtyard the principal range consisted of an ancient two-storey block with the 100-foot long great hall lying at first floor level; below lay the great buttery chamber, silver scullery and saucery. Facing into this same courtyard were a gatehouse and also a three-storey building with the top floor 'fitted with all thinges usefull for a chappell', the ground and first floors being occupied by the wine cellar and its staff. Adjoining buildings contained the queen's closet, a kitchen and poultry house, and two 'faire and large passages' each over eighty feet long and 'of singular use and speciall ornament to the fabrick of the whole house'. Yet another 'fayer and spacious Court' was enclosed by three ranges of brick-built lodgings for the officers of the household.

The privy garden was bordered on its north side by a range incorporating 'divers choyse and faier roomes both below stairs and above' and also a tennis court. To the south-east of the garden and the adjoining privy orchard lay a 200-yard long gallery block, open to the gardens at ground level and enclosed against the weather on the first floor. Here too were various sporting and gaming facilities, with 'houses of pleasure' built 'as well to use the said plays as to behold them so disportyng'. A few gaming boards and a billiard table appraised in 1649

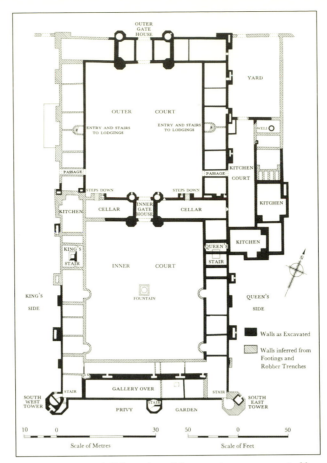

Figure 13 *Nonsuch Palace*: plan of the structures as excavated by Martin Biddle in 1959-60. Reproduced by courtesy of English Heritage.

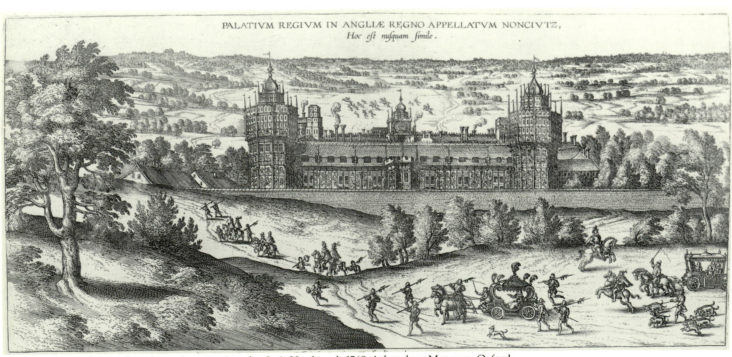

Figure 14 *Nonsuch Palace from the south*: engraving after Joris Hoefnagel, 1568. Ashmolean Museum, Oxford.

echo these pleasurable pastimes; otherwise the inventories are mainly concerned with the usual hangings, carpets, bedding and other furniture.

Under James I a new park was formed to the north of the palace approximating to the area of the Old Deer Park of today, while in 1634 Charles enclosed a larger area to the south-east, corresponding to the present Richmond Park. At the time of the survey there were 'no Deare at all' within the park, the herds having no doubt been annihilated in the turbulent years of the Civil War.

Parts of the palace were demolished during the Interregnum, and although enough survived to form an occasional residence for Henrietta Maria following the Restoration, by 1700 it had become 'an old and ruinated building' of which only meagre traces now survive.

Nonsuch Palace

On 22 September 1538 Henry VIII embarked on what was to be his most ambitious building project, on the site of the former manor house of Cuddington to the south-east of Kingston-upon-Thames. The ambitious scale on which he planned the residence was reflected in the name chosen for it – Nonsuch – while the estate was subsumed into the burgeoning Honour of Hampton Court. The palace, 'built with so great sumptuousnesse and rare workmanship that it aspireth to the very top of ostentation for show', remained incomplete at the time of Henry's death; it was visited only once by Edward VI and was disposed of under Mary to Henry Fitzalan, twelfth Earl of Arundel, to whom the task of completion fell. In 1560 he also acquired the surrounding park. On Arundel's death the entire estate passed to his son-in-law John, Lord Lumley, but overwhelming debts forced Lumley to surrender the palace to Elizabeth, bringing about its return to the crown estates.[77]

The property inherited by James I at Nonsuch (Figs. 13-14) fulfilled in every way the ambitions of its Tudor founder. In plan it was basically rectangular, with the accommodation laid out around two adjoining courts of almost equal size. By way of a gatehouse in the north frontage, access was gained to the first (outward) court, cobbled over most of its surface but with pathways of smooth Purbeck stone. The enclosing two-storey ranges were built of brick but faced with stone. Servants' quarters shared the ground floor with various domestic offices while more senior members of the household occupied the first floor. To the west of the court lay the privy stables and to the east the subsidiary kitchen courtyard. In the centre of the facing range lay a three-storey inner gatehouse, built of stone and with octagonal turrets at the corners, providing a striking focal point at the heart of the palace.

Passing by way of a flight of steps through the inner gatehouse and up into the inward or 'royal' court, a striking panorama met the eye. Here the inward-facing walls were of stone on the ground floor and timber-framed above. Lavish decoration covered this upper storey in the form of plaster panels fitted between the timbers and deeply moulded with ornament forming an ambitious inconographical programme; gods and goddesses, the arts and virtues, insignia and floral motifs ranged round the walls. The plaster panels were framed with gilded slate mouldings while the timbers too were hung with decorative panels of slate.[78] Battlements of wood covered with lead and braced with iron crowned the outer walls of the inward court and were in turn surmounted by carved representations of the king's beasts, each supporting a wind vane.[79] The courtyard itself was flagged with stone and had a 'fayer fountayne of whyte marble' at its centre.

On the upper floor of the inward court lay the royal apartments, the king's side on the west and the queen's on the east. The privy gallery linked these chambers across the south wing, whose 200-foot frontage was bisected by a tall and graceful bay window and flanked by five-storey octagonal corner towers.

The Renaissance themes of the palace decorations were echoed by the siting of a temple in the gardens and by a sculptured group representing Diana and Actaeon set about a spring in one of the groves. The gardens themselves were planted with a maze and a wilderness.

From the time of its settlement on Queen Anne in 1603, it took only a short while for a complaint to surface to the effect that the Queen 'cannot conveniently keep house at Nonsuch without she could procure the Great Park', and in 1605 Lumley duly surrendered his residual interest to the Crown. Extensive renovations were carried out in 1609-10 and more expenditure followed the granting of the palace in 1627 to Henrietta Maria.

At the time of the Parliamentary survey in 1650,[80] although the palace was judged to be 'in very good repayre and not fit to be demolished', the privy garden was showing signs of neglect; 'with a little labor', however, it was expected to 'answeare the expectatyon of a very hansome garden plot.' Some 2,800 trees in the park, on the other hand, were 'marked forth for the use of the Navie'. The list

416-18 [1-33]

of contents eventually sold reflects little of the original lavishness of the palace, being limited to £1,000-worth of pictures, twenty-four stools and a marble table. The palace itself was sold during the Interregnum to General Lambert, but restored to Henrietta Maria thereafter. Following the Queen-Dowager's death in 1669, Charles II made a gift of the palace to his mistress, the Duchess of Cleveland, who realized her asset in 1682 by demolishing the buildings and selling the materials.

Oatlands Palace

The manor of Oatlands, near Weybridge, was acquired by Henry VIII from Thomas Cromwell and by 1537 was annexed to the Honour of Hampton Court. Some £17,000 was then spent in transforming the manor house into a palace appropriate to the king.[81]

The familiar layout of adjoining quadrangles was adopted for the complex, built of red brick with stone dressings. Three major courtyards were constructed, 'the first two whereof are grene courts and the other is paved with rough freestone'. A modest entrance to the first of these (Great Court) contrasted with a massive four-storey gatehouse with octagonal flanking turrets which controlled access to Middle Court and a more elegant entry to Inner Court (where the royal apartments, great hall and chapel lay). A lofty octagonal tower, jettied and pinnacled, dominated the panorama of the palace (Fig. 15). Around the subsidiary Bakehouse Court were grouped the bakehouse, buttery and other offices, together with domestic accommodation.

Oatlands was soon supplanted among Henry's enthusiasms by Nonsuch, and played little part in the rest of his reign. Edward VI, Mary and Elizabeth were almost equally infrequent visitors, although cosmetic improvements were made during Elizabeth's reign by 'pencelling in Bricke Culloures all the gable endes and walles on the outsyde of the Queenes lodginges and gallery towards the garden', the joints being rendered in black.

Figure 15 *Oatlands Palace from within the main courtyard*: drawing by A. van den Wyngaerde, 1559. Ashmolean Museum, Oxford.

In 1603 Prince Henry was installed at Oatlands at the age of nine, cared for by his own household. The palace was formally granted to him in 1610, but the following year was settled on the Queen. Improvements made under Anne included the installation of a complex water system to bring water to the 'Queene's lobby' and the construction of a two-storey silkworm house. The Tradescants, father and son, later held successively the post of 'Keeper of His Majesty's Gardens, Vines and Silkworms' at Oatlands: some three score 'Oring Trees' sold off with the other goods in 1650 had no doubt been nurtured by them.

250 [34-9], 276-89 [1-179]

Under Charles I, Oatlands was granted to Henrietta Maria, who bore the King a son there – the future Duke of Gloucester, known as Henry of Oatlands. Improvements to the King's and Queen's chambers are recorded in 1637-8, but Henrietta Maria's most interesting innovation was perhaps the decoration of the eighty-foot gallery with painted views of eight of her houses.

During 1643 Oatlands served briefly as the residence and headquarters of Prince Rupert before relapsing into obscurity until 1647, when it served for ten days as Charles's prison before his removal to Hampton Court. On his escape from custody, Charles again made his way back to Oatlands whence a proclamation was issued that 'shortly brave things would come to pass', but these sentiments were abandoned along with Oatlands itself when Charles set out for Carisbrooke a few days later.

Under the Commonwealth the palace was largely demolished, the trees decimated for ship-building and the estate disparked.

Wimbledon

With only brief interruptions, the manor of Wimbledon in Surrey was held by the archbishops of Canterbury from the time of the Conquest until 1536, when it was acquired by Henry VIII and promptly granted to Thomas Cromwell. Four years later it was repurchased for the Crown and annexed to the Honour of Hampton

Figure 16 *Wimbledon House,* after an engraving by Henry Winstanley, 1678. Hope Collection, Ashmolean Museum, Oxford.

Court, but was later granted by Elizabeth to Sir Thomas Cecil (afterwards Earl of Exeter) and his heirs. Cecil built himself a magnificent new house there, which was added to the royal properties in 1639 when Wimbledon manor was bought for Henrietta Maria.

Cecil's innovatory mansion (Fig. 16) was laid out on an H-plan (with wings of unequal length), the first time such an arrangement had been used in polite architecture.[82] Much of our detailed knowledge of it comes from the Parliamentary survey of 1649:[83] the house was then described as of 'excellent good brick' with freestone dressings; most of the roofs were lead covered, the prominent stair turrets in the internal angles of the building being roofed with slate. On the ground floor the principal accommodation included a 'faier and large hall' and a spacious chamber termed the 'marble parlour', taking its name from the material in which it was finished and from the marble tables with which it was furnished – seemingly among those which were later to feature in the inventories. Large windows opened from the parlour on to a 108-foot long balcony overlooking the gardens. Also on the ground floor was an organ room with 'a rich payre of organs' (perhaps the same instruments sold for £6 in 1651), a chapel, a number of chambers (designated the King's, Queen's and Lord's), two bathrooms and various domestic offices. Grand staircases at either end of the central block led to the first floor, dominated by the 'greate gallery' with its cedar floor 'casting a pleasant smell'. The dining room and drawing room were on this level, as were the 'summer chamber' and further lodgings. Below stairs a full range of domestic offices is enumerated by the surveyors, most of them 'very light and pleasant'. Here too lay the 'stone gallery', running the length of the eastern facade under the balcony and opening directly on to the gardens; opening inwards from the centre of the gallery was a grotto, 'wrought in the arch and sides thereof with sundry sorts of shells of great lustre and ornament formed into the shapes of men Lyons Serpents antick formes and other rare devices', and with a marble-lined pool set in the floor.

Everything about Wimbledon speaks of charm and refinement. Internally many of the walls were 'spotted with starrs of gould' and crosses pattée; many ceilings were also painted or blazoned with arms and some of the floors were painted with 'cheker worke'. Elaborately conceived gardens surrounded the house, sheltering several dovecotes, 'shadow houses', a pheasant house and banqueting house. The park round about was stocked with deer and dotted with fishponds. In sum, the surveyors concluded,

. . . wee finde the scite thereof very pleasant, the roomes richly adorned, very commodious and fit for present use, the ayre sweete and open the church and market nere, and the convience and nearness of London of noe smale advantage, the gardens richly planted and compleately ordered being a seate of a large prospect every wayes usefull to the purchaser.

That purchaser was to be Adam Baynes, who sold it on to General Lambert *c.* 1653. In 1660 it was restored to Henrietta Maria, but within a year was sold again. The house was pulled down in the early eighteenth century.

Theobalds

The modest moated manor house of Theobalds in Hertfordshire, acquired by Sir William Cecil in 1564, provided its new owner with little more than temporary lodgings while a more splendid house was newly built alongside. Even this new mansion was begun, in the words of its founder, 'with a mean measure', but from 1571, the year in which Cecil was created Lord Burghley and Theobalds received its first visit from Queen Elizabeth, the original concept was radically revised and in the building work carried forward thereafter Theobalds 'was envisaged less as a nobleman's house than as the Queen's occasional palace'.[84]

The splendid brick-built mansion bequeathed by Burghley in 1598 to his second son, Robert Cecil, was ranged around two major quadrangles and some lesser courtyards (Fig. 17). The principal lodgings, including the apartments formerly occupied on the one side by Burghley and on the other by the Queen on her occasional visits were grouped around Middle Court. The second quadrangle, Conduit Court, was enclosed by ranges housing various rooms of

230 [228-30]
53 [-], 57-62 [1-32, 1-33]
217-18 [1-30], 296-7 [228-50]

Figure 17 *Theobalds from the south-west*: a sketch reconstruction, drawn by Malcolm Higgs. Reproduced from *Archaeologia* 97 (1959) by permission of Sir John Summerson and the Society of Antiquaries.

state and had at its centre a huge fountain from which it took its name. Great square towers, each with slate-hung corner turrets, rose from each angle of this courtyard. Entry to the house was gained through a smaller courtyard termed Dial Court, flanked by domestic offices on one side and by stables on the other. The house was surrounded by extensive 'Gardens, Fountaines, & Walks . . . perfected most costly, bewtyfully, & pleasantly'.[85]

In the course of James I's initial progress from Holyrood to Whitehall in 1603, he passed four days at Theobalds in the company of the Privy Council, 'with entertainment such and so costly as hardly can be expressed.'[86] Three years later Cecil sought to mount a further refined entertainment there for James and his brother-in-law Christian IV of Denmark, but some spirited carousing by the royal party reduced the occasion to one of the most celebrated and hilarious debauches in English history.[87] So taken was James with Theobalds that in 1607 he prevailed upon Cecil (now Earl of Salisbury) to convey the house with its surrounding properties to the Crown, the Earl receiving in return Hatfield House and several other manors.

On taking possession James immediately set about modifying the accommodation to conform with the formal requirements of the King's Presence, Privy and Withdrawing Chambers, while the Queen, on whom the house was formally settled, had her corresponding chambers on the other side of Middle Court. Accommodation for the increased household was found in premises built over new and existing structures or in lodgings converted from other use. Against considerable local opposition, the park was greatly enlarged and walled in around a circuit of nine miles.[88]

James died at Theobalds on 25 March 1625 and Prince Charles was instantly proclaimed King at the gates. The house held less appeal for Charles than for his father, however, and there are no records of any developments there during his reign. The inventories seem to reflect the house very much as it was at James's death, the pictures mostly undistinguished princely portraits (but including some representations of boar, stag and 'baboones') and the other contents including over a hundred pairs of antlers.

136 [22, 24], 393-6 [935-81]

396 [980-1]

The Parliamentary surveyors found the house in good repair and not appropriate for demolition,[89] but most of it was none the less pulled down within a short time of its disposal by the Commissioners.

Holdenby House

Many analogies can be drawn between the development, the brief flowering and the early extinction of Lord Burghley's seat at Theobalds and the history of the palatial mansion erected at Holdenby in Northamptonshire by Burghley's younger contemporary, Sir Christopher Hatton. Born in the ancient manor of Holdenby in 1540, Hatton rose in favour at Elizabeth's court to become Lord Chancellor in 1587. In many ways, Burghley the elder statesman provided an exemplar for Hatton to emulate and, just as Theobalds was remodelled to receive the Queen whenever she might favour it with a visit, so Holdenby was conceived *ab initio* less as a private residence than as a pavilion designed for the Queen's pleasure, whose purpose would be fulfilled, in Hatton's own words, only when

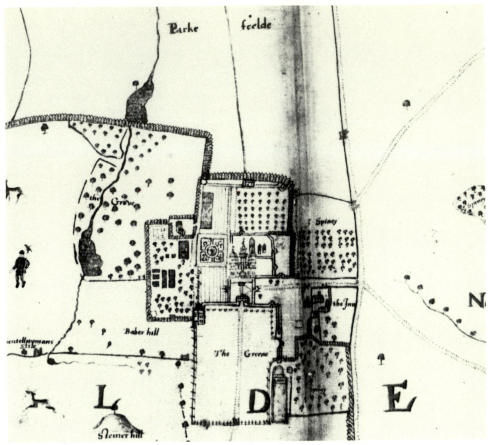

Figure 18 *Holdenby House*: detail from a survey of 1587 by Ralph Treswell. Photograph by Northamptonshire Record Office, reproduced with permission of the Trustees of the Winchilsea Settled Estates.

'that lady saint may sit in it to whom it is dedicated'.[90] Sadly, this was an ambition that was to remain unconsummated.

The great Northamptonshire mansion (Fig. 18) had the advantage over its model that its design was conceived from the beginning as a unified whole. All the building work was concentrated in the period of about five years leading up to its completion in 1583. Like Theobalds, the house was designed around two major courtyards, the main facade at Holdenby being longer by some fifty feet at 352 feet. The accommodation was 'double-built', some of the rooms looking outwards and others overlooking the internal courtyards, all of them well-lit with the most extravagant acreage of glazed windows in England. The south range, facing the gardens, was dedicated in the original scheme to the Queen and her court, Hatton's chambers occupying a corresponding position on the other side of the main hall. Six massive towers marked the corners of the adjoining rectangular blocks.[91]

Along the south frontage the ground was embanked to form a knot garden, with walks running the length of the house. Where the ground sloped away, terraces cut into the slopes transformed the 'craggye and unprofitable lande' into 'a most pleasante, sweete and princely place with divers walks', shaded with fruit trees and with many 'artificially composed Arbors'.[92]

With Hatton's death in 1591, his heirs were forced to sell off many of his properties in order to cover his debts and finally, in 1608, Holdenby and its estates fell to James I. Having been conceived as a palace fit to receive a Tudor queen, there was little the Stuart king had to do to adapt it to his own needs. The garden range, on which Elizabeth never set eyes, became James's lodgings, while Anne and her retinue occupied Hatton's own chambers. Neither they, nor later Charles and Henrietta Maria (on whom the house was settled), were frequent visitors, however, and by a twist of fate the full panoply of state descended on Holdenby only when Charles spent four months there in 1647 in the custody of the Parliamentary Commissioners. At this stage in his detention Charles was treated with every deference: all the officers and staff of the household occupied their appointed places, every formality of the court was observed and 'all the Tables were as well furnish'd as they used to be when his Majesty was in a peaceful and flourishing State'.[93] The Commissioners and their own attendants were also accommodated there, 'all within the king's House without straitning'. For weeks this situation, not wholly disagreeable, was to persist until the military intervened to convey the King under close arrest first of all to Newmarket and thence to London and his fate. By the time the contents of the house were inventoried by the Trustees, they had little to note but a few items of kitchen and brewhouse equipment, £5-worth of furniture and (outvaluing everything else) twelve head of livestock.

241-2 [283-305]

The Parliamentary survey of 1650[94] speaks in fair terms of the house and gardens at Holdenby. Despite the observation that it could easily be formed into 'several commodious habitations', most of the house was demolished immediately on its sale to the same Adam Baynes that purchased the manor of Wimbledon, who preserved only the kitchen wing as his own residence.

Bewdley

The manor of Tickenhill at Bewdley in Worcestershire housed various members of the royal family from as early as the fourteenth century and from the fifteenth century also served as the summer-time residence of the Lords President of Wales and seat of the Council in the Marches of Wales.

Few details of the manor house are recorded, although it is known to have been largely of timber-framed construction with stone-tiled roofs. Something of its character can be seen in a view of part of the eastern range, executed in 1712 by William Stukely (Fig. 19). In 1582, at the time of the improvements he wrought at Ludlow (p. 43), Lord President Sir Henry Sidney installed a piped water supply, culminating in 'a fayre lardge founteyne made with Lyme stone and ledd at the Howse, her Majesty's Armes with divers other Armes sett thereupon'.[95]

A survey of the manor was carried out in 1612, when it was held by the Prince of Wales but leased to a tenant, Ralph Clare. There seems to have been some dispute concerning responsibility for upkeep of the house, with the result that by 1641 it was almost ruinous. Charles I spent a few days there – presumably in some discomfort – in 1644, but on his return to Bewdley in the aftermath of Naseby in the following year he was forced to sleep in an inn in the town, so decayed was the manor. The Parliamentary surveyors in 1650 described the

Figure 19 *Bewdley (Tickenhill) House*: drawing of the gatehouse by William Stukely, 1721. Bodleian Library, Oxford (MS Top. Gen. d.13, f.32).

house as 'very much out of repair' and assessed it only for the value of the site and the materials.[96] The entire contents of the house, mostly kitchen and brewhouse equipment and a few sticks of furniture, sold for a mere £27 19s. 6d: the buyer was a local man from Bewdley, and it seems unlikely that the goods had ever left the manor house. Most of the surviving structure was pulled down in 1738.

238-9 [258-77]

Woodstock

Having supported a royal hunting lodge from as early as the reign of Aethelred II, Woodstock became a royal manor during the Middle Ages, successive monarchs being drawn to it for frequent and sometimes prolonged visits. Accommodation was found in the manor house both for the household and for the administration of the estate.

The medieval manor house, ranged around two courtyards and dominated by a large gatehouse, was extensively rebuilt by Henry VII and further improved under Henry VIII (when the water supply was upgraded and baths and fountains installed). There followed a period of neglect (the house being described as 'for many years decayed and prostrated' in 1551), so that it was barely fit to serve even as a prison for the Princess Elizabeth, detained there by Mary in 1554-5.[97]

Some degree of consolidation and even expansion followed under James and Charles (both of whom hunted from Woodstock). As well as suites for the queen and the king (including Presence, Privy and Withdrawing Chambers), there were rooms designated for the Prince (perhaps alluding to Henry, who was granted the manor in 1610), the Lord Chamberlain, the Lord Treasurer and various others. Further accommodation was contained in four lodges in the park, at some distance from the manor house.

During the Civil War the house was at first garrisoned by the royalists and later subjected to a damaging siege, leading to its surrender. In 1649 the Parliamentary surveyors found it 'much out of repaire' but yet 'fitter to stand than to be demolished'.[98] On 23 October 1650 the Trustees discovered there nothing but some 'Peeces of very old and decayed Tapistrie hangings', three lead cisterns and some scraps of furniture, other hangings having previously been removed to Whitehall and the remainder 'imbezelled by the Souldiers of yᵉ Garrison'. The manor house was sold in 1652 and partly demolished thereafter, the remainder crumbling away to become 'altogether ruinous' in the course of the next half century.

244 [316-21]

Royston

Royston in Hertfordshire has seemed to some an unlikely spot to be singled out for royal favour, 'the town itself being uninviting, the situation bleak, on the northern side of the open downs, and surrounded by a country described . . . as healthy and clean, but having no pleasant prospects and but few rural charms'.[99] Yet from the time of James I's initial encounter with the town on 30 April 1603, in the course of his progress to London to assume the crown, it was to become his favourite resort.

Returning to Royston even before his coronation, James initiated the process that led to the purchase of several properties, including two former inns, the Cock and the Greyhound, which in the following years were united, extended and adapted to the royal purposes. The informality of these arrangements seems to have been entirely suited to James's aims, for he had no thought of establishing there a palace in which the household in all its complexity could be installed:[100] Royston was to function instead as a hunting lodge, a private retreat from the demands of the capital and the duties of kingship, where the monarch could retire with his 'merry crew of hunters'.

In the course of 1604-5 the property was 'nowe made a convenient house for his highnes and his traine'. At this time the King's lodgings occupied the site of the Cock, while the Greyhound served as a guard chamber and as officers' quarters. Further ranges of privy lodgings were added between 1607 and 1610. Other properties were gradually absorbed into the complex, including a house known as Howletts which James converted as a lodging for Prince Charles;

further accommodation was added for visitors and equerries. Some visual coherence was imposed on these disparate structures by pencilling the brickwork throughout.

For the recreation of the King and his guests, gardens were laid out, a bowling green was formed and a cock-pit was built. The all-important facilities for the hunt included timber kennels for the King's hounds and stables for the horses, together with a smithy and 'shoeing place' for the farriers.

243 [306-15]

In contrast to his father, Charles I was rarely seen at Royston, the last occasion being involuntarily in 1648 in the custody of the Parliamentary army. By this time only the King's and Prince's Lodgings were in good repair, the remaining accommodation having been allowed to fall into decay. The few items inventoried from the 'Royston and Newemarkett Wardrobe' – evidently a single office – totalled a meagre £33. 17s. in value. Under the Commonwealth the property passed out of the royal domain and Royston relapsed into its former obscurity.

Newmarket

A convenient ride to the north-east of Royston lay Newmarket in Cambridgeshire, where James I's initiatives were to have a more lasting influence. James's first recorded visit to the town, for the enjoyment of the field sports, came in 1605.[101] Pleased with what he found there, the King acquired a small house at Newmarket in the following year, which was periodically extended and adapted throughout the remainder of his reign. In 1614-15, following some structural damage caused by subsidence, a new block of lodgings was built 'with a greate chamber presence etc and roomes both over and under the same for Noblemen, and Gentlemen of the bedchamb[er]'. Lodgings for other members of the household were incorporated from time to time into other new buildings: these included a tennis court built in 1615 'for the recreation and exercise of the nobility and others', which included rooms at either end, and a dog-house and stables, both with lodgings over. A more formal addition came in 1618-19 with a new Prince's Lodging (designed by Inigo Jones, newly appointed as Surveyor of the Works), connected by a gallery to the King's chambers.

James was a regular visitor to Newmarket until the end of his life, drawn there by good hawking and coursing as well as the racing which was already making the town a resort of the nobility. As with Royston, the absence of appropriately formal accommodation at Newmarket did not endear it to Charles I, although he occasionally lodged there, the last time in Parliamentary custody.

Following the Restoration the property was reclaimed and regularly used during the racing season by Charles II and his successors, until sold by the Crown in 1862.

Windsor Castle

Since the time of its adoption as a royal residence in the early twelfth century, Windsor Castle has been intensively occupied by the monarchy almost without a break. The early Stuarts were no exception, James using it frequently as a base for hunting excursions and Charles spending several weeks in residence every year in the late summer and autumn.

John Norden's 'topographicall delineation' of the castle and its immediate surroundings (Fig. 20), dated 1607, provides a clear impression of its extent and disposition at the time. Following St. John Hope's analysis of Norden's illustration,[102] entrance was gained by way of a bridge and gatehouse to the lower ward, largely taken up by St. George's Chapel (the scene of splendid investitures to the Order of the Garter in the early seventeenth century as at other times) and the cloisters and accommodation of the 'poor knights' and canons. A second gate gave access to the middle ward, dominated by a great motte crowned with a keep (heavily buttressed and battlemented), containing two-storey structures ranged around four sides of a central courtyard.

The royal apartments were disposed around three courts (rendered somewhat inadequately by Norden) in the upper ward, to which access was

Figure 20 *Windsor Castle*: 'topographicall delineation' by John Norden, 1607. Royal Library, Windsor: reproduced by gracious permission of Her Majesty The Queen.

controlled by a third gate. 'Lodginges for the Household' were built against and between the towers of the Norman walls. A survey undertaken in 1628-9 (in which many of the chambers, lodgings and offices are enumerated) revealed widespread dilapidation of these premises, demanding an extensive programme of repairs. In the centre of the upper court Norden includes a conventionalized representation of a fountain which was set up there in 1557-8; this was to be replaced in 1635 by a new fountain dominated by figures of Hercules and Antaeus.

In the face of a deteriorating situation, following the debâcle of his attempted arrest of the Five Members in January 1642, Charles quit London first of all for Hampton Court and then, briefly, for Windsor, where he might be 'more secure from any suddain popular Attempt'.[103] Later in that year the castle was occupied without resistance by Parliamentary forces who held it thereafter for the remainder of the hostilities. The most serious damage to the fabric seems to have been that inflicted by Colonel Venn and his troops on St. George's Chapel: the interior was comprehensively ransacked, the furnishings torn up, the organs and stained glass defaced.[104] Later again, the New Model Army that was to play a decisive role in the course of the Civil War learned its skills under General Fairfax in the pastoral surroundings of Windsor Great Park.

The King returned briefly in custody in the summer of 1647 and then again in December of 1648 under close arrest. There he stayed until 19 January 1649 when he was removed to St. James's and thence to Whitehall and the block. His remains were returned to Windsor on 7 February, Parliament having decided that he should be interred there 'in a decent manner, provided that the whole Expence should not exceed five hundred pounds'.[105] Those charged with his burial had difficulty in finding an appropriate vault in St. George's Chapel, for despite their former familiarity with it 'they found it so alter'd and transform'd, all Inscriptions, and those Land-Marks pulled down, by which all men knew every particular in That Church, and such a dismal mutation over the whole, that they knew not where they were'.[106] On 9 February they finally discharged their duty with all the dignity they were allowed, 'without any words, or other Ceremonies than the tears and sighs of the few beholders'.

In June of 1649 Parliament resolved that Windsor should be 'kept for the public use of the Commonwealth', though later it only narrowly escaped sale. Perhaps understandably, little appears in the inventories of the Windsor wardrobe to hint at its former richness: a few good-quality hangings were still to be found there (mostly among the reserved goods) and a splendid bed with Elizabethan arms merits special note. Ultimately the castle was returned to Charles II, proclaimed in Windsor on 12 May 1660.

290-95 [180-227]
293 [210]

Tower of London

From the time of its foundation as a royal stronghold by William I, the Tower of London took on many additional roles while its importance as a residence declined. Its functions at the end of the sixteenth century were summarized by John Stow:

This Tower is a citadell, to defend or commande the Citie: a royall palace for assemblies, and treaties. A prison of Estate, for the most daungerous offendors: the onely place of coinage for all Englande at this present. The Armorie for warlike provision: the Treasurie of the ornaments and Jewels of the Crowne, and generall conserver of the most aunciest Recordes of the kinges Courtes of justice at Westminster.[107]

The 'treasurie' functions mentioned by Stow were the province of the Jewel House, a term which comprehended both a department of the Chamber and also the place of safekeeping for the monarch's jewels and plate, placed in the charge of its officers. Since the time of Henry III this had been located in the Tower. Repairs were carried out to the building in 1528 and then in 1532, as part of a broader programme of 'nedeful reparacions' within the Tower, orders were issued for 'the offyce of the Juelle house to be newe made'.

From the *History of the King's Works*[108] we learn that the site of the new Jewel House lay to the north of the Great Hall and to the south of the White Tower (Fig. 21), adjacent to that of its predecessor (which survived alongside it for a time). The new building was a commodious two-storey structure of brick with stone dressings, with a flight of stairs leading up to the entrance; its security was enhanced by 'grete crosse barres of iron' set in the windows. Internally it was fitted out with cupboards and presses for the safekeeping of the jewels and plate, and with 'Long settyls to be closed above with lydds lycke unto chests to putt in records or enny other wrytyngs or juells into them'. When the contents were installed, the jewels and regalia[109] were placed on the first floor (which became known as the Upper Jewel House) while the plate occupied the ground floor (the Lower Jewel House).

During the period of the later Tudors and early Stuarts, the Tower is best remembered in its role as prison. James I's principal interest in it was as the home of his collection of wild beasts, but while entertaining Christian IV at the Tower in 1606, James took care to show his brother-in-law not only the lions, the mint, the

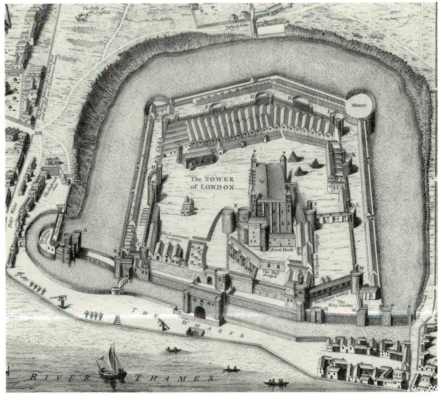

Figure 21   *The Tower of London*, with the Jewel House in the centre. From 'A true and exact draught of the Tower Liberties, surveyed in the year 1597', by Gulielmus Haiward and J. Gascoyne. British Library.

wardrobe and the ordnance, but also the Jewel House, 'where the most rare jewels and beautiful plate were shown to him'.[110]

The end of the Jewel House came with the Interregnum. By 1644 the regalia had already been moved to the Martin Tower. After dispersal of the remainder of the contents, appraised on 13-15 August 1649 at a total value of £13,430. 2s. 6½d. (including the beams and scales with which the plate was valued by weight), the building itself seems to have been demolished.

Also mentioned in the inventories are items from the Tower wardrobe, including over £18,500-worth of hangings and some £3,000-worth of cloths of estate and miscellaneous furnishings. The department of the Chamber designated the Wardrobe had its headquarters and depot in the Tower.

22-50 [1-61, 1-210, 1-13], 252 [63-72]
253 [85], 373 [665-6]

1-19 [1-83]

Carisbrooke Castle

The history of Carisbrooke as a royal stronghold reaches back to the Conquest and beyond, but it was not until the twelfth century that the castle, on the Isle of Wight, was extensively built in stone. The medieval buildings were evidently in a state of some decay by the late sixteenth century when a comprehensive rebuilding programme was initiated. The defences were further strengthened in 1587 with the threat from Spain in the offing, and the massive gatehouse with its twin drum towers was complemented by auxiliary defences designed in the latest Italian manner by Gianbelli in 1597.[111]

Having passed the whole of the early Stuart period in some obscurity, Carisbrooke suddenly entered the limelight on 13 November 1647 with the dramatic arrival of King Charles's companions Ashburnham and Berkley: they explained to the governor, Colonel Hammond, that the King, having taken flight from Hampton Court, was now close by and willing to place himself under Hammond's protection in return for an assurance that he would not be delivered up to Parliament. The King's trust proved ill-founded for, having given undertakings to the monarch and admitted him to the castle, Hammond immediately sent word of what had transpired to Parliament. Charles now found himself in confinement once again, and his liberties were further curtailed following an abortive local rising: thenceforth his exercise was limited to 'some six or eight circuits about the castle wall' after morning prayers and 'the like in the afternoon if fair'. This was to be the way of Charles's life at Carisbrooke until the end of November 1648, when he found himself suddenly removed to Hurst Castle on the Hampshire mainland and thence, three weeks later, to Windsor.

220-23 [39-75, 1-9], 275 [1-11]

Two groups of items from Carisbrooke appear in the inventories. The first, received by Anthony Mildmay 'for the use of the late Kings Childeren', comprises an adequate ration of furnishings and plate to serve the needs of the small household in whose charge they were placed; the second (a mere eleven items) consists of furnishings and hangings which were 'all sold to yᵉ Gover[nor] of the said Castle', the transaction presumably taking place on the spot.

Kenilworth Castle

Having served from the late twelfth century as one of the principal royal strongholds in the Midlands, Kenilworth in Warwickshire (Fig. 22) was granted first in 1553 to John Dudley, Duke of Northumberland, and later, after reverting to the Crown on the Duke's attainder, to his son Robert Dudley, created Earl of Leicester by Elizabeth. Extensive alterations to the fabric were begun by Leicester in 1570, when even the defensive keep was fitted with large ornamental windows. In time the castle passed to Dudley's brother and then to his son, Sir Robert Dudley, but James I contrived to reclaim Kenilworth for his own use on the grounds of doubts surrounding Dudley's legitimacy.

A survey of 1603[112] paints an impressive picture of the castle, its four gatehouses with walls up to fifteen feet thick and roofed with lead. 'The Roomes of great State within the same, & such as are able to receaue his Maty. the Queen & Prince at one tyme, built with asmuch uniformity and conveniency as any houses of later tyme, and with such stately Sellars all carried upon pillars and Architecture of free stone carved and wrought as the like are not within this Kingdome and also other houses for Offices answerable'. The surveyors ventured that 'the Circuits, Mannors, Parks, and Chase lieing round together

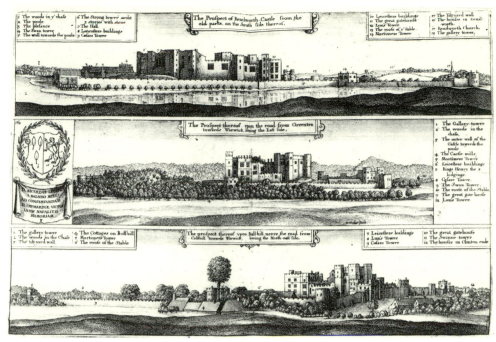

Figure 22 *Kenilworth Castle,* from Sir William Dugdale's *Antiquities of Warwickshire* (1656).

conteyne at least 19 or 20 miles in a Plesaunt Countrey, the like both for strength, state, and pleasure not being within the Realme of England'.

Negotiations were begun by Henry, Prince of Wales, to buy out Dudley's residual rights and, after Henry's death, the agreement was concluded by Charles. From 1624 the castle was leased to Robert, Lord Carey, with the remainder to his sons. It was occupied again by the soldiers of the Crown at the opening of the Civil War; Charles withdrew the garrison at an early stage, but the unopposed transfer of the castle to the Parliamentary forces failed to prevent its deliberate slighting in 1649. All that survived to be inventoried there were a few items evidently from the brewhouse and a 'Bell in Peeces', sold to a Mr Tanner in whose safekeeping it already was.

For a time thereafter part of the castle was occupied as a dwelling and later was inhabited by a colony of weavers, before falling utterly into ruin.

Ludlow Castle

Built on a rocky eminence as the principal stronghold of the Earls of March, Ludlow Castle (Fig. 23) became the seat of the Council in the Marches of Wales in the sixteenth century. Extensive improvements to the accommodation were instituted by Sir Henry Sidney, Lord President of the Marches from 1560 to 1586, fitting the castle for its new role as the Lord President's headquarters and residence (as well as an occasional lodging for judges on the Welsh circuit). These improvements included the 'making and repayring of twoe chambrs and divers other howses of offices, as kitchin larder and buttry at the gate over the Porters lodge', and fitting out of the former chapel as a court house, the construction of 'a ffayre Tennys corte . . . paving thereof with free stone and making the howses rounde about the same with Tymber', and the provision of an elaborate water system leading to a 'goodly large founteyne' within the castle, thence through the gardens and 'divers other offices' and out into a second fountain in the town below.[113]

These improvements evidently stood the castle in good stead, for no further works of a major character are recorded before the suspension of the Council in the Marches under the Commonwealth. The goods appraised there in late October and November 1650, although modest in value, give a more comprehensive picture of the furnishings than can be reconstructed from any of the other inventories. Although no doubt depleted to some extent, a range of domestic equipment and other chattels survives, all of it listed room-by-room in a

240 [278-82]

224-36 [76-240], 254 [94-8]

43   The King's Goods and the Commonwealth Sale

Figure 23 *Ludlow Castle*, from *The . . . Progress of His Grace Henry, the First Duke of Beaufort, through Wales in 1684*, a facsimile publication (London, 1888) from an original MS by Thomas Dineley.

particularly helpful manner, with the exception of £15-worth of pewter collected together and sold by weight. Also recorded, in the 'Court Howse of Justice', were 'The Seate of Justice, Tables, and Bennches', valued together at a mere 10s.

Following its reinstatement in 1661, the Council found itself with bills of £1,959 to replace the furnishings sold off by Parliament and a further £2,218 for repairs to the fabric. With the abolition of the Council in the Marches in 1689, the castle gradually fell into decay.

Other Properties Mentioned in the Inventories

In addition to the royal residences and castles already described, a number of other properties feature in the inventories. They are disparate in nature, as are the reasons for their inclusion.

Worcester House

The mansion in the Strand known during the Commonwealth as Worcester House had by that time already experienced a long history and several changes of name.[114] The salient facts concerning the house are encapsulated in John Stow's brief account of 1603: it was, he says,

sometime the Bishoppe of Carlisles Inne, which now belongeth to the Earle of Bedford, and is called Russell or Bedford house. It stretcheth from the Hospitall of Savoy, west to Iuie bridge, where sir *Robert Cecill* principall Secretary to her Maiestie, hath lately raysed a large and stately house of brick and timber.[115]

The marriage in 1600 of Anne, sole survivor of the Bedford line, to Henry Somerset, Lord Herbert (later first Marquis of Worcester), ultimately brought about a further change of name to Herbert House or Worcester House.

Figure 24   *Aerial view of the north bank of the Thames,* in the region of the Strand. Detail from a print *c.* 1650 after Wenzel Hollar. Reproduced by courtesy of the Trustees of the British Museum.

Figure 25   *Durham House, Salisbury House and Worcester House from the Thames, c.* 1650. Print after Wenzel Hollar. Reproduced by courtesy of the Trustees of the British Museum.

Worcester's willing support for the Crown and for the Catholic faith was to prove disastrous for him. The fate of his house in the Strand can be read in the 'Inventory of the goods of the Earle of Woster A Delinquent seized and taken the last daye of July 1643'.[116] The room-by-room inventory, together with other references and contemporary views (Figs. 24-5) combine to form a picture of a many-gabled house of some 'Threescore Roomes great and small, the greater p'te whereof are of an ancient structure', ranged around two quadrangles and with orchards and gardens leading down to the river.

From 1643 Worcester House was reserved for the use of Parliament and served as offices for an ever-increasing number of committees of the Council of State; these were to include the Trustees of Forfeited Estates and the Committee for the King's Goods, whose staff were assigned two rooms over the cellar.[117] Some twenty-three pieces of hangings and four damask curtains, totalling £310. 3s. 6d. in value, were sold from Worcester House in May 1650.

During the year 1659-60 Margaret, Countess of Worcester, successfully pressed her claim for restoration of the house, prompting the need for yet another committee to be set up to consider 'how to remove and where to place the Conveyances, Records and other Writings now remaining at Worcester House'. Eventually this gallimaufry of departmental offices was replaced by the Chancellery of England, established at Worcester House by the Earl of Clarendon following the Restoration.

After a final change of name to Beaufort House in 1682, the mansion was burned to the ground three years later. Its site is occupied today by the Savoy Theatre.

45   The King's Goods and the Commonwealth Sale

Durham House

Throughout the later Middle Ages, Durham house functioned as the London residence of the bishops of Durham. The house turned its back towards the Strand, its principal elevation facing the river (Fig. 25) where the bishops had advantage of a private landing stage. The Strand frontage, meanwhile, was occupied principally by stabling and by other out-houses.

The See of Durham was forced to cede the mansion to Henry VIII, but had it restored under Mary; Elizabeth reclaimed it for the Crown and in 1584 bestowed it on Sir Walter Raleigh, but twenty years later, at the instigation of Sir Robert Cecil, James I deprived Raleigh of the house and gave it back once again to the bishops of Durham. At this point the site of the Durham House stables, destroyed by fire in 1600, was purchased by Cecil, whose Salisbury House had recently been built on the plot immediately to the east (Fig. 24). Clearing away the ruinous out-houses, Cecil set up there the New Exchange, otherwise known as 'Britain's Burse'.[118]

A crude but informative plan of the complex survives, drawn up to help describe the course of a fracas which took place on 26 February 1626, 'betwixt ye Kings Officers, & the French Amb^rs followers by occasion of apprehending English Subjects Papists y^t resorted dayly to Masse to ye Embass^rs lying in Durham House'.[119] The principal buildings are shown grouped around a courtyard by the riverside, with lesser structures clustering around a larger courtyard towards the Strand and with other dwellings encroaching on the grounds. According to the Bishop's own testimony, the French ambassador (who had been lodged there at the King's request) occupied thirty of the best rooms while the Bishop made do by 'crouding up himself & his whole family being great into the worst and basest roomes of his house'.

In the same year the congregation of St. Martin-in-the-Fields, desperate for a larger place of worship, attempted to wrest from the Bishop the main hall of his house which, they claimed, was used only as a passage.[120] The hall, a severe crenellated edifice with stairs leading down to the water, occupies most of the river frontage in contemporary views.

In 1641 Philip Herbert, fourth Earl of Pembroke, obtained a lease on the property at £200 per annum. Pembroke had plans drawn up for the rebuilding of the house, but these had to be shelved on account of the Civil War. By the time the fifth Earl succeeded his father in 1650, Durham House had been occupied by the military and payment was made so that he could find temporary lodgings elsewhere. On 25 February 1650, however, the Commons decreed

that the Soldiers in *Duresme House* be forthwith removed: And that the Possession of the said House be delivered up to the Earl of *Pembroke* [and] forthwith put in as good Repair and Condition, as it was when the Soldiers entered into the said House.[121]

356 [410-16]   Hangings, bedding and a 'Crimson velvett Chaire' (the latter reserved for use at Whitehall) were appraised there in the lodgings of one Captain Lusons at £81. 5s. and sold in 1651.

Following the Restoration the house was cleared away to make way for residential developments which rapidly became overcrowded and squalid in the extreme. Before being cleared for a second time by the brothers Adam for their Adelphi development, it had become, in the architects' own words, 'a mere dunghill, a receptacle for filth, obscenity, and wretchedness, a scandal to a well-governed city'.

Syon House

Founded as the only English nunnery of the Bridgettines under Henry V, Syon in Middlesex became a royal house at the Dissolution. Following its granting in 1547 to the Duke of Somerset, over £5,500 was spent in converting the monastic buildings into a private mansion with well-planted gardens, a process set temporarily into reverse when the Bridgettines were re-established there briefly under Mary. For thirty-five years the house became a royal residence again under Elizabeth (who spent, however, no more than a few hours there in all that time), until leased in 1594 in a state of some neglect to Henry Percy, ninth Earl of Northumberland. Following Percy's entertainment of James I at Syon on two occasions in 1603, the Earl was granted the freehold in the following year in gratitude for his part in securing the King's succession.[122]

Secure in his tenure, Percy now set into motion a fifteen-year programme of reconstruction involving an expenditure of over £9,000. The mansion he had acquired was a three-storey structure of brick faced with stone, built as a hollow square with battlemented walls and with turrets at the angles and with a 'green court' in the centre. The south range housed the principal chambers while the west wing was taken up largely by the great hall with its associated buttery and pantry. A splendid 130-foot gallery occupied the east front, with a series of smaller rooms overlooking the courtyard from the same range. On his own evidence, the Earl drew inspiration for his developments from a wide range of influential contemporary buildings, most notably from Theobalds. The gardens were also expanded with exotic introductions, the Earl spending regular sums on further plants every year. By a sad irony, however, his personal enjoyment of all these improvements was curtailed by many years of imprisonment in the Tower.

Syon was to become a lodging for the three younger children of Charles I when they were placed in the custody of the tenth Earl. Quantities of plate were issued to the Earl in 1645 and in 1649 for the service of the royal children.[123] Their father was a regular visitor from his own place of detention at Hampton Court.

215-6 [1-22]   The items listed in the inventories, comprising some forty hangings (a number of them from Oatlands and Theobalds), twelve carpets and some curtains, were presumably issued from the Wardrobe for the benefit of the royal children and their household.

Much of the present-day appearance of the interior of the mansion derives from its splendid remodelling by the brothers Adam in 1762-9.

Mortlake

The origins of the tapestry works at Mortlake in Surrey can be dated with some precision to the year 1619 when Sir Francis Crane, a prominent member of the royal household, was granted a twenty-one-year exclusive right to tapestry production, with freedom from customs duty, in return for setting up the factory. The weavers were to be immigrant Flemish craftsmen, amongst whom the principals were to have the right to naturalization. Recruitment was carried out in great secrecy by the King's agents on the Continent (where there was already apprehension at the drain on Flemish expertise caused by a similar initiative by Henri IV), with the result that fifty weavers had arrived within the first year. In addition, Sir Francis undertook to train a number of apprentices selected from foundlings in the City hospitals.[124]

Responsibility for building and equipping the factory also fell to Sir Francis. The premises erected were of brick and stood three storeys high around a central courtyard. The two main workrooms, eighty-two feet by twenty feet and twenty feet by twenty feet, housed twelve and six looms respectively; they shared the first floor with a large studio, the 'limning room', presided over by the chief designer, Francis Cleyn. Cleyn occupied a detached house adjacent to the works, while accommodation for the weavers themselves was found on the ground and top floors of the factory.

The enterprise proved hugely successful from the point of view of the quality of its products, although it suffered cash flow problems almost from its inception. A year after the death in 1636 of Sir Francis Crane, his brother sold out to Charles I, the Mortlake factory thenceforth being known as the King's Works. Extracting payment for work done continued to be a problem: at the outbreak of the Civil War the royal patron himself was in debt to the works to the tune of £3,937.

After being surveyed in 1651[125] the works were exempted from sale. Steps were taken to put the premises in good order[126] and production was encouraged.

423 [1-17]   A number of 'Designes at Mortlack for makeing of Tapistrey hanginge', together with 'Loomes Scailes and weightes', were inventoried there, all of them 'reserved for Sale by order of Parliam^t dated ye 10th of October 1651'.

Following the Restoration a further grant was made towards the upkeep, but although production continued and the factory was reorganized for a time as a joint stock company, prosperity continued to decline. Finally, in 1703 Queen Anne revoked the restriction placed by Charles II on the uses to which the premises could be put, and tapestry production promptly came to an end.

Vauxhall

Although unremarkable in size, at a little over two acres, or in the range of resources it offered, the foundry complex by the Thames at Vauxhall formed the setting for some notable mechanical innovations and for more grandiose but ultimately unrealized developments in the mid-seventeenth century.

The primary activity at Vauxhall was directed towards the making of leather guns and the founding of cannon, but an 'Inventory of all his Ma[ts] Goods Engines and Materialls . . . at Vauxhall' compiled in 1645 reveals a much wider range of interest.[127] The foundry itself was controlled in Charles I's time by one William Lambert. Something of Lambert's position at Vauxhall is revealed in a petition he submitted to Charles II in 1665 in an attempt to re-establish himself there:

Your Petitioner was founder to His late majesty of blessed memory in Ffoxhall under the Marquis of Worcester, for guns and Waterworks, or any other thing founded in brass.[128]

The original mind of Edward Somerset, second Marquis of Worcester, is revealed in his *Century of Inventions*, published in 1663. The services of William Lambert, and those of a skilled mechanic of Dutch origin named Caspar Kalthoff, were employed by Worcester in translating new ideas into working models. That Vauxhall was destined for greater things than the production of mere mechanical curiosities is made plain in a letter from John Dury to Benjamin Worsley, dated 1649, containing 'A Memorandum for setting Faux-hall apart for Publick Uses': amongst the functions foreseen were 'To Keepe all manner of Ingenuities, rare Models and Engines w[ch] may bee useful for the Comon-wealth . . . to make Experiments and trials of profitable Inventions' . . . to bee a place of Resort whereunto Artists and Ingeneers from abroad and at home may repaire to meet with one another . . . and hold forth profitable Inventions . . .' The 'conveniences of forges, furnaces, mills, and all manner of tooles' were held to be of particular value to the establishment, which promised to become 'a treasurie of infinit and unknow'n Valew' to the Commonwealth. The origin of such an idea (a perfect expression of Francis Bacon's empirical approach to the advancement of scientific learning) is attributed by the author to Charles I who, he adds, 'did designe that place for such an use'.[129] The precise nature of the relationship at Vauxhall between work carried out for the King and that executed for the Marquis of Worcester is now obscure.

In 1648 Worcester had been forced to take flight for Paris. A year later Vauxhall was first appraised and then exempted from sale, with a resolution that the Act for sale of the royal 'Honors, Manors and Lands' of 16 July 1649 'shall not extend unto the House called . . . Vaux-hall, nor to the Grounds, Houses, Buildings, Models, Utensils, or other necessaries for practical Inventions therein contained, or thereto belonging; but that they, and every of them, shall remain and continue for the use of the Commonwealth'.[130] With a further change of heart by Parliament,[131] however, Vauxhall was sold in 1652 to John Trenchard of Westminster, in whose custody the 'Goodes remainenge att: Vaux hall reserved from Sale by Order of the Parliament' were eventually inventoried. Apart from an entry for 'one stilling for beare', some planks and a trough, all are concerned with engineering and founding equipment to the value of £95. Presumably it was Trenchard who later obtained an order of Parliament requiring the Trustees to return certain goods from Denmark House to Vauxhall, arguing, perhaps, that they were essential assets of his newly acquired property and not removable goods.[132]

424-5 [1-12]

On returning from Paris in the same year the Marquis of Worcester was promptly committed to the Tower, but on his release two years later he immediately resurrected his plans for Vauxhall. Samuel Hartlib informed Robert Boyle in 1654 that Worcester was buying back the foundry from Trenchard 'to bestow the use of that house on Gaspar Calehof . . . for he intends to make it a College of Artisans'.[133]

The property reverted to the Crown at the Restoration, hence Lambert's petition to the King. Charles granted the plea, decreeing that Lambert should 'abide in and possess to our use at Ffoxhall aforesaid together with the outhousing and appurtenances of the same and there proceed in the work as he formerly hath done'.[134] The foundry was not to flourish, however, and neither did the 'College of Artisans' ever see the light of day. Following the death of the

Marquis of Worcester in 1667 the premises were turned over to the baking of sugar.[135]

Scotland Yard

In John Stow's *Survey* of 1599,[136] Scotland Yard in Westminster is described as

. . . a large plot of ground inclosed with bricke . . . called Scotland, where great building hath beene for receipt of the kinges of Scotland, and other estates of that Countrie; for *Margaret* Queene of Scots and systar to king *Henry* the eight had her abiding there, when shee came into England after the death of her husband, as kings of Scotland had in former times, when they came to the Parliament of England.

Stow's matter-of-fact account not only perpetuates a myth (generated, it seems, in support of fifteenth-century claims of superiority of the English Crown over that of Scotland) but elaborates it with sixteenth-century detail. 'Scottesland', however, was nothing more than a stretch of open ground when in 1519, ony six years after the death of Margaret's husband James IV at Flodden, it was granted to Wolsey for incorporation into the grounds of York Place (see p. 21).[137]

From the time that the Cardinal's palace entered the royal demesne in 1529, the character of Scotland Yard was already established as a service area, given over largely to the uses of the Works.[138] As well as warehouses, offices and yards, the Scotland Yard complex included a dock, first excavated in 1532 and later enlarged 'for the easye commyng in of bargies and lighters', and stabling for the Works horses. The entire yard was originally protected by a thorn hedge and a stake fence, replaced by a brick wall, it seems, by the time of Stow's description.[139] Not only were new materials stored here but also elements from buildings which had been demolished in the course of redevelopment and which

252-3 [73-85] might serve for further use: the entries relating to £128. 12s. 6d.-worth of raw materials and worked stone inventoried there appear to comprehend both categories.

Westminster Abbey

The Abbey features in the inventories as the place where the coronation regalia were stored (all other regalia being kept in the Jewel House at the Tower). As early as 2 June 1643 the Commons resolved 'that the Dean, Subdean and Prebends, be enjoined and required to deliver unto Sir *Hen. Mildmay*, and Mr *Marten*, the Keys of the Treasury where the regalia are kept; that they may search that Place, and report to the House what they find there'.[140] The following day, the House ordered that 'the Locks of the Doors, where the *Regalia* are kept, in *Westminster* Abbey, shall be opened . . . and new Locks set upon the Door; and nothing removed, till the House take further Order'.[141]

49-51 [1-13, 1-9] Much of the coronation regalia was to perish under the Commonwealth, as recorded elsewhere (p. 261). Perhaps no group of items in the inventories more forcefully conveys the sense of the ending of an era that must have hung over the dispersal of the King's goods: the King's and Queen's crowns to be delivered to the mint for rendering into coin; the sceptres and staves of office broken and defaced by order of Parliament; some part of the residue of vestments in silk, lace and cloth of gold estimated at £4. 10s., the remainder valued at nothing.

Notes

Professor Gerald Aylmer and Mr Howard Colvin kindly commented on this chapter in the course of its preparation.

1. *Acts and Ordinances* II, pp. 160-8.

2. Interspersed with orders for the defacement of 'superstitious and idolatrous monuments' and for the royal plate to be 'sold, pawned, melted down and converted into coin', are to be found orders from the Commons for the safeguarding of, for example, the contents of Denmark House and Whitehall in 1643 and 1644 (*Lords Journals* VI, pp. 181, 415), the King's robes, watches and cabinet at Whitehall in 1645 (*Commons Journals* IV, pp. 265-6) and the 'Books, Manuscripts, and other Antiquities' also at Whitehall in 1648 (*Commons Journals* V, p. 436; *Lords Journals* IX, p. 666).

3. While acknowledging that most of the goods and properties concerned belonged to the Crown and not to the persons of the King, Queen or Prince, the Act deemed it appropriate that proceeds from the sale should go towards settlement of the private debts of the royal family, as well as those incurred as household expenses, provided that the creditors themselves were not delinquents. Specific provision was made in the Act for reservation of the first £30,000 raised to form a loan 'for supply of the present uses of the Navy': although due to be repaid to the Treasurers for the sale by 1 May 1650, the £26,500 eventually loaned remained outstanding three years later, to the chagrin of the creditors: see *A Remonstrance, manifesting the lamentable miseries of the Creditors and Servants of the late King, Queen and Prince* (London, 1653) pp. 1-2. [A copy of this pamphlet is in the British Library (Thomason Tracts E 693, 13)].

4. *Acts and Ordinances* II, pp. 546-8.

5. *Remonstrance* (op. cit. Note 3), p. 3.

6. For this information, as for so much here, I am indebted to Sir Oliver Millar's introduction to his volume on *The Inventories and Valuations of the King's Goods 1649-1651* (Walpole Society 43) (1972), hereafter abbreviated to *Inventories*. See also G. E. Aylmer, *The State's Servants. The Civil Service of the English Republic 1649-1660* (London, 1973), p. 218.

7. W.L.F. Nuttall, 'King Charles I's pictures and the Commonwealth sale', *Apollo* 82 (1965), p. 302.

8. PRO, SP 25/16, 43.

9. See p. 15.

10. *Remonstrance* (op. cit. Note 3), p. 9.

11. *Commons Journals* VII, pp. 250-1. For a counter-petition by the Trustees and Contractors, dated 5 January 1654, see *CSP Domestic* 1653-4, p. 348. Aylmer (op. cit. (Note 6), p. 164) suggests that Beauchamp's only crime may have been to harbour certain royalist sympathies: at the Restoration he pleaded vigorously that he had helped to save some of the King's goods and to keep watch over the fate of others.

12. *CSP Domestic* 1654, p. 278.

13. *Inventories*, p. xvii. The manuscripts listed are as follows: PRO, LR2, 124; Corsham Court MS (in possession of Lord Methuen); PRO, SP 29/447, 300-3; Society of Antiquaries MS 108.

14. *Inventories*, p. xviii.

15. Ibid., pp. xxiii-xxiv.

16. The copy is that referred to as '. . . sold at Sotheby's, 6 [December] 1955 (402), bt. John Hewett'. It formed part of a collection of 'Books from the Library of Sir Robert Walpole at Houghton Hall, Norfolk, the property of the Most Hon. the Marquess of Cholmondeley'; the sale catalogue suggests that it may have been the copy which once belonged to George Vertue (Sotheby & Co., *Catalogue of Valuable Printed Books, Literary Manuscripts and Autograph Letters* (London, 1955), p. 57). The manuscript was acquired by Lord McAlpine in 1986.

17. *Inventories*, pp. xxvii-xxviii.

18. Ibid., p. xviii. An investigation carried out in 1656 revealed, however, that half of these goods were not then in use in the Commonwealth service (ibid., p. xix).

19. PRO, SP 25/63, 102, 396.

20. *Inventories*, p. xviii.

21. *Remonstrance* (op. cit. Note 3), pp. 3-4.

22. *Inventories*, p. xv.

23. Nuttall, op. cit. (Note 7), p. 302. On 26 November 1649 a payment of £40 was made to Daniel Norman, one of the Contractors, for expenses in removing 'the goods from the houses or places where they now are . . . to Somersett house' (*Inventories*, pp. xvi-xvii).

24. *CSP Domestic* 1654, p. 255.

25. Nuttall op. cit. (Note 7), p. 303. The more pragmatic might also have foreseen something of the reverses that were to occur at the Restoration, when the most strenuous efforts were made to recover former crown property.

26. *Remonstrance* (op. cit. Note 3), p. 2. Some of the most desperate cases were said to be reduced to starvation for want of bread, and their plight was exacerbated by the delays and loss of revenue occasioned by the reservation of goods by the Council (*CSP Domestic* 1654, p. 104).

27. *Remonstrance* (op. cit. Note 3), p. 2.

28. Nuttall (op. cit. (Note 7), p. 305) lists fourteen such syndicates and gives details of some major purchasers and creditors.

29. A large number of receipted warrants relating to payments made on authority of these lists survives in the Public Record Office (SP 28/282-5). A record of such payments (in money or goods, in full or in part) also survives (SP 18/123, 89-96), concluding with a list of twenty 'Persons especially recommended by His Highness, the Council or Members thereof'.

30. *Remonstrance* (op. cit. Note 3), p. 4.

31. Nuttall, op. cit. (Note 7), p.305.

32. *CSP Domestic* 1654, p. 278.

33. Bod. Lib., MS Rawlinson D 695, f. 12ᵛ. The list is in the handwriting of Elias Ashmole.

34. PRO, SP 28/350, 56.

35. Some new owners of pictures never even collected their property: many paintings remained in the royal galleries until formally repossessed by Charles II at the Restoration (A. Blunt and M. Whinney, *The Nation's Pictures* (London, 1950), p. 8.

36. H.G. Hewlett, 'Charles the First as a picture collector', *The Nineteenth Century* 28 (1890), p. 209.

37. A high point was reached at the beginning of James I's reign, when many members of the Scottish household were added to the existing English establishment: see N. Cuddy, 'The revival of the entourage: the Bedchamber of James I, 1603-1625', in D. Starkey (ed.), *The English Court from the Wars of the Roses to the Civil War* (London, 1987), p. 176.

38. G. Aylmer, *The King's Servants. The Civil Service of Charles I 1625-1642* (London, 1974), p. 27.

39. Ibid., p. 29.

40. Ibid., Table 58.

41. The organization was ultimately of Tudor origin, its duties and offices enshrined in the Eltham Ordinances of 1526. See further the various essays in Starkey, op. cit. (Note 37).

42. Apart from a diminished necessity to maintain order by the physical presence of the monarch in every corner of the realm, the sanitary arrangements which required periodic removal of the court to allow emptying of garderobe pits and airing of rooms became less pressing as water-cleansed conduits were introduced in many Stuart palaces (see *King's Works* IV, passim).

43. See p. 38 and Note 100. In one year (1622) James is recorded as moving from house to house no fewer than twenty times between 29 June and 13 September: see (R. Ashton (ed.), *James I by his Contemporaries* (London, 1969), pp. 247-8.

44. See Cuddy, op. cit. (Note 37), and K. Sharpe, 'The image of virtue: the court and household of Charles I, 1625-1642', in D. Starkey (ed.), *The English Court from the Wars of the Roses to the Civil War* (London, 1987), pp. 232-3. See also H.M. Baillie, 'Etiquette and planning of the state apartments in Baroque palaces', *Archaeologia* 101 (1967), pp. 169-80.

45. Cuddy, op. cit. (Note 37), pp. 177-95 passim,

46. BL., Lansdown MS 736 ('A Survey or Ground Plot of His Majesty's Palace of Whitehall'). The survey dates from the reign of Charles II, but as observed by Sharpe (op. cit. (Note 44), p. 229 n. 13), the household of the time bore a strong resemblance to that of Charles I.

47. Sharpe, op. cit. (Note 44), p.233

48. At Newmarket, for example, where shortage of accommodation must always have been a problem, it seems likely that the lodgings incorporated into the ends of the tennis court and over the stable and dog-house (*King's Works* IV, p. 176) would have been pressed into service on occasion for those whose social standing would elsewhere have guaranteed them more genteel surroundings.

49. For a summary of these trends see *King's Works* III, pp. 225-32.

50. A list of eight 'houses of access' or 'standing palaces', 'so called because each had its own standing complement of furniture, which was never moved from one house to another' (*King's Works* IV, pp. 28-9) omits Nonsuch but includes Eltham. Eltham, however, was judged by James I himself to be 'farre in decay' and 'not fitt for our abode' in 1603; plans for a complete restoration were drawn up and a certain amount of work was carried out (ibid., pp. 84-6), but by the end of James's reign many buildings were again in a state of collapse and an air of neglect hung over it (see also B. Fletcher, *Royal Homes near London* (London, 1930), p. 57-8). Certainly there are no goods from Eltham in the inventories.

51. For Thetford see H.F. Killick, 'The King's House at Thetford, with some acount of the visits of King James Ist to that town', *Norfolk Archaeology* 16 (1905-7), pp. 2-30.

52. *Statutes of the Realm*, 28 Henry VIII c. 12.

53. See E. Sheppard, *The Old Royal Palace of Whitehall* (London, 1902); *King's Works* IV, pp. 300-25. The palace of Westminster was extensively damaged by fire in 1512 and from 1530 was entirely supplanted by Whitehall as the principal royal residence, Westminster becoming instead the seat of Parliament and of the Exchequer. For an account of the palace see L.W. Cowie, 'The Old Palace of Westminster', *History Today* 24 (1974), pp. 542-9.

54. G.S. Dugdale (*Whitehall through the Centuries* (London, 1950), p. 30) compares the twenty-three acre site of Whitehall with the seven acres of Versailles and the thirteen and a half acres of the Vatican. A 'Survey or Ground Plot of His Majestys Palace of Whitehall' (BL, Lansdown MS 736) gives the following figures for accommodation at or pertaining to Whitehall: rooms, 1161; closets, 55; garrets, 75; cellars, 26; kitchens, 13; shops, 2.

55. Externally, Whitehall appeared as 'nothing more than an assemblage of several houses, badly built, at different times and for different purposes [with] nothing in its exterior from which you could suppose it to be the habitation of the king' (*Travels of Cosmo the Third, Grand Duke of Tuscany, through England, During the Reign of Charles II* (London, 1821), p. 367, the description dating from 1669).

56. *King's Works* IV, p. 304.

57. See J. A. Gotch, 'The original drawings for the palace at Whitehall, attributed to Inigo Jones', *Architectural Review* (June, 1912), pp. 1-32.

58. *The Weekly Intelligencer of the Commonwealth* no. 223 (14-21 March 1653/4), p. 179.

59. In 1653 a complaint arose that some statues assigned earlier to creditors still had not been released from the gardens at Whitehall: see *Remonstrance* (op. cit. Note 3), p. 4.

60. J. Stow, *A Survay of London* (London, 1598), p. 374.

61. On St. James's see E. Sheppard, *Memorials of St. James's Palace* (London, 1894); B, Graeme, *The Story of St. James's Palace* (London, 1929); *King's Works* IV, pp. 241-52.

62. According to Sir John Summerson (*Inigo Jones* (Harmondsworth, 1966), p. 81), this took the form of a colonnaded gallery parallel to the Orchard wall with grilles set in the openings, whose roof was cantilevered over the gardens to provide a sheltered area in which the King might ride in inclement weather.

63. *Commons Journals* IV, p. 270.

64. J. Harris, 'Somerset House, London', *Country Life* 142 (1967), pp. 1248-52, 1340-3.

65. This was the largest sum expended on any palace since the reign of Henry VIII (*King's Works* IV, pp. 252-7).

66. J. Nichols, *The Progresses, Processions, and Magnificent Festivities, of King James the First, his Royal Consort, Family and Court* (London, 1828), III, p. 253. There are some indications that the name had been applied to the house some years earlier, but the evidence is equivocal: see R. Needham and A. Webster, *Somerset House Past and Present* (London, 1905), p. 69.

67. *Commons Journals* III, p. 27. Here the attentions of the committee appointed 'concerning the Removal of the Capuchins' were directed not only to the 'superstitious and idolatrous monuments' but also to 'the great Quantities of Beads, Crucifixes and other Superstitious Books and Pictures' to be found in the friars' quarters.

68. Ibid. IV, p. 270.

69. An order survives to the effect that the Lord General and his officers should 'forbear coming to Somerset House until the goods are sold, there being need to use [the rooms] for shewing the goods' (Needham and Webster, op. cit. (Note 66), p. 127).

70. For Greenwich see G.H. Chettle, *The Queen's House, Greenwich* (London Survey XIV) (London, 1937); Fletcher, op. cit. (Note 50), pp. 63-88; R.K. Dickson, *Greenwich Palace* (Greenwich, 1939); *King's Works* IV, pp. 96-123.

71. Work was suspended on the building on 30 April 1618 and was not completed until 1635, when it was occupied by Henrietta Maria.

72. *The Diary of John Evelyn* (ed. E.S. de Beer) (Oxford, 1955), II, 30 March 1652.

73. For Hampton Court see E. Law, *The History of Hampton Court Palace* II *Stuart Times* (London, 1888); *King's Works* IV, pp. 126-46; *VCH Middlesex* II, pp. 322-86. On the elaborate system devised to supply water to Wolsey's palace see J.W. Lindus Forge, 'Coombe Hill conduit houses and the water supply system of Hampton Court Palace', *Surrey Archaeological Collections* 56 (1959), pp. 3-14.

74. *King's Works* IV, pp. 144-5.

75. For Richmond Palace see *King's Works* IV, pp. 222-33; W.H. Hart, 'The Parliamentary surveys of Richmond, Wimbledon, and Nonsuch, in the County of Surrey, AD 1649', *Surrey Archaeological Collections* 5 (1871), pp. 76-103.

76. PRO, E 317 Surrey 37.

77. Hart, op. cit. (Note 75), pp. 142-56; *King's Works* IV, pp. 179-205. Particularly useful for Nonsuch is J. Dent, *The Quest for Nonsuch* (London, 1962), which includes some account of the extensive excavations carried out there in 1959-60.

78. Pepys (*The Diary of Samuel Pepys* (eds. R. Latham and W. Matthews) (London, 1972), 21 September 1665) further alludes to 'all the house on the outside filled with figures of story, and good painting of Rubens or Holben's doing,' but no confirmatory evidence exists for this statement.

79. In 1624 John de Critz, sergeant-painter, repainted ninety-one such beasts on the battlements and on the roof of the banqueting house (*King's Works* IV, p. 204).

80. PRO, E 317 Surrey 39-41.

81. For Oatlands see S.W. Kershaw, 'Oatlands in Weybridge', *Journal of the British Archaeological Association* new ser. 9 (1903), pp. 182-90; J.W. Lindus Forge, *Oatlands Palace* (Walton and Weybridge Historical Society Paper 1) (1966); Fletcher, op. cit. (Note 50), pp. 141-6; *King's Works* IV, pp. 206-17.

82. J. Summerson, *Architecture in Britain 1530-1830* (London, 1953), p. 39.

83. Hart, op. cit. (Note 75), pp. 104-42. See also *VCH Surrey* IV, p. 122.

84. J. Summerson, 'The building of Theobalds, 1564-1585', *Archaeologia* 97 (1959), pp. 107-26. Other sources for Theobalds used here are *VCH Hertfordshire* III, pp. 447-50; *King's Works* IV, pp. 273-8.

85. F. Peck, *Desiderata Curiosa* (London, 1732), I, *Lib.* I, p. 34.

86. J. Stow, *The Annales of England* (London, 1605), p. 1414.

87. Nichols, op. cit. (Note 66), II, pp. 72-3.

88. M. Phillips, 'Theobalds park wall', *Transactions of the East Herts Archaeological Society* 5 (1912-14), pp. 248-62.

89. PRO, E 317 Hertfordshire 26.

90. M. Girouard, 'Elizabethan Holdenby', *Country Life* 166 (1979), pp. 1286-9, 1398-1401, especially p. 1289.

91. The principal sources quoted here are A. Hartshorne, 'Holdenby, Northamptonshire; its manors, church and house', *Archaeological Journal* 65 (1908), pp. 90-120; *King's Works* IV, pp. 153-4.

92. J. Norden, *Speculi Britanniae, or a Delineation of Northamptonshire* (London, 1720), p. 51.

93. T. Herbert, *Memoirs of the Two last Years of the Reign of . . . King Charles I* (London, 1702), p. 11.

94. PRO, E 317 Northamptonshire 35.

95. *VCH Worcestershire* IV, p. 311. Also used in this account is J.R. Burton, *A History of Bewdley* (London, 1883).

96. PRO, E 317 Worcestershire 1.

97. *King's Works* IV, pp. 349-55. I have also made use here of the text of *VCH Oxfordshire* XII (forthcoming), and acknowledge the kindness of Dr Alan Crossley in making this available to me in advance of publication.

98. PRO, E 317 Oxfordshire 12.

99. J. Beldam, 'Royston Court House and its appurtenances', *Archaeologia* 40 (1866), p. 121. Apart from Beldam's paper, which includes a conjectural plan of the entire complex, the most useful sources are *VCH Hertfordshire* III, pp. 256-8, and *King's Works* IV, pp. 237-8.

100. We hear of James setting out for Royston on 14 January 1613 with a 'small train of forty persons', perhaps his accustomed entourage for such an excursion (*CSP Domestic* 1611-18, p. 167).

101. Nichols, op. cit. (Note 66), I, p. 495. The other principal sources used here are G.B. Mead, 'An account of the visits of King James I to Newmarket', *Cambridge Antiquarian Communications* 14 (1864), pp. 295-326; *King's Works* IV, pp. 175-9.

102. W. St. John Hope, *Windsor Castle. An Architectural History* (London, 1913), pp. 291-5. Also used here is *VCH Berkshire* III, pp. 5-19.

103. T. Hyde, Earl of Clarendon, *The History of the Rebellion and Civil Wars in England, begun in the Year 1641* (Oxford, 1702-4), I, p. 302.

104. *Commons Journals* III, p. 348. See also J.R. Tighe and J.E. Davis, *Annals of Windsor* (published privately, 1858), pp. 242-3.

105. Clarendon, op. cit. (Note 103), III, p. 199.

106. Ibid., III, p. 200. See also Tighe and Davis, op. cit. (Note 104), pp. 256-7.

107. Stow, op. cit. (Note 60), p. 46.

108. *King's Works* IV, pp. 265-9. See also D. Wilson, *The Tower 1078-1978* (London, 1978), passim; M. Holmes and H.D.W. Sitwell, *The English Regalia* (London, 1972), pp. 49-54.

109. The coronation regalia were kept separately, and stored at Westminster Abbey (see p. 49).

110. Nichols, op. cit. (Note 66), II, p. 78.

111. *VCH Hampshire and the Isle of Wight* V, pp. 222-5, 347-51.

112. J.H. Harvey, 'Side-lights on Kenilworth Castle', *Archaeological Journal* 101 (1944), p. 106. Other sources used here include W. Dugdale, *Antiquities of Warwickshire* (London, 1656), pp. 167-8; *VCH Warwickshire* VI, pp. 135-8; *King's Works* III, pp. 258-60.

113. See W. St. John Hope, 'The castle of Ludlow', *Archaeologia* 61 (1908), pp. 257-328; *King's Works* III, pp. 277-82.

114. See S.J. Madge, 'Worcester House in the Strand', *Archaeologia* 91 (1945), pp. 157-80.

115. J. Stow, *A Survay of London*, new edn. (London, 1603), p. 449.

116. PRO, SP 19/91, 1, reprinted in Madge, op. cit. (Note 114), pp. 170-80.

117. *CSP Domestic* 1656-7, p. 133.

118. See T.N. Brushfield, 'Britain's Burse or the New Exchange', *Journal of the British Archaeological Association* new ser. 9 (1903), pp. 33-48.

119. Reproduced in H.B. Wheatley, 'Original plan of Durham House and grounds, 1626', *London Topographical Record* 10 (1916), pp. 150-61.

120. C. Pendrill, *The Adelphi, or Old Durham House in the Strand* (London, 1934), p. 72.

121. *Commons Journals* VI, p. 371.

122. See R. Batho, 'Henry, Ninth Earl of Northumberland and Syon House, Middlesex, 1594-1632', *Transactions of the Ancient Monuments Society* new ser. 4 (1956), pp. 95-109; *VCH Middlesex* III, pp. 97-9; *King's Works* IV, p. 272.

123. *Seventh Report of the Royal Commission on Historical Manuscripts* pt. 1 (London, 1879), p. 594. See also *Commons Journals* IV, p. 270, where the resolution is recorded that the 'respective officers . . . shall deliver such Hangings, Plate, Silver Vessel, or such other necessary and fitting Accommodations, as [the Earl of Northumberland] shall require, for the Use of the King's children.'

124. J.E. Anderson, *A Short History of the Tapestry Works, Mortlake* (published privately, 1894); G.L. Hunter, *Tapestries, their Origin, History and Renaissance* (London, 1912), pp. 105-17; W.G. Thomson, *A History of Tapestry* 3rd. edn. (Wakefield, 1973), pp. 277-312.

125. PRO, E 317 Surrey 37.

126. PRO, SP 25/62, 547.

127. The inventory is reproduced by W.H. Thorpe, 'The Marquis of Worcester and Vauxhall', *Newcomen Society Transactions* 13 (1932-3), pp. 80-86.

128. *CSP Domestic* 1665-6, p. 153. For the Marquis of Worcester see H. Dircks, *The Life, Times and Scientific Labours of the Second Marquis of Worcester* (London, 1865).

129. Royal Society, Boyle Letters VII, 1. I am grateful to the President and Council of the Royal Society for allowing me access to this letter. The authorship of the original text transcribed by Hartlib has been variously attributed, most recently to John Dury (C. Webster, *The Great Instauration. Science, Medicine and Reform 1626-1660* (London, 1975), pp. 364-5). See also J.J. O'Brien, 'Commonwealth schemes for the advancement of learning', *British Journal of Educational Studies* 16 (1968), pp. 34-5.

130. *Acts and Ordinances* II, p. 190.

131. *Acts and Ordinances* II, p. 692.

132. *Remonstrance*, (op. cit. Note 3), p. 6. The goods in question are valued there at 'about £200', and the author of the pamphlet expresses the hope that they may be 'kept safe for the poor Creditors'.

133. For a recent discussion of some elements of the proposed college see A. MacGregor, ' "A magazin of all manner of inventions": museums in the quest for "Salomon's House" in seventeenth-century England', *Journal of the History of Collections* 1 (1989), pp. 207-12.

134. PRO, SP 29/142, 138.1.

135. C. ffoulkes (*The Gun-Founders of England* (Cambridge, 1937), p. 54) speculates that the Marquis may have died in the mansion at Vauxhall, where many of his ideas had been formulated.

136. Stow, op. cit. (Note 60), p. 374.

137. See G. Eborn, 'Scotland Yard and the Palace of Westminster', *Journal of the London Society* no. 400 (1975), pp. 11-19.

138. A plan of the area as it was in James I's time, compiled by G.P.V. Akrigg (*Jacobean Pageant, or the Court of King James* (London, 1962), p. 282 and plan following p. 398), indicates that a number of domestic offices (scalding house, spicery and bakehouse) were also located here, as were various living quarters for the Household.

139. *King's Works* IV, pp. 310, 317.

140. *Commons Journals* III, p. 112.

141. Ibid., p. 114.

2 Charles I and the Tradition of European Princely Collecting

Ronald Lightbown

Marginal numerals refer to page and entry numbers in the *Inventories* (see p. 11)

The collections of Charles I were at once a compound and culmination of European royal traditions of collecting and patronage. In the sixteenth century there had been a metamorphosis in the attitude of kings and princes to the arts. In general medieval kings and princes had collected only jewels and goldsmith's work and rich textiles, as a treasury of *jocalia* or precious things. These might also include objects of great curiosity or rarity – unicorn horns, carved ivory oliphants or hunting horns, gold cups that had belonged to Charlemagne or to St. Louis. As they were knights, they also collected ancient weapons that appealed to their sense of chivalric romance or heroism. The Emperor Henry VI sent King Richard I of England in 1194 the sword of Tristram; Henry III, Richard's nephew, owned Curtana, the sword of Ogier the Dane. In Spain the Kings of Castile were the proud possessors of Tizona and Colada, the swords of the Cid, and of La Lobera, the sword of St. Ferdinand, while the Kings of France believed themselves to own Joyeuse, the sword of Charlemagne himself. As for the Roman heroes of antiquity, Duke Philip the Bold of Burgundy owned at his death in 1404 a great silver-gilt cup 'which belonged to Julius Caesar'.[1]

This tradition was to persist to the end of the Middle Ages and into Renaissance and Baroque times. In 1499 the armoury of the French royal château of Amboise contained a collection of ancient arms and armour 'which of all time have been kept and caused to be kept by defunct kings until this present time'. It included an enchanted sword, said to have belonged to Lancelot of the Lake, the dagger of Charlemagne, and swords that had been the property of St. Louis, of Philippe le Bel, and of King Jean le Bon, as well as one once owned by a mythical king who had slain a giant on the island of Notre-Dame at Paris. There was an axe that had belonged to Clovis, and one that had belonged to Bertrand du Guesclin and a suit of armour worn by Joan of Arc.[2]

Renaissance tastes were less for fabled arms of chivalry and romance, which the age was not so credulous in accepting, and more for the arms and armour of kings and princes and great generals, or for richly ornamented weapons and armour, European or exotic. About 1600 the Medici maintained a special room off their *Galleria* in Florence as a 'sala dell' armi', in which were collected 'the ancient offensive and defensive arms of all nations, and those modern ones that are of exquisite fashion, even from the New World and India, and the finest Persian weapons of steel for infantry and cavalry'.[3] The same taste is found in Charles I's collections. He had a variety of arms. Some were exotic, like his scimitars, perhaps of oriental origin (see pp. 356-7) and supplied with rich silver-mounted scabbards of red velvet; others were antiquities or believed to be such, like 'One Ancient sword in a blacke scabberd', or 'A Saxon kings Mace used in War, wᵗʰ A Ball full of Spikes & the handle Coverd wᵗʰ gold plates and Ennamelled' or 'A Grecian Helmett of Steele, Upon the Topp A Dragon, of Silver gilt'. Some were rich, like a gorget of massy gold chased with a battle scene.

The collecting of pieces of goldsmith's work on a large scale as works of art as well as for use and display begins with the four great Valois princes of the later fourteenth century, all sons of King Jean le Bon of France: Charles V, Louis of Anjou, Jean, Duc de Berry and Philippe the Good of Burgundy. In his exclusive accumulation of wrought plate of gold and silver Louis of Anjou represents what may perhaps be described as a purely medieval taste in collecting; this is also true of his brothers King Charles and Duke Philippe, who were less truly connoisseurs of fine workmanship than Louis and his other brother Jean. It was the collections of Jean that set a pattern for future royal and princely collecting. A characteristic of Jean's taste was a passionate interest in precious stones and hardstone rather than in wrought plate, and in virtuoso techniques, such as the cutting and shaping of stone to make cameo portraits or naturalistic forms. In this he anticipates the tastes of the virtuoso princes of the Renaissance. He also had proto-humanist tastes, for he bought classical coins and medals, or what he believed to be classical coins and medals.[4]

With René of Anjou (1408-80), the great-nephew of these princes, we come to the first medieval king who seems to have practised the arts and worked in their

382-3 [780-87]

383 [797]
431 [73]

431 [76]
431 [75]

techniques, again strangely anticipating the virtuoso princes of the Italian Renaissance. There appears to be some evidence that he painted, and he certainly took a personal interest in goldsmith's work, for in a 'petite chambre' attached to his 'hault retrait' in his château of Angers was a complete goldsmith's workshop, with two furnaces, a lathe, a steel anvil and a goldmsith's bench set out with hammers and pincers. It is difficult now to realize the departure that such interests represented from the rigid conventions of the Middle Ages, by which the arts were divided into those that were liberal and those that were mechanical, and the mechanical arts were regarded with disdain because they involved manual work. Edward II of England had been heartily despised in early fourteenth-century England because of a taste for digging, carpentry, and gardening, and these attitudes to manual work on the part of the great were to persist for many centuries. René's 'petite chambre' is also the ancestor of the Renaissance court workshop, established within or close to the apartments of the prince himself.[5]

The collecting of arms and armour and the commissioning or purchase of rich pieces of goldsmith's work were to remain typical royal and princely tastes into the Baroque age. The Renaissance, however, greatly enlarged the range of what kings and princes collected and introduced a new spirit of scholarly antiquarianism into their collections. The characteristic Renaissance and Baroque taste for collecting antique coins and medals first appears in Verona, Venice, Padua and other cities of the Veneto. It was here too that the first important collections were formed of small antique bronzes, largely by great ecclesiastics. Collections of ancient gems and cameos were by contrast no novelty, for these had been eagerly sought for by kings and princes throughout the Middle Ages. But what was new was the humanist spirit in which they were now collected, as evidence for all aspects of antique history, life, culture and religion. It became the fashion during the later fifteenth century to furnish a *studio* or room for retreat and study with works of art of all kinds, both modern and antique. The first princely *studio* of which we have certain knowledge is that of the Marchese Lionello d'Este at Ferrara; the first of whose contents we have detailed knowledge is the celebrated *studiolo* of the Marchesa Isabella d'Este at Mantua. This came to be decorated with paintings by Mantegna, Perugino, Costa, and Correggio: its principal ornaments were two famous sleeping Cupids of marble, one attributed to Praxiteles, the other by Michelangelo, antique marble heads and other antique sculptures, and antique bronzes.[6]

By the end of the sixteenth century the term *studio* had come to mean more or less a collection: thus in 1621 Duke Ferdinando Gonzaga was in treaty for the 'studio' of a Roman canon named Pasqualini.[7] The *studiolo* of Cosimo I de' Medici in the Palazzo Vecchio, Florence, contained, according to Vasari, 'great numbers of ancient statues, of marbles and bronzes and small modern paintings, very rare miniatures and an infinity of medals of gold, silver and bronze most beautifully ordered'.[8] The *studio* was undoubtedly the origin of the seventeenth-century princely cabinet, in which paintings, antique sculptures, modern and ancient bronzes were gathered together, not so much as room decorations, but as works of art or rarities or curiosities, to be appreciated in an intimate setting for their superlative beauty or interest. The origins of the Northern cabinet have not been traced like those of the Italian *studio* but it seems possible that François I was already forming one in the 1520s.

The history of royal and princely collecting in the sixteenth century is in many ways the history of how the tastes of lettered humanists, partly clerical, partly lay, became the tastes of the great. Indeed this development was probably the consequence of the humanist doctrine that learning and the arts expel the vices of ignorance and idleness and are necessary adjuncts of nobility. There was also a majestic model from antiquity for royal and imperial collecting, for no less an emperor than Augustus was recorded by Suetonius as having collected curiosities – 'giants' bones' – and arms and armour that had belonged to heroes, in preference even to statues and pictures.[9] The first court north of the Alps to be strongly affected by Italian Renaissance tastes and styles was that of King Matthias Corvinus of Hungary (ruled 1458-90). Matthias appears to have been more of a pure patron than a collector, if we define a pure patron as one who primarily commissions works of art directly from artists and is not so concerned with assembling them by miscellaneous purchase. Possibly then the first royal collector to import the tastes in art of the Italian Renaissance north of the Alps was François I of France. According to Henry Peacham, writing in 1622, François was himself an amateur artist, being 'very excellent with his pencill', as was his sister Queen Marguerite of Navarre.[10] François was in many ways the prototype of the royal Renaissance patron and collector, both in his appetite for works of art of all kinds, and in the scale and lavishness with which he collected.

Already in late fifteenth-century Italy the Popes had imposed an embargo on the export of antique sculptures from Rome, and whenever they appeared on the market they were extremely costly. Even princely Italian collectors found themselves obliged to be satisfied with the plaster casts from the antique that artists had already been making for their own use in the 1450s.[11] The plaster casts of antique sculptures that François I imported from Rome for Fontainebleau were of course for casting in bronze to form decorations for the palace gardens.[12] This is a famous episode in the history of Renaissance art: less well known is the fact that François as early as 1529 had a cabinet in the Louvre containing exotic curiosities. Two of these, a bed-frame and chair inlaid with foliage in mother-of-pearl 'which had been made in the country of India', he bought from a French merchant living in Portugal. From the time of the great voyages of the 1490s which led to the discovery of America and of the sea-route to the East Indies, such things began to enter European collections though always remaining rare enough to be very highly prized. Again the inventory of Fontainebleau in 1540 lists 'a little box of ebony marquetried with mother-of-pearl, work of the Indies, on three jasper balls'.[13]

François also imported a long line of Italian artists to work for him in the most modern of Renaissance styles, as these styles rapidly succeeded each other during the swift evolution of Italian art in the first four decades of the sixteenth century. Early in his reign he took into his service Leonardo da Vinci, whose manner in painting was the most revolutionary of its day: in its latest decades, the 1530s and 1540s, he was employing artists like Rosso, Primaticcio and Benvenuto Cellini, who were working in highly advanced and sophisticated Mannerist styles. It was François's great *galerie* of Fontainebleau, now known as the Galerie François Ier, and the two other great *galeries* of the same palace, the Galerie Henri II and the Galerie d'Ulysse (1540-50) that were to be the inspiration of the architectural form of the *Galleria* of Florence, the first great princely gallery in our sense of the word.[14]

In England Henry VIII, François's neighbour and rival, attempted to vie with the brilliance of the French court by summoning artists from Florence and also from the North. As is well known, he succeeded in obtaining the services of two major artists, Pietro Torrigiani and Holbein, one Italian, one Northern. This duality of taste was to remain characteristic of the English court: in place of an exclusive admiration of Italian Renaissance art, an equal enthusiasm, even it may fairly be said, an intimate preference, was felt for the Northern Renaissance. It still appears in Charles I and Thomas Howard, Earl of Arundel, conscious though they were of the Italian Baroque, and is perhaps typical of the collectors of the Northern world of Germany, the Netherlands, England and Scandinavia, for we find the same enthusiasm for Dürer and Holbein even in a late sixteenth-century collector so greatly influenced by Italy as the Emperor Rudolf II.

With the universal triumph of Renaissance over Gothic taste Italy became the prime source from which Northern princes sought to obtain both antique works of art – sculptures, gems and medals – and modern ones – pictures, crystal caskets and other works in crystal and hardstones. This demand produced two curious sixteenth-century types, the antiquary who was at once a connoisseur and a dealer, and the merchant who dealt in pictures and works of art. The second type, as might be expected, preceded the first, and both, again as might be expected, found a natural home in Venice. Venetian merchants had travelled for centuries the courts of Northern Europe selling precious goldsmith's work and jewellery: indeed some had found their traffic with the fourteenth-century French court in works of art of this kind so lucrative that they had settled in Paris. Accordingly Venetian dealing in the new kinds of works of art demanded by Renaissance taste was only a natural extension of a long tradition. The correspondence of Isabella d'Este in the early sixteenth century is a rich source of information on what was in the hands of dealers in Venice.[15] In 1506 for instance, she was in pursuit of a painting of the *Passage of the Red Sea* attributed to Jan van Eyck and of an antique agate vase, both belonging to a Venetian dealer named Michele Vianello. On Vianello's death in the spring of that year, Isabella instructed her agents to bid for them at the sale of his effects by auction.[16] Fifty years later Cosimo I of Florence bought a large part of his admired collection of medals from a Jew of Venice named Jacobillo.

The representative antiquary-dealer of the sixteenth century was un-doubtedly Jacopo Strada (1507-88) whose portrait by Titian, painted in 1568, is now in the Kunsthistorisches Museum, Vienna.[17] Strada, who was probably of Flemish descent, was born in Mantua and trained as a goldsmith. In the course of practising his art he would almost certainly have dealt in gems and medals, and early in the 1540s he entered the service of the Fuggers, the great bankers of Augsburg, as their agent for the purchase of antique medals and sculptures in Italy. From 1546 he lived in Nuremberg, working in some sort of association with the great goldsmith Wenzel Jamnitzer, becoming in 1549 a citizen of the town. But he plainly aspired to greater things, and after compiling a treatise on classical medals, left in 1552 for Lyons, then a great international publishing centre, to see to its publication in 1553. After a second Italian purchasing mission for the Fuggers in 1556, he moved in 1558 to Vienna, where he was eventually taken into the service of the Habsburg court.[18] He was greatly valued there as an adviser on matters of art, and by 1565 his reputation as an antiquary was so great that the Emperor Maximilian lent him to Duke Albrecht V of Bavaria, so that he could give his advice on the design of the famous *Antiquarium* of the ducal palace. This was a special building (still surviving, though restored after war-damage) in which the Duke intended to house his existing collection and future acquisitions of classical antiquities.[19] It was actually begun in 1568, and was adjacent to the new *Kunstkammer*, built above the ducal stables. The antique sculptures were housed in a gallery on the ground floor, while the upper floor housed the new court library. In 1567 Albrecht sent Strada to Italy to make fresh purchases, especially in Rome and Venice. His judgment was sometimes questioned by his contemporaries; but he certainly had useful connections in the Venetian dealing world, and succeeded in making purchases from prime collections such as that of Cardinal Bembo, whose son Torquato sold him a number of pieces, though he had inherited them only on the understanding that they were never to be alienated.

Strada was also in touch with dealers like Niccolò Stoppio,[20] whose network of connections extended from Titian to the Duke of Bavaria. Stoppio trafficked in precious works of art, such as a casket of crystal and silver gilt that had belonged to Carlo della Serpa, a former chamberlain of Pope Julius, was later transferred to Titian, and finally sold to the Duke of Bavaria. In 1567 Strada was appointed Imperial Court Antiquary, and he remained in Imperial service until his death. The feverish pursuit of works of art by princes through such agents and speculators and dealers is richly documented in the later sixteenth and seventeenth centuries. Thus the Medici Grand Dukes made much use of the Florentine virtuoso Niccolò Gaddi for their incessant purchases of antique sculptures and other works of art in Rome. Another notable intermediary of the kind was the Augsburg *marchand amateur*, Philipp Hainhofer, who advised among others Duke Philip of Pomerania and Gustavus Adolphus of Sweden in the early seventeenth century.[21]

Ambassadors also played an important role in commissioning works of art for princes or bringing possible acquisitions to their notice and negotiating sales. In the late Renaissance they were often men of high cultivation, like Henry Wotton, for eloquence in speech and writing were still indispensable in diplomacy. The correspondence of Dudley Carleton, himself a collector, as English ambassador to the States General from 1616 shows how busily he was employed from England by various court patrons in negotiating with Rubens and other artists, and in the purchase of pictures and works of art. Figures like Daniel Nys, the French merchant settled in Venice who turned art-dealer and bought the Gonzaga collections for Charles I, or Balthasar Gerbier or the musician Nicholas Lanier (Pl. 3), who travelled in the Netherlands and Italy looking out for pictures and works of art for Charles I and Buckingham were operators of a long-established kind. Their advice and expertise lay behind a number of Charles's acquisitions, and a very busy world of traffic and speculation in works of art, ready-made, antique, or executed to commission, is disclosed by their correspondence.[22]

A novel direction was given to princely patronage and collecting with the appearance of the virtuoso prince, who himself carried out or promoted experiments to discover the secrets of nature and to explore or to improve the techniques of the arts. The virtuoso prince is first known to us in Italy, and Michael Vickers has suggested that the model for what in Italy too was a departure from rigid aristocratic prejudice against the mechanical arts was the example of such Hellenistic monarchs as Attalus of Pergamum, who is recorded as having invented a technique of interweaving gold in cloth.[23] The earliest virtuoso prince of the Renaissance appears to have been Alfonso I d'Este, Duke of Ferrara from 1505 to 1534, who set on foot a court workshop or pottery in his private apartments in the Castello of Ferrara. In this, researches were conducted into the secret of the manufacture of Chinese porcelain, long a perplexing mystery to the European virtuoso, and also into the means of improving maiolica glazes. The philosophy of all such investigations by princes into the secrets of the arts was well expressed c.1558 by Cipriano Piccolpasso, the author of the only Renaissance Italian treatise on the art of the potter, in his prologue to that now famous work. He explains that he is divulging the secrets individual master-potters have so jealously guarded so that they may escape from 'persons of small account' and 'circulate in courts, among lofty spirits and speculative minds'. Alfonso was also passionately interested in the art of founding cannon, and indeed appears leaning on one of his own cannon in a famous portrait by Titian.[24]

Emmanuele Filiberto, Duke of Savoy (ruled 1559-80) was another prince who was expert in the casting of artillery, and who assembled excellent masters and craftsmen of various kinds in workshops close to his palace 'where his Highness visited them at least once every day and worked now in one and now in another of those workshops', being extraordinarily expert in making the wheels of arquebuses after several fashions.[25] Henry Peacham cites him in *The Compleat Gentleman* in 1622 as a great prince 'who could draw and limne excellently'. But the chief virtuoso princes of the later Renaissance were undoubtedly the Medici Grand Dukes of Tuscany. The famous *studiolo* that Francesco I de' Medici made for himself in Palazzo Vecchio in Florence, with its paintings and bronzes celebrating the investigation of the occult secrets of nature has perhaps rather too much obscured the fact that the grand originator of the tradition was his father Cosimo. Piccolpasso writes of Cosimo:

he assembled men of worth, excellence and knowledge in all exercises...and not content with this, was willing to labour with his own hands in the fashion of a master craftsman, now working with the hammer, now printing, sometimes sculpting, now being a carpenter in artillery works; often a founder at the furnace, or alloying metals to see if bronze came out as a soft or hard alloy, or with his own hand making counterfeit stones and jewels to discover the deceits so many practise, or compounding remedies against poison, and most singular unguents for all sicknesses.

Among his other ventures Cosimo conducted experiments to discover a recipe for tempering chisels to sufficient hardness to make large-scale works in porphyry, a secret lost since antiquity. He succeeded in 1555, so founding a school of Florentine porphyry-workers. It was his custom to spend some part of every day in his workshops on these and similar tasks.[26]

Medici patronage of such investigations led to the conception by Cosimo during the 1560s of a grandiose princely mausoleum, later known as the Cappella dei Principi, to be erected in San Lorenzo with walls decorated internally with coloured marbles. Eventually this and other projects were to inspire the establishment of palace workshops collectively known as the Galleria de' Lavori, on the first floor of the Uffizi. Francesco de' Medici (ruled 1574-87), Cosimo's son, initiated them by gathering artists and craftsmen together in his newly rebuilt garden palace known as the Casino di San Marco, where jewellers, hardstone-carvers, makers of *pietra dura* and porcelain all worked side by side. It was also Francesco who began building in the Uffizi, constructed to serve as state tribunals and offices by his father, the great *Galleria*. Seemingly the first of its kind, this was intended to house the Medici collection of marbles. He also created in 1584 the famous *Tribuna*, a round room off the *Galleria*, with a dome of mother-of-pearl set in red lacquer, especially to house the choicest treasures of the collection. The word *galleria* was not in fact Italian, but was borrowed from the French, and Francesco's inspiration, as already noted, was probably the great *galeries* of Fontainebleau.[27]

The existence of the Medici workshops was first officially recognized in letters patent issued on 3 September 1588, the second year of his reign, by Francesco I's son the Grand Duke Ferdinando I. These letters appointed a superintendent of all the artists and craftsmen who were employed in the *Galleria*: 'jewellers, and engravers and carvers of every sort, cosmographers, goldsmiths, illuminators, gardeners and turners, sweetmeat-makers, distillers, artificers of porcelain, sculptors, and painters, and crystal-makers'.[28] New forms of art emerged from all this ferment of workmanship, notably the imitations of Chinese porcelain known as Medici porcelain and more durable and important, the making of reliefs in the mosaic technique known as *pietra dura*, in which semi-precious hardstones were largely employed. *Pietra dura* was to remain the Florentine court art *par excellence* for centuries and all the Medici took the keenest interest in improving its range and technique.[29] In 1601 Ferdinando I made a present to a Florentine virtuoso of a portrait of Pope Clement VIII in *pietra dura*, explaining proudly that the art of representing flesh tints in their proper colours as displayed in this portrait was his own invention.[30] The institution of the *Galleria* set up on a new footing, as a permanent establishment, what had before been a much more temporary form of patronage, in which princes with a taste for the arts, like Jean de Berry, surrounded themselves with artists and craftsmen of all kinds, at their own choice. This type of patronage, lasting no longer than the lifetime of the prince, was still to continue, indeed was to be that of Charles I, but it was to Florence and its *Galleria* that Colbert and Louis XIV were to look on setting up in the 'logements du Louvre' a French version of permanent royal patronage of the various arts.

The *Galleria* quickly became the draw to travellers and grand tourists that it has remained ever since. A description by Filippo Pigafetta *c*.1600 shows that the walls were hung with portraits of the Medici, living and dead. Above these, on the right, hung portraits of popes, of cardinals, of famous theologians and of writers on war, on the sciences, and on the arts, and of famous authors. On the left hung portraits of emperors, kings and princes, and of great generals and admirals. In front of these, along the floor, stood antique marbles and statues by Michelangelo and other famous modern sculptors. The *Tribuna* had walls lined with silk, studded with gold and silver. In the centre was a collection of Greek and Roman medals in an elaborate *tempietto*, while other precious works of art, ancient and modern, were ranged round the walls which were hung with precious paintings.[31]

The *studiolo* of Francesco I was known quite early in England. In 1594 the Elizabethan traveller Fynes Moryson describes its decorations and contents as

most faire pictures; two chests of Christall guilded over; divers statuas, not of brasse, but of mixt metals, shining here like silver, there like gold; a cup of Amber, a little Mountaine of pearles, wrought together by the hands of Duke Francis; a Pyramis of Pearles as they grow in oyster-shels; two knives set with Jewels, and a third Indian knife; a naile halfe turned into gold by Tomeser an Alchumist, the other part still remaining Iron; a piece of gold unpolished, as it was digged out of the Mines; two pictures of Flemings...a clock of Amber; a piece of Amber falling upon a Lizard, and retaining the lively forme thereof; a stone called Vergoara that cureth poyson; the head of a Turke all of pure gold; a most beautifull head of a Turkish woman; a Table of gold, and of Jasper stone, and other Jewells.

He also mentions a table in *pietra dura* which he saw in the Uffizi, still unfinished.[32]

In 1638 the young sculptor Nicholas Stone, son of the elder Nicholas, sculptor and master Mason to Charles I, made a few notes on the Florentine *Galleria*, into which he had hoped to be admitted in order to learn the art of making *pietra dura*. He found that the Grand Duke Ferdinando II 'would give no leave for the learning of inlayd worke in the gallery, but for to coppy the paintings and draw after the statues was free leave'. So jealously was *pietra dura* guarded as a court art. All Stone could do was admire such works in it as a table in a cabinet of the Uffizi 'of branches of honeysuckles, olives and other spriges, so curiously inlayd of precious stones y[t] itt doth almost deceive the eye to be naturall, being the best that ever was made'. And in 'one of the lapidaryes shopps' of the *Galleria* he also saw and admired '(being the best of them all) a Charytye of jasper relieue, the naked of a fleshy couleur, the drapery part of yellow and part of blew, very industriously done'. Nevertheless the persistent Stone, in spite of Ferdinando's refusal, found a Signor Serragli who was prepared to 'speake with [him]...concerning inlaying; after I had spoke with him he sent his man with me to a shopp to se the worke, where I appoint to come the monday following for to begin'.[33]

There is evidence that Charles I shared in this admiration for *pietra dura*, which is indeed one of the archetypal expressions of the princely workshop in the costliness and beauty of its materials and in the expensive virtuosity of its techniques – as well as in the jealousy with which they were guarded. Charles owned 'A Marble Table inlaied with stone of divers cullo[rs] upon a frame suiteable' together with a matching cabinet, described as 'A Cabbonett of Marble

121 [335]
121 [335]

120 [333]

428 [37]
428 [39]
428 [38]
418 [33]

suiteable to the Table' which were valued jointly at the high price of £60, and sold for £65. Again among the Queen's furnishings was 'One Marble Table inlaied with many cullo^rs upon a guilt frame square' which had been given to Henrietta Maria by Lady Banning. Presumably too a 'small Table of Lapis Lazula &c' and another of 'Serpentine Stone &c' listed in 1649-50 among the goods reserved from the sale of the King's goods were of *pietra dura*, while a third of porphyry was surely also from a Florentine or Roman workshop. At Nonsuch too there was 'A Marble Inlaid Table'.

Besides originating the permanent court workshop as a state institution the Medici also set a pattern for other European princes in the great collections they formed of pictures and statues. Like other forms of Renaissance collecting, the accumulation of pictures in order to make a collection rather than as ornaments for rooms was not princely or royal in origin. As with the collections of antique bronzes and gems of the *quattrocento*, it began among the lettered, and especially the lettered high clergy, such as bishops and cardinals. The first large collection of pictures was in fact a collection of historical portraits, that was formed in his villa at Como by the historian Paolo Giovio (1483-1552), Bishop of Nocera, a famous historian and *letterato*. It was put together for the sake of the sitters and not for the sake of the masters who had painted their portraits, though Giovio was able to include among his many copies some paintings by major artists, such as Botticelli and Titian. The collection then was iconographical, in that the subject-matter of the pictures was more important to the collector than their quality and attribution. Its inspiration was again antique, the lost *Imagines* of the famous Roman antiquary Varro.[34]

The collecting of portraits to make a historical series or a gallery of famous men was to remain a typical pursuit of Renaissance and Baroque virtuosi, whether royal, noble, or learned. Descriptions of Giovio's collection were very popular in the sixteenth century, and appeared in various versions and redactions from 1546 to 1567. Giovio's own description, the first to be published, was called *Descriptio musaei*, so inaugurating our modern usage of the word museum. The series was copied several times in the sixteenth century, for Cosimo I de' Medici, for the collections of the Archduke Ferdinand of the Tirol at Ambras, for Ippolita Gonzaga. It was almost certainly the initial inspiration of the grandiose princely collections of paintings of the Late Renaissance and Baroque and also of the tendency to collect or commission portrait series which became a characteristic of Late Renaissance and Baroque patrons. Thus in 1604 we find Duke Vincenzo Gonzaga of Mantua proposing to decorate a chamber 'with portraits of all the fairest ladies in the world, both Princesses and private ladies' and asking his agent in France for portraits of all famous French beauties.[35] Charles I's own 'Privie Galerie' at Whitehall was largely lined with portraits of the Kings and Queens of England as far back as a supposed portrait of Edward III. With a break for Henry IV and Henry V, it made up a complete series of English kings from Henry VI, intermingled with portraits of other members of the royal family, of the royal house of France and its offshoot the Dukes of Burgundy, of the Habsburg Emperors and their families, of the Grand Dukes of Florence and the Dukes of Savoy, and of Charles's own relations by marriage, the House of Orange. It even included some of the Kings and Queens of Spain.[36]

As an independent genre the portrait had not been in existence for more than about a century and a half before Giovio began making his collection, so that it was only in his generation that the very notion of a collection of historical portraits could begin to seem a valid possibility. Medici collecting of pictures on the grand scale as opposed to the commissioning or purchase of single works, began in 1552 when Cosimo I ordered copies to be made of Giovio's portraits and sent the painter Cristofano dell'Altissimo to Como especially to make them. During the late fifteenth century the Venetians had already anticipated the Florentines in the collecting of fine pictures by contemporary masters, but this was in order to adorn a small *studio*, and the collecting of pictures on a princely scale really begins only in the second half of the sixteenth century. Again some sixty years had had to pass of an immense production of pictures in styles acceptable to sixteenth-century eyes for the notion of collecting pictures by various hands to become a serious pursuit. The publication of Vasari's *Vite*, first in 1550 and in a second edition in 1568 undoubtedly stimulated the process, for it provided at once a guide to the history of painting and sculpture in Italy from the late thirteenth century and a critical canon in the shape of Vasari's scheme of the rise and progress of the art from Italo-Byzantine stiffness to its ultimate degree of perfection with Leonardo, Raphael and Michelangelo. It is noteworthy that in his *Compleat Gentleman* (first published in 1622), a guide for the aspirant to the cultivated life, Henry Peacham found it worthwhile to include in his chapter on art brief biographies of famous Italian artists, illustrating the rise and progress of painting. He took them from a Northern source, Karel van Mander's *Schilderboek*, for he had not seen Vasari's *Lives* and knew of only two copies in London, one belonging to Dr Mountford, a Prebendary of St. Paul's, the other to Inigo Jones.[37]

The collecting of pictures by the Medici was emulated by other Italian princes, such as the Farnese and the Gonzaga, and the later sixteenth and first half of the seventeenth century saw a veritable picture-mania with huge collections formed by voracious collectors. Again it is important to separate the first half of the sixteenth century from the second, for it must be emphasised that until the 1560s pictures, even when bought in bulk, were bought largely as room decorations, rather than as important works by famous masters. Thus when in 1535 Duke Federico Gonzaga acquired from Matteo de Nasar, probably a merchant, one hundred and twenty Flemish landscape paintings from a collection of three hundred that Nasar had put together on speculation in Flanders, his intention was to mount them in the walnut panelling of the new apartments he was making in the Castello, 'and this can be done very gracefully because all one hundred and twenty are of three sizes only'.[38] Even when collectors like Isabella d'Este in the first decade of the century were eagerly seeking single pictures and works of art these were intended to be hung in personal apartments. There was as yet no notion of a great princely collection of pictures housed in a special *galleria* and adding lustre by its completeness and beauty to the reputation of a princely house.

Indeed only from the accession of Duke Vincenzo I in 1587 did the Gonzaga begin an avid accumulation of pictures through agents or ambassadors in all the great cities of Italy and sometimes in smaller places as well. Pictures were bought singly or in numbers and in whole collections, patterns of purchase that we find repeated later elsewhere, not least in the collections of Charles I. Even so it was not until 1594 that Vincenzo embarked on the project of constructing a *galleria*. Painted armorial windows were already being ordered for it from a glass-painter of Murano in 1600-1, but work really seems first to have got under way both on the windows and the fabric in 1602-3. By June 1604 the Duke could order his court architect Antonio Maria Viani and Rubens, then his court painter, to make designs for the distribution of the pictures on its walls, but only in 1611-12 was his *galleria* finally completed. It was of course the acquisition of part of the Gonzaga collection some ten years later that was to give Charles I's collection of pictures and sculptures equality in range and importance with the other great royal and princely collections of his age.[39]

Such ardour for the collecting of pictures naturally gave rise to the arts of connoisseurship. It is in the later sixteenth century that patrons and collectors begin to insist on the execution of all or part of a picture by the hand of the artist himself. This in turn implied the development by the patron of something of an eye for the hand of the master and of a sharper sense of quality in the execution of details. It also implied the development of a critical sense of the merits and shortcomings of an artist or a work of art. There had in fact always been from at least the early fifteenth century lay (that is to say, non-professional) cognoscenti in the arts – though the judgment of pictures was often left even so late as the nineteenth century to the expertise of professional painters. But the Late Mannerist and Baroque ages saw the appearance of the virtuoso collector who trained his own eye to assess the quality of paintings.[40]

We find in Jacobean England too a sudden sharp critical awareness of the merits and defects of individual artists and of the importance of the hand of the master. From 1616 the correspondence between Dudley Carleton, English ambassador in the Low Countries, and his friends is full of observant notes on painters and their abilities: Cornelius Cornelisz of Haarlem 'doth excelle in colouring but erres in proportion', Hendrik Vroom is 'very rare' in his pictures of ships, while Goltzius's art 'decayes with his bodie'.[41] It is also full of bargains struck with Rubens about pictures and how much difference it would make to their price if Rubens painted the whole or instead only part of a picture. When Rubens painted in 1620 a picture of a *Hunt* to the commission of Lord Danvers for presentation to Charles, it was rejected by Danvers because 'in every paynters opinion he hath sent hether a piece scarse touched by his own hand, and the postures so forced, as the Prince will not admitt the picture into his galerye'.[42] We have a testimony to the quality of Charles's own connoisseurship from the Papal agent Monsignor George Conn. In February 1637 Conn reported that he had presented to Charles a painting of St. Michael sent him as a present by Cardinal Antonio Barberini and another he himself had bought from a certain Roberti. 'It passed for a thing of singular merit, but I would not risk giving it any other father than Il Sermoneta, by whose hand His Majesty had seen no other work before this. He recognized at once that the St. Michael was of the school of Guido Reni and at first hesitated whether it were not by his own hand, but then concluded absolutely that it was not, but praised it none the less excessively'.[43]

The late Renaissance passion for picture-collecting produced two new types who have haunted the world of art ever since, the forger and the copyist. In his lives of artists Giovanni Baglione has left us a vivid picture of the late sixteenth-century Roman painter Terentio da Urbino 'who was one of those who seek to pass off their modern paintings as ancient'. Terentio made a practice of searching out old worm-eaten and smoke-blackened panels and frames, with some rough old picture painted on them. These he would improve into something very much better as a picture, which he would then smoke and varnish with coloured varnishes into the appearance of age. Among other ventures of this kind he painted on an old panel in a fine gilt frame a Madonna that he tried to pass off on his patron Cardinal Alessandro Montalto as a Raphael, only to be exposed and disgraced. At least Terentio's activities were unequivocal in their endeavour to deceive: much more ambiguous was the status of the copy.[44]

The sixteenth and seventeenth centuries did not entertain quite the same scorn for the copy as later times. If a picture was greatly admired, it seemed only natural to have it copied. If the copy was by a good hand it was valued for its own sake though less, of course, than an original. Thus when an inventory was taken in 1618 of the pictures of Cardinal Federico Borromeo (1564-1631) the learned and saintly Archbishop of Milan, whose large gallery formed the foundation of the Ambrosiana collection, it was divided into sections of originals – including 'Originals by artists of importance' and 'Originals by less famous painters' – and a section of 'Copies made with diligence'.[45] And when Cardinal Francesco Barberini in Rome first received a suggestion from the Papal agent to Henrietta Maria, Gregorio Panzani, that Charles I's goodwill could be conciliated by gifts of pictures, he wrote back on 13 March 1635 'You enquired about pictures, but did not write if you want copies or originals, old or modern works'.[46] On the other hand some princely collectors wholly disdained copies of any sort or quality: in December 1600 the chancellor of Duke Vincenzo I of Mantua rejected a collection of copies offered to the Duke 'as not suitable for Your Highness, who has no need of copies, but rather desires originals by good hands that are worthy to stand among the many others Your Highness has by the most excellent painters'.[47] Princely and royal collectors, if they gave away or exchanged a picture, might often keep a small-scale copy of it as a reminder and record. Thus Charles I employed Henry Gheerardts to make a copy of a Domenico Feti from Mantua he had exchanged with the Duchess of Buckingham for a picture of the *Rape of Lucretia* by Giovanni Contarini, of which Marcus Gheerardts also made a copy, presumably for the Duchess.[48]

Outside Italy in the decades that preceded the Jacobean and Caroline age, the two great exemplars of collecting and patronage of the arts were both Habsburgs, the Emperor Rudolf II and King Philip II of Spain. They represented different patterns of their type. Philip was a connoisseur of pictures with a taste that embraced with equal appreciation Titian and Hieronymus Bosch. He also collected at his court Italian artists, painters such as El Greco, sculptors like Leone Leoni, medallists like Jacopo da Trezzo. During his reign an exquisite Renaissance refinement and cultivation introduced new tastes to a nobility and gentry that already had traditionally much love for poetry and much skill in its practice. In particular the doctrine, first made popular by Castiglione's *Cortegiano* (1528) well-known in Spain in the classic translation of the poet Juan Boscán (1534) that drawing and painting were not arts merely for mechanics, but fit for gentlemen, nobles, and even kings to practise, found ready adepts. Under this new impulse, Spanish collections became some of the largest and most important of Late Renaissance and Baroque Europe, all the more easily because Lombardy and Naples were Spanish possessions ruled by Spanish viceroys and because the King of Spain was the dominant power of late sixteenth- and early seventeenth-century Europe, whom all were anxious to conciliate by gifts.

There is however no evidence that Philip was in any sense a virtuoso prince. Rather he was the type of prince who assembled collections by commission, purchase and gift, including in his case paintings by Dürer and Brueghel from the Renaissance North, and by Leonardo, Raphael and Titian from Renaissance Italy, and gathered artists around him to execute works of art in established genres, such as portraits, altarpieces, room-decorations, tombs. Essentially his tastes and intentions in the patronage of secular art were those of François I, but brought up to date in their manifestations. By contrast his nephew the Emperor Rudolf II (ruled 1576-1612), who grew up at Philip's court, made his own court at Prague the apogee of the tradition of the virtuoso prince dedicated to the investigation of all the secrets of nature and the arts.[49] Rudolf was motivated not only by speculative curiosity, but by that sincere desire of the virtuoso to penetrate more deeply into the mysteries of creation and so admire the Creator in the wonders of his works. In common with other princes of his kind, Rudolf made no distinction between the mechanical arts and sciences and those arts that were dedicated to producing costly objects, executed in beautiful, but resistant materials, such as hardstone and crystal, and therefore combining in their realization a joint triumph of art and skill. To his court Rudolf brought painters from the Rhineland like Bartholomeus Spranger and Hans von Aachen and sculptors from the Netherlands like Adrian de Vries, all working in Northern versions of Late Mannerism. He also summoned goldsmiths from the Netherlands to work for him, again in various Mannerist styles – Erasmus Hornick, Jan Vermeyen, Jost Gelle, Hans de Vos and in the last years of his reign, Paul van Vianen, whose works were to be eagerly collected by Charles I and whose nephew Christian was to become Charles's court goldsmith.[50] The later sixteenth century was still an age when Netherlandish goldsmiths were among the leaders of their art. The principal court goldsmith of the Medici from 1573 until his death was the Dutchman Jacques Bylivelt of Delft, better known as Jacopo Biliverti (1550-c.1593), who became *Proveditore* of the *Galleria* in Florence.[51]

The Medici *Galleria* and its skills in working precious and semi-precious stones were plainly the model that Rudolf had before his eye in setting up his own court workshops. In 1588 he instituted a search throughout Bohemia for precious and semi-precious stones, and some of these he despatched c.1591-2 to Florence in order to have them set in a *pietra dura* panel. The costliness of such pieces can be judged from the report of a Venetian ambassador in 1597 that the materials and workmanship of this panel had cost the Emperor the huge sum of 20,000 *scudi*. By 1596 Rudolf had established in Prague his own workshop for *pietra dura*, employing at least one workman from Florence, Castruccio Castrucci.[52] Meanwhile in 1589 for making vessels in hardstones he had summoned from Milan Ottavio Miseroni (1567-1624), who belonged to a long-established Milanese family of rock crystal cutters. Miseroni inaugurated in Prague a family dynasty of imperial hardstone cutters which was to last until 1684. Rudolf established Ottavio in his imperial court workshop, which was again modelled on the *Galleria* of Florence. It was however less tightly disciplined: the court goldsmiths, for example, could offer their works for general sale in the great Wladislaw hall of the imperial palace of the Hradschin in Prague.

Rudolf's collections were housed in the Hradschin. Far from being the disorderly accumulations of wonders and curiosities and rich objects of their mythical reputation, they were most carefully arranged. The pictures were housed in a special gallery, known as the 'Spanisches Saal', constructed in the new north wing which Rudolf began adding to the Hradschin in 1590. The 'Neues Saal', adjoining the Spanisches Saal, was a great columned room, in whose walls, within a framework of blind panels and pilasters, were great niches displaying statues in stucco and bronze by Adrian de Vries. The *Kunstkammer*, or collection of objects, was arranged in vaulted rooms along a building that connected the new north wing with the main part of the Hradschin. Above the rooms housing these collections, pictures decorated a corridor that led from the Spanisches Saal to the Emperor's apartments. The whole recalls what was evidently its model, the Medici galleries in the Uffizi, and seems to have had at least some richly decorated ceilings. The collections of the *Kunstkammer* were under the supervision of Daniel Fröschl, the imperial antiquary, who compiled and maintained from 1607 to 1611, the last year of Rudolf's life, a systematic inventory of its contents and acquisitions.[53]

Nevertheless for contemporaries an atmosphere of mystery and seclusion shrouded Rudolf and his collections, especially after he had withdrawn himself from general view in the later years of his life. There was a suggestion too that erotic self-indulgence was one reason for his retirement from the world to pass his time among his treasures. Probably this image of him is best rendered in the much-read *Satyricon* (1605-1611) of John Barclay (1582-1661), a young Scot with French connections who was for a time in the entourage of James I and lived in London from 1606 to 1616. In Part II of *Satyricon* Rudolf appears as Aquilius. The hero is conducted to visit his private apartments by a courtier, Trifortitus, or Duke George of Leuchtenberg. He finds Rudolf in his chamber, an ageing man of middle-size, with a kindly but troubled air. The walls of the chamber are painted not with battle scenes, but with beautiful maidens, more beautiful than nature, recalling the pictures of courtesans painted by the Greek artists of antiquity. On a table stand a terrestrial and a celestial globe, with their proper figures. On enquiring who the craftsman was that had made them, he is told Aquilius.

Nothing is more industrious than this solitude of his, nor on giving up all sight of man has he ceased to labour. Instead he has gone over to the curious delights of certain arts. In these images and portraits of women you see not only his study, but his wealth. He prefers freedom in his loves to marriage, and weighs vagrant delights by his own caprice. For when lust feigns in his mind the loveliest forms of women, he transfers all to panel with learned colours, and following the lineaments of his imagination confesses his desires in a picture. Then he summons flocks of courtesans and virgins who esteem it an honour to lose that name to Aquilius. Himself the judge of their beauty, he compares their faces to the likeness in the image, and according to the nearness with which nature approaches that painted beauty, he bestows on them the favour of three nights. If any of them kindles love in him more ardently, if he has lost himself more sweetly in the embraces of any one of them, he decrees to her not a statue, but a portrait in his chamber, painted by his own hand. These terrestrial and celestial globes display an image of his imperial power, and the industriousness of the daily labour, by which he breaks into the hidden mysteries of nature, and overcomes the envy of the gods, whose will it was that most beautiful things should lie hidden from mortal men. Already can he compel crystal not to remain frozen in an eternal winter: from metals he can now wring their very soul, and convoke all the sun's miracles into a temperate fire, and even teach ignorant nature her own strength. Vital juices, such as provoke still more than Aesculapius's art the thunderbolt of envious Jove, are expressed by his arts. Not by my unartificial discourse to betray this wondrous art, these sciences were expecting Aquilius, disdaining to be loved by lesser men as unworthy.[54]

Rudolf's passion for the mechanical arts was not generally approved of in early seventeenth-century England. Henry Peacham warns his young readers to take up 'honest and commendable exercises savouring of vertue', and not to addict themselves 'wholly to trifles' like 'Alphonse Atestino Duke of Ferrara' who 'delighted himself onely in Turning and playing the Ioyner [or] Rudolf the late Emperour, in setting of Stones and Watches'.[55] But Charles I certainly knew much about his collections, if only through Abraham van der Doort (c.1575-80–1640) his own court antiquary, whose famous inventory of 1639 is the foundation of all studies of Charles I's collection. For Abraham, who seems to have begun life as an engraver of dies and a wax-modeller, specialities that suggest a training as a goldsmith, had made for Rudolf, who like other virtuosi was much interested in the technique of wax-modelling, a life-size head in coloured wax on a pedestal of black ebony inlaid with gold and silver. He seems to have produced this in England, for Prince Henry, Charles I's elder brother, had refused to part with either the bust or its maker. Instead 'promising that he – would give soe good entertaynment as any Emperor should', he offered Van der Doort the Keepership of his medals when the Cabinet Room that Inigo Jones had begun for him in 1611 was ready. Various notes in Van der Doort's inventory show that he was well acquainted with the names of the artists who had worked for Rudolf: Hans von Aachen is 'the Emperor Radolph Painter', Paul van Vianen is 'the Emperor Radolphs man in Chast worke', Daniel Fröschl 'the Emperor Rodolph's limner'.[56]

It will be obvious from what has gone before that in the scale and ambitiousness of his collecting and patronage Charles was importing into England a conception of the royal and princely gallery that had become current in Europe during the last decades of the sixteenth century. After the death of Henry VIII, neither Edward VI, nor Mary, nor Elizabeth renewed his traditions of royal patronage and the tastes of James were for learning rather than for the arts, at any rate in any deeper sense. It is generally recognized that the tastes which found their fullest expression in Charles had their first precocious manifestation in his elder brother Prince Henry. The mediators between Prince Henry and knowledge of the princely cabinets and galleries of Europe are not known, but it is probable that Inigo Jones was his chief adviser. Jones was in Italy c.1600, and must have known something of the collections of Venice, which he visited in 1601, and something also of the various princely collections of Italy. We can assume too that Henry learned of the princely fashion for cabinets of works of art from noblemen returned from the Continent, and from ambassadors, especially perhaps those who negotiated in 1610 for his marriage to Caterina de' Medici, sister of the Grand Duke Cosimo II of Florence.

Although in general English princes did not travel abroad, they, like other virtuosi, did have means of becoming acquainted with celebrated buildings and works of art, through engravings. Collections of engravings of ancient sculptures and of the buildings of Rome were already being issued from the second half of the sixteenth century – especially notable are the *Speculum Romanae Magnificentiae* (1575) of Antonio Lafréry and the *Romanae Urbis Topographia* (1597-1602) of J.J. Boissard. Lord Exeter gave Charles I 'a very greate Booke in folio of Prints beeing of severall Antiquities of statues and Roman buildings' which in 1639 the King kept in his new Cabinet Room at Whitehall. Moreover some famous pictures or cycles of pictures were on occasions reproduced in small-scale copies. The earliest examples of this practice known to the writer are all from the Veneto, where small-scale copies of Mantegna's Ovetari frescoes were already being made for collectors in the late fifteenth or early sixteenth century. Several sets of small-scale copies of Mantegna's *Triumphs* were also made during the sixteenth and early seventeenth centuries, a number of them for princely patrons, like the set in grisaille made for the Archduke Leopold Wilhelm, governor of the Spanish Netherlands from 1646 to 1656, which is now in Vienna. Advice from older collectors, like Thomas Howard, Earl of Arundel, and discussion with other court collectors and also with artists must have played an important part in Charles's education in art. That Charles was interested in more than the decorative value of works of art is plain not only from his appointment by James I in 1622 to found an academy to encourage education and the arts but also from the books, prints and drawings he had in his Cabinet at Whitehall in 1639 – Vesalius's *Anatomy*, Dürer's woodcuts of 'the Proportions of Men', drawings of 'Accions and postures invented by Michael Angell Bonorotto'.[57]

It is certain that models and plans of buildings or of notable features of buildings were also sent to English princely and noble patrons for their interest and information. Thus Prince Henry was sent a model of Michelangelo's staircase to the Laurentian Library in Florence, and in 1623 Thomas Howard, Earl of Arundel, is found asking Duke Ferdinando of Mantua for a model of Giulio Romano's Palazzo del Te,

but he would like it to be made with punctual care and by the hand of a person who understands these things, and that it should show every detail of it with a distinct narration of principal things that are inside it, that is of sculptures and pictures, thus in the *camera* and in the *sala* there are such and such things, and if he might have the selfsame model after which the building was made he would be even more grateful. His Excellency would also like a model of the courtyard of the Palazzo in Mantua that was built not long ago with a rustic order.

The task seems to have been entrusted to the Gonzaga court architect.[58]

Less exalted persons also bought plans or views of admired buildings. In 1623 during Charles's return from Spain after the abortive negotiations for his Spanish marriage, Sir Richard Wynn, a courtier not only made one of his household note down a careful description of the Escorial where Philip II's collections were partly housed, but bought 'the plat of the house . . . of a fryar for twenty ryales, very well set forth'. Charles himself examined with keen admiration the great Spanish royal collections in Madrid, as augmented by Philip III and even more by Philip IV, long to be his great rival as a royal collector and patron. He bought paintings, sat to Velazquez, and in recognition of his tastes Philip presented him with Titian's *Venus of the Pardo* (Pl. 13).[59] Again on his return journey, during his visit to the garden of the royal palace to Valladolid, he was presented with Giambologna's marble fountain of *Samson and the Philistine* (Fig. 31), which he later gave to the Duke of Buckingham. In the palace itself 'hee was much delighted with the pictures of Raphael de Urbino and Michelangelo'.[60] But as with most seventeenth-century kings and princes, for much of his knowledge of collections he must have depended on eyewitness accounts either by letter or by word of mouth.

We have seen that by the time of Charles's accession European princely fashions in collecting and patronage were well-established. A gallery of pictures and a collection of works of art had come to be a recognized advertisement of princely magnificence, and also, in that cultivated age, of princely knowledge and taste. Collecting had developed during the sixteenth century from the careful selection of single objects or a few objects in the same genre for a small *studio* into an omnivorous pursuit of pictures, of antique sculptures and of works of art, notably those wrought in precious hardstones and metals. Although princely collections or the pick of them might still be housed in a small *studio* or cabinet, the fashion more and more was to erect a special gallery and adjacent rooms in which to house and display them suitably. Princely patronage was more complex. On the one hand a king or prince might simply call artists – painters, sculptors, goldsmiths and their like – into his service and set them to work for him in recognized genres. On the other, he might set up court workshops, like the Medici and Rudolf II, for the production of costly objects in difficult techniques and rare materials.

Let us now see how these established norms of collecting and patronage affected Charles. As with most collectors and patrons, the works of art that he collected were largely in genres approved by current taste – antique medals and sculptures, paintings by the great masters of Italy and the North, and also by living masters of greatest reputation in the Netherlands and Italy, portraits, arms and armour, goldsmith's work, modern medals and sculptures. Let us glance briefly at each of these genres as it appealed to Charles.

The famous painting by Daniel Mytens of Thomas Howard, Earl of Arundel, seated and proudly pointing with his cane to a gallery lined with antique sculptures is a faithful image of the principal ambition, not only of Arundel, but of every great collector of the sixteenth, seventeenth and eighteenth centuries. From the late fifteenth century, antique marbles were more eagerly pursued than any other kind of work of art, more even than pictures. During the second half of the sixteenth century the Medici Grand Dukes incessantly bought antique sculptures in Rome, and Pigafetta's description of their *Galleria c.*1600 shows that it was these that were its principal feature, indeed that the *Galleria* was principally designed to display. Charles shared this taste to the full though the restored marbles of the Renaissance and Baroque age have so fallen from fashion that the importance of this aspect of his collection has lost the emphasis that is its due. In Peacham's famous words,

King *Charles* also ever since his comming to the Crowne, hath amply testified a Royall liking of ancient statues, by causing a whole army of old forraine Emperors, Captaines and Senators all at once to land on his coasts, to come and doe him homage, and attend him in his palaces of Saint *Iames*, and Sommerset-House.[61]

Most had belonged to the Gonzaga collection: others had been brought from the ruins of the Temple of Apollo on Delos by Sir Kenelm Digby. These two provenances illustrate the two main aspects of Caroline collecting of antique sculpture: purchase of collections already formed, and searches in the Levant for previously unknown pieces.

In the collecting of antique medals Charles had been preceded by Prince Henry (see pp. 411-12), but already while Prince of Wales he had bought five folio books 'Concerning Antiquity of Medalls'. On medals, as ancient coins were generally called, the Renaissance set the highest value, as being in Henry Peacham's words 'memorials of men and matters of elder times; whose lively presence is able to persuade a man, that he now seeth two thousand yeeres ago'.[62] Indeed in an eloquent later passage Peacham urges:

But would you see a patterne of the *Rogus* or funerall pile burnt at the canonization of the Romane Emperors? Would you see how the *Augurs* Hat, and *Lituus* were made? Would you see the true and undoubted modells of their Temples, Altars, Deities, Columnes, Gates, Arches, Aquaeducts, Bridges, Sacrifices, Vessels, *Sellae Curules*, Ensignes and Standards, Navall and murall Crownes, Amphy theatres, Civici, Bathes, Chorists, Trophies, Ancilia and a thousand things more; Repare to the old coynes, and you shall find them, and all things else that ever they did, made, or used, there shall you see them excellently and lively represented. Besides, it is no small satisfaction to an ingenuous eye to contemplate the faces and heads, and in them the Characters of all these famous Emperours, Captaines and Illustrious men whose actions will bee ever admired, both for themselves and the learning of the pennes that writ them.[63]

Charles had quite a collection of antique medals, and Van der Doort retained under him as part of his Keepership of the King's Cabinet Room the custody of both the King's own acquisitions and the medals he had inherited from Prince Henry. This was a very troublesome trust. We have a vivid picture, probably from 1636, of Charles going with Van der Doort into the Chair Room and showing him '27 goulden meddalls in black torned hoopes lyeing upon the table and Said looke Arbaham how comes these here. I answered I see by this that there is more keys than one which your Maiestie hath given me and he Said yes I have one'.[64]

Figure 26 *Papal medals of Urban VIII,* of the type known to have been presented by George Conn, the papal agent, to Henrietta Maria.

Charles certainly did not have the same passion for gems and costly works in hardstone or for a rich variety of sumptuous goldsmith's work as Italian and German princes. There is no record, for instance, of his employing a hardstone-cutter at his court. But such objects, particularly if antique, were very acceptable to him as presents. On 9 October 1636 George Conn, the second Barberini emissary from Rome to England, offered a small group of antique gems he had either been given by the famous Roman antiquary and connoisseur Cassiano dal Pozzo or bought on his advice – a cameo of young Nero with a Medusa head, an intaglio of Gordianus Pius, a Hercules and Deianira, and an Apuleius. Conn also bought from Rome a number of medals (Fig. 26), an antique agate vase, another of chalcedony and a small agate *tazza*.[65] A difficulty in defining Charles's own personal taste in hardstones, both in the nature and in the degree of his interests is that the royal treasure of plate and jewels he had inherited from his predecessors included many such objects, especially in mounted crystal and agate with some in mounted lapis-lazuli and mother-of-pearl. Seemingly he had only a little amber, a favourite material with Mannerist and Baroque connoisseurs – the 1649-50 lists include only two amber cups, an amber sconce, a standing cup and a double salt with six spoons, a gaming table of silver-mounted amber with men and dice, thirteen figures cut in yellow amber. Yet if there appears to be no evidence that among the many artists he patronized there were any workers in costly hardstones, it is at least interesting that the young Nicholas Stone, whose father the elder Nicholas was not only the most prominent sculptor of the day, but Charles's Master Mason, should have been so eager in 1636 to master the secrets of working *pietra dura*.

In modern sculpture Charles's patronage, like the patronage of the Emperor Rudolf and other late Renaissance princes, was partly directed to the creation of monumental and heroic sculptures, glorifying him as king and so exalting the monarchy itself. The two genres most favoured for these purposes in Late Mannerist Europe were the equestrian statue and the portrait bust, and the medium most preferred was bronze, which recalled the august equestrian sculptures and portrait busts of antiquity. Giambologna had made a bronze

40 [157], 42 [·174], 117 [301-3]

equestrian monument to Cosimo I for the Piazza della Signoria in Florence, and his pupil Pietro Tacca another of Philip III for the Plaza Mayor in Madrid. From the Netherlandish bronze sculptor Adrian de Vries, another pupil of Giambologna, who first came to Prague in the early 1590s, Rudolf commissioned bronze busts and bronze reliefs with imperial themes, as well as decorative sculptures. In the early seventeenth century, because of the prestige of Giambologna and his pupils, Florence enjoyed unequalled prestige for its bronze sculptures, and the bronze equestrian statue of Henri IV, erected in 1614 on the Pont-Neuf in Paris, had been begun by Giambologna and completed by Pietro Tacca. An equestrian monument of James I had been mooted in emulation in 1619, but it was only under Charles that the French sculptor Hubert le Sueur at last executed an equestrian monument of an English king (Fig. 55) – though not originally to Charles's commission – and a series of official bronze busts glorifying the king.[66]

Although it was Le Sueur's habit to refer to himself as Praxiteles, this self-estimate has not been endorsed by subsequent generations. It is a measure of Charles's keen judgment in sculpture as in the other arts, that as soon as unofficial relations had been opened with the Papal court in the mid-1630s, he began successful negotiations for a bust of himself by Bernini, the greatest sculptor of the age and also its greatest innovator in sculptural style (see Fig. 47).[67] His motive must have been the characteristic motive of the Late Mannerist and Baroque collector, to have something from the hand of a great artist, rather than merely yet another official bust of himself as a heroic monarch. This emphasis marks a stage in that slow but far-reaching shift in the taste of European patrons from recognition of excellence of workmanship in a set commission, to the creation of works of art as much for their aesthetic as for their social, decorative, or religious significance. That shift has proved one of the profoundest and most lasting consequences of the late sixteenth- and seventeenth-century passion for collecting.

Sculpture was also valued for purposes of decoration. Le Sueur cast a series of bronze sculptures from famous classical figures – the *Farnese Hercules* (Fig. 33), the *Borghese Gladiator* (Fig. 34), the *Diana of Ephesus* then in the Marble Chamber of the Louvre and now at Versailles – whose inspiration must have been the similar figures cast in bronze for François I at Fontainebleau. These were placed in the garden of St. James's Palace, for from the first moment it had learned that classical antiquity had placed statues in gardens, the Renaissance had decorated its own gardens with sculpture, both antique and modern.[68] Again the inspiration must have been French, for François I's bronze statues from plaster casts of the antique were also intended for the gardens of Fontainebleau. Large-scale fountains were another favourite feature of the Renaissance garden, but these had already been introduced into England under James I in their most elaborate Late Mannerist form by the Frenchman Salomon de Caus. Charles's patronage of the Florentine Francesco Fanelli as a sculptor of small bronzes is therefore more significant than his patronage of him as a maker of fountains. The reputation of Florence and its court-sculptors in the making of small bronze figures of all kinds had been paramount from the days of Giambologna, who had made himself the recognized master in the genre. His followers had continued this tradition, and we can still read of the surprise and delight with which Prince Henry received in 1612 a set of bronze statuettes cast by Pietro Tacca after models by Giambologna.[69] Fanelli made a number of small bronzes during his residence at Charles's court (Figs. 43-5), and Charles's encouragement of this aspect of his art presumably represents an attempt to import into England a genre in which Florence enjoyed – indeed was long to continue to enjoy – a European reputation for unequalled excellence.

In Charles's collecting of pictures we see him employing the same methods as other princely collectors of the age – large-scale purchases from a great collection, as in the case of the Gonzaga pictures and sculptures, or the block purchase of smaller collections, like that of William Frizell in 1637.[70] Very many pictures – and indeed quite a number of other works of art – were also offered to him as gifts by courtiers, diplomats and artists, either singly, or in some numbers, like those despatched by the Barberini from 1635 to 1640. Such presents were of course intended to gain the King's favour by appealing to his taste for art. Charles also exchanged quite a number of pictures with other collectors in his court circle – in this perhaps he was unusual among the collectors of his age. In his state commissions for paintings as in his commissions for sculpture we can trace the same heroicization of the monarchy, as in the Rubens ceiling of the Banqueting

House (Fig. 66), or the state portraits by Van Dyck (Pls. 18, 67-71). His other purchases and commissions from living artists illustrate clearly the omnivorousness of taste characteristic of the princely picture-collector, though plainly he had more than a penchant for the sumptuous mythologies and histories of Titian and Rubens, with their splendour of colour and vigour and freedom of handling. This catholicity of taste he shared with other collectors of his age and court: landscapes and portraits came from Dutch artists, while Gentileschi was imported from Italy to paint in the Caravaggesque manner.

Charles was also a patron of the miniature, the sole genre in which English late sixteenth- and seventeenth-century artists and virtuosi claimed surpassing excellence for their own country. In view of this claim it is perhaps not surprising that only in the very English genre of the portrait miniature do we find a new virtuoso technique being invented under Charles's direction. The portrait-miniature painted in enamel on gold, a genre invented or at any rate perfected by Jean Petitot and Jacques Bordier, two Genevan goldsmiths taken into court service c.1636,[71] was to prove a lastingly popular form, and its invention must be traced to the same spirit of innovation and experiment that had animated the workshops of Medici Florence and of the Emperor Rudolf II. This semi-scientific aspect of the promotion of the arts in England was undoubtedly encouraged by Charles, but it is also plain that unlike the Grand Duke Francesco I or the Emperor Rudolf, he was no personal investigator of technical secrets. His attitude, for all his enthusiasm and excellence of judgment in all kinds of art, retained a traditional aristocratic and princely detachment from their practice. In this he was unlike his contemporary Louis XIII of France, who like Alfonso d'Este and Emmanuele Filiberto in the sixteenth century, worked with his own hands to improve firearms. Yet we shall see in the history of the invention of the enamel portrait miniature that Charles was well able to conceive the notion and direct the execution of a new genre in art. It is in this aspect of his collecting and patronage that he becomes most nearly a virtuoso prince.

There was moreover at his court a virtuoso who was particularly interested in the secrets of the arts, no less a personage than his court physician, the Genevan Sir Theodore Turquet de Mayerne (1573-1655). Mayerne is another link between England and Florence, for it was with his help while he was teaching anatomy at the Spedale of Santa Maria Nuova in Florence that Lodovico Cigoli modelled his celebrated wax anatomical figure of a man, for two centuries or more a classic artist's model, of which Charles I owned a cast in bronze. His manuscript collections of technical secrets in painting, sculpture and dyeing, many obtained directly from artists and craftsmen, still survive in the British Library, and one of them *Pictoria, Sculptoria, Tinctoria*[72] has been twice printed in the twentieth century.

414 [124]

As with all innovations, a certain obscurity surrounds the credit for the first invention of the enamel portrait miniature. An improved technique of painting in vitrifiable colours which were subsequently fused by firing with a ground of white enamel is said to have been perfected by Jean I Toutin of Châteaudun and Blois in 1632. However, traces of the technique can be found in Limoges enamels of the sixteenth century, and it was certainly being used by other goldsmiths of Blois in 1630. But Toutin certainly made experiments to improve it, and took the decisive step of working on gold, instead of on copper. He applied it to the decoration of rings and jewellery so successfully that he moved to Paris at some date between 1632 and 1636 and became a court jeweller. The earliest surviving portrait miniature in enamel was painted in Paris by his son Henri, and is a portrait of Charles I, dated 1636, now in the Dutch royal collections (Fig. 27).

The Toutins were Huguenots, and all this milieu of French jeweller-goldsmiths was in fact to remain largely Protestant until the Revocation of the Edict of Nantes in 1685. Hence Jean Petitot, from Calvinist Geneva, may well have gravitated to the Toutins' shop in Paris, after he left Geneva at some date after November 1632. Here he would have learned their new technique, before coming over to England. His early biographers declare that he came to England, probably early in 1636, attracted by reports of Charles's generous patronage of the arts, and took service either with his court goldsmith or his court jeweller. The rings and jewels he enamelled were so much more brilliant in colouring and technique than anything Charles had seen before that he was greatly struck with the potentialities of this new medium. For this form of painted enamel allowed the enameller to achieve something of the same effect as painting in oil or water-colours, but in a medium that was much more durable and brilliant. Certainly by 1639 Petitot had executed for Charles a work of decorative enamelling which must

Figure 27   Henri Toutin: *King Charles I,* enamel miniature,
signed and dated 1636, Rijksmuseum, Amsterdam.

have appeared in the England of the mid-1630s as a striking novelty. This was a
'Curious Landskept' of a farm and a windmill on a hill done after a copy of a
landscape by the younger Brueghel which Peter Oliver had executed in
miniature. It was enamelled on a 'gould plate', and framed in a black ebony
frame.[73]

Work of this kind, after a miniature or painting by another hand, was to be
typical of the art of Petitot in England: like most seventeenth-century enamellers,
he was largely a translator from one artistic medium into another. But in an age so
passionately interested in techniques and in accomplishment of execution, this
was no serious aesthetic disability. According to the most reliable eighteenth-
century sources, writing up information from the Petitot family, it was Charles
himself who suggested either to his jeweller or directly to Petitot that the new
medium should be applied to portrait miniatures. Petitot made the attempt, and
the resulting enamel miniature so delighted King Charles that he showed it to
Van Dyck, who immediately offered to instruct Petitot in the finer points of
modelling and flesh-tones, in which the enameller, from lack of knowledge, had
made mistakes. Charles also commissioned Mayerne to discover new enamel
colours that would help Petitot to a fuller and more accurate range of flesh-tones.
We have no external confirmation that Van Dyck gave any training in portrait
drawing to Petitot, though Petitot's surviving English enamel miniatures
certainly emulate in their key and tones oil rather than miniature painting. But
there is external confirmation from Mayerne's own manuscripts that he was
closely involved with two enamellers, and invented several reds for their use, and
every reason to believe that those enamellers, who compiled a little treatise on
enamelling in French for him, were Petitot and Bordier.

Until further evidence appears, it must remain uncertain whether Charles
simply encouraged improvements to a genre invented by Henry Toutin in Paris,
or whether the invention of the enamel portraiture miniature was his own
inspiration. Certainly Petitot was already working at court in 1636, for a miniature
on vellum of Charles I and Henrietta Maria in the Northumberland collection is
signed and dated 1636.[74] And on 22 January 1637 George Conn, while at court
was shown by Lord Holland in the presence of Henrietta Maria 'a little portrait of
the King, in enamel, very curious' which was surely a work by Petitot, if only
because Petitot and Bordier were formally the Queen's servants.[75] It is always
possible, therefore, since the Toutin enamel portrait, though painted in Paris,
represents Charles I, that it was a copy of a portrait in enamels executed by
Petitot. The new genre certainly achieved its full perfection at Charles's court and
under his impulse, and is a typical expression in its costliness of gold and refined
virtuosity and brilliance of technique of the rarefied world of the court artist.

Charles also employed as his court goldsmith Christian van Vianen, nephew of Paul, who had been one of the most significant artist-goldsmiths employed by Rudolf II. His art is discussed elsewhere (pp. 237-42), like the work of other artists and craftsmen who have been considered here solely as part of the general pattern of Charles's collecting and patronage. In general, compared to the court galleries and palace workshops of Florence and Prague, more closely organized and controlled, there is a certain impression of diffuseness about Charles's collections and patronage. It may be that this is misleading: certainly in Abraham van der Doort he had his own court *antiquarius*, whose duties, as outlined on his renewed appointment on 21 April 1625 were very similar to those of Rudolf's *antiquarius*. He was to be Keeper of the King's Cabinet Room

in our Pallace of St. James, or wheare we afterwards shall think fitt to appoint the same, wth the Medalles and limbed peeces and all other rarities belonging therunto or hereafter may belong, and alsoe to have the colecting, receiving, delivering, soorting, placeing & remoaving and causing of making by our appointing such things as wee shall think fitt and alsoe to be a Register booke of them.[76]

Van der Doort's catalogue, completed in 1639, of Charles's collections is one of the most precious documents for the history of art and taste in England. It reveals that the collections were largely distributed in the King's private apartments or 'Privie Lodgings' as Van der Doort calls them, which included a 'Privie Gallerie' decorated with family and other royal and imperial portraits, like the *Galleria* of the Uffizi. To a 'new erected Cabbonnett' Charles had transferred all the pictures and rarities previously kept in the Cabinet Room at St. James. It was now lined with seventy-three of his finest smaller pictures, interspersed with seven reliefs and with thirty-six small sculptures, including some of the bronzes Charles had inherited from Prince Henry and some by Fanelli, together with a few exotic curiosities. One or two were set in windows, and others stood on a table. Cupboards contained miniatures, as cupboards at Mantua had also contained small works of art,[77] and Charles's books of special artistic interest – books on heraldry and the order of the Garter, of emblems, on medals, a French book of court portraits, patterns by Gentileschi for Mortlake tapestry, the King's books on anatomy and proportion, already mentioned. Probably the new great palace of Whitehall, for which designs were under meditation from about 1638, would have included a new great gallery and cabinet for the paintings, sculptures and works of art. Would it also have included court workshops, like those of Florence and Prague? We shall never know, for the years during which the King's modernity and sophistication of taste formed collections equal to those of the most advanced of Continental princely collectors and patrons were abruptly ended by the Civil War.

Notes

1. For the sword of Tristram see R.S. Loomis, 'Vestiges of Tristram in London', *Burlington Magazine* 41 (1922), pp. 54-64; for the other swords, Lord Twining, *A History of the Crown Jewels of Europe* (London, 1960), pp. 114, 115, 589; for Philip the Bold, R. Lightbown, *Secular Goldsmith's Work in Medieval France* (London, 1978), p. 61. *Cf.* also L. de Laborde, 'Glossaire', in *Notice des émaux, bijoux et objets divers exposés dans les galeries du Musée du Louvre* (Paris, 1853), p. 479, s.v. *Reliques historiques*.

2. Laborde, op. cit. (Note 1), pp. 481-3, s.(AG) 1499.

3. Filippo Pigafetta, cited in F. Bencivenni-Pelli, *Saggio istorico della Real Galleria di Firenze* (Florence, 1779), I, pp. 196-7.

4. For some notes on these princes and their collecting see Lightbown, op. cit. (Note 1), pp. 10-13 and *passim*.

5. A. Lecoy de la Marche, *Extraits des comptes et memoriaux du roi René* (Paris, 1873), pp. 244-5; Lightbown, op. cit. (Note 1), pp. 106-7.

6. For the history of the *studio* see now W. Liebenwein, *Studiolo: die Entstehung eines Raumtyps und seine Entwicklung bis um 1600* (Berlin, 1977). The inventory of Isabella's *studiolo* is printed by C. d'Arco, *Delle arti e degli artefici di Mantova* (Mantua, 1857), II, pp. 134-5, and by A. Luzio, in *Archivio Storico Lombardo* 4th series 10 (1908), pp. 413-25.

7. For the Pasqualini *studio* see A. Luzio, *La Galleria dei Gonzaga venduta all' Inghilterra* (Milan, 1913), p. 49.

8. Vasari, 'Degli Accademici del Disegno', in *Vite* ed. G. Milanesi (Florence, 1881), VII, p. 603.

9. Suetonius, *Divus Augustus*, c. 72.

10. H. Peacham, *The Compleat Gentleman* (London, edn. of 1622), p. 106.

11. For early plaster casts see R. Lightbown, *Mantegna* (Oxford, 1986), p. 18 (1455), p. 151 (1489).

12. For these casts *cf.* Laborde, op. cit. (Note 1), p. 132; S. Pressouyre, 'Des fontes de Primatice à Fontainebleau', *Bulletin Monumental* 127 (1969), pp. 223-39; B. Boucher, 'Leone Leoni and Primaticcio's moulds of antique sculpture', *Burlington Magazine* 123 (1981), pp. 23-6.

13. Laborde, op. cit. (Note 1), p. 345.

14. For François I as a collector of pictures see Musée du Louvre, *La collection de François Ier* ed. J. Cox-Rearick (Paris, 1972). For the *galeries* of Fontainebleau see A. Blunt, *Art and Architecture in France 1500-1700* (Harmondsworth, 1953), pp. 30, 35, 37, 65, 66; Comité française d'Histoire de l'Art, *Revue de l'Art*, numéro spécial, *La Galerie François Ier au Château de Fontainebleau* (Paris, 1973).

15. For Isabella's correspondence see C.M. Brown with A.M. Lorenzoni, *Isabella d'Este and Lorenzo da Pavia* (Geneva, 1982).

16. Luzio, op. cit. (Note 7), pp. 105-6.

17. Bencivenni-Pelli, op. cit. (Note 3), I, p. 75.

18. For Strada in general see J. Hayward, *Virtuoso Goldsmiths and the Triumph of Mannerism, 1540-1620* (London, 1976), p. 47; and T. DaCosta Kauffman, *Variations on the Imperial Theme in the Age of Maximilian II and Rudolf II* (New York, 1978), pp. 76-7.

19. For the Munich *antiquarium* see L. Seelig, 'The Munich *Kunstkammer*, 1565-1807', in O. Impey and A. MacGregor (eds.), *The Origins of Museums. The Cabinet of Curiosities in Sixteenth- and Seventeenth-Century Europe* (Oxford, 1985), pp. 76-7.

20. J.A. Crowe and C.B. Cavalcaselle, *The Life and Times of Titian* (London, 1881), II, pp. 367-9.

21. For Gaddi see Bencivenni-Pelli, op. cit. (Note 3), I, p. 135 and *passim*; II, pp. 83-4 note lxi (with references). For Hainhofer see Hayward, op. cit. (Note 18), p. 28, and H.O. Boström, 'Philipp Hainhofer and Gustavus Adolphus's *Kunstschrank* in Uppsala', in Impey and MacGregor, op. cit. (Note 19), pp. 90-101.

22. For Carleton's correspondence of this sort see W.N. Sainsbury, *Original Unpublished Papers illustrative of the Life of Sir Peter Paul Rubens* (London, 1859), pp. 9-65 and *passim*. For Nys see D. Howarth, *Lord Arundel and his Circle* (New Haven and London, 1985), pp. 39, 61.

23. Michael Vickers, personal communication. For Attalus see Pliny, *Naturalis historia* VII, 30.

24. For Alfonso see G. Campori, *Notizie storiche e artistiche della maiolica e della porcellana a Ferrara nei secoli xv-xvi* (Modena, 1873); C. Piccolpasso, *The Three Books of the Potter's Art* ed. R. Lightbown and A. Caiger-Smith (London, 1980), II, pp. 6-7; R. Lightbown, 'L'esotismo' in Einaudi (ed.), *Storia dell'Arte Italiana* X (Turin, 1981), p. 460.

25. C. Piccolpasso, *Le piante et i ritratti delle citta e terre dell'Umbria* ed. G. Cecchini (Rome, 1963), p. 244.

26. Ibid., p. 240. For porphyry see Vasari, *Vite* (ed. cit. Note 8), I; Bencivenni-Pelli, op. cit. (Note 3), I, p. 66; and Palazzo Pitti, *Splendori di Pietre Dure* ed. A. Giusti (Florence, 1988), pp. 10-11.

27. For Francesco see Bencivenni-Pelli, op. cit. (Note 3), I, p. 105, and L. Berti, *Il Principe dello Studiolo: Francesco I dei Medici e la fine del Rinascimento Fiorentino* (Florence, 1967).

28. This document is printed in Bencivenni-Pelli, op. cit. (Note 3), II, pp. 119-23, and also in G. Zobi, *Notizie storiche sull'origine e progressi dei lavori di commesso in pietre dure* (Florence, 1852), p. 162-5.

29. For the whole subject of *pietra dura* see now the exhibition catalogue *Splendori di Pietre Dure* (op. cit. Note 26).

30. Bencivenni-Pelli, op. cit. (Note 3), I, p. 117.

31. Filippo Pigafetta, cited in Bencivenni-Pelli, op. cit. (Note 3), I, pp. 193-5. For the Tribuna see Berti, op. cit. (Note 27), pp. 133-5.

32. Fynes Moryson, *An Itinerary* (Glasgow, edn. of 1907-8), I, pp. 321-2.

33. The diary of Nicholas Stone the Younger is printed by W.L. Spiers, in *Walpole Society* 7 (1919). The references in the text are on pp. 162-4.

34. For the Museo Gioviano see J. von Schlosser, *La letteratura artistica* 3rd. edn. ed. O. Kurz (Florence, 1964), pp. 195-7, 199.

35. Luzio, op. cit. (Note 7), pp. 39-40.

36. *Van der Doort's Catalogue, passim.*

37. Peacham, op. cit. (Note 10), pp. 117-37.

38. Luzio, op. cit. (Note 7), pp. 29-30.

39. Ibid., pp. 41-3.

40. There is no comprehensive study of this interesting subject.

41. Sainsbury, op. cit. (Note 22), pp. 12-13.

42. Ibid., pp. 57-8.

43. Vatican Library, MS Barb. Lat. 8645, f. 287.

44. G. Baglione, *Le vite de' pittori scvltori et architetti* (Rome, 1642), pp. 157-8.

45. [A Ratti], *Guida sommaria per il visitatore della Biblioteca Ambrosiana* (Milan, 1907), pp. 132-40.

46. Vatican Library, MS Barb. Lat. 8633, f. 226.

47. Luzio, op. cit. (Note 7), p. 38.

48. *Van der Doort's Catalogue*, p. 123.

49. For Rudolf see T. DaCosta Kauffman, *Variations on the Imperial Theme in the Age of Maximilian II and Rudolf II* (Outstanding dissertations in the Fine Arts) (Garland, 1978), and the exhibition catalogue *Prag um 1600. Kunst und Kultur am Hofe Kaiser Rudolf II* (Vienna, 1988).

50. Hayward, op. cit. (Note 18), pp. 269-71.

51. Ibid., p. 152.

52. For the Prague *pietra dura* workshops, see the essay by D. Heikamp in Giusti, op. cit. (Note 26), pp. 232-7.

53. For the arrangement of Rudolf's collections see Kauffman, op. cit. (Note 49), pp. 105-7, 113-18, and E. Fučíková, 'The collection of Rudolf II at Prague: cabinet of curiosities or scientific museum?', in Impey and MacGregor, op. cit. (Note 19), pp. 47-53, especially pp. 48-9.

54. Of the many editions of Barclay's *Satyricon* I have used that of Leyden, 1674, pp. 265-7.

55. H. Peacham, *The Gentleman's Exercise* (London, 1634), p. 124.

56. *Van der Doort's Catalogue*, pp. 12, 76, 108, 154.

57. M. Whinney and O. Millar, *English Art 1625-1714* (Oxford, 1957), p. 3 note 4; *Van der Doort's Catalogue*, pp. 125-6.

58. Howarth, op. cit. (Note 22), p. 227; Luzio, op. cit. (Note 6), p. 68.

59. J. Nichols, *The Progresses, Processions, and Magnificent Festivities of King James the First* (London, 1828), IV, p. 914; Whinney and Millar, op. cit. (Note 57), p. 3.

60. Nichols, op. cit. (Note 59), IV, p. 918.

61. H. Peacham, *The Compleat Gentleman* (London, edn. of 1634), pp. 107-8.

62. Howarth, op. cit. (Note 22), pp. 119-20; *Van der Doort's Catalogue*, pp. i, 124-5; Peacham, op. cit. (Note 61), p. 105.

63. Peacham, op. cit. (Note 61), pp. 123-4.

64. *Van der Doort's Catalogue*, p. 135.

65. Vatican Library, MS Barb. Lat. 8639, f. 118.

66. Concerning Le Sueur, see C. Avery, 'Hubert Le Sueur, the "unworthy Praxiteles" of King Charles I', *Walpole Society* 48 (1982), pp. 135-209.

67. For Charles I's bust by Bernini, see R. Lightbown, 'Bernini's busts of English patrons', in *Art the Ape of Nature: Studies in Honor of H. W. Janson* (New York, 1981), pp. 439-52.

68. For these the *locus classicus* is Peacham, op. cit. (Note 61), pp. 104-11.

69. For these see K. Watson and C. Avery, 'Medici and Stuart: a Grand Ducal gift of "Giovanni Bologna" bronzes for Henry, Prince of Wales (1612)', *Burlington Magazine* 115 (1973), pp. 493-507.

70. For the Frizell collection see B. Reade, 'William Frizell and the Royal Collection', *Burlington Magazine* 133 (1947), pp. 70-7.

71. For Petitot and Bordier at the English court see R. Lightbown, 'Jean Petitot: étude pour une biographie et catalogue de son œuvre', *Genava* new ser. 18 (1970), pp. 81-103.

72. BL, MS Sloane 2052.

73. *Van der Doort's Catalogue*, p. 127 [3]; p. 221 [97].

74. B. Long, *British Miniaturists* (London, 1929), p. 339.

75. Lightbown, op. cit. (Note 71), p. 79.

76. Sainsbury, op. cit. (Note 22), pp. 349-50.

77. Luzio, op. cit. (Note 6), p. 117.

3   Charles I, Sculpture and Sculptors

David Howarth

Marginal numerals refer to page and entry numbers in the *inventories* (see p. 11)

In 1957 Margaret Whinney and Oliver Millar published their *English Art 1625-1714* which remains the authoritative survey of the fine arts under the Stuarts. In this book the authors gave Inigo Jones an entire chapter whereas sculpture was coupled with tapestries, a decorative art, because:

English sculpture of the seventeenth century is far less lively than English architecture, nor does it rise to the level of contemporary painting, for though several foreign sculptors worked here, they . . . were not of the stature to found a school . . . Moreover, in sculpture the general standard of taste had been formed on Flemish rather than on Italian or antique models.[1]

After thirty years much new research has been undertaken to modify their views. The authors chose the accession of Charles I in 1625 as their starting point and that was also the time when more English sculptors and their patrons began to absorb the classical style directly from Italy rather than encountering it, modified, through north European mannerisms. The influence of Netherlandish sculpture on English tradition remained very strong, though it is easy to underestimate the widespread appreciation of classical sculpture which had been established since the reign of Elizabeth. The statesman and philosopher Sir Francis Bacon was intrigued by sculpture in a way which he was not by painting.[2] The poet William Drummond of Hawthornden was not only inspired by the thought of Virgil's tomb, but composed or translated poems on the figures and busts of Venus, Adonis, Amphion, Medea, Medusa, Alcides and Nero. The scholar Sir Robert Cotton had the busts of philosophers and poets in his library, and Lord Lumley an equestrian statue at his castle.[3] In 1615 the Earl of Somerset, short-lived favourite of James I, tried to prop up a fading image by negotiating for a major collection of sculpture from Venice;[4] an exercise in the social manipulation of art which was to be repeated ten years later by his successor in the King's affections, the Duke of Buckingham.

Nicholas Stone, the most talented native-born sculptor of the period, died a rich man. Commissions for monuments poured into his workshop: in 1638 he received £400 for a monument to a Chief Justice of the King's Bench,[5] the same amount as Hubert Le Sueur, a French sculptor settled in England, contracted with Archbishop Laud for making bronzes of Charles and Henrietta Maria.[6] Evidently in England in 1630, sculpture was a vocation in which a man could do exceptionally well; in 1635 Charles I sold over two hundred acres in Somerset for far less than a sculptor might receive for an ambitious monument.[7]

Stone had three sons who were variously connected with sculpture, architecture and monumental stone-work, of which the most talented was also called Nicholas. The younger Nicholas died before he had accomplished much, but when he was in Rome in 1638, he attracted the notice of Bernini who thought he had talent. Stone recorded in his diary how, on 26 October, he introduced himself to Bernini in St. Peter's and

he fauoured me so farr as to show me the statua that he had under hand in that church, and told me that for a while he should be bussy thaire, but when he had done and that he was att his housse I should be welcome to spend my time with the other of his disciples.[8]

They met again on 11 December when they walked back together from St. Peter's to Bernini's house and

[I] showed him some drawings yt I had coppyed after Raphyells with 3 orders of archytecture of my own caprycio; he was uery well pleased to see them and told me that 15 dayes hence he should haue finisht his statua then under hand and then if I would come to him he would first haue practice after some thinges he had and I should se his manner of workeing and then worke my selfe . . .[9]

The worldy success enjoyed by the elder Stone and the encouragement given to the younger, suggests that the art may have been more flourishing and ambitious than has been thought. An examination of the collection of sculpture which belonged to Charles I, shows that this was indeed the case.

Whinney and Millar's account of foreign artists working in England is also challenged by the recent discovery of more works by François Dieussart; the most promising foreign sculptor to come to England before the Civil War. The best of Dieussart suggests that some of his sculpture was outstanding by international standards. Dieussart arrived in 1635 to work for the Earl of Arundel and he developed into a major figure with a European reputation whose work was surpassed only by Bernini, Algardi and Duquesnoy.[10]

The collections of antique and modern pieces possessed by Charles I and Arundel were surpassed only by the Vatican, the Medici and Farnese holdings. But those Italian collections had been accumulated over generations, whereas Charles's acquisitions represented the enthusiasm of one man over a period of twenty years: it comprised hundreds of antique statues or busts, and modern works by or attributed to Antico, Torrigiano, Michelangelo, Sansovino, Giambologna, Vittoria, Tacca, Bernini, Duquesnoy, Fanelli, Dieussart, Le Sueur and the Vianen family.

Charles had first shown this love for sculpture when only eleven. In 1611 his elder brother Henry, Prince of Wales, had been presented with examples of the most fashionable sculpture in Europe: fifteen table bronzes from the workshops of Giambologna sent from Florence as part of the negotiations which it was hoped would lead to marriage between Henry and Caterina de' Medici, sister of Cosimo II.[11] A suggestion that a walking horse from this consignment would make a suitable present for Charles, was however rebuffed by Henry, but the sight of these child-sized bronzes was a critical moment in awakening an appreciation of sculpture in the young boy (Fig. 28).[12]

Scattered references over the next decade suggest that Charles built upon that covetous experience. Van der Doort noted the purchase of 'the head of Nero' which was acquired from the painter Geldorp when Charles was Prince of Wales and for which he later got Hubert Le Sueur to 'make a buske – and a Peddistall to it'.[13] While yet Prince of Wales, Charles seems already to have had ambitions as patron, not just as collector: he was probably the moving figure behind approaching Pietro Tacca to cast a bronze equestrian monument of James I.[14] The project was never realized but it would have put the English monarchy on the

Figure 28   Giambologna [after]: *A Bird-Catcher*. Florentine, *c*. 1610. Bronze. Reproduced by courtesy of the Board of Trustees of the Victoria and Albert Museum, London.

same pedestal as the Medici and the kings of France, since they already had such images of themselves.

The experience of seeing and handling the bronzes belonging to Prince Henry was certainly important for the development of Charles's tastes, but then so were certain people. Christian IV of Denmark, his uncle, was establishing one of the most ambitious and splendid Renaissance courts in northern Europe at this very time.[15] Christian had visited London in 1606 and then came again in 1614 when Charles, by now adolescent, was at his most impressionable. Charles's fastidiousness and love of art came from the Danish side of the family, through his mother, Anne of Denmark.

There is much circumstantial evidence to suggest that Christian may have adopted the role of tutor to his nephew despite the Danish monarch's robust, not to say, saturnine temperament, which must have grated with that of Charles. When Christian had been in London in 1606, Sir Walter Cope had borrowed works of art to dress up his cabinet in preparation for a private visit from the Danish king.[16] As it was, Christian had long looked to England for creative talent: John Dowland certainly, and Inigo Jones possibly, worked at the Danish court.[17] However, what is of particular interest in the context of Charles's response to sculpture, is that Christian was much preoccupied with it at the time of this second visit to London in July 1614.

Christian believed that he had emerged from the Kalmar War with Sweden of 1611-13 as the figurehead of a Denmark ordained to rule the Baltic and northern seas. Consequently he had decided to commemorate this with a series of commissions from artists of which the most eye-catching was to be a Neptune fountain at Frederiksborg Castle, symbolizing the apotheosis of Denmark's new role in the northern world. In May 1614, just two months before coming to London, Christian had sent his mint master Nicolaus Schwabe to Prague, where he had commissioned the Neptune fountain from Adrian de Vries. Thereby Christian had obtained the services of the most celebrated sculptor of northern Europe for a major propaganda coup – a lesson in the political use of sculpture which was surely not lost on his young English nephew. Furthermore, at the time of Christian's visit his stonemason, Hans Steenwinckel – recorded in Van der Doort's inventory as having presented Charles I with an 'imboast sitting figure'[18] – was not only assembling the Neptune fountain but also building a grandiose two-storey marble gallery in front of the King's Wing at Frederiksborg to house sculptures from Hendrick de Keyser's workshop in Amsterdam. In 1613 Nicholas Stone the Elder, who was to do so much for Charles I as builder, fountain designer, sculptor and restorer of antiquities, had just returned to England from Amsterdam. He had been there since 1606, improving his skills as a sculptor under the guidance of Hendrick de Keyser, whose daughter Maria he had just married.

Some years after the project to get Tacca to cast a bronze equestrian statue of James I, moves were made which eventually resulted in Charles acquiring virtually all the statues which had belonged to the court of Mantua – famous during the Renaissance for its patronage of the visual arts.

That extraordinary sale was the result of negotiations which began when the Countess of Arundel was returning in 1623 from the Veneto, where she had been educating her children. Married to a famous collector and a connoisseur in her own right, to whom Titian's grandson had just dedicated his *Life* of the painter,[19] she was a natural choice for Duke Vincenzo II of Mantua to approach when, desperate for money, he had decided to jettison a famous collection. She responded in July 1623 by asking for a model of the Ducal Palace with descriptions of its contents.[20] Although, regrettably, that fascinating object has not survived, it had the desired effect because matters began in earnest in 1625. Daniel Nys, a dealer, bought from the Gonzaga and then sold to Charles I, whose interests were represented by Nicholas Lanier. The negotiations lasted, one way and another, for almost a decade.

Nys is an important but shadowy figure in the early history of collecting who seems to have been French by birth but had been domiciled in Venice since 1598. There he had established a position as Swedish consul and as the person to whom English dispatches were entrusted. Nys had also been an art agent for at least ten years before the Mantuan sale and had by then considerable experience in dealing with English clients: he had sold antiquities to the Earl of Somerset in 1615. Lanier had been a servant of Prince Henry's and was a prominent musician and art dealer at the English court. As a dealer, he made frequent trips abroad to buy for the king and to speculate on his own behalf.

It is difficult to assess the cost of the Mantuan sculpture and so to make assumptions about how it was valued in England, as compared with the paintings. £10,500 was paid for the sculpture but included within that sum was an unknown amount for Mantegna's *Triumphs of Caesar* (Fig. 69), and other unspecified pictures. This compares with £7,780 which Charles either had paid or would pay for the majority of the paintings. All that can safely be said is that the Mantuan sculpture was no less highly regarded than the paintings which included some of the greatest masterpieces of the Renaissance: the Mantegnas themselves, Titian's *Entombment* (Pl. 8) and Correggio's *Allegory of Love* (Pl. 16).

What is clear, however, is that the acquisition of sculpture and paintings periodically created serious financial problems for the crown.[21] A commitment to pay £15,000 for the Mantuan collection was made at a time when desperate attempts were being made to extricate the Duke of Buckingham's expeditionary force, sent to relieve the Protestants of La Rochelle. Filippo Burlamachi, money-lender to the King, thought the purchase interfered with more important priorities, as he made clear to the courtier Endymion Porter in a letter of October 1627:

By the letters I send you this morning you mai have seene Ni. Laniers demand. Hier bi the notes and descriptions send to mee. I praie lett me know his Ma[ts] pleaseur, but above all where monie shall by found to pay this great somme. Iff it where for 2 or 3000£ it could be borne, but for 15000£, besides the other Engagements for his Ma[ts] service, it will utterli put me out off ani possibilite to doe ani think in those provisions wiche are so necessari for mi Lord Ducks relieve. I praie lett me know what I must trust . . .[22]

Burlamachi was essential to Charles I as his principal money lender, but he was neither close to him nor interested in art. Thus he failed to see that for Charles, these acquisitions were an arm of policy; a necessary adjunct of his greatness as a Renaissance prince.

As it was, such irresponsible extravagance (as Burlamachi saw it) had its compensations, or so Nys claimed. He wrote of how the sculptures had created a sensation when put on public view in Venice and sent a servant to London to make known to

all the grandees that the statues and pictures of his Majesty are daily visited here in Venice by all the great people of the city, as well as by foreigners. That all speak in admiration of their beauty and rarity, observing that the King of England will possess the most beautiful works in the world.[23]

Possession was not, however, something that Charles was able to achieve easily; it took over four years for all the sculpture to arrive in London. This was partly Charles's fault; he frequently delayed in paying Nys who then had to incur a heavier burden of debt to service interest on bills of exchange issued by Burlamachi on the Venetian market. It was probably because Nys frequently doubted that he would ever be reimbursed the £18,280. 12s. 8d. paid out on behalf of Charles for the Mantuan pictures and statues, that he kept back significant holdings of the sculpture, intending, if things went against him, to sell what remained to other interested parties. However, a substantial consignment of sculpture was sent in twenty-five cases aboard the *Margaret,* the *Unicorn* and the *Pearl*. These Nys described as 'the refuse', in a letter sent to Charles from Venice on 26 July 1630.[24] But in order to reassure his client, Nys added that 'The most beautiful have to come'. Actually this was far from true. On 25 October 1630, Thomas Rowlandson, acting ambassador in Venice, wrote to Lord Treasurer Weston, whose dealings with Nys over the Mantuan sculpture, may well have induced him to commission the Le Sueur equestrian statue of Charles I, now in Trafalgar Square (Fig. 55):

As I gave y[r] L[p] addvertissement of the shipping of severall chestes of his Ma[tyes] Statues and pictures upon the Rebecke and the London soe shall please your L[p] to understand that I have lately consigned unto Mr Richard Haddock, M[r] of the Industrye, other 30th chestes of statue and two of pictures, there remaining no more pictures, and onlye 16th great statue, wich shall be sent, God willingh, in the Peeter Bone-venture layng now at an anchor in this port . . .[25]

But there were still more statues to be disgorged. On 13 June 1631, Nys wrote to Thomas Carey, a Groom of the Bedchamber, relating how he had been bankrupted: the implication must be (if indeed the claim was true) that it was because Charles had not paid him. According to Nys, the creditors had been rummaging in the back of his house to see what they could find and had come

Figure 29   Anonymous: *Crouching Venus and other Mantuan statues*. North Italian, 1627. Pencil and bistre wash, and red chalk and pale brown wash. Royal Library, Windsor; reproduced by gracious permission of Her Majesty The Queen.

Figure 30   Anonymous: *Sleeping Cupids*. North Italian, 1627. Pencil and bistre wash, and red chalk and pale brown wash. Royal Library, Windsor; reproduced by gracious permission of Her Majesty The Queen.

across three Titians and a Raphael, as well as 'A large figure in antique copper, very rare; a 'Figure of a woman sitting in marble; some say *Venus delli Ely*, others *Helen of Troy* [Fig. 29]. It is the finest statue of all, and estimated at 6000 *escus*'; and in addition, three *Sleeping Cupids* by Michelangelo, Sansovino and Praxiteles respectively (Fig. 30). These 'three children', Nys added, 'are above price, and are the rarest things which the Duke [of Mantua] possessed'. All, Nys then declared disingenuously, forgotten by him, but certainly 'belonging to the King my most gracious Master'.[26] Nys took these embarrassing revelations in his stride, however, and it was not until over a year later – on 4 August 1632 – that these, the last of the Mantuan sculptures, left Venice on board the *Assurance*. It had been a long saga from which none of the parties emerged with credit, except perhaps the harassed officials at the English embassy in Venice: they sent the *Assurance* away with the fervent prayer that 'God send her a good voiagge home'[27] and the hope that they would not have to be involved with the King's collection again.

Clearly Nys was not to be trusted and, even by the standards then prevailing, his exaggerations would have been manifest when all the sculpture had eventually arrived in London. As for its intrinsic quality, there was little which would now be regarded as exceptional. Most of the pieces were Hellenistic or late Imperial; though the Commonwealth inventories of the King's goods describe a number of rarities which do indeed suggest that there was a proportion of pieces which were unusual. Some of these may have come from Mantua, for example: three 'Grecian Buskes' and a 'Jupiter in black Marbell'.[28]

But the Mantuan piece with the most romantic provenance was Michelangelo's *Sleeping Cupid*, which appears alongside those versions of the same subject attributed by Nys to Praxiteles and Sansovino respectively, on one of the sheets of drawings now at Windsor – drawings dispatched by Nys early in February 1629 to give Charles an impression of what he would be acquiring, were he to buy the Mantuan sculpture as he had done the paintings. The Michelangelo *Sleeping Cupid* had been carved in the antique style in 1496 and then acquired by the dealer Baldassare del Milanese who had offered it for sale as a genuine antique. Eventually it was sold to Cesare Borgia and later came into the collection of Isabella D'Este. There it was displayed as a work by Praxiteles, proudly shown off to a select few whom Isabella allowed into her *grotta* within the ducal palace at Mantua.[29]

143 [79], 144 [92-3], 146 [145]

Of the pieces which arrived via Venice between July 1630 and August 1632, it is difficult to identify more than a handful with specific statues and busts in museums and private collections today.[30] This is partly because some of the pieces were almost certainly wrongly restored either by sculptors in the employment of the Mantuan court, or by Charles I's own restorer who was sent from London to help prepare the sculpture for shipment.[31] Some of these will have had that restoration removed so that they will now bear little relation to what can be seen in the drawings. Another difficulty is that many of the busts were mundane versions of a standard type of which many identical examples still exist. It might be possible to make headway even with some of these, but the Nys drawings are on relatively small sheets and sometimes details which would help with identification are imprecise. Furthermore, Nys was not above enhancing his stock by giving pieces an elevated but bogus status, as indeed was the case with the *Crouching Venus* discovered, much to his surprise, in the purlieus of his house, and today still in the Royal Collection. Although Rubens had admired it when he had been keeper of the Mantuan collections, it was certainly not the *Venus de Milo* or *Helen of Troy*, as Nys had claimed.[32]

Adolf Michaelis, the nineteenth-century German archaeological scholar, could identify only one example of Greek sculpture from the collection of Charles I, and that was not a free-standing statue, but a round altar with figures in relief.[33] Although there were certainly more Greek pieces in the collection than Michaelis believed, the small number of pre-Roman works was in marked contrast to what could be seen at Arundel House. There was to be found a collection famous throughout Europe, which contained not only Greek marbles but also bronzes such as the third-century BC head of *'Homer'* now in the British Museum.[34] Furthermore, Charles and Arundel were far from being alone in collecting antique sculpture, since the Duke of Buckingham was also an assiduous collector who had started buying in Asia Minor as the Mantuan sale got under way. When he also acquired Rubens's collection of statuary in 1628, what the King owned became only one – and then not the best – of a number of collections which made up the most remarkable concentration of Greek and Roman sculpture assembled in modern times outside Rome.

Charles loved sculpture as a connoisseur but exploited it as a king. However splendid and eloquent a painting may be, it cannot be displayed outside. By contrast, sculpture can. At a time when access to royal palaces was confined to the rich and the privileged who, for the most part, were supporters of the King, paintings impinged on those who needed no persuasion. Sculpture on the other hand, exposed the person and the *idea* of the King to all – rich and poor, sympathetic and disaffected alike. Thus it may well be that Charles valued the work of his second-rate sculptors as highly as the paintings of his consummate master, Van Dyck.

In 1634, the social historian Henry Peacham published a new edition of his popular *Compleat Gentleman*, which contained for the first time a chapter on antiquities in response to the interest provoked by the influx of classical statuary from Italy. Peacham wrote that Charles I testified to 'a Royall liking of ancient statues, by causing a whole army . . . to come and doe him homage, and attend him in his palaces of Saint Iames, and Sommerset-house'.[35] Peacham's testament is important: it suggests that people thought of St. James's and Somerset (or Denmark) House as the main repositories of the sculpture collection after everything from Mantua had arrived. Indeed it confirms the impression gained from other sources; that Whitehall was not such an important location for sculpture, at least as far as full-scale marbles and bronzes were concerned. Greenwich came to have some of the very best items from the sculpture collection but, from what Peacham writes, it may be assumed that that it was only after the Queen's House was completed (shortly after the new edition of Peacham's book appeared) that Greenwich came to be especially favoured as a venue for sculpture.

The use of the adjective 'Royall' in this passage is also significant because it implies that there was something different about a monarchical attitude to sculpture. Although Peacham is being whimsical, he is also being serious in the sense that he perceives that the rhetoric of sculpture was useful to a monarch, just as the rituals of the coronation enhanced the deistic image of the king. For Peacham, as for Charles, sculpture was as much the art of eloquence as proportion; a means of persuasion in a society to which the art spoke in ways now hard for us to grasp.

Machiavelli had perceived the social and political significance of owning sculpture in his preface to Book I of *The Discourses*, where he wrote:

When, therefore, I consider in what honour antiquity is held, and how – to cite but one instance – a bit of an old statue has fetched a high price that someone may have it by him to give honour to his house . . . [36]

Sir Henry Wotton, who had been much involved in buying sculpture for English collectors when ambassador in Venice during the second decade of the century, went further than Machiavelli in seeing a direct connection between art, society and politics. Wotton finished his diplomatic career just as the Mantuan sale got under way and from then on his writing kept him closely in touch with the King. What Wotton had to say about statuary reflects the values of Charles himself: Wotton argued that the monuments of the ancients were not 'a bare and transitory entertainment of the Eye . . . But had also a secret and strong influence, even into the Advancement of the Monarchy, by continual representation of virtuous examples, so as in that point, Art became a piece of state'. [37]

In contrast to Wotton, there were those like Burlamachi who felt that because of the chronic state of royal finances, the King's extravagance was vitiating the effectiveness of government. But Wotton was right: the Mantuan purchase was a more successful expedient in projecting the image of Charles I than conventional initiatives in foreign policy. Marie de' Medici and her chief minister, Cardinal Richelieu, became eager to acquire the Mantuan statues for their respective collections, and so the wholesale acquisition of this famous Renaissance collection was to be an important coup for England. [38]

The Mantuan collection is known to have affected London sculptors after its arrival from the summer of 1630 onwards. Nicholas Stone became involved in his capacity as a restorer as soon as it began to be unloaded. The statues and virtually all the pictures had undergone the hazards of the long voyage from Venice, and although pictures were more obviously vulnerable to the movement of cargo during storms and to the spillage of dangerous substances like quicksilver or olive oil, the marbles were not immune; evidently some were damaged. The royal accounts for 1629-30 include a payment for work done at St. James's in 'mending statues damaged by sea'. [39] The restoration undertaken by Stone gave him a close acquaintance with the classical sculpture and at the time the last consignment arrived from Venice a radical response is observable in his work. In the monument of 1634 to John and Thomas Lyttleton at Magdalen College, Oxford, [40] for example, the boys lean like melancholy supporters of a coat of arms, contemplating their own funeral tablet; they wear togas, the folds of which reveal a close scrutiny of classical drapery.

But despite the thorough-going influence of classical statuary on Stone's execution of the Lyttleton monument, there is a danger in over-estimating the effect of the Mantuan sculpture on the artist. Even before its arrival, he had adapted his style to what he could already see of classical works in London: for example, the Holles monuments in Westminster Abbey, which were carved before the advent of the Mantuan sculpture, reveal a somewhat gauche pastiche of Michelangelo and the antique. [41] In this case, the patron, the Earl of Clare, may have influenced Stone decisively. He was an intimate political ally and fellow conspirator of Arundel against Buckingham; frequent meetings between the two at Arundel House exposed Clare to the classical statues which had come to London following Arundel's return from Italy in 1614. [42]

Nevertheless, the advent of the Mantuan pieces gave fresh impetus to Stone's ambition and new coherence to his commissions. Hitherto he had only been able to graft classicism on to the individual figure, but after his appointment as Master Mason to the King in 1632, and the privileged access that post allowed to the King's sculpture, the influence of classicism extended beyond the single figure to affect the design of whole monuments. The point is made by comparing a Stone monument executed before the arrival of the Mantuan sculpture with one made after. The monument to Lady Knatchbull at Mersham of 1626 seems like an ingenious clock rather than a structure that has been designed as an integral whole; two angels in sagging contrapposto draw back a veil to show a kneeling figure – as a curtain might suddenly part to reveal Vulcan striking the hour upon the town hall. [43] This contrasts with the monument to Lady Catherine Paston of 1636 in Oxnead. [44] The Paston effigy is set upon a pedestal which has been designed as the centrepiece towards which everything else gravitates. The ensemble has a quite new simplicity and coherence which could be accounted for by Stone's involvement in the display of Charles's classical statuary; something with which Arundel was surely asked to help. Arundel liked to group busts and architectural fragments in his gardens and the Paston monument is reminiscent of an ensemble which had originally been set up in Arundel House garden and which George Vertue saw reconstructed at Easton Neston in Oxfordshire in the eighteenth century.[45] It is tempting to suggest that a consequence of the reconciliation which took place between Arundel and the King in the autumn of 1628 after the death of Buckingham, and which was given public expression with a three-hour tour of Arundel House, was that Charles commissioned tableaux like those he had seen in Arundel House gardens. These would have been supervised by Stone, which would account for a much enhanced architectural coherence in his work during the 1630s.

There are half a dozen other Stone monuments indicating the change which antique sculpture wrought upon his practice; one of the most adventurous is the tomb of Dudley Carleton, Viscount Dorchester, of 1640 in Westminster Abbey.[46] The tomb is a sophisticated variation upon the theme of the ancient Roman funeral effigy. Here, Carleton is propped up on his right elbow, dressed incongruously in his Viscount's regalia while lying on a *triclinium*, contained within an aedicule of Jonesian purity.

Stone executed surprisingly little new work for the King and what there was seems to have been confined to Windsor Castle, where Stone may have had something of a proprietorial attitude as a consequence of his appointment in April 1626 as 'Master Mason and Architeckt for all our buildings and reparations within our house and castle of Windsor'.[47] The most interesting item at Windsor, which was probably destroyed in the Civil War, was Stone's 'carved piece that stands over the Gate of Diana or chast love taking her repose having bereaved Cupid of his bow and arrow and turned him to flight'.[48]

However, the Diana relief would have been overshadowed by a fountain, the subject of which was 'the Statues of Hercules worrying of Antaeus as if by squeezing of him, the water comes out of his mouth', commissioned in July 1635 but abruptly cancelled in December of the same year.[49] This very subject had been chosen already by Sir John Danvers for one of two fountains, the other being a *Cain and Abel*, which had been executed by Stone's assistant John Schorman, for Sir John's famous garden in Chelsea.[50] In the light of this, the cancellation of the Windsor project is understandable: Charles, at the time of commissioning, may have been unaware that Stone's assistant had already carved such a group but was then told, and, in a competitive world, was reluctant to have one of the same subject himself. Alternatively, perhaps he had not seen the design of the Chelsea fountain before he ordered one himself, but then did not like what he saw.

The Schorman statues represented the response of Stone's workshop to the great masterpieces of Italian fountain sculpture created by the Mannerist artists Giambologna and Niccolo Tribolo. The work of the Italians, because of its brilliant inventiveness, became the chief inspiration for English seventeenth-century sculptors of large-scale commissions.

Just before his death in 1550, Tribolo had conceived a fountain design depicting Hercules wrestling with Antaeus – now known as *The Fountain of Hercules* – for the Medici villa of Castello in the Valdarno. Although Tribolo died before the project had really got underway, it was completed by Ammanati. This was the sort of monument which became the model for English sculptors.[51]

Stone and Schorman were also very much aware of Giambologna's *Samson and the Philistine*, one of the most celebrated of the master's works (Fig. 31). Known after it had left Italy as *Cain and Abel*, it had been erected in the gardens of York House, Buckingham's principal London residence, in the summer of 1624. There, virtually within walking distance of Danvers' property, it became one of the most celebrated monuments in London.

Stone, together with the circle of sculptors associated with him, periodically turned to the royal collection for inspiration. Pembroke's garden at Wilton, the most splendid of the period, was much loved by Charles I and it may be no coincidence that the statues which surmounted the four fountains in the *parterres de broderie* suggest sculpture from the royal collection: the *Venus and Cupid* fountain at Wilton seems to derive, in part at least, from a *Venus and Cupid* and a *Venus with a Dolphin*, both from Mantua and both included on the Nys sheets, while the *Susanna* fountain, also at Wilton, takes the famous *Crouching Venus*, about which Nys had made such inflated claims, as its starting point.[52]

Figure 31   Giambologna: *Samson and the Philistine. c.* 1566. Marble. Reproduced by courtesy of the Board of Trustees of the Victoria and Albert Museum, London.

Edward Marshall who was to succeed Stone at the Restoration as Master Mason to the King, was not as talented as Stone himself, but he too responded to the wealth of sculpture then in London. One of his best works is the monument to Henry Curwen of 1636 in Amersham church. The standing shrouded figure seems to have been inspired by Giambologna statuettes such as *The Venus Urania*, which may have been in the royal collection.[53]

Although Nicholas Stone, more than others, was affected by Charles's sculpture, its influence was not confined to him and his workshop. There was Marshall and also Hubert le Sueur, a Frenchman probably brought over from Paris by Buckingham in 1625, who established himself at court as an efficient but second-rate bronze caster. He probably first got to know the King's sculpture through his work as a restorer. That activity also involved him in providing plinths and pedestals for the display of sculpture, which in turn, led him to Rome to take moulds of antiques for casting in bronze.

However, it is only with a commission of 1633 that the influence of the royal collection on Le Sueur can be detected in work which was neither connected with restoration nor involved a cast after the antique. In that year he signed a contract for a posthumous monument to Admiral Sir Richard Leveson. What survives of the Leveson monument in St. Peter's, Wolverhampton, suggests he was unable to accomplish with any conviction, composition requiring free-standing groups. The life-size standing figure of Sir Richard is pretentious with its contrived and mannered contrapposto and shows that the artist has only partially understood the mechanics of statues like the *Shepherd* or *Eros* illustrated in the Nys drawings at Windsor.[54]

A bust of Catherine Bruce, Countess of Dysart which might be associated with her marriage in 1636, to judge from her revealing dress, again suggests the influence of the Mantuan examples on Le Sueur. Although the worried drapery of the Dysart bust is markedly unclassical, the way the left arm is placed across the right breast is reminiscent of *Mario Catone* on one of the Nys sheets and the top left hand unidentified bust on a separate Nys sheet.[55]

The statues and busts which were available in London by the early thirties caused an undoubted reaction – though this was not always favourable. Sir Isaac

Wake was involved in the Mantuan negotiations in his capacity as ambassador in Venice. In the summer of 1625 he wrote to a friend while Lanier was in Venice, negotiating for the Mantuan collection. Wake referred in his letter to:

Some in England who have taken unto themselves a monopolye of passing their verdict upon all things of this nature, so that if a man do not baptise his picture or statue at the font of their censure he cannot be admitted into the Church.[56]

Wake was highly articulate – he had been Public Orator of Oxford University – but, like many educated Englishmen, seems to have felt that the courtier-collectors were remote, even mildly comical figures. Charles I and his circle certainly developed a passion for antique statuary but this was a new and sophisticated taste which was slow to extend beyond the italianized court.

Courtiers reacted against painted statues in favour of marble or bronze because they assumed that antique statuary had been monochrome. The shift can be traced in the literature of the period. Whereas Shakespeare's statues in *The Winter's Tale* and *Cymbeline*, were in the English tradition of coloured figures and the literary tradition of 'counterfeits of nature',[59] by the 1630s things had changed. Ben Jonson favoured what one might term 'court' as opposed to 'city' taste, in his play *The Magnetic Lady* (1632):

RUTLAND: I'ld have her statue cut, now, in white marble.
INTEREST: And have it painted in most orient colours.
RUTLAND: That's right! all Citie statues must be painted:
Else, they be worth nought i'their subtile Judgements.[58]

Sir Henry Wotton was a more significant influence on Caroline taste than his distinguished if unspectacular public career might suggest. He too, did much to create a fashion for marble. As a long-serving ambassador in Venice he had entertained scores of rich young men whose tastes he helped to form. Thereafter he published *The Elements of Architecture* (1624), the most accessible and popular of all interpretations in English of Italian palace design. Then he had become Provost of Eton, where he lived under the shadow of Windsor Castle to which he had access when Charles I was in residence. Wotton gave Charles a number of paintings and sculptures and also, no doubt, the benefit of his incomparable experience of classical and Renaissance art, seen at first hand in Italy. As for the Eton boys:

He was a constant Cherisher of all those youths in that School . . . for whose encouragement he was – besides many other things of necessity and beauty – at the charge of setting up in it two rows of pillars, on which he caused to be choicely drawn, the pictures of divers of the most famous Greek and Latin Historians, Poets, and Orators . . .[59]

Wotton's biographer, Isaak Walton, described him as 'a most dear Lover and a most excellent Judge' of the visual arts who thought 'the Fashion of *colouring, even Regal Statues* . . . an *English Barbarism*'.[60] He was strategically placed to persuade the court, and those who aspired to be courtiers, of his strong views on the proper treatment of sculpture and he was surely one of that band of advisers who persuaded the King to acquire the Mantuan statues after he had bought the pictures.

John Earle was a popular writer whose work survives not on literary merit but for its value to the social historian. Earle dissected Caroline society in his best-seller – *Micro-cosmographie*, in which he analyzed the different types to be found in society. The book was licensed at the Stationers' Hall on 5 June 1628,[61] before any of the Mantuan statues had arrived, but probably about three weeks after Titian's series of *Emperors* had arrived from Venice on the *Margaret*.[62] In *Micro-cosmographie*, Earle betrays that vein of good-natured scepticism, tinged with a trace of contempt, which Wake had felt when in the company of Nys and Lanier. Earle brings on the antiquary who:

. . . is of our Religion because we say that it is most ancient; and yet a broken statue would almost make him an idolater . . . His estate consists much in shekels and Roman coins, and he hath more pictures of Caesar than James and Elizabeth.[63]

Peacham was all in favour of this new 'religion', and as a self-proclaimed friend of Inigo Jones,[64] his instruction to poets and those who worked with them, as to how they were to respond to statuary, is of particular interest in the light of the Mantuan collection. Peacham instructs playwright and poet to converse with the statues of antiquity:

for the presentation of comedies, tragedies, masques, shows, or any learned scene whatsoever, the properties whereof can neither be appointed nor judged of but by such as are well seene in statue-craft.[65]

It would seem that Jones agreed with Peacham because his designs for masques and pastorals of the 1630s show many more classical allusions than do those of the previous decade. Scenes of atria, arcades and fora, suddenly become more abundant. Furthermore, there is a higher proportion of costume design based on what Jones understood of classical dress, as he interpreted it from his own extensive collection of prints and from his examination of the statues belonging to Charles I, Arundel and Buckingham.

Jones was jointly responsible with Aurelian Townshend for *Albion's Triumph* (1631) which was performed shortly after the first consignment of sculpture had arrived from Venice. Jones's scenes represent the most evocative tribute to the new Arcadia which seemed to have sprung up in the galleries and gardens of the great London palaces. The designs show him at his very best.[66] The basis for the setting for Scene 1, *A Roman Atrium*, may well have been the background to Mytens's stage-like painting of *Lord Arundel in his Gallery* where there is an enfilade of statues.[67] *Albion's Triumph* is a tribute to the classical world which the King as Apollo, and Henrietta Maria as Diana, had begun to inhabit not only in the masques themselves, but also in their gardens, where they were accompanied by their statues. In addition to the design for the atrium for *Albion's Triumph*, there are a number of costume sketches for characters who might have stepped off podia in St. James's Palace: *The Vestal Virgin, A Sacrificer, Flamen* and *Cytharoedus*.[68]

The following year saw a production of the pastoral, *The Shepherds Paradise*, which again seems to suggest the spirit of the King's sculpture.[69] In this case it is perhaps hardly surprising because here Jones was collaborating with Walter Montague, a great buyer of art,[70] who had been responsible for obtaining permission for Le Sueur to take moulds of famous antiques in Rome. One of three shutter designs associated with *The Shepherds Paradise*, is heavily indebted to a print by Callot of *Le Grand Parterre de Nancy* where the background has a raised terrace supported by a wall with niches containing statuary; a type of arrangement which might by then have been in the making at St. James's and which was probably put into effect for Henrietta Maria some six years later at Wimbledon House,[71] As with *Albion's Triumph*, so here too in *The Shepherds Paradise*, individual characters seem to have an enhanced classical air suggesting that in the early thirties, Jones was particularly conscious of the 'whole army of old forraine Emperours, Captaines, and Senators', which Charles had caused 'to land on his coasts'.[72] After Jones's designs for *The Temple of Love* (1635), where the costumes for *A Noble Persian Youth* and *Sunesis* have a classical feel to them, the presence of sculpture seems much less in evidence.[73] But by then, the novelty of the Mantuan sculpture had worn off.

Mantua provided the nucleus of the royal sculpture collection and it had a profound effect on the development of Charles's taste, as well as a marked impact on the visual arts in general. By the early thirties, Charles had become the most active royal patron of sculptors in Europe. The Mantuan sculpture greatly stimulated his appreciation and he became absorbed by pieces in Italy which were not for sale.

Charles combined a disinterested appreciation with an awareness of the propaganda value of sculpture. In the late 1620s he made attemps to acquire some of the most famous statues in Rome and when that failed sent 'ingenious Master Gage' to Italy to acquire a mould of the *Borghese Gladiator* which was cast in bronze by Hubert le Sueur in London.[74] The transplant seems to have been a success, for Le Sueur himself was in Italy in the summer of 1631, helping Walter Montague supervise the shipment of a further collection of moulds which Montague had procured in Rome. Inigo Jones, always as involved in the King's collections as he was with his buildings, wrote to Sir Henry Garway in November 1631:

Sir,
The King's Majesty having ordered certaine mouldes to be made at Rome, of such statues and other things as he desireth to have since the originalls are not to be got for money, the which mouldes being all made up and well packt up and sent for Lighorne by Mr Walter Montague who procured them from whence they are to be shipt for England, his Maj commanded me to signify his pleasure unto you, which is that you, as conveniently as you may doe write unto your factor at Livorne to see the said moulds carefully shipt and sent

away by the first ship that come for England and because the said Cases of mouldes will be of some bulke his Maj will give order for the discharge of the fraite when they come here, thus desiring your answer for the satisfaction of his Maj desire herein I rest,
Readie to do you service,
Inigo Jones

The 19 day of 9bre
In Whitehall

To the Right Worth:
Henry Garway Esq., one
of ye Aldermen of the cittie of London.[75]

The venture appears to have been successful, since there are a number of bronzes by Le Sueur which are copies of famous Roman antiques. These were displayed either at Greenwich, as with the *Antinous of the Belvedere* or in the Privy Garden at St. James's, as in the case of the *Farnese Hercules*, the *Borghese Gladiator* and the *Spinario* (Figs. 32-5). To the modern eye there is a vacuity, almost idiocy, about the faces and a rubbery tonelessness in the muscles of Le Sueur's bronzes which give them an unattractive appearance. His work was, however, avidly sought after by powerful figures at court. Among those was the Earl of Pembroke, who was able to obtain his own bronze of the *Borghese Gladiator* from Le Sueur's moulds; it has been suggested that this was a special favour because, as Lord Chamberlain, he was intimately involved in the royal palaces and their decoration.[76] He may not have been so extraordinarily privileged however, since a bill submitted to Charles I in 1637 by Le Sueur for 'renewing all the moulds' suggests that others followed suit.[77]

Charles I's wish for bronze copies provides an interesting parallel with François I of France. In the 1530s he too had wanted original bronzes and marbles to decorate his palace at Fontainebleau but had to fall back on sending Primaticcio to Rome, as Charles sent Le Sueur exactly a century later.[78] However, the moulds ordered by Charles I may not have been the first collection of its type in England. Descriptions of the palace of Nonsuch suggest that Henry VIII may have reacted at once to what his great competitor François was doing at

Figure 32   Hubert le Sueur, after the antique: *Antinous of the Belvedere*. *c*. 1633. Bronze. East Terrace Garden, Windsor Castle. Photograph courtesy of the Courtauld Institute, London: reproduced by gracious permission of Her Majesty The Queen.

Figure 33   Hubert le Sueur, after the antique: *Farnese Hercules*. *c*. 1633. Bronze. East Garden, Windsor Castle. Photograph courtesy of the Courtauld Institute, London: reproduced by gracious permission of Her Majesty The Queen.

Figure 34   Hubert le Sueur, after the antique: *Borghese Gladiator.* c. 1633. Bronze. East Terrace Garden, Windsor Castle. Photograph courtesy of the Courtauld Institute, London: reproduced by gracious permission of Her Majesty The Queen.

Figure 35   Hubert le Sueur, after the antique: *Spinario. c.* 1633. Bronze. Old State Bedchamber, Windsor Castle. Photograph courtesy of the Courtauld Institute, London: reproduced by gracious permission of Her Majesty The Queen.

Fontainebleau. Paul Hentzner, tutor to a German nobleman travelling in England in 1598, thought that there was at Nonsuch:

> . . . an excess of magnificence and elegance, even to ostentation; one would imagine that everything that architecture can perform to have been employed in this one work; there are everywhere so many statues that seem to breathe, so many miracles of consummate art, so many casts that rival even the perfection of Roman antiquity, that it may well claim and justify its name of Nonesuch.[79]

Charles I's wish for bronze copies provides an interesting parallel with other items in his collection. When Charles had been in Madrid in 1623, the Titians had created a lasting impression on him, but the originals, like the statues of Rome, had also been unobtainable. However, he responded in much the same way in each case: just as he sent Gage and Le Sueur to get moulds from Rome, so too he had copyists in Madrid and kept reductions by English miniaturists of some of the most famous Titians belonging to his courtiers. Whereas people pursue original works of art for many reasons, knowlingly to spend money on copies suggests the disinterest of the real devotee.

Hubert Le Sueur produced an exceptional amount for the royal collection. There is evidence of nearly fifty varied commissions executed for the King alone in less than twenty years. It has been suggested that what made Le Sueur attractive to Charles I was technical virtuosity gained from his years as an apprentice armourer at the French court and it does indeed seem that the King himself was aware of Le Sueur's artistic shortcomings; on one occasion Charles petulantly reduced the amounts on a Le Sueur account.[80] A tension may have existed between them; partly the result of Charles being nearly always late in paying his bills, but also because of the frustration of having to deal with the second-rate; great artists simply would not leave Rome to commit themselves to a small and isolated northern kingdom. Nevertheless, even though Le Sueur's work was rarely inspired, it was always forthcoming. His output was continuous from the moment of his first recorded commission at court for modelling twelve figures for the catafalque of James I between October 1626 and September 1627, until his departure from England shortly after January 1641.

The most important part of his practice was the construction of tombs, of which the most grandiose and ambitious was that erected for the Duke and Duchess of Buckingham (1634) in Westminster Abbey.[81] Although no documentation for the commission survives, Buckingham was the only man to whom Charles ever gave his heart and the initiative was therefore surely Charles's. The figures of Buckingham and his wife seem to have reverted toward a Renaissance or even earlier type of funeral effigy; the type of Renaissance monument which Pietro Torrigiano had evolved more than a hundred years before at the early Tudor court of which examples then existed not only in the Abbey but in Old St. Paul's. Here Le Sueur may have been adapting his style to suit a taste for the art and artefacts of the Tudor Age, a taste which was entwined with that new sophisticated Italianism also favoured by Charles. If the character and reputation of the great Duke himself is taken into account, it may well be that Le Sueur was being more fashionable than has been thought.[82]

Sculptors of public monuments commemorate aspirations as well as achievements and the way Buckingham and his wife are cast in old-fashioned poses, may be a response to the myth which had surrounded the Duke. Admirers had often likened him to Scipio Africanus but they had also seen him as an exclusively British hero, cast not in the role of St. George, like the King himself, but as a knight-errant sent on crusade to rescue England's Protestant brethren from the Anti-Christ of Rome just as, in past ages, English heroes had defeated the Infidel or anticipated Buckingham in fighting for English honour upon French soil.[83] Buckingham had been assassinated while preparing for a crusading battle on behalf of the beleaugered Protestants of La Rochelle and perhaps Charles wanted a martial but specifically English type of representation suggesting the Christian knight. So the Duke and Duchess lie upon their catafalque in poses reminiscent of crusader effigies. The way that people related Buckingham to their country's past does suggest that his archaic appearance may have been a positive choice and that this was not a case of Le Sueur being unable to do better. Such a view is given credence by the more adventurous and classical rendering of the attendants at the four corners of the monument.

By the mid-thirties, Charles had become a very active patron of sculptors; Henrietta Maria's role as a patroness of the arts seems to have reached a crescendo at much the same time. In 1636 she had a huge reredos in stone and paint by François Dieussart, representing a 'Glory of Angels', inserted into her chapel at Denmark House.[84] While much work was going on inside the palace, Le Sueur and Nicholas Stone the Elder were working together in the grounds making two separate fountains crowned by statues of Mercury and Arethusa respectively.[85] The choice of theme for these can hardly have been fortuitous since the court had something of a proprietorial attitude to Mercury if not to Arethusa. In 1628 Honthorst had painted for Charles I what turned out to be the most sophisticated and ambitious allegory created in England since the age of Holbein: the *Apollo and Diana* in which Buckingham as Mercury leads on the seven liberal arts, come to pay homage to the King as Apollo and Henrietta Maria as Diana (Pl. 59).[86]

The Mercury fountain was broken up, though the central figure may be the single free-standing *Mercury* by Le Sueur which still exists (Fig. 36).[87] By contrast, the *Arethusa Fountain* has fared somewhat better since most, if not all, the bronze components are in Bushey Park, outside Hampton Court, where it is usually referred to, erroneously, as the *Diana Fountain* (Fig. 37).[88] As it now stands, the bronze pieces of the *Arethusa Fountain* have been mounted insensitively on a base too massive for a relationship between Arethusa and her train of alternating putti and mermaids; the figure of Arethusa, is lofted amongst the clouds like a crocket on a buttress. Before the fountain was moved to Bushey Park, Cromwell had had it re-erected at Hampton Court and his reconstruction was almost certainly faithful to the original appearance of the fountain as it had first been installed at Denmark House. A description of what it looked like in 1659, makes it clear that, as in the case of Stone and Schorman's work for Danvers at Chelsea, Le Sueur had been dependent to a marked degree on Italian Mannerist fountain designs of eighty years earlier:

[it was] composed of four syrens in bronze, seated astride on dolphins, between which was a shell, supported on the foot of a goat. Above the sirens on a second tier, were four little children, each seated, holding a fish, and surmounting all a large figure of a lady – all the figures being bronze and the basin of marble.[89]

Figure 36   Hubert le Sueur, after a lost original by Giambologna: *Mercury*. 1636. Bronze. Private collection.

Figure 37   Hubert le Sueur: *Arethusa Fountain*. 1636. Bronze and marble. Bushey Park, Middlesex.

Originally the *Arethusa Fountain* bore a close relationship to Giambologna's *Fountain of Neptune*, in the Piazza Nettuno, Bologna; for instance Le Sueur has copied Giambologna's conceit of having mermaids squeezing water from their breasts.[90] Indeed so close is the dependence of the one on the other, that the 1659 description of the *Arethusa Fountain* provides an adequate description for that of Giambologna. Besides the fecund mermaids common to both, each fountain has children seated on an upper tier, squeezing fish until water comes out of their mouths. But Le Sueur did not look to a single source for his inspiration: the figure of Arethusa herself appears to have been derived from one of the Mantuan statues, the *Venus with a Dolphin*.[91]

Evidently, then, Le Sueur's design for the *Arethusa Fountain* was fundamentally derivative, as we should expect from a sculptor who was never original. But he was an industrious student of other men's work, and it may well be that on this occasion, he was able to rise above plagiarizing figures to grasp that real revolution in fountain design which had been the achievement of Tribolo and Giambologna. This 'animation of the fountain' as it might be termed, occurred first with designs by Tribolo of the mid-sixteenth century for Medici villas in the Valdarno. The first, the *Fountain of Hercules*, referred to above, has Hercules squeezing Antaeus so hard that water spouts from Antaeus's mouth as he struggles desperately to evade his antagonist's clutches. The second, the *Fountain of the Labyrinth*, is surmounted by a figure of Venus Anadyomene wringing from her hair the water which then descends into the basin below.[92]

In the case of Le Sueur's fountain, Arethusa holds a fish in her right hand and it would be interesting to discover whether water originally spouted from its mouth. If it did so, then it would demonstrate how Le Sueur had animated each section of his fountain; the sculptural figures were no longer inert but all reacting to the water – water, the *raison d'être* of the ensemble, the life source and, in the realm of art, the source of life for the bronze figures themselves. Thus in the *Arethusa Fountain*, – designed for the delight of Henrietta Maria – Le Sueur introduced a theatrical note to fountain design for the first time in England, a legacy of the Italian Mannerists which Bernini was then so brilliantly exploiting in Rome.

Figure 38   Hubert le Sueur: *Bust of Charles I*. 1631. Marble. Reproduced by courtesy of the Board of Trustees of the Victoria and Albert Museum, London.

Figure 39   Hubert le Sueur: *Bust of Charles I in a helmet with a dragon crest*. c. 1638, Bronze. Stourhead, Wiltshire.

The most constant demand on Le Sueur was for royal busts and statues, which in themselves are rather monotonous but fascinating for what they reveal about attitudes to sculpture at the time. The prototype for the busts is probably the marble of Charles I signed and dated 1631, now in the Victoria and Albert Museum (Fig. 38), the only marble portrait of the King by the artist to have survived. Although much of the detail has been lost (the bust clearly having been outside for part of its life), it was never a very inspired work. In contrast to this is the gilded bronze bust of Charles I at Stourhead, 'after the Auncient Roman fasshion', which is in a class by itself (Fig. 39).[93] It has been suggested that by the time the Stourhead bust was made, Le Sueur was having to come to terms with the more talented François Dieussart and with Bernini, whose own bust of Charles I had recently arrived. If that is correct, the Stourhead portrait is dateable to after July 1637 when the Bernini came to London.

The Stourhead bust is exceptional in Le Sueur's *œuvre* not only in its beauty but also in its iconography. Charles wears an antique helmet with a dragon crest; an allusion to the King's penchant for seeing himself as a latter day St. George. He had already been commemorated in this role by Rubens, in a painting the King had acquired in the early thirties, and it was a theme to which Francesco Fanelli was to pay tribute in a small table bronze of *St. George and the Dragon* (see Fig. 43).[94]

Altogether five types among Le Sueur's bronze busts of Charles I can be distinguished which, for the purposes of cataloguing, may be described as the Stourhead, Oxford, Wentworth Woodhouse, Chichester and Woburn types, according to the best examples of each. Though none of these latter four match the quality of the Stourhead example, as a group they are of the greatest interest.[95]

What was doubtless an example of one of these types, probably the Oxford image (Fig.40), was erected on the Square Tower in Portsmouth and although it has been lost, a study of its context allows us to speculate about the attitude of Charles to sculpture. Correspondence regarding it survives and this suggests that the distribution of these quasi-official images was carefully considered. Lord

Figure 40   Hubert le Sueur: *Bust of Charles I with lion mask pauldrons*. 1636. Bronze. Bodleian Library, Oxford.

Figure 41   Hubert le Sueur: *Bust of Charles I with crown, Order of the Garter and ermine cape*. 1636. Bronze. The Council Chamber, Chichester (from Chichester Cross). Photograph courtesy of *The News*, Portsmouth.

Wimbledon, Governor of Portsmouth, at the time the bust was erected, wrote to the Mayor and Corporation on 22 October 1635 to complain that the image of the King which had been placed on the Square Tower looking up the High Street was being 'outfaced' by signs and that because 'any disgrace offered His Majesties figure is as much as to himself',[96] the signs should be taken down. Evidently, to a courtier like Wimbledon, busts were not merely 'brazen images' but real presences.

Portsmouth had been privileged to receive the King's image because, according to the inscription carved beneath the niche, it was there that Charles had safely landed after returning from Spain in 1623. However, what the inscription does not record was that the perspective from the Square Tower was a tragic scene for Charles I and one to which his thoughts often returned in the 1630s. The Duke of Buckingham had been the evil genius behind that visit to Spain and it was surely Buckingham's ghost that could have explained the private but compelling reason for placing the King's bust in that particular position. The bust which Wimbledon claimed was the very presence of the King, could clearly 'see' the house in which Buckingham had been assassinated on 23 August 1628; a house which lay beyond St. Thomas's Church, also visible from the Square Tower, where Buckingham's heart lay in an urn placed at the east end in what appeared to some to be a substitute for an altar. To the left of the bust as it looked up the High Street lay the docks which Buckingham had refurbished in his capacity as Lord High Admiral, an office he had filled with great commitment and effectiveness.

This bust, therefore, may have been erected as a tribute to the King's chief minister and companion of his carefree days. However, by the time the bust was put up, Buckingham's memory was execrated in a town which had suffered greatly in a war for which Buckingham was held responsible, and he could be remembered only covertly. Thus private grief had to be concealed beneath public rejoicing.

Chichester has another Le Sueur bust of Charles (Fig. 41), which was placed on the Market Cross at the Restoration, but there is circumstantial evidence to suggest that it may have been sent to the city before the Civil War.[37] The bust differs from the other surviving examples in having the crown, the collar of the Order of the Garter and an ermine cape. The Portsmouth bust was probably a martial image because the town was a naval and military centre, whereas Chichester was a cathedral city and here the King appeared as the supreme head of the Church, a right invested in him by virtue of his Coronation, part of the regalia of which he wears. Why, though, did Charles permit his image to appear in Chichester but not apparently in the other cathedral cities of his kingdom?[98] The answer is perhaps to be found in the politics of the city during the mid-1630s.

Richard Montagu, Bishop of Chichester, became the figure-head of English Arminianism after the death in 1628 of Lancelot Andrewes, Bishop of Winchester. The Arminian party within the Church of England stood 'in the gapp against puritanisme and popery, the Scilla and Charybdis of Ancient Piety' as Montagu himself put it.[99] Arminians argued against one exclusive orthodoxy and they promoted decent ceremonial. Despite such apparent tolerance however, their figure-head became the most hated prelate after Archbishop Laud. Montagu was called before the House of Commons, and described as 'an animal scarce rational' in a pamphlet of 1629.[100] Despite the controversy provoked by his ministry and writing, Charles had promoted him to the see of Chichester the previous summer.

Montagu set about his job with provocative efficiency which culminated with his primary Visitation of the see of Chichester in 1635. That gained him the approval of the King but the hatred of his flock, and, in 1636, a bitter dispute arose which, in another age, would surely have inspired Trollope.

It began when the Mayor and Corporation claimed jurisdiction over the Cathedral and Close; it then descended to a less constitutional level when they complained at not having sufficiently important seats in the Cathedral. The parties were unable to come to terms and the dispute went to the Privy Council. Although the King was of the same persuasion as Montagu and the dean, Dr Richard Steward, Montagu had always been a controversialist and Charles manoeuvred between the parties with unusual tact. The Privy Council came down in favour of the clergy over the issue of jurisdiction within the Close but then tried to sooth the wounded pride of the Mayor by ordering that he and his Corporation should be given the pews formally occupied by knights. The judgment then finished by directing 'that this present mayor ... should by some act under the seal of the city, be engaged that neither he nor his successors should disturb or affront the dean or his deputy in the church or close for matter of precedency, as lately this mayor did'.[101]

If indeed the bust was in Chichester before the Civil War, then its presence may be explained by these local issues. After Charles had adjudicated he may have decided to make his presence felt in that troubled community and it may be significant that the Chichester bust is dated 1637, that is, to within months of the King's judgement in council.[102] By having his bust sent down, Charles was thus setting his seal on what he hoped would be a new start in the same way as, in other circumstances, he might have presented the city with a new Royal charter. In the context of what had been going on in Chichester, it was most appropriate for the King to appear in the role of law-giver, as the head of both church and state, rather than as commander of his armies as he had already done in Portsmouth. Therefore a new type of bust was evolved to create an image more consonant with one who had authority in lay and ecclesiatical matters. Whether that is what actually happened is a matter for speculation, but what is certain is that in 1637 Charles was much exercised about church-state relations. On 9 July he wrote to Bishop Mainwaring of St. David's: 'What great inconveniences must arise both to Church and Commonwealth, if the authority of bishops be not supported as it ought'.[103]

It is important in understanding the attitudes to sculpture of seventeenth-century Englishmen to think about why objects were placed where they were. For instance, the Earl of Strafford had a Le Sueur bust of Charles. Although it is possible that it may always have been kept (as now) at Wentworth Woodhouse, Strafford's seat in Yorkshire, it may for a time have been given an elevated status in Dublin Castle, the official residence of Strafford as Lord Deputy of Ireland. Strafford and Laud were the main executors of the King's policy during the Eleven Years Tyranny.

Another significant act may have been the placing in St. Paul's, Hammersmith, of another bust of *Charles I* by Le Sueur. The notes taken by Laud at his trial in Westminster Hall in 1641, include the following entry: 'They object

Figure 42   Hubert le Sueur: *Bust of James I*. 1639. Bronze. Banqueting House, Whitehall. Crown copyright: reproduced with permission from the Controller of Her Majesty's Stationery Office.

against me the Consecration of Churches and Chappells as a Popish innovation...for consecrating...the Chappell of Hammersmith, where they alledge, I consecrated the first stone when it was layd...'[104] If indeed the bust at Hammersmith was presented by Laud – and he certainly did give one to the Bodleian Library – its presence could only have served the King's enemies who were doing all that they could to associate him with popery.

There were two Le Sueur sculptures at the Banqueting House at Whitehall. A bust of *Charles I* installed 'Above the door which leads into the room, and which is opposite the royal throne', while a colossal bust of James I (Fig. 42), still to be seen in the building, was originally placed in the corresponding position to Charles on the outside of the entrance.[105] For the *James I*, Le Sueur was paid £120 on 5 November 1639.[106] This was an unusually generous amount, due, perhaps, to Charles being in an expansive mood having at last seen the installation of Rubens's canvases on the ceiling of the Banqueting Hall. That installation marked the completion of the great work begun during the reign of his father. In his turn, Rubens had been rewarded with the full payment of £3,000 and a golden chain in June 1638.

Palme suggests that Le Sueur based his likeness of James on the effigy on the King's hearse of 1625, which had been worked up by Jones, Maximilian Colt and Le Sueur in collaboration.[107] John Williams, Lord Keeper and Bishop of Lincoln, had preached the sermon at James's funeral and the text shows in dense and allusive prose so characteristic of that age, how men believed that the soul inhabited the bronze:

As *Spartianus* therefore reports of *Traian*, that after his Death, he triumphed openly in the Citie of Rome, *In Imagine*, in a Liuely *Statue*, or Repræsentation inuented by Adrian for that purpose: soe shall this *Salomon* of *Israel* doe at this time in the Statue, and Repræsentation of our *British Salomon*. Truly me thinkes (si nunquam fallit imago) the resemblance is very liuely'.[108]

It was not only the busts of Charles I which involved Le Sueur in a sequence of variations on an image for he also produced a number of full-length statues of

Charles. These were paired either with James I or with Henrietta Maria, and the inspiration for them seems to have come from Laud.

In 1636 Laud was enjoying the summit of his prosperity as Archbishop of Canterbury and Chancellor of the University of Oxford, in which capacity he fêted the King in August. The setting was St. John's College, where he had just erected the Canterbury Quadrangle to commemorate his former presidency of the college. He had prepared well for the King's visit because in December 1634 full length statues of Charles and Henrietta Maria by Le Sueur had been installed in the niches on the east-west axis of the quadrangle.[109]

Possibly as a result of Laud's example at Oxford, Charles ordered Le Sueur to provide a number of similar full-length statues to be placed in various prominent positions within the cities of London and Westminster. Many were destroyed after Charles's execution, and of these, the most conspicuous and provocative was one which was paired with a *James I*. They were placed in the centre of the balustrade of Inigo Jones's portico at St. Paul's, where they were supposed to have been joined with statues of other benefactors of the Cathedral; in the event, these others never materialized. If the project had been fulfilled, the effect would have resembled the appearance of the sky-line on the west front of St. Peter's, where Maderno had placed the statues of the apostles in 1614. Jones had been in Rome on that occasion and, as a result, may have suggested the idea of a balustrade of statues at St. Paul's some twenty years later. The two kings presided over St. Paul's because James had tried to improve general building standards in London, and because Charles had encouraged Laud to make the building a Temple of Solomon, cleansed of the prostitutes, merchants and booksellers who frequented the west end in search of custom.

As it transpired, the statues turned out to be a disastrous advertisement for the monarchy. Money for cathedral repairs had been extorted from a resentful community and the venture contributed to the alienation of the City in the years before the Civil War. Even Peter Heylyn, who as a chaplain to Charles I might be thought to have been prejudiced in favour of the policy, admitted that the way in which the citizens of London had been pressurized into making financial contributions had 'met with many rubs, and mighty enemies'.[110]

The iconoclasts of the Civil War could do nothing about dismantling the portico after Charles's execution – the stones were so massive that before the war some, not then positioned, had been used as ship's ballast – but they set about the statues with a vengeance. On 31 July 1650 the Council of State ordered 'The statues of King James and the late King, standing at the west end of Pauls' to be thrown down and broken to pieces, and the inscription on the stone work under them deleted'.[111]

Charles's statue at the Royal Exchange was decapitated in what may have been a macabre and symbolic re-run of his execution. The Royal Exchange was the commercial heart of London where, before the war, there had been a series of statues of English monarchs along the first floor on the inside of the courtyard which had culminated in the *Charles I*. Order was given that this 'statue of the late King... [was] to be demolished, by having the head taken off, and the sceptre out of his hand, and this inscription to be written *"Exit tyrannus Regum ultimus, anno primo restitutæ libertatis Angliæ 1648"*, and this to be done between this and Saturday next'.[112]

There was also a full-length bronze of the King at St. Paul's, Covent Garden which I would suggest was a site hardly less important in the eyes of Charles than the Royal Exchange. The church to which the statue was closely related, had been designed by Inigo Jones in 1631 as the frontispiece to an elegant Italian piazza. St. Paul's Covent Garden was the first church to be built on a new site since the Reformation. As such it demanded the presence of the Defender of the Faith and accordingly, the bronze of Charles was erected in the churchyard. Originally the church was approached from the west, not, as it is today, from the east, and accordingly the parishioners would have passed the statue as they came through either of two gateways into the churchyard and up to the main, west door of the church itself. Hollar's aerial view of London of *c*.1640 (Fig. 24) shows a small figure in the middle of the path which bisected the churchyard and this probably represents the statue.[113] Thus the King stood before what to some was the only true Protestant church in London, and in front of the most elegant and commodious square in his kingdom.

There was, however, another good reason why Charles I might have wished to have his statue in Covent Garden. An important document on the building of

Covent Garden has been published recently which reveals that Charles, in consultation with some of his Commissioners for New Buildings, intervened at a late stage in the planning of the scheme, changing aspects of the project in significant ways.[114]

But despite the sympathetic Italianate elegance which surrounded this particular image of Charles, Covent Garden in the 1630s was a somewhat hostile environment. The Puritan Francis Russell, fourth Earl of Bedford, had commissioned Jones to design the piazza as a speculative venture which provided investors with 'houses and buildings fitt for the habitacons of *Gentlemen* and men of ability'.[115] But although Bedford could appreciate Jones's brilliance, he could not extend his sympathy to the Court, from which he absented himself with ostentatious rectitude, alienated by what he saw as repellent values and suspect religion. Bedford's large town house lay to the south of the piazza and it may be thought that the King wished to impose his presence in an environment which he had already helped shape decisively but by this time one which was dominated by his rich, powerful and disloyal subject.[116]

The fate of the Covent Garden statue is uncertain. On 16 October 1650, the Council of State ordered the Sergeant 'to make enquiry after the statue of the late King in Covent Garden, and that at Greenwich, both being cast in brass, and report in whose custody they now are.'[117] Despite that instruction however, nothing was done at Covent Garden because in July 1655, Major-General Desborough, Cromwell's brother-in-law, was summoned before the Council to 'state the matter of fact touching the statue in the churchyard of Covent Garden, and to report', after which no further mention is made in the official papers.[118]

At an unspecified date images of Charles I and Henrietta Maria had also been put up in Queen Street, probably because this was one of the most fashionable areas in London inhabited by courtiers like the Earl of Northumberland and Sir Kenelm Digby. The statues themselves appear to have been destroyed. On 27 January 1651, perhaps in preparation for the anniversary of the King's execution three days later, Colonel Berkstead was told to 'take care for the pulling down of the gilt image of the late Queen, and also of the King'. The order suggests that Charles faced Henrietta Maria, since his image was at 'the upper end of the same street, towards Holborn,'[119] and that he was influenced by Laud's arrangement at Oxford where the royal couple gaze at each other from richly encrusted niches.

The Council of State's response to the discovery of images of Charles and Henrietta Maria seems inconsistent, since in one part of London they ordered the destruction of images which in another, they sold off. However, these decisions may have been more logical than they appear: the Council may have been guided by a distinction between public busts and statues and those which had been ordered for the royal collection.

In this chapter it has been assumed that most of the 'public' images of the King and his consort, whether busts or statues, were casts from a standard type made by Le Sueur, but there were other sculptors working for Charles I of whom Francesco Fanelli, the 'one eyed Italian' as Van der Doort called him, was one. Fanelli came into contact with Charles I in the early 1630s; there is no evidence that Charles was responsible for bringing him to London. With the arrival, first of Fanelli and then of Dieussart, Le Sueur no longer had the field to himself. Indeed it must soon have become apparent to his more sophisticated patrons that Le Sueur could not compete with the new arrivals in vivacity or finesse of detail and that he could only better them, if at all, in technical competence and reliability of output.

The first documentary record connecting Fanelli with Charles I is the grant of a pension by the King in 1635, which suggests that he had probably been in London for some time before then.[120] His work consisted mostly of table bronzes and in the Royal Collection there is a *St. George and the Dragon* already referred to, and a group of *Two Cupids with a Horse* (Figs. 43-4). In addition, and presumably for Charles, Fanelli produced a much reduced cast after one of the three marble versions of *The Sleeping Cupid* which was probably after the marble ascribed by Nys to Praxiteles. The Victoria and Albert Museum version (Fig. 45) follows the Praxitelean prototype in general design though there are significant differences; for example Fanelli has omitted the club which was held by the cupid in the Mantuan marble.[121] Although Charles must have seen that Fanelli was superior to Le Sueur, it was not he but the Duke of Newcastle who became the sculptor's most consistent patron. For him Fanelli cast at least nine bronzes of which the *Charles, Prince of Wales* is unique in being signed. This is the most interesting and

Figure 43   Francesco Fanelli: *St. George and the Dragon. c.* 1635-42. Bronze. Reproduced by courtesy of the Board of Trustees of the Victoria and Albert Museum, London.

Figure 44   Francesco Fanelli: *Running Horse with Cupids. c.* 1635-42. Bronze (damaged). Reproduced by courtesy of the Board of Trustees of the Victoria and Albert Museum, London.

Figure 45   Francesco Fanelli: *Sleeping Cupid*. *c*. 1635-42. Bronze. Reproduced by courtesy of the Board of Trustees of the Victoria and Albert Museum, London.

indeed the most accomplished of Fanelli's bronzes and a comparison of this with Le Sueur's portrait busts reveals the latter's inadequacy to devastating effect.[122]

The possibility that Bernini might make a bust of Charles I was raised in a letter of 13 June 1635, from Gregorio Panzani, papal envoy to Henrietta Maria, to Cardinal Francesco Barberini, nephew of Urban VIII and Protector of the English Nation. In his letter, Panzani relates how pleased the King was that permission had been granted for Bernini to proceed, and matters went smoothly thereafter. Nine months later, on 17 March 1636, Charles himself sent a flattering letter to Bernini in which he asked him to proceed with the bust, using the famous triple portrait of himself painted by Van Dyck (Fig. 46) which then went to Rome. The bust (Fig. 47) was executed during the summer of 1636 and sent from Rome to England where it was received with great enthusiasm at Oatlands Palace in July 1637.[123] Hitherto, English connoisseurs could have obtained only a faint inkling of Bernini's brilliance, from a reliquary he designed which had been installed in one of the Queen's chapels about a year before the Charles I bust arrived. The reliquary, executed by Francesco Spagna and containing relics of St. Helena, had been brought by George Conn from Rome in the early summer of 1636 when Conn came to replace Panzani as envoy to Henrietta Maria.[124]

The bust, the first Bernini had executed of someone outside the Roman orbit, must have struck its admirers with all the freshness and force of the Rubens *Self-Portrait* (Pl. 22) which had been presented to Charles in 1623, when he was Prince of Wales. The Rubens had created a sensation by revealing artistry of a different order to anything most patrons had encountered in England before, and so too, fifteen years later, the bust displayed the powers of contemporary sculpture with magical force. Such paradigms of the arts of painting and sculpture were decisive in the nurturing of English taste, and in the European context, once again Charles had beaten the field. He had become the first ruler outside the Vatican to have himself immortalized by the dominant figure of the world's artistic capital and what he accomplished others emulated: Cardinal Richelieu, Duke Francesco I D'Este, and Louis XIV.

The bust was installed at Greenwich where it was regarded as one of the greatest treasures of the King's collection. Bernini questioned Nicholas Stone the Younger about reactions to it. Although Bernini was pleased to hear that it was greatly admired, he was worried about how it was kept, despite good intentions

Figure 47 (above and far right) Thomas Adye, after Bernini: *Bust of Charles I*. Eighteenth-century. Marble. Royal Collection: reproduced by gracious permission of Her Majesty The Queen.

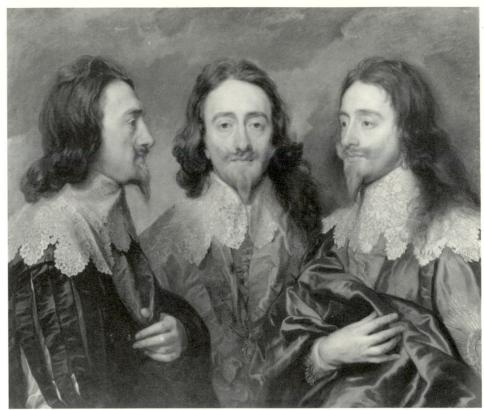

Figure 46 Van Dyck: *Charles I in three positions*. 1636. Royal Collection: reproduced by gracious permission of Her Majesty The Queen.

on the part of the royal household. What Stone had to tell Bernini made it all sound rather precarious:

being in a uery good umour hee askt me whether I had seene the head of marble wch was sent into England for the King, and to tell him the truth what was spoken of itt. I told him that whosouer I had heard admired itt nott only fr the exquisitenesse of the worke but the likenesse and nere resemblance itt had to the King countenannce. He sayd that diuers had told him so much but he could nott beliue itt, then he began to be uery free in his discourse to aske if nothing was broke of itt in carryage and how itt was preserued now from danger. I told him that when as I saw itt that all was hole and safe, the wch (saythe) I wonder att, but I tooke (sayth he) as much care for the packing as studye in making of itt; also I told him that now itt was preserued with a case of silke, he desyred to know in what manner. I told him that itt was made like a bagg getherd together on the top of the head and drawne together with a strink under the body with uery great care, he answered he was afraid thatt would be the causse to breake itt for sayes he in my time of doing of itt I did couer itt in the like manner to keepe itt from the flyes, but with a *grea-a-t* deale of danger, because in taking of the casse if itt hangs att any of the little lockes of hayre or one the worke of the band itt would be presently defaced, for itt greiue him to heare itt was broke, being he had taken so great paines and study on itt. . .[125]

The artist need not have worried, however, because it came through the Civil War unscathed only to be destroyed in the fire at Whitehall in 1698.

The Queen, for whom the Charles I bust was made, was so delighted with Bernini that she sent him a diamond worth 4,000 *scudi* and planned that he should make a portrait of her as a companion to her husband's. Three separate Van Dyck portraits, as opposed to the three heads in one canvas provided for her husband's bust, were ready to be sent to Rome by August 1638. For some unknown reason however, it was not until June 1639 that she wrote asking Bernini to proceed. There were then further delays; the portraits appear never to have been sent and the Civil War intervened before anything further could be done. So the last significant act of royal patronage in the field of sculpture ended in frustration.[126]

Although the Henrietta Maria project faltered, the Bernini bust of her husband was a triumph to be savoured with the Rubens ceiling, the series of Van

Dyck royal portraits and the acquisition of the Mantuan collection. But what made the arrival of the Bernini peculiarly gratifying was that Arundel, who had always offered his advice on artistic matters whether asked for or not, now followed suit by sending a portrait of himself by Van Dyck as a guide to be used by an unknown sculptor in Florence from whom he wanted a portrait group. On 9 October 1636 Arundel wrote to William Petty, his most trusted agent, who was then in Italy:

I send by Francesco a Picture of my owne and my little Tom: bye me, and desire it may be done at Florence in Marble Basso relievo, to trye a yonge Sculptor there whoe is sayde to be valente Huomo, Francesco hath his name I could wish Cavaliere Bernino, or Francesco Fiamengo, might doe another of the [sam]e.[127]

Although on this occasion Arundel was following rather than leading, he was being characteristically more contrived and sophisticated in the demands he made on his artist than those who had approached Bernini because he wanted to set up a rivalry between painting and sculpture. The Van Dyck double portrait of *Arundel and his grandson Tom* is not simply an analysis of feature and character as is *Charles 1 in three positions*, however sensitive and penetrating that may be, but a response to the challenge of classical sculpture which Van Dyck saw at Arundel House; a variation upon the theme of the Roman funeral reliefs which decorated the gardens at Arundel House. Arundel was trying to be 'anciently modern and modernly ancient', to borrow Pietro Aretino's phrase about Giulio Romano.

The relationship between Charles 1, Arundel and the various foreign sculptors employed in London during the 1630s is far from clear. Dieussart, the best of them, who had first come to London to work for Arundel, had talents which Arundel guarded jealously, but there were occasions when it was plainly impolitic to prevent him doing work for the royal family, as in the case of the 'Glory of Angels' for Denmark House chapel; in any case, allowing Dieussart out of the confines of his studio at Arundel House could also bring tangible benefits. 1636 was the year of the Denmark House chapel reredos, but it also happens to

Figure 48   Antico: *Hercules and Antaeus*. c. 1500. Bronze. Kunsthistorisches Museum, Vienna.

Figure 49   Antico: *Hercules and the Ceryneian Hind*. c. 1500. Bronze. Kunsthistorisches Museum, Vienna.

mark the high point in relations between Charles and Arundel. In that year, Charles sent Arundel to the Emperor at Vienna to try to obtain restitution of the Palatinate for his dispossessed nephew, Charles Louis. Although Arundel returned empty handed, reports of the negotiations made it clear that he had behaved like 'a right English earl'.[128] Charles throughout thought that Arundel had put his nephew's case most effectively and it may be that Dieussart's bust of Charles, at Arundel Castle, which is dated 1636, was commissioned by Charles I from Dieussart while Arundel was away. It might then have been presented to Arundel as a gesture of appreciation for the way in which he had upheld the honour of the English crown.

While most of the Mantuan sculpture consisted of life-size antiquities, there were many smaller Renaissance and Mannerist bronzes, and of these, among the finest was Charles's outstanding holding of works by Antico. Pier Jacopo Alari Bonacolsi, nicknamed Antico, is traditionally paired with the Paduan *bronzisto* Andrea Riccio as the two great masters of the early Renaissance table bronze. Both were profoundly influenced by Andrea Mantegna, the presiding artistic genius of Renaissance Mantua. But, as Radcliffe has aptly put it, their styles differed greatly: 'Antico (was) all form and Riccio all expression'.[129]

We can be certain that Charles owned at least five bronzes by Antico; all of which were later acquired at the Commonwealth sales by Archduke Leopold Wilhelm von Habsburg, Governor-General of the Spanish Netherlands. These consisted of *Hercules and Antaeus* (Fig. 48), a *Satyr, Atropos, Hercules* and *Mercury*, all now in the Kunsthistorisches Museum, Vienna. They are the work of 'the perfect court artist', calculated to appeal to a connoisseur of such refined and fastidious tastes as Charles I. They originated from Isabella d'Este's famous *grotta* in the ducal palace in Mantua. The subjects had first been worked up by Antico about 1498 for Bishop Lodovico Gonzaga's residence at Bozzolo. Twenty years later, Isabella had approached Antico for her own set. Splendid though the pieces of the Isabella set were, they had none of the fire-gilding and silver-inlay which makes Antico's *Venus Felix*, also at Vienna, such a de luxe object. Nevertheless, Charles's holding of Antico statuettes was superior to the Habsburgs' in one respect: Charles had the three circular reliefs mentioned in the 1627 inventory of Duke Ferdinando Gonzaga as 'Tre tondi di bronzo con le forze di Ercole' The subjects were *Hercules and the Ceryneian Hind* (Fig. 49), *Hercules and the Erymanthian Boar* and *Hercules and the Hydra*.[130].

Wonderful though the Anticos must have been, the single most spectacular object in the entire sculpture collection was Giambologna's *Samson and the Philistine* (Fig. 31). But this, presented to Charles while he was returning from Spain to England in 1623, he immediately gave to Buckingham, who had taken Charles to Spain to get him a Spanish bride. As a method of conducting foreign policy it was an act of consummate folly, but as a way of bolstering the confidence of the Prince, a prodigious success. In Spain, Charles emerged from the shadow of an alien father to appear, in his own eyes at least, an heroic prince in the mould of a chivalrous knight; a match for any danger which crossed his path. He owed his release to Buckingham and as soon as he was given the Giambologna, he passed it on in a compulsive gesture of thanks.

By 17 June 1624, the group was installed as a fountain in the garden at York House, Buckingham's principal London residence, where it became one of the most admired works of art in the capital. Buckingham had acquired York House from the disgraced Lord Chancellor, Sir Francis Bacon, who had not only meditated upon the effects of statuary in gardens but had actually created a notable garden at this very house. Thus Buckingham had the evidence of Bacon's own intitiative to illustrate what his luckless predecessor had written on the subject and he would surely have agreed with that passage in Bacon's essay in which he wrote about the effect of 'princely gardens':

for great princes, that for the most part taking advice with workmen, with no less cost set their things together; and sometimes add statua's, and such things, for state and magnificence . . . [131]

Buckingham would have been gratified by the vicarious credit he acquired from the admiration gained by his famous Giambologna, a fame given both public and private expression. Henry Peacham wrote of York House gardens in his *Compleat Gentleman* that 'they will be renowned so long as John de Bologna's Cain and Abel stand erected there, a piece of wondrous Art and Workmanship'.[132] Before then, however, no less a figure than Thomas Wentworth, later to become Earl of Strafford, was more taken with the statue

Figure 50   Francesco Fanelli: *David and Goliath*. *c*. 1635-42. Bronze. Metropolitan Museum of Art, New York, The Jack and Belle Linsky Collection, 1982.

than with the new buildings which provided a back-drop to it. Wentworth referred to it as 'a goodly statue of Stone set up in the garden before the new building, bigger than the Life, a Samson with a Philistine betwixt his legs Knocking his brains out with the Jaw-bone of an Ass'.[133]

But it would seem that while Buckingham exploited the prestige of his collection, he was himself persuaded by its eloquence because within four months of the installation of the *Samson and the Philistine*, he had started to collect sculpture himself. On 1 October 1624 he wrote to Sir Thomas Roe, the English Ambassador in Constantinople:

That if you find among those people (who prize not those rarities of art that are of great esteem in other countries) any statues of excellent workmanship which in the judgement of those that have skill may be worth the buying. . . you would do me the favour . . . to make choice thereof. . .[134]

Thus the most magnificent piece of sculpture Charles was to possess went out of the royal collection as soon as it had entered it, but it seems to have inspired one of the greatest English collectors of the day.

The King's sculpture was distributed among the various royal palaces, though of the scores of rooms in which it was housed, we have a detailed account of only two. Some of the best of the small table pieces were to be found in Whitehall, concentrated in the Chair Room and New Cabinet Room. Here the windows provided platforms upon which to sit small busts and statuettes, while the walls were reserved for a dense selection of some of the finest paintings in the royal collection. The Chair Room may have been relatively small since it had only two windows housing twelve pieces of sculpture. In the first window there were seven items: a Le Sueur bust of Charles – probably the bust now at Stourhead; an East Indian idol; a bronze of a 'little Statua where David overcomes Goliah',[135] which may have been by Fanelli (Fig. 50); one of the two large 'brazen' horses made by Tacca for Prince Henry; a small head of a woman, acquired with the help of Arundel; a head of 'Giatto' and another female head. The second window had five pieces: a head of *Nero* bought by Charles when Prince of Wales, for which Le Sueur had been commissioned to make a bust and pedestal; a *Nessus and*

Dejanira; a *Faustina*; 'a bald headed ould Grecian mans head', and an *Adonis, Venus and Cupid*.[136]

The Chair Room also housed a few items of furniture of which the most interesting was a table of 'black ebbone woodden laied in wth white Ivory'. This had a compartment beneath into which were inserted white ivory trays, made to hold 'all the meddalls [and] agotts' which had belonged to Prince Henry. The table had previously been kept in 'the little store roome' off the School Chamber at St. James's. However, Thomas Carey had removed the contents and the key, neither of which he had returned by the time Van der Doort came to compile his inventory in 1639. Carey's negligence appears to have had unfortunate consequences for it seems that Van der Doort's anxiety about what had happened to this exceptional collection of medals and agates,[137] contributed to a breakdown which led to suicide.[138] Besides the empty medal cabinet, there was also a table, a yard and a half long, 'covered with silver engraved plate'. The plates were probably a selection of the silver bas-reliefs made by the Van Vianen family; those not on show were housed in cupboards in the room.

The Chair Room contained a variety of sculpture both ancient and modern. Faustina was an extremely common subject in antiquity, but what makes the version of this bust noteworthy, was that it had been brought out of Spain along with Giambologna's *Samson and the Philistine* and was presumably, therefore, regarded as remarkable. The *Nessus and Dejanira* was one of the fifteen bronzes which had been presented to Prince Henry as part of the Florentine marriage negotiations. The *Adonis, Venus and Cupid* is likely to have been a small bronze group which can now be attributed with some confidence to Fanelli (Fig. 51).[139]

The New Cabinet Room, with nearly twice as many pictures as the Chair Room, must have been a more impressive space and indeed may have been conceived as a sort of *Tribuna*.[140] However, it is easy to over-estimate its significance, for Whitehall is the only royal residence for which there is a detailed inventory dating from before the Civil War. The New Cabinet Room contained no

Figure 51   Francesco Fanelli: *Venus, Adonis and Cupid. c.* 1635-42. Bronze. Reproduced by courtesy of the Board of Trustees of the Victoria and Albert Museum, London.

Figure 52 Anonymous: *Negro Venus*. Late sixteenth-century. Bronze.
Kunsthistorisches Museum, Vienna.

less than seventy-four paintings and eighty-eight sculptures consisting of: thirty-eight small-scale statues, seven roundels of stories taken from Ovid's *Metamorphoses*, probably by the Van Vianens, and, in addition, another forty-three bas-reliefs of various shapes and sizes. The room contained sixteen out of the eighteen 'florentine brazen statuas' which Charles had inherited from Prince Henry. Van der Doort describes one of these as 'upon the wainscott Cornish' which suggests that a number were displayed at eye-level, much as Paduan bronzes appear in Carpaccio's painting of *The Vision of St. Augustine* or Lotto's portrait of *Andrea Odone*. Some of the best bronzes in the entire royal collection were concentrated in the Chair and Cabinet Rooms; yet only seventeen appear to have been bought or commissioned by Charles; the others came either through inheritance or gift.

The most significant gift housed in the Cabinet Room, was the group of thirty-five bas-reliefs which had been entrusted to Lord Cottington, by a person unknown, to give to the King. Most of these were by members of the Van Vianen family (see pp. 234-40) whose work was greatly admired by English collectors. [141]

Cottington also presented Charles with a 'standing blackamore woeman houlding her left hand downwards, and her right hand upwards like as if shee were to hold some drapery', which was thought 'to bee an Antiquitie'. [142] This is known as *The Negro Venus* (Fig. 52) and is currently thought by some to be by Danese Cattaneo, a sixteenth-century Tuscan sculptor. Another gift was a *Sleeping Cupid* by Francesco Duquesnoy, [143] bought in Rome by Sir Henry Mildmay, who became Master of the Jewel House. Duquesnoy was one of the leading contemporary sculptors and it says something for the breadth of Charles's tastes that he seems to have had a number of works either by Duquesnoy or after his designs. [144] As it was, there is a sad irony attached to Duquesnoy's *Sleeping Cupid*, since Mildmay later deserted the King to become a most significant figure in the dispersal of the royal collection. The *Sleeping Cupid* must have been of particular interest since it made a fascinating contrast, not only to the three larger marble versions sent from Mantua by Nys, but also with Fanelli's copy after the Michelangelo, which Charles had ordered for his

Figure 53   Antonio Susini: *Venus and a Satyr*. Bronze. Private collection.

collection (see Fig. 30). Other gifts housed in the New Cabinet Room included 'the Statua of Laocon wᵗʰ his two-Sonns' presented by the Marquis of Hamilton which, conceivably, might have been a version of the bronze reduction in the Victoria and Albert Museum. There was another East Indian idol given by the Earl of Denbigh; doubtless brought back from his embassy to the Great Moghul. Sir Henry Vane gave an intriguing item; 'A woemans head in brasse blakt over wᵗʰ black vernish being soe big as the life upon a black Tutchstone square Peddistall said to be an Antiquity of Piety'. Sir Henry Wotton presented a little farmhouse carved in wood, which he had acquired when ambassador in Venice. Mrs Heriot, the widow of the King's jeweller, gave items from her husband's collection: a 'Sitting Venus blinding Cupid', and a 'strugling mercurie standing upon one-legg' which was probably by or after Giambologna. Another bronze almost certainly by Giambologna or his follower Antonio Susini, is described as 'a naked woeman lying on her back a sleepe wᵗʰ a Satirr by, being in bras' (Fig. 53). This was given by a 'Dutch Merchant'. A 'head of Moses being in brasse blackt', had been the gift of William Murray, A Gentleman of the King's Bedchamber, from whom Charles had also acquired an oval of *Venus and Cupid* by Rottenhamer. [145] A Mr Goodman had donated a 'little Eve' carved in peartree. Finally, amongst the gifts housed in the Cabinet Room was 'a standing Countryman leaning wᵗʰ both his hands upon a Spade', carved in wood. The donor is unspecified.

The New Cabinet Room also contained the Fanellis of *St. George and the Dragon* (Fig. 43) and a *Running Horse with Cupids* (Fig. 44), presumably commissioned by Charles himself. There were too, a number of works by Le Sueur: a bust of Charles I, though of the less ambitious type than the Stourhead version; an equestrian statuette which made the King look like a lead soldier rather than the Emperor of Van Dyck's equestrian portrait; and a pair of *Minerva* and *Bacchus* by an unknown artist. Lastly there were some curiosities. There was a full-length portrait of Henry VIII on a miniature scale, made of a type of hone-stone which is found only in Germany, and therefore, probably carved either on the Continent or in England by a foreign sculptor during the Tudor period (Fig. 54). [146] It was later owned by Horace Walpole when it acquired a romantic attribution to Holbein. [147] It was one of the many relics of Tudor art that were to be found in Stuart collections. The Cabinet Room probably also housed a pair of ivory reliefs of boys fighting; the description suggests that the pair in the Louvre by Gerard Van Opstal may be these. [148] Here there was also an unusual Vianen relief: 'under the peece aforesaid [a *St. Jerome* by Lucas van Leyden] a peece done by—Paule Van Vianan who was the Emperoʳ Radolphs man in Chast worke . . . a silver plate in a—black frame being or lady and Christ and some Sᵗ with a paire of pinchers where she houldeth a Tooth with'. [149] This was a relic and as

Figure 54   Anonymous: *King Henry VIII*. German, mid sixteenth-century.
Private collection: photograph, British Museum.

such, might have been destroyed during the Commonwealth. The room also had
a single silver candlestick bought by Charles from Christian van Vianen. [150]

It is not known how the pictures were selected for the two rooms, though
some may have been hung with sculpture in mind or vice-versa. For example
there was a wooden statue of Lucretia which Van der Doort specifically mentions
as having been copied from a painted version of this subject attributed to Titian,
then in the royal collection. It may be no coincidence that one of the two large
'brazen' horses from the Prince Henry gift was in the Chair Room, which also
contained Van Dyck's modello for the equestrian portrait of Charles I,[151] both
ultimately derived from the equestrian statue of Marcus Aurelius on the Capitol
in Rome. In the Chair Room there were also those bronze groups of *David and
Goliath*, *Nessus and Dejanira* and *Adonis, Venus and Cupid* which would have been
nicely contrasted with small-scale works such as the *Diana and Calisto* by
Poelenburgh.[152] The New Cabinet Room contained Raphael's *St. George and the
Dragon* as well as the bronze of the same subject by Fanelli (see Fig. 43). It would
be interesting to know whether the one was placed below the other. For the most
part however, it would seem that the pictures in these two rooms were chosen to
hang in relation to one another and without regard for the sculpture.

There is no painted record of the appearance of either the Chair or Cabinet
rooms at Whitehall, but it may be that Charles wanted to create a rich ensemble in
the style of a European *Kunstkabinett*; the most famous was Rudolf II's at Prague.
Evidence that he was thinking in this way, may be thought to be provided by the
existence in the Chair Room of a painting, possibly by Frans Francken II,
described by Van der Doort as: 'a peece of painting of a Cabbonett wherein all
sorts of painting are painted as if some pictures were hanging at the wall as also
of all severall sorts, of drawings soe well in redd as in black Chalke Boxes w^th
books and manie other things painted upon Board.'[153]

The Chair Room and the New Cabinet Room housed most of the sculpture at
Whitehall, though other rooms also contained pieces. The Adam and Eve Stairs
Room had a collection of eight Limoges enamels which were hung above the
paintings and below the ceiling: an unidentified Roman emperor; two enamels

representing Hector and Jonathan on horseback; and several profile portraits including a marble of Aristotle which had been given by the Earl of Salisbury, [154] a description of which suggests that it may have been a work by Torrigiano. Of more interest was a polychrome plaster of Henry VIII.[155] Here there was also 'the Picture of Cavellero John de Bollonia the famous Sculptor to the granduke of fforanc done in a litle ruff: and In a furrd gowne' by an unidentified artist and given to the King by the Earl of Ancrum.[156]

Nys evidently thought of the Mantuan paintings and sculpture as one decorative ensemble, since he had written to Endymion Porter in May 1629: 'As companions to these pictures it will still be necessary to have the Marbles of the Duke of Mantua'.[157] However, Charles did not try to relate pictures and large-scale sculpture as Nys would have approved. At Whitehall, the Long Gallery and the adjacent Privy Chamber housed thirty-five marbles and a large number of paintings with no attempt being made to create a classical ambience.[158] This was in contrast to the contemporary appearance of the Louvre, where, as an English visitor to Paris in 1625 noted:

. . . the principal beauty . . . of this so much admired Palace . . . is a low plain room, paved under foot with brick, and without any hangings or tapestry on the sides; yet being the best set out and furnished, to my content, of any in *France*; it is called *La Salle des Antiques*, and hath in it five of the ancientest and venerablest pieces of all the *Kingdom*.[159]

Evidently Charles had a much less purist attitude to the display of his sculpture collection than the French monarchy. But the description of France from which this passage is taken, is valuable in providing a corrective to the assumption that the French had an altogether more sophisticated appreciation of antiquities. After dealing with the *Salle des Antiquités* at the Louvre, the same writer went on to compare France with England in such a way as to suggest that there were many in England who responded to Charles's initiatives as a collector of antique statuary:

For the *Nation* generally is regardless of antiquity, both in the monuments and in the study of it; so that you shall hardly find any ancient inscription, or any famous ruine snatched from the hand of time, in the best of their *Cities* and *Churches*. In the *Church* onely of *Amiens* could I meet with any ancient Character . . . So little also did I perceive them to be inclining to be *Antiquaries*; that both neglects considered (*si verbis audacia detur*) I dare confidently averre, that one *Cotton* for the Treasury, and one *Selden* (now Mr *Camden* is dead) for the study of Antiquities, are worth all the *French*.[160]

Although Whitehall had splendid interiors, there was only one relatively undistinguished Privy Garden with no sculpture, whereas St. James's, Greenwich and Denmark House all had more extensive grounds which contained some of the best marbles and bronzes in the royal collection. Arundel had been the first Englishman to conceive of his grounds as an extension of the house and, thereby, a means to frame and display sculpture. Sir Francis Bacon, that passionate student of the art of gardening, had been fascinated to see the transformation Arundel had made after his return from Italy in 1614. He was so taken with the crowd of statues gesticulating on their symmetrically placed plinths that he quipped 'My Lord, I see the Resurrection is upon us!'[161] Bacon's conceit may have been intentionally ambiguous because his host was resurrecting a method of display favoured in antiquity and the Renaissance, but hitherto unknown in England. In any event, what Arundel had done at his own palace was the inspiration for the extensive embellishments of the royal palace gardens a decade later.

There were two gardens at St. James's, though these were modest when compared with what Danvers had done at Chelsea and Pembroke was doing at Wilton. One was an elaborate embroidered parterre in box, the second a walled orchard which also contained an arcade for sculpture designed by Jones. It consisted of a Tuscan colonnade—of fifteen columns with grilles in the openings – which was always a feature of a larger whole, never a garden in its own right. Thus to define it as 'a museum garden', as has recently been done, is more misleading than helpful.[162]

Henrietta Maria rather than Charles I has recently been credited with thinking of the royal gardens as theatres for sculpture and certainly it was through her connection with the court of France, that André Mollet was brought over to work at St. James's.[163] Mollet's father, Claude the Elder, had built celebrated gardens, such as Saint-Germain-en-Laye for Henri IV, and consequently there was a distinctly French feel to what his son did in London.[164] The English had favoured geometrical borders, but Mollet introduced scroll-like forms and, specifically for the purpose of setting off the royal sculpture, *compartiments de gazon*. It was probably the imminent arrival of the Mantuan statues which inspired Henrietta Maria to make these improvements at St. James's, since the main phase of work there started just after the first shipment from Mantua and was not finished until 1633, by which time everything had come from Italy.

The Sieur de la Serre, a French nobleman visiting London in the entourage of Marie de' Medici in 1637, described St. James's in some detail. When he came to the gardens, he did not specify statues actually within the parterres themselves, but did refer to the gallery in the orchard garden 'where one may see the rarest wonders of Italy in a great number of stone and bronze statues',[165] the most spectacular of which were some of the set of casts by Le Sueur.

The inventories and valuations of Charles's collection, drawn up shortly after his death, fill out de la Serre's tantalizingly brief description of St. James's and suggest that the sculpture must have extended beyond Inigo Jones's gallery into the main body of the gardens themselves. As it was, de la Serre had not been looking at palace embellishments which had received their definitive form. The royal accounts show that work went on at St. James's throughout the 1630s: payments were made to Andrew Durdaunte 'for his paines Travell and care in lookeing to the safe landing and carriage of divers statues and marbles and for takeing severall Notes of them in a Booke by way [of] Inventory' and the accounts also record a payment for 'mending and repainting three Marble Statues viz: Apollo Bacchus and Cupid'.[166]

From the manuscript copies of the sale inventories it is unclear exactly what was displayed at St. James's and what at Greenwich, and consequently the holdings at these two palaces are best taken together. That being done, there appear to have been 395 pieces divided between St. James's Palace, the armoury at St. James's, and the buildings and grounds at Greenwich. They comprised: whole statues, fragments of statues, busts, plaster heads, chimney pieces, terms, urns, pedestals, bits of architectural decoration and, finally, stones – perhaps for use in restoration work. There were 117 statues, 227 busts, of which twenty seven were Le Sueur's bronze 'philosophers',[167] eight reliefs, six terms, one urn, twenty-one loose pedestals, six blocks of marble, one 'fragment' and '10 broken figure 6 of plaster 4 of wax'.[168]

140 [10, 25]
140 [3]
Fifteen statues either from St. James's or Greenwich, fetched £200 or more, with a 'Sellena. hole. figure bigger than yᵉ life' and a 'sabyna fugitiva soe big as yᵉ life' making £600 a piece and a 'Tiberio bigger then yᵉ life' fetching £500. Of the busts, the Bernini of Charles I was more expensive than anything else in the entire sculpture collection. This was bought for £800 by Emmanuel de Critz, a third-rate artist working in London, who turned himself into one of the shrewdest dealers at the Commonwealth sales where he headed a syndicate.

138 [16]
139 [23, 26]
Besides buying the Bernini, de Critz also acquired a 'Persius' for £200, and 'Adonus' for £150, and an 'Exculapis Daughter' for £80. It is impossible to tell what was antique and what modern at St. James's and Greenwich. The inventories do reveal that there were thirty-two bronze statues and busts – including the 'philosophers' – all of which were surely modern.

The most important site for royal sculpture within London itself, after Whitehall and St. James's, was Denmark House. This became Henrietta Maria's principal London residence where Inigo Jones was employed on extensive alterations and additions, some of which, like the building of the new Cabinet Room to the west of the Cross Gallery, were intended to provide better settings for works of art, including sculpture.

136 [17]
136 [16]
131 [22]
The Contractors for the sales of 1649-51 disposed of 143 sculptural items from Denmark House, not including the dismantled pieces of the *Arethusa* and *Mercury* fountains 'wch did belong to, ye uppr, ground'. These 143 lots consisted of: seventy-seven statues, fifty-five busts, four pieces of marble, a marble table, a marble bedstead, '2 carved Chymne peces', 'a fragment' and 'diverse peeces' which may conceivably have been small quantities of rare marble and semiprecious stone, such as Arundel's sculptors used to restore antiquities. Although the inventories specify that twelve of the statues were in the gardens, only one – a 'herculus and his Clubb' – was described as 'brass', but there were certainly more bronzes than that. Of the statues, 'Augustus Cezar bigger than yᵉ life', was the most valuable at £200, while a 'Young. Comidus' made £150. There was one

132 [63]
136 [19]

419 [7], 420 [18]
421 [19]

287 [144]
395 [966]
395 [967]
395 [968, 970]
229 [145]

247 [1-8]

247 [389]

181 [264]
182 [290]

183 [293]
184 [320]

197 [195]

anomaly in the form of a statue with a biblical subject – a *St. John the Baptist* which made only £1. Le Sueur's *Arethusa* fountain was sold for £500, together with 'yᵉ figure of. Mercure in brass'.

The Queen took an interest in her palaces until the very outbreak of Civil War. She recalled Mollet from France to transform Wimbledon House which Charles had bought for her in 1639 and there is a record of a payment to him of £50 as late as April 1642, some two months after Henrietta Maria herself had fled abroad.[169] Had she had more time, much sculpture would surely have been deployed both within those sumptuous rooms with their blue and gold wainscots and grey marble fireplaces, and in the Italianate gardens with terraces of orange and cherry trees. As it was, however, only five statues were listed in the inventories as having come from Wimbledon, though the Parliamentary surveyors admired 'a faire banqueting house . . . handsomely arched within which, thirteene heades or statues guilded, stand in a circular forme adding very much to the beautie of the whole roome . . .'[170] If war had been averted Wimbledon would have been used as much as Greenwich, where Inigo Jones had finished his work on the Queen's House only in the 1630s.

In contrast to Whitehall, St. James's, Denmark House, and Greenwich, the palaces and houses of Nonsuch, Oatlands, Theobalds, Richmond, Woodstock, Royston and Ludlow Castle seem to have contained little sculpture. Possibly a 'Diana in Allabaster' sold for £2. 10s. came from Nonsuch, with a 'little Marble Statue' and 'Eight Sculptures in Gold Cases one is iron and one is Silver'. Although both Inigo Jones and Nicholas Stone worked on embellishments at Oatlands, it does not seem to have contained any sculpture of note, merely one of the ubiquitous 'brass figures' of Charles I which was sold for £5. Theobalds was more interesting: in the garden was 'A great fountaine of marble and lead', which made £50, and another fountain in the inner court which made £30. In addition, there were 'two old figures in the garden' and twelve marble statues. The hall at Ludlow contained '2. Woodden figures of Beasts' which sound as if they may have been Tudor heraldic animals such as Henry VIII had placed in the Privy Garden at Whitehall. Ludlow also contained a series of portraits in wax and silver of James I which may have been silver relief plaques placed on walls. In addition it also housed a 'King Henry halfe Figure less in Brasse', which may have been a Torrigiano.

Hampton Court was a favourite palace of Charles I but very little is known of the sculpture that must have been there. Although extensive inventories of the pictures and hangings survive, the equivalent for the sculpture has not. One or two items are to be found buried under cushions and curtains; a pair of alabaster figures which were sold to De Critz for £3, three brass andirons which might conceivably have been of Renaissance workmanship since they fetched £7; one cabinet of velvet with the history of Hercules, which was not very impressive compared with the cabinet of white ivory and the two cabinets of ebony since it fetched only £6 while they made £75 as one lot. Within the inventory of pictures is one solitary sculpture simply described as 'A Marbell. peece on a Cupboard', which was sold to De Critz for £10.[171]

The holdings at St. James's and Greenwich compare with the thirty-two statues and 128 busts which a visitor would have seen at Arundel House. Although Charles had more than three times as many statues and nearly twice as many busts at St. James's and Greenwich alone than Arundel had at his house, many were works made by contemporary sculptors whereas the majority of the Arundel statues were Roman or Hellenistic, with a sizeable holding of Greek originals. Furthermore, only eight items from St. James's and Greenwich may be construed as bas-reliefs, whereas Arundel had 250 bas reliefs, sarcophagi, inscriptions and fragments of classical monuments. It was the difference between a garden to please the eye and one to instruct the mind or as Peacham put it when describing the Arundel House gardens, a garden that 'will afford you the pleasure of a world of learned lectures'.[172]

Charles I left London in 1642 and Parliament gained access to the royal palaces where virtually everything remained *in situ*. The palaces were placed under the supervision of the Earl of Northumberland, who had been a distinguished patron of Van Dyck. Of this hazardous period for the royal collection, Millar has written:

. . . During the war works of art were constantly in danger from the hands of the iconoclast, the Puritan zealot and parliamentary troops. Works of art were also assailed by official action, often directed by the Committee, under the chairmanship of Sir Robert Harley, for demolishing superstitious monuments.[173]

However, although there was clearly potential danger, it is possible to see the period of the Civil War and the Interregnum, as it affected the royal collection, in a rather different light. What is remarkable is just how little was destroyed. Many aristocrats had joined the Parliamentary cause in 1642 and they saw themselves not as the King's enemies but as men appointed by providence to rescue their sovereign from evil counsellors. Many were great landowners, and all were believers in the laws of property.

At the time of the break-up of the collection seven years later, events had taken a very different course. The first Parliamentary leaders had died or been superseded, the King had been executed and power now rested with Cromwell and his future major-generals who were, for the most part, middle-class puritans. But still there was much less destruction than might have been expected. One of the mysteries of the Civil War is why so few works of art with relipious subject matter from the royal collection were destroyed. Objects which it might be imagined would have been hammered to pieces, as had happened to Charing Cross, were put up for sale along with the lascivious pictures: from Wimbledon House a 'hermitt on Marble', 'Christ Mary & Joseph' and 'Mary. in ye Cloudes', both also in marble, were sold and not destroyed; a 'Peter. on ye Sea. done on Marbell' from either Denmark House or Whitehall, fetched £10 on 8 October 1651; and another, 'Mary Christ & Joseph', specified as having come from Denmark House, £12. Rubens's altarpiece from Denmark House chapel had indeed been thrown in the Thames and Dieussart's reredos demolished, but that had been the action of the mob at a dangerous and volatile moment before Parliament had had time to assert its control over the royal palaces. The royal chapels in particular attracted the attention of the zealots, but a significant amount of the Denmark House chapel sculpture survived to be sold off: 'Mary ye Childe & 5 persons wth Angells' in marble was coupled with a 'Christ and an Angell' in the same material, and both went for £3 each.

While it is noteworthy that so much sculpture with religious subject matter came through unscathed, it is less surprising that the antiques survived since the Puritans admired classical art; high prices for statues and busts were consistently obtained at the Commonwealth sales. During the Interregnum, a number were either reserved for the use of the state or, as the Protector settled into government, bought back to give to Hampton Court something of the dignity it had had before the war. It became a weekend retreat for Cromwell, who had a number of the best of Charles's statues placed in the gardens including Le Sueur's *Arethusa* fountain, 'brazen statues' of *Venus* and *Cleopatra* and marble figures of *Adonis* and *Apollo*.[174] But Hampton Court was by no means the only royal residence where this happened. In April 1654 Cromwell moved into Whitehall with his wife and by October, Clement Kynnersley, who had been one of the most important of the Contractors at the sale of the King's goods, claimed that he was owed £500 for 'doing his best service' to decorate Whitehall with works of art from the late King's collection.[175] John Evelyn, a man of starched rectitude, was decidedly shocked to find Whitehall 'glorious and well furnished' when he saw it again after many years in February 1656.[176]

Only a few bigots were outraged at all this purloined splendour. One maniac attacked a statue in the Privy Garden at Whitehall, while a certain Mrs Nethaway was so provoked by the nakedness of the Hampton Court statues that she wrote to Cromwell: 'This one thing I desire of you, to demolish these monsters which are set up as ornaments in the Privy Garden,'[177] and told him that by preserving them he would invite the wrath of God as the idolatrous Israelites had done. However, she was not supported and the attitudes of Bulstrode Whitelocke and John Milton were much more typical of the times. Whitelocke became a leading figure at Cromwell's court to whom the Protector turned when considering whether to take the Crown, and he had been one of the four members of the Inns of Court who in 1634 had orchestrated *The Triumph of Peace*, the most splendid of the Caroline masques and the most effective in reconciling government and people. That experience not only made him an obvious choice as keeper of statues and pictures at St. James's, but taught him 'the sweet persuasion' of the arts for the conduct of more serious affairs. As for Milton, it is well known that he was passionately fond of music but he also admired sculpture: a short tract in praise of classical statuary, with practical advice as to where statues were to be found and how they could best be transported, has been attributed to him.[178]

A number of leading Puritans therefore admired the royal collection, and although there were those who disapproved of either works of art or their ostentatious display, they are not easily categorized. Charles had given much

61 [18, 21]
60 [12], 309 [165]
310 [186]

413 [98]

thought to the placing of statues of himself, but there were doubts about such propaganda exercises even from within the ranks of his own supporters. Heylyn, who after all had been a chaplain to Charles, had been unimpressed by the sight of kings parading themselves in brass and marble. He wrote of the statue of Henri IV in Paris which had been the inspiration behind that abortive attempt to obtain an equestrian monument of James I:

In the midst of it [the Pont Neuf] is the *Statua* of the said *Henry* the fourth all in brass, mounted upon his barbed Steed of the same mettal. They are both of them very unproportionable to those bodies which they represent, and would shew them big enough were they placed upon the top of *Nostredame Church*: What minded *King Lewis* to make his *Father* of so *Gigantine* a stature I cannot tell. *Alexander* at his return from his *Indian* expedition scattered armours, swords, and horse-bits far bigger than were serviceable, to make future ages admire his greatness: Yet some have hence collected, that the acts he performed are not so great as is reported, because he strived to make them seem greater than they were. It may also chance to happen, that men in the times to come, comparing the atchievements of this *King* with his brasen portraiture, may think that the *Historians* have as much belyed his valour, as his *Statuary* hath his person.[179]

Heylyn was not alone, since James Howell, also a royalist, reacted in much the same way. He had been in Paris five years before Heylyn and expressed much the same sentiments: 'tho' *Henry* the Great himself lies Centinel there in Arms, upon a huge *Florentine* Horse, and sits bare to every one that passeth; an improper posture methinks to a King on Horseback'.[180]

Charles I and Cromwell were united in believing that sculpture and pictures were necessary adjuncts of greatness and so a nucleus for the reconstruction of the royal collection survived. When the monarchy was re-established under Charles II in May 1660, many of those who had benefited from the Commonwealth sales were eager to come to terms and a significant number of statues and busts were retrieved. A Committee of the House of Lords encouraged Colonel Hawley to bring in as much as he could find by offering him a fifth of their value.[181] He was notably successful. He was able to return between 200 and 250 items of sculpture as well as many notable paintings. The sculpture included most if not all Le Sueur's bronze copies after antique statues and his heads of 'philosophers'. In addition, a number of Fanellis came back into the collection: *St. George and the Dragon*, a *Venus and Cupid* and also, probably by the same artist, a *Venus and Adonis*.[182] Hawley also returned a number of Duquesnoys: a work described in the Hawley inventory as 'A Lucres in Marble halfe as big as ye life of ffrancisco ffamelo', which is not otherwise recorded as having been in the royal collection, and what was probably *Cupid Shaving his Bow*, itself an ivory after the marble. Also probably by Duquesnoy were: 'Two Boyes wth a goate in Ivory', and 'A Rame and a goate wth three Boyes done in Ivery'. By far the largest proportion of sculpture returned, consisted of ranks of Roman emperors and empresses, but there were other things of more interest. These included: 'A curled dog done in marble', two Mercurys, a Bull and a Hercules, all in brass; and, in the realm of fantasy, 'A Boy in Clay done by Tititian' and 'Thomas Ebecits stafe made of unicorns horn ye head of it inlaid with precious stons'. What is surprising given that both Philip IV and Cardinal Mazarin bought extensively at the Commonwealth sales, is how many of the best Mantuan statues had stayed in London. Of these, Hawley managed to locate at least seven; including the 'sabyna fugitiva' which had been sold to the upholsterer Ralph Grynder, for £600 on 23 October 1651.

Hawley was not the sole inquisitor. The committee of which he was a member, met in the Queen's Council Chamber in Denmark House.[189] There they would interview those suspected of possessing the late King's property. Among the miscreants were the painters Geldorp and Michael Wright, the sculptor Edward Marshall and the jeweller Jasper Du Aults, all of whom attended because they were supposed to have bought or dealt in objects from the royal collection. Hawley's committee sat at least until the winter of 1664, when Elias Ashmole was ordered to deliver to Mr Rhemy, 'ye picture of the late King on Horseback now in his Custody'. By such means the royal collection sprang to life again.

In the spring of 1660 there had been almost universal sympathy towards the martyred figure of Charles I. On 16 March 1660 Major Henshaw informed the Earl of Clarendon that 'last evening the detestable motto on the Exchange under the last King's statue was expunged' by the City painter.[184] In the light of a new-found reverence for the monarchy, Edmund Waller's poem, *On the Statue of King*

Figure 55   Hubert le Sueur: *Equestrian statue of Charles I*. 1629. Bronze. Trafalgar Square, London.
Photograph courtesy of the Courtauld Institute, London.

Charles I at Charing Cross, (Fig. 55) provides a sad, not to say, ironic commentary
upon Charles I's love of sculpture:

That the First Charles does here in triumph ride,
See his son reign where he a martyr died,
And people pay that reverence as they pass,
(Which then he wanted!) to the sacred brass,
Is not the effect of gratitude alone,
To which we owe the statue and the stone;
But heaven this lasting monument has wrought,
That mortals may eternally be taught
Rebellion, though successful, is but vain,
And kings so killed rise conquerors again.
This truth the royal image does proclaim,
Loud as the trumpet of surviving fame.[185]

Notes

I would like to thank the following for their help: Dr Charles Avery of Christie's; Malcolm Baker, Department of Sculpture, Victoria and Albert Museum; Michael Bury, Department of Fine Art, University of Edinburgh; Philippa Glanville, Department of Metalwork, Victoria and Albert Museum; Arthur MacGregor, Department of Antiquities, Ashmolean Museum; Tony Radcliffe, Department of Sculpture, Victoria and Albert Museum; Tim Wilson, Department of Medieval and Later Antiquities, British Museum.

1. M. Whinney and O. Millar, *English Art 1625–1714* (Oxford, 1957), pp. 104-5.

2. J. Spedding, R. L. Ellis and D. D. Heath (eds.), *The Works of Francis Bacon* (London, 1858) VI, pp. 481–5 and 485–92: 'Of Building' and, 'Of Gardens'.

3. L. Cust, 'The Lumley Inventories', *Walpole Society* 6 (1917-18), pp. 15-35, pl. VII.

4. W.N. Sainsbury (ed.) *Original Unpublished Papers Illustrative of the Life of Sir Peter Paul Rubens* (London, 1859), pp. 237-8.

5. For Stone's contract for Sir Edward Coke's monument in St. Mary's, Tittleshall, Norfolk, see; W.L. Spiers, 'The Note-Book and Account Book of Nicholas Stone', *Walpole Society* 7 (1918-19), p. 75.

6. For Le Sueur's contract with Laud, see C. Avery 'Hubert Le Sueur, "The unworthy Praxiteles of King Charles 1"', *Walpole Society* 48 (1980-82), p. 203.

7. PRO, SP 16/312, 21 January 1635-6.

8. Spiers, op. cit. (Note 5), p. 171.

9. Ibid, p. 171.

10. For accounts of Dieussart in England see: C. Avery, 'François Dieussart, portrait sculptor to the courts of Northern Europe' in C. Avery, *Studies in European Sculpture* (London, 1981), pp. 205-35. See also, D. Howarth, *Lord Arundel and his Circle* (New Haven and London, 1985).

11. For Prince Henry's bronzes see C. Avery and K. Watson, 'A Grand Ducal gift of "Giovanni Bologna" bronzes for Henry Prince of Wales (1612)', in Avery, op. cit. (Note 10), pp. 95-114.

12. Ibid., p. 103.

13. *Van der Doort's Catalogue*, p. 72.

14. Avery and Watson, op. cit. (Note 11), p. 98.

15. For Christian IV as art patron, see Steffen Heiberg (ed.), *Christian IV and Europe* (Herning, 1988), *passim*, especially pp. 73-150.

16. K. Sharpe, *Sir Robert Cotton 1586-1631* (Oxford, 1979), p. 68.

17. J. Summerson *Inigo Jones* (Harmondsworth, 1983), p. 16.

18. *Van der Doort's Catalogue*, p. 94.

19. Tizianello, *Breve Compendio della Vita del famoso Titiano Veccellio di Cadore* (Venice, 1622).

20. For Lady Arundel as collector and patron see M.F.S. Hervey, *The Life Correspondence and Collections of Thomas Howard Earl of Arundel* (Cambridge, 1921), and Howarth, op. cit. (note 10), passim.

21. R.M. Smuts, in *Court Culture and the Origins of a Royalist Tradition in Early Stuart England* (Philadelphia, 1987), pp. 131-3, suggests that 'the expense of artistic and literary patronage remained relatively modest' under Charles I. However the author bases his argument simply on the amount of money issued by the Exchequer for the purchase of works of art and he makes no reference to the important testimony of Burlamachi quoted above. As it was, art was often paid for through rather informal means.

22. Sainsbury, op. cit. (Note 4), p. 323.

23. Ibid., p. 334.

24. Ibid., p. 333.

25. Ibid., p. 336.

26. Ibid., p. 336.

27. Ibid., p. 339.

28. All of these were inventoried at St. James's (*Inventories*, pp. 143-44, 146).

29. L. Goldscheider, *Michelangelo: Paintings Sculpture Architecture* (London, 1964), p. 5.

30. For accounts of items in present day collections which were part of the Mantuan collection see D. Chambers and J. Martineau (eds.), *Splendours of the Gonzaga* (Victoria and Albert Museum, London, 1982), pp. 229-31, and A. Scott-Elliot, 'The statues from Mantua in the collection of King Charles I', *Burlington Magazine* 101 (1959), pp. 218-27.

31. On 30 July 1629 Rowlandson wrote [to recipient unspecified]; 'Nr Niss is calling up his Maties scolture for to send them with the first opportunity of shipping' (Sainsbury, op. cit. (Note 4), p. 332).

32. Ibid., p. 337.

33. A. Michaelis, *Ancient Marbles in Great Britain* (Cambridge, 1882), p. 28.

34. British Museum, Bronze no. 847. D.E.L. Haynes, *The Arundel Marbles* (Windsor, 1975), p. 20, where the author writes: 'Traditionally known as the "Arundel Homer", the head is more probably that of Sophocles'.

35. Avery, op. cit. (Note 10), p. 189.

36. Machiavelli, *The Discourses* (ed.) B. Crick, (Harmondsworth, 1970), p. 97.

37. P. Palme, *Triumph of Peace* (Uppsala, 1957), p. 267.

38. For references to interest shown by other collectors see Sainsbury, op. cit. (Note 4) pp. 320-40.

39. Whinney and Millar, op. cit. (Note 1) p. 110, and R. Strong, *The Renaissance Garden* (London, 1979), p. 232.

40. Spiers, op. cit. (Note 5), pl. xxxii, a.

41. Ibid., pls. xiv, c and d.

42. See K. Sharpe 'The Earl of Arundel, his circle and the opposition to the Duke of Buckingham, 1618-1628', in K. Sharpe (ed.), *Faction and Parliament* (Oxford, 1978), pp. 209-45.

43. Spiers, op. cit. (Note 5), pl. xxvi, c.

44. Ibid., pl. xxvi, a.

45. See Haynes, op. cit. (Note 34), p. 15 and M. Vickers, 'Germanicus's tomb', *The Ashmolean* 15 (Spring 1989), pp. 6-8.

46. Spiers, op. cit. (Note 5), pl. xxxv, a.

47. Whinney and Millar, op. cit. (Note 1), p. 110.

48. Ibid., p. 110.

49. Spiers, op. cit. (Note 5), p. 107.

50. For Danvers's garden at Chelsea, see Strong, op. cit. (Note 39), pp. 176-81.

51. See J. Pope-Hennessy *Italian High Renaissance and Baroque Sculpture* (London and New York, 1970), pp. 71-8 and fig. 92.

52. For gardens and fountains at Wilton, see Strong, op. cit. (Note 39), pp. 147-61. The Nys *Venus and Cupid* and *Venus and a Dolphin*, (of which Nys sent over four versions), are Royal Library Windsor, Nys Drawings: R.L. 8913 and 8905, 8907, 8909, 8910.

53. For the Giambologna see C. Avery and A. Radcliffe (eds.), *Giambologna 1529-1608 Sculptor to the Medici* (Arts Council, Great Britain, 1978), p. 68, pl. 12. For Marshall's Curwen monument see Whinney and Millar, op. cit. (Note 1), pl. 29a.

54. For the Leveson monument see C. Avery, op. cit. (Note 6), pls. 62b and 42c. For the *Shepherd*, Royal Library, Windsor, Nys Drawing R.L. 8903.

55. Royal Library, Windsor, Nys Drawings R.L. 8886 and R.L 8922.

56. See D. Howarth, 'Charles I and the Gonzaga', in Chambers and Martineau, op. cit. (Note 30) p. 97.

57. Stephen Larrabee, *English Bards and Grecian Marbles* (New York, 1943), p. 46.

58. Ibid., p. 46.

59. Walton's *Lives* [no ed.] (London, 1858), p. 146.

60. Larrabee, op. cit. (Note 57), p. 46.

61. E. Arber (ed.), *A Transcription of the registers of the Company of Stationers of London 1554-1640 AD* (London, 1877), IV, p. 164.

62. On 12 May 1628, Nys wrote to Endymion Porter; 'The ship Margaret must now be far advanced on her voyage. I have not as yet heard that she has arrived at London, so that his Majesty may see so many beautiful and exquisite pictures. Among them . . . are the twelve Emperors of Titian . . . ' Sainsbury, op. cit. (Note 4), pp. 325-6, where the date is wrongly transcribed as, 'Venice, May 12, 1639'.

63. H. Osborne (ed.), *Microcosmography* (London, n.d.), pp. 20-21. Osborne considered that Earle was referring to coins in using the word 'pictures'.

64. Howarth, op. cit. (Note 10), note 44, p. 237.

65. Ibid, p. 120.

66. S. Orgel and R. Strong, *Inigo Jones and The Theatre of the Stuart Court Masque* (London, Berkeley and Los Angeles, 1973), II, pp. 453-79.

67. I am grateful to John Peacock of The Department of English, Southampton University for first pointing out the connection between the Mytens portrait and Jones's design for *A Roman Atrium*. For the Mytens portrait see Howarth, op. cit. (Note 10), colour pl. 2.

68. Orgel and Strong, op. cit. (Note 66), II, pls. 199-202.

69. Ibid., II, pp. 505-37.

70. Reeves wrote to Lord Feilding, ambassador in Venice, on 8 November 1638 of 'Mr Mountegues great collection of pictures wch Mr Fitton bought for him at Rome, are nowe also in the Downes, where they have escap'd 20 to one the casting away; at their arrivall heere, there will [be] great vying of good peeces'. (Warwickshire County Record Office, CR2017).

71. Orgel and Strong, op. cit. (Note 66), II, pl. 252 and fig. 90.

72. Avery, op. cit. (Note 10), p. 189.

73. Orgel and Strong, op. cit. (Note 66), II, pp. 598-629 and pls. 312, 317.

74. Avery, op. cit. (Note 6), p. 149.

75. Florence, Archivio di Stato, MS. Galli-Tassi, 1789.

76. F. Haskell and N. Penny, *Taste and the Antique* (New Haven and London, 1981), p. 35.

77. Avery, op. cit. (Note 6), p. 149.

78. B. Boucher, 'Leone Leoni and Primaticcio's moulds of antique sculpture', *Burlington Magazine* 133 (1981), pp. 23-6.

79. J.A. Gotch, *Early Renaissance Architecture in England* (London, 1914), pp. 34-5.

80. Avery, op. cit. (Note 6), p. 205.

81. Ibid., pls. 38b, 41c, 44a, 44c, 45a, 45c, 46a, 46b, 46c, 46d.

82. Howard Colvin remarks on 'mixed styles' in *The Canterbury Quadrangle St John's College Oxford* (Oxford, 1988), pp. 15 and 19.

83. See R. Lockyer, *The Life and Career of George Villiers 1st Duke of Buckingham* (London, 1981) *passim* for a full account of how contemporaries saw Buckingham.

84. For a description of the reredos see: T. Birch, *The Court and Times of Charles I* (ed.) R.F. Williams (London, 1848), II, pp. 311-13.

85. Spiers, op. cit. (Note 5), p. 105.

86. For analyses of this picture see: C. White, *The Dutch Pictures in the Collection of Her Majesty The Queen* (Cambridge, 1982), cat. no. 14, pp. 53-6; G. Parry, *The Golden Age Restor'd: The Culture of the Stuart Court, 1603-1642* (Manchester, 1981), pp. 225-7.

87. Avery, op. cit. (Note 6), pls. 50f, 51e.

88. Strong (op. cit. (Note 39), p. 189) was the first to identify the figure as Arethusa, because she is so described in the Commonwealth Inventory of 1659. Strong accepts the conventional attribution of the fountain to Fanelli which dates from a remark made by Evelyn in 1662. Avery however, has convincingly re-attributed it to Le Sueur: Avery, op. cit. (Note 6), pp. 151-3. An identification with Diana is also improbable because Le Sueur's figure does not have the crescent moon in her hair; an invariable attribute. The identification of the main figure on the fountain with Arethusa is surely correct because she is an appropriate subject: she was turned into a fountain by Artemis to escape the advances of Alpheus (see P. Levi (ed.), *Pausanias Guide to Greece, Southern Greece* (Harmondsworth, 1971), II, p. 213.

89. Strong, op. cit. (Note 39), p. 189.

90. Pope-Hennessy, op. cit. (Note 51), fig. 94.

91. Royal Library, Windsor, Nys Drawing, R.L. 8907.

92. Pope-Hennessy, op. cit. (Note 51), fig. 93.

93. See also p. 354 below.

94. For the Le Sueur bust see C. Avery 'Hubert Le Sueur's portraits of Charles I in bronze at: Stourhead, Ickworth and elsewhere', in Avery, op. cit. (Note 10), pp. 189-205. For the Fanelli see J. Pope-Hennessy, 'Some bronze statuettes by Francesco Fanelli', *Burlington Magazine* 95 (1953), pp. 157-62, pls. 10-12.

95. Avery, op. cit., (Note 6), pls. 58a and 58c, 55a, 55d and 55e, 56d, 57a, b, d and e, 56a.

96. Ibid., p. 184.

97. In *V.C.H. Sussex*, III, p. 73, it is stated that the bust appeared on the Market Cross at the Restoration. But George Vertue, on a tour 'round Kent, Sussex and thro Hampshire' in 1738, noted: 'at Chichester − an ancient Cross in the middle of four great cross streets but in King Charles the first's time a bust in brass of his head was put up in a nich. and taken down in the War time and buried till after the restoration. This head is much like some others done by le Sueur or rather Fanelli' (Vertue, *Note Books* VI, p. 90). However, earlier in the same volume (p. 38), Vertue states that the bust was first placed in its niche at the Restoration.

98. There were full-length Le Sueur statues of Charles I and James I on Inigo Jones's choir screen in Winchester Cathedral, but there is no known record of a bust of Charles I by Le Sueur strategically placed in a cathedral city as happened at Chichester in 1637.

99. *Dictionary of National Biography* XIII, p. 713, under Montagu, Richard.

100. Ibid., XIII, p. 715.

101. PRO, SP16/325, 60, 6 June 1636, Order of the King in Council.

102. PRO, SP16/331, 14. The Dean and Recorder of Chichester were both present in August 1636 at St. John's College, Oxford when Charles first saw the statues of himself and Henrietta Maria.

103. PRO, SP16/363, 80.

104. William Prynne, *Canterburies Doome* (London, 1646), p. 497. Avery thinks the bust has no connection with Laud; '[it] was set up in the former church (the last, incidentally, consecrated by Archbishop Laud), probably as a thank-offering after the Restoration (1661), by Sir Nicholas Crispe; it is incorporated in a wall monument with an urn containing the baronet's heart' (Avery, op, cit. (Note 6), p. 157). There is no documentary evidence for this statement which therefore may not be correct.

105. Avery makes no mention of the Charles I bust which Count Magalotti described in his *Travels of Cosimo the Third, Grand Duke of Tuscany, through England, During the Reign of Charles II* (London, 1821), p. 367; 'Above the door which leads into the room, and which is opposite the royal throne, is a statue of King Charles 1, whose majestic mein delights the spectator, while he is at the same time saddened by the remembrance of the mournful catastrophe which took place in this very room'.

106. Avery, op. cit. (Note 6), doc. no. 83, p. 207.

107. Palme, op. cit. (Note 37), p. 267.

108. Ibid., p. 268.

109. Colvin, op. cit. (Note 82), p. 27.

110. Peter Heylyn, *Cyprianus Anglicus* (London, 1671), p. 209.

111. PRO, SP, Council of State, Day's Proceedings, vol. IX, 6, 31 July 1650.

112. Ibid., vol. IX, 7, 31 July 1650.

113. For a full discussion of the building of both church and piazza, see Summerson, op. cit. (Note 17), pp. 83-96.

114. Smuts, op. cit. (Note 21), p. 128.

115. G. Parry, *Hollar's England* (Wilton, 1980), text to pl. 32.

116. For Bedford's relations with the King see M. Butler, *Theatre and Crisis 1632-1642* (Cambridge, 1984), pp. 147-8, where the author provides further information which might encourage the view that Charles wished his presence to be felt within what was an 'alien' environment: 'It [the Covent Garden development] was also a challenge to Laud's conforming ministry. Covent Garden church was the first church to be built in London since the Reformation and the puritan earl reserved the patronage to himself, resisting the attempts of the vicar of St Martin-in-the-Fields to control the living.'

117. PRO, SP, Council of State, Day's Proceedings, vol. XI, 13, 16 October 1650.

118. Ibid., vol. XCIX, 23, 31 July 1655.

119. Ibid., vol. XV, 24, 27 January 1651. Vertue refers to a bust of Charles I, now gone, which was in Westminster Hall – another critical site: 'Bust of K. Charles I in Brass on a pedestal that has stood many many years, over an Arch or gate within Westminster hall, near the King's Bench and when Scaffolds etc. is there erected it is usually taken down, so it was now, when I saw it. [Aug. 27 1740] in the clerks of the works office – and having well observd it. I do not think it is a cast from Berninis Bust of Marble as is said – but rather younger. the face well repaird and ye Armour curiously wrought with ornaments and masks. it is much the likeness of face as in the Family picture by Vandyke. K. Ch. his Queen and 2 Children at Kensington – no mark or name or Artist on it nor date' (Vertue, *Note Books* IV, p. 178). Vertue's description suggests that it was another Le Sueur bronze.

120. Pope-Hennessy, op. cit. (Note 94), p. 158.

121. For a full discussion of the Fanelli see Chambers and Martineau, op. cit. (Note 30), cat. no. 279.

122. Whinney and Millar, op. cit. (Note 1), pl. 31a.

123. For the Bernini documents see R.W. Lightbown, 'The journey of the Bernini bust of Charles I to England', *Connoisseur* 169 (1968), pp. 217-20. The bust perished in the fire at Whitehall in 1698.

124. Vatican Library, MS, Barberini Latina, 8639, ff. 1 seq: 'Nota di robbe consegnate al Sig Giorgio Coneo portarle in Inghilterra. Adi 15 Maggio 1636'; f.15: 'e piu un Reliquiario con Reliquie di S Elena fatto da Fran Spagna con desegno del Bernini alto un palmo et mezo cioe del mezo in su tutto d'oro fatto ornato in mezo con Cristalli di Venetia et sopra una Corona piena di robini diversi et uno spiede d'argento dorato con un cherubino con 4 ale posto sopra un triangolo.' Francesco Spagna II had a pension of 6 scudi a month as jeweller to the Pope, 1628-1640. He is recorded as having produced work for Carlo and Antonio Barberini.

125. Spiers, op. cit. (Note 5), p. 170.

126. O. Millar, *The Age of Charles I* (London, 1972), p. 63.

127. F. C. Springell, *Connoisseur and Diplomat* (London, 1963), p. 262.

128. PRO, S.P. 16/343, 3.

129. For Antico see A. Radcliffe, 'Antico and the Mantuan bronze', in Chambers and Martineau, op. cit. (Note 30), pp. 46-51.

130. M. Leithe-Jasper, *Renaissance Master Bronzes*, (London and New York, 1986), cat. no. 10 and, Chambers and Martineau op. cit. (Note 30), cat. nos. 58-61.

131. Bacon, op. cit. (Note 2), VI, p. 492.

132. See M. Baker, 'A peece of wondrous art: Giambologna's Samson and a Philistine and its later copies', *Antologia di Belli Arti*, nuova serie 23-4 (Vincenza, 1984), pp. 62-72. Another hitherto overlooked reference suggests that the Giambologna was not something that simply attracted attention when first erected. Right up to the Civil War it was regarded as the finest object in an outstanding collection. Peter Mundy, perhaps the most travelled of all early Stuart adventurers, noted in his diary on an unspecified day in 1639; 'I was allsoe att Yorckhouse, where I saw sundry rare ritche pictures, statues, roomes, curiosities thatt was in it: Cain and Abell off Marble on a Mountt in the gardein, which was taken From a Fountaine in the King of Spaines gardein at Valladolid in Castile. Att my beeing there I saw the basis or place whereon itt stood, and then, they told mee what became off the reste". Sir Richard Temple (ed.), 'The Travels of Peter Mundy', *Hakluyt Society*, second series IV (London, 1925), p. 45.

133. J. Pope-Hennessy, *Catalogue of Italian Sculpture in the Victoria and Albert Museum*, (London 1964), II, p. 462.

134. Howarth, op, cit. (Note 10), pp. 197-8.

135. *Van der Doort's Catalogue*, p. 71: 'Item Cast in brass and blackt over wth black vernish a little Statua where David overcomes Goliah being a little intire figure. Bought by ye king. Mr Endimion Porter'. This corresponds to bronzes in the Pushkin Museum, Moscow and the Linsky Collection, The Metropolitan Museum, New York, which are attributed to Fanelli by Radcliffe.

136. For items which were in the Chair Room see *Van der Doort's Catalogue*, pp. 70-75.

137. For these, from the cabinets of 'Abraham van Hutton' and Hans von Dirbige, see R. Strong, *Henry Prince of Wales* (London, 1986), pp. 198-9.

138. *Van der Doort's Catalogue*, p. xvi.

139. This corresponds to the appearance of a bronze in the Victoria and Albert Museum (A96-1956), which Radcliffe attributes to Fanelli.

140. For items which were in the Cabinet Room see *Van der Doort's Catalogue*, pp. 92-102.

141. For a definitive account of pieces by the Van Vianens in the royal collection during the reign of Charles I, see J.R. ter Molen *Van Vianen* (Rotterdam, 1984), cat nos: 108-111, 117, 127, 131, 132, 134-9, 177, 375, 399, 538, 582, 610-13, 619, 634-41, 794, 802 and 848. For Christian in England, see R.W. Lightbown, 'Christian Van Vianen at the court of Charles I', *Apollo* 87 1968, pp. 426-439.

142. H.R. Weihrauch, *Europäische Bronzestatuetten* (Braunschweig, 1967), p. 145.

143. *Van der Doort's Catalogue*, p. 94: '19 Item more imboast in earth a little Childe lying a sleepe being done by the Sculpter ffrancisco ffeamingo at Roome who is in Conquerence with-Caveleero Barnino.'

144. There are a number of ivory pieces itemized within the inventory of pictures in the Cabinet Room which suggest Duquesnoy. (a) *Van der Doort's Catalogue*, p. 86: '54. Item a leaping Goate whereon is a Child and-another Child standing by, pulling by a stringe being set upon a black velvett in a black ebone frame' (b). Ibid., p. 87: '56. Item a little Cuppid who is a shaveing his bow being Carved in white Ivory set upon black velvett in a black ebbone frame'; this may have been after the damaged marble by Duquesnoy now in the Staatliche Museen Skulpturen-sammlung, East Berlin, or, alternatively, it could have been an Italian Mannerist piece after the painting by Parmigianino. (c) Ibid., p. 88: '62. Item a peece Cutt in white Ivory where a Goate is-runing along over a Child, and on the Goats backe-an other Child falling, and the Third runinge-behinde takeing hold of a lock of haire of the Goate sett upon black velvett in a black ebbone frame'; this and (a) (above) would seem to have been from the putti series designed by Duquesnoy of which there were six. See Victoria and Albert Museum, London, nos. 1059-1064-1853.

145. *Van der Doort's Catalogue*, p. 76-97. For the identification of this bust and its significance in the English collectors' world of the 1630s, see Katharine Eustace's Catalogue entry no. 68 in D. Howarth and N. Penny (eds.), *Patronage and Collecting in the Seventeenth Century. Thomas Howard Earl of Arundel* (Ashmolean Museum, Oxford, 1985).

146. Ibid p. 78; 'Item a Picture carved in a greish soft stone, being the peece of king Henry the 8th at length a-little intire figure, in a curious little carved frame wch yor Matie had when you were Prince. Carved in kinge Henry the 8ts time wch yor Matie had when you were Prince'.

147. I examined the hone stone relief in the British Museum, and found that the measurements correspond extremely closely with those given by Van der Doort: $5\frac{7}{8} \times 3\frac{7}{8}$ inches compared with his $5\frac{3}{4} \times 3\frac{3}{4}$ inches. The relief has the following note on the back, inscribed in Walpole's hand: 'Henry the 8th modelled by Holbein; bought at the auction of Lady Elizabeth Germain in 1770 and came out of the Arundel Collection.' Despite what Walpole writes however, nothing corresponding to it appears in the Germaine sale catalogue. Walpole's claim that the relief was in *both* the Arundel and the royal collection is unlikely to be true. If the object at The British Museum is indeed that which Van der Doort describes, then it was still in the royal collection in 1639; by which time Arundel was in serious political and financial difficulties and therefore unlikely to be acquiring things from the royal collection. Walpole was probably therefore confused as to where he had acquired it. It was sold for £67 4s. at the Strawberry Hill sale of 1844. It appears in the sale catalogue as item no. 52, p. 199. It passed into the collection of Mrs Dent of Sudeley. She lent it for the *Exhibition of the Royal House of Tudor* (London, 1890) no. 1074. In the catalogue entry there is a reference to

'Two other figures carved in stone by Holbein [which] were in the Museum of Tradescant at Lambeth'. There is, however, no trace of these ever having been in the Tradescant collection.

148. *Van der Doort's Catalogue*, p. 152: '16 Item a Carved peece in white Ivory sett upon black velvett in a square ebbone frame Two sitting Children-a fighting. Bought by yor Maty of Mr Endimion Porter'; '17 Item a fellowe peece of thaforesaid, being also Carved in white Ivory-sett upon a black vellvett in a-black ebbone frame Two other-Children standing fighting. Bought by yor Maty of Mr Endimion Porter.' See *De Beeldhouwkunst in de eeuw van Rubens* (Brussels, 1977), cat. no. 215, for a discussion of these reliefs which are in the Musée du Louvre, Paris, no. M.R. 361.

149. *Van der Doort's Catalogue*, p. 76.

150. Ter Molen, op. cit. (Note 141), cat. no. 610; 'To Cristian van Viane of Utrecht. By order dated vlto April 1633 the some C1 viz 1 for one Candlestick by him sold vnto his Matie and C wch his Matie is pleased to allow vnto him for his charges and expenses in remouing and transporting himself and his family from Utrecht hither.'

151. *Van der Doort's Catalogue*, p. 62.

152. Ibid., p. 63: 'Item a little Landskipp peece wherein is painted Diana who is pulling Calista by the haire whereby Three Nimphs are with her in a black frame. Don by Pullenbourch bought by ye king.'

153. Ibid., p. 65.

154. For sculpture in the Adam and Eve Stairs Room see ibid, pp. 12-14.

155. Ibid., p. 13: Item the second the peece of king Henry the 8.th done in a plaister painted over wth oyle Cullors in a black Capp. so big as the. life in a woodden frame; being only a head'.

156. Ibid., p. 13.

157. Sainsbury, op. cit. (Note 4), p. 326.

158. *Van der Doort's Catalogue*, p. 202 for the sculpture in the Long Gallery. Van der Doort mentions three busts of Bacchus, 'A Young Romane head', An 'Entire Cupid', 'A Childs head', 'A young mans head', 'On Twenty Three Wooden-Petticke stanes Twenty Three Severall heads of Marble vizt' and there the list ends.

159. P[eter] H[eylyn], *The Voyage of France or A Compleat journey through France* (London, 1673), p. 155.

160. Ibid., pp. 155-6.

161. Howarth, op. cit., (Note 10), p. 120.

162. Strong, op. cit. (Note 39), p. 189.

163. For André Mollet and the royal palace gardens see Strong, op. cit., (Note 39), pp. 188-97.

164. For Claude Mollet the Elder see ibid., pp. 83-4 and pp. 187-8.

165. Ibid., p. 188.

166. Ibid., p. 232, note 53. Stone and others were also involved in reparations and the making of pedestals at Greenwich at this period. G.H. Chettle, *The Queen's House, Greenwich* (14th Monograph of the London Survey Committee) (n.p., 1937), pp. 104-5, mentions [1637-8] 'Taskeworkes viz. To Nichās Stone Mʳ Mason for working and squaring of iiijᵉʳ Pedestalls of Purbecke stone & setting them vpp the king finding stuffe at XVᵈ the peece'; [1639-40] '. . . working & making Tenn carved Pedestalls to sett marble Statuaes on, setting those Statuaes on them in the gᵗ. roome at the sd. building. . . To Robert Peeke & Vᵉ other Masons for raising of Statuaes & setting them on Pedestalls at the new Buildings; xxviijˢ: xjˡⁱ xixᵈ . . . Zachary Tailer Carver for carving Tenn Pedestalls of timber for marble Statuaes to stand on with Bulls heads festons fruites leaues & flowers att 1xˢ the peece . . . To Nichās Stone for altering & new carving the thighes legs and feete of a marble Statua of a young man, for iron cramps to fasten some members & for cemᵗ straw to pack it & carr. of it from London Iˢ: xxxixˡⁱ ijˢ vᵈ, John Hooker Turner for turning Xᵉⁿ great Pedestalls of elme timber with their bases & capitalls at xijˢ the peece'.

167. I have followed Avery in assuming that all bronze heads in the Armoury at St James's can be assumed to have been by Le Sueur. Avery, op. cit. (Note 6), cat. no. 22, p. 180; *Inventories*, pp. 155-6.

168. For statues at St. James's and Greenwich see *Inventories*, pp. 139-50, 155-6, and 138-50.

169. For Mollet's work at Wimbledon House see Strong, op. cit. (Note 39), pp. 191-7.

170. W.H. Hart, 'The Parliamentary surveys of Richmond, Wimbledon, and Nonsuch, in the County of Surrey, AD 1649', *Surrey Archaeological Collections* 5 (1871), pp. 120-21.

171. 'Mary sitting in a Marbell seate', which De Critz bought for £1 (*Inventories*, p. 196 [180]), might have been a piece of sculpture.

172. Howarth, op. cit. (Note 10), p. 120.

173. *Inventories*, p. xi.

174. E. Law, *The History of Hampton Court Palace* II *Stuart Times* (London, 1888), p. 302.

175. A. Fraser, *Cromwell Our Chief of Men* (London, 1973), p. 459.

176. Ibid., p. 459.

177. Ibid., p. 460.

178. The Columbia University edition of Milton includes a tract, 'Of Statues and Antiquities', which is described as 'Perhaps by Milton': see F.A. Patterson (ed.), *The Works of John Milton* (New York, 1938), XVIII, pp. 258-61.

179. Heylyn, op. cit. (Note 159), pp. 121-2.

180. James Howell to Richard Altham, Paris, 1 May 1620: J. Jacobs (ed.), *Epistolae Hoelianae, The Familar Letters of James Howell* (London, 1890), I, p. 45.

181. BL, Additional MS, 17, 916. 'A Boke conteining severall of his Maties Goods brought into his Maties Closet and Wardrop by Coll Wm Hawley by ye order of A Committe of Lords in April 1660. Whitehall June 1 1660'.

182. I have assumed that this *Venus and Adonius in brasse*, as it is described, was by Fanelli because it is listed after *A St George A Horsebacke in Brasse* and *A Venus and Cupid in brasse*, on f.74ʳ of BL Additional MS 17, 916.

183. See Bod. Lib., MS Rawlinson A111, for further evidence of Hawley's work of reconstruction.

184. Bod. Lib., Clarendon State Papers, 94-5 and 181b.

185. G.A.E. Parfitt (ed.), *Silver Poets of the Seventeenth Century* (London, 1974), p. 41.

4 The Limnings, Drawings and Prints in Charles I's Collection

Jane Roberts

Marginal numerals refer to page and entry numbers in the *Inventories* (see p. 11)

Abraham van der Doort (d.1640), whose name is mentioned on so many occasions throughout this volume, served as Keeper of the newly-built Cabinet Room at Whitehall from 1625, but had already occupied this position for some years before that date. By the terms of his appointment, Van der Doort was given charge of 'the Meddalies and Limbed pecees and all other rarrities belongeng or hearafter may belong'. His responsibility for the pictures in Charles I's collection was distinct from the Keepership of the Cabinet Room, in which were kept the majority of the precious small-scale artefacts of the collection, whether miniatures, drawings, books, medals, coins, or other miscellaneous articles.[1] The practice of making (and collecting) portrait miniatures was introduced to England in the reign of Henry VIII. Van der Doort's inventory of Charles I's collection, and particularly of the Cabinet Room, is a crucial document in the early history of the portrait miniature in England. Its authority is enhanced by the fact that it was compiled by the curator of the collection himself.

The core of the collection of around eighty miniatures in the Cabinet Room was formed by the portraits of English monarchs and their families. There were two rectangular frames containing respectively seven portraits of monarchs and their consorts from Henry VII to Queen Elizabeth, by Holbein, Hilliard and others,[2] and eight portraits of the descendants of Mary Queen of Scots, by Hilliard, Isaac Oliver and others[3] – in other words, of Charles I's Tudor and Stuart progenitors. In due course, the contents of each of these two frames were valued for sale at £100. In addition, there were several independent portraits of members of Henry VIII's family, attributed to Holbein and Hilliard; these included four tiny portraits set in a gold and enamelled jewel.[4] Other early miniatures were kept in turned ivory boxes. Four portraits each of Charles I's

257 [31]

257 [30]

Figure 56   John Hoskins: *Queen Henrietta Maria* (watercolour and bodycolour on vellum). 89 × 76mm. Royal Collection: reproduced by gracious permission of Her Majesty The Queen.

Figure 57   *a* Daniel Fröschl: *Emperor Rudolf II* (watercolour and bodycolour on vellum).
130 × 102mm; *b* back of frame; *c* back of frame with slide removed to show Charles I's brand and the
back of the vellum on which the miniature is painted. Reproduced by permission of Sam Fogg.

Figure 58   Isaac Oliver: *Henry, Prince of Wales* (watercolour and bodycolour on vellum).
130 × 120mm. Royal Collection: reproduced by gracious permission of Her Majesty The Queen.

elder brother, Prince Henry (by Isaac and Peter Oliver, and by Hilliard), of their sister the Queen of Bohemia and of Queen Henrietta Maria, 'in sundry bignes' (by Hoskins [Fig. 56] and by Peter Oliver), were accompanied by portraits of the King and Queen together, and of the King alone, by Hoskins.[5] Finally, there were portraits of important figures such as the Emperor Rudolf II (Fig. 57) and one-time court favourites such as the Earl of Essex.

247 [371]

With the exception of the majestic portrait of Prince Henry in armour by Isaac Oliver (Fig. 58), which measured five and a quarter by four inches, the majority of the portrait miniatures were less than three inches in height (or two inches in width). However, the Cabinet Room also contained a new and larger type of miniature, with religious or even secular subject-matter, as characterized by Edward Norgate. The fact that Norgate had been employed specifically to teach the art of limning to the two sons of Thomas Howard, Earl of Arundel, is symptomatic of the new importance attached to this art. According to Norgate's *Miniatura or the Art of Limning* (originally written in 1620 but revised *c*.1650),

Histories in Lymning are strangers in England till of late Yeares it pleased a most excellent King [Charles I] to command the Copieing of some of his owne peeces, of Titian, to be translated into English Lymning, which indeed were admirably performed by his Servant, Mr Peter Oliver.

The most important of these copies were the ten 'lim'd peeces . . . in dowble shutting cases with Locks and keys and glasses over them',[6] which consisted of miniature copies by the younger Oliver of Italian paintings of the High Renaissance, almost invariably from the King's own collection. The list was however headed by an independent collaborative piece (now lost) by Isaac and Peter Oliver of the Burial of Christ, measuring eleven and a half by fifteen and a half inches. The smallest of the copies (Peter Oliver's version of Correggio's *Holy Family*) measured five by four inches; the largest (the same artist's copy of Raphael's *St George and the Dragon*: Fig. 59) measured nine and a half by seven inches. These copies, many of which survive in the Royal Collection, are dated

258 [40]

117   Charles I's Limnings, Drawings and Prints

Figure 59   Peter Oliver, after Raphael: *St. George and the Dragon* (watercolour and bodycolour on vellum). 223 × 166mm Royal Collection: reproduced by gracious permission of Her Majesty The Queen.

Figure 60   Peter Oliver, after Holbein: *The Duke* from *The Dance of Death* (watercolour and bodycolour). 63 × 53mm. Royal Collection: reproduced by gracious permission of Her Majesty The Queen.

247 [368]   between 1628 and 1639. The tiny copy of Holbein's *Duke* from the *Dance of Death* (Fig. 60) was elsewhere in the Cabinet Room. Other large-scale religious limnings were listed in the Queen's apartments in Somerset House.[7]

Although Norgate identified Peter Oliver (at the instigation of Charles I) as the originator of the new large-scale miniature copies, his father, Isaac Oliver, surely had some influence (look, for instance, at his large-scale 'narrative' portrait miniatures), just as he did in the evolution of the drawing as an independent art form in England. In his will, dated 4 June 1617, Isaac Oliver mentions 'all my drawings allready finished and unfinished and lymning pictures', which were bequeathed to his eldest son Peter.[8] The fact that Oliver distinguished between finished and unfinished drawings demonstrates that he was not referring to preparatory studies or sketches. It should come as no surprise, therefore, to find that drawings are occasionally described as limnings 'in black and white'. They were similar in several respects (generally small-scale framed items, often painted on vellum), but were in monochrome rather than the jewel-like colours of a true limning. The fashion for drawings that were finished (and therefore usually framed) is first documented in England during the years of Isaac Oliver's maturity. In the second (enlarged) edition of Henry Peacham's treatise, published in 1612 with the title *Graphice or the Most Auncient and Excellent Art of Drawing and Limning*, practical advice is given to the 'young learner' of this most demanding art. A small group of works by Isaac Oliver, including subjects from classical mythology, had probably passed into Charles I's collection from his mother, Anne of Denmark. These included three finished drawings by Oliver which are noted by Vertue, but were listed neither by Van der Doort nor by the compilers of the inventories: at Denmark House they may have been somewhat out of range. The drawings of 'Nymphs and Satyrs' (Fig. 61) and 'Moses striking the Rock' remain in the Royal Collection.[9] The third drawing, of the 'Rape of the Sabines', is not recorded after the late seventeenth century.[10] With other items from the Royal Collection, it may have perished in the Whitehall Fire of 1689.

The following references appear to relate to other framed drawings (or limnings?) in Charles I's collection. Among the contents of the Little Store Room

246 [357] off the Bear Gallery, Whitehall, Van der Doort noted 'an our La[dy]: hugging. Christ. in her armes halfe figures done and hatched [by the King's engraver, Robert van Vorst] with a penn uppon a white vellam in a black arched [or octagonal?] ebbone frame',[11] and a 'head of Christ Crowned with thornes' after Dürer, 'upon blew paper drawen in black and white . . . very Curiously done set in a black frame wth a shiver', measuring eleven by nine inches.[12] Another religious subject, the significance of which is uncertain, was also in the Little Store Room off the Bear Gallery: 'Item In a frame Some drawing peece uppon paper bin de chusment auffte michel angelo bonarotis jusment Wij is in pijnting so big als ta hol sijd aufft pops chapel at rom'.[13] Was this a copy of Michelangelo's *Last Judgement*, or a fragment of Michelangelo's cartoon for that painting?

247 [378] Another drawing noted by Van der Doort (but which was described as a print in the inventories) showed 'Marcus Courchus liping in the fiery Pitt at Roome', 'a little drawing wth a Penn in a black frame'.[14] The name of the artist was not specified. It sold for £5 in the Commonwealth sales.

The subject-matter of other drawings was both more traditional and more personal. Above a door in the Privy Chamber, Whitehall, Van der Doort noted 'In
271 [244] a Litle wodden frame the Princees arms Being the 3 ffeathrs made aboute with a collor of roasees Being done with a penn uppon white parchmt Sett uppon
246 [358] board': it raised 1s. in the Commonwealth sales.[15] Elsewhere in the Whitehall inventory Van der Doort listed 'a drawing in little of Prince Henry where hee is playing wth a lance beeing side faced in a black frame with a shiver' by Isaac
63 [59] Oliver (now lost, but known from copies: see Fig. 62).[16] and 'another drawing wth a penn upon white vellam yor Mats owne Picture on horsback'.[17] These were sold respectively for 1s. and 2s. 6d. The entry immediately following in Van der Doort's lists is more enigmatic: 'Don by Juliano [or julio] the Italian . . . under a glasse being larg that hath bin a lookeing glasse a larg drawing upon vellam conteyning manie little figures beeing kinde of a part of a Citty'.[18]

Figure 61   Isaac Oliver: *Nymphs and satyrs* (black ink with white heightening over black chalk, on discoloured brown paper). 205 × 357mm. Royal Collection: reproduced by gracious permission of Her Majesty The Queen.

Figure 62   Simon van der Passe, after Isaac Oliver: *Henry, Prince of Wales* (engraving).
Royal Collection: reproduced by gracious permission of Her Majesty The Queen.

Other items which appear to be framed drawings are listed in the inventories: 'The drawing of a Candlestick. don by van Melly', sold to De Critz on 18 November 1651 for 2*s*.; 'a drawing after Raphaell. of ye 3 Kings pasted on a desk', valued at £5; and 'A Draught of A Shipp', valued at 10*s*. The 'One peece of writeing done by holben' is particularly hard to visualize: it was sold (to Colonel Webb) in 1649 for the relatively large sum of £10, while few other drawings fetched over £1.

A small number of framed prints are also mentioned, occasionally both by Van der Doort and by the compilers of the inventories. Among the contents of the Little Store Room in the Bear Gallery was Dürer's great woodcut *Triumphal Arch of Maximilian* (later valued at £2),[19] 'the picture in a print of the Kinge and Queene together'[20] (possibly Van Vorst's engraving after Van Dyck's double portrait), and a print of the *Battle of Leipzig*.[21] In addition the inventories list 'The 8. picture prints', sold for 10*s*. in 1651, and 'A Print of Judith and Holophernes' valued at £1. A rather separate category is formed by the four 'redd Copper . . . engraven plates for to print prints with', noted by Van der Doort in Whitehall.[22] Three of these engraved plates (later valued at between £5 and £20) reproduced paintings (by Titian, Annibale Carracci and Honthorst) in the Royal Collection. The fourth plate (which was excluded from the inventories) reproduced Lord Arundel's painting of the *Burial of Christ* by Parmigianino. The engravers were Robert van Vorst and Lucas Vorsterman.

Thus far, the majority of the drawings and prints noted were doubtless of almost equal status to the paintings and limnings with which they hung: they were finished works of art in their own right, rather than working pieces. Even the designs for the candlestick and ship were probably highly worked drawings, made for presentation to a patron. The following items, kept in volumes or portfolios, probably in the Cabinet or Library, may present a rather different aspect. Once again they include pieces submitted by artists and designers to the patron, but they are more in the manner of working drawings, or pictorial compendia on specific subjects. As such they constitute the first hints of an accumulation or collection of drawings by 'old masters', valued as collectors'

151 [1]
151 [3]
419 [9]
63 [46]

312 [219]

271 [243]
246 [355]
246 [350-2]

Figure 63 Hans Holbein the Younger: *An unidentified gentleman* (black and coloured chalks, with black ink and wash, on paper coated with a pink preparation). 274 × 211mm. Royal Collection: reproduced by gracious permission of Her Majesty The Queen.

items. Although the latter aspect may now be considered to be the most important, neither Van der Doort nor the inventories provide much relevant information. This may be partly because, as we shall see, their notes on the contents of Charles I's library are far from complete. Alternatively, it may be because King Charles's collection of prints and drawings was somewhat limited in both its scope and its extent.

One of the few items known once to have belonged to Charles I and which is still to be found in the Royal Collection today is Holbein's 'great booke' of portrait drawings (e.g. Fig. 63), which appears to have passed from the Lumley collection to that of Henry, Prince of Wales, and thence (via James I) to King Charles I. In 1627, a volume of drawings by Holbein was shown by Charles I's surveyor, Inigo Jones, to the German biographer, Joachim von Sandrart. Although Sandrart described the drawings as being 'in pen and ink', omitting to mention the addition of colour (in chalk or watercolour), it is possible that this reference does indeed relate to Holbein's 'great booke'.[23] In the same year (or the year following) the volume was exchanged by the King for Raphael's painting of *St. George and the Dragon*, then in the collection of Lord Pembroke who 'imediatly soe soone as hee receaved it [the Holbein volume] of yor Matie gave it to my Lo: Marshall', Thomas Howard, Earl of Arundel.[24] Therefore by the time of Van der Doort's inventory the Holbein volume was no longer in the Royal Collection, although by 1675 it had returned to royal ownership and has remained there ever since.

A small number of volumes of drawings and prints were included among the fifty-four books listed by Van der Doort in the Cabinet Room, Whitehall. One of these was a folio volume, purchased by Charles I (before his accession) from the Duc de Liancourt: 'Item one Booke with . . . Pictures by the life don in dry Cullors of the Cheifest Nobility and famous men at the tyme in ffraunce where at the end some . . . drawings'.[25] The variant copies of Van der Doort's inventory differ as to whether there were forty-nine portraits ('in dry Cullors') plus five other drawings ('in blak and Wijt'), or forty-six portraits plus four other drawings. The group of twelve drawings at Windsor (attributed to Clouet and François Quesnel: see Fig. 64) may represent the surviving contents of this album, which was later valued at

274 [286]

Figure 64   Attributed to François Quesnel: *An unidentified lady* (black and coloured chalks, with watercolour). 307 × 229mm. Royal Collection: reproduced by gracious permission of Her Majesty The Queen.

£10.[26] Compared to these, the contents of the other volumes listed in Charles I's Cabinet Room appear to have been insignificant: a small book containing six (or eight?) designs, on blue paper, by Francis Cleyn and John Hoskins, for the great seal;[27] and a 'Booke in larg folio: white vellam wherein some .8. little drawings of Horatio Jentellesco', presented to the King by the artist and used to provide designs for the Mortlake tapestry factory.[28] 'Item a painted Booke in quarto in browne Leather wth your Mats Armes upon it when you were Prince Conteyning sev'all Accons and postures invented by Michaell Angello Bonorotto' might appear at first to describe a volume of drawings, but a variant of Van der Doort's text describes the contents as 'printts'.[29] Other volumes of engravings included 'Prints of Ulysse', bound in white vellum,[30] a copy of Vesalius' *Anatomy* bound in brown leather,[31] 'a Booke in folio of wood Prints of Alberdure being the inscription in high dutch of the Proportions of Men', presented to the King before his accession by Van der Doort himself,[32] and 'a very greate Booke in folio of Prints. beeing of severall Antiquities of statues and Roman buildings'.[33] There were also books of emblems, doubtless printed rather than manuscript. One is specified as 'a Booke of severall spirituall Emblems in the shape of .2. Children don by Octavo van venan whereby the interpretacon thereof in fower severall Languages printed'.[34] The inventories list 'A great Boock wth Prints' (possibly the antiquarian prints noted above) and three other volumes of prints, one of which is specified 'with Catts [or cuts] faces'.

The clues as to the extent of Charles I's collection of prints and drawings gleaned from Oliver Millar's invaluable editions of Van der Doort's lists and the later inventories and valuations are meagre indeed. There is much duplication between the two listings and it would appear unlikely that those who compiled them missed very much. However, as we might also expect to find references to volumes of drawings in the inventories of Charles I's books, it may be worth examining the contents (and fate) of his library, albeit fleetingly.

The fifty-four books listed (and itemized) by Van der Doort in the Cabinet Room, Whitehall (which may have been included among the fifty-six books from Denmark House, sixty from Richmond, and seventy-five from Oatlands noted in the inventories), evidently constituted only a small fraction of the Royal Library at that date.[35] We know that Charles I inherited from his father part of the library of John, Lord Lumley, which had been acquired by Henry, Prince of Wales and which included numerous important volumes. These and Prince Henry's other books were kept in the new library at St. James's, specially fitted out for this purpose in 1609/10. They were cared for by the King's librarian, Patrick Young, from this date until the time of Charles I's execution. And even thereafter, in 1649, Young was asked (by the Council of State) to draw up an inventory of the King's books.[36] It was intended that the books should be available 'for the Public Use'. By 1651 John Durie (appointed by the Council of State to the post of 'Library Keeper of the Books at St. James's') reported that the books were in a dangerous condition, exposed to weather and vermin. In the following year they were to be moved back to Whitehall.[37] The list of reserved goods drawn up in 1651 included the contents of the libraries at Whitehall, St. James's and Richmond, totalling £6,166. 5s.[38] Detailed catalogues of these libraries have survived only in fragmentary form.[39] From these it has however been possible to establish that the majority of Charles I's library is still extant in the 'Old Royal Library' in the present British Library. A rapid search through the mid-seventeenth-century lists has not revealed any albums of drawings or prints. It is also worth pointing out that the volume containing Holbein's portrait drawings (now in the Royal Collection) was included alongside oil paintings in the Lumley Inventory of 1590, the only volume to be mentioned therein.[40] It appears that our early seventeenth-century antecedents already recognized albums of drawings as a distinct element within the quantities of volumes (both printed and manuscript) under their care.

To the evidence of Van der Doort and the inventories should be added that of contemporary commentators. These include various suggestions of Charles I's ownership of drawings by Leonardo da Vinci. During his visit to Spain in 1623 to woo the Spanish Infanta, Charles (then Prince of Wales) is known to have made several important purchases of paintings. In the correspondence of Galeazzo Arconati relating to his compilation of Leonardo's writings for Cassiano dal Pozzo, who died in 1647, there is a note (datable c. 1634-9) stating that no reference has been made to Leonardo's drawings for the 'treatises on anatomy and natural things, and to colour', as these treatises (or drawings?) are in the hands of the King of England.[41] In addition, Carducho claimed that Charles bought many of the finest things at the posthumous auction of Pompeo Leoni's collection in Spain.[42] The binding which formerly contained all the six hundred or so drawings by Leonardo now in the Royal Collection bears the name of Leoni, who died in Madrid in 1608. However, after a thorough examination of the evidence Kenneth Clark concluded that 'it seems unlikely that Leoni's heirs should wait till 1623 . . . to auction his possesions; and even supposing Charles bought anything at Leoni's sale, it is unlikely that he bought the Leonardo drawings . . . There can be little doubt that the Windsor volume was brought to England by Thomas Howard, Earl of Arundel', and that Charles I was thereafter not himself in a favourable position to purchase it either in 1641 (when Arundel left England) or in 1646 (the year of Arundel's death).[43] It does not now appear possible to find the evidence on which these two reports from overseas were based.

As we have already seen, there is not so much as a hint concerning the King's ownership of the Leonardo drawings in Van der Doort's inventories, nor in those made for the Commonwealth government. The earliest certain reference to the presence of the Leoni volume in the Royal Collection occurs in the diary of Constantin Huygens, secretary to William III, for 22 January 1690. Huygens had joined his royal employer in London, where he recorded many happy hours spent looking at drawings in private houses, attending auctions, and making a number of purchases for his own art collection. On the day in question Huygens 'went in the morning with his friends Berghesteyn and Sonnius to the rooms underneath the King's Closet [at Whitehall Palace], where we saw four or five books with drawings, among others Holbein's and Leonardo da Vinci's'.[44] On 31 August Huygens reported that 'the Queen [Mary] sent for me, saying that she wanted me to put the books with the King's drawings in good order'. The following day 'In the morning at nine o'clock, when I was still in bed, the Queen sent for me again, and together we went through the whole of the book by Leonardo da Vinci and one by Holbein'.[45] In the absence of any certain account of the means, method or date of acquisition of these drawings for the crown, it appears most likely that they were acquired after, rather than before, the Restoration of the monarchy in 1660.[46]

From these somewhat inconclusive contemporary accounts we should progress to those of a generation or two later. The first writer to suggest that Charles I had a considerable collection of drawings appears to have been George Vertue, in the first half of the eighteenth century. He explained the significance of the two star marks which appear on those drawings which had once belonged to Nicholas Lanier (1588-1666), Charles I's court musician (Pl. 3). The large five-pointed star was 'the mark of Laniere on the drawings which he had collected for the King', whereas the smaller five-pointed star was 'the mark on the Arundell collection drawings', for which Lanier had also acted as agent.[47] Later in the century Walpole ascribed a star with eight (rather than five) points, in two different sizes, to the same collections.[48] In the event, the most common star marks are the large eight-pointed and the small five-pointed.[49] Vertue and then Walpole made two important claims: first that Lanier collected drawings, as well as paintings, for the King, and secondly that these drawings were identifiable by a particular mark.

Although both these claims are inherently plausible, some caution should be used in accepting them whole-heartedly. Furthermore, it should be noted that Jonathon Richardson believed that the two sizes of star marks did no more than distinguish the drawings belonging to Nicholas Lanier from those of other members of his family.[50] Lanier's activity as a collector of drawings is well-known. The numerous drawings bearing star marks (which surely indicate Lanier's ownership, even if the connection with Arundel and Charles I has to be reconsidered) are testament both to Lanier's energy and to his connoisseurship. In a letter sent on 29 June 1663, and therefore within Lanier's lifetime, from Christian Huygens (in London) to his brother Constantin (in The Hague), the writer records having seen 'ces jours passez une partie des desseins de Lanier et entre autres une grande quantité de Raphael qui sont incomparables'.[51] Roger North (who was executor to another great collector of drawings, Sir Peter Lely) stated that drawings

were not much esteemed in England until Nicholas Laniere was employed by Charles I to go abroad and buy pictures, which he loved. He used to contract for a piece, and at the same time agree to have a good parcel of waste-paper drawings, that had been collected, but not much esteemed, for himself. This and the Arundel Collection were the first in England.[52]

The suggestion that one of the star marks relates to Lanier's purchases for Arundel is possibly supported by the fact that we have documentary evidence that Lanier was involved with Arundel's activities as a collector of both drawings and paintings.[53] It would be interesting to know whether any of the surviving drawings etched by Hollar and Van der Borcht as in Arundel's collection bear a Lanier star. Preliminary research (on the Parmigianino drawings, for instance) suggests that they do not.[54] Lanier was also closely involved in Charles I's purchase of the Mantuan picture collection, with Daniel Nys. However, Van der Doort's notes on the provenance of the few drawings in the King's collection nowhere mention Lanier as the supplier.[55]

There appears to be no means of either proving or disproving Vertue's suggestion that Lanier purchased drawings for the King nor that these purchases were identified by a large star mark. It has long been recognized that the backs of the paintings from the King's collection were branded with the crowned initials CR.[56] In most cases the frames concerned have been adapted, even re-made. However, the miniature portrait of Rudolf II from Charles I's collection (listed by Van der Doort in the Cabinet Room at Whitehall) has recently been identified in its original frame (Fig. 57). As the miniature was painted on vellum fixed around the edges to a fine wooden stretcher, the brand is in this case on the frame itself.[57] The printed books from the King's library were similarly marked with his armorial block (or rather, series of blocks).[58] The use of stamps or marks to distinguish drawings from a particular collection was first established in England in the later seventeenth century. In the case of the drawings gathered together by Sir Peter Lely, it is clear from the accounts of his executors that the mark was applied shortly before the dispersal of the collection.[59] So far as I am aware, no item either mentioned by Van der Doort or listed in the inventories has come down to us bearing the large star mark, let alone any other collector's mark: this is hardly surprising, however, as collectors' marks tend to be used to identify loose rather than framed drawings. Likewise, of the few drawings that have come down to us bearing an inscription relating to Charles I's ownership, it is unlikely that any were annotated before the time of Vertue and Walpole.[60] The inscriptions may therefore have been added following an examination of the star marks, using the (false?) information about the marks supplied by these authorities. No drawing from Charles I's collection appears to have been reproduced (in etching or engraving) when in his possession.[61] We therefore have nothing to equal the valuable evidence of the etched copies of some of the drawings in Arundel's collection, commissioned by Arundel himself from Wenzel Hollar and Hendrik van der Borcht.[62] Unfortunately the present location of drawings bearing the different Lanier star marks does nothing to support Vertue's statement. Although there are many drawings with the small five-pointed star (Lugt 2886), the large eight-pointed star (Lugt 2885) and a six-pointed star (not cited by Lugt) in the Royal Collection, a number of other drawings with these same marks are also scattered among other long-established drawings collections such as those at the Ashmolean, the British Museum, Chatsworth, Christ Church and the Fitzwilliam.[63]

In a recent important discussion of the history of the Royal Collection of drawings,[64] it was suggested, at least partly on the basis of the Lanier stars, that the twenty-three 'Books of Drawings and Prints' listed in a Bureau in Kensington Palace c.1728 included many items from Charles I's collection.[65] However, No. 8 on this list ('Prince Charle's Book with a few Drawings') may have belonged to either Charles I or Charles II,[66] whereas No. 3 (the Holbein drawings) had temporarily left the collection well before Charles I's death. Meanwhile the album of French portraits listed by Van der Doort, the partial contents of which may still be at Windsor, is omitted. Without discussing this list in detail I would once again suggest caution in accepting the proposal. The late eighteenth-century compiler of 'Inventory A', listing the contents of George III's drawings collection, wrote of two drawings ascribed to Raphael that they were 'found in an Old Bureau at Kensington which contained part of the Collection of K. Charles ye first where also was preserved the Volume of Leonardo de Vinci', and thus apparently provided early evidence for the Charles I/Kensington Bureau theory.[67] (The writer also, incidentally, implied that the Leonardo drawings were *not* part of Charles I's collection.) However, of the two drawings concerned, which are still today in the Royal Collection, only one is marked with a Lanier star, and that star is not of the large 'Royal' type but of the small 'Arundel' variety.[68]

Although it is not strictly relevant to our discussion, as circumstantial evidence we will now look forwards to such information as may exist concerning the Royal Collection of drawings following the Restoration. The contents (both general and specific) of Charles I's Cabinet Room were reinstated in the King's Closet at Whitehall by Charles II, although the new King lamented that 'it was not half of what his father had owned'.[69] The small-scale treasures were there cared for (and guarded) by the Keeper of the King's Closet, a position occupied by Thomas Chiffinch (who had acted as page to both Charles I and the exiled Charles II). In April 1666 he was succeeded in this task by his younger brother William.[70] From the following references it appears that among the items cared for by the Keepers of the King's Closet were a number of drawings. The diary of the miniaturist Mary Beale, transcribed by George Vertue and since lost, includes the following two notes: 1674 'Novem. borrowd of W.m Chiffinch Esq. eleven of his Majesties Italian drawings', and 1677 February 'borrow 6 Italian drawings out of the Kings Collection for my sons to practice by'.[71] Malvasia included the name 'Carlo Stuart' among those who owned drawings by members of the Carracci family.[72] The inventory of James II's collection (published by Vertue in 1758) includes a number of independent (presumably framed) drawings which do not appear in the Charles I lists. Again, the diary of Constantin Huygens, which has provided such vital evidence concerning the presence of the Leonardo drawings in the Royal Collection, contains valuable information on other drawings (contained in at least four albums) in the collection at this time. A week after first seeing the Holbein and Leonardo drawings, Huygens and Berghesteyn 'looked at some more of the King's drawings in a chest, lying upstairs, containing many drawings with single figures by Parmigianino, and several other good ones'.[73] Seven months later, after recording that Queen Mary had asked him to reorganize the King's drawings, and that she had personally shown him the volumes of studies by Holbein and Leonardo, Huygens noted seeing 'other books of Italian drawings, which looked as if they had been robbed, and it was said that Lely, borrowing the books from Chiffinch, had busied himself in an enormous manner by taking out originals and putting back copies, made by his people etc.'[74] Huygens appears to have been occupied for much of the first half of September reorganizing the drawings. On 5 September he noted: 'spent the morning in the King's Closet where I separated the good drawings from the bad in about two or three books'.[75] Peter Lely's role in the formation (and possible spoliation) of Charles II's collection is still far from clear. His own collection of drawings rivalled that of Lord Arundel, both in size and quality, and as the King's Principal Painter from 1661 Lely was obviously in very close contact with the Royal Collection. It has been plausibly suggested that the Leonardo drawings entered the collection through Lely's agency.[76] The return of the Holbein drawings to royal ownership shortly before 1675 surely indicates a high level of interest in the acquisition of drawings at this time.

Item 5 on the Kensington Bureau list is a volume of 'Prints by Hollar', which relates to another possible aspect of Charles I's collection. A small number of printed works listed by Van der Doort and in the inventories have already been noted, but nowhere is Hollar's name mentioned as the artist responsible. The origins and history of the fine collection of etchings by Hollar now at Windsor are not known, but it does not appear likely that Charles I owned any considerable body of his work.[77] Walpole's editor, Dallaway, stated categorically that 'King William the Third began what is now styled the Royal collection, greatly augmented and completed by his present majesty, when Prince Regent'.[78] Meanwhile Charles I's contemporaries such as the Earls of Pembroke and Arundel (and Inigo Jones) amassed much more considerable collections of prints, along with their collections of paintings.

On numerous occasions in the above discussion the collection of Thomas Howard, Earl of Arundel has been mentioned. There appears to be little to support another oft-repeated claim that Arundel (like Lanier) acted as Charles I's agent in the purchase of drawings as well as paintings. A drawing (Fig. 65) from the school of Cranach in the Louvre is inscribed to the effect that on the occasion of the King's visit to Arundel House, London, in 1637 he was allowed to choose six or seven drawings (of which the Louvre drawing is one) from a volume of hunting scenes that the Earl had acquired during his recent visit to Germany.[79] (Incidentally, the drawings do not appear to be mentioned in any of the inventories of Charles I's collection, nor do they bear a star mark.) This episode, which may well be pure fabrication, suggests that the relationship between King and Earl was quite other than that of patron and agent. Arundel's collection of drawings was incontrovertibly superior to the King's and does indeed stand at the beginning of the history of the collecting of drawings in England.[80] Arundel's son confirmed that the Earl 'chiefly affects drawings', in spite of his obvious passion for paintings, antiquities and other works of art. Another contemporary,

Figure 65   School of Lucas Cranach: *Hunting scene* (pen and ink). 190 × 310mm. Département des Arts Graphiques, Musée du Louvre, Paris: copyright Réunion des Musées Nationaux.

Sir Edward Walker, considered that Arundel's 'Collection of Designs' was larger than that of 'any person living'.[81] By the end of the first quarter of the eighteenth century the collecting of drawings had reached such a level that Jonathon Richardson could claim that whereas 'l'Italie est le principal Apartement de la grande Collection du Mond, l'Angleterre est le Cabinet des Desseins'.[82]

At around the time that the above words were published, the inventory of the contents of the Kensington Bureau was made, listing what may justly be claimed to be the 'true core' of the collection of old master drawings in the Royal Collection. The detailed relationship of those drawings with the collection of Charles I will probably never be settled. It should be clear from the foregoing, however, that neither Charles's cabinet nor his library were filled with bulging portfolios of drawings and prints,[83] and that those drawings that he did own do not compare either in quality or in quantity with his collection of paintings. There are moreover several factors which suggest a positive lack of interest in drawings (and prints) on the part of Charles I. A study of the graphic work of those artists who were patronized by Charles I (Isaac Oliver, Inigo Jones, not to mention Rubens or Van Dyck) indicates what was available, but in no case were sketches by these artists acquired by the King.[84] Apart from the volume of French portraits, the historical piece by 'Juliano', and the large drawing related to Michelangelo's *Last Judgement*, all the drawings mentioned in the inventories had apparently been given to the King, rather than having been pursued and purchased by him. The fact that he exchanged the Holbeins, often considered the greatest treasure of the present Royal Collection of drawings, for a painting by Raphael, surely indicates the true significance that the King claimed for drawn as opposed to painted artefacts.

Notes

1. *Van der Doort's Catalogue*, p. xiii.

2. Ibid., pp. 109-10 [24-31]. This frame survives intact in the collection of the Duke of Buccleuch.

3. Ibid., pp. 110-12 [32-9].

4. Ibid., pp. 112-17 [40-53].

5. Ibid., pp. 105-8 [11-20].

6. Ibid., p. 102.

7. Ibid., p. 123.

8. J. Finsten, *Isaac Oliver* (New York and London, 1981), I, p. 31. See ibid., pp. 141-5. for a discussion of the early history of drawing in England. L. Stainton and C. White (*Drawing in England from Hilliard to Hogarth* (London, 1987), pp. 13-28) also provide a full and fundamental discussion of the subject.

9. A.P. Oppé, *English Drawings — Stuart and Georgian Periods — the Collection of His Majesty The King at Windsor Castle* (London, 1950), nos. 460 and 459; Finsten, op. cit. (Note 8), nos. 182 and 181. See Vertue, *Note Books* IV, p. 93, and W. Bathoe [and G. Vertue], *A catalogue of the Pictures &c belonging to King James the Second* [and] *in the closet of the late Queen Caroline* (London, 1758), pp. 56 [638] and 55 [636].

10. Finsten, op. cit. (Note 8), no. 226. Vertue, *Note Books* I, p. 62, and IV, p. 93; Bathoe, op. cit. (Note 9), p. 53 [612]. Four drawings by Isaac Oliver are included in the inventory of Charles II's pictures (Royal Collection Department).

11. *Van der Doort's Catalogue*, p. 178 [43]. What appears to be the same drawing was also mentioned amongst the 'silver gilt peeces': ibid, p. 145 [7]. In both accounts the drawing is said to have been given to the King by Van Vorst, the artist.

12. Likewise listed twice: ibid., pp. 145 [8] and 178 [44]. Presented by the King's jeweller, Heriot.

13. Ibid., p. 175 [19]. Described as 'A Mantua Peece'.

14. Ibid., p. 153 [22].

15. Ibid., p. 26 [23].

16. Ibid., p. 153 [23]: 'Given to yor Maty by Mr Surveyor', i.e. Inigo Jones. The Ashmole MS adds 'vor a patron tu bi ingraffing bij'. The drawing was the basis for the engraving by Simon van de Passe.

17. Ibid., p. 153 [24].

18. Ibid., p. 153 [25].

19. Ibid., p. 174 [15]: purchased by the King from Abraham der Kindron.

20. Ibid., p. 176 [27]: given to the Queen.

21. Ibid., p. 178 [45].

22. Ibid., pp. 148-9 [1-4]. The plate for Vorsterman's print after Lord Arundel's Parmigianino was apparently excluded from the inventories.

23. J. von Sandrart, *Teutsche Academie* (Nuremberg, 1675), pt. II, Bk. III, p. 251.

24. *Van der Doort's Catalogue*, p. 79 [14]. For the Holbein drawings see K.T. Parker, *The Drawings of Hans Holbein . . . at Windsor Castle* (Oxford and London, 1945); reprinted, with an Appendix by Susan Foister (New York and London, 1983).

25. *Van der Doort's Catalogue*, p. 125 [42].

26. A. Blunt, *The French Drawings . . . at Windsor Castle* (London, 1945), nos. 2 and 9-19, and idem, *Supplements to the Catalogues of Italian and French Drawings . . . at Windsor Castle* (London, 1971), p. 3.

27. *Van der Doort's Catalogue*, p. 153 [21].

28. Ibid., p. 126 [49].

29. Ibid., p. 126 [47].

30. Ibid., p.125 [43]: given to Charles I 'by my Lo: of Suffolke'.

31. Ibid., p. 125 [44]: the author's name is given as Vasari (in several different spellings). The variants of Van der Doort's text differ as to whether the book was given by Suffolk or by Inigo Jones.

32. Ibid., p. 125 [46]. This reference has been related to the copy of Dürer's *Menschlichen Proportion* in the British Library (C.82.g.9), bearing the arms of Charles I when Prince of Wales (M.J. Foot, 'Some bindings for Charles I', in *Studies in Seventeenth-Century English Literature, History and Bibliography*, ed. G.A.M. Janssens and F.G.A. Aarts (Amsterdam, 1984), p. 102).

33. *Van der Doort's Catalogue*, p. 126 [50]: given to Charles I by the Earl of Exeter. Foot (op. cit. (Note 32), p. 96, note 11) suggests a tentative identification of this volume with the *Speculum Romanae Magnificentiae* (Rome, 1519-75) in the British Library (C.77.9.11) which must be correct. Besides the 118 plates it has 58 additional ones. (I am indebted to Professor T.A. Birrell for this and other information concerning Charles I's Library.)

34. *Van der Doort's Catalogue*, p. 126 [52]: given to Charles I. Identified by Millar as the *Amorum Emblemata* of Otho Vaenius. The four-language edition (Antwerp, 1615) is rare: only four copies are known. The present British Library copy is from Sir Hans Sloane's collection.

35. For Charles I's library see G.F. Warner and J.P. Gilson, *British Museum: Catalogue of Western Manuscripts in the Old Royal and King's Collections* (London, 1921), pp. xx-xxv, and Foot, op. cit. (Note 32), pp. 95-106.

36. This inventory (countersigned by John Durie), survives in the British Library (Royal MS App. 86). Over three hundred of Lumley's manuscripts can be identified, among the 'Royal' manuscripts in the British Library: see Warner and Gilson, op. cit. (Note 35), p. xix, and *The Lumley Library. The Catalogue of 1609*, ed. S. Jayne and F.R. Johnson (London, 1956).

37. These events may explain the following (undated) statement: 'all the rarities in the Kings Library at St. James's are vanished': Vertue, *Note Books* IV, p. 183.

38. *Inventories*, pp. xii, xiv and xx.

39. Apart from the inventory mentioned in Note 36 (above), there are two copies of the lists of the books at St. James's (divided into five parts, the last of which covered the Closet there), of which one is sub-titled 'the Bookes that were brought from Whitehall, 1651' (British Library, Department of Printed Books, C.120.h.6(1) and (2)). See also *The Lumley Library* (op. cit. (Note 36), pp. 292-6).

40. L. Cust, 'The Lumley Inventories', *Walpole Society* 6 (1918), p. 27.

41. K. Clark and C. Pedretti, *The Drawings of Leonardo da Vinci at Windsor Castle* (London, 1968), I, p. xii.

42. V. Carducho, *Dialogos de la Pintura* (Madrid, 1633), pp. 155-6.

43. Clark and Pedretti, op. cit. (Note 41), I, pp. xi-xii.

44. *Journal van Constantijn Huygens den zoon*, in *Werken van het Historisch Genootschap* n.s., no. 23, (Utrecht, 1876), I, p. 227. I am indebted to Beatrijs Brenninkmeyer-de Rooij for providing translations of this and the following passages in Huygens' diary.

45. Ibid., pp. 325-6.

46. Clark and Pedretti, op. cit. (Note 41), pp. xiii-xiv.

47. Vertue, *Note Books* I, pp. 45 and 47.

48. H. Walpole, *Anecdotes of Painting in England* (with additions by the Revd. James Dallaway), ed. R.N. Wornum (London, 1849), III, p. 273.

49. F. Lugt, *Les Marques de Collections des dessins et d'estampes* (Amsterdam, 1921); *Suppléments* (The Hague, 1956). Both volumes include crucial discussions on Lanier's activity as collector, under numbers 2885 and 2886.

50. J. Richardson, *Traité de la Peinture et de la Sculpture* (Amsterdam, 1728). For Richardson's notes on early collecting see also F.J.B. Watson, 'On the early history of collecting in England', *Burlington Magazine* 85 (1944), pp. 223-8.

51. Christian Huygens, *Œuvres complètes publiées par la Société hollandaise des sciences* IV *Correspondance, 1662-3* (The Hague, 1891), pp. 362-3.

52. *The Autobiography of The Hon. Roger North*, ed. A. Jessopp (London, 1887), p. 202.

53. See Lugt, op. cit. (Note 49) [1st edn], pp. 533, and D. Howarth, *Lord Arundel and his Circle* (New Haven and London, 1985), pp. 212 and 246, note 18.

54. It is also interesting to note that some of Hollar's etched reproductions of items in Arundel's collection have asterisks included as part of the etching: see G. Parthey, *Wenzel Hollar* (Berlin, 1853); expanded by R. Pennington, *A Descriptive Catalogue of the Etched Work of Wenceslaus Hollar* (Cambridge, 1982), no. 271A.

55. See *Van der Doort's Catalogue*, pp. 11 and 39 (note 6) for further references to Lanier's activity in supplying paintings to the Crown. Lanier was also a keen purchaser at the Commonwealth sale.

56. Examples of these brands have been frequently illustrated: see, for instance, O. Millar, *The Queen's Pictures* (London, 1977), pp. 33 and 46. It was presumably brands such as these that Bainbridge Buckeridge had in mind when he made the following statement: Nicholas Lanier 'was employed by king Charles I beyond sea, to purchase that collection made by him, the first Prince we ever had that promoted Painting in England, to whom he was closet-keeper. He gave a particular mark, by which we distinguish all the things of this kind which he brought over' (B. Buckeridge, 'Essay towards an English School', in Roger de Piles, *The Art of Painting* (London, 1750 [etc.]), p. 401). However Walpole interpreted the statement as referring to drawings, and added a sketch of a six-pointed 'Lanier' star mark (op. cit. (Note 48), III, p. 362 (note 3)).

57. S. Hindman, *Medieval and Renaissance Miniature Painting* (exh. cat., Ohio and London, 1988-9), no. 40.

58. For Charles I's bindings see Foot, op. cit. (Note 1) and T.A. Birrell, *The Panizzi Lectures 1986: English monarchs and their books: from Henry VII to Charles II* (London, 1987). Foot's study is based on bindings in the British Library, most of which were part of the gift of the 'Old Royal Library' in 1757 (Foot, op. cit. (Note 32), p. 95).

59. See Lugt, op. cit. (Note 49), *sub numeri* 2092-4 and BL, Additional MS 16174.

60. For drawings inscribed with Charles I's name see, for instance, a study by Schiavone in Edinburgh (D 1764; K. Andrews, *National Gallery of Scotland. Catalogue of the Italian Drawings* (Cambridge, 1971), p. 113, fig. 787), and one by Girolamo da Carpi in the Frits Lugt collection, Paris (J. Byam Shaw, *The Italian Drawings of the Frits Lugt Collection* (Paris, 1983), no. 130).

61. A cryptic reference in Vertue's notebooks to 'Van der Borcht who grav'd many of the Arundell & King's Collection. at Arundell House in the year 1637' (Vertue, *Note Books* I, p. 47), should be noted here.

62. See Parthey/Pennington, op. cit. (Note 54), pp. xxvii-xxix, and Howarth, op. cit. (Note 53), pp. 171-82.

63. I am indebted to the researches of my former colleague Olivia Hughes-Onslow (now Mrs Michael Winterton), for this analysis of the Lanier stars. See also Lugt, op. cit. (Note 49), nos. 2885 and 2886.

64. Blunt, op. cit. (Note 26 [Supplements]), pp. 1-18. Blunt's conclusions concerning Charles I's collection of drawings have been generally accepted: e.g. Stainton and White, op. cit. (Note 8). The present author is no exception to this statement (J. Roberts, *Master Drawings in the Royal Collection* (exh. cat., London, 1986), pp. 9-11 and 49).

65. The Kensington Inventory (BL, Additional MS 20101, f.28) is reproduced in Roberts, op. cit. (Note 64), p. 12.

66. Blunt (op. cit. (Note 26 [Supplements]), p. 3) suggested that this may be the volume of prints after Michelangelo noted by Van der Doort (see above).

67. Ibid., p. 3. The suggestion that the contents of the Kensington Bureau were chiefly from Charles I's collection was repeated in H. Reveley, *Notices Illustrative of the Drawings and Sketches . . .* (London, 1820), p. 43.

68. The marked drawing is A.E. Popham and J. Wilde, *The Italian Drawings of the XV and XVI Centuries . . . at Windsor Castle* (London, 1949), no. 850; the second drawing is ibid., no. 808. See also Blunt, op. cit. (Note 26 [Supplements]), pp. 3-4.

69. Millar, op. cit. (Note 56), p. 69. The detailed description of the miniatures included in the Inventory of Charles II's Pictures (Royal Collection Department) supports this statement. The volumes of drawings are omitted from this inventory.

70. Ibid., p. 69.

71. Vertue, *Note Books* IV, pp. 172-3. William Chiffinch was Charles II's confidential servant.

72. C.C. Malvasia, *Felsina Pittrice* (Bologna, 1678), I, p. 478.

73. Huygens, op. cit. (Note 44), I, p. 230: 29 January 1690.

74. Ibid., I, p. 326: 1 September 1690.

75. Ibid., I, p. 327.

76. A Scott-Elliott, 'The Pompeo Leoni volume of the Leonardo drawings at Windsor', *Burlington Magazine* 98 (1956), pp. 11-17.

77. Parthey/Pennington, op. cit. (Note 54), p. lviii.

78. Walpole, op. cit., (Note 48), III, pp. 891-2.

79. Howarth, op. cit. (Note 53), pp. 202 and 245 (note 35). The drawing is catalogued in L. Demonts, *Musée du Louvre: Inventaire General des Dessins des Ecoles du Nord* (Paris, 1937), no. 96 (Inv. 18719).

80. Howarth, op. cit. (Note 53), pp. 182-5. It is perhaps worth noting here the very large number of items described as drawings in the 1655 Arundel inventory. These were presumably framed items and included works by Bronzino, one of the Carracci, Correggio, Jean Cousin, Dürer, Jan van Eyck, Holbein, Ligozzi, Raphael, Rubens and Rembrandt. The drawings in volumes (which would have included those by Holbein, Leonardo and Parmigianino) were not mentioned. For this inventory see M.F.S. Hervey, *The Life, Correspondence and Collections of Thomas Howard, Earl of Arundel* (Cambridge, 1921).

81. See Stainton and White, op. cit. (Note 8), p. 18.

82. J. Richardson, *Traité de la Peinture et de la Sculpture* (Amsterdam, 1728), III, p. 9.

83. However, see W.G. Hiscock, 'The Charles I collection of drawings by Leonardo and others', *Burlington Magazine* 94 (1952), pp. 287-9. Hiscock discussed the late nineteenth-century 'Inventory' by M. Guéraut of the 1,392 drawings (in nineteen portfolios) at Christ Church, which purported to constitute the 'Collection de Charles I formée par le comte d'Arundel'. Byam Shaw concluded that Guéraut's document was no more than a 'jeu d'esprit' on the part of the Librarian, Professor York Powell, and his friend M. Guéraut (J. Byam Shaw, *Drawings by Old Masters at Christ Church Oxford* (Oxford, 1976) I, p. 2 note 3).

84. The '8 little drawings of Horatio Jentellesco' were indeed the work of one of Charles I's artists, who presented them to the King: see Note 28 (above).

Plates

Plate 1   Antonio Mor [after]: *King Philip II of Spain*. Royal Collection: reproduced by gracious permission of Her Majesty The Queen.

Plate 2 Titian: *Emperor Charles V with a Hound*. Museo del Prado, Madrid.

Plate 3 Van Dyck: *Nicholas Lanier*. Kunsthistorisches Museum, Vienna.

Plate 4   Rubens: *Peace and War*. National Gallery, London.

Plate 5 Rubens: *Daniel in the Lions' Den*. National Gallery of Art, Washington.

Plate 6 Jacopo Bassano: *Jacob and his Family*. Royal Collection: reproduced by gracious permission of Her Majesty The Queen.

Plate 7   Titian: *Venus* [?] *with an Organ Player.* Museo del Prado, Madrid.

Plate 8   Titian: *The Entombment of Christ*. Musée du Louvre, Paris: copyright Réunion des Musées Nationaux.

Plate 9   Titian: *First Altarpiece of Jacopo Pesaro*. Musée Royal des Beaux-Arts, Antwerp.

Plate 10 Titian: *Allocution of Alonso de Avalos, Marqués del Vasto.* Museo del Prado, Madrid.

Plate 11   Titian: *The Supper at Emmaus.* Musée du Louvre, Paris: copyright Réunion des Musées Nationaux.

Plate 12   Titian: *Nude Girl in a Fur Wrap*. Kunsthistorisches Museum, Vienna.

Plate 13 Titian: *Venus del Pardo*. Musée du Louvre, Paris: copyright Réunion des Musées Nationaux.

Plate 14   Lorenzo Lotto: *Three Views of a Man's Head*. Kunsthistorisches Museum, Vienna.

Plate 15   Titian: *Doge Andrea Gritti*. National Gallery of Art, Washington.

Plate 16   Correggio: *Mercury instructing Cupid before Venus*. National Gallery, London.

Plate 17   Raphael: *The Virgin and St. Elizabeth with Jesus and the Infant St. John the Baptist (The Madonna della Perla).* Museo del Prado, Madrid.

Plate 18   Van Dyck: *Queen Henrietta Maria*. Royal Collection: reproduced by gracious permission of Her Majesty The Queen.

Plate 19   Cornelis van Poelenburgh: *The Seven Children of the King and Queen of Bohemia*. Reproduced by courtesy of the Board of Directors of the Budapest Museum of Fine Arts.

Plate 20   Honthorst: *The Duke of Buckingham with his Family*. Royal Collection: reproduced by gracious permission of Her Majesty The Queen.

Plate 21 Rosso: *The Challenge of the Pierides*. Musée du Louvre, Paris: copyright Réunion des Musées Nationaux.

Plate 22   Rubens: *Portrait of the Artist*. Royal Collection: reproduced by gracious permission of Her Majesty The Queen.

Plate 23   Titian: *The Rape of Europa*. Isabella Stewart Gardner Museum, Boston.

Plate 24 Titian: *Diana and Callisto*. Duke of Sutherland Collection, on loan to the National Gallery of Scotland, Edinburgh.

Plate 25   Titian: *Diana and Actaeon*. Duke of Sutherland Collection, on loan to the National Gallery of Scotland, Edinburgh.

Plate 26   Orazio Gentileschi: *The Finding of Moses*. Museo del Prado, Madrid.

Plate 27 Artemisia Gentileschi: *Allegory of Painting*. Royal Collection: reproduced by gracious permission of Her Majesty The Queen.

Plate 28   Orazio Gentileschi: *Allegory of Peace and the Arts under the English Crown*. Department of the Environment, Crown copyright: reproduced with permission of the Controller of Her Majesty's Stationery Office.

Plate 29   Caravaggio: *Death of the Virgin*. Musée du Louvre, Paris: copyright Réunion des Musées Nationaux.

Plate 30   Correggio: *Allegory of Virtue*. Musée du Louvre, Paris: copyright Réunion des Musées Nationaux.

Plate 31   Correggio: *Allegory of Vice*. Musée du Louvre, Paris: copyright Réunion des Musées Nationaux.

Plate 32 Raphael: *St. George and the Dragon*. National Gallery of Art, Washington.

E COSI DESIO ME MENA·

Plate 33   Holbein: *Allegory with Horse and Rider*. 1530, oil on panel, 45×45cm.
J. Paul Getty Museum, Malibu.

ÆTATIS · SVE · 88 ·

Plate 34   Holbein: *Portrait of Dr John Chambers*. Kunsthistorisches Museum, Vienna.

Plate 35   Holbein: *Portrait of Erasmus*. Musée du Louvre, Paris: copyright, Réunion des Musées Nationaux.

Plate 36   Leonardo da Vinci: *St. John the Baptist*. Musée du Louvre, Paris: copyright Réunion des Musées Nationaux.

Plate 37 *The Wilton Diptych*. National Gallery, London.

Plate 38 Titian: *Tarquin and Lucretia*. Musée des Beaux-Arts, Bordeaux.

Plate 39 Domenico Feti: *The Vision of St. Peter.* Kunsthistorisches Museum, Vienna.

Plate 40   Dürer: *Portrait of the Artist*. Museo del Prado, Madrid.

Plate 41 Dürer: *Portrait of the Artist's Father*. National Gallery, London.

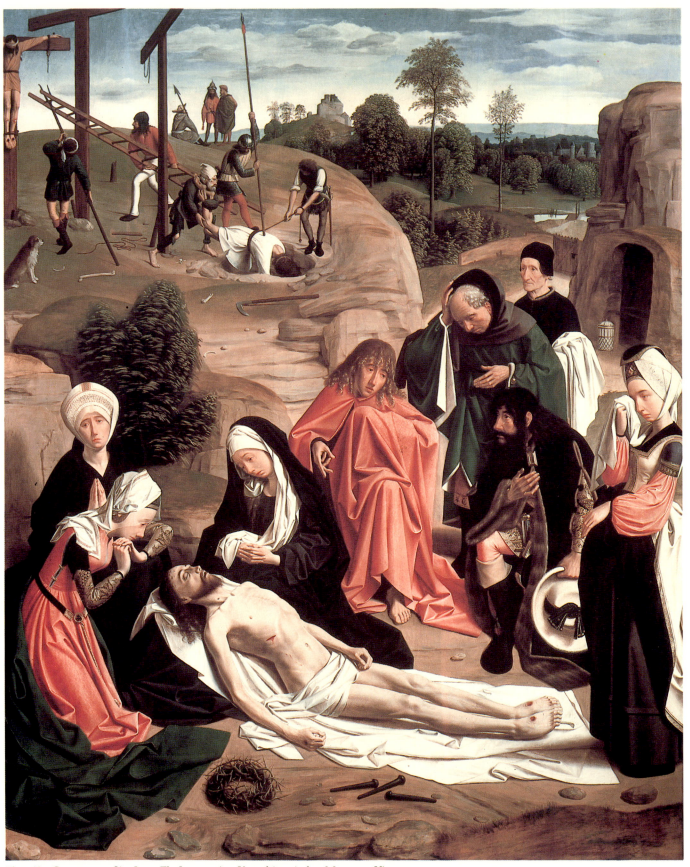

Plate 42 Geertgen tot Sint Jans: *The Lamentation*. Kunsthistorisches Museum, Vienna.

Plate 43   Geertgen tot Sint Jans: *The Burning of the Bones of St. John the Baptist*. Kunsthistorisches Museum, Vienna.

Plate 44   Lucas Cranach: *Adam and Eve*. The whereabouts of Charles's painting are uncertain: the copy shown is merely representative of Cranach's work on this theme. Staatliche Museen Preussische Kulturbesitz, Berlin (West).

Plate 45   Giorgione: *Laura*. Kunsthistorisches Museum, Vienna.

Plate 46   Giorgione: *Three Philosophers*. Kunsthistorisches Museum, Vienna.

Plate 47   Antonello da Messina: *San Cassiano Altarpiece*. Kunsthistorisches Museum, Vienna.

Plate 48 Vecellio: *The Mystic Marriage of St. Catherine*. Royal Collection: reproduced by gracious permission of Her Majesty The Queen.

Plate 49   Tintoretto: *The Virgin and Child*. Royal Collection: reproduced by gracious permission of Her Majesty The Queen.

Plate 50 Mabuse: *Adam and Eve*. Royal Collection: reproduced by gracious permission of Her Majesty The Queen.

Plate 51   Attributed to Aertgen van Leyden: *St. Jerome*. Rijksmuseum, Amsterdam.

Plate 52   Rembrandt: *Portrait of an Old Woman*. Royal Collection: reproduced by gracious permission of Her Majesty The Queen.

Plate 53   Domenico Puligo: *Portrait of a Lady*. Royal Collection: reproduced by gracious permission of Her Majesty The Queen.

Plate 54   North Italian school: *Diligence*. Royal Collection: reproduced by gracious permission of Her Majesty The Queen.

Plate 55　North Italian school: *Fame*. Royal Collection: reproduced by gracious permission of Her Majesty The Queen.

Plate 56　Dosso Dossi (or copy after): *Soldier with a Girl*. Royal Collection: reproduced by gracious permission of Her Majesty The Queen.

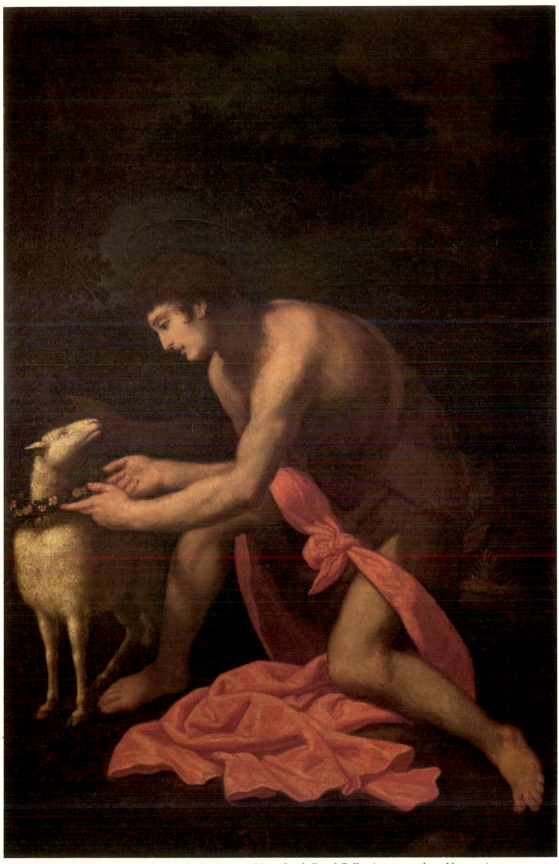

Plate 57 Giovanni Baglione: *St. John the Baptist wreathing a Lamb*. Royal Collection: reproduced by gracious permission of Her Majesty The Queen.

Plate 58   Giovanni Baglione: *Virgin and Child with Angels*. Royal Collection: reproduced by gracious permission of Her Majesty The Queen.

Plate 59   Honthorst: *Apollo and Diana*. Royal Collection: reproduced by gracious permission of Her Majesty The Queen.

Plate 60   Rubens: *Landscape with St. George and the Dragon*. Royal Collection: reproduced by gracious permission of Her Majesty The Queen.

Plate 61   Van Dyck: *Rinaldo and Armida*. Baltimore Museum of Art, Jacob Epstein Collection, BMA 1951. 103.

Plate 62   Mytens: *Portrait of the Artist*. Royal Collection: reproduced by gracious permission of Her Majesty The Queen.

Plate 63   Mytens: *King Charles I and Queen Henrietta Maria*. Royal Collection: reproduced by gracious permission of Her Majesty The Queen.

Plate 64   Mytens: *King Charles I and Queen Henrietta Maria*. Royal Collection: reproduced by gracious permission of Her Majesty The Queen.

Plate 65 Mytens: *King Charles I*. Royal Collection: reproduced by gracious permission of
Her Majesty The Queen.

Plate 66   Mytens: *King Charles I*. Royal Collection: reproduced by gracious permission of Her Majesty The Queen.

Plate 67 Van Dyck: *King Charles I and Queen Henrietta Maria with their Children*. Royal Collection: reproduced by gracious permission of Her Majesty The Queen.

Plate 68   Van Dyck: *King Charles I on Horseback with M. de St. Antoine*. Royal Collection: reproduced by gracious permission of Her Majesty The Queen.

Plate 69   Van Dyck: *King Charles I on Horseback*. National Gallery, London.

Plate 70   Van Dyck: *King Charles I in Hunting Dress*. Musée du Louvre, Paris: copyright Réunion des Musées Nationaux.

Plate 71   Van Dyck: *Cupid and Psyche*. Royal Collection: reproduced by gracious permission of Her Majesty The Queen.

5   Charles I's Collection of Pictures

Francis Haskell

Marginal numerals refer to page and entry numbers in the *Inventories* (see p. 11)

When, on the afternoon of 30 January 1649, Charles I stepped through one of the windows of Inigo Jones's Banqueting Hall in Whitehall on to the adjoining scaffold,[1] he can hardly have had the chance to peer through the twilight at the ceiling high above him into which, fourteen years earlier, had been fitted Rubens's set of nine allegorical canvases glorifying the rule of his father, James I (Fig. 66). The principal political achievements which they celebrated were the *Unification of the Kingdoms of England and Scotland* and *The Peaceful Rule of the King*, while smaller flanking canvases depicted *Royal Bounty overcoming Avarice* and *Temperance* [or *Reason*] *overcoming Intemperance* and similar themes.[2] These claims could hardly have seemed less appropriate in current circumstances. It had been the break between England and Scotland which had led to the destruction of peace and the triumph of intemperance, and on a more specific level even *Royal Abundance* had not been much in evidence when Rubens's canvases had been left waiting in Antwerp for a full year before the King had paid for their transport to England (the artist himself had had to wait much longer for his payment). This, however, had been uncharacteristic, for Charles was always keen to lay hands as quickly as he could on the paintings he had ordered. Moreover, many years earlier, Rubens seems to have been the first living artist from whom he had commissioned a picture.

The Banqueting Hall was the only modern feature of the palace of Whitehall,[3] but in its heyday, and probably still at the moment of Charles's execution, it contained a substantial proportion of the finest collection of pictures ever assembled in this country. Unfortunately, we have no adequate plan or even description of the internal lay-out of the palace, but the individual rooms were given names and their contents were recorded, and it is thus possible to get some idea of the arrangement of the collection.[4]

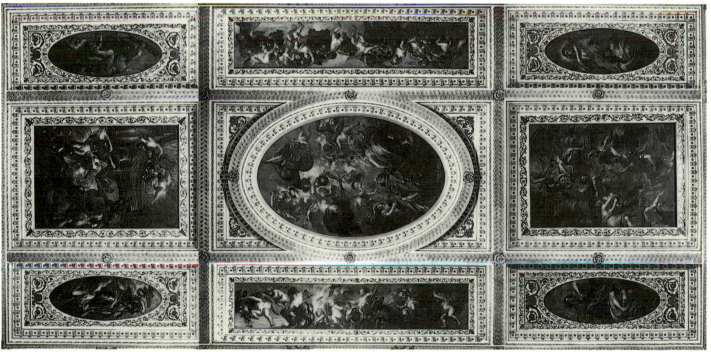

Figure 66   Rubens: *Ceiling decoration,* Banqueting House, Whitehall. Crown copyright: reproduced with permission of the Controller of Her Majesty's Stationery Office.

69 [4]
269 [203]
70 [26]
70 [25]
70 [27]
299 [17]
70 [33]
70 [31]
70 [32]
*206 [332]
310 [184]
300 [36]
71 [36]
323 [20]
305 [113]
206 [337]
264 [130]
310 [189]
267 [181]

In the Bear Gallery hung thirty-five pictures, of which twenty-eight were portraits. With one or two notable exceptions, such as an Antonio Mor of *King Philip II of Spain* (Pl. 1) which Charles had been able to acquire from Lord Arundel before becoming king and Titian's grand *Charles V with a Hound* [5] (Pl. 2) which had been presented to him by Philip IV, these portraits were by contemporary court artists—chiefly Van Dyck, Daniel Mytens and Paul van Somer—of living or only recently deceased members of the English royal family, its related members in Europe and some of its principal courtiers. By far the most beautiful of these, Van Dyck's *Nicholas Lanier* [6] (Pl. 3), Master of the King's Music and part-time agent in building up the royal collection, had (as we will see) played an extremely important part in the lives of both the King and Van Dyck. Among the other seven pictures in this room were two major works by Rubens, *Peace and War* (Pl. 4) (which he himself had given to the King) and the large but not very convincing *Daniel in the Lions' Den* (Pl. 5).

In the Adam and Eve Stairs Room—so-called because outside the door was 'a defaced ould picture [of] Addam & Eve'—were twenty-four pictures, divided almost equally between religious paintings and portraits. It is difficult to discern much logic in the arrangement, and of the pictures which we can identify to-day only one—Jacopo Bassano's *Jacob and his Family* (Pl. 6)—strikes us as a real masterpiece.

It was in the Privy Lodging Rooms—a sequence of relatively private apartments which were not used for official functions such as the reception of foreign ambassadors and which were not, therefore, easily accessible—that Charles kept his most highly-prized paintings. In the first room, for instance, were twelve pictures, of which eleven were attributed to Titian and one to Correggio. No special concern was shown with subject matter, so that Titian's erotic 'naked woeman Lyeing along uppon her velvett gowne and a litle dogg by And also a gentleman In a black habbitt with a swoard at his Side Sitting and playing uppon yᵉ Organs in a Landskipp' [7] (Pl. 7), was placed almost next to his *Entombment of Christ* (Pl. 8). Other masterpieces by him in the same room were the *Pesaro Altarpiece* (Pl. 9), the *Allocution of the Marqués del Vasto* (Pl. 10) the *Supper at Emmaus* (Pl. 11) and the *Nude Girl in a Fur Wrap* (Pl. 12).

None of the other apartments could quite rival this one in splendour, but the second room was almost as spectacular in concept—if not in reality. Of its nineteen pictures eight were attributed to Titian, four to Polidoro da Caravaggio and six to Giulio Romano. In fact only one of the 'Titians' seems to have been a real one—the so-called *Venus del Pardo* (Pl. 13)—though, both because of its size and beauty and because it had been given to Charles by the King of Spain from the royal collection (in which it had been a particular favourite of the King's father, Philip III) [8] it must have been of special importance to him; and another of the pictures believed to be by Titian was the magnificent *Three Views of a Man's Head* (Pl. 14), now recognized as by Lorenzo Lotto, and among the Giulio Romanos and Polidoros were some of high quality.

In the third, and last, Privy Lodging Room were fifteen pictures, also by the most renowned masters. Three were attributed to Titian (among them his fine portrait of *Doge Andrea Gritti*) (Pl. 15), three to Correggio (including the famous *Education of Cupid*) (Pl. 16), two to Andrea del Sarto, but the most celebrated and admired picture in this room, and indeed probably in England, was Raphael's *Virgin and St. Elizabeth with Jesus and the Infant St. John the Baptist* (Pl. 17), which when it was later acquired by the King of Spain, was described as being 'the pearl' of his collection.

If we now move to the Privy Gallery we find ourselves in a far more public part of the palace, where correspondingly the decoration was much more traditional. Of the seventy-three pictures at least seventy were portraits of named figures, the overwhelming majority of them of deceased royalty. Some of these were given ambitious attributions, and some were indeed pictures of the highest quality (by Mabuse and Van Dyck, for instance), but it is quite clear that in a state room of this kind it was the sitters rather than the artists who were of primary importance.

There were ten pictures in Charles's bedroom, and five of these were portraits of his family—his wife *Henrietta Maria* by Van Dyck [9] (Pl. 18); his sister Elizabeth (the 'Winter Queen') and her husband Frederick, King of Bohemia, [10] both painted by Honthorst, and their children depicted as childish hunters in Arcadian costume (Pl. 19); and (by Mytens basing himself on a miniature by Isaac Oliver (Fig. 58)) his elder brother, *Prince Henry*, [11] whose death in 1612, at the age of eighteen had led to Charles inheriting the throne. One other portrait group,

Figure 67   Titian: examples from the series of *The Twelve Caesars*. Engraved after the original paintings by Aegidius Sadeler.

also by Honthorst, found a place, next to those devoted to his closest family, in this, the most intimate of the King's rooms: that of the Duke of Buckingham, favourite of his father and his own bosom friend, together with his wife and children[12] (Pl. 20). Apart from the emotional importance to the King of the two men represented by posthumous portraits in his bedroom, both had played a very significant part in the creation of his art collection. It was from Prince Henry that (as we will shortly see) he had inherited his first pictures; while it was with the Duke of Buckingham (assassinated in 1628) that he had visited the court of Philip IV in Madrid and acquired his first great masterpieces. Three of the remaining pictures in the bedroom were (in varying degrees) devotional in character—a *Holy Family* given to Parmigianino, a *Virgin, Child and St. John* said to be by Raphael, [13] and a *Mary Magdalen* which even at the time was recognized as having been over-cleaned and unlikely to be by Correggio despite its attribution.[14] Finally there was 'the picture of the Nyne naked Muses and Nyne other Musees in apperell, with some Poeticall gods by in the clouds. Little Intire figurs' (Pl. 21). This picture, then believed to be by Perino del Vaga but (both before and since) attributed to Rosso, had been bought in Madrid for Charles by Lord Cottington who had been there with Charles in 1623.[15] It represents a story to be found in Ovid's *Metamorphoses*: the challenge made by the nine mortal Pierides to the Muses to take part in a song contest in front of a Jury of Nymphs—later, when the Pierides lost, they were punished for their presumption by being turned into jackdaws. We are specifically told[16] that (as might indeed be expected) the choice of pictures to be hung in the King's bedroom had been decided by him in person, and it is almost impossible not to believe that this selection of themes—family and friend, religion and the arts (both the latter being enlivened with a touch of female nudity) brings us close to his most deeply felt values.

299 [14]
205 [326]

It would be possible to go through most of the rooms in Whitehall palace in this way and record the paintings to be seen in them, but this is hardly the place to conduct such a lengthy, but very fascinating, investigation. On the other hand, we do need to stress that not all the pictures were kept at Whitehall. Charles maintained at least seven other palaces—St. James's, Denmark House, Hampton Court, Richmond, Greenwich, Nonsuch and Oatlands—and they too had to be fully decorated, often with works of the highest importance (which have not always been adequately recorded). Thus we know that it was in St. James's Palace that Charles kept his set of *Caesars* by Titian (Fig. 67), and we will later discuss the adornment of Greenwich: but so huge was Charles's collection that no attempt will be made in these pages to do more than indicate its nature.

Most of what we can learn about the pictures owned by the King and the way they were arranged is due to the existence of what has been described by Sir Oliver Millar as 'perhaps the finest inventory of its kind ever compiled in England',[17] drawn up by Abraham van der Doort who seems to have come to this country in 1609 and to have been employed by Prince Henry in the organization of his coins, medals and other works of art. He worked in various capacities (including that of portraitist) for other members of the royal family, and when Charles came to the throne in 1625 his role as surveyor of the royal collections was more or less regularized. This did not, of course, mean that he was actually paid regularly or even that he was able to keep full control over the objects entrusted to his care: indeed, it was apparently distress over the unsettled nature of his employment which led him to commit suicide in 1640—a decade before the collections which he had catalogued in such exemplary detail were to be finally dispersed.

Van der Doort was not able to record all the pictures in the royal collection, but nonetheless from the information supplied by him and from various other sources we can form a tolerably accurate and complete notion of its formation and can even follow up various clues indicating the part played by Charles's own taste in its constitution and appearance.

Charles was not, of course, alone in collecting pictures in England during the first half of the seventeenth century. His elder brother Prince Henry (whose memory he always revered) had been the first member of the royal family since Henry VIII to show any real awareness of artistic developments on the continent of Europe, but although we will see that his embryonic collection played its part in stimulating that of Charles, more important impulses came from elsewhere. Ambassadors in Venice and in the Low Countries, such as Sir Henry Wotton and Sir Dudley Carleton, bought pictures for themselves and for noblemen in London, of whom none was more enthusiastic than Lord Arundel. A proud, difficult man, some fifteen years older than Charles (with whom his relations were not always easy), Arundel was probably the most perceptive collector in seventeenth-century England.[18] He had a strong, but thwarted, sense of dynastic loyalty which no doubt played its part in stimulating his passion for the portraits of Holbein (which included masterpieces recording the association of his own family with the Tudor monarchy), while his diplomatic missions to Germany and Austria were to make him very conscious of the art of Dürer and the cult which surrounded it in Central Europe. Such attention to Northern art was to appear rather old-fashioned to many collectors (including, one suspects, the King), but he became celebrated throughout Europe through his intense commitment to the sculpture of antiquity (a commitment which was never fully to be matched by that of Charles). In this field he proved himself a real pioneer, for he was one of the very few collectors of his time to send agents to the Near East in search of marbles. It may well have been his wife, even more than he, who showed a special feeling for Venetian painting–though his actual love of Italy probably surpassed hers: it was almost certainly through her that he acquired what has in recent years come to be looked upon as one of Titian's greatest masterpieces, *The Flaying of Marsyas*,[19] and he owned superb pictures by many of the leading Venetian painters of the Renaissance. Both Lord and Lady Arundel (whose own relations were not always very harmonious) were also remarkable patrons of contemporary art: Rubens and Van Dyck, who are so indelibly associated with the court of Charles I, were both employed by them well before being taken up by the King.

The example of Arundel can hardly be over-rated, but he was never really close to the King. No-one, however, was closer to the King than the man whose dazzling beauty and charm had first intoxicated Charles's father, James I. The meteoric rise to power of George Villiers, as from 1623 first Duke of Buckingham, combined with his somewhat meretricious glamour, extraordinary political ineptitude and early death, have made it difficult for historians to take his commitment to art as seriously as it deserves.[20] And yet his collection was an amazing one–not just because of the masterpieces it contained but because of its adventurous quality: thus, as early as 1621, he had acquired paintings by such modern artists as Manfredi, Guido Reni and Baglione, and we will see later that (like Arundel) Buckingham played a very important role in bringing contemporary painters to the attention of the King. Even more spectacular was his collection of Old Masters. Well before his visit to Madrid with Prince Charles–a decisive moment in the formation of the royal collection–Buckingham owned at least one Titian (the *Ecce Homo*)[21] which could compete in quality and importance with any belonging to Arundel, and it is not surprising that the two men were serious rivals.

It is always difficult, often impossible, to understand either the motives or the extent of understanding shown by extravagant, upstart and extremely successful collectors. How much of their achievement should be credited to a true love of art, which has suddenly been given the means to realize its full potentiality, and how much to a desire to follow a socially acceptable fashion? We know very little about Buckingham's aesthetic sensibility–but to a large extent the first half of the question is irrelevant. For it was he, more than anyone else, who actually set the fashion. Arundel (who was of course no upstart and whose means were by no means unlimited) was too isolated at court, too proud, too quirky, to set the tone; Prince Henry had too little time and too few possibilities to amass a really significant group of pictures. But Buckingham understood that on the Continent of Europe a splendid art collection contributed to the owner's prestige and even power, and he introduced that concept into England where, for much of the century, it was eagerly taken up both by those, such as Charles I, who truly did love painting and by those, such as Charles II, who evidently had little if any feeling for it.

Buckingham certainly owed much of his success to his agent, Balthasar Gerbier, who came to England from Germany in 1615 and who worked indefatigably for him between 1620, when both men were aged 28, and 1628 when Buckingham was assassinated; after which he transferred his excellent services to other collectors. As early as 1625 he could write with justified pride that out of 'all the amateurs and princes and kings, there is not one who has collected in forty years as many pictures as Your Excellency has in five', and in 1629 (the year after Buckingham's death and hence when no question of flattery could arise), Rubens was ready to put his collection on a par with that of Charles himself: he had, he wrote, 'never seen such a quantity of pictures by great masters as in the palace of the King of England and in the gallery of the late Duke of Buckingham'. Among those pictures was a ceiling canvas and a wonderful equestrian portrait, both painted by himself.

Another superb collection belonged to the third Marquis [later first Duke] of Hamilton[22] – a greedy, ambitious and elegant Scottish nobleman who gravitated to the English court where he appears to have made a conscious effort to replace the murdered Buckingham in Charles I's affections. He married Buckingham's niece, he moved into Wallingford House, a residence that had once belonged to Buckingham; and, with the King's active encouragement, he began to collect pictures. Within a few years he had acquired some six hundred, of which half were Venetian – more in number, and more distinguished in quality, than those which were still the property of Buckingham's heirs. But although his collection included such masterpieces as the *Laura* (Pl. 45) and *Three Philosophers* (Pl. 46) by Giorgione and Titian's late *Nymph and Shepherd*,[23] we can now see from the extraordinarily interesting letters which have recently been edited and published by Paul Shakeshaft that Hamilton's attitude to his collection was somewhat ambiguous – to say the least. In one letter he would write that he is 'much in love with pictures' and then, soon after, maintain that he does not much care for them. Indeed, it is very tempting to single out Hamilton as a man who – far more than Buckingham – was following a fashion which was by now already established. One of his great ambitions seems to have been to build up a better collection than Arundel, and he pulled off a particularly satisfying coup by purchasing from the aged Procurator Priuli in Venice (who then 'entangled his foot in his gown, fell down a pair of stairs and died') a *St. Margaret*,[24] then attributed to Raphael, on which Arundel had set his heart. Hamilton was in a good position to build up his collection because his brother-in-law Basil, Viscount Feilding, was in 1634 (possibly at Hamilton's prompting) made Ambassador in Venice, a great centre (as had been well appreciated by his predecessors) for the art market in general, and in particular for those pictures by Titian and other masters which were specially loved in England.

The concentration of art in London was very remarkable, for the main collections were nearly all within a walking distance of about half an hour. One could start, for instance, at St. James's Palace (where, as we have seen, the King kept some of his most important pictures, and also his ancient statues) and then move across the park to Wallingford House, on the site of the present Admiralty (where rooms were being made ready for Hamilton's masterpieces). From here there was an excellent view of the Banqueting Hall adjoining the complex of buildings which made up Whitehall Palace and extended down to the Thames. Proceeding along what is now the Strand one would have passed one mansion after another with gardens overlooking the river: York House, where the Duke of Buckingham's pictures remained more or less undisturbed for many years after his death; Denmark House, another royal palace richly furnished with pictures; and then, a little further on (just after what is today Aldwych underground station), was Arundel House, its contents as splendid as any of the others. And there were, of course, a number of other collections of less grandeur, but still very striking: that in Northumberland House at Charing Cross was soon to become resplendent, as Lord Northumberland trod his careful way between warring factions; while much further down the river at Blackfriars Van Dyck himself kept a group of Titians which were as superb as any belonging to his noble patrons. Associated with these noblemen was a conspicuous set of agents (themselves often collectors) who tended to combine the accumulation of pictures with the practice of espionage: Balthasar Gerbier, Endymion Porter and Nicholas Lanier were among the most prominent of them, but there were many others. No discussion of the formation of Charles I's collection can be of much value if it fails to acknowledge the significance of those belonging to his exemplars and his rivals. It is with this in mind that we must return to its origins, and hence to the role of his elder brother.

Prince Henry, who died in 1612, had been much encouraged by his circle of advisers to form an art collection and he received a number of gifts – of varying quality and importance – from courtiers and foreign diplomats.[25] The pictures he thus acquired seem to have been much admired by his contemporaries, and it is true that by the standards of what was to be seen in England during the first two decades of the seventeenth century the effect that they made must have been striking. Among the three dozen or so pictures mentioned was one attributed to Tintoretto, while the subjects included 'Bacchus, Ceres, and Venus, with fauns, nearly the size of life, very artistically painted' and 'The history of Tityus, how he lies, and the eagle picks out his heart, which is also large'. It was a far cry from the dry ancestral portraits which formed the main stock of English galleries at the time and which would have been more familiar to most visitors to the houses of the nobility and royalty. Yet, although it is very difficult to identify most of the paintings owned by Prince Henry, there is reason to believe that there were few, if any, masterpieces among them except for two portraits by Holbein, and that Charles (who, as we will see, was not particularly attracted to Holbein) did not feel any special admiration for his brother's pioneering efforts to bring recent Italian and Northern painting to England. It is true that Charles's own collection was necessarily built around this nucleus – though it was to be some years before he took it over, for he was aged only twelve when his brother died – but in some cases the fact that a picture in it had once belonged to Prince Henry was forgotten, while in others a painting from that source was exchanged for something more desirable or disposed of in some other way. And the same fate seems to have been met by the pictures inherited by Charles from his mother, Queen Anne, who died in 1619.[26]

It is, in fact, very soon after his mother's death that we first hear of Charles, at the age of twenty-one, expressing a personal interest in art and exerting a strong initiative in the realm of picture collecting. The episode is a revealing one. By 1621 Rubens, who was already famous in Antwerp and even Italy, though he had not yet 'conquered' France and Spain, had been in touch with English diplomats and art lovers for some years; and in 1620 he had, at the special request of Lord Arundel, painted the magnificent group portrait of Lady Arundel and her retinue as she passed through Antwerp on her way to visit their sons at Padua University.[27] We know that by this time Prince Charles already owned a *Judith and Holofernes* said to be by Rubens, but as this was disowned by the artist himself as an insignificant painting of his youth. Lord Danvers was keen to acquire for the Prince another, finer, picture by Rubens and, through the mediation of Sir Dudley Carleton, he eventually obtained a *Lion Hunt* (Fig. 68).[28] But this picture too was not a success – everyone agreed that it had been 'scarce touched by his own hand and the postures so forced, as the Prince will not admitt the picture into his gallery'. As a result of Charles's decision the painting was returned to Rubens, who agreed to paint another *Hunt* 'entirely of my own hand without admixture of the work of anyone else, which I will undertake to you on the word

Figure 68   Rubens: *Tiger, Lion and Leopard Hunt*. Galleria Corsini, Rome.

of a gentleman'; moreover, as requested, he would also make the lions look rather tamer. Rubens had already pointed out, reasonably enough, that a picture painted entirely by him would be more expensive than one painted by a pupil and then touched up in his own hand, and he now hoped that 'the Picture for His Royal Highness, the Prince of Wales, [could] be of the largest proportions, because the size of the picture gives us painters more courage to represent our ideas with the utmost freedom and semblance of reality'. He made the same point again in the same letter in his enthusiastic response to an approach which had evidently been made to him, on behalf of Prince Charles as well as of King James I, to decorate the Banqueting Hall, then being built by Inigo Jones: 'I confess myself to be, by a natural instinct, better fitted to execute works of the largest size rather than little curiosities. Everyone according to his own gifts. My endowments are of such a nature that I have never wanted courage to undertake any design however vast in size or diversified in subject'. It seems that the new *Hunt* was not, in fact, painted, and it was to be many years before Rubens set to work on his canvases for the Banqueting Hall, but it is clear that, after a brief moment of trouble, his relations with the Prince had begun well. This was shown not long afterwards when Charles commissioned Rubens (once again through Lord Danvers) in the most flattering terms to paint for him a *Self Portrait* (Pl. 22)—and he hung this at first in his palace of St. James and, later, when he became King, at Whitehall.[29] As early as January 1625, nearly three months before Charles's accession, Rubens could write to a friend that 'Monsieur le Prince de Galles est le prince le plus amateur de la peinture qui soit au monde'.[30]

272 [250]

Indeed, while negotiating with Rubens the Prince's intermediaries had claimed that by 1621 he already owned a collection containing 'many excellent . . . works of all the best masters in Christendom'.[31] This was no doubt something of an exaggeration—'a note of all such pictures as yo.r Highness hath at present, done by several famous masters own hands, by the life',[32] which seems to have been drawn up a year or two later, lists only twenty-one pictures, nearly all of them portraits and some obviously inherited: they include, however, a full-length portrait of Charles V said to be by Titian, and a 'head of a Venetian Senator' by Tintoretto. The Venetian Ambassador in London wrote that 'he loves old paintings, especially those of our province and city'.[33] This was no doubt true, but just eleven years earlier a predecessor of this Ambassador had written almost exactly the same about Prince Henry,[34] and we cannot assume that in either case a royal love of Venetian paintings was matched by the opportunity to possess them. However, all this was now to change.

Charles, accompanied by Buckingham, arrived in Madrid in March 1623 in a reckless attempt to woo the Infanta Maria, sister of King Philip IV of Spain. They stayed for less than six months. It was clear even before the end of that time that the marriage plan would come to nothing, but it was also clear that, in other respects, Charles had not wasted his time. The King of Spain's picture collection was, at this date, incomparably the greatest in Europe. Philip, who had come to the throne two years earlier at the age of sixteen, had inherited the paintings which had been acquired by his forebears during a century of imaginative patronage. He was thus the owner of a remarkable set of Flemish paintings, which included major works by Bosch and Brueghel, though on his visit fifteen years earlier Rubens had been employed primarily by the Duke of Lerma, the favourite and chief minister of his father, Philip III. Charles may indeed have seen the equestrian portrait which Rubens had painted of Lerma in emulation of Titian's great painting of the *Emperor Charles V at the Battle of Mühlberg*, which belonged to the King: within only a few years Charles himself and Buckingham would join these rulers in being immortalized in equestrian portraits of fully comparable quality. It was Titian who made the greatest impact on the Prince, for a very large number of quite superlative works by this artist were to be seen in Madrid: portraits, religious paintings and mythologies. Two of these, *The Emperor Charles V with a Hound* and the so-called *Venus del Pardo* were presented by Philip to Charles and were taken back by him to England; and a number of others, including *The Rape of Europa* (Pl. 23), *Diana and Callisto* (Pl. 24) and *Diana and Actaeon*[35] (Pl. 25) were (incredibly) also offered to the Prince, but were left behind when negotiations for the royal marriage showed signs of breaking down. That Philip IV, whose passion for painting was at least equal to that of Charles, should have proposed such amazingly generous gifts shows how eager he must have been to wed his sister to the heir to the throne of England.

269 [203], 310 [184]

Charles also tried to buy works of art from private collectors while he was in Madrid. He was unable to persuade Juan de Espina to part with two volumes of drawings and manuscripts by Leonardo da Vinci,[36] but he was more successful with the Conde de Villamediana from whom he obtained, among other things, Titian's *Nude Girl in a Fur Wrap*. And he also commissioned copies to be made of other Titians which he saw in the King's palaces.[37] He was painted by Velazquez who arrived in Madrid during his stay there, but the picture does not appear to have been taken to England.[38] Finally, it was while he was still in Spain that he was able to complete arrangements, which had already been entered into at an earlier date (perhaps on the advice of Rubens) for the purchase in Genoa of the cartoons designed by Raphael for a set of tapestries to be woven in Flanders and hung in the Sistine Chapel (Fig. 89). The acquisition of these was purely functional: they were to serve as models for the production of further sets of tapestry by the workshop which had recently been set up at Mortlake. They were cut up into vertical strips, and when not in use at Mortlake as a source for copies, they were kept in storage at Whitehall, and were not displayed as works of art in their own right.[39]

70 [32]

72 [61]

It can be seen that when Charles I, by now betrothed to Henrietta Maria of France, ascended the throne two years later in 1625 he already owned a number of outstanding pictures of his own as well as the many portraits which he had inherited with the crown. One of his very first moves was to try to bring to London an Italian painter of the first rank. His first attempt was unsuccessful. Guercino refused his invitation both because he did not wish to work for heretics and because he did not welcome the prospect of having to put up with the English climate;[40] but nonetheless within less than a year of his accession Charles's part-time agent, Nicholas Lanier, had obtained a licence to have two paintings by Guercino–a *Prophet* and a *Landscape*–exported from the papal states.[41] And not long afterwards the King and the Duke of Buckingham managed in October 1626 to persuade Orazio Gentileschi, a one-time follower of Caravaggio, to move from Paris (where he was employed by Marie de' Medici, mother of Charles's wife Henrietta Maria) and to settle in London, where he served on diplomatic missions as well as becoming court painter.[42] Gentileschi, whose presence in England aroused violent opposition from other artists and agents working for the King, painted many pictures for Charles and Henrietta Maria during the remaining thirteen years of his life, all of which he spent in England. It has been argued that the over-refined atmosphere of the English court was responsible for the increasing bloodlessness of his painting. His most beautiful single picture of this period, however, a *Finding of Moses* [43] (Pl. 26) was a brilliant venture into the manner of Veronese, and it is not quite clear whether it was actually produced for the King (who, as will be seen, did not particularly admire this artist), for with Charles's full authority it was sold by Gentileschi to the King of Spain. Gentileschi's most important commission in England was for a series of nine canvases to be fitted into the ceiling of the Queen's House at Greenwich, and it was only completed shortly before his death, perhaps with the assistance of his daughter Artemisia, who may have presented to the King her beautiful self portrait in the guise of an *Allegory of Painting* (Pl. 27). The theme was the *Allegory of Peace and the Arts under the English Crown* (Pl. 28), and here–as in another canvas which was painted by Gentileschi probably for the King but which can now no longer be traced–great prominence was given to the Nine Muses, a favourite subject of Charles (as we have already seen).

263 [124], 203 [294]

191 [97]
137 [3]

316 [286]

Less than a year after Gentileschi had settled in England, his two sons, Francesco and Giulio, were sent to Italy to join Nicholas Lanier in Genoa and to make arrangements with him for the purchase of a collection of pictures there on behalf of the King.[44] Much confusion ensued, and the plan seems to have come to nothing, although Lanier–who within weeks of the King's accession had been ordered to go to Italy incognito 'to provide for him some choice Pictures'[45]–had certainly been very active in buying works of art in various towns.[46] However, by the time the Gentileschi brothers arrived a project was already under way which would soon put all the King's previous acquisitions in the shade.

Vincenzo II, last of the main line of the Gonzagas, succeeded his brother Ferdinando as Duke of Mantua in October 1626.[47] Whether his character was quite as vicious as Italian historians have made out is not altogether certain, but he was certainly unhealthy (he was to die at the age of thirty-three) and his duchy was heavily in debt. He had, however, inherited one of the most spectacular art collections in Italy, famous above all for a concentration of major works by Mantegna, Titian and Giulio Romano which paid homage to the world of antiquity. Mantegna had worked in Mantua for nearly half a century. Some of the grandest paintings which he produced for the Gonzagas–the frescoes in the 'Camera degli Sposi' of the ducal palace–were, of course, immovable, but he had also painted many smaller pictures (including the *Parnassus* and *Expulsion of the Vices* for Isabella d'Este's grotto), and–most famous of all–the set of nine *Triumphs of Caesar* (Fig. 69) which ever since the Renaissance itself have been considered the most powerful and evocative recreations ever attempted of ancient Rome. Rubens was much struck with them, and indeed they were among the very rare works of the *Quattrocento* whose fame remained undiminished in later centuries. The eleven *Caesars* (there was no space for the twelfth) which Titian had painted for Federico Gonzaga were equally well known and were repeatedly copied, and as the originals were burnt in 1734 it is only from such (sadly feeble) interpretations that we can get any impression of their original appearance. They were inserted into a specially designed 'Cabinet of the Caesars', and below them was a series of scenes from the Lives of the Caesars based on Suetonius, painted by Giulio Romano and his pupils. Giulio Romano's most splendid work for the Gonzagas–principally the Palazzo del Te which he designed and decorated–could not be disposed of, but he also painted for Federico a number of portraits and historical and mythological paintings, which hung in his gallery, and some altarpieces. And, quite apart from the *Caesars*, Federico had also commissioned many other paintings from Titian. Correggio too had been much employed by the Gonzagas–he had painted two of the pictures for the grotto of Isabella d'Este, Federico's mother, but his most beautiful paintings for Federico–*The Loves of Jupiter*–had been ceded to the Emperor Charles V in 1530 (or 1532). In more recent times, Vincenzo I (who ruled from 1587 to 1612), the reigning Duke's father, had been a passionate, though not always discriminating, art lover. Perhaps his most famous gesture had been the award of a marquisate to Count Canossa in return for Raphael's *Virgin and St. Elizabeth with Jesus and the Infant St. John the Baptist*;[48] but he had also been patron of Franz Pourbus and of Rubens, each of whom was put in charge of his pictures, and it was through the intervention of Rubens that he bought the greatest of his modern masterpieces, Caravaggio's *Death of the Virgin* (Pl. 29) Duke Vincenzo II's elder brother, Ferdinando (who ruled from 1612 until 1626), had also been a lavish patron, and it was thanks to him that the collection contained a large number of pictures by Domenico Feti.

In 1623, while Ferdinando still ruled over his beautiful but impoverished duchy, his chamberlain received an indirect request from Lord Arundel (conveyed by his wife) for 'a model of the palace of His Highness, the Duke of Mantua, called the Palazzo del Te. . . and if it were possible to acquire the original model which was used for the design of the building he would be much more grateful. . . and also a model of the courtyard of the palace of Mantua with its rustic order constructed not long ago'.[49] In itself this was not particularly strange, for Giulio Romano's architecture was admired throughout Europe, and the Arundels (who were special patrons of Inigo Jones) were deeply interested in spreading the taste for Italian designs to England. However, some of the details required were a little more surprising: 'He would like the model to be made as accurate as possible by a skilled craftsman and that it should make every detail clear and should be accompanied with a clear description of the principal things to be seen inside, as regards sculpture and painting–i.e. what is in what room and how it is arranged'. It is almost inconceivable that (as has sometimes been suggested) this was a preliminary move by Arundel in an attempt to acquire the Gonzaga collections for Charles who was still only Prince of Wales, though he may have had eyes on some of the pictures for himself. But it certainly meant that the English were unusually well-informed about what was to be seen in Mantua, and this may have stimulated the steps taken by Charles to acquire the whole collection almost as soon as he became King two years later.

We have seen that Nicholas Lanier was sent to Italy in 1625. In Venice he stayed with Daniel Nys, a merchant of French or Flemish origin, who had had much experience over a long period of doing business with the English and who was very familiar with the workings of the art market. In August Lanier went to Mantua with a letter of introduction from Nys, explaining that he was an acomplished musician with a great love of pictures and that the King of England would be very grateful for any hospitality shown to him. Three weeks later Lanier returned to Venice 'in ecstasy . . . at the honours with which he had been welcomed' in Mantua, and then went back to London presumably to give an account of his visit to the King. Soon afterwards Nys approached Duke Ferdinando with an offer for his pictures. On the surface this was a surprising

186 [–]

270 [219]

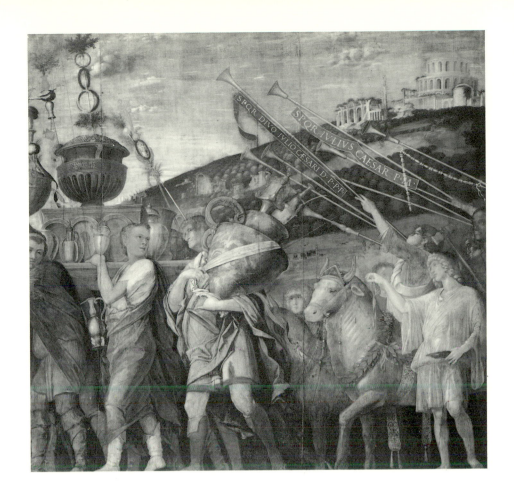

Figure 69   Mantegna: *Triumphs of Caesar*. Royal Collection: reproduced by gracious permission of Her Majesty The Queen.

move, for Ferdinando had been as enthusiastic about his inheritance–to which he had made notable additions–as had been his predecessors. None the less he was in great financial straits and he seems to have agreed in principle to some sort of sale; and then at the end of October 1626 he suddenly died. By the middle of November negotiations had been resumed with his brother Vincenzo II, and early in the following year lists were drawn up of the pictures to be disposed of and the valuations placed on them. Matters were made particularly complicated by the (perhaps well-founded) suspicions of the Mantuan authorities that Nys was trying to cheat them and was acting not, as he claimed, for the King of England but for the Duke of Parma or the Grand Duke of Tuscany; and also by their fear that the sale would attract bitter indignation–as indeed it did on a scale that they had not even imagined possible. Moreover, the Duke himself felt some

186 [–] scruples, and he refused to sell the Mantegna *Triumphs* explaining that he had had two new rooms specially built for them. None the less, most of the remaining pictures were sent in secrecy to Nys's house on the island of Murano. Sir Isaac Wake, the British Ambassador in Venice, obtained customs clearance from the local authorities,[50] and, in April 1628, the *Margaret* set sail for London (through a heavy and extremely damaging storm) carrying on board

the twelve Emperors of Titian, a large picture of Andrea del Sarto, a picture of Michelangelo di Caravaggio; other pictures of Titian, Correggio, Giulio Romano, Tintoretto, and Guido Reni, all of the greatest beauty–in short so wonderful and glorious a collection, that the like will never again be met with; they are truly worthy of so great a king as his Majesty of Great Britain.[51]

Meanwhile Nicholas Lanier travelled to England by land taking with him the two Correggio temperas (Pls. 30-31) from Isabella d'Este's grotto, which it was feared would suffer from a sea journey, and the Raphael.[52]

Duke Vincenzo II had died on 25 December 1627 (before the final departure of his pictures from Italy) after having ruled for little more than a year. He was succeeded by Carlo di Nevers of the collatoral branch of the family. Carlo was embroiled in continuous war in order to secure his rights to the duchy, and in any case he felt none of the twinges of loyalty to his forebears or his subjects which had inhibited Vincenzo from disposing of two of the special glories of the collection: Mantegna's *Triumphs of Caesar* and the ancient statues. Although Daniel Nys had declared of his acquisitions to the King that 'Since I came into the world, I have made various contracts, but never a more difficult one than this, and which has succeeded so happily', in fact–as he was later to acknowledge–he was 'touched to the core' by his failure to buy the Mantegnas.[53] 'The best-informed persons told me that I had left the most beautiful behind, and that, not having the Triumphs of Julius Caesar, I had nothing at all'. In a vivid letter to Lord Dorchester, who as Sir Dudley Carleton had been ambassador in both Venice and The Hague, Nys described the interest shown by the Grand Duke of Tuscany and the Queen of France in acquiring what still remained behind in Mantua, and reported that the agent of the Duke of Nevers had repeatedly urged him to make a deal himself for the statues and pictures. 'And I answered, "Let them take them who will, I will not" [*pigli chi voel, io non le voglio*].[54] To which he then replied, "And what if I were to get for you the nine pieces of Andrea Mantegna, that is the Triumph of Julius Caesar? Would not that persuade you to make up your mind, because I know that Duke Vincenzo would not give them to you?".'[55] And so, Nys explained, in order to forestall rival bidders he had himself bought the antiquities and the Mantegnas on behalf of the King of England–even though he had received no instructions or commission to do so. It is difficult to catch all the nuances in the extensive and disingenuous correspondence concerning this matter. Nys was (understandably) desperate to be reimbursed for the huge sum of more than £10,000 which he had spent, and for this purpose he was ready to play off rival collectors against each other, to cheat and to lie. On the other hand, Charles's willingness to accept the Mantegnas and the antiquities, combined with his extreme reluctance to pay for them, is hardly more edifying–and it led to Nys's ruin; but the Mantegnas are still in the royal collection.

Charles I's acquisition of the Gonzaga paintings (and sculptures) was certainly the most remarkable transaction of its kind that had yet been seen; and ironically the only other transfer of works of art on a similar scale in the seventeenth century was to be the dispersal of most of those same pictures and sculptures within twenty years or so. Meanwhile, however, their presence transformed the whole nature of the royal collection, so that within less than a decade of Charles's return from Madrid to London, his palaces could rival those of Philip IV in the magnificence of their contents—indeed the Spanish took a keen and natural interest in what had happened.[56] We have already had a brief glimpse at their arrangement, and we must now try to look more closely at Charles's involvement with his recent, and earlier, acquisitions in order to try to understand his own individual tastes.

Investigations of this kind are always difficult in the case of large-scale collectors, particularly royal ones, who necessarily have certain obigations—to the expectations of their courtiers and subjects, to the traditions of their ancestors, to the Church, even to the cause of ostentation itself—which may stand in the way of their expressing a more personal discrimination. And, naturally enough, the purchase *en bloc* of a whole collection, which had been built up over several generations by a foreign dynasty whose circumstances bore no relation to those prevailing in England, make it even more complicated for us to try to ascertain how much of Charles's feelings we can discern in the pictures which

Figure 70   Holbein: *The Triumph of Poverty*. Drawing after original painting by Lucas Vorsterman the Elder. Reproduced by courtesy of the Trustees of the British Museum.

Figure 71   Holbein: *The Triumph of Riches*. Drawing after original painting by Lucas Vorsterman the Elder. Ashmolean Museum, Oxford.

215   Charles I's Collection of Pictures

surrounded him. Nevertheless, there are certain clues which can be tentatively followed up, but before we do so, it has to be emphasised that there is conclusive evidence that the King (and certain members of his entourage) had a real understanding of painting and were not just following that fashion for extravagant collecting which, as we have seen, was so widespread at the time. The evidence comes not, of course, from the flattering panegyrics of courtiers, but from confidential reports and from references to conversations in which there could have been no conceivable reason for not telling the truth: thus the papal agent in London, an English Benedictine monk in the Queen's circle and Van Dyck himself were all agreed that Charles had a 'good nose for pictures' and that he had 'a perfect understanding of painting' (*esquisitamente intende della pittura*).[57]

It has already been made clear that both before and during Charles's reign there were many other lavish art collectors in London, and it was therefore natural that they tended to exchange pictures with each other. In such circumstances it seems reasonable to assume that royalty usually gets its own way.

Shortly after his accession, Charles gave a volume of Holbein's portrait

258 [33]   drawings to Lord Pembroke in return for Raphael's small, early *St. George and the Dragon* (Pl. 32), and Lord Pembroke in turn gave the Holbeins to Lord Arundel, one of whose ancestors had once owned them.[58] It is true that this particular Raphael held a special significance for the King, for he must surely have been aware of the tradition that it had originally been commissioned by the Duke of Urbino as a present to Henry VII in gratitude for having been made a member of the Order of the Garter. But the royal associations of the Holbein drawings were equally strong, and in fact Charles's exchange was probably prompted by the fact that (until the purchase of the Mantua pictures) he found it extraordinarily difficult to lay his hands on any Raphael: certainly he was later to say that Raphael was his favourite painter.[59]

Many other pictures by Holbein passed from Charles's possession into other collections, most notably that of Lord Arundel, who had a passion for the artist: the two very large allegories, for instance, of *The Triumph of Poverty* (Fig. 70) and *The Triumph of Riches* (Fig. 71), which were considered to be his masterpieces and which had been painted for the guildhall of the Hanseatic merchants in London and had then after various peregrinations reached Prince Henry.[60] The Petrarchan *Allegory of Desire* (Pl. 33), inscribed 'e cosi desio me mena', which had belonged to Prince Henry, may also have reached Arundel through the King,[61] and this applies to the *Portrait of Dr Chambers* (Pl. 34) as well. In addition to all these Charles gave away another beautiful Holbein (which may or may not have belonged to his brother), the *Portrait of Erasmus* (Pl. 35),[62] as well as what was, apparently an important Titian *Madonna*, which had belonged to the poet John

268 [192]   Donne, to the Duc de Liancourt in return for Leonardo da Vinci's *St. John the Baptist* (Pl. 36).[63] There is therefore a good deal of circumstantial evidence to suggest that Charles by no means shared Arundel's enthusiasm for Holbein. Indeed, the comparatively few pictures by him in the royal collection, all of them portraits, were for the most part acquired by gift or inheritance. To the King their appeal, such as it was, must have been one of ancestral piety—as was the case with another picture, the so-called *Wilton Diptych* (Pl. 37), which portrayed Richard II and which was also presented to him.[64]

Charles's love of Titian is by contrast particularly well attested, but before giving examples to demonstrate this it is essential to point out that this love was indeed shared by Lord Arundel and by all the other collectors attached to the Stuart court, as well as by princes in France, Spain, Germany, Italy and elsewhere: an admiration for Titian was one of the hallmarks of noble collecting in the seventeenth century. It was from Arundel (whether as a gift or in exchange for some other piece is not certain) that Charles acquired his 'defaced' version of

298 [4]   Titian's *Tarquin and Lucretia* (Pl. 38),[65] despite the fact that he already owned (or was soon to get) another picture of the same subject attributed to Titian;[66] and he also acquired, by exchange, yet another *Rape of Lucretia* (by Simone Cantarini) from the widowed Duchess of Buckingham.[67] From the Duchess he obtained a further picture believed to be by Titian, which was described in Van der Doort's

70 [32]   inventory as 'a Sitting naked woeman with both her hands putting on her Smock'[68] and also a Veronese 'Leda Lyeing naked on a Bedd with Jupiter upon, her in the shape of a white Swann'.[69] In return for this the Duchess was given Domenico Feti's *Vision of St. Peter* (Pl. 39) from Mantua.[70] As we are told by the Duke of Hamilton, who was certainly in a position to know, that Veronese was 'a master not very much esteemed here by the King',[71] it was probably the nature of the subject which appealed. This seems confirmed by some of the other pictures

that Charles acquired by exchange: a few have already been mentioned, and to them we can add the 'full faced painted younge womans picture in her yellow haire with her left breast naked and her smock over her other right breast . . . Done by John: Bellin' which was obtained by him when he was still Prince of Wales.[72] In return for this, and also a Parmigianino, Charles gave Lord Pembroke a little *Judith* which he believed to be by Raphael, that most sought-after of Old Masters.[73]

Charles's taste was therefore hardly an austere one. He does not seem to have been much more interested in Dürer than he was in Holbein, though like all collectors he owned some of his prints, most of which had been given to him, when still Prince of Wales, by Van der Doort.[74] Similarly, of the three paintings which he owned two, the *Self Portait* (Pl. 40) and the *Portrait of the Artist's Father* (Pl. 41), had been presented to him by the City of Nuremberg through Lord Arundel who travelled there in 1636.[75] It must have been particularly galling for Arundel to be forced to act only as a conveyor in this instance, for he really did care deeply for Dürer. Fortunately, the city of Würzburg gave him a picture of the *Madonna*, which he considered to be 'more worth than all the toys I have gotten in Germany',[76] but this too nearly went the same way as the Nuremberg portraits. When the King and Queen visited Arundel House, Lady Arundel (whose relationship with her husband never seems to have been a very happy one) made a proposal which she, and everyone else, knew would cause him the utmost distress. She wished, she said, to give to the Queen a present of 'a most beautiful altarpiece by the hand of Dürer'. The Queen became embarrassed, especially when, in her presence, Arundel objected to the idea of his collection being dismantled in this way, and the plan seems to have come to nothing–perhaps because the King did not pursue it, as he surely would have done, had Lady Arundel offered him a Venetian nude. The papal envoy was present–it is from him that we hear the story–and, in what appears to be his only recorded joke, Arundel explained that 'he was most ready to support the doctrine of free will in everything except in the matter of giving away pictures'.[77]

Further evidence of the nature of Charles's taste is suggested by the gift which he made to Hamilton of the two beautiful paintings by Geertgen tot Sint Jans of *The Lamentation* (Pl. 42) and *The Burning of the Bones of St. John the Baptist* (Pl. 43) which had been presented to him by the States General of the United Provinces.[78] It is true that in return for these (or other) pictures Hamilton gave the King two German paintings, both by Cranach–but of these one, a *Portrait of Luther*, was obviously of considerable historical interest, while the other two 'intire figures' of Adam and Eve ('Adam is eating the Apple') (Pl. 44), was certainly as erotic in content as are all Cranach's known representations of this theme.[79] It seems reasonable to agree with one of the cataloguers of the Royal Collection[80] that

from the pattern of his collecting–and there is no more direct kind of evidence–it would appear that Charles I as a young man took some interest in early Netherlandish painting and particularly in mid-sixteenth-century portraits. As his fondness for classical art increased, however, and as his love for Italian, and especially Venetian, painting developed, his taste for Netherlandish art seems to have diminished. His most interesting acquisitions came as gifts or rather unexpected inclusions in the consignment from Mantua. Two of the outstanding masterpieces, the panels by Geertgen, he gave away; and he may have planned to give away two more, the panels by Van der Goes. The prejudice against northern art and in favour of Italian Renaissance and Seicento painting . . . is already apparent in Charles and in many of the collectors who were his contemporaries.

Among these contemporaries, we may note, Queen Christina of Sweden who, in 1649, was to write to Paolo Giordano Orsini of her collection of pictures in Stockholm that it contained

an infinite number of items, but apart from thirty or forty original Italians, I care nothing for any of the others. There are some by Alberto Dürer and other German masters whose names I do not know, and anyone else would think very highly of them, but I swear that I would give away the whole lot for a couple of Raphaels, and I think that even that would be paying them too much honour.[81]

Another indication of Charles's taste may perhaps be found in the copies that were made for him of pictures in his collection–though as the purpose of these copies is by no means clear too much reliance cannot be placed upon them as evidence. It has recently been emphasised that quite remarkably few copies were made of portraits of the King during the period of his personal rule, 'though the

259 [65, 64]

258 [46]

situation changed dramatically after the Civil War began'.[82] The portraits by Van Dyck were certainly not reproduced in bulk, either on canvas or in the form of engravings, as was the practice in most European states. It almost seems as if their significance for the King was essentially a personal one. As from about 1628, however, Charles employed Peter Oliver (son of the miniaturist Isaac) to make small copies, mostly in watercolour, of about a dozen pictures, some belonging to him and some to be seen elsewhere.[83] These copies were kept in cupboards in one of the rooms in Whitehall, and they can presumably be thought of as tributes (though hardly very pleasing ones) to the beauty of those paintings which the King most admired—or at least wished to have recorded for some special reason. Among them were Raphael's *St. George* (which he had acquired from Lord Pembroke in exchange for the album of Holbein's drawings) and a *Holy Family*, four or five Titians, of which two belonged to him—*The Allocution of the Marqués del Vasto*, probably from Mantua, and *The Mystic Marriage of St. Catherine*, acquired—as we will see from William Frizell—while two were unavailable, though doubtless very desirable—the *Venus of Urbino*, then as now in Florence and presumably known to Oliver through a copy, and a version of *Venus and Adonis* [84] which belonged to Lord Arundel; there were three Correggios—the *Venus, Cupid and Satyr* and *The School of Love* [85] from Mantua, and a *Holy Family* in the Buckingham collection. There were also copies of two Holbeins—the *Portrait of Dr Chambers*, which he had given to Arundel, and the *Portrait of Edward VI*. Peter Oliver was also required to copy the portrait by his father Isaac of *Prince Henry*. And there were other copies both by Peter Oliver himself and by various less significant artists.

258 [35]
256 [12]

Charles's artistic tastes are, of course, most evident in his patronage of contemporary painters, but before we turn to these it will be necessary to emphasise that his collecting of Old Masters by no means came to a sudden end with his acquisition of the Mantua pictures, though both the quality and the scale of his outright purchases inevitably declined. In 1635, however, another astonishing prospect appeared to open before him. He heard that the Ludovisi, owners of one of the greatest collections in Rome, were thinking of selling their beautiful pictures 'by Raphael, Correggio, Titian and Leonardo da Vinci' and he at once showed an interest.[86] But this time it was his rival, King Philip IV of Spain who, in 1637, was able to obtain—as a gift, arranged by his Viceroy in Naples—the two supreme masterpieces on offer, Titian's *Andrians* and *Worship of Venus*.[87] And, despite frequent rumours, no other important picture from the collection became available at this time.

Even more enticing was the very well-known collection which had been built up by the Venetian merchant Bartolomeo della Nave and which came on to the market in 1637, possibly following his death.[88] It contained wonderful paintings by Giorgione (the *Laura*, Pl. 45, and the *Three Philosophers*, Pl. 46), Antonello da Messina (the *San Cassiano Altarpiece*, Pl. 47), and considerable numbers of pictures attributed to Titian and all the other great Venetian masters of the Renaissance. The King was 'so extremely taken' with the list of the paintings in the collection, which was sent from Venice by Lord Feilding, that he persuaded Hamilton to buy it *en bloc*, on the understanding that he (the King) would be able to acquire from it what he wanted for his own gallery.[89] However, by the time the pictures reached England, Hamilton was already in Scotland as Charles's commander against the rebellious Covenanters, and Charles himself was no longer in a position to buy any of them.

Compared to such possibilities the actuality of Charles's last bulk purchase must have seemed a little disappointing. In 1637 he was able to obtain not the Ludovisi Titians nor the della Nave Giorgiones, but some twenty or so lesser (but still notable) Italian paintings which seem, for the most part, to have been assembled in Naples. Their owner, usually called William Frizell, was a mysterious figure whose identity has never been clearly established, but who was certainly in the employment of Lord Arundel and who may have been related to Daniel Fröschl, a miniaturist in the service of the Emperor Rudolf II at the beginning of the century.[90] The most important of the paintings were nine panels by Polidoro da Caravaggio (Fig. 72), which may once have adorned a suite of bedroom furniture: three of them represent episodes from the story of Psyche while the remaining, much narrower, ones are conceived of as decorations 'all'antica' and depict putti, satyrs and so on.[91] Among the more interesting of the other pictures acquired at this sale were a *Mystic Marriage of St. Catherine* (Pl. 48) attributed to Titian[92] which (as we have seen) was copied for Charles I by Peter Oliver and a *Virgin and Child* (Pl. 49) by Tintoretto.[93] There was also a curious

268 [194]

Figure 72 Polidoro da Caravaggio: examples from his *Nine Panels*. Royal Collection: reproduced by gracious permission of Her Majesty The Queen.

Figure 73   Guido Reni: *The Labours of Hercules*. Musée du Louvre, Paris: copyright Réunion des Musées Nationaux.

315 [263]   painting, perhaps representing *The Calling of Saints Peter and Andrew,* whose attribution to 'an imitator of Caravaggio' by Van der Doort has been accepted in part by many modern scholars, who have seen in it a possible copy of a lost original.[94]

Although Charles I bought fewer Old Masters at this time, he continued to receive important gifts–often prompted by political motives. In 1636 the States General of the United Provinces presented him with four pictures removed from a suppressed convent.[95] Of these he presented the two masterpieces (the Geertgen panels) to Hamilton almost immediately, but he retained Mabuse's *Adam and Eve* [96] (Pl. 50) and a *St. Jerome* (Pl. 51), then attributed to Lucas van Leyden.[97] Other Dutch pictures–including three Rembrandts (Pl. 52) (the first to leave the Netherlands)–also came to Whitehall as gifts, particularly from Sir Robert Kerr, who had been with Prince Charles in Madrid and who in 1629 visited Amsterdam (where he was eventually to die).[98]

204 [304]
64 [63]

Of more interest to Charles must have been the paintings sent to London from the papal court. Officially these were intended for the Catholic Henrietta Maria, but we know that the Pope's nephew, Cardinal Francesco Barberini, who was the most important art patron in the Rome of his day, had the King in mind when making a selection of what to send: 'as soon as he knew the King's taste he would despatch them to the Queen so that she could give them to the King';[99] and the Queen herself said that, much as she liked the presents which had arrived for her, 'she would not be able to keep them, as the King would steal them from her . . .'[100] The papal agent in London reported to Rome that it did not matter whether the pictures chosen were old or modern, but that he himself thought that old ones would be more acceptable because of their rarity. In fact, both old and new paintings were sent at various times,[101] and we have a vivid eye-witness account of the arrival of one consignment in January 1636.[102] The Queen was resting in bed as they were shown to her, but Charles came at once, accompanied by Inigo Jones, by Lord Holland (a special favourite of the Queen) and by Lord Pembroke: not long afterwards Lord Arundel also came to see what had arrived. Both the King and Inigo Jones, who threw off his cloak, put on his eye-glasses and took up a candle, examined them very closely. They agreed with Henrietta Maria in showing particular enthusiasm for a *Portrait of a Lady* (Pl. 53) by Andrea del Sarto [103] and a Leonardo da Vinci which Inigo Jones believed to be a portrait of Ginevra Benci; while the King and Jones were also very keen on a picture–or pictures–believed to be by Giulio Romano (Pls. 54-5).[104] Another painting in the same group of a *Soldier and a Girl* (Pl. 56), which Cardinal Barberini had attributed to Giorgione, seems not to have attracted any attention.[105]

308 [159]

319 [333]

306 [131]

The papal agent thought that of modern artists Guido Reni would be the most welcome, but that something by Lanfranco, Ribera or Annibale Carracci would also be acceptable.[106] As far as we know, however, the Queen (and hence the King) had to make do with a *St. John the Baptist wreathing a Lamb* (Pl. 57) and a *Virgin and Child with Angels* (Pl. 58) by Giovanni Baglione. She was, however, obviously pleased with her paintings from Rome, for she put all the religious ones on display in her chapel at Denmark House, and the Baglione *Virgin and Child* was hanging in her bed chamber in France at the time of her death.[107]

304 [104]
320 [350]

Royal enthusiasm for Guido Reni was no doubt stimulated by his superb *Labours of Hercules* (Fig. 73) which came to London from Mantua; and it was natural therefore for the Queen to turn to him in 1637 when she wished to order a large mythological painting for the ceiling of her bedroom at Greenwich,[108] for the main Hall of which Orazio Gentileschi was probably preparing his ceiling canvases at this very time. The commission was transmitted from the papal agent in London to Cardinal Barberini, who–as we have seen–had already sent her a number of pictures. Indeed, it is an indication of her satisfaction with these that she asked him to choose the subject. The Cardinal at first decided on *Cephalus and Aurora* and then changed his mind and asked Reni instead for a *Bacchus and Ariadne* (Fig. 74).[109] It was not completed for more than three years, and when the Cardinal eventually saw it in August 1640 he got a shock.

274 [280]

Both as regards the story and as regards the way in which the painter has chosen to depict it, the picture appears to me to be lascivious. I hesitate to send it for fear of further scandalising these Heretics, especially since the subject of the work was chosen here in Rome. I will have a sketch made and sent to you [the papal agent], and if these things bother neither the Queen nor Father Philip [the Queen's chaplain], we will have to let it appear that Her Majesty ordered everything and that I was solicitously carrying out her commands.

Both for the light it it throws on the sophisticated court of Rome and for the information it gives about likely English reactions, the letter is wonderfully revealing; but – although the Short Parliament had been summoned four months earlier and there had been demands that the law against Roman Catholics should be strongly enforced – the Queen was not worried about the picture's possible indecency. She had heard that it was exceptionally beautiful and she was keen to receive it. Cardinal Barberini still hesitated: 'The figures are not as well draped as I should like,' he wrote in February 1641, 'especially in these parliamentary times' *(massime in questi tempi di Parlamento)*. His instinct was probably right: in any case the time for buying pictures of any kind was now over, and this one probably never even reached London.

English patronage of Italian art had thus been very limited indeed; but Charles fared better with Northern painters, although (partly perhaps because it was impossible for him to travel abroad once he had come to the throne) most of the really important foreign artists who were employed by him in England had first been invited to this country by other patrons. Thus it seems to have been Buckingham who was primarily responsible in 1628 for bringing Honthorst to London from the Low Countries,[110] just as, two years earlier, he had persuaded Gentileschi to come from Paris. Honthorst had, in fact, been 'discovered' in about 1620 in Utrecht (to which he had recently returned after a very successful decade in Italy) by Sir Dudley Carleton, and Carleton had sent a picture by him to Lord Arundel; but although Arundel expressed great admiration for this, and noted the impact on it of the style of Caravaggio, he did not commission anything for himself.[111] Honthorst did not, in fact, stay in London for long, perhaps because of the assassination of Buckingham which took place only a few months after his

299 [14] arrival, but we have seen that the elegant portrait which he painted of the Duke, together with the Duchess and their two children, was later to hang in Charles's

264 ['130] bedroom, as were portraits by him of Charles's sister, the exiled Queen of Bohemia, and brother-in-law which he painted for the King after he had left England (at the very end of 1628) and settled, for a time, in The Hague. All these favoured friends and relatives of Charles were included in the two very ambitious (and somewhat ludicrous) mythologized portraits which Honthorst painted for him – or which were given to him. In *Apollo and Diana* (Pl. 59),[112] which was kept (understandably enough) in store at Whitehall, Mercury – in the guise of the Duke of Buckingham – and Grammar – personified by his bare-breasted wife – lead Logic, Rhetoric and the other Liberal Arts to pay homage to Apollo and Diana (the King and Queen) who sit on a cloud above them; and in

300 [35] *Seladon and Astraea*,[113] the King and Queen of Bohemia appear as the shepherd

Figure 74   Giovanni Bolgnini after a painting by Guido Reni: *Bacchus and Ariadne on the Island of Naxos*.
Royal Collection: reproduced by gracious permission of Her Majesty The Queen.

and shepherdess of those names who were the protagonists of Honoré d'Urfé's hugely popular sentimental romance, the publication of which in four parts had only recently been completed. Fortunately for Charles's reputation as patron it was just at this time that he was able to make arrangements for introducing into England a decidedly more convincing example of the most sophisticated aristocratic art of contemporary Europe.

We have seen that when still Prince of Wales he had been in touch with Rubens and had hinted to him that there was a potential commission open for him to decorate the new Banqueting Hall, which was then still under construction. Rubens had responded with enthusiasm, but for nearly a decade no precise offer was made: during these years Rubens had painted, in the Palais du Luxembourg in Paris, his series of twenty-four canvases depicting the adventures of the widowed Marie de' Medici and had also planned–but not executed–some of the matching series to be devoted to her husband Henri IV; he had also produced major works for the Habsburgs and for religious institutions in Spain. But his contacts with England had not been wholly severed and in May 1625, when he was in Paris to hand over and put the finishing touches *in situ* to the last of the canvases commissioned by Marie de' Medici, he met Buckingham, who was acting as proxy for the newly-crowned Charles I at his marriage ceremony with Marie's daughter Henrietta Maria. Rubens and Buckingham engaged in negotiations to bring to an end the war between England and Spain which had broken out as a direct result of the collapse of Charles's proposal of only two years earlier to the Infanta Maria–a proposal which had also been made with the full backing of Buckingham. Rubens designed a magnificent equestrian portrait of Buckingham,[114] and after a few months they met again in Antwerp to which Buckingham had been sent on a diplomatic mission, and there he persuaded the artist to sell him a substantial part of his private collection of paintings and sculpture. Two years later (by which time Buckingham had been assassinated) Rubens came to London in order to negotiate an exchange of ambassadors between England and Spain as a preliminary step to the restoration of peace. He arrived on 5 June 1629, and on the following day he was received by the King at Greenwich.

Rubens stayed in London for nine months, and although the main purpose of his visit was political, he was also able to visit the principal art collections, which made a considerable impact on him, and to paint a few pictures of great beauty and importance: among them a superb three-quarter length portrait of Lord Arundel in armour.[115] But Rubens's most significant relationship was with the King for whom he painted as a gift an apposite political allegory of *Peace and War* (Pl. 4) in which Minerva, the goddess of Wisdom, is shown protecting Pax and her beneficiaries from Mars, the god of War. Rubens also painted for himself a *Landscape with St. George and the Dragon* (Pl. 60) which he 'sent home into Flanders to remain there as a monument of his abode and employment' in England: in this picture St. George and the Princess appear to have been given the features of the King and the Queen. This form of compliment was not unusual at the time, but it is surprising that Rubens never painted a direct portrait of Charles: in any case this chivalric fantasy was acquired by the King from the artist a few years later.[116]

The most important outcome of Rubens's stay in London was the confirmation of the tentative proposals made many years earlier that he should decorate the Banqueting Hall (Fig. 66). He probably made a preliminary sketch for this before leaving London in March 1630.[117] This depicted, in a very general way, some of the themes that Rubens was later to develop in detail and was probably discussed with the King and Inigo Jones. No specific programme has survived (or was perhaps ever made) and much of the imagery is of a conventional kind, however magnificent the fantasy with which it was conveyed.[118] Thus in the largest and central (oval) canvas we are shown the *Apotheosis of James I* to whom are attributed the standard virtues ascribed to all rulers–Piety, Wisdom and so on–even if these cannot always be identified with absolute certainty. On the other hand it is clear beyond doubt that Charles and his advisers must have told Rubens what were the principal achievements of his father's reign (and, by implication, of his own) which were to be celebrated in the other two main spaces of the ceiling: the successful cultivation of Peace and Plenty by the King, in the guise of a new Solomon, despite the threats of his enemies and (the only feature of the whole decoration which applied exclusively to a specific political event) the Union of the Crowns which had been brought about by accession of James VI of Scotland to the throne of England as James I.

70 [25]

Here too James is portrayed as a Solomonic figure at whose behest an infant Great Britain is held up by personifications of England and Scotland to be crowned by Minerva. Rubens made a number of oil sketches of the scheme, and the canvases themselves were completed, with the help of assistants, in August 1634, though they were only shipped to London from Antwerp more than a year later.

Long before this, when Rubens was painting Lady Arundel and her retinue in 1620, her husband's secretary had written to him that Rubens's pupil Van Dyck (who was then aged only twenty-one) enjoyed a reputation almost as great as that of his master, but that it was unlikely that he would want to leave Antwerp where he stood to make a good deal of money.[119] The implication seems to be that Arundel might well be interested in trying to lure him to London. Whether or not this was the case, a year later Van Dyck did make his first visit to England: it lasted for only three months, but during the course of it he appears to have found time to paint a portrait of Arundel and, above all, a major picture for the Duke of Buckingham. Nothing is known of any work he did for the King, but he was paid £100 for some unspecified 'special service'.[120]

For the next eleven years Van Dyck was in Antwerp and Italy, but he retained the occasional contact with English patrons, and in 1630 Charles, by now King and owner of the Gonzaga pictures, commissioned from him a *Rinaldo and Armida* (Pl. 61), which proved to be one of his greatest masterpieces. Two years later Van Dyck himself came back to England, invited—so it was said—because Charles was so impressed by the (indeed incomparable) portrait which he had painted of Nicholas Lanier[121]—probably at the very moment when Lanier had arrived in Antwerp bringing with him the Correggios and Raphael from Mantua on the way to London. With one short break, Van Dyck was to remain in England for the rest of his life.

70 [26]

The portraits painted by him of Charles and his family and courtiers are so famous and have for so long been thought of as quintessential representations of a refined and doomed culture at its peak that it will hardly be necessary here to do more than refer very briefly to a few of them in order to set them within the context of prevailing Stuart portraiture as it was to be seen in this country when Van Dyck arrived.

While still Prince of Wales, and during the first few years of his reign, Charles had been portrayed above all by Daniel Mytens, an artist from Delft who came to England, probably on the invitation of Arundel, in about 1618.[122] This was two years after the arrival of Paul van Somer (who, however, had worked more particularly for Charles's parents, James I and Anne of Denmark), and seven years after the failure of Prince Henry to attract Michiel van Miereveld, also from Delft.[123] Charles admired Mytens: he helped him to settle in London and, on his accession, he appointed him 'one of our picture-drawers of our Chamber in ordinarie' for life;[124] moreover, he hung a self-portrait by him (Pl. 62) in the same little room in Whitehall in which were hung others by Rubens and Van Dyck.[125] Yet although Mytens painted many portraits of Charles I and Henrietta Maria (Pls. 63-6) the King did not (as has been pointed out by Sir Oliver Millar) retain any of them for himself. This lack of any personal enthusiasm assumes particular significance when we take into account another observation of Sir Oliver's: many of the portraits of the King and Queen by Van Dyck, to which great prominence was indeed given in the royal palaces, are essentially brilliant reinterpretations of the conventions of state portraiture as they had been devised by Mytens, Paul van Somer and earlier artists. It was not so much novelty of concept as sheer aristocratic distinction of pose and gesture which so delighted the King in such famous works as the 'great piece of our royal self, consort and children' (Pl. 67) placed at the end of the King's Long Gallery.[126] The same applies to a far greater extent to Van Dyck's two superb images of the King on horseback (Pls. 68-9) for which an English precedent of a kind could be said to exist in Robert Peake's dignified but somewhat lifeless representation of *Prince Henry*, though of course the true comparison was with the equestrian portraits of Titian and Rubens (most recently of the Duke of Buckingham) which were certainly familiar to Charles I. It is, however, astonishing that what seems to us to be the most wonderfully imaginative and poetical of all Van Dyck's portraits of the King—the one described as 'Le Roi a la Ciasse' (Pl. 70)—was commissioned, but not apparently retained, by him in any of the royal palaces, and was in fact probably sent as a present to some fortunate but unknown recipient in France where it was not to re-emerge until the eighteenth century.[127] This curious fate is one of the reasons for doubting whether the Van Dyck who was so deeply admired by the King was the artist who captivates us to-day.

264 [129]

306 [132]
273 [279], 316 [283]

For, wonderful as are the best of his English (and especially royal) portraits, the employment by the King of this great artist must finally leave us with a feeling of disappointment – as indeed it did Van Dyck himself. It seems incredible that a patron as in love with Venetian art as was Charles could have commissioned from the painter of *Rinaldo and Armida* only one other figure painting of a similar nature: the ravishing *Cupid and Psyche* (Pl. 71), which probably dates from late in Van Dyck's career and may well have been painted primarily for the Queen's House at Greenwich (although it was kept, unframed, in the King's gallery at Whitehall).[128] Such neglect of Van Dyck's talents as a creator of 'poesie' is inexplicable in the light of present-day taste. Nor is the problem made any easier for us by the information given by the artist's first biographer, Giovan Pietro Bellori, that Van Dyck *did* in fact paint a number of mythologies for the King among them a *Parnassus*, an *Apollo and Marsyas* and some *Bacchanals*.[129] Bellori learned about Van Dyck's English period from Sir Kenelm Digby, and Digby was a friend (and patron) of the artist, as well as a devoted courtier of Charles I with whom he had been in Madrid in 1623. Moreover Digby was in England in the 1630 s, and although what he told Bellori is not always strictly accurate it is hard to believe that he would have given him a whole list of titles of pictures which had never in fact been painted. On the other hand, not a single one of these pictures is recorded in Van der Doort's inventories, in the sale catalogue of the royal collection or in any other source. It seems probable that Bellori's notes may have got somewhat confused, but it is in any case difficult to decide which possibility is the more distressing: the failure of the King to allow Van Dyck to develop a gift which would surely have added a number of masterpieces to his œuvre or the failure of such masterpieces, assuming that they were ever painted, to have survived. That Van Dyck was indeed disappointed by having to concentrate for so long on portraiture is clear enough – not only from the declining quality of some of his later works in the genre, but also from the fact that he himself is reported (once again by Sir Kenelm Digby) to have proposed designing a set of four large tapestries, perhaps to decorate the walls of the Banqueting Hall, which would illustrate the history and ceremonial of the Order of the Garter. This ambitious plan never advanced beyond the stage of a compositional oil sketch,[130] and Van Dyck was equally unsuccessful in his hopes of being given the commission in January 1641 to decorate the Grande Galerie of the Louvre – the task was entrusted to Poussin himself (who never in fact wanted it). Van Dyck returned to England in March, and died in December, one month before the departure of the King from London.

217 [1]

151 [2]

Charles had continued to collect and to commission art almost to the end, although as his political and economic position worsened he was compelled to settle for less than the best. Thus for the decoration of the Queen's House at Greenwich, which was under way in 1639 and 1640, he turned to Jordaens rather than to the much more expensive Rubens for twenty two paintings of *The Story of Psyche* which were to adorn the walls and ceiling of one of the rooms.[131] But even the employment of Jordaens presented complications. Balthasar Gerbier, who was entrusted with supervising the commission, was told to make sure that neither his chief negotiator, the Abbé Scaglia, who lived in Brussels, nor Jordaens himself should know from whom the commission had come, for knowledge that it was a royal command would certainly lead to an increase in price. The Abbé Scaglia agreed 'very willingly and cheerfully' to this humiliating condition, but Gerbier himself was thoroughly dismayed by the notion of employing Jordaens rather than Rubens, who was not only a far greater painter, but also his personal friend: he was indeed concerned that Rubens would be offended once he heard that he had been passed over for the commission. Gerbier therefore did everything he could to get the decision changed. Both artists, he acknowledged, were Dutchmen and well able 'to represent robustrious boistrous drunken-headed imaginary Gods', but Rubens was certainly 'the gentilest in his representations; his landskipps more rare, and all other circumstances more proper', and he tried at first to insist that the difference in price between them was not a significant one. If the commission had to be given to Jordaens, he then argued, it would be desirable to tell him to make 'the faces of the women as beautiful as may be, the figures gracious and svelta'. He then came up with a suggestion for a compromise: perhaps the two artists could collaborate in some way – thus Rubens could produce just the ceiling canvases, for Jordaens might well be relieved not to have to cope with all the difficulties presented by foreshortening. Whatever happened, Gerbier emphasised, it would be advisable to consult Rubens as to the compositions. That all these proposals came to nothing was due not merely to the financial crisis but also to the sudden death of Rubens on 30 May 1640. Even Jordaens had time to complete only eight of his canvases before the Civil War put an end to the whole scheme – and incidentally to payments due to the artist.

137 [4]

It has recently been pointed out[132] how extraordinarily haphazard and improvised was Charles's patronage of the arts. During fifteen years he and his circle had transformed England from the most artistically impoverished to the richest nation in Europe, and yet no new institutional framework had been created and the collections remained attached exclusively to the persons of their owners. And it has also been stressed that, despite appearances, the sums involved in acquiring pictures were relatively modest and can have made little real impact on the King's finances as a whole. But appearances can be as important as realities, and contemporaries did not see matters in this light. When the pictures arrived from Mantua in 1628, Filippo Burlamachi, the King's money-lender, is said to have complained that as a result of the payment of £15,000 which he had had to make he was no longer in a position to equip Buckingham's army which was hoping to raise Richelieu's siege of the Huguenots in La Rochelle.[133] Whether true or not such stories must have spread and they proved to be of real importance when it came to dispersing the King's collection, for despite what is still widely believed it is not at all easy to come across any objections to the collecting of pictures (as distinguished, for example, from the staging of plays) on grounds of religion or morality or politics in these years.[134] It is true that half-hearted threats were made – but fortunately never carried out – to destroy paintings which were in any way 'superstitious', but absolutely nothing was ever done to deface or destroy the wonderful portraits of the King or his family by Van Dyck, Bernini and other masters, even if public monuments were sometimes vandalized. To those who had no feeling for art the one message that was as clear in 1649 as it is to-day was that pictures can make money. And so, very soon indeed after the King's execution, Parliament decided to sell off his collections – and, unlike the situation in Mantua twenty years earlier, on this occasion there were no signs of public regret or protest.

On 1 February 1649 the House of Commons appointed a special committee to take care of the King's possessions and to have them locked up.[135] A few weeks later it was agreed to sell them to pay off the King's debts, reserving only what was necessary for the State (see pp. 15-16). Commissioners were appointed to draw up full inventories, and to put a valuation on the individual items so that these could be sold, for contrary to what is often claimed there was never any question of an auction though it was recognized from the first that prices would be much higher if foreign purchasers showed an interest.

It is hard to exaggerate the skill with which the Commissioners tackled the incredibly difficult problems facing them. Only one of their number could lay claim to any serious knowledge of the works of art to be listed. This was Jan van Belcamp, a minor Dutch painter and copyist, whose qualifications were excellent, though one might detect a certain conflict of interest, or at least of loyalties, in a man some of whose own works were represented in Charles I's collection; who, as one of the King's creditors, was entitled to acquire pictures from it for himself; and who, as Keeper of the King's pictures since 1640, and been responsible for seeing that the collection remained intact during this most alarming phase of its short existence. Van Belcamp had worked under Van der Doort before succeeding him in this post, and it is hard to believe that he did not have access to the inventory of his great predecessor when helping to draw up his own necessarily far more superficial sale catalogue.[136] It has been held against the Commissioners that the prices they attached to the King's pictures were so extraordinarily low, despite Parliament's desperate need for money, that they proved themselves ignorant and inefficient. It is true that foreigners were sometimes astonished at the cheapness of some of the pictures, but in many other cases they were deterred by what they thought of as excessively high valuations. And we must also remember that the glut of works suddenly thrown on to the market was unprecedented, and that not only England, but most of Europe also, had hardly begun to recover from a series of devastating crises and wars.

305 [113]
271 [241-2]

By far the most expensive item in the sale was the Raphael from Mantua, which was valued at £2,000. The Correggio *Allegories of Vice and Virtue* from Isabella d'Este's grotto in Mantua, which had been brought to England by Lanier with the Raphael, were rated at £1,000 each. £500 was asked for Giulio Romano's

72 [57]

Nativity with Saints, but for those with less money to spare Van Dyck's beautiful portrait of Nicholas Lanier was available for £10 (and was not surprisingly bought by the sitter), and the *Head of an Old Woman* by Rembrandt was offered for £4.

Sales to the public began in October 1649, and among the first to take advantage of them was Colonel John Hutchinson who had played an active part in the Civil War on the side of Parliament and had been one of the judges who had passed the death sentence on the King. Thereafter his involvement with politics became more obscure, and in her famous *Memoirs* his wife was to paint a charming picture of him on his country estate, hawking, playing the viol and looking after his 'neat cabinett' of pictures,[137] which included, among many others, Titian's *Venus del Pardo* and *Venus with an Organ Player*, as well as Holbein's *Portrait of Frobenius*. Other army officers did well for themselves also,[138] though Cromwell's choice of what to retain was a very eccentric one with the supreme exceptions of Mantegna's *Triumphs* and Raphael's *Tapestry Cartoons*.

We have seen[139] that the money raised in this way was first to be lent to the Navy and then used to assist those of the King's retinue who had remained, unpaid, in parliamentary London or who had at least not compromised themselves by actively supporting the King; but it soon became apparent that the demand for the King's pictures was simply not great enough to raise the sums needed. It was therefore decided to draw up a list of those who were in the greatest difficulties and to pay them in goods from Charles's estate rather than in cash which would be disbursed only when absolutely essential. The pictures had, of course, already been valued when it had been hoped to sell them all directly, and consequently a royal plumber who was owed £903 for repairs to various palaces and the Tower of London might find himself being given £400 in cash, and then being allowed to choose up to £500 worth of pictures—among them, for instance, Titian's *St. Margaret triumphing over the Devil*.[140] From the government's point of view the plan had obvious attractions, but for the plumber the Titian naturally served only one purpose: that of being transformed into currency as soon as possible.

After the most urgent cases had been dealt with, a Second List of the King's Creditors was drawn up, and particular care was taken to verify the authenticity of individual claims. Even more than with the First List, debts were to be settled in furnishings or works of art rather than in cash, and to cope with this most of the creditors organized themselves into Syndicates (which were called Dividends). Each one was led by one individual who, in collaboration with the Trustees for the Sale, chose what to acquire up to a limit of about £5,000 in the interest of his group. Within each Syndicate the objects were divided among members through the casting of votes: thus in theory each member became the owner of some painting or item of furniture and could do what he liked with it; in practice most members realized that it was not all that easy to turn a Correggio into ready cash, and therefore tended to leave such items with the head of the Syndicate and ask him to arrange for its sale on their behalf, presumably on the basis of a commission. These Syndicates, which were often led by men with some experience of the luxury trade, managed to acquire some of the great masterpieces from the royal collection—partly, no doubt, because such items were too expensive for all but extremely few individuals buying on their own. Thus the Syndicate headed by Thomas Bagley, the King's glazier, was able to acquire not only rich saddles to the value of £2,000 and twenty-two antique statues, but also Correggio's *The Education of Cupid*, which had been valued at £800.

It is impossible here to pursue the results of the royal sales in any detail, but it is worth emphasising one surprising consequence of the procedures which had been decided on by Parliament. For the very first (and for the very last) time a huge range of great artistic masterpieces was widely distributed among the ordinary citizens of England. Had matters rested there the whole course of this country's aesthetic experience might well have been irrevocably changed. But, of course, matters did not rest there. Within four years Colonel Hutchinson was letting it be known that he was so attached to Titian's so-called *Venus del Pardo* (which had cost him £600) that he did not want to part with it; but that if he were offered £7,000—exactly the sum, so he claimed, that he had paid for it—he would be prepared to sell the picture to M. de Bordeaux, Cardinal Mazarin's representative in England.[141] A profit of eleven hundred per cent was too great to resist—and very few indeed of the new breed of art collectors, which had come into being so suddenly after 1649, even tried to hold on to their possessions in the face of temptations of this order. Already in August 1653 the Council of State had instructed the Commissioners of Customs 'to permit the Spanish ambassador to

70 [26]
265 [156]

310 [184], 299 [17]
260 [66]

186 [–], 72 [61]

316 [287]

323 [20]

export, free of duty, twenty-four chests of pictures, hangings and household stuff' for his own use. [142]

It is true that, after the Restoration of the Monarchy in 1660, such works of art from the former royal palaces as still remained in England (although they were not many or of the very highest quality compared to what had once been in them) were taken back to Whitehall – where many were to be destroyed by fire in 1697 – but it is also true that the shipping across the Channel of those twenty-four chests marks the symbolic conclusion of Charles I's collection of paintings which had first come into existence not much more than twenty years earlier.

Notes

1. C. V. Wedgwood, *The Trial of Charles I* (London, 1967), pp. 213-4.

2. See below, Note 118.

3. See, for example, the opinion of it from Charles II's reign quoted on p. 51 (Note 55).

4. For this whole section see *Van der Doort's Catalogue*. Some items had changed location by the time the sale inventories were compiled: Van der Doort's catalogue reflects more accurately the disposition of the pictures during the King's lifetime.

5. In the *Inventories* (p. 269 [203]) the picture is listed at St. James's.

6. On Lanier see p. 391, below.

7. *Van der Doort's Catalogue*, p. 15 [5].

8. V. Carduchi, *Dialogos de la Pintura* (Madrid, 1933), p. 155ᵛ.

9. In the *Inventories* (p. 206 [337]) at Hampton Court.

10. In the *Inventories* (p. 264 [130]) at St. James's.

11. In the *Inventories* (p. 267 [181]) at St. James's.

12. Not all these portraits can now be traced with certainty: the Van Dyck *Henrietta Maria* is in the Royal Collection; the Poelenburgh *Children of the King of Bohemia* is in the Museum of Fine Arts, Budapest; the Honthorst *Duke of Buckingham with his wife and children* is in the Royal Collection.

13. In the *Inventories* (p. 205 [326]) at Hampton Court.

14. In none of these cases is it certain which version of these paintings was owned by Charles.

15. This picture is now in the Musée du Louvre. A. Brejon de Lavergnée (*L'inventaire Le Brun de 1683. La collection des tableaux de Louis XIV* (Paris, 1987), pp. 139-40, no. 62) discusses its earlier history in some detail, but Sainsbury's dating to 'about 1614' of the 'Note given me by James Bapᵗᵃ Cresentio, touching pictures' (W.N. Sainsbury, *Original Unpublished Papers Illustrative of the Life of Sir Peter Paul Rubens* (London, 1859), pp. 354-5) is surely much too early, and it is extremely unlikely that — as this would imply and as Brejon states — the picture was acquired for James I rather than Charles I.

16. *Van der Doort's Catalogue*, p. 36.

17. *Van der Doort's Catalogue*, pp. xi, xiii-xvii.

18. For Arundel see N.F.S. Hervey, *The Life, Correspondence and Collections of Thomas Howard, Earl of Arundel* (Cambridge, 1921); D. Howarth, *Lord Arundel and his Circle* (London and New Haven, 1985) and Ashmolean Museum, Oxford, *Patronage and Collecting in the Seventeenth Century: Thomas Howard, Earl of Arundel* (Oxford, 1985-6).

19. Now in the Statnzamek, Kromeriz (Kremsier).

20. For Buckingham's collection and the part played by Sir Balthasar Gerbier in its formation see especially L. Betcherman, 'The York House collection and its keeper', *Apollo* 92 (1970), pp. 250-9; R. Davies, 'An inventory of the Duke of Buckingham's pictures, etc. at York House in 1635', *Burlington Magazine* 10 (1907), pp. 376-82; G. Martin, 'Rubens and Buckingham's "fayrie ile"', *Burlington Magazine* 108 (1966), pp. 613-18; I.G. Philip, 'Balthazar Gerbier and the Duke of Buckingham's pictures', *Burlington Magazine* 99 (1957), pp. 155-6.

21. Now in the Kunsthistorisches Museum, Vienna.

22. For Hamilton's collection and its sources see E.K. Waterhouse, 'Paintings from Venice for seventeenth-century England: some records of a forgotten transaction', *Italian Studies* 7 (1952), pp. 1-23; S. Savini-Branca, *Il Collezionismo Veneziano nel '600.* (Padua, 1965); and, especially, P. Shakeshaft,' "To much bewiched with thoes intysing things": the letters of James, third Marquis of Hamilton and Basil, Viscount Feilding, concerning collecting in Venice 1635-1639', *Burlington Magazine* 128 (1986), pp. 114-32.

23. All these pictures are now in the Kunsthistorisches Museum, Vienna.

24. Now in the Kunsthistorisches Museum, Vienna where it is usually attributed to Giulio Romano following a design by Raphael.

25. For this whole section concerning the contents of Prince Henry's art collection, see T.V. Wilks, *The Court Culture of Prince Henry and his Circle, 1603-1613*, unpublished D. Phil. thesis (Oxford University, 1988). I am most grateful to Dr Wilks for allowing me to draw on the researches of his work.

26. J. Steegman, 'Two unpublished paintings from Charles I's collection', *Burlington Magazine* 99 (1957), pp. 379-90.

27. Now in the Alte Pinakothek, Munich.

28. For all this episode see Sainsbury, op. cit. (Note 15), pp. 57-61.

29. In the *Inventories* (p. 272 [250]) it is back at St. James's. See O. Millar, *The Age of Charles I: Painting in England, 1620-1649* (London, 1972), p. 22 no. 15.

30. Letter to Valavez of 10 January 1625.

31. Sainsbury, op. cit. (Note 15), p. 58.

32. Ibid., p. 355 (where, however, the suggestion is made that the pictures belonged to James I). The date of this well-known list presents many problems. The reference in it to a portrait of 'The Emperor at whole length by Titian' has suggested to many scholars that the document must have been drawn up after Charles's return from Madrid, on the assumption that the Titian is the *Charles V with a Hound*, now in the Prado. On the other hand, many major pictures which we know to have belonged to the Prince at that date are not mentioned at all, and the portrait of the Emperor may well have been a copy. I prefer to date the list somewhat earlier.

33. Millar, op. cit. (Note 29), p. 21.

34. See Wilks, op. cit. (Note 25).

35. See V. Carduchi, op. cit. (Note 8), p. 156ʳ.

36. Ibid., p. 156ᵛ.

37. Ibid., p. 22ʳ.

38. See references in O. Millar, *The Queen's Pictures* (London, 1970), p. 226 [Chapter 3, note 7] and E. Harris, 'Velázquez and Charles I', *Journal of the Warburg and Courtauld Institutes* 30 (1967), pp. 414-19.

39. J. Shearman, *Raphael's Cartoons in the Collection of Her Majesty the Queen and the Tapestries for the Sistine Chapel* (London, 1972), pp. 145-7.

40. C.C. Malvasia, *La Felsina Pittrice* (Bologna, 1841), II, p. 261.

41. D. Mahon, 'Guercino's paintings of Semiramis', *Art Bulletin* 31 (1949), p. 221, note 41.

42. For all references to Gentileschi's paintings in England see W. Bissell, *Orazio Gentileschi and the Poetic Tradition in Caravaggesque Painting* (University Park and London, 1981).

43. Now in the Prado, Madrid.

44. Sainsbury, op. cit. (Note 15), pp. 311-13.

45. Ibid., p. 321.

46. Ibid., p. 320.

47. Unless otherwise indicated all references to the Gonzaga collection and its dispersal are taken from A. Luzio, *La Galleria dei Gonzaga venduta all' Inghilterra nel 1627-28* (Rome, 1913), and D. Chambers and J. Martineau (eds.), *Splendours of the Gonzaga* (London, 1981-2).

48. Luzio, op. cit. (Note 47), pp. 90-1.

49. Ibid., pp. 68-9.

50. Sainsbury, op. cit. (Note 15), pp. 324, 326.

51. Ibid., p. 326.

52. Ibid., p. 325.

53. Ibid., pp. 325, 328.

54. Luzio, op. cit. (Note 47), p. 160.

55. Sainsbury, op. cit. (Note 15), p. 328 – slightly corrected and amended translation; Luzio, op. cit. (Note 47), p. 160.

56. Carduchi, op. cit. (Note 8), p. 18ʳ.

57. R. Wittkower, 'Inigo Jones – "Puritanissimo Fiero"', *Burlington Magazine* 90 (1948), pp. 50-1, and R.W. Lightbown, 'Van Dyck and the purchase of paintings for the English Court', *Burlington Magazine* 111 (1969), pp. 418-21.

58. *Van der Doort's Catalogue*, p. 79 [14]. The Raphael is now in the National Gallery of Art, Washington. The Holbein drawings returned to the Royal Collection at some later date.

59. Lightbown, op. cit. (Note 57).

60. See J. Rowlands, *The Paintings of Hans Holbein the Younger. Complete Edition* (Oxford, 1985), pp. 223-4, nos. L13 A and L13 B. These Holbeins were subsequently destroyed.

61. For the history of this picture, now in the J. Paul Getty Museum, Malibu, see B.B. Fredericksen. 'E cosi desio me mena', *J. Paul Getty Museum Journal* (1982), pp. 21-38. Rowlands, op. cit. (Note 60), p. 238, no. R47, rejects the attribution to Holbein.

62. See E. Foucart-Walter, *Les peintures de Hans Holbein le Jeune au Louvre* (Paris, 1984), pp. 72-3.

63. *Van der Doort's Catalogue*, p. 89 [71]. The Titian can no longer be traced, and the Leonardo is now back in the Louvre.

64. Ibid., p. 161 [11].

65. Ibid., p. 14 [1].

66. Ibid., p. 22 [15]. The picture, now in the Royal Collection, is described as a 'competent but stiff copy' of a Titian in the Kunsthistorisches Museum in Vienna: see J. Shearman, *The Early Italian Pictures in the Collection of Her Majesty The Queen* (Cambridge, 1983), p. 259, no. 274.

67. *Van der Doort's Catalogue*, p. 48 [32]. This picture cannot now be traced: see M. Levey, *The Later Italian Pictures in the Collection of Her Majesty the Queen* (London, 1964), p. 68.

68. *Van der Doort's Catalogue*, p. 15 [4]. This picture, in the Royal Collection, is described as a partial copy of a lost *Venus disrobing* by Titian (Shearman, op. cit. (Note 66), p. 274. no. 297; see also H.E. Wethey, *The Paintings of Titian. Complete Edition* (London, 1975), III, p. 234, L-II.

69. Ibid., p. 59, no. 98. The whereabouts of this picture are uncertain.

70. See Millar, op. cit. (Note 38), p. 46, for the label on the back of this picture.

71. Shakeshaft, op. cit. (Note 22), p. 124, letter xxi.

72. *Van der Doort's Catalogue*, p. 79 [15]. For this picture, now attributed to Catena, see Millar, op. cit. (Note 38), p. 227 [Chapter 3, note 17].

73. *Van der Doort's Catalogue*, p. 79 [15].

74. Ibid., p. 125 [46].

75. Ibid., pp. 68 [30] and 159 [11].

76. F. Springell, *Connoisseur and Diplomat – The Earl of Arundel's Embassy to Germany in 1636* (London, 1963), p. 264. This picture cannot now be traced.

77. Hervey, op. cit. (Note 18), p. 399.

78. See L. Campbell, *The Early Flemish Pictures in the Collection of Her Majesty the Queen* (London, 1985), pp. xxxviii-xxxix. Both pictures are now in the Kunsthistorisches Museum, Vienna.

79. *Van Der Doort's Catalogue*, p. 86 [51] and p. 90 [76]. For Cranach's treatments of the theme see M. Friedlander and J. Rosenberg, *The Paintings of Lucas Cranach* (New York, 1978).

80. Campbell, op. cit. (Note 78), p. xxxix-xl.

81. F. Haskell. *Patrons and Painters* 2nd edn. (London and New Haven, 1980), pp. 97-8.

82. J. Richards, ' "His Nowe Magestie" and the English monarchy: the kingship of Charles I before 1640', *Past and Present* 113 (1986), pp. 74-5.

83. *Van der Doort's Catalogue*, pp. 102-6. Also see A.P. Oppé, *English Drawings – Stuart and Georgian Periods – the Collection of His Majesty The King at Windsor Castle* (London, 1950).

84. In the *Inventories* (p. 258 [35]) at St. James's.

85. In the *Inventories* (p. 256 [12]) at St. James's.

86. Wittkower, op. cit. (Note 57), p. 50, note 8.

87. Wethey, op. cit. (Note 68), p. 147. Both pictures are now in the Prado.

88. For this collection see Waterhouse, op. cit. (Note 22), and Savini-Branca, op. cit. (Note 22).

89. Shakeshaft, op. cit. (Note 22), p. 125, letter xxvi.

90. B. Reade, 'William Frizell and the royal collection', *Burlington Magazine* 89 (1947), pp. 70-5.

91. See Shearman, op. cit. (Note 66), pp. 196-200, nos. 198-205.

92. This picture is now attributed to Francesco Vecellio (ibid., p. 278, no. 303).

93. Ibid., p. 236, no. 253.

94. *Van der Doort's Catalogue*, p. 181 [12]; Levey, op. cit. (Note 67), p. 69, no. 424.

95. C. White, *The Dutch Pictures in the Collection of Her Majesty the Queen* (Cambridge, 1982), p. xxxv.

96. See Campbell, op. cit. (Note 78), p. 51, no. 33.

97. Now attributed to Aertgen van Leyden: see White, op. cit. (Note 95), p. xxxv.

98. Ibid., pp. xxxvi-xxxvii.

99. Wittkower, op. cit. (Note 57), p. 50.

100. Ibid.

101. Levey, op. cit. (Note 67), pp. 18-19.

102. Wittkower, op. cit. (Note 57).

103. Now attributed to Domenico Puligo: see Shearman, op. cit. (Note 66), p. 205, no. 213.

104. These are perhaps the *Diligence* and the *Fame*, now in the Royal Collection, which were attributed by Cardinal Barberini himself to Garofano and are now believed to be by two different North Italian artists: see Shearman, op. cit. (Note 66), pp. 164-5, nos. 162-3.

105. Now believed to be by Dosso Dossi (or a good copy of a picture by him): ibid., p. 91, no. 83.

106. Wittkower, op. cit. (Note 57).

107. Levey, op. cit. (Note 67), pp. 18-19, and 51-2, no. 352.

108. For this whole episode, see S. Madocks, ' "Trop de beautez découvertes" – new light on Guido Reni's late "Bacchus and Ariadne" ', *Burlington Magazine* 126 (1984), pp. 544-7.

109. The picture was subsequently destroyed in France, but its appearance is known through an engraving.

110. White, op. cit. (Note 95), p. xxiv.

111. Sainsbury, op. cit. (Note 15), pp. 291-2.

112. See *Van der Doort's Catalogue*, p. 172 [6]; and White, op. cit. (Note 95), pp. 53-6, no. 74.

113. See White, op. cit. (Note 95), pp. xxvi-xxvii and fig. 4.

114. This was later destroyed by fire, but an oil sketch survives at the Kimbell Art Museum: see J.S. Held, *The Oil Sketches of Peter Paul Rubens* (Princeton, 1980), I, pp. 393-5, no. 292.

115. Now in the Isabella Stewart Gardner Museum, Boston.

116. See Millar, op. cit. (Note 29), pp. 56-7, no. 84.

117. Held, op. cit. (Note 114), I, pp. 187-210.

118. The most recent discussion of the iconography of the ceiling is that by Roy Strong, *Britannia Triumphans. Inigo Jones, Rubens and Whitehall Palace* (London, 1980) (with reference to the earlier literature). I have relied heavily on this, but – as will become clear – I have not been able to accept all of Strong's conclusions.

119. Hervey, op. cit. (Note 18), p. 175.

120. O. Millar, *Van Dyck in England* (London, 1982), p. 14.

121. W.H. Carpenter, *Pictorial Notices: consisting of a Memoir of Sir Anthony van Dyck* (London, 1844), pp. 22-3, and Millar, op. cit. (Note 120), pp. 45-6, no. 6.

122. O. Millar, *The Tudor, Stuart and Early Georgian Pictures in the Collection of Her Majesty The Queen* (London, 1963), p. 84.

123. Wilks, op. cit. (Note 25); White, op. cit. (Note 95), p. xvi.

124. Millar, op. cit. (Note 122), p. 84. The self-portrait is catalogued at St. James's in the *Inventories*.

125. *Van der Doort's Catalogue*, pp. 37-8.

126. Millar, op. cit. (Note 120), pp. 46-7, no. 7. The picture is now in the Royal Collection.

127. Now in the Louvre. Van Dyck's list was first published by Carpenter, op. cit. (Note 121), pp. 66-9.

128. Listed in the *Inventories* (p. 217 [1]) at Wimbledon House. Millar, op. cit. (Note 120), pp. 97-8, no. 58.

129. G.P. Bellori. *Le Vite de' Pittori, Scultori e Architetti Moderni* (Turin, 1976), p. 281.

130. Millar, op. cit. (Note 120), pp. 86-7, no. 43.

131. For this whole episode see the documents in Sainsbury, op. cit. (Note 15), pp. 211-30 and R.-A. d'Hulst, *Jacob Jordaens* (London, 1982), p. 26.

132. M. Smuts, 'The political failure of Stuart cultural patronage', in G.F. Lytle and S. Orgel (eds.), *Patronage in the Renaissance* (Princeton, 1981), pp. 165-87.

133. Chambers and Martineau, op. cit. (Note 47), p. 99.

134. But for the comments of William Prynne, see Millar, op. cit. (Note 38), p. 53.

135. For all this section see Millar, op. cit. (Note 29), and W.L.F. Nuttall, 'King Charles I's pictures and the Commonwealth sale', *Apollo* 82 (1965), pp. 302-9.

136. Though Sir Oliver Millar, in *Inventories*, p. xviii, points out that 'there is no evidence that the Trustees had access to any of Van der Doort's manuscripts'.

137. L. Hutchinson, *Memoirs of the Life of Colonel Hutchinson, Governor of Nottingham Castle and Town* (London, 1806), p. 334.

138. Such as, for instance, Colonel Webb and – more surprisingly – Colonel Wootton, who was a Leveller.

139. See above, p. 50 (Note 3).

140. See, for instance, John Emery (Nuttall, op. cit. (Note 135), p. 306). The picture is now in the Prado.

141. G.-J. Cosnac, *Les Richesses du Palais Mazarin* (Paris, 1885), pp. 189-98, 200-3.

142. *Inventories*, p. xxii.

6   Charles I and the Art of the Goldsmith

Ronald Lightbown

Marginal numerals refer to page and entry numbers in the *Inventories* (see p. 11)

Goldsmith's work was for the seventeenth century still an art in which beauty of form and ornament and skill of hand in the various techniques of the goldsmith – chasing, engraving, casting – were highly valued by patrons. To understand the taste of Charles I in silver we must first see what a departure it was from the taste of his predecessors. In the sixteenth and seventeenth centuries royal plate still essentially retained its two medieval functions. On the one hand it was required for household use – in eating at table, for the service of drink, for the washing of the hands before and after meals, for the toilet. And on the other it was required for display. From the fifteenth century onwards it had become the custom to range rich plate on rows of shelves on a cupboard of estate. The greater the number of shelves, the richer and the more elaborate the plate that was crowded upon them, the more complete the satisfaction of the spectators with these shining proofs of the prince's wealth and magnificence. There were besides certain kinds of precious materials, exotic curiosities and rarities that were traditionally mounted in silver or gold as cups and vessels for just such shows of magnificence – ostrich eggs, coconuts, nautilus shells, Chinese porcelain, crystal, hardstones, alabaster, mother-of-pearl – in order to give them a recognizable form. These were all accumulated in the royal Jewel House at the Tower, where they served several other purposes. For besides being an indispensable part of royal household life and royal display, plate and jewels were required for issue to members of the royal family, for issue to ambassadors going abroad, and for presents to visitors of importance such as foreign ambassadors or foreign princes visiting England.[1]

The sixteenth century was a luxury-loving age, and richness of materials and of design and ornament came more and more to please its taste in plate as in other forms of art. Travellers in the late sixteenth century admired in the English royal palaces many sumptuous objects made or decorated with silver that must have been monuments of Late Mannerist virtuosity of form. In 1597 for instance, the young Bohemian traveller, Baron Waldstein, admired in Whitehall three globes, a ship made of gold and silver with an awning woven of gold thread and silk, a sundial in the form of an elephant, caskets of mother-of-pearl.[2] The impression is of curiosities, of rarities, of intricately wrought show-pieces, in which richness of material was married to complexity of form. James I, though he took steps to declare certain jewels inalienable heirlooms of the crown, was obliged in the pursuit of his foreign policy to give away many important pieces of the royal plate.[3] Yet although he had drawings made of the splendid pieces of goldsmith's work presented as gifts to the Spanish ambassador Don Juan Fernandez de Frias and his suite on the conclusion of the Treaty of London in 1604 in order to have replicas made of them, there is no evidence that he had anything more than a conventional taste in goldsmith's work. It is true that in a warrant of 7 May 1608 ordering his Lord Treasurer to fill the gaps in the royal collection of plate his Spanish presents had created by accepting pieces different in design from the pieces given away, he commands 'let nothinge be omitted either in the curiousnes of the workmanshipp or quantitie of the peces tht may adde either grace or bewtie unto them'. But in the end what he seems to have acquired as replacements were massy pieces decorated with devices and symbols such as thistles and marigolds, in a heavy heraldic taste.[4] Shortly after his accession, pressed by his financial commitments to the King of Denmark, Charles disposed in 1626 of much or all of the plate he had inherited from his father that was used for display in 'his Majestye's great gilt cupboard of estate' to his royal goldsmith John Acton.[5] It was Acton who had the duty of maintenance of the royal plate, but there is no record of his receiving any commission for goldsmith's work, at any rate of importance, beyond the very routine services of repair, refurbishment and replacement which his office of royal goldsmith required. It is quite clear that Charles had no taste for the dull magnificences which had contented his father and which maintained in Late Mannerist guise traditions in the forms and ornamentation of plate that went back to the fifteenth century and even earlier.

The styles of goldsmith's work in which Charles was interested, the Late Mannerist auricular style of Utrecht and the Baroque classicism of Antwerp, were very different. To begin with, in contrast with Jacobean goldsmith's work, they were strikingly modern. The auricular style was the product of some of the most sophisticated court workshops of the late sixteenth century, those which the Emperor Rudolf II established at his court in Prague. There can be no doubt that during the second half of the sixteenth century the impetus of stylistic innovation in goldsmith's work passed from Italy to the Netherlands and Germany. However it was in High Renaissance Italy that classical forms and ornaments had first been applied to the traditional types of ceremonial plate inherited from the Middle Ages – the ewer and basin, the salt, the standing-bowls now called *tazze*, which were used for handing round sweetmeats. Because the application of these novel forms and ornaments required more knowledge of the antique than was usually possessed by goldsmiths trained in the Gothic tradition, we find that designs for plate in the new style were now often first commissioned from painters. Mantegna, Raphael, Giulio Romano all designed plate for princes and cardinals. This also became the practice in the North, where we find designs for plate made among other artists by Dürer and Holbein. As painters of this sort were not quite so hide-bound in their designs by workshop tradition as goldsmiths, the consequence was a liberation of the fancy in the shapes and ornaments of plate which stimulated an ever greater freedom and sophistication of design and ornament.[6]

Since many elaborate pieces were intended solely for display, practicality of form was in any case a secondary consideration in their design. For princes and great men goldsmith's work was still the form of art in which their magnificence and taste could be most easily and boldly advertised, and their delight in the beauty and richness of its materials and workmanship was not checked by any puritanism or sobriety, save in exceptional cases. Under the stylistic influence of Mannerism, whether that of Fontainebleau, of Antwerp, of Italy or Germany, ever greater capriciousness of form and ornament was applied to the design of plate, so that works of extreme elaboration were executed in which the essential shape of a vessel became little more than a theme for elegant variations. Yet in consonance with the Mannerist theory of congruity, a theme related to function was still frequently observed through all these complexities of design and ornament: for instance mythological figures and motifs associated with water were often chosen for the decoration of ewers and basins. Because such pieces were conceived either to impress the eye at a feast or to delight it in a princely cabinet by their rarity of fancy and intricacy of form, the impulse of style throughout the later sixteenth century and into the early seventeenth was always in the direction of further innovation and refinement.

At the court of Rudolf II Late Mannerism entered into its ultimate phase of sophisticated variation on set formal themes. Although an intricate richness of surface decoration is one of the characteristics of Late Mannerist goldsmith's work, as of other types of Late Mannerist decorative art, nevertheless it had always employed ornament as a composition of separately realized motifs, whose articulation, if not immediately distinct on a crowded surface, was nevertheless clear to the more closely inspecting eye. Under some impulse whose exact place of origin is still controversial but was either the Netherlands or Prague, a stylistic movement began for the interfusion of ornamental forms, for their dissolution into fleshy shapes that suggested, rather than figured such favourite motifs as grotesque masks, scrolls, and lobes. In place of the cherished Renaissance principle of symmetry these audacities substituted an asymmetry that became ever more pronounced as they developed into a self-sufficient style. This style, known as auricular because of an imaginary relationship between its flowing, abstract, scrolling, dimpling forms and the cartilaginous forms of the ear, was initially applied purely to ornament. It was first used in Rudolf's workshops by the influential goldsmith Adam Schweinberger, who worked in Prague from 1587 until 1603. In Schweinberger's surviving works the style is perhaps best described as proto-auricular and its fuller development was the work of two Dutchmen who rank among the greatest goldsmiths of Late Renaissance Europe, Paul van Vianen of Utrecht, and his elder brother Adam.[7]

Paul van Vianen, the first of the two brothers to take up the style, was born *c*.1570. The family was one of goldsmiths, and Willem Eerstensz of Vianen, a small village near Utrecht, the father of the two brothers, was well-known in his day. According to Joachim von Sandrart, the seventeenth-century historian of German and Netherlandish art, Adam and Paul were taught by their father to

Figure 75   Adam van Vianen: *cup and cover,* silver gilt, 1614. Height 25.5cm. Photograph courtesy of National Museums of Scotland. The cup and cover are now in the Rijksmuseum, Amsterdam.

draw, model in wax and work in silver. But it seems that in fact Paul was trained by another goldsmith of Utrecht, Bruno Elhardz van Leyenberch. He then went to France, and from France in all probability to Rome in order to study from the antique. Paul was already working for the Electoral court at Munich in 1596, but in 1601 he moved to the court of the Archbishop of Salzburg, Wolf Dietrich von Raitenau, a patron of art and especially of goldsmiths. In December 1603 he entered the service of the Emperor Rudolf II in Prague as a court goldsmith and remained in it until his death in 1613. Paul's earlier works in the auricular style, such as a silver tazza of 1607 now in the Rijksmuseum, essentially apply auricular ornament to conventionally designed vessels, dissolving the rigid profiles of knop and foot, rather than shaping them into auricular forms. His later works, like the great ewer of 1613, also in the Rijksmuseum, still observe this principle, but with increasing resolution of individual parts, as in the foot and lip and handle of the ewer, into sinuously flowing surfaces and scrolls whose asymmetrical caprice subordinates all expression of the function to the creation of a decorative complexity of abstract ornamental forms.

It was Paul's brother Adam (*c.*1569-1627) who developed these stylistic premises into a complete plastic fullness, in which the shape of a whole vessel rather than of single parts became totally an expression of the auricular style (*cf*. Fig. 75). In one sense Adam's invention remained tied to the shapes that the Renaissance had evolved for the classic showpieces of sixteenth-century plate – the ewer, the basin, the tazza, the salt. For the intention of his art was to play on these shapes, sometimes creating from them forms of fanciful strangeness, sometimes effects of grotesque humour. Rigid definition of the separate parts of such vessels is almost completely abandoned in favour of an overall unity, animated by contours of softly capricious irregularity, in which scroll-forms or other less definite motifs suddenly curl into lobe-like shapes, and swell into unexpected curves. The definition of decorative motifs is equally elusive in its play between suggestion and abstraction. Thus apparently abstract swirls of ornament may suddenly metamorphose themselves into a huge mask, perceived to be such only because of two eyes that lower to either side of a ridge.

What Adam seeks is essentially an extreme mobility of elision, whose inspiration Sandrart well defines as a search for 'chimerical', that is to say for unsubstantial, shifting, monstrous, non-realistic effects. Adam, he says, earned as great a reputation as his brother 'because from a single mass of silver by the skill of his hammer he could happily ornament ewers, basins, salts, knife-handles and other things of the same kind, that were purchased not only in Amsterdam, but throughout all Holland'.[8] In the full plastic form given to it by Adam, the auricular style remained essentially a Dutch style. Purely as ornament, however, it had a strong vogue in Germany, France and England throughout the middle decades of the seventeenth century and was much used in the ornamentation of works in other media, such as the decorative carved woodwork of picture frames. As we shall see, under Charles's patronage the style was to be carried in the 1630s in its full form to England by Adam's son Christian, but here it remained a court style, rather than becoming a general fashion.

Before discussing Christian van Vianen and his work at Charles's court however, we must return to Paul and another aspect of the art of the Van Vianens, more especially of Paul, their production of the delicate small reliefs often known as plaquettes. Adam, according to Sandrart, preferred to work in the round, whereas 'Paul took especial delight in human figures and in histories, and made his journey to Rome in order to penetrate to the deepest knowledge in these by studying from the works of the ancients'. In Rome he acquired such skill 'that by his hammer he wrought from single pieces of silver great vessels, most beautiful ewers and other things of this kind, and made among other things the Bath of Diana with naked nymphs and various animals and fitting landscapes, all with perfect expression, correctest drawing and wonderful beauty'. By this work he earned great praise which, says Sandrart, 'is confirmed by his figures of the Blessed Virgin, and various poetical fables, and especially his Argus, with other designs cast by his hand'.[9]

Paul's speciality was in fact the production of silver reliefs by chasing, that is by the goldsmith's technique of raising the design by the use of a hammer. His skill in figure-subjects in this technique attained to the most refined virtuosity in the subtle modulation of sculptural planes: his hammer raises a principal figure in smooth bold high relief with graceful modelling of musculature, a subordinate figure in lesser relief and a setting in exquisitely sharp delicacy of low relief, even to the light billows of cloud in the sky. Paul van Vianen's great sensitivity to landscape – also evident in his drawings – gives a curiously poetical and atmospheric suggestiveness to his subject compositions, more especially to those from his years in Prague, which is enhanced by the soft glitter of the silver that is their medium. In counterpoise a direct sensuality, also typical of the court art of Prague, on occasion emerges. Chased silver was far more highly valued in the seventeenth century than cast silver, no doubt because the age appreciated the technique's directness of skill. In 1624 for instance, Lady Carleton, wife of Sir Dudley Carleton, Charles I's ambassador to Holland, was sent to Flushing to make purchases from a Spanish vessel belonging to the Viceroy of Naples which had been taken as a prize. She writes to her husband of '2 delicate basiones they saye of hammered worke but I thinke they are but cast'.[10]

Charles bought or acquired a number of silver and bronze reliefs by Paul van Vianen, which in 1639 were set round the walls of his new cabinet in Whitehall.[11] Charles's seven bronze reliefs were all circular plaquettes in black frames, representing stories from Ovid's *Metamorphoses*, always a favourite source of decorative mythological subjects in Mannerist and Baroque art. Two were evidently a pair – Phaeton kneeling before his father Phoebus who is seated on his throne, and its companion piece of the Fall of Phaeton, with horses and chariot tumbling from the clouds. Four reliefs depicted the story of Mercury, Argus and Io – Jupiter transforming his mistress the nymph Io into a cow in order to protect her from the jealousy of Juno, Mercury despatched by Jupiter to cut off the head of Argus, Mercury piping Argus asleep, and finally Mercury cutting off Argus's head. A seventh relief showed the jealous Juno beating the nymph Callisto, another of Jupiter's loves, and transforming her into a bear.

These bronze reliefs had all been given to Charles at various times in the three years before 1635 by that experienced diplomat, his Chancellor of the Exchequer, Lord Cottington. It is probable that they were casts or adaptations from reliefs by Paul van Vianen, rather than original works by him. Such copies were produced early: thus there is a copy in bronze signed *CB* in the Deutsches Museum, Berlin, of Paul's famous silver relief of the sleeping Argus, executed in

Figure 76 Paul van Vianen: *plaquette,* silver, signed and dated 1610. Argus, charmed by Mercury, falls asleep, and Mercury approaches to kill him; in the background, Io transformed into a cow. 13.2 × 15.6cm. Rijksmuseum, Amsterdam.

1610, now in the Rijksmuseum (Fig. 76).[12] We can form an image of others either from lead versions or from actual silver plaquettes by Paul van Vianen: Mercury piping to Argus and Mercury with the head of Argus are figured in two companion lead plaquettes which appear to be early works and in two silver plaquettes of 1606. A series of four lead plaquettes made in Prague (Figs. 77-9) may well represent the compositions that belonged to Charles, since they figure Jupiter and Io, Jupiter ordering Mercury to descend to earth to kill Argus, Mercury piping Argus to sleep, and Mercury after he has slain Argus. Similarly the composition of Juno chastising Callisto and transforming her into a bear is recorded in a lead plaquette in the Rijksmuseum (Fig. 80). Charles appears to have owned its pendant, in which Jupiter, disguised as Diana, seduces Callisto.[13]

Subjects of this kind, with their direct or romantic Ovidian eroticism, delighted the sophisticated taste of the age for an elegant sensuality. But Paul van Vianen also executed reliefs in which the religious fervour that was the counterpoint to this sensuality was figured with the same elegance of style. Charles owned one of these, of a Virgin and Child in the clouds, with a female saint kneeling below, holding a tooth in pincers, evidently St. Apollonia. It was framed, like most such precious silver reliefs, in a frame of black ebony and had been bought by Charles himself. Such reliefs were highly typical of Counter-Reformation devotional taste, which used the same costly materials of ebony and silver, so popular for the caskets and other appurtenances of wealthy domestic life, for devotional ends, to which their sobriety and discretion of richness made them extremely appropriate. Mannerist goldsmith's work of any pretensions is richly gilt: the extreme sophistication of the auricular style is revealed not least in its preference for plain silver, with its greater softness and subtlety of surface when modelled.

From Christian van Vianen, Adam's son, Charles obtained both works in the round and reliefs in the styles practised by his father and by his uncle Paul. Christian was born at Utrecht in 1598, and was Adam's eldest son by his second wife Catherine van Wapenweld. Unlike his father and uncle, he was not an innovator or inventor in matters of style, but was content, in the words of

Figure 77   Paul van Vianen: *plaquette,* lead, *c.* 1608. Jupiter commands Mercury to slay Argus, whom Juno has set to watch the nymph Io, Jupiter's mistress, who has been changed into a cow. Diameter 20.5cm. Rijksmuseum, Amsterdam.

Figure 78.   Paul van Vianen: *plaquette,* lead, *c.* 1608. Mercury piping Argus to sleep. Diameter 17.5cm. Rijksmuseum, Amsterdam.

Figure 79.   Paul van Vianen: *plaquette,* gilt lead, *c.* 1608. Jupiter raises his hand as Juno rises on her peacock car into the sky after changing the nymph Io, Jupiter's mistress, into a cow; in the background, Io fleeing from Jupiter. Diameter 20.5cm. Museum für Angewandte Kunst, Cologne; Clemens Collection.

Figure 80   Paul van Vianen: *plaquette,* lead, *c.* 1608. The jealous Juno chastises Callisto; in the background Arcas prepares to shoot his mother Callisto, changed by Juno into a bear. Diameter 20.5 cm. Rijksmuseum, Amsterdam.

Sandrart, to 'adhere tenaciously in the steps of his father's art'.[14] It was probably the family's European reputation that persuaded Charles to entice him into his service, unless Christian himself came over the water to seek royal patronage, rather as his uncle Paul had sought service at various courts. Charles's growing reputation as a patron and his father's death in 1627 may well have urged him to try his fortune at the English court. The subtlety and refinement of the auricular style as practised by the Van Vianens plainly appealed very considerably to Charles, not least because they were so different from the humdrum or conservative Late Mannerist style of English goldsmith's work. For if Christian was not an innovator, yet he was at his best a most excellent workman in the auricular style. In whatever way he came to Charles's notice, it is certain that he had entered his service by April 1630, when the King's accounts record the grant to him of an annual pension of £30, to be paid quarterly, and to begin from 'Our Lady Day last', in other words from 25 March previous. In the same accounts he was paid £40 'for his Majesty's service'.[15]

It seems however from pieces which bear Christian's mark together with Utrecht marks for 1631 and 1632 that he did not remain long in London on this first visit. But he must have returned here in 1632 or early in 1633. Perhaps he had only been settling up his affairs in Utrecht, for on 30 April 1633 he was paid the large sum of £100 not only for a candlestick he had sold to Charles, but for 'his charges and expenses in removing and transporting himselfe and his family from Utrecht hither'. The candlestick sold to Charles was undoubtedly the silver candlestick by Christian that the King kept in his Cabinet Room at Whitehall as a work of art. It is virtually certain then that it was an elaborate example of the auricular style in the round. The document that records the payment does not make it clear whether Christian had already moved to London or was only preparing to do so – possibly the latter, for it is only from 1634 that he is recorded as living in the house in Chapel Street, by the New Chapel near Tothill's fields, next to the house of the Countess of Brandford where he was to live until 1642.[16] This house seems to have become something of a resort for artists from the Netherlands. Cornelis van Poelenburgh lived there from 1638 to 1641 and the house seems to have been occupied in 1642, after Christian's departure, by the miniaturist Georg Geldorp. Christian was certainly settled in London early in 1634, for in April that year he was paid an advance of £600 to begin work on the altar plate of the Order of the Garter. His pension, however, was renewed only on 26 February 1636.

The altar plate of the Order of the Garter must await discussion until the second half of this chapter, when we come to Charles's association with Anglican church silver. Meanwhile let us see what documents record of Christian's work for Charles. On 16 February 1636 he was given a warrant for the sum of £326. 11s. 6d. for a ewer and basin delivered to Charles on 14 June 1635. They weighed 313 ounces, at 5s. 6d. the ounce, exclusive of the fashion and cases, and were 'beaten wth the Hammer', that is chased. Christian received a later payment of £156 for them on 29 June. The sum granted by the warrant included the purchase from Christian of a 'Landskipp' by Alexander Keirincx, a Flemish artist who worked for Charles, as well as arrears of pension and a sum towards the expenses of a workshop which Christian was either building or proposing to build. Christian employed a number of workmen; one of them, a certain Levin Brinckmayr, a 'High German', was in prison in December 1640 in the Gatehouse of Westminster and obtained his liberty only on Christian's guarantee that he would leave England within fourteen days.

Christian also made reliefs, probably in large part copies or versions of his uncle Paul's designs, for two of four silver reliefs that he sold Charles in 1637 were identical in subject with two by Paul that we have already encountered. All four were inventoried by Abraham van der Doort as 'don hir'. Two represented Mercury piping Argus asleep and Mercury cutting off Argus's head; in this second subject was also figured Io brought to Juno and Juno setting Argus's eyes in her peacock's tail. The other two reliefs were of the *Judgment of Paris*. In one Mercury pointed out Venus to Paris, while Juno and seven other figures were in the distance. In its companion Mercury pointed to Paris, as he gave Venus the apple. All four were oblong, and measured six inches long by four inches deep. Probably made either for Charles or for a loyal subject were two small silver portraits by Christian of Charles and Henrietta Maria, last seen by Vertue in the late 1730s. He describes them as 'two curious silver embossed oval plates chasd. …both extraordinary high relievo – calld alto-relievo. and finely done. the faces from Vandykes pictures most likely – the ornaments or dress band hair very neat and well finisht in a good Taste – the oval plates about six inches upon the back of each was graved CV'. Small silver portraits of this kind are known to have had a certain currency among the English gentry and nobility – not perhaps surprisingly given the popularity here of the small portrait either as miniature or engraved medallion.

Like so many dependants on royal patronage Christian found it wise to supplement the irregular payments of the court by commissions from other patrons. It is plain that a number of patrons in the court circle shared the King's taste for the conceits and caprices and subtleties of modulation of the auricular style. Christian's work is now known to us only from pieces executed for such patrons, rather than for the King, since all the royal plate was melted down or sold during the Civil War. As a royal servant Christian appears not to have had to register a mark at Goldsmith's Hall, and it is probable that the only piece from his hands to bear ordinary London hall-marks, those for 1639, was sponsored for him through Goldsmith's Hall by the 'AJ', possibly the assaymaster Alexander Jackson, whose mark it bears. It is a notably large and handsome silver standish (Fig. 81), equipped with holders for candles supported by pairs of addorsed cherubs, and resting on lion feet. It is richly ornamented with cherubs and mythological or festive scenes in relief within auricular cartouches and scrollwork.

The patron for whom he made a unique silver covered bowl, perhaps all that survives from a larger set of plate, is by contrast known. He was Algernon Percy (1602-68) tenth Earl of Northumberland. This bowl can be securely dated between 1636 and 1642 because one of the pair of badges it bears is engraved with an anchor, Algernon's device either as admiral, *Custos Maris* and Governor-General of the Fleet, which he became on 23 March 1636, or as Lord High Admiral of England which he became on 13 April 1638, only to be dismissed on 28 June 1642. The design of the bowl was probably the invention of Christian's father Adam, whose drawings appear to have provided much of Christian's inspiration – indeed he was later to publish a collection of engravings of them at Utrecht in 1650 with the title of *Modelles Artificiels*. True to the auricular style's preference for the lobe, the bowl has a four-lobed form. Each lobe is boldly pronounced, while the spaces between them are decorated with monster masks, and a border of wavy auricular ornament runs round the base of the bowl. The foot is a regular octofoil of lobes, but each lobe has a swelling profile which creates a supple swerve and irregular play of light on its surfaces. Dimpling lobes and masks, reduced to abstractions of scrolls and protuberances, decorate the lid, while the sinuous handles are formed as serpents whose twin heads divide from a neck shaped as an auricular mask. The sophistication of taste represented by the quiet modulations and sliding ripple of surface of such a piece makes the loss of the plate executed by Christian for Charles all the more disastrous.

The other surviving piece certainly executed by Christian during his stay at Charles's court is the magnificent silver basin, signed *C. d. Vianen fecit 16.35*, now in the Victoria and Albert Museum (Fig. 82). Of the few surviving early works from his hand it is the one which best represents the mobile asymmetry which is a cardinal principle of the auricular as a plastic style. Its border uses a favourite auricular motif of two dolphins whose forms emerge from broad asymmetrical curves to form a fountain-head. Across the bowl ripples of water flow with marvellous effectiveness and dexterity of technique, while two sea-monsters struggle in it with a ferocity of naturalism that is already far from the stylizations of Mannerism. The motif is a savage one, for one monster seizes the other as its prey. There is occasionally in the figural imagery of Adam van Vianen a suggestion within the infinitely delicate and subtle play of surface ornament of something either discordantly coarse or as here discordantly fierce, and a taste for such motifs was plainly part of the inheritance of Christian.

With the collapse of Charles's power in 1643 Christian withdrew to Utrecht. He was not the only goldsmith from the Low Countries whom Charles patronized. For if Charles admired artists from the Dutch Netherlands, commissioning paintings from Honthorst and employing Mytens and Poelenburgh and Christian van Vianen, Antwerp, still one of the great artistic capitals of Europe because of Rubens and his circle, also attracted him, for its goldsmith's work as well as for its pictures. The Baroque silver of Antwerp has only recently begun to be studied and published, but pieces in museums or which have passed through the market show that at its best it was magnificent in design and facture. English magnates and Charles himself were always commissioning paintings or negotiating for the purchase of works of art in

Figure 81 Christian van Vianen: *standish,* silver, 1639. Reproduced by courtesy of Messrs Christie, Manson and Woods.

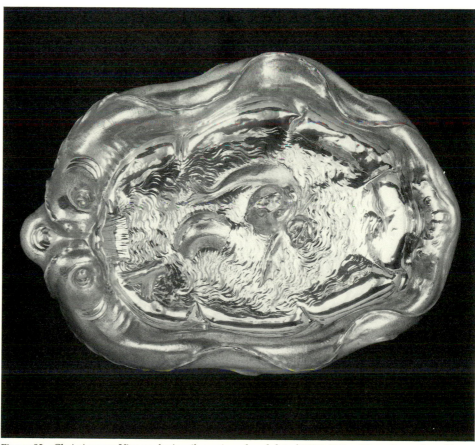

Figure 82 Christian van Vianen: *basin,* silver, signed and dated 1635. 48.5 × 35cm. Reproduced by courtesy of the Board of Trustees of the Victoria and Albert Museum, London.

Antwerp, in this continuing a tradition that went back to the reign of Henry VIII. Among the city's goldsmiths Charles certainly thought highly of Théodore Rogiers, whose name is in this version a Flemish form of the French de Rasier or de Rasières. Théodore was born at Antwerp in March 1602, the son of the goldsmith Rombaut de Rasier. It seems that he became a friend of many of the city's famous painters, including Rubens and Van Dyck, and in 1631 he was admitted into the Gilde de Saint-Luc as a 'dryver' or chaser. For his reputation too was founded on his skill in chasing: the engraving by Clouet after the portrait Van Dyck painted of Rogiers describes him as *caelator in argento*, chaser in silver.[17]

It was in silver that Rogiers chased a ewer and basin which Rubens had designed for Charles I. Rubens's invention survives in two forms, a grisaille painting of the basin in the National Gallery, London, and an engraving by Jacob Neeffs published by Gillis Hendrincx at Antwerp, which shows the basin and one side of the ewer (Fig. 83). The scene on the side of the ewer is repeated in an engraved strip at the bottom, with the addition of the figures and setting that completed it on the other side. The inscription *P. P. Rubens pinxit pro Carolo I magnae Britanniae Franciae et Hiberniae Rege* suggests that it was designed by Rubens for Charles at the King's request.[18] In this Charles was continuing the Renaissance tradition of commissioning a special design from a painter for a work that required a serious knowledge of the antique. It has been rather strangely argued that the basin and ewer were never executed, because they are not mentioned in Van der Doort's inventory of Charles's collection. But then neither are the costly ewer and basin that Christian van Vianen is documented as executing for Charles in 1635, and the presumption must be that this sort of plate for display was listed with other plate and jewels, according to time-honoured practice, and not with the King's pictures and works of art. For those aware that there still remain documents undiscovered or unpublished about art at the Caroline court, not to mention those that are lost, there is also no substantial argument against the ewer and basin to be found in the silence of the published documents. The etching by Neeffs has, it is true, been dated after 1660, when Neeffs, whose date of death is untraced, was still living, because the inscription refers to Charles as Charles I.

All these arguments have little or no plausibility. Why should Neeffs have invented a ewer and basin and published an etching of them as if they had existed? We shall see too that the iconography of ewer and basin does not bear out the strange case brought against them. But first let us see what was figured on them. In spite of its cult of the *capriccio* and the conceit, we saw that an underlying canon of Mannerist art was always some congruity of decoration with function, even in vessels which were purely for display, like these. As so often then with Mannerist ewers and basins, some of the themes of ornament and decoration that Rubens chose were connected with water. In the centre of the bowl is the Birth of Venus, not in the form known as Venus Anadyomene, or Venus rising from the sea, as in Titian's famous picture in Edinburgh, but in the second episode of her birth, that preferred by Roman art, in which her first landing on the shore is depicted. The shore is either that of Cythera or that of Cyprus – antique myths differ as to whether she first landed on the one island or the other. She is attended by three nymphs, probably to be identified as Nereids or the Graces. Above the head of Venus a winged female figure and an Amor hold a garland. These are to be explained as Peitho, the goddess of Persuasion, and Cupid, for the motif was surely suggested by the description in Pausanias of the relief on the base of the statute of Zeus by Phidias at Olympia. In this Eros was shown welcoming Aphrodite as she rose from the sea and Peitho crowning her with a wreath.

Behind, in a motif inspired by Mantegna's famous *Battle of the Sea Gods*, a bearded hippocamp, bearing a nymph on his back blows a conch-shell in sounding triumph and indeed the theme is partly rendered as a Triumph of Venus, resembling Raphael's famous fresco of the *Triumph of Galatea* in the Farnesina. In the border, which is separated from the central scene by an edging of sea-shells, punctuated by foliage at the centre top and a sea urchin in the centre base, Neptune and Amphitrite preside over an urn emptying water which then flows around the border. Swans, Cupids riding sea-horses, nymphs riding dolphins and sea-monsters disport themselves in its stream. A pair of figures, a winged youth and a winged girl in amorous disport occupy a key position in the centre of the base: they figure Cupid and Psyche.

The same festive mythological amorousness animates the figures on the ewer, for they represent scenes from the Judgment of Paris, again as related by Ovid. On one side Jupiter bids a goddess take a garland. Mercury stands behind

Figure 83 *Basin and ewer,* designed by Rubens and executed in silver by Theodore Rogiers of Antwerp for Charles I. Etching by Jacob Neffs, mid-seventeenth-century.

Paris holding up an apple as Paris sits meditatively on a rock, gazing at the rival beauties of the three goddesses, Minerva in front, attended by an owl, Venus in the middle, with Cupid clinging to her leg, and Juno in the rear, attended by her peacock, which is perched on a tree. In the background are the walls, houses and temples of Troy – the judgment took place on Mount Ida, outside Troy. Probably then the river god who sits by his urn among rushes, attended by nymphs, is the personified Scamander, the river that flowed below Troy. On the upper part of the body two putti sit on classical swags, while a third is perched in the spout, which like the handle is formed as classical acanthus stems and foliage. The octofoil foot echoes the watery symbolism of the basin, for on it, supporting or reclining against a low stem that supports the body, are two fish-tailed sea nymphs. The whole, in striking contrast with the subtleties of auricular goldsmiths' work, is full of the robust borrowings from antique art so characteristic of Rubens's classicism.

According to specialists in the art of Rubens the design for the basin and that for the scene on the ewer were not made at the same time. The design for the basin is generally dated to the early 1630s, while that for the scene on the ewer has been related by Julius Held to the *Judgment of Paris* which Rubens began in 1638 for Philip IV of Spain. But this argumentation can concern only the date when Rubens first made the designs from which the scenes on basin and ewer derive: there is no need to suppose that he made entirely novel designs for the two pieces, instead of using or reworking old ones. Held has correctly noticed that the imagery of the basin has nuptial overtones and indeed the theme of the birth of Venus is that of the birth of love, while Cupid and Psyche figure the perfect union in marriage of body and soul. Indeed the presence of Cupid and Psyche in union will hardly allow of any other interpretation of the imagery. Consequently Venus must be intended to figure as the bride, and this is why a garland is to be set on her head, in allusion to the marriage-garland that was placed on the head of brides. What has also been overlooked is that in the context of the basin the theme of the Judgment of Paris, with its compliment to Venus as the most beautiful of all three goddesses, and with its despatch of a garland by Jupiter himself is also nuptial, in that it figures symbolically a compliment to the bride implying her selection as most beautiful by the groom. Presumably then ewer and basin were intended as a magnificent marriage-gift. If the stylistic distinction between the dates of the scenes on basin and ewer is a correct one, presumably the designs for them were made *c.*1639, and in any case before Rubens's death on 20 May 1640. Perhaps then as a bridal gift they never entered Charles's collections at all, but on the other hand several rich basins and ewers are listed in the sale of his goods in 1650.

Charles also owned ten circular chased reliefs by Rogiers which again were probably in a noble classical style. One, of a drunken Bacchus carried by two satyrs with three other satyrs attending, perhaps inspired by the well-known Bacchic engravings of Mantegna, was a gift from his court jeweller Jacques Duart. It was quite large – nine inches in diameter – and another description of it suggests that it may in fact have represented Bacchus led by a male and female satyr with ropes or vine. Another relief, eight inches in diameter, figured Europa and the Bull, with Europa being carried to sea while her waiting women lament on the shore. A third was a pastoral landscape, with a hart, two oxen and a he- and she-goat, followed by a child and a satyr playing bagpipes, with a woman in a landscape behind carrying a basket on her head. A fourth figured a hermaphrodite in a pool beside which were two women and a child, a fifth Pyramus and Thisbe, with Pyramus lying dead by a well, a dog beside him, and a distraught Thisbe approaching.[19]

The ecclesiastical silver that Charles commissioned, and in especial as we shall see, the set of communion plate made for the Feast of the Order of the Garter at St. George's Chapel, Windsor, by Christian van Vianen, was an expression of his own sincere and fervent attachment to the ideals of High Church Anglicanism. It might be expected that Charles, with his love of art, would prefer a movement in the church that favoured the use of art and imagery to the bareness of Puritan austerity. But his preference was not merely one of taste, but an affirmation of a new Anglicanism, whose doctrines in matters of style and imagery were a rejection of the iconoclasm of the Elizabethan past and of contemporary Puritanism. Church plate became in fact a matter of raging controversy under Charles, with one church party flagrantly provoking the other by the form, type, style and decoration of its vessels. What in a museum case or on a church altar may now seem of inoffensive handsomeness was in fact a passionate expression of convictions that we must explore if we are to understand Charles as a patron of plate for use in that church of which he was the Supreme Head.

In opposition to the Puritans, whose ambition was a radical break with the medieval past, High Anglicans saw their church as one that was continuous with the past, but purged of its gross errors of doctrine and practice, such as transubstantiation and the worship of saints and of relics. In particular they remained attached to episcopacy as the best and most proper form of church government. Both movements drew their inspiration from the doctrine and practice of the early Christian church which all were agreed represented the Church as instituted by Christ in its primitive integrity, before the corruptions and errors introduced by Romanism. But whereas the Puritans rested their version of the doctrines and order of church discipline and practice by which Christians ought to live exclusively on what they found in Scripture, the High Anglicans regarded the first centuries of the Church as preserving authentic traditions of how the Church should be governed. Consequently they studied the Greek and Latin Fathers of the first five centuries of the Church for evidence of what they had regarded as lawful.[20]

The general position of the two parties in regard to the use of imagery in churches was irreconcilable. The iconoclasm of the Reformers had found vigorous expression in the *Homilies* which the Elizabethan church published for reading in churches. *An homily against Peril of Idolatry, and superfluous decking of churches* declared uncompromisingly:

the corruption of these latter daies, hath brought into the Church infinite multitudes of images, and the same, with other parts of the Temple also, have decked with gold and silver, painted with colours, set them with stone and pearl, clothed them with silks and precious vestures, fancying untruly that to be the chief decking and adorning of the Temple or house of GOD, and that all people should be the more moved to the due reverence of the same, if all corners thereof were glorious and glistening with gold and precious stones. Whereas indeed they by the said images, and such glorious decking of the Temple, have nothing at all profited such as were wise and of understanding: but have thereby greatly hurt the simple and unwise, occasioning them thereby to commit most horribly idolatry.

Against which the homily alleges 'the most manifest Doctrine of the Scriptures', 'the usage of the Primitive church, which was most pure and incorrupt', and 'the sentences and judgements of the most ancient, learned and godly Doctours of the Church'.

Official Elizabethan doctrine condemned then the lavishing of money on church decorations, and the introduction of images into churches. By this doctrine a virtual proscription of all figural religious art in churches was implied, though not a proscription of all art, or even of all religious subjects. Particular detestation was felt for representations of the Trinity, of God the Father, and of the Holy Ghost, because Scripture says that God is a spirit, whom no man can know, and because of the Second Commandment. And although Christ had put on humanity, since no authentic likeness of him had been preserved, representations of Him in his humanity were equally to be proscribed. Crosses, with or without crucifix figures, and the sign of the Cross were abhorrent. No pardon was of course extended to the images and painted histories of the multitude of saints whom the Reformers discarded as figments of Popery.

Especial horror was felt for sculptured images, whether of stone, wood, gold or silver. The homily recounts how paintings first came notably into the Western church during the fifth century, with the paintings commissioned by St. Paulinus, Bishop of Nola, and by others to instruct their unlettered congregations.

And so by this example came in painting, and afterward Images of Timber and Stone, and other matter, into the Churches of Christians. Now and ye well consider this beginning, men are not so ready to worship a picture on a wall, or in a window, as an imbossed and gilt Image, set with pearl and stone. And a process of story, painted with the gestures and actions of many persons, hath another use in it, than one dumb idol or image standing by itself. But from learning by painted stories, it came little by little to idolatry.

In opposition to this radical rejection of a thousand years of church art, in favour of primitive purity, High Anglicans sought to retain what they felt to be valid in the medieval church. Their High Anglican conviction, that the Church was linked to the past by a continuous tradition, even if it was one that had been muddied by error and ignorance, found one of its most significant expressions in the remarkable revival in the early seventeenth century of the Gothic style both in architecture and in church plate.[21] The Anglican Church of Edward VI and Elizabeth, much more Calvinistically inclined than the Jacobean Church, had ruthlessly melted down all the mass plate that the Dissolutions of Henry VIII had spared. Chalices had been converted with ruthless thoroughness into communion cups, whose remarkably standardized forms and decoration were very close to those of contemporary secular cups. This approximation was deliberately made in order to express the Reformation's conception of communion as a commemoration, in opposition to Roman Catholic doctrine of the Mass as a sacrifice and of the consecration of the Host as a perpetual repetition of the miracle of transubstantiation. No longer was the chalice by its special form and name to declare the special nature of the rite in which it was employed. The altar cross and all other representations of Christ Crucified naturally disappeared. Candlesticks also disappeared with their candles as too closely associated with the idolatrous worship of the past and its vain ceremonials. The standard communion plate of an Elizabethan cathedral or rich church became a communion cup and cover which often served as a paten, with a pair of basins for alms and a pair of flagons for wine. For the fixed altar of the Middle Ages was substituted a moveable communion table, again from Reformation abhorrence of the doctrine of the Mass as a sacrifice performed on an altar. These tables too were made to resemble secular tables and were set not at the east end, but in the chancel or even the nave of the church.

We have no written record or explicit declaration of why or when the High Church of the early seventeenth century began to restore the chalice, not only in name but in a Gothic form and style that deliberately emphasised a continuity with the past. This silence in words is in sharpest contrast with the eloquent explicitness of doctrinal allegiance that was conveyed by the form and style of such objects; it was certainly motivated by discretion and a wish to avoid the bitterness of religious controversy. The style itself, so much at variance with Renaissance principles of design and ornament, is what may be called a distancing style: it separated and marked as holy the vessels of communion, and set them apart from the plain cup and paten of Elizabethan times, which commemorated the Last Supper in something that Christ might be imagined as having drunk and eaten from when he instituted communion. The revived Gothic style also expressed in visible form the conviction of High Churchmen that all such communion vessels ought to be consecrated, like everything else associated with the altar. The chalice which Thomas Howard, Earl of Arundel, like King Charles an ardent High Churchman as well as a collector and connoisseur, gave to Canterbury Cathedral, has a Latin inscription which reads in English: 'Thomas Howard, Ambassador to the Emperor of the Most Serene King of Great Britain, as he passed on 7 April 1636 most humbly offered this votive gift to the altar of this cathedral'. Puritans, however, regarded the consecration of 'Altars, Flagons, Altar-clothes and other Altar-furniture' as 'merely from the Roman *Missal* and *Pontifcal*, and from no better nor higher Antiquity'.[22]

The forms of High Anglican communion plate were imitated from those of English late medieval chalices. They are a visible expression of the High Anglican resolution of the dilemma that confronted all the Reformers. If the medieval church had been absolutely corrupt, then what was there to link the Church of the present with the pure and primitive church of the early Christians? The Puritans were driven to find their link in the survival of the Waldenses in Piedmont, whose tiny church in its Alpine valleys had, so they thought, preserved 'thy truth so pure of old when all our Fathers worship't Stocks and Stones' in the words of Milton's famous sonnet.[23] The High Anglicans, in contrast, saw themselves as the descendants of a past that, whatever its corruptions, still stretched back in authentic ascent to the early church. It was necessary to purge that past of its errors and distortions, but it could not be rejected as the Puritans rejected it, wholesale.

Such High Church views were held largely by high prelates, by the King and by great nobles close to the King, and by those who came beneath their influence. They were identified with the University of Oxford and with some of the colleges of Cambridge, where the clerical leaders of High Anglicanism had studied and reached their first eminence, and with the royal court. Even under Elizabeth the royal chapel and the royal foundation of Westminster Abbey had aroused Puritan suspicion and hostility because they preserved some of the ornaments of the medieval past, such as crosses, copes, and stained glass, with their religious imagery undamaged by Protestant iconoclasm. Elizabeth herself, a convinced Anglican, incurred the disfavour of her Calvinistic bishops for retaining a cross and candlesticks in her chapel.[24] The Gothic style as revived by High Anglicanism is generally called Laudian because it was under the ascendancy of William Laud (1573-1645), Archbishop of Canterbury from 1633, that the High Church party began to promote far more openly the restoration of some of the ornaments and imagery of the Middle Ages. But as with architecture and stained glass, so in church plate it made its first appearance rather earlier, under the reign of James I, who by learning and temperament leant to High Churchmanship.

It seems that its introduction into church plate is principally to be associated with one of the most famous and learned of early seventeenth-century Anglican divines, Lancelot Andrewes (1555-1626), successively Dean of Westminster, Bishop of Chichester, then of Ely, and finally of Winchester. Andrewes was one of the most influential personages of the Jacobean church, and can be regarded as the founding father of High Anglicanism. He was a man with the reverence for the past that was characteristic of the movement: it is typical of his affection for its inheritance of tradition that he should bequeath to his old college, Pembroke Hall, Cambridge, copies he had had specially made of three pieces of plate given by the college's foundress in order to preserve some memory of them in case of accident to the originals.[25] It was Andrewes who with true High Church care for the beauty, dignity and decorum of Church services introduced the notion that the proper furniture of the communion table was not the simple cup and paten of the Elizabethan days, but a service of communion plate. This conception which was to prove so influential throughout the seventeenth century, was in fact a novelty, for even in the Middle Ages, with its fervent devotion to the Host, the altar plate used in the mass had never really been conceived as a uniform service of liturgical vessels and instruments matching in form, proportion and ornament. Plainly Andrewes was moved by his belief that the solemnity of the communion service ought to be enhanced by a dignified set of communion plate which should signal the reverence that ought to be felt for so holy a sacrament. He might well feel justified in his innovation by the example of Solomon's temple, for the wise king had caused to be made in gold not only the altar and table, but also the ritual vessels of the Temple – the ten candlesticks, the flowers, the lamps, the tongs, the bowls, the snuffers, the basins, the spoons and the censers. But by such stately services of plate he was separating from that more extreme Protestant usage which had sought to establish for its own doctrinal reasons as little distinction as possible between communion plate and secular plate. All the two parties had in common was the belief that only precious silver was suitable for communion plate: in their choice of type, design and ornament they diverged violently, from opposing convictions. Accordingly such services of communion plate became an object of Puritan offence. Moreover, it was Andrewes who first reintroduced the practice of consecrating church plate, much to the fury of the Puritans as we have just seen.

A stately set of communion plate, arranged in seemly order was only a part of the High Anglican scheme for the restoration of a reverent richness in churches and chapels, and particularly in everything that had to do with the sacrament. The Holy Table for them was the altar of the Old and New Testaments, and they preferred to set it end-wise against the east wall and to rail it in with a rich wooden railing, so as to enhance its sanctity. It was their custom to bow to the altar – at Laud's trial he was accused of bowing and of allowing his chaplains to bow at their approach to the altar before celebrating communion.[26] Again the Puritans objected to this as a mere revival of an idolatrous Popish ceremony. The originator of this new conception of the nature and significance of church furnishings was once more Lancelot Andrewes. In 1645 Archbishop Laud was to admit that he had modelled his own renovation and refurnishing of Lambeth Palace chapel on Andrewes' chapel.[27] The plan of Andrewes' chapel still survives and shows an altar on a raised foot-board, set against the wall covered with a Turkey carpet and railed off in front above an ascent of two steps.[28] On it at the back was a cushion, flanked by two candlesticks with tapers, and with an alms-basin resting against it. A cushion on the left was to support a service book. There also stood on the altar a silver-gilt canister for the communion wafers, and a silver tun on a stand for the communion wine. Between them was the chalice, with before it two patens, and a round silver ball with three pipes, called the *triconale*, for mixing the water with the wine.

In the right corner stood a credence or side-table for use before the service began: on it were placed the canister and tun, a ewer and basin for washing before consecration, and a towel. On a music table in the nave of the chapel stood a three-cornered censer, into which frankincense was put when the first lesson was read, and an incense-boat. Behind this a stepped pedestal supported a lectern with a great Bible, and behind the lectern again a faldstool for kneeling to read the Litany. All this breathes the true spirit of High Anglicanism, in which piety is expressed by means that for Andrewes at any rate were purified of all the superstitions of Papistry, yet honoured ancient Christian tradition. Much of it was inspired by no less a Scriptural exemplar than Solomon's Temple, whose decorations justified to the High Church its belief that the house of God ought to be adorned with becoming richness, though without superfluity of ornament.[29]

At times this spirit was pushed to extremes. After his appointment to Durham in 1617 Bishop Richard Neile, Laud's old patron and one of the most ardent of Jacobean High Anglicans – significantly he had been Dean of Westminster – together with the Dean and Prebendaries one of whom, John Cosin, was later to be a leader of the High Anglicans, 'cast the Communion-Table out of the . . . Cathedral . . . Church, and erected a high Altar at the East end of the Quire, of Marble stones, with a carved screen most gloriously painted and guilded, which cost about two hundred pound'. As if this were not enough, 'they did likewise set up fifty three glorious Images and pictures over the Bishops throne, and about the Quire in the said Church'. These were apparently medieval images restored, and offence of offence, included a stone statue of Christ with a gold beard, blue cap, and sun-rays on his head. A Puritan Prebendary, Peter Smart, protested bitterly in 1629 that Bishop Neile and his chaplains 'have taught the People in their Sermons, that too much cost cannot be bestowed upon Christ that is the Church, and Church-ornaments, brave Altars, rich Altar-furniture, gorgeous Vestments, Sumptuous organs, glorious glasse-windowes, painted, gilded, and garnished images and other unnecessary bravery'.[30]

Far more characteristic of High Anglican piety in its restraint and sobriety of richness was the redecoration of the London church of St. Giles-in-the-Fields by Alice Lady Dudley, later Duchess Dudley (died 1669), one of the most representative figures of Caroline High Anglican piety and patronage of churches. St. Giles, which was greatly decayed, had been rebuilt by subscription from 1623 to 1631, and on completion was consecrated by Laud, then Bishop of London. Alice Dudley determined that its 'large goodly Fabrick' should be decorated with corresponding dignity. Accordingly she had the chancel paved with marble and gave hangings of taffeta bordered with a fringe of silk and silver thread to cover its east end. For the altar she provided a rich green velvet hanging embroidered in gold with the Sacred Monogram *IHS*, and another green velvet cloth with a gold fringe to cover the altar on Sundays. She also gave an altar-cloth of cambric edged with lace, and another of damask, and two cushions richly embroidered in gold to support the service books or alms-basin when laid out on the altar. To cover the altar on week-days she gave a large Turkey carpet. She also gave two organs, in a richly gilt case – organs were instruments that always incurred deep Puritan detestation – and 'Very Costly handsom Rails, to guard the Altar or Lord's Table from profane abuses'. Finally she gave as her crowning gift a set of communion plate in silver gilt 'which is as large and Rich as any in the City and Suburbs'. The doctrinal significance of all these ornaments did not escape the Puritans, and during the Civil War they were demolished and sold 'being counted Superstitious and Popish', under the very modern excuse of a 'pretense of relieving the poor out of the Mony received for them'. Only the communion-plate escaped, but it too has since disappeared.[31]

Typical then of High Anglicanism was a stately set of communion plate, handsomely arranged on a table that was treated as an altar, providing a vista of gleaming beauty in the choir for the worshippers. This in turn helped to promote the conception of the table as an altar. It did not promote it universally, for we know that some patrons who gave rich gifts of seemly sets of church plate in the Laudian Gothic style still retained the Elizabethan belief that the Holy Table must not be treated as an altar, that is, railed off and set against the east end of the church, but placed in the chancel or nave. Nevertheless in 1633 Archbishop Laud decided that the communion table must now stand permanently where the high altar had formerly stood.[32]

Besides giving the communion cup the aspect of the late medieval chalice, the High Anglicans revived the altar candlesticks of the Middle Ages as part of the communion service. These were anathema to the Puritans and had been expressly condemned both in the Elizabethan *Homilies*, issued as we saw to serve as a body of doctrine for the guidance of the newly established Anglican church, and in Elizabeth's injunctions for the church.[33] Their revival was certainly due to Andrewes, who felt authorized to use them by the practice of the Primitive Church, which had used lights for its services in the catacombs, and then kept them in its churches above ground to show its communion with the faith of the ancient Christians 'by the communion of the former usages'.[34] For him then and for the High Anglicans who followed him, they were a potent symbol of the continuity in faith of the Church. At his trial in 1645 Laud was formally charged with having set the communion table of his Lambeth chapel 'Altarwise, with the ends of it North and South against the wall' having furnished it 'with Basons, Candlesticks and other furniture, and hanging a cloth of Arras behind it, with the Picture of Christ and his Apostles eating the Lords Supper together'.[35] William Prynne, mouthpiece of Puritan hatred for Laud and historian of his trial, expressly singles out the candlesticks in his reinforcement of this charge. After condemning Laud's altar and the 'new costly Raile' that hedged it in, he attested as an eyewitness that

vpon this new Altar he had much superstitious Romish furniture never used in his Predecessors dayes, as namely, two great Silver *Candlestickes*, with Tapers in them, besides *Basons* and other *Silver Vessels* (with a costly Common *Prayer-Booke* standing on the Altar, which some say had a Crucifixe on the bosses).

Prynne was able to show from a Parisian edition of 1633 of the *Caeremoniale Romanum* as published by Clement VIII the damning fact that silver candlesticks containing tapers were expressly prescribed by the Popes as altar furniture, together with a cross and crucifix, while they also suggested that an arras or tapestry showing images of Christ, the Virgin or the saints might be hung above the altar.[36]

There can be no doubt that Charles was in fullest sympathy with the High Anglican conception of what a communion service ought to be. In 1631 a Yorkshire squire was fined the huge sum of £1,000 for committing adultery, then technically incest, with his married niece. The Dean and Chapter of York petitioned the King to grant them the fine for 'repaireing the ruines of the said Cathedrall Church, for setting up a new organ, for furnishing and adorning the altar, and ennabling them to mainteyne a library keeper'. On 28 November 1632 Charles granted them the £1,000 by letters patent, and Richard Neile, now Archbishop of York, laid out part of it in London in 1633 on the purchase of a set of silver-gilt communion plate engraved with the cathedral arms, consisting of two chalices and three patens, two gilt flagons, a basin and a pair of candlesticks. This nomenclature is that of the cathedral inventory of 16 January 1634: as was pointed out by Oman, it suggests that the whole was in Laudian Gothic style, as indeed the composition of the service and its purchase by Neile himself would suggest. It was much admired by contemporaries: three travelling gentlemen from Norwich speak of the 'rich plate wee saw wch is kept also in the vestry, & was given by our now most gracious soveraigne'. Although Charles did not choose the actual pieces himself, he must have approved of the proposal to furnish the altar with so significant a service of communion plate.[37]

We have no detailed description of the chapel plate of the royal palaces, and indeed as our only inventory was drawn up by the Commissioners appointed by the Commonwealth for the sale of Charles's goods, its real nature is surely disguised under a Puritan nomenclature. But the large Bible and Book of Common Prayer with covers mounted in silver gilt which the commissioners inventoried in the Tower must have come from a typically High Anglican set of plate for the Holy Table, especially as their mounts were rich and heavy. Certainly if the communion plate matched the furnishings and vestments of textile of the Denmark House chapel, it must have been of a seemly richness.

The High Anglicans were also at bitter issue with the Puritans over the matter of religious imagery. In searching the Bible and the early Fathers they found authority for modifying the extreme Elizabethan position. There was first of all the greatest work of Jewish architecture described in the Old Testament, Solomon's Temple, raised in all its glory by the piety of an exemplary king to whom God himself had granted the gift of wisdom in a dream. Although the Temple had contained no sculptured figure of Jehovah, yet there could be no doubt that it had been built and decorated with the richest of woods and substances – cedar and pure gold – and had contained sculptured figures. Had not Solomon set two cherubim of olive wood overlaid with gold each ten cubits high, with wings that were each of five cubits' span, within the oracle, so that their wings touched? And had he not also had the walls around the doors into the oracle carved with figures of cherubim and palm trees and open flowers?[38] Here then was ample scriptural justification for the use of sculptured cherubs as decoration in the innermost sanctuary of the Lord's House. Following the example of Solomon, cherubs also appear on High Anglican Gothic plate, adding often a delightful Late Mannerist or Baroque twist to their aspect, and giving yet further idiosyncrasy to the style.

Then there was evidence from the Fathers that the early Church had pictured Christ as the Good Shepherd on chalices, for in a famous passage, cited by Laud in his own defence at his trial, Tertullian had alluded to Christ as 'that shepherd whom you depict on the chalice'.[39] Andrewes laid especial hold on this motif and on its use in the early Church, which justified his timid and tentative revival of religious iconography, so carefully grounded on generally accepted authority from Scripture or the Fathers. He mentions it in 1590 in a sermon delivered before Elizabeth at Greenwich and again in a draft sermon for Easter 1625 in which he says: 'You may see him in the parable, coming with His lost sheep on his shoulders. That one sheep is the image of us all. So careful he was, as He laid him on His own neck, to be sure; which is the portraiture or true representation of his *anagoge*'.[40] The bowl of the chalice in his own chapel was engraved with the Good Shepherd, described as 'Christ with the lost sheep on His shoulders'.[41] At his trial in 1645 Laud, refuting the charge that he had set up 'Popish Images and Pictures' in the windows of his chapel in Lambeth Palace, not only defended himself by saying that he had simply had the existing windows repaired, but declared: 'the Primitive Christians approved, and had the Pictures of Christ himself: *Tertullian* recording, that they had the Picture of Christ engraven on their Chalices in form of a Shepherd carrying home the lost sheep on his back'.[42] An engraved figure of the Good Shepherd is recorded on a church flagon from as early as 1619, and continued to be a favourite motif with High Anglicans throughout the seventeenth century, certainly from this sanctified association with the early and pure Christian church.[43]

The Roman Catholic reverence for saints later than the Apostles and the centuries of the pure and primitive church was particularly abhorrent to Protestants, because of their belief that God's saints could not be identified by human judgement, but would be revealed only at the last day. But for the High Anglicans representations of the Apostles, and of saints whose cult was authorized by the early church were not open to any such objections: only

24 [45]

indeed to the objection, which was in fact made by the Puritans, that we could not know their true appearance. Thus at his trial in 1645 Laud told his accusers that they could have no legitimate objection to the picture of saints they had found in his gallery at Lambeth, described by Prynne as 'a glorious costly Picture in a very large frame of the foure Fathers of the Church, Saint *Ambrose*, Saint *Chrysostome*, Saint *Austin* and St. *Hieram*, all in their *Pontificalibus*, with the Picture of the *Holy Ghost* in the form of a Dove, hovering over their heads, and from this beake distilling the rayes, streames and influences of his graces severally upon them'. Laud stoutly declared that in the first place it was a gift from a friend, and secondly that as representing the four Latin Fathers of the Church 'there can be no harm or Popery in it, being only the Picture of Saint *Ambrose, Augustine, Jerome* and *Gregory* the first, which may be lawfully made and reserved'.[44]

Nor in the High Anglican view could any exception be taken to representations of scenes and figures from the Old and New Testament, for the reality of the personages they represented and the truth of the episodes they figured were vouched for by Scripture itself. In understanding the Puritan objection to this High Anglican view, it is important to remember that Puritans might well allow pictures from Scripture history as illustrations to books or as decorations in their houses, or even collect paintings of 'scripture histories' – Robert Dudley, Earl of Leicester, Elizabeth's favourite, though a patron of the Puritans could nevertheless own two Netherlandish pictures of the *Nativity* and *Christ calling St. Matthew*. What they most abhorred was the representation of such figures and scenes in churches, and indeed from the reign of Elizabeth there survive only very few painted figural decorations in churches and none of a very controversial kind.[45] The reintroduction of figures of saints on the church plate by the Anglicans was therefore audacious, though only very tentative. St. Peter appears on a chalice belonging to St. Werburgh, Bristol, of 1619, while on a covered paten given in 1623 to a Warwickshire church by Lady Dudley, the munificent donor of communion plate to churches whom we have already encountered, is a representation of St. John the Evangelist. But these were Apostles, of whose sanctity, so a High Anglican would have argued, there could be no doubt. The Puritans, however, were of a different opinion, for among the plate that has disappeared from Peterhouse College, Cambridge, a principal centre of Laudianism in the 1630s, is a flagon engraved with a figure of St. Peter that was supplied in 1638 to the Master John Cosin, whom we have already met at Durham as one of the leaders in doctrine and art of High Anglicanism. It was part of a set of plate for the college chapel. Of course St. Peter's image could if necessary always be defended by Cosin and his supporters against Puritan critics as merely emblematic of the college's name.[46]

We also find scenes, particularly from the New Testament, engraved on High Anglican church plate. The Nativity, so beloved of the Middle Ages, reappears in the form of the star that guided the wise men to Bethlehem. In a sermon preached before James I in 1620, Andrewes declares 'in the old Ritual of the Church we find on the cover of the canister, wherein was the Sacrament of his body, there was a Star engraven to show that now the star leads us thither to His body there'.[47] And accordingly the cover of the chalice on the communion table in his own chapel was engraved with 'the wise men's star'. Here then was another symbol authorized by Scripture and early usage, and it too makes an occasional appearance on High Anglican plate. Another symbol, the *IHS* or Sacred Monogram, had been used uninterruptedly from the Middle Ages, without inconsistency, since it was a formula devised expressly to render Christ by letters, rather than by a figure. But to it High Anglicans added a cross and three nails, recalling the late medieval cult of the Instruments of the Passion as favourite symbols of affective piety. Other medieval imagery also made its appearance, including, most surprisingly, the Crucifix, which is found on three chalices ranging in date from 1607 to 1638. On the covered patens given by Lady Dudley to three churches in 1638 it is even accompanied by the Instruments of the Passion, a choice of imagery that was at once a conscious imitation of the imagery of the fifteenth century and of contemporary late Renaissance and Baroque Catholic devotional imagery. The Last Supper a subject of obvious appropriateness is figured on a chalice of 1625: more recondite and also more medieval in its imagery is the Sacrifice of Isaac, found on a chalice and paten of 1635 made for St. Botolph, Aldgate, for the Sacrifice of Isaac was the Old Testament antitype of the Sacrifice of Christ. Another medieval symbol that makes a single appearance in 1633 is the Pelican: the bird was believed to wound her own breast to draw blood to feed her young, and so had been a favourite medieval figure of Christ's sacrifice of himself on the Cross.[48]

Yet this imagery, though so remarkable as a rebellion against the accepted Protestant iconoclastic doctrine of the sixteenth century, is infrequent and in execution relatively inconspicuous. This must be borne in mind when we consider the most important set of church plate commissioned by Charles I, the great communion service for use at the Feast by the Order of Garter. For this was not only a matching service of the kind introduced by Lancelot Andrewes, it was also richly decorated with scripture histories, more richly it would seem than any earlier High Anglican communion plate known to us either from records or from survival. It was therefore in all probability the fullest affirmation of the doctrines of High Anglicanism concerning the validity of religious imagery on church plate that was ever realized in the first half of the seventeenth century.

From its foundation by Edward III in the 1340s the Order of the Garter had been one of the prime royal chivalric orders of Christendom, and by the early seventeenth century it could be described by the great antiquary John Selden as having 'precedency of antiquity, before the eldest rank of honor of that kind any where established'.[49] Its Sovereign was always the King himself, and in number the knights never exceeded twenty-five. The Order had survived through all the dynastic vicissitudes of the fifteenth century to become under the Tudors an even more exalted royal companionship of honour, bestowed in general only on great noblemen, great officers of the royal court and on foreign emperors, kings and princes. Its seat was at Windsor, where it had in St. George's Chapel a magnificent Late Gothic chapel especially constructed for its ceremonies and dedicated to the Order's patron saint. From the first the Order met there annually on the 22 April, the Vigil of St. George's Day, for the celebration of divine service. According to its statutes, as last drawn up in 1522 under Henry VIII, on the afternoon of the Vigil the knights were to attend Evensong, and on St. George's Day itself they were to attend matins, 'procession' (what later under Protestantism became morning service), mass and a second Evensong.[50]

Provision, however, was always made for proroguing this ceremony, if it so pleased the Sovereign, and it seems that Edward VI set his successors the example of neglecting to hold the feast, almost certainly, as Ashmole suggests, from 'the common calamity of that Age, wherein most Ceremonies, solemn or splendid, either (chiefly such as related to Divine Services) came under the suspicion of being superstitious, if not idolatrous'. Edward later in his reign seems to have allowed some sort of feast to be held, but 'without any regard to the ancient and usual place, the Castle of Windesor'.[51] Elizabeth went further, and on St. George's Day 1567, issued a decree in a Chapter of the Order held at Whitehall declaring that the Feast could be held wherever the Sovereign might happen to be, irrespective of whether the place was Windsor or not. The decree even established that no solemnity of the Order need be held at Windsor, except when some especially illustrious personage was to be installed. As a result no annual feast was held at Windsor for the rest of her reign, and it was only under James I that the ancient order of things, by which the feast was always to be held at Windsor, was restored. No doubt James was anxious that as at his coronation so in the affairs of the Garter ancient custom should be followed or reinstituted.[52]

Charles, even more than his father, was 'a great restorer of the ancient Solemnities and Discipline of this Order, punctual even in circumstances of Honor'.[53] The seriousness of his interest in it appears from Van der Doort's list of his personal library in his Cabinet at Whitehall, where some two-thirds of the fifty volumes were in some way concerned with the Order. Almost all of them he had acquired before his accession. A quarto book, bound in gilt green leather 'Concerning the order of ye Garter', was stamped with his arms as Prince of Wales. Thirty-six of the other books, some with bindings enriched with mounts and clasps of silver-gilt, two with bindings of purple velvet and one with a binding of green velvet, are described as 'Concerning the garter', or according to another inventory 'concerning the orders of the Garter and Harroldry'. They had been given him by his mother Queen Anne of Denmark, surely in order to encourage in him an interest in the Order. A likely date for the gift might be after the death of Charles's older brother Prince Henry in 1612: it must have been made before Queen Anne's death in 1619.[54] Later, at the disposal of his possessions, '17ᵉⁿ Bookes of Armes of Knights of the Garter in redd vellvett Cases bound with gold Galloone' were among the 'Goodes receaved from Mʳ Wheeler'; valued at £14, they sold to Bass. 'Twoe Table of yᵉ ordʳ of yᵉ Garter' which were 'In yᵉ custody of Coll. Whitchcote. Governʳ. of windsor Castle' (more evidence of

246 [349]

294 [223]

Charles's devotion to the Order), are of uncertain nature. They were not furniture, and must have been either pictures or else lists of the knights with arms.

From the first, Charles plainly wished to reinform the Order with its first spirit of religious dedication. The preamble of Henry VIII's Statutes emphasised that the Order was founded

To the onnoure of almighti God, and of the blessed and immaculate Virgyne marie, and the blessid Martir Seinte George, Patron of the right noble Roialme of England, and of Saynt Edwarde, Kyng and Confessour; to the exaultation of the holy Faith Catholique.

But by the reign of James I what had originally been conceived as a chivalric and religious fraternity had become in reality a companionship of secular honour. Like so much else in the Caroline age, the first movement towards reviving the spiritual life of the Order and providing St. George's Chapel with a seemly set of plate really began before Charles's accession. For it was James I who 'taking into his pious thoughts the nakedness of this *Altar,* and considering how decently sacred *Utensils* would become the Service of *God,* made some convenient provision for the adorning thereof'.[55]

At the Chapter of the Order held on 23 April 1618 it was accordingly decreed that all the existing Knights-Companions of the Order and all who were admitted into it afterwards should give a piece of plate, to the value of at least £20, 'for the use of the Altar'. This remained however, purely a good resolution. Charles manifested his own determination to reinstitute the Feast at Windsor in all its ancient solemnity and splendour, but as an essentially religious ceremony, on 24 November 1625 at the very first chapter of the Order held after his accession. At it he revived his father's proposal for the donation by each Knight of a piece of plate to the value of at least £20. As Bishop of Winchester, Lancelot Andrewes was Prelate of the Order, but he was a dying man and his place was taken by Charles's favourite, Laud, then Bishop of London, who tried to stimulate the Knights into making their contribution by offering to donate a piece of plate himself.

In spite of this lead and the renewal of the proposal at successive chapters of the Order in 1628 and 1630, subscriptions came in very slowly. The Dean and Canons of the College of Windsor were even empowered by the Chapter of 1630 to demand the money, and in February 1631, to set an encouragement by example, Charles donated £100 from his Privy-Purse. The first Knight to make his offering was, as perhaps might be expected, Thomas Howard, Earl of Arundel, who gave £20 to the Dean. But as late as November 1633 a number of subscriptions were still in arrears, and it was resolved to impose a fine on all the recalcitrant Knights.[56] This draconian measure having successfully produced funds, Christian van Vianen, so 'excellently skill'd in chasing of Plate', was commissioned to make a communion service.[57] The actual agreement with him was made by Lord Arundel, acting as Earl Marshal of England, by Sir Francis Windebanke and Sir Francis Crane, Chancellor of the Order, and stipulated that the payment was to be at 12s. an ounce, a very high rate which shows how ambitious was the workmanship demanded. Accordingly on 24 April 1634 Charles ordered the payment of £600 to Christian as an imprest towards making the plate, 'after the receipt of which, he forthwith disposed himself to the work', so says Ashmole, our principal authority for the whole story. By June 1637 Christian had finished a service of nine pieces, consisting of two small candlesticks, chased and gilt, two large plain candlesticks, two chalices, four patens, a large alms basin and two small ones. The small candlesticks were for wax candles, the large ones for tapers, and news of them must have given horrible offence to the Puritans. Equally offensive were the basins, for these 'contained the whole History of Christ, in chased Work'.

Christian delivered the whole to Windsor on 3 July, and was paid £142, being what was due to him over and above the £600. At first it was arranged that the new plate should be taken to Croydon or Lambeth to be consecrated by Laud in person, but for some reason it was decided to defer the ceremony of consecration until the next Feast of St. George, which had been prorogued until 3 October 1637. Here it was 'to be offered the next morning at the *Altar,* and there to be consecrated to *God* and his *Service* for ever, by the *Prelate* of the *Order'.* The whole ceremony, Ashmole tells us, 'was performed with great veneration, and all due reverence, his late Majesty being a high promoter of Ecclesiastical decency and holy discipline'. At a certain point in the second service of the day, at the versicle *Let your light so shine before man,* the Bishop of Winchester, as Prelate, standing before the altar 'read certain select *Verses* out of the Old *Testament,* concerning the dedication of *Solomons* Temple, and the Riches thereof' and other appropriate verses. From Exodus (35: 3) he read 'Take from among you an offering unto the Lord: whosever is of willing heart, let him bring it, an offering of the lord; gold, and silver and brass'. From further in the same chapter of Exodus he read verses 21-22 describing the offerings of jewels and precious objects of gold made by the Jews to the newly instituted tabernacle. These were justifications of the new service from the Old Law: from the Gospel of St. Matthew he then read a verse (2: 11) describing the offerings of gold, and frankincense and myrrh offered by the Magi to the new-born Christ.

The Bishop now made ready for the offering, while Charles descended from his throne as if to make an offering and bowed three times in the choir to the altar – an action as we saw peculiarly repugnant to the Puritans, who persecuted Laud at his trial on this very question of bowing to the altar, as being idolatrous. Charles then moved on to the steps of the altar, where he knelt down and offered the great alms basin, 'devoutly saying, *Part of thy bounty to us, O Lord Almighty, I offer to thee and to thy Service*'. The Bishop received the basin and set it on the altar, after which all the Knights-Companions present each offered 'his piece of dedicated Plate, with the same words, and in like manner'. The Bishop arranged them all on the altar, touched each one as a sign that he received them on God's behalf, and then spoke prayers of consecration and benediction.

As a set of communion plate, however, the service was still incomplete, for it lacked flagons. Accordingly, when Prince Charles, later Charles II, was installed as a Knight of the Order on 22 May 1638, he offered two great gilt silver flagons for water weighing 387 ounces, which were also chased with histories, and again had been made by Christian van Vianen. Even after this complementary gift the King was plainly determined to enlarge and enrich the service still more. He found that arrears of £137. 4s. had been produced by a forceful letter sent out on 9 November 1637 to the Knights warning them that any delay in paying their subscriptions to the service would be penalized by a monthly fine of a third part of the sum due. Shortly after this happy result had been declared on 23 May 1638 Christian was again commissioned to make more plate for the altar and was paid these arrears as an earnest, receiving a further sum of £200 for the work on 27 March 1638. The new plate was completed before 8-10 October 1639, the Feast of St. George, when it was offered on the altar. It consisted of two great candlesticks, weighing 471 ounces, a book-cover for the Bible, and another for the Book of Common Prayer, and two great flagons, all of silver-gilt. In all the seventeen pieces of the whole service cost the enormous figure of £1,564. 6s., and weighed in total 3,580 ounces.

All were chased with histories, whose iconography had been most carefully devised.[58] We already know the three earlier alms-basins were chased with the 'whole history of Christ', which they would have figured in sequence laid out side by side against cushions, with the large basin in the centre. On the foot of one of the new large candlesticks of 1639 was chased the Sermon on the Mount, whose beatitudes are the pattern of the Christian life. On the other were the parables of the lost goat and the lost sheep, both of which commend perseverance and diligence in the pursuit of salvation. On one of its covers the Bible had two scenes, Moses bringing down the Tables of the Law from Sinai, representing the delivery by God of the Old Law, and David and the Ark, certainly chosen to figure royal reverence for the things of God, for David had not hesitated to dance before the Ark, though a king, when he and the house of Israel brought it up from Gibeah to Jerusalem.[59] On the other cover were three scenes which figured three key moments in the delivery and preaching of the New Law, again the Sermon on the Mount, with its annunciation of the Beatitudes, Pentecost, or as Ashmole calls it, 'the sending of the Holy Ghost', and St. Paul falling from his horse at the moment of his conversion.

The *Book of Common Prayer*, as the cornerstone of the ritual life of the Anglican Church and as the expression of the divinely ordained authority of its Supreme Head, also had covers decorated with significant scenes. On one side was the Angel of Incense, that is the angel who is described in Chapter 8, verse 3 of Revelations: 'And another angel came and stood at the altar, having a golden censer; and there was given unto him much incense, that he should offer it with the prayers of all saints upon the golden altar which was before the throne'. This was a very High Anglican motif, chosen to decorate the *Book of Common Prayer* in order to emphasise the continuity of the prayers of the present church with the prayers of the early Church. In his *Answer to Cardinal Perron*, a controversial work against the Roman Catholics composed in 1620, Andrewes accepted the use of incense as lawful because it was used by the Primitive Church when they held their meetings 'in caves and grots under-ground', to sweeten the air. Like the use of tapers and candles, they retained it after they had churches above ground, 'to show themselves to be the sons and successors of those ancient Christians which in former times had used them (though upon other occasion) showing their communion in the former faith, by the communion of the former usages'.[60]

Even more remarkable was 'the *King* healing the *Evil*', a scene deliberately chosen to exalt the semi-sacred character of the monarchy. It illustrated the strange belief, current from at least the early twelfth century, that by virtue of their anointing the Kings of England, like those of France, had the power by the touch of their hands to heal the King's Evil or scrofula. This belief inspired under Charles the introduction of an official service for the rite of touching into the 1633 edition of the *Book of Common Prayer*, a testimony to the importance that he and his High Church advisers attached to the royal touch as a vindication of the divine right of kings.[61] On the other cover of the Prayer-Book were scenes representing the Anglican manner of preaching and of christening, preaching being a vital element in the life of the Anglican Church, with its emphasis on the exposition of God's word to the people, while christening is the sacrament that admits to the Christian life. The whole was therefore an exposition of the origins of the Church under the Old Law and the New, and an exaltation of the King and the Anglican Church. In its massiveness of form, intricate richness of surface, and enhancement of treble gilding, this great service must have shone with high magnificence of array on the altar of St. George's chapel, moving the minds of the worshippers to a solemn disposition of piety with a truly Anglican seemliness of ornament. We are told that Van Vianen's workmanship was excellent: 'to give him due praise in this undertaking', writes Ashmole in 1672, 'he discovered a rare ingenuity and happy fancy, as the skilful did judge while the Plate was in being, and the designs of each piece yet to be seen (among the present *Soveraign's* rare collection of Draughts and Sketches) can sufficiently manifest'. The fact that Van Vianen's drawings for the plate were in the collection of Charles II surely suggests that they were made for Charles I and submitted to his approval. Van Vianen indeed expended so much time and labour on this great service, that he complained 'he was a great loser, at the rate agreed upon; so much and so good work had he bestowed on them above the rest'.[62]

In the Garter Plate we come very close to Charles's inner conception of sacred royalty and of the purity of the Church over which he had been set as Supreme Head, now for a century purged and cleansed of the disfigurements of error, and so made ready to be robed in the state and trappings that became her beauty. Such was not the opinion of his Puritan enemies, for whom the works of art that Charles saw as an expression of pious reverence were horribly superstitious and idolatrous. On 23 October 1642 Sir John Seyton seized Windsor Castle for Parliament, whereupon a certain Captain Fogg went at once to the College and demanded the keys of the Treasury. When the three keepers of the keys could not be found, he had the doors battered down and carried off all Van Vianen's plate, which no doubt disppeared shortly afterwards into the melting-pot. The service was never again to appear at a Garter Feast before the hangings of crimson velvet and gold which decorated the east wall of the Chapel during Charles's reign, or below the two pieces of arras, one figuring St. George, the other the Assumption of the Virgin, that Charles had ordered at a Chapter held on 6 November 1634 should be brought out and hung up over the altar at the Grand Feast and other festivals of the Order.[63]

Notes

1. A.J. Collins, *Jewels and Plate of Queen Elizabeth I* (London, 1955), p. 68.

2. L.W. Cross (ed.), *The Diary of Baron Waldstein* (London, 1981), p. 45.

3. Collins, op. cit. (Note 1), p. 136.

4. Ibid., pp. 165-6

5. Ibid., p. 165.

6. C. Hernmarck, *The Art of the European Silversmith 1430-1830* (London, 1977), I, p. 54.

7. For the Van Vianen family see J.R. ter Molen, *Van Vianen: een Utrechtse familie van zilversmeden met een internationale faam* (Leiden University thesis, 1983). See also the exhibition catalogue, Centraal Museum, *Zeldzaam Silver uit de Gouden Eeuw: De Utrechtse edeesmiden Van Vianen* (Utrecht, 1984-5).

8. J. von Sandrart, *Academia nobilissimae artis pictoriae* (Nuremberg, 1683), p. 340.

9. Ibid., p. 340.

10. W.N. Sainsbury, *Original Unpublished Papers illustrative of the Life of Sir Peter Paul Rubens* (London, 1859), p. 306.

11. For Charles's reliefs by Paul van Vianen see *Van der Doort's Catalogue*, pp. 76 [3], 207 [5], 213 [36].

12. J.W. Frederiks, *Dutch Silver* I. *Embossed plaquettes, tazze and dishes . . .* (The Hague, 1952), p. 149, no. 88.

13. Ibid., pp. 114, nos. 60-61; p. 131, no. 75-6, pp. 139-41, nos. 80-3, p. 142, nos. 84-5.

14. Sandrart, op. cit. (Note 8), p. 340. For Christian see R.W. Lightbown, 'Christian van Vianen at the court of Charles I', *Apollo* 137 (1968), pp. 426-39; ter Molen, *op. cit.* (Note 7), pp.24-5.

15. For all documents about Christian's sojourn at Charles's court see the article by Lightbown, (op. cit., Note 14) unless otherwise specified.

16. The Countess of Brandford is unidentified. The exact address was identified by ter Molen, op. cit. (Note 7), p. 25, who also found the documents about Poelenburgh and Geldorp.

17. For Rogiers see the article 'Rasières, Théodore de', in Académie Royale des Sciences, des Lettres et des Beaux-Arts de Belgique, *Biographie Nationale* XIX (1907), cols. 813-5; Rubenshuis, *Antwerps Huiszilver uit de 17ᵉ en 18ᵉ eeuw* (Antwerp, 1988-9), p. 30.

18. For Rubens and these designs see G. Martin, in *The Flemish School c.1600-1900*, (National Gallery Catalogues) (London, 1970), pp. 187-93; A. Braham, *Rubens* (Themes and Paintings in the National Gallery, no. 8) (London, 1973), pp. 35-8; J. Held, *The Oil Sketches of Peter Paul Rubens* I (Princeton, 1980), pp. 355-8, no. 265. The identification of the source of Peitho and the Amor in Pausanias (v,ii) is due to Held.

19. For these reliefs see *Van der Doort's Catalogue* pp. 149 [5-7] , 150 [8-10].

20. For the High Anglican movement in general see G.W.O. Addleshaw, *The High Church Tradition* (London, 1941).

21. For Laudian or Revived Gothic Church plate see C.C. Oman, *English Church Plate* (London, 1957), pp. 145-8.

22. W. Prynne, *Canterburies Doome* (London, 1646), pp. 65, 502. For Arundel's chalice see Oman, op. cit. (Note 21), pp. 204-5

23. Milton, *Poetical Works* ed. H.C. Beeching, (Oxford, reprint of 1952), p. 84.

24. Oman, op. cit. (Note 21), pp. 175-6, 246.

25. L. Andrewes, *Two Answers* (Oxford, 1854), p.xxi and *cf.* Oman, op. cit. (Note 21), p. 145.

26. Prynne, op. cit. (Note 22), pp. 63-4, pp. 49-70.

27. Ibid., pp. 467-8, 499.

28. In BL, Harleian MS 3795. Engraved in Prynne, op. cit. (Note 22), p. 122 and Andrewes, op. cit. (Note 25), pl. facing p. xcvii.

29. Andrewes, op. cit. (Note 25), pp. xcvii-xcix.

30. There was quite a controversy over the Durham altar and decorations. The quotation is from Peter Smith, *The Humble Petition*, (London, 1640), pp. 1, 7, 10. *Cf.* also Smart's own *A short Treatise of Altars, Altar-furniture, Altar-cringing . . .* (London, 1629).

31. For Duchess Dudley's chapel, see B. [R.], *A Mirrour of Christianity and a Miracle of Charity, or, A true and Exact Narrative of the Life and Death of the most Virtuous Lady, Alice Dutches Duddeley*, (London, 1669), pp. 21-4.

32. For this see Oman, op. cit. (Note 21); Addleshaw, op. cit. (Note 20).

33. See Prynne, op. cit. (Note 22), p. 62, for Puritan offence.

34. Andrewes, op. cit. (Note 25), pp. 373-4. For the Puritan point of view see Prynne, op. cit. (Note 22).

35. Prynne, op. cit. (Note 22), p. 466.

36. Ibid., p. 62.

37. Surtees Society, *Fabric Rolls of York Minster* (Durham, 1858), pp. 307, 316, 319n, 321-22. Oman, op. cit. (Note 21), p. 157.

38. 1 Kings 6.

39. Tertullian, *De Pudicitia*, X.

40. L. Andrewes, *Works*, (Oxford, 1841) II, p. 29; III, pp. 89-90.

41. Andrewes, op. cit. (Note 25), p. xcvii.

42. Prynne, op. cit. (Note 22), p. 463.

43. Oman, op. cit. (Note 21), pp. 226-7. The Flagon is at Severn Stoke, Worcestershire (ibid., pl. 123a).

44. Prynne, op. cit. (Note 22), pp. 67-472.

45. E. Croft-Murray, *Decorative Painting in England*, (London 1962), p. 31.

46. Oman, op. cit. (Note 21) pp. 227-8. *The Correspondence of John Cosin, D.D.* I (Surtees Society 52) (London, 1868) p. 224.

47. Andrewes, op. cit. (Note 41), I, p. 247.

48. Oman, op. cit. (Note 21), pp. 225-7.

49. Selden, cited in E. Ashmole, *The Institution, Laws & Ceremonies of the Most Noble Order of the Garter* (London, 1693), p. 187.

50. See ibid., appendix V for the Statutes of Henry VIII.

51. Ibid., pp. 473, 474.

52. Ibid., pp. 474-5.

53. Ibid., p. 477.

54. *Van der Doort's Catalogue*, p. 124 [19-36].

55. Ashmole, op. cit. (Note 49), p. 491.

56. Ibid., pp. 491-2 for the collection of funds.

57. What follows is from ibid., pp. 492-6, where Ashmole gives documents concerning the commission, the history of the plate, and the subjects that decorated it. *Cf.* also Oman, op. cit. (Note 21), pp. 157-9.

58. The iconography of the Garter plate has not previously been studied.

59. 2 Samuel 7.

60. Andrewes, op. cit. (Note 25), p. 34; *cf.* also P.O. Welsby, *Lancelot Andrewes 1555-1626* (London, 1958), p. 129.

61. For all this see the classic work by M. Bloch, *Les rois thaumaturges* (Paris and Strasbourg, 1924), cited here in the English translation, *The Royal Touch*, (London, 1973). See especially p. 208 and pp. 399-40.

62. Ashmole, op. cit. (Note 49), pp. 492, 494.

63. Ibid., p. 499.

7 The King's Regalia, Insignia and Jewellery

Ronald Lightbown

Marginal numerals refer to page and entry numbers in the *Inventories* (see p. 11)

The Regalia of England was left by Charles as it had been constituted by time.[1] There had been from the twelfth century at least two regalias. One was the personal or semi-dynastic regalia belonging to the kings, which was from *c.*1300 preserved in the Tower of London, first in chambers deputed for the purpose, then from the sixteenth century in a specially constructed Jewel House adjoining the south-front of the Tower (Fig. 21). The other, even more potent and venerable as a collection of symbols of the monarchy, was the regalia of St. Edward the Confessor, preserved since the twelfth century under the perpetual custody first of the Abbots, and then after the Reformation, of the Deans of Westminster. As the first two Stuart monarchs attached prime importance to all that was ancient in the rituals and ornaments of the coronation, it is this Westminster regalia that must claim our attention first. Its original nature and the purpose with which it was constituted are two of the thorniest problems of English history. Some of it at least – the Crown, a gold Sceptre topped by a cross, two Rods, one topped by a dove and one of iron, a great Chalice whose bowl of antique hardstone or glass was mounted in gold and the accompanying Paten, also of gold – had probably been made for the Confessor, and deposited by him in the Abbey either for safe custody, according to a well-documented custom of the early Middle Ages, or for perpetual use at all future coronations, as Westminster Abbey was already claiming in the 1130s. To it were added from time to time by later kings other insignia and robes required for the coronation. A Stole had already been added at some date between the early thirteenth century and 1308 when Edward II is recorded as wearing it for his coronation. An ivory Rod and a gold Sceptre topped by a dove for the Queen also entered it during the thirteenth or more probably the early fourteenth century. In 1388 Richard II contributed a Ring to be used in perpetuity at coronations, while in 1483 Richard III deposited the Ampulla containing the Holy Oil of St. Thomas à Becket, used for anointing the kings from the coronation of Henry IV, the first Lancastrian king, in 1399. From 1559, and probably before, the Abbey also held in its custody the Spurs. After his own coronation, as we shall see, Charles was to add the Swords.[2]

From the canonization of St. Edward in 1161 the Westminster regalia had acquired the status of holy relics and indeed before the Reformation the robes of St. Edward which it contained were exhibited annually in the Abbey on his feast-day. After the Reformation this status as relics became an embarrassment. On the one hand lineal descent from the kings of the past was as strongly claimed by the Tudors as by previous royal houses, and we shall see that images of two royal English saints, the Confessor himself and St. Edmund, appeared on their Imperial State Crown. But if Edward was still regarded as a holy king by the new Church of England, it could not encourage the superstitious worship of his relics, for the veneration of relics was one of the practices of the medieval church most fiercely reprobated by the Reformers. Accordingly from the coronation of Edward VI, held in 1547 and devised by Archbishop Cranmer and Lord Protector Somerset, there was a tendency to diminish the unique significance of St. Edward's Crown in the ceremony. No longer did the Archbishop of Canterbury crown the king solely with St. Edward's Crown: no longer did the King solemnly lay it on St. Edward's altar before his shrine – indeed the shrine had been destroyed by Henry VIII. Instead Edward was crowned with three crowns, first with St. Edward's Crown, then with the great Imperial State Crown, and finally with a small crown made specially for him by the goldsmith Everard Everdyes. This from its lightness was much more comfortable for wear during the remainder of the service and the procession and feast that customarily followed. Nevertheless the numinous sanctity that St. Edward's Crown had acquired during five centuries of association with the sainted King and his shrine was still something of an embarrassment to Anglicans. Accordingly we find a revival of the belief, once current in England and particularly in Westminster Abbey during the fourteenth century, that St. Edward's Crown was in reality the crown of King Alfred. On the strength of a passage in the *Flores Historiarum* of the thirteenth-century chronicler Roger of Wendover, it was believed that when the little Alfred had been sent to Rome in 854 by his father King Aethelwulf of Wessex for confirmation by Pope Leo IV, he had been crowned and anointed King by the Pope. Alfred, so it was said, had kept the regalia with which he had been crowned and brought it back to England, where he constituted it as the regalia of the kingdom and bequeathed it to be worn by all his successors.[3]

Belief in Alfred's coronation and unction by the Pope was confirmed in Elizabethan times by what appeared to be the incontrovertible testimony of Bishop Asser, Alfred's friend and counsellor, whose biography of the king, when printed in 1574 by the great Elizabethan antiquary Archbishop Matthew Parker and again in 1603 by the even more celebrated William Camden, was found to contain a passage claiming that Pope Leo had indeed crowned and anointed Alfred. Accordingly Jacobean and Caroline antiquaries encouraged themselves to believe that St. Edward's Crown was in reality Alfred's crown. One of the earliest students of Anglo-Saxon antiquity, Sir John Spelman, in his biography of Alfred, written in 1643, but printed only in 1709, was confident that the crown was indeed that of Alfred, for the special box that contained it bore when he saw it the Latin inscription *Haec est principaliter Corona cum qua coronabantur Reges Alffredus, Edwardus &c* (this is the Crown with which Kings Alfred Edward &c were chiefly crowned). He reports that it was 'of a very ancient Work, with Flowers adorned with Stones of somewhat a plain setting'. We know from other sources that it was of imperial form, that is to say, it was surmounted by arches, and this is the form it was given when it was resurrected – admittedly from memory and brief inventory descriptions – for Charles II at the Restoration. Persuaded by the inscription on the box, Spelman declared that the Crown was the Crown of Alfred and his successors, and

...is to be supposed to have been made by him, and that when he was become Universal King of the *Heptarchy*. In which respect, and for the value of the Jewels (then and long after very rare in these parts) as also for the venerable Esteem which (for the Original and Author) succeeding Ages have ever had of it, seems deservedly to be accounted the most principal Crown.[4]

The story that Alfred was crowned and anointed by Pope Leo was dispelled only in the nineteenth century, when Leo's original letter to Aethelwulf appeared and revealed that he had given Alfred only the honorary rank of consul. In the absence of this document, however, it was widely, though not universally, believed. Another crown appears to have found its way into the Westminster regalia between 1359 and the mid 1450s, by which last date it was passing as a 'good crown' which the Confessor had left for the coronation of the Queen, and this also came to be assigned to King Alfred. It was supposed to have been the crown of his consort Queen Edith, and so acquired during the early seventeenth century the name of Queen Edith's Crown. These illustrious associations, though entirely the result of wishful thinking, were highly acceptable to true Anglicans, aureoling the two crowns as they did with all the prestige of being the original crown of the first king of all England, as Alfred was believed to have been, and of his queen, and conferring on them both a venerableness of antiquity independent of all prestige as holy relics.

Besides the Westminster regalia Charles had inherited as his personal – or rather semi-dynastic regalia – the royal regalia of the Tudors.[5] This consisted in the 1520s of a gold imperial state crown for the king, a gold imperial state crown for the queen, a sceptre of gold topped by a dove and a gold rod for the king, another smaller gold sceptre for the Queen, also topped by a dove, a pair of gold bracelets, and a gold orb. The crowns and bracelets were jewelled, whereas the sceptres, rods, and orbs were plain. In order to understand the nature of this regalia it is important to realise that although some of its components, such as the two state crowns, the sceptres and the rod were used at coronations, the whole was also intended to be used when the king appeared in his estate. The sixteenth and seventeenth century, however, seem to have seen the abandonment of many medieval court customs connected with the wearing by the king of robes and insignia in his estate. In 1494 Henry VII could require the bracelets and orb to be produced for him to wear every Twelfth Night, whereas after his coronation in 1626 Charles simply ordered them to be left together with the Swords among the Westminster regalia, which were never used in full except at coronations, while only one or two items of it, such as St. Edward's Sceptre and Staff, were ever used on other occasions. In Charles's time the Westminster regalia were kept stored in the Chapel of the Pyx, described by the Westminster prebendary Peter Heylyn as 'a secret place of *Westminster* Abbey, not easily accessible to any, but such as know the mystery of it: never brought forth but at the Coronation of a

King, or his going to Parliament'.[6] And indeed it was now principally when the Sovereign went in state to open or close Parliament that he wore some of the regalia – as indeed is the practice of modern times.

From the early sixteenth century, this personal regalia, kept in the Tower, as we saw, had acquired a fixed, dynastic, hereditary character, which the Middle Ages had failed to achieve for the personal regalia, in spite of partial and abortive attempts by Edward I and Edward III. The only significant addition made to the royal crowns in the sixteenth century was the small imperial crown made by Everard Everdyes for Edward VI in 1547, and this too was kept among the regalia.[7] This relative stability of the regalia must in itself have been an act of deliberate policy on the part of the Tudors and Stuarts, intended to sustain the impression of a stable dynasty and state which they were so anxious to present after the savage dynastic conflicts and rivalries of the fifteenth century. From the early seventeenth century indeed the legal doctrine was enunciated by Sir Edward Coke that 'the ancient jewels of the crowne are heirloomes and shall descend to the next successor, and are not devisable by testament'. He made however one exception to this rule: the King might grant them away during his lifetime, by letters patent made under the Great Seal or Privy Seal. The kings moreover could point to a long history of pawning of their treasures to meet financial necessities, and it was no doubt with knowledge of these vicissitudes that in 1605 James I had declared 'The Imperial Crowne of this Realme of Gould' and the Queen's Crown to be among the 'Roiall and Princely Ornaments and Jewells' which were forever 'annexed to the Kingdome of this Realme'. And certainly there was a popular conviction, though it was not shared by those in office, that the jewels of the Crown were inalienable.[8]

The form of the state crowns was imperial, that is to say they were closed crowns with the arches, surmounted by a ball and cross, which had of old been the distinguishing feature of imperial crowns. Into the imperial crown of the Holy Roman Empire of the fourteenth century had been incorporated a mitre to indicate the clerical status of the Emperor, and the two had been fused into a high, rather conical crown which it is thought Henry V saw on the visit of the Emperor Sigismund to England in 1416 and imitated in his own crown. The principal reason why the English kings wore imperial crowns was not so much that they claimed to rule over several kingdoms and lordships, though this was certainly one reason why they did so, as because they claimed to be immediately subject to no other ruler, but only to God. Edward the Confessor had an imperial crown for this very reason. Writing of St. Edward's Crown in 1643, Spelman implies that it was of flatter form than the modern Imperial Crown: he calls it an 'Imperial Crown, which though not of the Form, that by way of Distinction we at this day call Imperial, yet was it of a more August and Imperial Form than had formerly been in use in this Kingdom'.[9]

The conical form of imperial crown had established itself for both King and Queen during the fifteenth century. From the reign of Henry VI at any rate such imperial crowns were decorated with crosses, generally alternating with fleurons. The Imperial Crown inherited by Charles I was of this design. Neither the date when it was made nor the king for whom it was made are known, though there is a possibility that it was made for one of the Tudors, either Henry VII or more probably Henry VIII. When it first becomes known to us, in 1521, it consisted of a circlet from which rose five fleurons of the usual fleur-de-lis design alternating with five crosses. Each of the fleurons bore a holy figure, Christ, the Virgin and Child, St. George, the patron saint of England, and two figures which from other descriptions can be plausibly identified as the two most universally revered of the sainted kings of England, St. Edmund and St. Edward the Confessor. The iconography of the crown then invoked on the king the protection of Christ, of the Virgin, and of the especial saints of England and of the royal line, and simultaneously proclaimed the descent of the king from sainted ancestors. One reason for thinking that this crown may have been made for Henry VIII is that in the Vigil or Riding Procession through London which, as was customary, took place the day before his coronation, he was followed by three men wearing tabards of the arms of St. Edmund, St. Edward and St. George. The crown was richly jewelled with balas-rubies, sapphires, emeralds, diamonds, and pearls, and although there was some variation in the quality of the stones – no unusual feature of English royal crowns – there was plainly an attempt to achieve some uniformity or at any rate harmony of size, design, and colour in their setting. This is the crown with which Charles is shown in Daniel Mytens' portrait of Charles I (Fig. 84), for a figure of the Virgin and Child is

Figure 84 Mytens: *King Charles I*. National Portrait Gallery, London.

represented on the upper leaf of one of the fleur-de-lis fleurons. Unfortunately there is every reason to distrust painters' representations of royal crowns, but the presence of this verifiable detail suggests that Mytens has given us a more accurate representation than was usual. It was of course worn with a cap: that fitted in 1574 was of purple velvet – purple was a royal colour – lined with black satin.

The Queen's Crown had plainly been made to match this crown, though it was much lighter and its stones were many fewer and of rather inferior quality. It too had crosses alternating with fleurons, in this case six of each, not five, and though surmounted by imperial arches, these were plain, not set with diamonds and pearls like the arches of the king's crown. Above it rose a cross. The whole suggests a richness carefully adjusted to the inferior status of the queen, in keeping with the traditions of the monarchy. It too was fitted with a cap of purple velvet. We have no representation of it: the crown shown in the portrait after Van Dyck of Henrietta Maria, in the National Portrait Gallery (Fig. 95), which had been claimed as depicting it is certainly of the same general type, but cannot be an exact reproduction, for it has no crosses, and its arches are rimmed with pearls. Its style, moreover, suggests the late sixteenth or early seventeenth century, whereas the queen's crown was already in existence by 1521.

Although the framework of these crowns remained so to speak stable, stones were sometimes removed from them permanently or temporarily, usually for mounting in other ornaments. On some occasions stones were added. The crown that suffered most from pillaging was Everard Everdyes's crown. This was a small imperial gold crown surmounted by a little cross enamelled blue over a great pierced balas-ruby which may have been the Black Prince's ruby. Made for the coronation of Edward VI in 1547, its original pearls had in any case been taken from the caps and collars of Henry VIII. By 1649 it had been so altered and its stones had been stripped in such numbers that without a certification from the Master of the Jewel House it would be unrecognizable from the inventory description as the crown of Edward VI. When the king's 'Imperiall Crowne of Massy gold' was valued after its confiscation by the Commonwealth in August 1649, it was still set with fifty-eight rubies, twenty-eight diamonds, nineteen sapphires, two emeralds and one hundred and sixty-eight pearls and its gold

43[-]

weighed 7*lbs*. The queen's crown was still much lighter, weighing only 3*lbs*. 10*oz*. and still much more lightly jewelled, being set with only twenty sapphires, twenty-two balas-rubies (spinels) and eighty-three pearls. Even in his worst extremities then, though driven to pawn in 1641 the richly jewelled circlet which James I had had made for Charles's 'late Deare Mother Queen Anne', and had designated as an heirloom, Charles seems to have respected the integrity of the old regalia.[10]

The regalia, and more especially the Westminster regalia, still possessed for royalists and High Church Anglicans a potent aura of the ancient greatness of the monarchy. Lamenting its destruction by the Commonwealth, Thomas Fuller writes in 1655 of the Westminster regalia:

Posterity conceived so great an opinion of King *Edward's* Piety, that his Cloaths were deposited amongst the *Regalia*, and solemnly worn by our *English* Kings on their Coronation. never counting themselves so fine, as when invested with his Robes; the Sanctity of Edward the first Wearer excusing, yea adorning the modern Antiquenesse of his Apparell. Amongst these is the *Rod* or *Sceptre*, with a *Dove* on the Top thereof (the Emblem of Peace) because in his Reign *England* enjoyed Halcyon *dayes*, free from *Danish* Invasions: as also his *Crown, Chair, Staffe, Tunick, close Pall, Tuisni hosen, Sandalls, Spurres, Gloves*, &c. Expect not from me a Comment on these severall Cloaths, or reason for the wearing of them. In generall, it was to mind our Kings, when habited with his Cloaths, to be cloathed with the habit of his vertuous Endowments: as when putting on the Gloves of this Confessour, their Hands ought to be like his, in moderate taking of Taxes from their Subjects...But now *Edward's Staffe* is broken, *Chair* overturned, *Cloaths* rent, and *Crown* melted; our present Age esteeming them the Reliques of Superstition.[11]

Both James I and Charles I were exceedingly anxious to be crowned according to the ancient forms of the Kingdom. The principal authority for the order of service of the Coronation was now the *Liber Regalis*, an illuminated manuscript order of service especially prepared at Westminster Abbey *c*.1390 as a guide to royal ceremonials of coronation and interment, and in the seventeenth century so precious that it was kept with the regalia. During medieval times and the storms of the Reformation the prescriptions of the *Liber Regalis* had on occasions been honoured very much in the breach as well as in the observance, but James appears to have been anxious that his own coronation should be conducted in accordance with time-honoured tradition. Accordingly, and perhaps too because almost forty years had passed since Elizabeth's coronation, so that there was no other authority to which to refer, the *Liber Regalis* commanded unquestioned ceremonial and liturgical prestige. There was however one major departure from the past at James's coronation. The order of service of the *Liber Regalis* was rendered into English and was no longer recited in its original Latin, as had been the case even at the coronation of that convinced Anglican, Elizabeth I, in January 1558. This in itself testifies to a new spirit of confidence in the Church of England, fortified as it now was by the great *Ecclesiastical Polity* of Richard Hooker, published in 1594-7 and by the forty years of the Elizabethan Settlement. To this feeling of assurance the growing influence of the High Church party may have contributed, with its insistence on the Anglican Church as a purified, rather than a novel institution, for this doctrinal position preserved a sense of continuity with the past.

James's coronation was held on 25 July 1603.[12] He entered the Abbey preceded by the great gold chalice of St. Edward, according to a custom which had been observed from 1236 until the Coronation in 1547 of Edward VI, whose ritual marks the high water-mark of extreme Protestant influence on the ceremony. After the anointing, he was clad in the vestments of St. Edward, again a ritual that seems to have been omitted from 1547, though of this it is rather more difficult to be certain. And instead of being crowned with three crowns, St. Edward's Crown, the Imperial State Crown, and finally the little crown of Edward VI, he was crowned with St. Edward's Crown, and with the Imperial State Crown – or so it would seem – only putting on a light crown when he changed into his processional robes at the end of the ceremony. Yet Peter Heylyn, a High Anglican prebendary of Westminster Abbey, a royal church always detested by the Puritans for maintaining ornaments, music and customs from the medieval past, was later to say that 'the ritual was drawn in haste, and wanted many things which might have been considered in a time of Leisure'.[13] Accordingly Charles was informed on succeeding in 1625 that his father's coronation order had been too hastily compiled. His own coronation was put off for some time, at first on account of Charles's forthcoming wedding to Henrietta Maria and then on account of the plague. Only towards the end of 1625 did

Charles appoint Archbishop Abbott and a number of bishops and magnates to revise the coronation order. It is significant that he instructed this Committee to ensure that 'ancient custom was observed'. The day chosen for the ceremony was 2 February, the feast of the Purification of the Virgin Mary, originally perhaps in order to honour Henrietta Maria, who in the end was to refuse as a Roman Catholic to take part in the heretical ritual, and contented herself with watching the procession from the window of a house.[14]

The Committee of Bishops met for the first time on 4 January 1626, but by 16 January William Laud, then Bishop of St. David's and also a prebendary of Westminster, had been appointed by Charles to act as Dean at the Coronation, the real dean, Bishop John Williams of Lincoln, until recently Lord Keeper, being now in deep disgrace. Next day Williams himself formally appointed Laud to act as his deputy. According to Laud himself the form of the coronation was agreed by the whole Committee 'according to a former book' which he was given by Archbishop George Abbott of Canterbury, to whom as Primate pertained of old the right of crowning the king. At his trial he claimed that 'strictly speaking...he was but a Minister to the Committee'. But as acting Dean of Westminster the principal responsibility for compiling and directing the ceremony devolved on him, as four hundred years or more of tradition prescribed, and it was he who corrected and altered the 'former book', a copy of the ritual used for James I. He must have laboured hard, for at first, before Henrietta Maria refused to take part, the coronation was to have been a joint coronation of Charles and Henrietta Maria, and a draft survives for the ceremony in this form, with provision for the anointing and crowning of the Queen and a French form of the Royal Oath for her to swear.[15] After her decision to absent herself, Laud must have been obliged to revise his work. On completion and after receiving royal approval he caused the new order to be written out at least twice with rubrics in red – these last most offensive to the Puritans as a revival of medieval practice. One of these copies, now in the Library of St. John's College, Cambridge,[16] is a little book handsomely bound in green leather gilt, with gilt edges and with red lines ruled for the margin. According to a tradition recorded by Archbishop Sancroft c.1685 this was 'ye very Book which the King held in his Hand at ye great solemnity'. Laud's own copy[17] is even smaller, and is bound in yellow calf, with gilt edges, and tied by blue silk strings. Laud carried out the King's instruction that 'ancient custom' should be observed by bringing the ritual into as close conformity with the *Liber Regalis* as possible. He did this in consultation with Charles, for on 18 January he took the notes he had made about the ceremony for the King to review. On 23 January he recorded in his diary 'I perfected the book I had prepared for the ceremonies of the Coronation, according it in all things with the *Liber Regalis*'.[18]

On 24 January the traditional Court of Claims was appointed to hear the suit of those who claimed the right to perform honorary offices and services at the coronation, such as holding a sword, or bearing the crown. On 31 January the Committee of bishops and the great noblemen who composed the Court of Claims attended the King by his command for consideration of the ceremony. Sir William Segar, Garter King of Arms, had already prepared a list of the 'Necessaries to be provided by the Mr of the Jewell House the daye of the King and Queens Coronacion', which included 'The Orbe, the Scepter, the Armill, and such other Regalls as he hath in his Custodye'.[19] The whole regalia, both the items from Westminster and those from the Tower, were brought to the palace where the King inspected them in the presence of the Committee of the Court of Claims. It must have been on this occasion that an incident recorded by Thomas Fuller, the great Caroline divine and historian, took place. It appears that the dove which surmounted the Queen's gold sceptre from the personal regalia had been damaged, and lost its left wing. Fuller writes:

The Day of the King's Coronation drawing near, His Majesty sent to survey and peruse the Regalia, or royal Ornaments, which then were to be used. It happened that the left wing of the Dove on the Sceptre was quite broken off, by what casualty God himself knows. the King sent for Mr. Acton, then his goldsmith, commanding him that the very same should be set on again. The Goldsmith replied that it was impossible to be done so fairly but that some mark would remain thereof. To whom the King in some passion returned, 'If you will not do it, another shall'. Hereupon Mr. Acton carried it home, and got another Dove of gold to be artificially set on; whereat when brought back, his Majesty was well contented, as making no discovery thereof.[20]

In a marginal note he adds that Acton's son, 'succeeding his father in that place of goldsmith, and then present, attested to me the truth hereof'. It seems that the dove had lain unrepaired for quite a few years, for the damage to the wing was probably that which was caused to the sceptre when Anne of Denmark had carried it at a court masque, on which occasion the dove is known to have lost a wing.

Charles also tried on the vestments of St. Edward, and commanded Laud to read out the rubrics from the order of service he had devised, so that the occasion was as nearly as possible a rehearsal. When the reading was finished, the regalia were taken back to Westminster and put away in the Chapel of the Pyx. Meanwhile a great square scaffold, railed in at the top, was being erected according to tradition between the choir and the high altar of the Abbey, between the four great pillars of the crossing. On this the King would be shown to his people at the beginning of the ceremony, and would later be enthroned and receive the homage of the spiritual and temporal peers. Again according to tradition it was covered with red cloth, and on it was placed the Chair of State, or throne, on a pedestal five steps high covered with cloth of silver. A 'traverse' or closet in which the King could take off the vestments of St. Edward and put on the ceremonial robes he wore in the final procession from the Abbey to the Palace of Westminster was set up well behind the altar on the right. A chair of state was placed by the south side of the altar but below it, while in a corresponding position on the north side was set the chair containing the Stone of Scone made for Edward I which is now known as the Coronation Chair. In this chair, then called St. Edward's Chair, Charles was to receive anointing and crowning.

One departure from precedent in a ceremony otherwise punctiliously conducted according to medieval ritual was the compounding of a special oil for anointing the King. From the coronation of Henry IV in 1399 to the coronation of James I it had been the custom to anoint the king with the holy oil miraculously delivered, according to early fourteenth-century legend, by the Virgin to St. Thomas à Becket while he was in exile in France. Perhaps none was left – the oil as delivered by the Virgin was contained in a very small stone phial – or perhaps it was thought dangerous to expose the King to Puritan censure by using an oil tainted with Popish superstition. Charles himself may have been reluctant to associate himself with a relic of the Papistry of which he sincerely believed the Church of England should be purified, all the more as his recent marriage to a Catholic made him more than usually vulnerable to accusations of crypto-Catholicism. Accordingly his court physicians, or perhaps only one of them, the celebrated Sir Theodore Mayerne, compounded oils of orange and jasmine, distilled roses, distilled cinammon, oil of been, ambergris, musk and civet to make an unguent that must have been more notably sweet-smelling than the holy oil of Becket, of which Queen Elizabeth complained in 1559 that it 'was grease and smelt ill'. The oil was hallowed by Laud, in virtue of his office as Bishop of St. David's, for by ancient Church usage only a bishop could hallow holy oils.[21]

In accordance with the prescriptions of the *Liber Regalis*, on the evening before the coronation Laud exhorted Charles to give himself up to contemplation and prayer. The traditional vigil procession had been abandoned for the same reason that James had also found himself compelled to abandon it, namely the prevalence of the plague, and Charles was brought next morning from the Tower by barge to the Parliament Stairs. This caused a mishap, for Sir Robert Cotton was waiting at his own stairs, where Charles had been expected to disembark, in order to greet him with one of the greatest treasures of his famous library, the Gospel-Book of King Athelstan, then believed to be the book 'upon which for divers hundred years together the Kings of England had solmnelie taken their Coronation Oath'.[22] In spite of this contretemps, Cotton managed to deliver the book in time for use at the ceremony. Although modern scholarship has disproved its claim to be the ancient coronation gospel-book, its use at Charles's coronation shows how anxious he and his entourage were to introduce into the ceremony all that was august by reason of its venerable association with the coronation and with the ancient kings who had made England a kingdom and founded the royal line. From chroniclers like William of Malmesbury it was known that the Anglo-Saxon kings had generally been pious monarchs, numbering several sainted kings, and several saints among their daughters and relations, and these associations were much cherished by pious antiquarian royalists and by High Anglicans.

Charles and the peers robed in the Palace of Westminster and then came into Westminster Hall. In the middle of this great room a high stage had been erected surmounted by a throne. After the King had been set up in the marble chair at the upper end of the hall, a very ancient ceremony, he mounted this stage and seated himself on the throne. The Archbishop of Canterbury now appeared leading a procession composed of bishops, of clergy, including Laud as Dean and the prebendaries of Westminster, and of the singers of the Chapel Royal and also of Westminster Abbey. They brought 'the ancient ornaments and Ensignes of Honour vsed in the Coronations of the Kings of England'. They presented these insignia from the Westminster regalia to the King who received them and handed them one by one to his favourite George Villiers, Duke of Buckingham, who as Lord High Constable laid them on a table beside the throne.[23] Once the regalia were set out, and after the procession of clergy had withdrawn, one by one they were brought to Charles by Buckingham, who handed them to him on bended knee. The King then delivered them to the individual noblemen and bishops who were entitled either by hereditary right or by royal favour to carry them in the opening procession from Westminster Hall to the Abbey with which every coronation began. Charles took off his hat after Buckingham had delivered the crown, and in the procession walked bareheaded along a cloth laid on fresh gravel from the door of Westminster Hall, the traditional means of marking the processional way. He too broke with earlier tradition by wearing under his rich coronation robes only the humble white of a postulant as prescribed by the *Liber Regalis*, imitating his father James I by not wearing the red shirt in which his predecessors had been clad over the white shirt. The white dress of a postulant had been from early medieval times the ritual garb in which the uncrowned king entered the Abbey for his coronation, Henry IV and his successors had broken with both the appearance and the spirit of this dress by wearing magnificent royal robes of red in the opening procession. When Fuller says that Charles's motive in wearing white was 'to declare that Virgin Purity with which he came to be Espoused unto his Kingdom', this was probably merely sentimental royalism in that loyal divine, for the truth was that the red shirt was regarded as useless, and superfluous. (For further discussion of the coronation dress, see pp. 325-7).

The regalia were carried into the Abbey in this procession, again according to ancient custom, recorded as early as 1189. St. Edward's Crown, St. Edward's Sceptre, St. Edward's Rod, St. Edward's Staff and the great Chalice known as the Regal, together with its Paten, belonged to the Westminster regalia, while the 'Orbe of Rule' and the three Swords, the Curtana, or Sword of Mercy, the 'pointed sword of temporall Justice', and the 'sword of spirituall Justice' were from the personal regalia. Other items from the personal regalia were also brought from the Tower by the Master of the Jewel House, such as the Imperial State Crown, sceptres and bracelets, for use in the closing procession, when the King after changing out of the vestments of St. Edward into royal robes, returned in state to Westminster Hall. The procession in which the regalia and King were escorted into the Abbey was opened by the Aldermen of London, by the great law officers, by the Knights of the Bath whom according to custom the King had newly created in honour of his coronation, by the Master of the Jewel House, and by the Privy Councillors. Next came the Gentlemen of the Chapel Royal and the Prebendaries of Westminster, all singing as they walked. Then followed the barons in their parliament robes and the bishops in scarlet gowns and lawn sleeves. After them walked the viscounts and earls in their velvet 'Creation', that is, peers' robes, bearing in their hands the crimson coroneted caps of maintenance they would wear in the closing procession. This part of the procession was punctuated by heralds.

Now advanced the great lords or officers of state bearing or accompanying the regalia. First came the Earl of Montgomery bearing the Spurs, followed by the Earl of Salisbury bearing St. Edward's Sceptre. Then came the three Swords, Curtana in the centre, as its primacy demanded, the Sword of Temporal Justice on the left, the post of lesser honour, and that of Spiritual Justice on the more honourable right. They were borne respectively by the Earls of Essex, Kent and Dorset. Then came the Lord Mayor of London, holding his mace, Garter King of Arms and a Gentleman Usher, all walking before the Great Chamberlain, Lord Worcester. After him came the Marquis of Hamilton as Earl of Cambridge, bearing 'the sword in the scabbard', the King's ordinary Sword of State, with Buckingham as Constable on his left and Thomas Howard, Earl of Arundel, Earl Marshal, on his right. St. Edward's Rod borne by the Earl of Rutland and St. Edward's Crown, borne by the Earl of Pembroke and the Orb borne by the Earl of Sussex came next, followed by St. Edward's Chalice borne by the Bishop of

London and its Paten borne by Laud. Then followed the King, his train borne up by two noblemen. He was supported as tradition demanded by the Bishops of Bath and Wells and walked under a canopy borne by the representatives of the Cinque Ports, known for the day as Barons. The procession was closed by his gentlemen and other household officers and by Sergeants at Arms.[24]

Archbishop Abbott was lame with gout, and instead of following the custom by which the procession of clergy from the Abbey to Westminster Hall fetched the King and headed the opening procession, the clergy were distributed instead in various sections of the procession. At the door of the Abbey, Charles was received by Laud in his role as acting Dean, and by the prebendaries all vested in rich copes. In order to do so, they must have waited at the door, leaving the rest of the procession to enter the Abbey. Laud now 'delivered into his Majesties hand the Staff of King Edward the Confessor'. The Staff, a tall wooden rod with an iron pike in its lower end was topped by a dove and plated on its lower-half with silver-gilt and on its upper half with gold. It was part of the Westminster regalia and one of the objects which may genuinely have had an association with the Confessor. From the fifteenth century it was occasionally used at coronations and at other great ceremonies; it was carried in Mary's coronation procession in 1553 and again in that of James I in 1603. By 1540 it had also come to be used as a ceremonial staff which was delivered to a king when he entered Westminster Abbey in state. This was presumably because Edward was regarded as the real founder of Westminster and as each king was in turn Edward's successor, he inherited his rights and privileges as founder, of which the Staff was evidently regarded as a symbol. Among the sceptres and rods of the Westminster regalia, which all had a powerful symbolism as emblems of an aspect of royal power, the Staff alone could be used to figure this relationship between the Abbey and the kings without confusion.

Charles mounted the scaffold, attended only by the lords, and was then presented bare-headed and standing by the Archbishop according to custom to the north, west, east and south, each time with the customary request first to the people on the north and south and then to the lords on the east and the clergy on the west of the choir for consent to his coronation. After being acclaimed King, Charles seated himself on the Chair on the scaffold while the Archbishop vested – he could not yet, of course, sit on the throne. Other regalia were already laid out on the altar and the Puritans were greatly offended when they saw standing on it the 'old Crucifix' as they called the *Crux Natans* or Swimming Cross, so named because it was said to have presented itself to Edward floating on the water on his return from his Norman exile to England in 1041. It too was part of St. Edward's Regalia, and it was tradition as well as High Anglican sentiment that had caused Laud to place it on the high altar. Meanwhile the Master of the Jewel House laid the Imperial State Crown in the traverse in readiness for the closing procession.

The regalia borne in the procession were offered up on the altar by the lords who had borne them, after the King had descended from the scaffold, attended by the Constable and Marshal, to make his customary offering of a pound of gold and of a pall to the church, and had then seated himself in the Chair of State set up on the south side of the altar. After the sermon and the Litany, Charles came to the altar and kneeling took the oath on the Gospel-Book of Athelstan, as the Archbishop repeated its clauses to him. He was now stripped of his robes, which were offered up at the altar, and then stood for a time in his hose and doublet of white satin – the doublet having special openings, fastened by ribbons, for the anointing. He was then led to the Coronation Chair by the Archbishop and by Laud, again acting as Dean. Here, while two lords held a canopy over him, he was anointed to the ancient coronation chant of *Zadok the Priest* which recalled the anointing of Solomon, on the hands, breast, between the shoulders, the elbows and crown of the head. Abbott and his Committee had determined that on the head 'the Unction was to be performed in *forma crucis*, after the manner of the Cross', in other words, after the old medieval fashion, which must have been abandoned at least for James I on account of Protestant abhorrence of the sign of the cross, as a piece of Papistical superstition. Its restoration was the most solemn, if private sign of the High Anglicanism that pervaded the service, partly no doubt under the influence of Laud, whose attempts to restore from the past what he thought doctrinally justifiable were soon to bring disaster on himself and his Church. It was the same spirit that inspired Charles to order the service to be conducted in accordance with 'ancient custom'. Although the Puritans were later to be refuted over the particular accusations they brought against some of the changes made in the prayers of the service, their sense that it restored more of the spirit of the medieval past than they could accept or tolerate was certainly justified. The anointing of the King as he sat in a chair was also a reversion to ancient practice: Henry VII and Henry VIII had both knelt before the Cardinal Archbishops of Canterbury, who had anointed them sitting in a chair. After the anointing of his head, Charles's hair was combed with the ivory comb which was part of St. Edward's regalia.[25]

After the anointing and combing, the traditional white coif was put on his hair to protect the oil, which would be washed off ceremonially only after eight days. Charles, still only in doublet and hose, was then led up to the altar where Laud, who as Dean of Westminster was the custodian of the Westminster regalia, 'brought forth the ancient Habiliments of King *Edward* the *Confessor*, and put them upon him'. These consisted first of the *colobium sindonis* formed like a dalmatic, then the supertunic or long close ankle-length robe decorated with great gold figures before and behind, then the gold brocaded hose and the sandals of cloth of gold. The hose Charles insisted upon putting on over the shoes he was wearing, so Laud records, complaining in a marginal note 'wch had almost indaingered ye tearing of ye old Tinsin Hose. It is safer to vnlase them before hand when they be vsed againe'.[26] The Duke of Buckingham, as Master of the Horse, fastened the Spurs on to the King, and then the Sword, described by Laud as the King's 'Ordinary Sword of State', which had been laid on the altar at the end of the procession, was given to him by the Archbishop and bishops and girded on to the King with its own belt by a peer. He was then vested in the stole so strangely used at Westminster as a substitute for the armills or bracelets demanded since the twelfth century by the coronation ritual, and in the great mantle, wrought with gold eagles, which was also part of the vestments of St. Edward's regalia. Both again were put on by Laud as Dean. The King now seated himself in Edward I's Coronation Chair. Laud presented St. Edward's Crown to the Archbishop who put it on the king's head as he sat in the Chair.

After this most solemn part of the investiture, Charles rose and went up to the altar wearing the vestments and crown. Here he received the first of the lesser ornaments, the ring, which was placed on the fourth finger of his right hand. Then linen gloves, specially preserved among the Westminster regalia, were put on his hands to protect the holy oil with which they were anointed, after which the King took off the Sword and offered it up on the altar, as a sign that he offered up this principal ensign of his secular authority to Almighty God. It was redeemed by the Marquis of Hamilton for £5 (a hundred shillings), who drew it out of its sheath and carried it thenceforward naked before the King for the rest of the ceremony. Then as the King stood at the altar, the Archbishop put St. Edward's Sceptre of gold, topped by a cross, into his right hand, then St. Edward's Rod, which was topped by a dove, into his left. The Earl of Pembroke, as Lord of the Manor of Worksop, had put the glove on the King's right hand, and now supported the hand as it held the Sceptre.[27]

Charles once more seated himself in King Edward's Chair, and the bishops came singly and in turn blessed the King while the pious Anglican Charles 'in King Edward's robes with the Crown upon his head rose from his Chaire and did bow severally to every Bishop apart'.[28] Charles also kissed each of the Bishops, as Samuel kissed the king whom he had anointed.[29] Then the King returned from the altar to the scaffold, escorted by the peers who had put on their caps of estate of crimson velvet at the solemn moment when the King was crowned, and by the Bishops. While the choir sang the *Te Deum* the King rested in a Chair of State set in front of the throne, and was then solemnly enthroned by the Archbishop, bishops and great nobles. The Archbishop now recited the address 'Stand and hold fast' in which the King was adjured in the words of the ancient Latin formula *Sta et retine* to hold fast to

. . . his inherited office, which is now delivered to him by the authority of Almighty God and by the hands of the Archbishop, Bishops and Clergy. He is to remember that he must give the greater honour to the clergy because they are nearer to the altar, so that he may be established by Christ, the Mediator between God and Man, as the Mediator between the Clergy and the Laity.

Later at his trial, Laud was to be challenged by the Puritans with having borrowed the words of his formula, so perfectly adapted to the High Anglican view of the king as ruling by divine right and as the Supreme Head of the

Church, from the Roman Pontifical. Laud admitted that he had done so, 'yet if it be good (as it is) there is no hurt', forgetting that the prayer was in the *Liber Regalis* and had been used at all English coronations from the tenth century.

Now as he sat 'in his Majestie the Drummes and Trumpets sounding, and the Church and aire filled with frequent Acclamations of the people', Charles received the homage of the Archbishop, who performed it kneeling, and in order to abridge an already long ceremony on behalf of all the bishops, who in Laud's disgusted words 'wear to slowe to keepe vp their owne order and dignitye'. The temporal peers by contrast insisted on their privilege of doing homage singly. The Duke of Buckingham as Lord High Constable for the day took the oath of homage, after which he swore 'all the nobility to be homagers'. Then as many of the peers as could crowd round laid their hands on the Crown and swore to maintain Charles and his heirs. All were supposed to kiss the King on the left cheek, but Charles told Laud that he would not have this ceremony performed by the bishops, 'nor did ye ArchBp. challenge it. So ye Temporall Lds. only did it'.[30] Charles in fact was no doubt eager to keep a lengthy ceremony as brief as possible, especially as throughout it he had to wear the heavy crown, ornaments and vestments. When the homage was over, he gave back the Sceptre and the Rod, which he was still bearing, to the lords who had carried them in the procession.

The ceremony of enthroning now being over, it only remained for the King to take Communion. The Archbishop descended from the scaffold and returned to the altar, where he began the Communion service. After the Creed and the Offertory, the King came down from the scaffold and made his traditional offerings of bread and wine for the Communion. Instead of returning to the scaffold, he then sat down in his chair to rest, and after resting, made his second traditional offering of a mark of gold (8*oz.* troy). The Archbishop received the gift, and proceeded to the consecration of the Sacrament while the King, instead of going to the altar as ritual allowed, in his piety remained kneeling on the altar steps. He took Communion with 'the faire Ordinary Towell wch he vses att White Hall' held before him by four bishops, the Archbishop administering the bread on St. Edward's Paten and Laud as Dean of Westminster the wine in St. Edward's Chalice.[31] Charles returned to his throne on the scaffold, and the Archbishop read the final prayers.

The King was then escorted in state from his throne on the scaffold into St. Edward's Chapel. Here he first took off his crown and laid it on the altar there, and then withdrew into his traverse, where he took off St. Edward's vestments, which Laud as Dean took and laid on the altar of the chapel, and put on, according to Fuller, a 'short Robe of red Velvet girt unto him lined with ermine'. He then returned from the traverse to the altar of the chapel, where the Archbishop put the Imperial State Crown on his head, which Fuller describes as 'narrower and higher' than St. Edward's Crown.

In the closing procession, when the King returned in state to Westminster Hall, Charles carried, not the Sceptre and Rod of St. Edward, as prescribed by the ritual, but the Sceptre and the Rod of the personal regalia, kept in the Jewel House in the Tower. The Sceptre and Rod of St. Edward were 'carryed before him by ye same Lords, to whom they were delivered att ye first. And thiss they all sayde was ye Custome', so Laud noted.[32] Ordinarily the King returned only the Westminster regalia to the Dean after the coronation feast, but as no coronation feast was to be held, no doubt on account of the plague, Charles restored them to Laud after they had once more mounted the stage in Westminster Hall. Charles also gave Laud Curtana and the other two swords that had been carried before him with their scabbards of cloth of gold, and ordered him to keep them with the rest of the Westminster regalia and to put them into the inventory of the regalia. Laud took the other ornaments from the Westminster regalia and the swords back to the Abbey, where he offered up the three swords on the altar 'to the perpetual use of the Kingdom and to the honour of the Church' – an action for which he was to be bitterly censured at his trial. He then put them away in the Chapel of the Pyx with the rest of the regalia, noting 'I left ye Inventorye of ye Regalia perfected: nothinge lost nor broken', and in the margin 'And the 3 swords added'.[33]

The ceremony had lasted from ten until three, but Laud recorded with great satisfaction that the day had been fine and sunny, and that he had heard earls who were walking with Charles in the closing procession say the ceremony was the quietest and best ordered of any they had ever attended.[34] This was not to be an augury of the future either of Charles and Laud, or of the regalia itself. The potency of monarchical symbolism which invested the Westminster regalia marked it down for the attentions of the rebellious Parliament. On 3 June 1643 the Commons, after rejecting the previous day a motion enjoining the Dean and Chapter of Westminster to deliver up the keys of the Chapel of the Pyx to Sir Henry Mildmay, Master of the Jewel House, who had taken the Parliamentary side, and to Henry Martin, MP for Berkshire and a future Regicide, passed a second motion by one vote ordering the Chapel to be broken open and the regalia inventoried, after which new locks were to be affixed and nothing removed except by order of the House. Mildmay and Martin were to put this resolution into effect. The scene that followed is vividly described by Heylyn. Mildmay and Martin, accompanied among others by the poet (and future Trustee of the Commonwealth sale) George Wither, tried to force the Sub-Dean to give up the keys, and when he refused, had the doors forced. In this way Martin

. . . made himself Master of the Spoil. And having forced open a great Iron Chest, took out the Crowns, the Robes, the Swords and Scepter, belonging anciently to K. EDWARD the Confessor, and used by all our Kings at their Inaugurations. With a scorn greater than his Lusts, and the rest of his Vices, he openly declares, *That there would be no further use of these Toys and Trifles.* And in the jollity of that humour, invests *George Withers* (an old *Puritan Satyrist*) in the Royal Habiliments. Who being thus crown'd, and Royally array'd, (as right well became him) first marcht about the Room with a stately Garb, and afterwards with a thousand Apish and Ridiculous actions exposed those Sacred Ornaments to contempt and laughter.[35]

Nevertheless St. Edward's regalia was left unharmed at Westminster until after the execution of Charles I in January 1649 and the subsequent passing of the Act for the abolition of kingship in March. Once this had been enacted, the Commonwealth felt itself entitled to dispose of all the former royal property, either as justly forfeited, or as belonging to the Crown, whose rights it now enjoyed. By another Act of 23 March Trustees were appointed to trace, inventory and value all the royal goods. The Council of State was empowered to decide on the retention or sale of all those valued at less than £10,000, but the actual disposal was entrusted to special commissioners. The Commonwealth, as might be expected, was bent on the wholesale destruction, rather than the sale of the regalia. St. Edward's regalia were inventoried once more, and although the vestments were left for the time being in their iron chest at Westminster, the rest of the ornaments, including St. Edward's Crown, Queen Edith's Crown, the gold chalice and paten, the ampulla, the mounts of the stole, the sceptres, staffs and rods, the spoon and the spurs, and all that had value as gold and pearls from the vestments were removed to the Jewel House in the Tower and marked for destruction along with the personal regalia already kept there. The only exception was the Cross, which later also took the same road to the Mint. On 9 August 1649 the gentlemen appointed by the Commons to be custodians of St. Edward's regalia were ordered to deliver it up to the Trustees, who were to have it broken up along with the regalia from the Tower and 'melt down the Gold and Silver of them, and to sell the Jewels for the best Advantage of the Commonwealth'. The Trustees had to overcome the resistance of the Clerk of the Jewel House, but in September they broke into the Jewel House and took away 'three crowns, 2 Sept(res), bracelets, globe, &c.' By the end of January 1650 the venerable regalia of the Confessor and the imperial crowns and ensigns of the Tudors were no more. Their metal had been melted down and sent to the Mint, their stones and pearls sold in parcels. The only item to escape was the silver-gilt anointing spoon, which was saved by its insignificance as a symbol of royal power and authority.[36]

The term jewels was still applied in the seventeenth century as it had been during the Middle Ages to much more than the small and precious ornaments for which we reserve the word. It included all goldsmith's work of an especially rich kind – most notably vessels of mounted crystal and hardstone and plate wrought in gold. As with Charles's treasure of goldsmith's work, it is difficult to resist the impression that his jewels in our sense were largely an inheritance from his father and from the Tudors. There were, it is true, court jewellers, George Heriot and the Frenchman Jacques Duart, but the financial crises of Charles's reign no doubt prevented him from lavish expenditure on jewellery. Probably he had relatively little interest in the jeweller's art as such, perhaps because he could not

49-50 [1-13]

50 [11]

afford the great stones and pearls which were such an inducement to the creation of magnificent jewellery and on which his extravagant mother Queen Anne of Denmark had spent such sums. For these, when worn, were an advertisement of the wealth and greatness of the prince and of his magnificence, and when not worn, were invaluable either as pledges or as royal gifts. Thus James I had offered Charles a great collar of thirteen gold links each set with a balas-ruby alternating with thirteen knots of pearls as a gift for the Infanta in 1623, requesting him to bring it home again if he did not think fit to give it to her, for it was a present 'not fitte for subjects'. Early in his reign Charles was to pawn it to the King of Denmark.[37]

Again James still owned one of the most famous of Burgundian jewels, the Three Brothers, now known to us only from a miniature in Basel (Fig. 85) and from portraits of James, who often wore it in his hat. Probably made for Duke Jean sans Peur of Burgundy c.1410, it was composed of three large table-cut balas rubies or spinels, to give them their modern name – the Three Brothers of their title – and of a great pointed diamond and four pearls. Captured by the Swiss from Duke Charles the Bold at the battle of Grandson in 1476, it was sold by Berne to the Fuggers of Augsburg, and from their hands passed into those of Edward VI who acquired it in Antwerp in May 1551. Along with another great jewel, known as the Mirror of Great Britain, made c.1605 of gold and set with the Sancy diamond and a lozenge-shaped diamond called the 'lettre H. of Scotlande' it was among the 'Roiall and Princely Ornaments and Jewells' which James declared on 27 March 1605 to be inalienable for ever from 'the Kingdome of this Realme'.[38] However, James himself gave it to Charles to take to Spain to wear during his courtship of the Infanta. And it was among the rich jewels and plate of the Crown that Charles pawned in Amsterdam in 1626 in order to finance his ill-starred intervention in the Thirty Years War. It led an undignified existence in the hands of various Dutch moneylenders until 1637, when it was redeemed along with

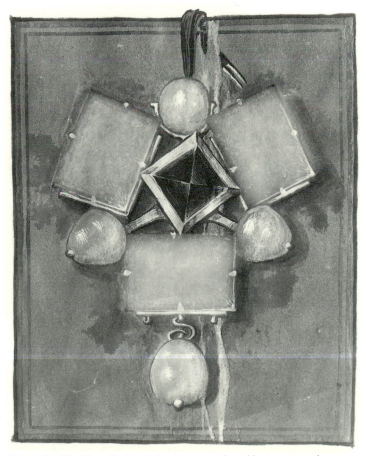

Figure 85 *'The Three Brothers'*: drawing reproduced by courtesy of the Historisches Museum, Basel.

other magnificences and brought back to England. We lose sight of it again in the 1640s, when it seems to have been once more in use as a pledge during the grave financial stresses of the Civil War.[39]

The history of the Three Brothers encapsulates in little the history of Charles I's jewellery, which appears in general to have been a pledging of the rich ornaments of the past. It is true that there was now in the later 1620s and 1630s much less encouragement from fashion to wear a rich array of jewels than during the late sixteenth and early years of the seventeenth century, when men wore much costly jewellery and women's dress was heavily decorated with ornaments of gold and pearls and precious stones, when women's headdress too was stiff with gold and jewels, and when ropes of pearls or chains of gold hung round their neck, rings loaded their hands, and rich earrings their ears. The fashions in jewellery of Charles's reign were far simpler and soberer, in keeping with the greater simplicity and sobriety of costume, with its relative emphasis on looseness and freedom and amplitude, compared to the stiffness and rigidity, splendidly patterned with jewelled ornament of the previous age. For men the hat-badge seems to have gone gradually out of fashion, and chains or ribands with their pendants were worn largely as badges of rank or office. The buttons fastening the coat or doublet might be of pearls. In 1642 Henrietta Maria wrote to Charles from Holland that she had finally pawned his fine pearl buttons: 398 in number they had already been pledged in Amsterdam once before, in 1626, along with Charles's other jewels and rich plate, and had been among the jewels redeemed in 1637. Now they served to raise money for the purchase of powder and carbines.[40]

Women's dress was equally simple, loose and flowing, and their jewellery showed the same restricted taste for pearls – colour was sought from ribbons rather than from precious stones. A short pearl necklace round the neck above the low bodice was now the favourite ornament, and this could be supplemented by pearl-earrings, usually drops, by a baldric or narrow girdle of pearls, and by a rope of pearls wound through the back of the hair. So much the portraits of Van Dyck reveal, with only an occasional bodice trimmed with pearls (Fig. 95), or a jewelled breast ornament, or rope of pearls worn over the shoulders and fastened to the breast ornament or to the side, or a pearl-mounted bracelet, or a hat-ornament to vary this insistent simplicity. At times we find indications of a rather more jewelled splendour, as in the Vienna portrait of Thomas Howard, Earl of Arundel, and his Countess Alethea in their peers' robes, in which the Countess wears a chain of jewelled links fastened to a jewelled breast ornament, but even here pearls dominate her necklace and small coronet. So strong and so apparently restricted a preference for pearls must have restricted patronage of the jewellers' art. No longer were the elaborately complex mounts of the Late Renaissance, rich with stones, pearls and enamels, wrought with richness of ornament and fantasy of motif or symbolism, required from the goldsmith-jeweller. Even the pendant, that cherished focal point of the rich collars and chains of the sixteenth century was no longer in such high fashion, although the wearing as pendants of miniatures of a beloved person in rich enamelled and jewelled cases remained popular.

The great exceptions to this change were as just noted the badges of rank or office that the King and the great wore. In the case of Charles, the two great royal badges were the insignia of the Order of the Garter and the Collar of SS. The Order of the Garter, founded by Edward III in the 1340s, had as its original ensign an actual garter, worn on the left leg, consisting of a blue riband with mounts of precious metal which on occasions were jewelled. This was sometimes embroidered or otherwise decorated with the Order's famous motto HONI SOIT QVI MAL Y PENSE. The other insignia of the Order instituted by Edward III were the mantle, surcoat and hood, which from the first were always of blue, like the garter itself. The hood was later supplemented by a black velvet cap which by the time of James I had become a black velvet hat. By the reign of Charles I it was generally plumed with white feathers, with a hat-band 'set thick with Diamonds . . . And sometimes the Brims have been tacked up with a large and costly Jewel' says Ashmole. There is evidence from c.1364 of a badge of the Order in the form of a garter bearing the motto and encircling a motif, for one is listed in the inventory of that year of Louis, Duke of Anjou. But unlike other late fourteenth- and fifteenth-century orders of chivalry, the Garter badge was not worn from a collar, chain or riband until the reigns of Henry VII and Henry VIII. The introduction of a collar was perhaps prompted by imitation of the Burgundian Order of the Golden Fleece and the French Order of St. Michel. The precise date when the collar was first instituted is unknown, but it was certainly in existence by 1507. Equally certainly it was Henry VII who chose for it the Tudor devices of white and red roses, which were intended to signal the reconciliation in the new dynasty of the rival houses of Lancaster and York.[41]

It was Henry VIII who in his statutes for the Order of 1522 regulated the wearing of the collar and badge of the Order and their form.[42] The collar was to be of gold weighing thirty ounces troy, composed of links shaped as garters encircling alternately a white and a red double rose. From it was to hang a pendant in the shape of a figure of St. George, the patron of the Order and also of the English kings from the time of Edward III, who had chosen him as a warrior saint and therefore a patron of knighthood. This was the collar for the great feasts of the year: on other days the knights were allowed to wear a small gold chain from which again was to hang an image of St. George. In war this could be hung from a simple silk lace. It was forbidden to set the collar itself with precious stones, but the pendant of St. George could be enriched at the pleasure of each individual knight. The links of the Garter collar, according to Ashmole, were generally enamelled blue, with the letters of the motto reserved in gold, and the number of the links was twenty-six, corresponding to the fixed number of knights composing the Order, their fraternal unity being figured by the gold knots that joined each pair of links together. This number of links, however, was often theoretical, rather than actual, and it must be said that some variation seems to have occurred in these motifs during the sixteenth century. The statutes of Edward VI of 17 March 1553 required only red roses, and the pendant was to be a massive gold figure of St. George, seated on horseback, holding a drawn sword, and encircled with the Garter. These Edwardian statutes however were never put into effect. The George that was worn with the great collar of the order was known as the Great George. 'It is allowed', writes Ashmole in 1672, 'to be garnished with Diamonds, and other enrichments, at the pleasure of the *Knight-Companion* who owns it; and upon that license, hath been frequently adorned with variety of costly art, whereon the Diamonds and other precious stones are so disposed, as may upon its motion and agitation cast out the greater lustre'. By the reign of Charles it generally took the form of St. George on horseback, tilting with his spear at the dragon. Made in gold, cast in the round, and in the sixteenth and seventeenth centuries often gaily enamelled, it was not encircled by a border of the Garter, like the Lesser George, which was the more everyday badge of the Order, worn pendant from a gold chain or by the reign of Charles I more usually from a riband.

Originally the colour of the riband had been optional, though black was usual and had been prescribed by the abortive statutes of Edward VI. In 1622 James I enacted that

. . . whereas the colour of the ribband had not been particularly expressed in any article of the statutes, and the blue or sky-colour had been used for some years past, the ribband shall in future always be of a blue colour and not other; nor, in time of mourning for any of the knights-companions, of what degree soever, shall the colour be changed[43]

It was said that Elizabeth's favourite, the Earl of Essex had introduced this fashion after a visit to France, where he saw the badges of the French royal orders of St. Michel and the Saint Esprit worn from blue ribands. Ashmole records in 1672 that 'the ordinary manner of wearing this *Ribband* in time of peace, was (till of late) about the neck, down to the middle of the breast, where the *Lesser George* hung' and this was the fashion in which Charles I wore it, as can be seen in Van Dyck's portrait of him in his Garter robes (Fig. 101).[44] In armour, however, he and the other knights wore it suspended from a small gold chain, as in other Van Dyck portraits of him at Arundel, Longford Castle, and in the Hermitage, and he was represented wearing it in this fashion on the gold coins he issued at Oxford during the Civil War. In the early seventeenth century the Lesser George was usually an oval pendant, whose frame was the Garter, enclosing a figure of St. George.

The ensigns of the Order of the Garter were presented by the King as Sovereign of the Order to foreign princes and kings who were admitted as knights, and on their death these were solemnly to be returned to him, at least in theory. They were always rich and costly, as might be expected, and those presented by Charles I were no exception, as can be seen from the account of the stones set in the Garter Collar, Greater George and Lesser George he sent to Gustavus Adolphus, the great King of Sweden and defender of Protestantism, when he was made a Knight of the Garter in 1627.[45] The stones set in them were inventoried by Charles's order on 24 May 1635, after the death of Gustavus Adolphus and their solemn return that April,[46] when they were handed over to the custody of the Dean and Chapter of St. George's Chapel, Windsor, 'to be preserved there in memory of that famous King'. On the Garter the motto was picked out in letters and stops composed of 292 small diamonds, while 113 more, both large and small, decorated a star and a cross and the four buttons, chape, buckle and hinge with which it was fastened. Some of these last were faceted or table-cut, and square or oblong in shape. The Great George was also set with 'large and resplendent Diamonds': ten small ones decorated the three gold chains by which it hung; others the feather in the Saint's cap and and his forehead. Faceted diamonds, some quite large, were set on his armour, from breast-plate to foot, while the horse's head, crest, mane, neck, shoulders, rear and leg and his bridle and trappings were also set with diamonds. The dragon too was set with diamonds on his forehead, wings and body. These jewels were buried in St. George's Chapel for safe-keeping at the beginning of the Civil War, but were 'discovered' by a certain Cornelius Holland, and brought away to London by John Hunt, Treasurer to the Trustees appointed by Parliament in 1649 for the sale of the King's Goods, and sold, according to Ashmole, to Thomas Beauchamp, the Clerk to the Trustees.

Charles I's own Garter, 'which his said late Majesty wore upon his Leg at the time of his Martyrdom' also had the motto picked out in diamonds, 'to the number of 412'. It came into the hands of Captain Preston, one of Cromwell's Captains of Horse, who delivered it to the Trustees. They in turn sold it to John Ireton, a Lord Mayor of London, for £205. At the Restoration, Ireton was summoned before the Commission appointed to discover the whereabouts of Charles's regalia, plate and jewels, but Ireton, though not denying he had bought the Garter, refused all composition and after a lawsuit was fined £205 and £10 costs. This must be the 'Garter of blue Velvett sett with 412 small Diamonds formerly in Captain Prestons Custody and now in the Clossett at Somersett house', valued in the inventories at £160 which was sold by the Trustees to Ireton on 3 January 1650, for, as Ashmole records, £205.

Charles also had a number of other Georges.[47] One, a Great George found in the Jewel House at the Tower, had figures of the saint and the dragon in the round of enamelled gold, set on a base or 'ground' of silver gilt and enamelled green. The figures were valued at £99, the base at £10, and both were sent to the Mint. Another, recorded by the Trustees as a 'george of gold sett wth dyamonds' was valued by them at £70: it had come from Colonel Thomlins or Thomlinson and was bought on 17 May 1650 by William Widmore. Ashmole also records other Georges that were sold by the Trustees. One valued at £60 and sold for £71. 2s., was set with 161 diamonds, and was again 'discovered' by Cornelius Holland in the hands of Lady Leicester. A Little George set with only a few diamonds was valued at £8 and sold for £9, another, set with five rubies and three diamonds was sold with eleven diamonds in a box for £11, again a pound more than its valuation, and another cut in a garnet was sold for £8, having been valued at £7.[48]

Fortunately Ashmole caused Hollar to engrave in 1665 for his book on the Garter the most interesting of all these Georges, that worn by Charles 'at the time of his Martyrdom' (Fig. 86). He describes it as

…curiously cut in an *Onix*, set about with 21 large Table Diamonds, in the fashion of a *Garter*: on the back side of the *George* was the picture of his *Queen*, rarely well limn'd, set in a Case of Gold, the lid neatly enamel'd with Goldsmiths work, and surrounded with a like number of equal sized Diamonds, as was the foreside.

This was presumably the 'George cut in an Onix, with 41 Diamonds in the Garnish' which was valued by the Trustees at £35, and sold by them for £37.[49]

Although Charles in no way modified the jewels of the Garter, ever anxious for the honour of the Order, he promulgated an ordinance on 27 April 1626 ordering all the Knight Companions to wear the Cross, which as the arms of St. George formed the badge of the Order, encircled by a Garter on the left-side of 'their Cloaks, Coats, and Riding Cassocks' whenever they were not wearing their robes. In this way it would always be plain that they belonged to so honourable an Order, and not merely on its great feast days. The 'escutcheon' was not however to be 'enriched with Pearls or Stones', which Charles no doubt thought unbecoming to a Christian knight. Ever anxious too, to infuse into the Order a revived spirit of piety, as we have seen when discussing the Communion plate made for the Garter, he ordained in 1629 that the badge was to become a star by

52[1]

45[-]

324[34]

Figure 86 *The 'Habit and Ensigns' of the Order of the Garter,* engraved by Wenzel Hollar for Ashmole's *Institution . . . of the Garter.* In the centre at the bottom are three views of 'The George which his . . . late *Majesty* wore at the time of his Martydom . . . curiously cut in an *Onix'.* Ashmolean Library, Oxford.

the addition of rays of glory issuing from the cross and forming a star-shaped aureole around the whole badge (Fig. 101). This change is commemorated in a medal struck in 1629 with the crowned bust of Charles on the obverse, wearing the collar of the Order over an ermine mantlet and on the reverse the new star-shaped badge with the motto PRISCI DECUS ORDINIS AUCTUM (The Ornament of the Ancient Order Enhanced). He is again shown wearing the badge in this form in portraits by Van Dyck. Presumably, however, such badges were always embroidered.[50] (See further p. 343.)

The other ensign worn by Charles on occasions was the ancient royal livery collar of SS. This now consisted of a number of links shaped in the form of a letter S—originally when the collar had first come into use as the livery badge of John of Gaunt, probably in the 1360s or 1350s, it had been a riband to which metal letters had been affixed. The significance of the letter S is a mystery, still unexplained. The collar of SS had become the livery collar of the royal house in 1399 when Henry of Lancaster, John of Gaunt's son, usurped the throne from Richard II and became Henry IV. In 1401-2 he promulgated an ordinance regulating its wear in his presence and absence. As a Lancastrian badge the collar of SS fell from favour under the Yorkist kings, Edward IV and Richard III, but was resumed again by the Tudors, in pursuit of their policy of blazoning their claim to have reconciled in their own dynasty the rights and claims of the two rival houses. The collar seems to have been given in the fifteenth century by the Lancastrian kings to those they wished to raise to the rank of gentleman, of which a collar was regarded as a principal ensign. In the sixteenth and seventeenth centuries it had lost all significance as a political or feudal badge, but was still a traditional royal collar, and could be worn by all knights who wished to blazon loyalty. As a badge of office it was worn by the Lord Mayor of London in a Tudor form, with the S links alternating with a white rose on a red, all linked by knots, and with the Tudor badge of the portcullis as its pendant. It was also worn by judges, notably the two Lord Chief Justices of the Benches and by the Chief Baron of the Exchequer, in the form of SS linked by knots with a rose in the middle at front and back, each rose set with pearls. Closely similar collars of SS were also worn by the Heralds. In observation of a medieval etiquette of distinction among the precious metals, certainly dating from the fourteenth century, if not before, plain esquires were entitled only to a collar of SS of silver, while knights wore one of silver-gilt. The King himself wore one of gold: presumably it was also worn by the especially privileged in this rich form. Charles's collar of SS was inventoried for the sale of his goods as 'One Coller of Esses of gould formerly in Collonell Harrisons Custody and now being in the said Clossett' (of Denmark House). It weighed 35½ ounces of gold, and so was of considerable weight as well as price. It was not sold, but valued at £3 an ounce, making £106. 10s. and despatched to the Mint. In the desperate circumstances of 1646 Charles had already pledged another 'Coller of Esses', from which hung a Lesser George, the whole set with some 800 diamonds, presumably mostly small, for £500 to Thomas Hamond, Lieutenant-General of the Artillery under Sir Thomas Fairfax.[51]

52[2]

Notes

1. This chapter incorporates some of the research undertaken for the compilation of the forthcoming catalogue of the Crown Jewels, to be published by Her Majesty's Stationery Office. A useful general introduction to the subject of the regalia is given by the two books by Lord Twining, *A History of the Crown Jewels of Europe* (London, 1960), and *European Regalia* (London, 1967).

2. For lists of the Westminster regalia see the inventory of 1359 (published by J. Armitage Robinson in the introduction to his edition of John Flete, *The History of Westminster Abbey* (Cambridge, 1909), p. 19). For Flete's own list see ibid., p. 71. The list of Richard Sporley (mid fifteenth-century) and the inventories of 1605 (repeating an earlier document of 1559) and of 1649 can be consulted in L.G.W. Legg, *English Coronation Records* (London, 1901), pp. 191-2, 242-4, 272-5.

3. See the treatise of Walter of Sudbury in Richard of Cicencester, *Speculum historiale* (Rolls Series), ed. J.E.B. Mayor (London, 1863-9), II, pp. 26-39.

4. J. Spelman, *The Life of Alfred the Great* ed. T. Hearne (Oxford, 1709), p. 29.

5. Much the best account of the personal Regalia of the Tudors is given by A.J. Collins, *Jewels and Plate of Queen Elizabeth I: the Inventory of 1574* (London, 1955), pp. 264-8, nos. 1-6; 271, no. 16. His remarks on the constitution and use of the regalia (pp. 17-18) show the usual confusion. But his annotations to the inventory of 1574 are invaluable for the history of the personal Regalia.

6. P. Heylyn, *Cyprianus Anglicus* (London, 1671), pp. 147-8.

7. For this crown see Collins, op. cit. (Note 5), p. 7.

8. For these references and a discussion of the legal position of the Crown jewels in the official and popular mind see Collins, op. cit. (Note 5), pp. 168-9, 174-5.

9. Spelman, op. cit. (Note 4), p. 29.

10. For all this see Collins, op. cit. (Note 5), pp. 266-7, nos. 1, 4, and p. 12.

11. T. Fuller, *The Church-History of Britain* (London, 1655), Bk. II, p. 144.

12. For the coronation of James I see J. W. Legg, *The Coronation Order of King James I* (London, 1902), which collects the sources. The Order of Service as given by William Prynne in his *Signal Loyalty* (London, 1660), Pt. ii, pp. 263-302, is reprinted by C. Wordsworth, *The Manner of the Coronation of King Charles the First of England* (Bradshaw Society) (London, 1892), pp. 106-37, who also prints a manuscript account of it from BL, 6284, Pl cxx.A.f.36.

13. Heylyn, op. cit. (Note 6), p. 145.

14. The sources for the coronation of Charles I are collected in Wordsworth, op. cit. (Note 12). A manuscript draft of the service in BL, Hare MS 5222, was edited by Legg, op. cit. (Note 12), pp. 245-71: it is for a joint coronation of King and Queen. The account of Thomas Fuller in his *Church-History* should be controlled from Wordsworth's documents: its accuracy was contested by Heylyn immediately after publication.

15. Lambeth Palace, London, MS 1076.

16. St. John's College, Cambridge, MS L.15.

17. St John's College, Cambridge, MS L.12.

18. See Wordsworth, op. cit. (Note 12), pp. viii-ix (date of 23 Jan misprinted as 13); *cf.* William Laud, *The History of the Troubles and Tryal . . . of William Laud* ed. Henry Wharton (London, 1695), pp. 26-8.

19. Cited by Collins, op. cit. (Note 5), p. 16, no. 2 from BL, Cotton Vespasian cxiv, f.136.

20. Fuller, op. cit. (Note 11), Bk.XI, p. 109 [*sic*] i.e. p. 121-4.

21. Wordsworth, op. cit. (Note 12), pp. xx-xii, 4. The herald John Bradshaw (in ibid., pp. liii-vi) is clearest about the Chairs and their arrangement.

22. Letter from Sir Simonds D'Ewes, printed in H. Ellis (ed.), *Original Letters illustrative of English History* (London, edn. of 1825), III, pp. 213-9. The claims of the Athelstan Gospel-Book were exploded by F. Wormald, 'The so-called Coronation Oath-Books of the Kings of England', *Beiträge für Georg Swarzenski* ed. O. Goetz (Berlin etc., 1951), pp. 233-7.

23. For these details see the account of the Coronation by John Bradshaw, in Wordsworth, op. cit. (Note 12), pp. liii-vi.

24. For the order of the procession and the complex question of the regalia I follow the official order of procession as recorded in PRO, SP Domestic King Charles I, xx.8, printed by Wordsworth, op. cit. (Note 12), pp. xlix-liii.

25. Ibid., p. xlv.

26. Ibid., p. 36, note 5; *cf.* also p. xlv.

27. For these details I have compared Bradshaw, in Wordsworth op. cit. (Note 12), pp. liii-vi, with Laud, in ibid., p. 41.

28. Fuller, op. cit. (Note 11), Bk. XI, p. 123 para. 24; *cf.* also Wordsworth, op. cit. (Note 12), p. 43.

29. 1 Samuel X, 1.

30. Fuller, op. cit. (Note 11), Bk. XI, p. 123 paras. 25-7; Wordsworth, op. cit. (Note 12), p. 46, n. 6.

31. Wordsworth, op. cit. (Note 12), p. 52.

32. Ibid., p. 54, note 2.

33. Ibid., pp. 54-5.

34. Ibid., p. x.

35. Heylyn, op. cit. (Note 6), pp. 147-8.

36. For events see *Inventories*, pp. xiii-xiv; Collins, op. cit. (Note 5), p. 190-1; and the literature they cite.

37. Collins, op. cit. (Note 5), p. 181.

38. Ibid., pp. 168-9.

39. *Notes and Queries* 10th series 3 (1905), p. 429; Collins, op. cit. (Note 5), p. 172.

40. Collins, op. cit. (Note 5), pp. 180-1.

41. Still invaluable is the lengthy chapter 'The Habit and Ensigns of the Order', in Elias Ashmole, *The Institution, Laws & Ceremonies of the most Noble Order of the Garter* (London, 1672), pp. 202-34; for the hat see p. 215.

42. Ibid., Appendix, f.h.i. art. xxxviii.

43. G.F. Beltz, *Memorials of the Most Noble Order of the Garter* (London, 1841), pp. xcix, cvii. Collins, op. cit. (Note 5), p. 566.

44. Ashmole, op. cit. (Note 41), p. 227.

45. For the insignia sent to Gustavus Adolphus see ibid., pp. 222-3, 228.

46. For their return see Beltz, op. cit. (Note 43), p. cix.

47. Ashmole, op. cit. (Note 41), p. 204.

48. Ibid., pp. 228, 202.

49. Ibid., p. 228. This Garter Badge was last recorded in the possession of James II: for its history and attempts to identify it see A. Payne–Gallwey, *A History of the George worn on the Scaffold by Charles I* (London, 1908), and The Duke of Wellington, 'The scaffold George of Charles I', *Antiquaries Journal* 33 (1953), pp. 159-68.

50. Beltz, op. cit. (Note 43), p. cviii; Ashmole, op. cit. (Note 41), pp. 215-6.

51. There is an extensive literature on the collar of *SS* and I have investigated its early history in my forthcoming *Medieval Jewellery*. For the collar of *SS* as seen by the antiquaries of the late sixteenth and seventeenth centuries see W. Camden, *Remains concerning Britain* (London, edn. of 1870), p. 210; John Selden, *Titles of Honor* 3rd edn. (London, 1675), pp. 691-2; and Ashmole, op. cit. (Note 41), pp. 224-6. For Charles's collars see Collins, op. cit. (Note 5), pp. 178-9.

8 'Shadows, not substantial things'. Furniture in the Commonwealth Inventories

Simon Jervis

Marginal numerals refer to page and entry numbers in the *Inventories* (see p. 11)

The furniture described in the inventories made after Charles I's execution poses grave problems for the historian and commentator. Because relatively little furniture of royal quality has survived from the early seventeenth century, it is difficult to match inventory entries with surviving objects. Because the more or less detailed descriptions such as are found in inventories are scarcely ever accompanied by illustrations, certainty as to the original form of the objects described is all too often unattainable, and the distinctions between different terms can rarely be fixed.[1] The language used by those who made the inventories was moreover often a kind of short-hand jargon, not dissimilar to that used by the modern auctioneer, and similarly liable to imprecision and to local and personal variation, not to say inaccuracy. Because so many of the terms used remain current, it is sometimes difficult to discern their original significance through the confusing filters of later usages. And because so much of the furniture surviving from this period is provincial oak, the recreation of a complex hierarchy, in which rich and exotic materials, above all textiles, and sophisticated ornament were vehicles of display, involves the radical modification of obstinately persistent images derived from such works as Joseph Nash's *Mansions of England in the Olden Time*, from oak-filled stately homes, from collectors' manuals, and from museums and antique shops.[2]

The strategy adopted here comprises first a description and evaluation of the various furniture types included in the inventories, and second some remarks on their combination and arrangement, in so far as these can be reconstructed.

Chests, Coffers, Trunks, Standards

Chests are the most basic form of furniture for storage, although they can also be used for seating. If of iron they provide extra security. The regalia at Westminster Abbey were listed 'in an Iron Chest where they were formerly kept'. 'A Chest wrought wth Iron, and lyned wth Peach culloure sattine', later described as 'The Iron Chest' and valued with 'three more Chests of the same makeing' at £8, was used to store textiles at Denmark House. Two iron chests at Hampton Court were valued at £5 each. It seems reasonable to assume that such iron chests, and a broken one in the Tower Jewel House, valued at £2, were more or less stock items of no unusual size or complexity, although their material made them much more valuable than a normal wooden chest. Another iron chest in the Tower Jewel House, valued at £20, must have been an object of a different size or order, probably the latter, as a 'great Iron. Chest in y[e] tow[r] over y[e] Coale house' at Windsor was valued at only £1. 'One rich Iron Chest' in Captain Blackwell's lodgings at Whitehall, valued at £25, was clearly something special and probably represented luxury as well as security. 'Two little Iron Truncks with 2 little Effigies', received from Mr Jolly and valued at £2. 10s., were probably also luxury items but much smaller.[3]

All these objects were probably covered in iron, although with a wooden core. 'One greate Trunke bound about wth Iron' from Wimbledon, valued at £1, a 'Woodden Boxe barred with iron' at Denmark House, and 'One old Coffer bound wth yron' in the Windsor wardrobe, valued at £1, represent a different and less secure type, only partly covered in iron. In 1639 Thomas Hardwicke, trunk-maker to the Queen, delivered 'a large trunk bared and plated wth Irons to keep her ma.ts gownes', priced at £1. 10s. and probably an example of the type completely covered in iron.[4]

Iron or iron-bound chests form only a small part of those listed. But already a problem of nomenclature has arisen. What is the difference between a 'chest', a 'coffer', and a 'trunk'? The different terms must have had different meanings, however confused and interchangeable in practice. In a study of predominantly seventeenth-century West Country inventories it has been observed that when they occur in the same inventory they always occur in the same order, viz. chest, coffer, trunk, suggesting a hierarchy as well as a distinction.[5] According to

The marginal references read:

51 [-] , 105 [-]

107 [190]
183 [298-9]

252 [69]

252 [63]

295 [225-6]
343 [2] 2

419 [3]

58 [16]
112 [249], 293 [32]

Randle Holme's *Academy of Armory* a chest had a flat lid and a coffer a rounded lid.[6] The difference reflects a craft demarcation. Chests were traditionally the preserve of the joiner whereas coffers were made by coffer-makers (who were members of the Leathersellers' Company) and were originally a travelling type, covered in leather, hence the rounded lid to throw off the rain.[7] The term 'trunk' also refers to a type made by coffer-makers, and therefore normally of leather. At Wimbledon were 'Two Sumpter trunks wth Locks', valued at £2: these were trunks to be carried by a pack animal. In 1637 Thomas Hardwicke delivered 'A p[air] of large Sumpters Covered wt. neats leather wt. good locks & ironwork to carry her Ma.ties lynnen in Removes', priced at £3. 10s.[8] A fourth closely related term is 'standard', which meant a large portable chest related to coffers and trunks and usually covered in leather: it is not to be confused with the textile type of standard, which also crops up in the inventories.[9] 'A blacke Leather Standard' valued at 15s. was listed at Denmark House as was 'A square Standard of leather' valued at £1. 10s.[10] In its squareness the latter presumably departed from the norm, as must have done 'A Flatt Standard, and a flatt Coffer', valued together at 10s., in their flatness. The appearance at Windsor of 'One old Chest covered wth leather', valued at 6s., demonstrates that any simple equation of chests with wood breaks down.

Most of these containers and the many chests, standards and trunks listed without qualification are likely to have been plain. It is a relief to turn to those with some decorative interest. A first category is provided by four cypress chests at Denmark House, two of which, valued at £4 together, contained Queen Anne's parliament and coronation robes, while the other two, valued at £2 and £1. 10s. respectively, contained further rich textiles. Cypress, with its pleasant smell, was regarded as a protection against moths: in the *Taming of the Shrew* cypress chests contained 'arras counterpoints'.[11] Such chests were imported from Northern Italy, and, to judge from surviving examples, were almost invariably decorated, usually, in the seventeenth century, with pen-work grotesques and armorials.[12] Sir Thomas Fairfax had a 'cyprus coffer' in his bed-chamber at Walton in 1624 and Lady Dorothy Shirley had 'One cipres chest of coverings for stooles and window cloathes' in the Great Chamber at Farringdon in 1620: in such positions these are unlikely to have been undecorated objects.[13]

Leather was not always plain. In 1619 to 1620 John Lewgar, royal coffer-maker, supplied Charles I, then Prince of Wales, with 'ij wainscot Boxes covered with red leather gilt' for £1. 4s.[14] It is likely that 'A redd leather guilt Chest', valued at £1. 5s., at Denmark House, where it contained rich textiles, was not dissimilar. Elsewhere in the inventories are 'a guilt redd leather Case', containing a green jasper cabinet, and another similar containing rock crystal bottles, a 'black leather guilt Case' and a red similar, both for looking glasses. Here the type of furniture supplied by coffer-makers merges with the custom-made leather containers of a type made to contain goldsmiths' work and similar precious objects since the Middle Ages.[15] In 1637 Edward Cordell, the queen's cabinet-maker, delivered 'a greatt read Spanish leather Cass for a greatt tortis shell standishe lyned wth fyne Carnascyon callicoe with ribine poyntes of Carnascyon scyllck for her maijs. bead-chamber', priced at 12s.: it must have been a leather container of this kind.[16] And there were probably close connections with bookbinding. The outer case of Lord Ellesmere's travelling library, in the form of a book, gives an idea of the probable appearance of such cases.[17] It is probable that although such items as 'a redd leather chest lyned with Crimson sattine', which contained a crystal cabinet at Denmark House, a 'redd leather Case', containing a white cabinet 'of Counterfeite stones', another containing a fan, a 'blacke leather Case' containing a lute, and a 'leather Case', which held a mounted porcelain basin, all lacked gilded ornament, they were small, tailor-made and to a degree decorative. 'Two redd leather Chests wth drawers' may by contrast have been furniture proper: the Victoria and Albert Museum possesses what would now be called a trunk with brass nail ornament including the monogram of William and Mary, which incorporates two drawers.[18] Such forms were highly conservative and this example is close to a trunk from Rushbrooke Hall in Suffolk, which has a traditional association with Charles I and bears his monogram.[19] In 1639 Thomas Hardwicke, the trunk-maker, delivered 'a large tronke haveing 4 draws. & couvrd. wt. Russia leather wt. good locks & Ironworke', priced at £4, and 'a less tronke wt. hoggskyn haveing 2 drawers 7 p[ar]titions in them; & double locks', priced at £3: these may have been trunks of this type.[20]

Leather was the staple of the coffer-maker, but coffers could be of many materials, including wicker.[21] The most regular variation was to cover coffers in textiles. Thus in 1563 the royal coffer-maker John Grene delivered a 'Coffer of waynescott with Diverse tylles in it and a room above covered with purple ffustian of Naples…',[22] while in 1601 the contents of Lady Shrewsbury's bedchamber at Hardwick included 'a little coffer covered with black velvet'.[23] In the Charles I inventories are 'A Greene vellvett Coffer' containing six shirts belonging to Henry VIII and 'Two. Coffers covered wᵗʰ black fustian'. Chests, boxes and cases were also covered in more or less rich textiles. Thus at Denmark House were 'a Crimson vellvett Chest' valued at £1, 'A small Chest of Crimson sattine enbroydʳᵈ with gould and silver', valued at £1. 10s., 'A flatt Chest of Arras worke' valued at 15s. and 'A Boxe of redd velvett enbroydered with gould and silver' valued at £1. Cases were of black, watchett (light blue), murray (purple), and green velvet. Many such objects must have been ornaments in their own right to an even greater degree than the leather cases mentioned above. Thus the 'Crimson vellvett Case' containing a wonderful crystal galley at Denmark House valued at £100, was itself protected by a 'blacke leather boxe'. In 1637 Edward Cordell, cabinet-maker to the queen, supplied 'a greatt Coup Cass Couffered Insyd and outtsyd with Crymson vellet and lassed wᵗʰ golld lasse with greatt Coper Joyntes ringes loupes and rosis and gyllte with golld for her maijs. Coupe', at £1. 5s., and 'a spoune and knife Cass Couffered wᵗʰ vellett and lassed with gold lasse', at 10s., presumably cases of this luxurious type.[24]

Sometimes it is difficult to say whether a case is a solid object or a loose cover. If chairs have 'caises of red Cotton' or 'a Case of Crimson Bayes' there can be little doubt that these are loose protective covers. The same seems probable but not certain with 'a leather Case lyned with redd Cotton' accompanying a tortoiseshell cabinet.[25] But when a mirror is listed with 'a Case of russett Sattine enbroydered with gould Twist and seede pearles' and 'an old Case of Carnacon Taffaty' definite conclusions are even more elusive.

So far this account has been mainly concerned with containers which were either relatively plain and functional, or whose decorative interest was less than that of the objects which they contained. 'An Indian Chest', valued at £10, 'An Indian Truncke', also valued at £10, and another 'Indian trunke', valued at £10 with its contents, viz. '7 boocks a straw hatt' were clearly of a different order. 'Indian' was a very flexible term: according to Purchas writing in 1613, 'The name of India is now applied to all farre-distant countries, not in the extreme limits of Asia alone'.[26] However the probability must be that these are Japanese lacquer objects, such as were directly imported to England by the East India Company from 1613 to 1623 and indirectly through the Dutch East India Company thereafter.[27] The cargo of the first trading ship, *Clove*, included two 'small trunckes or chests of Japan stuff guilded and set with mother of pearl', sold in 1614 for £4. 5s. and £5.[28] 'The peece. wᵗʰ Mother. of pearle & 2 dores' among the paintings at Hampton Court, valued at £40, could have been an exported triptych in this style.[29] But even allowing for price fluctuations it seems likely that the chests and trunks at Denmark House would have been larger, and, if later, probably lacked the mother-of-pearl.[30] They may have resembled the 'two very fine chests covered with gold and Indian varnish' given to the Duke of York by the Dutch East India Company which Samuel Pepys saw in 1661.[31] More problematic is 'one Indian box wᵗʰ an Indian Armor in it' which was almost certainly in the Indian Chamber at St. James's Palace. Armour and box were valued together at £10, so the latter was probably much less ambitious than the chest and trunks discussed above. Japanese lacquer is known to have been exported to India, particularly for presentation to the Great Mogul, but in view of the character of the armour it contained (see p. 353) it seems more likely that this was a direct import from Japan.[32]

The 'Case of woodd painted' which contained a copper and silver fountain valued at £60, and 'A painted Case', which contained a coral, silver and mother-of-pearl confection, valued at the surprisingly low figure of £2, may have been European equivalents of these exotica, perhaps painted with grotesques, but they may equally have been merely coloured versions of the 'white Woodden Boxe' which contained thirteen amber images. On the other hand 'A Boxe of Eboney' was by its very material fashionable and exotic. It is tempting to suggest that 'Two. small coffers. garnished wᵗʰ glasse', valued at 5s, may have been of ebony or ebonized wood decorated with *verre eglomisé* and produced in South Germany.[33] Equally, 'Two. casketts of steele', also valued at 5s, could also have been South German, and perhaps similar to those produced in some quantity by Michel and Condradt Mann in Nuremberg.[34] But their values are so low and the descriptions so brief that all speculation must be kept in check.

104 [164]
183 [297]

111 [–], [234], 112 [252]
112 [254]
112 [247]
111 [241], 115 [280-81]
117 [301], 118 [312]

117 [299]

288 [153], 120 [330]

123 [359]
115 [282]

121 [339]
129 [408]
251 [49]

202 [281]

154 [49]
154 [48]

117 [308]
118 [309]

117 [303]
113 [258]

181 [265]

180 [240]

'A smaller Coffer of Carnacon vellvett all studded with silver guilt with 4 Lyons now newe covered with greene vellvett' was by contrast valued at £50, and sold for £51.[35] This must have been an ambitious and luxurious item. An elaborate jewel casket in the Victoria and Albert Museum, of steel covered in red velvet with pierced and engraved brass and steel ornament, bearing the monogram of William and Mary, provides a later comparison.[36] In 1558 John Grene was supplied with 'asmoche crimsen Satten as will serve to lyne certen tylles of a Jewelle Coffer the whiche is covered with Tawnie velvett edged with pasamayne lace of gold & gilt Iron worke', an earlier parallel, unless that at Denmark House was, as seems possible from the circumstance of its having been re-covered, a sixteenth-century coffer.[37] If the four lions formed its feet, as seems likely, there is a direct comparison in the table clock of about 1610 by David Ramsay, clockmaker to James I, in the Victoria and Albert Museum, incorporating an anti-papal engraving.[38]

Dressers, Cupboards, Presses, Cabinets

In the Charles I inventories, dressers are utilitarian objects to be found in the kitchens and offices at Hampton Court, Bewdley House, Holdenby House and Wimbledon House. They have little value, three at Wimbledon House being appraised at 15s. It is unclear whether these dressers had superstructures with shelves for dishes, in the tradition of the late medieval dresser or buffet, on which plate was displayed on grand occasions, and which was more usually called a cupboard in England, or whether they were simple kitchen side-tables.[39] The 1641 inventory of Tart Hall lists in the milk house 'A Dresser and two Shelves' and in the kitchen 'A Frame Dresser of Deale & two other Dressers standing upon Tressells, whereof one a thicke one'.[40] This usage seems to imply that the dresser is simply a flat surface, on which vessels are set or food prepared, which needed a frame or trestles to support it. On the other hand John Price, an Oxford cook, had 'a Dresser of five shelves' in 1637.[41] The Charles I inventories also include three 'dresser boards' in the kitchen at Theobalds, valued at 10s., and 'Two old Dresser boards' among sundry goods received from 'Mr Willis'. There may have been little difference between these and dressers as described at Tart Hall. However Richard Percival in his *Bibliotheca Hispanica* of 1591 translated 'tajon' as 'a boord to cut flesh on, a dressing boord', suggesting the possibility of a restricted meaning for dresser boards.[42]

Furniture historians have laboured endlessly on the interpretation of the term, cupboard, which perhaps reaches its most confused stage in the seventeenth century.[43] Like dressers, to which they are, as noted above, closely related, cupboards listed in the inventories are low-value objects, even at first sight startlingly so, as with 'Foure Cupboard Joyned. wth doores and 20 ordenarie Cupboards' at Hampton Court, valued at £3 only. Often in the mid seventeenth century, cupboard seems to have implied a piece of furniture with a storage space enclosed by doors.[44] But in this entry there is a clear implicit distinction between four of that type and twenty presumably without doors. A plausible explanation is that these twenty were very simple side-tables, which could have been covered with cloth and used for serving and the display of plate, like the 'Court-Cubbords' shown in Ashmole's illustration of a Garter banquet.[45] Holbein's *Ambassadors* of 1533 in the National Gallery is an excellent illustration of a simple court cupboard. A plate in the 1672 Robert Pricke translation of Du Breuil's *La Perspective Pratique* illustrates two three-tier sideboards, one with a small recessed cupboard between its upper tiers.[46] In the original French they are called *buffets*, one with a 'petit Cabinet, ou Armoire . . . au milieu'; Pricke calls them 'Court-Cupboards' and describes that with the 'petit cabinet' as a 'Cupboard' with a 'little Cabinet . . . in the midst'.[47] Less usefully the later English translation by E. Chambers published in 1726 describes them as a 'Buffet' and a 'Buffet' with a 'little Cabinet or Locker'.[48]

In the Charles I inventories '3 old Court Cupboards' are listed at Wimbledon House, valued at a mere 5s., and 'One old Court Cuppboard' is listed among the goods received from Mr Willis. Apart from these probably outworn objects the term is confined to provincial contexts of Ludlow Castle in Shropshire and Bewdley in Worcester where little in the way of refurbishment seems to have taken place since the death of Sir Henry Sidney in 1586.[49] At Ludlow ten court cupboards were widely distributed from the Prince's Bedchamber to the

185 [333], 238 [259]
241 [293], 297 [236]

395 [973], 420 [7]

182 [287]

296 [229]
420 [2]

224 [80]

112 [253]

228 [126], 229 [145], 227 [124]
238 [259, 270]
239 [272]

239 [273-4, 276]

182 [287]

197 [195]

114 [272]

114 [269]

183 [294], 238 [267]
239 [272], 285 [135]

296 [229]
182 [284-5]

394 [949], 213 [75]

182 [287]

114 [269, 272]

114 [270-71, 273]

182 [286]
394 [952]

282 [100]

296 [228], 293 [-]

48 [210]

153 [37], 154 [40, 51-2]
225 [87]

Governor's Kitchen and the Hall, and only one, in the Governor's Quarters is described as 'old'. At Bewdley are three, one in the kitchen, the others in chambers. One of the latter is accompanied by 'One small Presse Cuppboard', clearly of the contrasting type with an enclosure: presumably this made up most of their combined value of £1. Randle Holme lists among the other items necessary to a dining room 'Side tables, or Court cubberts'.[50] It thus seems possible that a 'syde Cuppboard' and two others listed in chambers at Bewdley may have been variations on the court cupboard.

If the suggestion made earlier that the '20 ordenarie Cupboards' at Hampton Court were side tables is adopted, it seems reasonable to infer that any object described as a cupboard in these inventories should on balance be regarded as a non-enclosed piece of this type, unless of course the entry provides some evidence for enclosure. The mention at Hampton Court of 'A Marbell. peece on a Cupboard' in the middle of an inventory of paintings suggests that this cupboard too was a relatively simple support. Equally 'A wainscote Cuppboard with twoe leaves' at Denmark House sounds more table than enclosure, as does 'A Cuppboard of Wainescote guilt, standing upon a frame', an object comparable perhaps to the 'Frame Dressers' at Tart Hall mentioned above.[51] On the other hand a 'Cupboard Cabbonett' at Hampton Court, valued at 10s., another 'Presse Cuppboard' at Bewdley, and a 'Close Cubboard of wainescott' at Oatlands, valued at 8s., are clearly cupboards in the modern sense. Prices may provide assistance in distinguishing the two basic types: there would normally have been less wood and work in a open than in an enclosed cupboard, and the former would have been cheaper. The three old court cupboards at Wimbledon were valued at 5s. It would thus seem likely that 'Four old Cupboards' and 'one little 3 Corned Cupboards', presumably to stand in a corner, listed at Hampton Court and valued at 8s. and 2s., respectively, were of the open type, whereas a cupboard at Theobalds valued with a table at 8s. and another at Richmond valued at 6s. were enclosed. This statistical approach may be applied to the 'Foure Cupboard Joyned. wth doores and 20 ordenarie Cupboards' at Hampton Court, valued at £3: a reasonable calculation is that the twenty were priced at 2s. each, and the four at 5s. each.

There are two problems in the application of such a formula. First most of the cupboards are not individually priced, and second several which are priced are described as being of wainscot, that is high quality imported oak, and/or gilded, both factors which may have increased their value.[52] Hence despite their relatively high values of 5s. each the cupboard with a frame and that with leaves at Hampton Court, which were of gilded wainscot and wainscot respectively, may have belonged to the open category as proposed above, and if these were open it seems likely that two others of 'plaine Wainscot' and one of 'Wainscot guilt' listed alongside them, with less revealing entries, but also valued at 5s. each, may also have been open. By contrast the values of 'One wainescott Cupboard' at Hampton Court and 'One guilded Cupboard' at Theobalds, £2 and £1 respectively, are are so high that it seems likely that both were of the closed type. However 'Twelve ioyned Cupboards of sundry sorts' at Oatlands valued at £2 defy analysis.

The term press cupboard has already been noted and interpreted as meaning a cupboard with an enclosure. In the seventeenth century a press was usually a large storage cupboard, sometimes subdivided, sometimes with pegs for hanging clothes, the equivalent of the modern wardrobe.[53] Confusingly the Pricke 1672 translation of Du Breuil's 'Grandes Armoires' is 'great Cabinet': Chambers in 1726 provides the more straightforward 'large Presses or Cupboards.'[54] Examples of the first type can be identified in the Charles I inventories, as 'One great Press. wth 4 roomes' at Wimbledon House, valued at £1, and 'One old press. in y[e] wardrobe wth boxes' at Windsor, valued at 10s. The rooms in the former were presumably open compartments behind the doors. The boxes in the latter may have resembled those behind the doors of 'The New Cubborde of Boxes' made by Lawrence Abelle for the Corporation of Stratford-on-Avon in 1594, but it is possible that the Windsor press had no doors and was a frame containing drawers, resembling late medieval prototypes.[55] Only in the cases of a press in the Upper Jewel House in the Tower containing 'All the Knives and Cases . . . (the Cases being 16.) whereof 4. of them being silver', of two presses in the Armoury at St. James's Palace, valued at 10s. each and containing respectively ten and thirty 'burding peeces', and of a 'Presse' in the wardrobe at Ludlow Castle, which contained spare pieces of the gilt leather and green kersey hangings from the Shovel Board Chamber there, is there direct evidence of function, although

230 [148]
183 [301]

'One large Presse with Locke and keye', in Lord Berkeley's Chamber at Ludlow, was presumably a particularly secure specimen. And only one example, 'A Large press gilded wth Leather' at Hampton Court, valued at £1, can be described as a luxury object.

225 [87, 92], 227 [124]
228 [126], 230 [148, 156]

234 [219], 235 [234], 228 [126]

The only location containing presses in any number was Ludlow Castle, where twelve were widely distributed from the Chief Justice's Chamber to the Governor's and Marshal's Quarters. It should be noted, however, that press, like standard, is an ambiguous term: in the Governor's Kitchen at Ludlow were 'one Presse, & one smaller Presse to presse Lynnen'. Joseph Moxon, who in 1670 copied the plates of Hendrik Hondius I's *Instruction en la Science de Perspective* of 1625, described, the linen-press shown in one simply as 'a Press'.[56]

While remote Ludlow Castle abounded in court cupboards and presses, it contained not a single cabinet. Of the thirty-seven cabinets listed in the Charles I inventories no less than thirty-one were at Denmark House, and of the remainder five were at Hampton Court and a singleton at Wimbledon. Cabinet is another ambiguous term. It can signify, among other things, a small private room, an executive council of state, and a collection of arts and antiquities, all meanings current in the seventeenth century. By the second quarter of that century the cabinet, as a piece of furniture, normally connoted a box, large or small, filled with small drawers, usually with doors, but sometimes with a fall-front or no doors.[57] It was the most fashionable and conspicuous furniture type of the age. But cabinet could also mean a rich case, usually subdivided, for the reception of small and often precious articles. Thus the 1614 inventory of the Earl of Northampton included 'three bowles of gold in a cabonett of redd velvett' and 'one cabinett of purple velvett with a chesse boord and men sutable laced with gold lace'.[58] Randle Holme illustrates a cabinet of this sort, and a particularly elaborate example is shown in the foreground of a cabinet piece by Frans Francken II.[59]

183 [294]
111 [241]

A 'Cupboard Cabbonett', at Hampton Court, valued at only 10s., and a 'Cabbonett of Pomander', at Denmark House, valued at £5, are cases apart, the former presumably a wooden cupboard of the closed type with numerous drawers, the second probably deriving its high value from its precious and aromatic contents. A cabinet 'of steele worke', valued at 10s., is likely to have been a relatively modest object comparable to the steel caskets mentioned earlier. The next category comprises 'A Cabbonett of Cloth of silver lyned wth Orringe Tawney vellvet enbroydered with gould silke and spangles, and garnished with silver', valued at £2, 'A. Tawney Cabenett enbroid^d', valued at £2. 10s., and 'One Cabbonett of vellv^t wth the History of Hercules', valued at £5. The first two may either have been rich cases or small cabinets with drawers, resembling in form the many English stump-work and embroidered boxes and cabinets surviving from the seventeenth century, most of them unprofessional products.[60] Their decoration may have resembled bookbindings, such as a prayer-book of black velvet with silver and enamel mounts, given by Christian IV of Denmark to Kirsten Munk in 1617, or a richly and professionally embroidered *Book of Psalms of David*, illuminated by Esther Inglis in 1624 and presented to Charles I when Prince of Wales, both now at Rosenborg in Copenhagen.[61] The third cabinet, with the story of Hercules, seems likely, from its value, to have been larger: although covered in velvet it may have resembled a group of ebony cabinets with fine professionally embroidered doors and drawer-fronts which have been attributed to Antwerp.[62]

112 [246]
180 [240]
112 [243]

412 [79]
183 [293]

122 [351]
112 [242]

'One square Cabbonett of stone lyned wth Crimson Taphatie', valued at £5, and 'Two Cabbonetts one . . . white of Counterfeite stones with a Crowne on the Topp . . . The other of Greene Jaspers garnished with silver guilt', valued together at £20, are difficult to pin down.[63] Stone cabinets, apart from those of inlaid marble, are not common. At Schloss Ambras is a very elaborate architectural cabinet mainly of alabaster and marble, but also decorated with wood, silver, gilt-bronze, and semi-precious stones. It was in the 1596 probate inventory of Archduke Ferdinand, and was probably made for him in Augsburg, as was an ebony cabinet of similar form now in the Kunsthistorisches Museum in Vienna.[64] Venetian lacquer boxes and cabinets sometimes included marble plaques but do not seem to fit the above descriptions.[65] A 'Cabinett of Artificial stone with Drawers' which stood on an oval table at Tart Hall in 1641 provides a comparison.[66] The green jasper cabinet may have had a specific function: according to a lapidary of 1609 the stone, found in many parts of Germany and Bohemia, was considered efficacious against epilepsy.[67]

'A Marble Table inlaied with stone of divers collo^{rs} upon a frame suiteable' and 'A Cabbonett of Marble suiteable', valued together at £60, are clearly objects of a different scale and importance. The Luttrell inventory of 1590 illustrates a number of inlaid marble tables, square, circular, octagonal and rectangular, and Jacob Rathgeb, the Duke of Wurtemberg's secretary saw 'tables of inlaid work and marbles of various colours' at Theobalds in 1592.[68] At Hatfield House are two tables with inlaid marble tops, one of which may be '1 square table of stone inlaid with colours' listed in the 1621 Hatfield inventory, and quite possibly transferred to Hatfield from Theobalds.[69] In the library of Canterbury Cathedral is an octagonal marble table with inlaid scenes from Ovid made for Dr John Bargrave around the middle of the seventeenth century.[70] There is some evidence that the combination of cabinet and table was a contemporary one: the Victoria and Albert Museum possesses a tortoiseshell cabinet and a table *en suite* which probably belonged to the first Earl of Craven, and in 1683 'My Lord Huntingtower's Chamber' at Ham House contained 'One Cabinet, glasse table and stands of Inlaid wood'.[71] The 1664 inventory of the Maréchal de la Meilleraye lists a similar combination.[72] It is impossible to be certain as to the form or provenance of the Charles I table and cabinet, but it is most likely that they were of Florentine manufacture, possibly with drawer fronts decorated with birds and flowers such as John Evelyn purchased from Domenico Benotti in Florence in October 1644 and which were standard by the mid-century.[73] 'A Cabbonett of yellowe Amber garnished wth silver guilt with an Eboney Boxe', valued together at £20, was probably a comparatively small object, perhaps similar to a small amber cabinet in the Swedish Royal Collection or another with silver mounts formerly at Mentmore.[74] Amber cabinets could be of considerable size: at Nuremberg is an example over a metre high, which may perhaps have been made as a wedding present for the future Friedrich Wilhelm I of Prussia in 1706 or might even be the large cabinet sent to Queen Mary of England by the 'Duke of Brandenburgh whose country, Prussia abounds with amber cast up by its see' which Evelyn saw in 1687.[75] The whole range of amber objects, cups, game boards, house altars, statuettes, handles for cutlery and so on, were produced in Königsberg, where Georg Schreiber was the leading master from about 1610 to 1643, in Danzig, which Philipp Hainhofer used as a source of supply, and in Stolp, all on the Baltic, and examples are noted in most seventeenth-century princely collections (and in the 1656 catalogue of the Musæum Tradescantianum): for example 'Een ambre cabinet off cofferken seer cierelyck gemaeckt' was in the possession of Frederick Henry, Prince of Orange, in the Hague, in 1632.[76]

Seven mother-of-pearl cabinets are listed in the Charles I inventories. From their values, £1 and £1. 10s. respectively two were clearly small objects, perhaps comparable to 'a little deske of mother of pearle' in the Best Bed Chamber at Hardwick in 1601 or to the 'little boxe inlaid with mother-of-pearle' which Dorothy Lady Shirley bequeathed to her niece, Gertrude Gibbes, in 1634.[77] Their form may have resembled that of a mother-of-pearl casket with magnificent Parisian silver-gilt mounts in the Rennaissance style, probably of 1532, now in the cathedral of Mantua, or a similar mother-of-pearl casket with seventeenth-century silver mounts, which was exhibited in Amsterdam in 1936, or a simple mother-of-pearl coffer with seventeenth-century gilt bronze mounts at Waddesdon.[78] A spectacular mother-of-pearl basin in the Grünes Gewölbe in Dresden, mounted with silver-gilt in Nuremberg in about 1580, a mounted bowl in Hamburg, from the possession of the Rákóczi family, and a similar bowl in the Victoria and Albert Museum, both seventeenth-century, all display the same mother-of pearl technique, which is found on a large number of objects in the Topkapi-Museum in Istanbul, suggesting an Ottoman origin or at least inspiration for this type of artefact.[79] But it has been proposed that their origin may lie further east in the Kingdom of Cambay (Gujarat) in India.[80] It is possible that a table-top of mother-of-pearl with details of tortoiseshell at Hatfield House, which could be the survivor of those 'richlie inlaid with pearls' described in a 1629 inventory, may also represent these Indian or Turkish exports.[81] Another mother-of-pearl cabinet at Denmark House, which stood upon a frame of 'blacke woodd', presumably ebonized, and was valued at £8, was perhaps a larger version of those mentioned above, as may have been another valued at £13, some of which must have been accounted for by the mass of silver and 'other gummed flowers' stored in its lower drawer. 'Three Cabbonetts of Mother of Pearle garnished with silver guilt, and meane stones', valued at £60, must represent a different order of luxury, and it is tempting to associate them with 'the little tables

121 [335]

111 [240]

112 [245-6]

111 [237]

382 [775]

111 [238]

and the boxes that are encrusted with mother-of-pearl and gems in Sinde', which are mentioned by the Italian travel-writer, Clemente Tosi, in 1669 and must have had some resemblance to Mughal jade vessels inlaid with gems.[82]

From about 1640 tortoiseshell, usually backed with vermilion, became an increasingly fashionable decorative material for cabinets.[83] However, boxes and caskets of tortoiseshell were seen at Whitehall in 1600 and as early as 1632 Sir Richard Boyle, first Earl of Cork, noted 'A Cabbonett of Torties shell', and the 1638 inventory of Anne, Viscountess Dorchester, included a little cabinet of 'tortas shell'.[84] Presumably 'A small Cabbonett of Tortesse shells' in the Charles I inventories, valued at £3, resembled the latter. 'One large Cabbonett of Tortesse shell in an Eboney frame', valued at £30, was evidently a much more substantial object. Already at Tart Hall in 1641 was 'A little Ebony Square Table inlayde with Torteaux shells', and in the same year the Parisian craftsman, Pierre Lallemant, contracted to make an ebony cabinet engraved with flowers and with 'un panneau d'escaille de tortue' on each of its doors.[85] In 1645 Marie Fourmenois, widow of an Antwerp dealer in glass and ebony, Cornelis de Wael, had in her possession 'schelpen van schilpaeden' and a large tortoiseshell mirror.[86] She and her husband, Matthijs Musson, were subsequently to sell many tortoise-shell cabinets, and in 1651 Robert Spencer, commissioned by a friend to buy her an ebony cabinet, recommended instead a tortoiseshell cabinet, of which 'the best choice is at Antwerp.'[87] From at least 1652 the Antwerp firm of Forchondt was also to export many tortoiseshell cabinets.[88] However given that the large cabinet at Denmark House was probably purchased around 1640 at the latest, the case for Antwerp attribution is non-proven.

'An Ivory Cabbonett with a paire of Playeing Tables in them, and a lookeing Glasse with sundry Emptie drawers', valued at £40, and another 'Cabbonett of white Ivory', valued together with two ebony cabinets at £70, may have resembled an ivory cabinet which has certainly been at Skokloster since 1728.[89] With enamelled scenes of the Passion in gilt ovals on its drawers, this cabinet was probably made at Augsburg in about 1630: there is a similar example in the Victoria and Albert Museum.[90] Also at Skokloster is a somewhat later ivory cabinet, introduced in about 1841, which was probably made in Augsburg, as may have been an ivory casket decorated with polychrome engraving and set with gems in the Castello Sforzesco in Milan.[91] Writing in 1610 Philipp Hainhofer stated that 'gar schöne schreibtisch von Ebenoholz, helfenbein, und anderm holtz' were then being exported from Augsburg to Prague, France, Italy and Spain.[92] The great monuments of the genre are three ivory cabinets in the Bayerisches Nationalmuseum, one, with richly carved decoration and a parquetry outer case, made in Munich by Christoph Angermair, who had earlier worked for Hainhofer in Augsburg, for Maximilian I of Bavaria from 1618 to 1624, and two others, which are, for all their splendour, simpler, made in Augsburg by Melchior Baumgartner, whose father, Ulrich, had also worked for Hainhofer, in 1646 and 1655.[93] In an English context the grandiose 'Ivorie Cabinet' listed in 1677 in the North Drawing Room at Ham House and still there merits a mention, although it probably dates from about 1660.[94] The cabinets at Denmark House and Hampton Court are unlikely to have competed with such masterpieces.

The thirteen ebony cabinets in the Charles I inventories constitute by far the largest category of cabinets. In 1614 Henry Howard, Earl of Northampton, had owned a cabinet 'of ebony inlaied with white bone' and 'an Ebony Cabinett inlaied with mother of pearle'.[95] In 1623 the Duke of Buckingham paid £8 in Spain for a 'Spanish Cabonett of Ebony', and in 1629 John Webster wrote from Amsterdam offering Lord Carlisle '2 cabinetts which are made heere the one of Ebony wood, and the other of marble wood both very curiously made and valued about 150 l or 120 l star.'[96] Frederick Henry, Prince of Orange, had 'Een cabinet van ebbenhout met verscheyden laeykens' in The Hague in 1632.[97] Already in 1588 the Augsburg cabinet-maker Bernhardt Seydler claimed that he and his colleagues worked exclusively in ebony, which was claimed to be 'nicht für den gemeinen Mann sondern fur Standespersonen'.[98] In October 1605 Jean Heroard, the doctor of the Dauphin, the future Louis XIII, described his charge, then barely four years old, playing with his toys and 'à un petit cabinet d'Allemagne, fait d'ébène, baisse et rebaisse le couvercle, l'ouvre et le ferme à la clef'.[99] And as late as 1637 the Parisian cabinet-maker Jan Bolt contracted to finish 'un cabinet d'esbeine fasson d'Allemagne' for the widow of Jehan Senapre, a cabinet-maker of the Faubourg Saint-Honoré.[100]

Ebony cabinets were thus an international fashion by the 1630s, although Germany, and in particular Augsburg, was still the leading focus of production and imitation. It is possible that German style cabinets were being produced in London by 1625 when 'Cabbynett-makers' attended James I's funeral among the 'Artificers of the Roabes'.[101] Edward Cordell, cabinet-maker to Henrietta Maria, may also have made German style cabinets. His bills of the 1630s do not mention his making any cabinets of this type, although Cordell did supply leather cases for ebony cabinets, and oak cabinets covered with gilt leather, which may have resembled an earlier 'cabinet' now in the Victoria and Albert Museum, possibly made for Edward VI.[102] Indeed, most of Cordell's deliveries seem more appropriate to a trunk-maker or even an upholsterer than to a cabinet-maker proper. The less valuable cabinets in the Charles I inventories seem to have been plain, apart from one decorated with a dog and a monkey, valued at £2. 10s.[103] But they seem not to have been particularly small: another valued at £2. 10s. is described as long and 'with many Boxes in it', two valued together at £5 had '2. plaine black Tables to sett y^{em} on', while a plain cabinet 'with Drawers and a Frame suiteable' was valued at £7. Of the more expensive ebony cabinets valued from £25 to £60, five are given disappointingly summary descriptions apart from the information that one is large and has 'a Frame suiteable'. However 'One blacke Eboney Cabbonett with 5. silver Images curiously wrought with silver Supporters, and studds' valued at £30, would seem to fit into a known category of Augsburg cabinet, including one of about 1600 by Boas Ulrich in the Victoria and Albert Museum.[104] Another 'garnished with brasse worke guilt upon a Frame suiteable with a Cover of leather lined with redd Bayes' valued at £50 may have been a larger and more elaborate variation. However 'A rich Cabbonett of Eboney inlayed with silver with flowers and Beasts, and a Clock in the Topp &c . . . having one Serrindge Three Combes one paire of gould scalles 12 silver Instruments 2. paire of Sizers with one instrument more of silver', valued at £150, is clearly in a different class. It seems possible that this cabinet may have resembled those produced by Philipp Hainhofer in Augsburg from about 1610 to 1630 and including the *Pommersche Kunstschrank*, destroyed during the last war in Berlin, which was delivered to Duke Philipp II von Pommern in 1617, the *Stipo Tedesco* purchased by Leopold, Grand Duke of Tuscany in 1628 and still in the Pitti Palace, and the cabinet presented to Gustavus Adolphus by the City of Augsburg in 1632 and now in Uppsala, all of which were fitted up with instruments and rarities of every description.[105] However the cabinet is more likely to have been a more standard Augsburg product on the scale of a smaller cabinet in the Rijksmuseum in Amsterdam, probably delivered by Hainhofer to Duke Augustus of Brunswick-Lüneburg in 1631, or an undocumented cabinet in his style, now in Vienna but until 1806 in the possession of the Von Konigsmark family in Sweden.[106]

'A rich Cabbonett of Cristall with silver guilt and Copper guilt, in a redd leather chest lyned with Crimson sattine', valued at £100, does not fit into any standard category of cabinets. However the description could well fit a crystal and lacquer casket of a type produced in Venice around 1600: one of the most spectacular examples, a reliquary in the Basilica of Santa Barbara in Mantua which was probably presented by Duke Vincenzo I Gonzaga, was described in 1610 as 'capsa magna ex cristallo miro artificio fabricata, ac multis columnis ornata'.[107] The framework of such cabinets is of ebony with lacquered decoration in the Ottoman style, but they also incorporate silver gilt and gilt bronze elements. In the case of 'One rich Cabbonett haveing a Prospect in y^e and embossed with silv^r', valued at £40, a letter of 1640 from André de Saintes in Lisbon to the Forchondt firm requesting of cabinets he had ordered that 'elck moet binnen syn spiegels hebben int prospectiva hoe groeter hoe better' and another of 1652 from Ralph Harrison in London ordering three cabinets 'with pictures and a prospective' indicate that the prospect was the central niche with a perspective, often mirrored, typical of mid seventeenth-century cabinets.[108] The fact that this cabinet had embossed silver decoration may also suggest an Antwerp provenance: in 1646 the Antwerp silversmith Th. Rozier offered Frederick Henry, Prince of Orange, four cabinets with embossed silver plaques.[109]

Tables

The Charles I inventories contain a very large number of tables. At Ludlow Castle, for example, were over fifty tables listed without any qualification except,

229 [145]

238 [259]
296 [225]
420 [5]

249 [27]
285 [131]

in some cases, the adjective 'old'. There were also several tables at Ludlow and elsewhere qualified as long, large, square, small, little, wainscot, or deal. There is little prospect of divining their precise form or function from such summary entries, although their position may sometimes provide obvious clues: 'Two long Tables' in the hall at Ludlow are likely to have been long dining tables of the standard hall type and '2 small tables' in the kitchen at Bewdley are likely to have been kitchen tables. Such tables were given low values: for instance '4 deale tables' at Wimbledon were valued at 10s. and 'Five old Tables' received from Mr Willis were valued at £1. 10s. Some descriptions of what sounds like relatively utilitarian furniture are more specific: 'A drawin table at TB' [Theobalds] valued at 15s., and 'Two. drawing tables. of wainscott' at Oatlands, valued at £1, were presumably of the type with extra leaves which draw out from each end, but it is impossible to determine whether they resembled designs in Paul Vredeman de Vries's *Verscheyden Schrynwerck* with term- or baluster-shaped legs with stretchers, or another in Crispin de Passe II's *Oficina Arcularia*, with terminal standards carved with a winged sphinx and a pelican in its piety, united by an arcaded central support, or followed a different or, more probably, simpler

225 [88], 296 [230]
113 [263]
172 [144], 213 [77]
241 [294], 249 [26]
287 [145], 395 [959]

model.[110] 'One Large shovell Board Table' at Ludlow, 'One Shovell board table', valued at £3, at Wimbledon, 'A Billiard Board' at Denmark House, valued at £5, and others at Hampton Court, valued at £4, at Richmond, valued at £5, in the Gallery at Holdenby, valued at £2, at Greenwich [?], valued at £2. 10s. at Oatlands, valued at £2, and at Theobalds, valued at £2. 10s., were all presumably substantial fitments: a shovel board at Chartley Castle, described in Plot's *Staffordshire* of 1686 (see p. 410, below), was 'ten yards, 1 foot and an inch long', while a French late seventeenth-century billiard table was '12 pieds de long 6 pieds de large'.[111] Apart from turning on the legs all their bases are likely to have been relatively plain.

241 [293]
240 [281]

56 [28]

'One Planck table in the Hall' at Holdenby is likely to have been similar to the long tables in the hall at Ludlow, while 'Sixe Plancks for Tables' at Kenilworth Castle, valued at 15s. 9d., may have been the tops of a smaller set of hall tables there. Of these large wooden tables only 'One Long Table standing upon Antique tressells' from Greenwich, valued at £1, is described as decorated: the supporting trestles, sporting some type of grotesque ornament, may have resembled those supplied to the hall at Hatfield in 1611.[112] 'A wainscott table with Degrees for Boockes' at Oatlands, valued at 10s., does not correspond to any surviving object. It may have resembled a design by one of the Smythsons for a stepped cupboard for the display of plate, with a base formed as a table two feet nine inches high.[113] In the 'Chaplaines Chamber' at Standon in 1623 'one Table in the Studdie' is immediately succeeded by 'ffive shelves', suggesting that a table/shelf association or combination, as at Oatlands, may have been normal.[114]

114 [267]

'A Wainscote Table wth Drawers' at Denmark House, valued at 15s., is difficult to categorize but recalls 'A square Table of Wanscote therein a Drawer' in 'my Lordes Roome' at Tart Hall in 1641, and the 'two dressing tables wth drawers' for which

114 [268]

Sir Edward Dering paid 10s. in 1652.[115] The next entry is for 'A small lowe Table wth 2. draweing Boxes painted and guilt', valued at 10s. This must have been a gaudy little object, but it is difficult to know what it looked like and why the old-fashioned term, drawing box, was used here: perhaps it was a small dressing table and perhaps the drawers had lids. However 'Reache the cards, which thou shalt find in the drawer of the table', a line from *Campo di Fior*, a multilingual primer published in 1583, suggests that card tables also had drawers.[116] The

113 [260]
129 [407]

inventories include 'A greene vellvett Table wth Boxes and Drawers garnished with lace, and freindge of gould, and silver', valued at £1. 10s., 'A Greene vellvett Table enbroydered with gould and silver with Drawers', valued at £2. 10s., and

182 [278]

'One olde. table covered wth greene vellvt', valued at 5s. It seems probable that these were card tables. Pull-out card tables in a billiard table designed for the Prince de Condé at Chantilly later in the century are labelled 'velours vert'.[117]

181 [266]
182 [279]
182 [283]

Perhaps 'One fouldeing table wth greene Cloth', valued at 5s., and 'Thirteene old tables covered wth cloth' valued at £3. 5s., all at Hampton Court, were less luxurious card tables, while 'Eight paire of old broken tressells' may have been the survivors of the latters' original supports.

85 [51]

'One Table covered with the like Cloth of gould the frame painted and guilt', *en suite* with a canopy, recalls the tables, almost invariably covered with a cloth, which support hats or helmets in state portraits where the curtains of the canopy are regularly depicted, but rarely the canopy itself.[118] But what were 'One long.

172 [140]
172 [141]

table covered. wth yellow vellvt' and 'One. low table. like a forme. covered wth vellv^t', each valued at 10s.? Perhaps the latter was very like a form indeed. Abraham Bosse's engravings often show stools doing service as tables.[119]

212 [66]

234 [219], 285 [133]

Du Breuil's *Perspective Pratique* of 1642 has a plate of 'Certains Meubles qui se plient, qu'on fait servir pour des Sieges, des Tables et des Licts'.[120] 'One old fouldeing table' at Richmond, two more at Ludlow and 'One fouldeing feild table' at Oatlands presumably fit into this category with X-supports. Spanish tables were a specific folding type with iron struts which braced the legs in position.[121] Three formed part of a bedroom suite 'at Mas^{tr} Withers', and there were pairs in two separate bedroom suites at Oatlands, where 'A Carpett' of yellow damask 'for a Spanish. fouldeinge table' is also listed. But what of the 'french folding Table' which formed part of a bedroom suite at Carisbrooke Castle? Were the other French tables listed, at Denmark House two valued at 12s. and three 'belonging to the French Bedd', valued at 18s., and from Whitehall two valued at 10s. and 6s. respectively, also folding tables? This folding group may also have included '1 great foulding table with a crosse frame to brush the Queenes Clothes upon' and '1 little foulding table to putt bookes upon', priced at £1. 10s. and £1 respectively, delivered by the joiner Charles Goodyleare in 1637.[122] Illustrations are little help in this enquiry as the table cloths or carpets, which are listed in such profusion in the Charles I inventories and which are outside the scope of this essay, tend to conceal the structure of tables, as shown accompanying French beds by Bosse, Marmion, or, in another plate, Du Breuil.[123]

255 [127]

286 [140]

287 [152], 287 [147]

222 [64]

58 [15]

124 [370], 342 [212], 377 [723]

In 'The greate Roome or Hall next to the Pranketing House' at Tart Hall in 1641 the Countess of Arundel had 'A greate Ovall table of Wanscote with folding sides'.[124] 'One Ovall fouldeing table of spotted virgina wodd' at Oatlands, valued at 15s., could also have been a dining table, presumably of gate-leg form, and perhaps similar to a surviving table at Ham House, where in 1654 there was a round folding table in the 'parler' and in 1677 'two ovall Cedar tables' in the 'Marble Dining Roome'.[125] There was also 'An Ovall table of Wallenuttree painted wth silver and other culloures' valued at 10s. at Denmark House. 'Two Ovall Boards' at Oatlands, valued, with an iron bolt, at a mere 2s. 6d., may perhaps have been simple oval table-tops.

285 [129]

113 [259]

218 [26]

The 'Two old Oyster Tables', received from Mr Willis and valued at 4s., may have been of a circular type with a hole in the middle for the oyster shells.[126] The nature of 'ye Italian Table in ye somer romes' at Oatlands, which seems to have been *en suite* with 'Twelve blew. stooles of wood gilt' is a mystery. The simplest explanation, that it was an import, seems the likeliest. At Petworth House is an imposing Italian table with the Percy crescent, perhaps dating from the late sixteenth century, while at Tart Hall in 1641 there were 'Eighteen Italian Wooden Chayres gilt' in the 'South gallerie' and 'Nyne great Italian Wooden Chayres of Walnutt tree with Armes' in 'The greate Roome or Hall'.[127] A final puzzling table type is the 'square window table' at Wimbledon. A square table is shown in front of a window or on the pier between windows in more than one engraving by Bosse: perhaps such tables were an ingredient in the development of the late seventeenth-century window-pier triad of table and looking-glass flanked by candlestands.[128]

420 [3]

287 [152]

296 [231]

A table of 'spotted virgina wodd' has already been noted. This may have been an usually figured specimen of Virginia walnut, which was certainly imported by 1630 and was recommended by Evelyn in his *Sylva* of 1644.[129] 'A Table of Corall. in waves' at Windsor, valued at 10s., may possibly have been of coral-wood, another import from America already known in the seventeenth century.[130] Walnut, although not exotic, cost more than the standard oak or deal. An oval walnut table has already been noted at 10s. A small walnut table and 'A plaine Wallnuttree Table wth a frame painted', also at 10s., each, and 'A Walnuttree Draweing Table upon a frame' valued at 15s., must have been smaller than their equivalents in common woods, for example the drawing table at Theobalds, presumably of oak, also valued at 15s.

285 [129]

293 [-]

113 [259]

113 [264-5]

114 [266]

249 [27]

Ebony was used for tables as well as cabinets. 'An Eight square Table of Eboney inlayed with sundry stones of divers culloures with 4. feete suiteable', valued at £20, may have incorporated panels of marble inlay manufactured in Florence such as Hainhofer used in his cabinets.[131] The octagonal form is unusual and it is tempting to associate it with the octagonal base of Hainhofer's *Stipo d'Alemagna* in Florence.[132] Could the grandest of cabinets in the inventories, that valued at £150, have been octagonal in plan? Certainly it shared 'a Clock in the Topp' with the *Stipo d'Alemagna*. Could this octagonal table have been its base? 'A Table of Eboney inlayed all over, and on the feete inlayed wth Mother of pearle

113 [256]

111 [232]

113 [257]

standing upon 4. round Bases much defaced', valued at £3, and 'A Table of Eboney wth Crosse Feete inlayed wth Mother of pearle', valued at £2, are in a different class. It is tempting to draw a parallel with the tables of black marble inlaid with mother-of-pearl by the Amsterdam craftsman, Dirck van Rijswick, which were praised by Joost van Vondel.[133] But these were highly valued objects. It seems more likely that the two tables at Denmark House were exotic imports, possibly from Japan, but more probably from India, where round or bell-shaped projecting feet are found in Mughal depictions of thrones and tables.[134]

'One faire table. of walnutt tree garnished wth Mother of pearle. & silv^r gilt', valued at £3, very probably belongs to the group of Turkish or Indian exports discussed in connection with mother-of-pearl cabinets, and may have resembled the table still at Hatfield 'richlie inlaid with pearls'.[135] 'One China gilt Table' at Oatlands, valued at £1. 10s., may perhaps have been a Javanese carved gilt table similar to the surviving 'Tea table, carv'd and guilt' which was in 1683 in 'Her Graces private Closset' at Ham House.[136]

When marble tables were discussed above in connection with the matching cabinet and table with inlaid marble decoration at Denmark House, the marble tables illustrated in the 1590 Lumley inventory were mentioned.[137] The Charles I inventories list only one 'Marble Inlaid Table', valued at £20, at Nonsuch, which may well have survived from Lord Lumley's time and been illustrated in his inventory.[138] Some of the other entries for marble tables are also tantalisingly brief – at Denmark House 'A Marble Table', valued at £10, and 'A Marbell table', from the banqueting room, also valued at £10, at Wimbledon in the banqueting room 'one Marble Table', valued with four chairs at £3. 10s., and at Theobalds in the gallery 'One marble table, valued at £15. But 'A small square Table of White Marble, bordered with Ebboney with white flower deluces in ye Corners, and 4. Ovalls standing upon foure Balles of Eboney', valued at £10, might be recognizable. 'One Marble Table inlaied with many cullo^rs upon a guilt frame square', valued at £40, is likely to have been a more elaborate product, probably Florentine. The inventory also notes that it was 'Given to the Queene by ye Ladie Banning'. This may be Anne Glemham, daughter of Sir Henry Glemham and a grand-daughter of the first Earl of Dorset, who married Sir Paul Bayning, a prodigiously wealthy London merchant, who was a benefactor of Syon College and died in 1629, a year after having been created successively Baron and Viscount Bayning.[139] Within a year his widow married Sir Dudley Carleton, who had been created Viscount Dorchester in 1628.[140] Perhaps the gift of a table to the Queen may have smoothed the path of this rapid new alliance. An equally plausible 'Ladie Banning' is her daughter-in-law Penelope, daughter of Sir Robert Naunton, secretary of state to James I, and a grand-daughter of the first Earl of Essex, who married the second Viscount Bayning in 1634, was left a widow in 1638, and in 1639 married Philip Herbert, later fifth Earl of Pembroke.[141]

At Wimbledon 'one ovall Marble Table', valued at £2, 'A Black Marble Table wth Marble. tressells wth 4 stooles of wood', valued at £28, and 'A square white Marble table wth wodden Tressells. painted white and black', valued at £10, are followed by the square window table already noted, which was 'painted black. wth white tressells'. The marble trestles, at least, may have resembled those on the celebrated Farnese table, now in New York, whose design has been attributed to Vignola.[142] A strong play of black and white was clearly achieved, and reinforces the impression that marble tables played a conspicuous role in the decoration of Charles I's palaces, particularly in galleries and banqueting rooms. And also in gardens: a black marble table was in the garden at Denmark House and it seems likely that 'One great blacke marble Table of Irish Touchstone', valued at £30, was in the garden at Theobalds.[143] This is likely to be the table seen in a summer-house in the garden at Theobalds by Frederick, Duke of Wurtemberg, in 1592.[144]

A problem arises with a group of eight tables of more or less semi-precious materials, including lapis lazuli, porphyry, serpentine, agate, blood stone and Egyptian stone, which seem to have been in the Upper Jewel House. Their values range from £3. 10s. for a serpentine table to £35 each for two agate tables and £5 for the octagonal Egyptian stone table 'wth divers figures in Relivo'. As well as its standard modern meaning, table could also signify a slab, even one as small as a table-cut diamond.[145] The context of the Jewel House is not helpful in distin-guishing the nature of the table in question. It can only be suggested that 'A small table of Lapis Lazula &c' at £20, probably a specimen of Florentine marble inlay, and the two agate tables at £35 each could all have been table tops. The octagonal Egyptian 'Table', on the other hand, defies even tentative identification.[146]

113 [262]

172 [139]

285 [130]

121 [335]

418 [33]

56 [32], 325 [47]

297 [245]
393 [935]
113 [261]

120 [333]

296 [228-9]
296 [230]

296 [231]

136 [12]
395 [969]

428 [37-41], 429 [43-5]

428 [37]

428 [40-41]
429 [45]

274 [291]

'A silv^r Table. and frame. all laid over wth silv^r & a p^r of andiernes', valued at £120, represented a princely height of luxury. Although little silver furniture has been noted in England before this date, two late sixteenth-century Italian table-tops covered in embossed silver survive, and in 1640 Frederick Henry, Prince of Orange, owned an embossed and engraved silver table valued at 15,000 guilders.[147] Silver andirons were also an established type: Henry VIII owned some, as did Cardinal Mazarin, and fire dogs 'garnisht with silver' survive at Ham house, where they were listed in 1679.[148]

118 [314-15]

When the term, a pair of tables or playing tables, is used in the Charles I inventories it means a folding double games-board with backgammon on the inside, which also acted as a container for the men (see further p. 411).[149] It should be noted that their rich materials, ebony, mother-of-pearl, cloth-of-gold, silver, glass and cedar, were also the materials of luxury furniture. 'One table to play at Trolle Madam', valued at 10s., was a larger furniture type, and an early example of a table specifically designed for this purpose: in the seventeenth century the set of arches through which the balls were rolled to score at *trou-madam* seems usually to have been a separate entity to be set on a table.[150]

172 [143], 212 [62, 64]
419 [2], 282 [97], 212 [63], 172 [142]

294 [223]
280 [75]

'Twoe Table of ye ord^r of ye Garter', at Windsor, must have been a table in the sense of a list on a notice-board and 'A table wth Itallian verses' at Oatlands must have been something similar. Frame has already been noted as meaning a stand for a cabinet or a base for a table, often decorated, as with 'a Table painted on ye frame & gilt' at Denmark House. It could also mean a stand of any kind as 'one frame for a Bason' or 'Fowre Woodden painted Frames to sett Candlesticks upon', the latter perhaps similar to a surviving candlestand at Knole.[151] But it could also mean an inner frame-work, as 'a frame of wood of Iron to beare up' a cloth of estate, or the wooden structure of a piece of furniture, as 'A frame for Couch'. And it could also, of course, mean a picture frame, as 'An Ebony Frame for an Eight Square Lymned peece.'

57 [3]

226 [95], 118 [317]

283 [110]
413 [92]
247 [374]

Pedestals, sometimes qualified as round, square, high or little, were almost invariably associated with sculpture: the exception is a 'pettistall' at St. James's for a chimney clock in the Jewel House at Whitehall. Desks, which at this date were small, portable, sloping table-top desks, are conspicuous by their absence. There were only 'a board of an old desk of Nedlework' at St. James's and at Hampton Court 'One standing deske wth printers. leather', the latter, to prove the rule, a lectern-desk, its top presumably covered with leather by a book-binder.[152] Perhaps the 'deske for his Lordship covered with black leather' for which the ninth Earl of Northumberland paid £3 in 1585/6 was similar.[153]

133 [68, 74], 135 [6], 145 [131]
385 [815]

151 [18]
178 [225]

Chairs, Stools, Forms, Benches

111 [232]
111 [235]
356 [413]
402 [1059-60, 1062]
81 [43-4], 82 [45]

81 [44], 167 [97]
72 [61]

The most expensive single piece of furniture so far mentioned was the rich ebony cabinet valued at £150; only the rich crystal cabinet valued at £100 approached that level. The highest value given for an individual chair in the inventories was £5. This statistical comparison is striking but misleading. Only stray chairs were valued singly. The chair was normally valued as part of a suite. A standard grouping comprised a canopy or cloth of estate, a high chair, two high stools and a footstool. The value of such a suite could reach £100, or even – and this example included only one high stool – £500. As a point of comparison the Raphael Cartoons were valued at £300. The value lay in the rich textiles, and, in the case of the £500 suite, in pearls and precious or semi-precious stones.

It should be emphasised that this valuable furniture was furniture of state, an essential component of court ceremonial wherever the king or his representative might be.[154] Thus when the Garter feast was held in the Presence Chamber at Whitehall in 1636 tapestries were brought in and 'the rich State, Chair, Cushens, and Stools belonging to the *Queen's* Privy-Chamber'.[155] Similarly Anne, Lady Fanshawe, related that when her husband, Sir Richard Fanshawe, was appointed Ambassador to Portugal in 1662 he had 'by His Majesty's order, out of the wardrobe, a crimson velvett cloath of state fringed and laced with gold, with a chaire, a foot stoole, 2 cushions, and 2 other stooles of the same with a Persia carpett to lay under them, and a sute of fine tapestry hangings for that roome . . .'[156] She concluded, a little grudgingly perhaps; 'But there wanted a velvett bed which he should have had by custome.'[157] This constant movement meant that although upholstered furniture might be made in matching suites, large or small, the combinations and permutations varied

127 [399]

according to circumstance.[158] Thus an entry on a canopy at Denmark House notes 'one Couch thereto belonging is taken off to compleate a suite of Chayres &c'. Suites were sometimes supplied in quantity; thus under James I the upholsterers Anthony Lacenbury and John Baker submitted a bill for 'three lardge Charyes, vj highe stooles and Three ffootestooles all Covered wth Crimson velvett', which must have constituted three of the standard suites described above.[159] It should be noted, incidentally, that from the early seventeenth century the upholsterer rather than the coffer-maker was responsible for furniture of this type.[160]

342 [204], 251 [48], 85 [53]
90 [72], 284 [117], 284 [113]

The inventories use a variety of terms for the chair which was the focus of such suites; 'Chaire of state', 'great Chaire', 'high Chayre' (most frequent), even 'Middleing chaire' and 'low. Chaire', or, often, simply 'Chaire'. The traditional form for such chairs was X-framed with curved legs and arms, a type which goes back to Dagobert's throne and beyond.[161] The term, chair, normally implied the existence of arms. Anomalies occur. What was a 'high Chaire with Elboes' or an

18 [83]
384 [808]

'elbow Chaire'? If chairs had always come with arms (elbows) why was there any need to specify? A possible explanation is that such descriptions refer to a newly fashionable type in which arms were added to the back stool or back chair, which was essentially the standard four-legged high-stool with its back legs extended and linked by a rectangular upholstered back.[162] Perhaps 'Two French Chayres'

123 [365]
255 [127]

at Denmark House, and '3 french. Chaires' at 'Mas^tr Withers' were also of this pattern.[163]

226 [102]
287 [142]

Back chairs or back stools occur in considerable numbers in the inventories. At Ludlow Castle, for instance, were 'Tenn Turkey worke Back Chaires', valued at £3, and in the Queen's Gallery at Oatlands there were 'Tenn. Back. stooles. of greene vellv^t freindged wth greene silke', valued at £8. The next entry lists

287 [143]

'Twelve Fouldeing stooles. suteable', valued at £6, and states that 'all. ye s^d Chaires & stooles are Caised wth greene Cotten', 'Chaires' clearly referring to the 'Back. stooles' in the previous entry. Stools without backs were even more

82 [46], 84 [49]

prevalent. A crimson velvet canopy suite and another of green velvet, which had belonged to Anne of Denmark, included 'Twoe and Twenty highe stooles suiteable the frames painted and guilt' and '14 highestooles . . . suiteable',

287 [143]
126 [388], 288 [153], 255 [120]

respectively. Twelve folding stools have already been noted at Oatlands. These would have had X-frames with no curves, and seem to have been supplied in sets of six, eight or twelve, but no more.[164]

97 [112], 128 [404], 331 [70]

Back stools, high stools, and folding stools are seen in quantity in the prints of Abraham de Bosse, forming a more or less continuous border to the room.[165] In the Charles I inventories high stools are occasionally called simply stools, but foot stools and low stools were evidently distinct types. Foot stools were an essential complement to the high chair which was the focus of a state suite: thus

283 [110]

at Oatlands 'One high Chaire, one long Cushion. & one seate Cushion, One footestoole all. suteable to ye said State. & garnished wth ye like. lace'. Only old footstools which had accumulated over the years were listed in quantity: in

171 [134]

Hampton Court wardrobe, for example, were 'Two. foote. stooles wth Needleworke. ye ground redd. & H:R:', valued at £1, which must have belonged

371 [637]

to Henry VIII, and Clement Kynnersley had '6 broken foot-stooles of velv^t' from the Whitehall wardrobe. The form of footstools could follow that of the curved X-frame high chair, to judge from surviving examples at Knole.[166] Those in the inventories were almost invariably covered in rich textiles: the exception, 'one

12 [53]

footestoole of wallnuttree', had purple velvet upholstery embroidered with gold.

83 [47], 283 [111]
90 [72]
90 [70-71]

Low stools form a separate category which sometimes crops up in state suites, where they follow high stools in the standard hierarchy. Exceptionally 'One Middleing chaire' with Anne of Denmark's initials has 'Two middleing stooles' as supporters. 'Square lowe stooles' and 'square stooles' are also occasionally found. The state suite of which these were sometimes components

284 [117]
83 [47]

was not a straitjacket. The high chair might be matched by a low chair, and it might be accompanied by two back stools as well as high and low stools, and as the suite grew the insignia of precedence and ceremonial merged into the trappings of luxury, comfort and fashion, to such an extent that one entry lists a

82 [46]

suite including no less than thirty-four pieces of seat furniture.

169 [111]

The seat furniture so far considered depended on rich and colourful textiles for its impact. Even when some wood was exposed, as with 'One Chaire of wood carved. wth rich cloth. of gould. purple tissew. haveing the Armes. of England.

171 [129]

houlden by beasts' or 'Two. square stooles. of wallnuttree. of cloth. of silv^r Tissued', all at Hampton Court, the textiles were what mattered. A possible

56 [20]

exception is 'One Low Back Chaire wth a gilt frame', at Denmark House, valued at 10*s*. However there are six groups of seat furniture which seem to be definite exceptions. At Denmark House were 'Nyne formes. and 19 stooles. of wainscott Carved. and gilt uppon ye edges', valued at £13. 2*s*. and 'Twenty fowre woodden stooles with Backs painted and guilt', valued at £12. At Oatlands were '12 Carved stooles gilt & Collored', valued at £10. 16*s*. and 'Twelve blew. stooles of wood gilt of ye Italian Table in ye somer romes'. At Wimbledon were '4 stooles of wood' listed with a black marble table with marble trestles. And at Nonsuch were 'Twenty fowre Back Stooles of Wood Carved and Gilt', valued at £18. It has already been suggested that the Italian table at Oatlands may have been an Italian import, and the 'Eighteen Italian Wooden Chayres gilt' in the 'South gallerie' at Tart Hall in 1641 have been cited.[167] Before and after the twenty-four painted and gilt back-stools at Denmark House are listed inlaid marble tables. The gilt and blue stools at Oatlands were not only associated with an 'Italian' table; they also stood in the summer rooms. At Wimbledon wooden stools are associated with a marble table, while the next entry is for another marble table with trestles painted white and black. And finally at Nonsuch the twenty-four carved and gilt back-stools are followed by an inlaid marble table. Although proof is lacking it seems reasonable to suggest that this group of seat furniture was of an Italianate character and was considered particularly appropriate as an accompaniment to marble tables. The well-known portrait of the Countess of Arundel by Mytens depicts her sitting in a high chair of the curved X-frame type before a picture gallery opening into a garden.[168] Visible at the end of this summery Italianate room are two *sgabello* chairs or, in seventeenth-century parlance, back-stools. Francis Cleyn, who was very much in the ambit of Inigo Jones, designed similar chairs for Holland House and, possibly, Ham House.[169] It is not improbable that Denmark House, Oatlands, Wimbledon and Nonsuch should all have contained comparable chairs and stools, Italian or Italianate.

There are a few chairs that do not fit into the categories already established. At Denmark House were 'Two scrowle or Backd chaires of the same stuffe, the ground Tynncell garnished with freindge of silver' valued at 10*s*. 'The same stuffe' refers to the previous entry for two high chairs, eight high stools and two foot stools 'of stript stuffe in cullo^rs'. 'Scrowle' probably refers to the termination of the back uprights in a scroll, as seen in a design by Crispin de Passe II.[170] 'One fouldeing Chaire 8 foulding stooles. suiteable' from a yellow damask suite at Oatlands introduces a folding chair. In principle, of course, all curved X-framed high chairs could fold, but in practice their flexibility was residual at most.[171] It seems probable that the Oatlands folding chair was of the type with the curved X-frames set laterally rather than at front and back. An example was illustrated by Hendrik Hondius I in 1625, and called 'a Folding-chair' when Joseph Moxon copied Hondius's plates in 1670.[172]

'One Turned Chaire' is listed in a miscellaneous lot in the 'Inward Wardrobe' at Ludlow Castle, valued at 15*s*., and also including 'one Feather bolster, 3. necessary stooles with Panns, one Batheing Tubb with other odd Lumber'. Perhaps it may have resembled the provincial 'turned chair' illustrated by Randle Holme.[173] At Denmark House were 'A Chaire with wheeles of Crimson vellvett enbroyd^rd with Twist and spangles with a large footestoole suiteable, and a Board to ye same covered with Crimson vellvett', and 'One Orringeculloure Turneing chaire with a Back Chayre with wheeles both of Irishe stitch', valued at £5. All these chairs may have resembled the wheeled chair designed by Mathurin Jousse and published in 1627.[174] The 'Board' belonging to the first chair may have been some sort of foot rest.[175] 'One sleepeing Chayre of redd vellvett' may have belonged to the same chair family: the characteristics of a sleeping chair seem to have been an adjustable reclining back and head-rests or wings, such as are shown in the Jousse designs.[176] Perhaps 'A large Chaire of Deliverance covered wth crimson vellvett with a footestoole, and Winges suiteable to the same with a Case of Crimson Bayes thereunto', valued at £5, and, at Ludlow Castle, 'One Barbors Chaire' in the 'Wainescott Closett', close to the Prince's Bedchamber, were related forms.[177]

'Three Carrying Chaires 2 of Crimson & one of greene velvett' at St. James's, valued at £3, are very probably ordinary chairs with iron fitments for the insertion of carrying poles, simpler versions of a carrying chair in the Escorial once associated with Charles V and now with Philip II.[178] Simple *chaises à porter* were used by Catherine de' Medici and others in Paris around 1600, but the introduction of the sedan chair proper to Paris seems to have been a fitful process.[179] In 1623 a pamphlet urged the introduction of *'chaises portantes à la mode d'Italie'*, but in 1639 the invention was said to come from England. 'One large

57 [5]
120 [334]
279 [62]
287 [152]
296 [229]

418 [32]
287 [152]

120 [333-4], 121 [335]

296 [230]

418 [33]

91 [80]

91 [79]

287 [148]

232 [188]

91 [81]

128 [403]

128 [406]

120 [330]

225 [86]

362 [491]

Chaire letter fashion Covered all over wth leather' at Whitehall, valued at £15, would seem to be a sedan. In 1635 the playwright, Richard Brome, referred to 'one o' the new Hand-litters: what call ye it, a Sedan' and in 1641 the first Earl of Cork bought a 'new sedan'.[180] In 1645 John Evelyn credited their introduction to Sir Sanders Duncombe.[181] A sedan chair is illustrated on the title of Henry Peacham's *Coach and Sedan Pleasantly Disputing for Place and Precedence; the Brewers-Cart being Moderator*, of 1636.[182]

55 [11]
100 [131]

120 [331]

392 [919]

The inventories list twenty-seven close or necessary stools, some with pewter pans. At Denmark House 'One Close stoole Trunke fashion of redd vellv^t', valued at 15s., was reserved for Cromwell's service and three of four 'Murrey culloured vellvett' close stools were sold to the Council of State. They were sometimes *en suite* with beds, as 'A Necessarie stoole of Wainescott covered all over with a Tawney vellvett, enbroydered suiteable to a Tawney Bedd', valued at the remarkable sum of £10. One crimson velvet close stool at Theobalds, valued at £5, had a leather cover. It must have resembled 'i greatt nyght box of wyndshott xxviii Inchis longe and xx Inches brode and xx Inchis hiye covered with crymson vellett and lassed with gold lass and lyned with quillted taffety' supplied to the queen by Edward Cordell in 1636/7 for £3, together with 'a great Casse of read russiy leather lyned with fyne bayes' at 15s. In 1639 Cordell delivered a similar 'greatt nyght bose' for the queen's bedchamber, and in 1638 another, covered in gilt Spanish leather and incorporating a drawer, for Lady Denbigh, the queen's first lady of the Bedchamber.[183] A surviving close stool at Hampton Court, in the form of box with a hinged lid, covered in crimson velvet, may be one of those in the inventories.[184] It is possible that some of these close stools may have been of the armchair form of a black velvet close stool supplied to Henry VIII in 1547 and as illustrated by Abraham Bosse.[185]

226 [99]
230 [155], 234 [219]

225 [88-9]
230 [154]
226 [95]

182 [288]
241 [293]
282 [101]
394 [951], 296 [227]

At Ludlow Castle 'a Joyned Chaire' in 'ye Clerke of ye Kitchin's Chamber', '2 Wainescott Chaires' in the Marshal's Quarter, and 'Twoe old Woodden Chaires' among the furnishings of the Chaplain's Chamber exemplify the sturdy oak furniture which was ubiquitous in provincial settings in the early seventeenth century.[186] '7 little Joyned formes' and 'twoe old Joyned stooles' in the Shovell Board Chamber, '3 Joyned Formes' in the Marshall's Quarter, and '3. ioyned stooles' in the Stewards Chamber, were probably of the same ilk. But while joined chairs and stools without upholstery scarcely crop up outside Ludlow, there were 'Twenty joyned Formes' at Hampton Court (immediately after '20 ordenarie Cupboards'), 'Twoe long Formes in ye Presence' at Holdenby, 'Tenn Joyned formes' at Oatlands (with, exceptionally, '6 Joyned stooles'), 'foure formes in ye p^rsence' at Theobalds, and 'One wainescott table and 12 formes & benches' at Wimbledon. From these entries it is evident that forms were widely used when seating was required in quantity, particularly in formal contexts. (It should also be stressed that, while some joined oak furniture was provincial and old-fashioned and perceived as such, neat practical furniture of this type was admitted anywhere). But what of benches? They occur in the Wimbledon entry just quoted, as 'The Seate of Justice, Tables, and Bennches' in the 'Court Howse of Justice' at Ludlow, and at Bewdley in the hall ('2 bennches') and in a bedroom ('one small Bench'). The distinction between a form and a bench is confused and was so in the seventeenth century: Randle Holme supplies a caption, 'Joint forme, or bench' and Pricke's translation of DuBreuil includes similarly 'a Form or Bench'.[187] Nonetheless the traditional distinction, also valid in France, seems to operate in the Charles I inventories: the bench had a back, the form did not.[188] Settles do seem usually to have had backs, but the two in the inventories, one in the 'Stewards mans Chamb^r' at Ludlow, and the other at Hampton Court, provide no clues. The seat of justice in the court house at Ludlow must have been a formal seat with a back: 'Two large Armes for a Seate of the wholle Coate of Denmarke' in a cypress chest at Denmark House may have been for something similar. Finally at the end of the arbour at Oatlands were 'Two. Stone Sundyalls. wth a wodden seate'. It would be rash to speculate as to the form of the latter.

231 [163]
238 [263]
239 [273]

226 [97], 182 [281]
231 [163]
110 [230]

250 [37]

Cloths of Estate, Canopies, Sparvers, Pavilions, Couches, Beds

The category of furniture now to be considered consists predominantly of textiles, and thus its principal materials and means of display are outside the scope of this essay. However a brief account must be given of the cloth of estate, or state as it was often known, and of other canopies and beds, as these were the key foci of court ceremonial, symbolizing in concrete form the separate and superior station of the monarch.

The cloth of estate consisted in essence of a flat canopy, the ceilour, which projected from the wall above the king, and a tall hanging, the tester, which hung on the wall behind the king. In the seventeenth century, confusingly, the ceilour came to be known as the tester and the tester as the headcloth. However the Charles I inventories usually employ the traditional nomenclature which is adopted here.[189] The ceilour of a cloth of estate was often embellished with double valances, and all elements were usually richly fringed. 'A frame to fix the State upon with screwes and four lyars of threed to hang it up withall' or 'a frame of wood of Iron to beare up ye same' might be required: a cloth of estate could be a heavy and bulky structure. The tester could be a special section of the hangings of a room, which then merged into the cloth of estate. Thus a set of hangings in the Tower wardrobe included a piece with 'the Armes of England with two beasts within a Garland richly embrod^rd . . . This is entred among the States being suitable to a Ceeler of the same stuff and embroidery which being semed together will make a Compleat State'.

The cloth of estate, although often very rich in materials and decoration, was structurally the simplest of a family of suspended canopies. The canopy proper was distinguished from the cloth of estate by two curtains and by a 'Topp' instead of a ceilour, and a 'Back' instead of a tester. The top could be square, circular or semi circular in plan, and its form was that of a pyramid, dome or half dome decorated inside and out, edged with valances. The back was often very similar to a tester, for instance 'enbroydered with the Armes of Denmarke cont 2 ^yrds ¼ in depth and in breadth 1. y^de', but when the canopy was round a back was not practicable. Like the cloth of estate the canopy proper could require a frame. In 1637 the joiner Charles Goodyleare delivered '1 large canopy frame with Screues for her Ma.tis suite of figured velvett with a cloth of tissewe ground'.[190] Another type of canopy was the sparver, which had a ceilour, tester, and valances, and a varying number of curtains, from two to five. When there were only two curtains a 'mantle' was also present; this would seem to have been a bedspread. Sparvers seem usually to have been rectangular in plan and to have been curtained all the way round. They were closely related to the canopy proper as is evident from an entry describing 'One Cannopie, Sparver fashion, Cont 4 Curtains, Tester & head Cloth, double Vallance wth 5 Cupps'. (It will be noted that here tester is used for ceilour and headcloth for tester).

The interpretation of pavilion is difficult. In France the term often means a circular canopy suspended above a bed.[191] However 'A Pavillian or Tent of printed Callicoe blue with Images and flow^rs being in foure peeces for the lower part of it and on the topp of the said stuff with foure painted posts and Lyo^rs to the same and all things fitting to sett it up and a Cover of blue and red Callicoe for the same the Pavillian was p^rsented to King James by the Russian Ambassador', in the Tower wardrobe, valued at £8, seems to have been a square [?] tent with posts and pulleys. On the other hand although a large and luxurious pavilion at Denmark House, valued at £90, had four curtains, it was probably a round canopy, as its valance 'of the like silver Tynncell garnished about wth an open silver lace and a Cawld freindge of silver and silke' is said to be '12. yds ½ in length', which sounds like a measure of circumference, as the next entry is for 'One other little round Pavillion'. This latter, valued at £10, had six short curtains, and contained 'A lowe stoole of woodd' covered *en suite*. 'One furniture of flowred grogran for a pavillian' at Oatlands is even more problematic: the presence of cantoons and a bedstead makes it probable that this was some sort of domed top for a bed with posts. 'Y^e Images belonging to a pavillian', valued at £10 and said in the copies to be gilded, sound as if they might have been figures or beasts to set on the painted posts of the Russian tent mentioned above, or something similar.

There are far too few pavilions for any conclusions to be drawn about their function: as one had a low stool *en suite* and another a bedstead they would seem to have been versatile. Much the same holds for sparvers. The only clear association is that between a sparver of green velvet laced with gold, and a high chair, two square stools and a foot stool of the same material, although it seems likely that others, particularly those with mantles, may have been for beds. However 'One Cannopie, Sparver fashion' was for a couch. Couches were often associated with canopies proper. Chairs, often high, are even more common, but

19 [83]
283 [110]

3 [11]

86 [56]

127 [399], 85 [53], 86 [54]

85 [52]
85 [53]
119 [321], 129 [411]

169 [109], 98 [114], 97 [113], 292 [199]

422 [5]

18 [82]

89 [68]

90 [69]

287 [151]

412 [85]

90 [69], 287 [151]

127 [396-7]

169 [109], 292 [199]
422 [5]

beds less so. As noted earlier the chair under a canopy could be the focus of an extensive suite, for instance 'One Chaire . . . and one Footestoole . . . Two other highe Chayres, 6 Backe Chaires . . . and 2. Footestooles . . . Twoe and Twenty highe stooles suiteable', the whole suite valued at £95. The couch under the canopy might also have its satellites as 'One skreene cloth . . . Two Chaires, and six Foulding stooles suiteable'. A canopy 'to be hangd over a square standing bedstead' implies a self-contained unit, but 'One round Cannopie to hang over a Bedd with a woodden Crowne guilt' also had 'One highe Chayre & two highestooles' *en suite*. With 'One flatt bedd. wth a Cannopie . . . one great. Chaire 2 high stooles. & a footestoole . . . & one. Close stoole. one tabell' the furnishings of a complete bedroom, valued at £20 and thus of some opulence, are focused round the bed and its canopy. By contrast three canopies, all 'halfe round' and in one case little, had only a table and a long cushion *en suite*; these may have been attributes of state in a standing position.[192]

The standard accompaniment to a cloth of estate in the inventories was a high chair, two high stools and a foot stool: they were never associated with beds or couches. But most, for instance 'One old State. of King Clowis of France wth flow^r de luces', had no accompanying furniture.

The couch has cropped up more than once. It is a difficult furniture type to pin down. 'One Seate Couch fashion' under a canopy with 'Twoe lowe stooles', or even one under a canopy without the accompanying stools seems very likely to have been double-ended and similar to one surviving at Hardwick.[193] (This incidentally was probably an item of small value; 'The Tymber of a rich Couch, and the Frame of a Cannopie' were valued together at £1). 'A Couch chaire', accompanied by 'Two square lowe stooles & one highe stoole', also sounds double-ended, and, perhaps, shorter. Several suites are listed, for example 'One Couch of Carnacon vellvett trymmed with a gold & silver plate lace, and Freindge, with six Foulding stooles, Two Chayres and Two Cusshions suiteable', valued at £50, or 'A Couch and six Foulding stooles of Crimson vellt trymmed with gowld lace and freindge', valued at £25, where only a double-ended couch would have worked satisfactorily in a formal arrangement. That fixed arrangements existed seems probable from the mention of a couch belonging to a canopy being 'taken off to compleate a suite of Chayres &c'. And formality seems likely when 'One couch, Two Chayres, Six stooles, & Eight Cusshions' form a part of a suite of cloth of gold hangings valued at the very high figure of £388. Suites of rich hangings of crimson china satin and gilt leather for the Queen's Cabinet Room and the Queen's Gallery respectively at Oatlands also included couches. Being relatively low, with inconspicuous outlines, and covered in the appropriate material they may well have fitted in with such schemes particularly well. Certainly Edmond Marmion depicted a double-ended couch in a fashionable setting without a canopy.[194]

It is also the case, however, that the single-ended daybeds shown in DuBreuil's *Perspective Pratique* and called by him 'petits Lits de Repos' were in 1672 translated by Robert Pricke as 'little Couches to rest in'.[195] Perhaps 'One low Couch. of greene sattine' was of this type albeit accompanied by 'six fouldeinge' (*sc.* stools). Finally there are two couch bedsteads, one described as having 'the head posts. post. and feete thereof richlÿ guilt wth gold', and valued at £15. This must have been a luxurious bed with low posts and without an integral ceilour.[196]

Beds and bedsteads have already been broached. The most fashionable type is represented by 'A large rich French Bedd . . . cont a Tester, Headcloth double vallances, Cantoones, Curtaines, and Bases, the Pillars and Cupps thereof being of greene sattine enbroydered . . . ' at Denmark House, which, together with three chairs, two carpets, and a 'faire large Cannopie', itself with an extensive complement of 'Ceeler Back, and two Cantoones, 4. Curtaines, and double vallances with 4. Cupps suiteable' and a screen cloth, was valued at £1000.[197] At Ludlow Castle, on the other hand, 'One French Beddstedd with greene seye Curtaines & Vallances' was valued at £1. What made these two different beds French? Firstly when their curtains were closed they presented a neat box-like appearance, and secondly the wooden structure was completely or almost completely concealed. (The description of another, at Theobalds, begins 'One french bedsted posts covered').[198] The term, French bed, occurs only three times in the inventories. Yet many other beds from 'One Crimson vellv^t Bedd. ye furniture lined wth Cloth. of gould and silv^r richly enbroid^rd wth gold and silv^r Cont ye Ceeler Vallances. Tester Covers. for ye posts & 4 knobs. for ye bedd stead. all Richly enbroidered. wth 4 Cantoones' at Denmark House, valued, with three chairs and six stools, at £500, to repetitive and brief entries of 'Furnitures for beds' such as 'A Ceeler. Tester. Six single valance & 3 bases of greene cloth of gold Tissue wth roses & po^rtcloses: 5 Crimson & white damasque Curtaines' at Richmond, valued at £15, must have been more or less correct variations on the French bed theme. The latter example may have been less correct more because of the jangle of colour between the curtains and the remaining hangings, rather than for any deviation in form.

At this point it should be noted that the term bed, as used in the Charles I inventories, is ambiguous. A bed could mean, as above, the furniture or hangings of a bed. But it could also mean the bedding of a bed, as with 'Fowre downe bedds and boulsters and 4 pillow to the bedds', valued at £20. Neither of these usages subsumed the bedstead, which was treated as a separate entity, as when 'One faire bed of watchett velvett' and its suite, comprising chair, two high stools, foot stool and close stool, were valued at £120 and 'the beadsted' at £10. Nor did the bedstead subsume its furniture or hangings, or its bedding: when they were listed together, as 'One bedsted Carved and gilt apparelled wth greene velv^t wth silver lace Cont. Curtaines vallance Tester and head Cloath wth a Counterpart suteable a fether bed and boulster an old quilt one paire of blanketts and one other boulster', the distinction between the solid wooden bedstead and its textile furnishings is maintained. Thus when bed hangings are described and the bedstead is not mentioned it should be assumed *prima facie* that the former are in store, and equally when, for instance, 'One halfe headed beddstead' is listed at Bewdley without any note of hangings, it is probable that it was in an undressed state.

The French bed was one generic type, apart from those with independent canopies already mentioned. Another related model was the slope bedstead, of which three are listed in the inventories. All seem likely to have conformed to the basic pattern of a bed in Stockholm probably made in Paris in the 1690s for Count Carl Piper, which had a short straight section at the head and a slope to the feet.[199] The entry for 'One Slope Bedd of rich Cloth of silver' at Denmark House valued, despite its 'Vallance being lost', at £20, lists the ceilour and headcloth (or tester), but also makes reference to 'The 2. head curtaines' and 'The other 3. Curtaines'; this fits the Piper model which has two side curtains at the head, corresponding to the short straight section of the ceilour, and then two curtains for the sloping part of the sides, and a foot curtain. The other slope beds in the inventories, one with its bedstead and 'foure knobbs of wood painted and guilt', also had five curtains.

Another model, closely related to both the French bed and the slope bed, was the field bed. There are three in the inventories. One, although 'altered into a Tester Bedd fashion' and not finished, was 'Apparrelled with crimson sattine verie richly enbroydered all over with gould and ragged pearles' and valued, together with a high chair, two high stools, and a footstool, at £400 'haveing a Chest, and the Beddstedd therein'. The second field bed was valued at £50 with a high chair, two stools, a foot stool and 'A Closet with the Beddstedd therein'. Both had two head curtains, like the slope bed described above, so it would seem that the distinguishing feature of this type was that bed and bedstead could be packed into a 'Chest' or 'Closet' for portability in the field.[200] The third field bed was an old one at Ludlow Castle.

Most of the bedsteads in the inventories are listed without any very revealing qualification, 'One old Joyned Beddstead' for instance, and serve only to support hangings and bedding. It may be assumed that most of these were relatively simple structures of four-poster conformation, the frameworks of more-or-less French beds. 'One old. Bedstedd of. wainescott. Turned' at Oatlands may have had posts of some eleboration, but it was valued at only 12s. with its hangings. 'One highe beddstead' at Ludlow, valued at £1, together with seven other substantial pieces of furniture, may simply have been tall. Two beds at Carisbrooke Castle and one 'In the Prince his Beddchamber' at Ludlow were described as standing bedsteads. Their rich hangings were all of the French bed type, and the term, standing bedstead, seems to convey only that they were unusually impressive in their provincial surroundings.

At Ludlow there were no less than fifteen half-headed bedsteads and a few others were scattered at Bewdley and elsewhere. These were probably bedsteads with a fixed canopy projecting about half the length of the bed; one is described as 'with a Darnix Cannopie' and another as 'with a darnix Cannopy and 2. Curtaines'.[201] Exclusive to Ludlow was 'one old settle Bedd', presumably a large settle which could double as a bed: at Tart Hall in 1641 there was 'a greate settle Bedsted of Wood put up in Fashion of a Fourme'[202] And also at Ludlow there

177 [206]

403 [1073]

333 [88]

239 [273]

96 [111]

17 [79], 336 [135]

95 [108]

96 [110]

230 [148]

227 [124]

281 [91]

230 [156]
220 [39], 222 [64], 224 [76]

226 [97], 232 [186]
225 [93]

227 [106-7], 230 [154]
231 [164]

were three trundle bedsteads, low wheeled beds designed to fit under the principal bed, and 'One Liverie beddstead' with 'Curtaines of Kydderminster stuffe freindgd about the Bedd', a difficult entry to interpret, but perhaps a small servant's bed.[203]

293 [209]

292 [203]
129 [411], 333 [88]
292 [203]

293 [210]

A small group of bedsteads listed in the inventories evidently had decorative pretensions. At Windsor was 'One old. bested. of wallnuttree. wth 4 wodden cupps', valued with its damask hangings embroidered with Queen Elizabeth's arms at £3. A minor object, no doubt, as must have been 'One inlaied Beddstead at Denmark House, valued together with two canopy frames at £1. 'One bedsted Carved and gilt' at Whitehall sounds more imposing. But 'One Beddstead of wood. painted & hatch^t wth gold wth 7 Cupps' and incomplete hangings, valued at £26, and 'One verry faire bedsted. haveing 4 pillars A headpeece. of wallnuttree. cull^r gilt wth gold. & silv^r ye Jaume peeces. servinge for ye sydes & feete' which was valued together with its rich velvet hangings embroidered with Queen Elizabeth's badges at £40, both at Windsor, must have been elaborate and ambitious. The latter bed in particular sounds as if it may have resembled designs by Jacques Androuet DuCerceau.[204] Although it is described as bearing Queen Elizabeth's arms, the description of this bed is remarkably close to that of a bed at Windsor listed in the 1547 inventory of the Wardrobe of Henry VIII: moreover, the £26 bed with incomplete hangings is close to another in the same document.[205] A

210 [33]

tantalizing entry is for 'Celler and narrow vallance of haire cullo^r Tincell 8 cupps 7 curtaines of sea water greene . . . all wch is for a ship bed'. Could this have been similar to the 'ship bedstead Carved and guilt' listed at Hardwick in 1601?[206] And might both have resembled the ship beds, one decorated with dolphins and seahorses, also designed by DuCerceau?[207] Sea-green curtains would seem appropriate. At all events this small group seems to have survived from the previous century when in 1590 a hierarchy of four 'Bedsteades gilt', twenty-three 'Bedsteades of walnuttre and markatre', and forty 'Bedsteades of waynskot' were listed in Lord Lumley's houses.[208]

412 [85]

172 [145], 286 [140]

393 [933], 25 [56]

120 [332]

Some small non-textile ornamented elements have already been noted on the odd canopy or bed, the gilded 'Images belonging to a pavillian' for instance. The cups or vase-shaped finials which decorated canopies and beds formed another category, as '10 cups of wood. 10 plumes. of feathers' and '4 Cupps wth spriggs' associated with beds at Hampton Court and Oatlands respectively. At Theobalds there was even 'One large box for Cupps & feathers'. '12 Canopy Standes' of silver in the Lower Jewel House at the Tower, valued at £72, may have been another textile accessory, perhaps for use when a canopy was carried above the king in procession. But closer to furniture proper are 'A Rayle and Ballaster to incompasse round ye Bedd silvered and varnished over', valued at £12 and associated with the £1,000 French bed suite at Denmark House. There were two

124 [375], 412 [84]
184 [308]

more bed rails at Denmark House, both gilt and valued at £12 and £5. '2 wainescott Railes' at Hampton Court, valued at £1, could be simpler examples. Such rails or balustrades had a long history. A print of the Emperor Ferdinand I dining in Vienna in 1560 under his cloth of estate shows a balustrade right across the room.[209] According to Ashmole, when the Garter Feast was held at Whitehall in 1633 'the *Tables* for the *Knights-Companions* were (like the Soveraign's) fenced in with rails', which foiled 'the troublesome (yet usual) croud and rapine of the people'.[210] The same principle applied to altars, which Laud had commanded to be railed in 1634 (see p. 247), and, of course, to state beds.

101 [143]

154 [55]

'A Leather Cradle covered with Carnacon vellvett . . . very old' makes a fitting postscript to so many beds. It would be tempting to add a possible link between the wrought-iron 'cunabula Henrici Sexti' in the Tradescant collection and 'An Iron cradell on wheeles' in the armoury at St. James's but this latter must have been a gun carriage.[211]

Miscellanea

183 [301], 402 [1065]
178 [225]
413 [97]

226 [95]

A cradle of leather has just been mentioned. Leather chests and cases were discussed earlier and a gilt leather press, a leather sedan chair and a desk 'wth printers. leather' have been noted. Leather was sometimes a relatively utilitarian material. For example 'five old leather Chaires' at Denmark House, valued at 15s., were probably neat but unostentatious, and the same may hold for 'one Leather Chaire and stoole' and 'one other Leather old Chaire' in the Steward's Room at

227 [123]
126 [389]

229 [146]

225 [87]

288 [154]

228 [155]

219 [32]
135 [5]

143 [80]

424 [8], 424-5 [12]
234 [220], 422 [31]
117 [298]

23 [18]
24 [39], 47 [199], 46 [193]

118 [317]

218 [22]

197 [191-3]

321 [353]
202 [272]
247 [374]
427 [26]

285 [132]
231 [166], 229 [140]
229 [145]

226 [96]
121 [342]

Ludlow Castle, where another room's furniture included 'one leather Chaire'. But 'Six Back Chayres, and six high stooles of black leather with a Border of silver on the Edges' from Wimbledon, valued at £6, may have been extremely stylish. Leather, gilt and stamped, was also used for wall-hangings. Thus at Ludlow the Withdrawing Chamber had a 'Suite of Watched Cloth Hangings paned wth gilt leather', that is in light blue panels with gilt leather borders, and the Shovell Board Chamber had 'Nyne Peeces of Greene Kersey hangings paned with guilt leather 8 Windowe Curtaines suiteable 5. Windowe peeces, & a Chimney peece of ye same'. These were two of the grandest rooms at Ludlow and the fashionable nature of their hangings is attested by those from the Shovell Board Chamber being reserved for Cromwell in Whitehall. However the most spectacular use of leather was at Oatlands. 'A furniture of gilt leather. for ye Queenes. Gallerie cont. 5 peeces . . . one window. peece . . . A foote Carpett & a table Carpett suteable. A Couch of ye same. Three low: stooles of blew Cloth. bordered wth gilt leather', valued at £30, and 'Two window. Curtaines of Blew Cloth. bordered. wth gilt leather but verrÿ old', valued at 10s., must have created a splendid ensemble of blue and gold.[212] Perhaps this suite was produced by Rowland Buckett, who in about 1635 supplied 'guilt leather hangings and guilt stools and Chaires for the parlour' at Althorp at a cost of £68. 10s. 3d.[213]

Gilt leather is a material which bridges furniture and interior decoration. The hangings of the Shovell Board Chamber at Ludlow Castle included 'a Chimney peece'. Such a hanging, and 'Fowre Chymney Peeces', probably of tapestry, valued at £13, were overmantel ornaments. But what of '2 carved Chymne peces' in the garden at Denmark House, valued at 14s.? The low value would tend to indicate wood, but the context points to stone. It is possible that these may have been fragments of early Stuart palace decoration, to compare with a chimney-piece in the dining-room at Charlton House, Greenwich, which has convincingly been assigned a Queen's House provenance.[214] At Greenwich was 'a. Chimney peece – men horses & Bulls in it', valued at £10, which might well have been the overmantel to such a chimneypiece. Alternatively, all the chimneypieces in the inventories, whether textile or carved, may have been decorated valances to hang round the lower edges of projecting fireplace hoods.[215] In this fire-place context it is worth noting that only three pairs of bellows crop up in the Charles I inventories, apart from those in the foundry at Vauxhall, one in a domestic setting at Ludlow, the second clearly from its juxtaposition with anvils for a smithy, but the third, at Denmark House, 'inlayed with Mother of pearle' (see also p. 379).

Major lighting fitments are few: '4 large hanging Wall Candlesticks' of silver and two singletons form exceptions as may '2. great brazen Lampes' valued at 6s., although they sound from their context as if they were Roman or Renaissance bronzes rather than modern lighting devices.[216] 'Fowre woodden painted frames to sette candlesticks upon' have already been noted (see also p. 380). Picture frames represent a form of wall decoration. Unsurprisingly they attract scant attention in the inventories, although occasionally a phrase such as 'the frame and all' is used with a painting. The order of cost may be gauged from the 13s. 4d. charged by 'a Joyner' for a frame and a case for a portrait of a 'Cataia or Iland' man painted by Cornelis Ketel in 1576 or the 8s. charged for a frame for a similar Ketel portrait by 'Peter Gilbart, Dutchman' in 1577.[217] Nonetheless a few independent entries make it clear that frames could be expensive: '3 picture frames gilt' were valued at £9, and 'A picture frame carved & gilt' at £1. The odd frame for miniatures is listed, for example the 'Ebony Frame for an Eight Square Lymned peece' already mentioned; but this was valued at a mere 2s. The 'Silver and gilt frame' of a portrait of Mary Queen of Scots when young must have contributed to its value of £5.

A wainscot table with degrees for books at Oatlands was mentioned earlier. At Ludlow there were also 'small shellves' in the scullery, 'Severall Cheese Racks' in the dairy house, 'Racks for Armo^r' in the hall, presumably supporting a decorative arrangement, and, in the closet next to the steward's chamber 'twoe frames to to hang Cloathes upon'.[218] All of these are likely to have been simple practical devices. However 'Nyne Woodden hanging shellves turned and guilt' at Denmark House, valued at £9, were clearly decorative: they are listed before a large assembly of porcelain, which they may have served to display. Suspended shelves with turned gilt columns are shown supporting blue-and-white porcelain in a 1716 painting of an Antwerp interior, but the type is already recorded in the seventeenth century.[219]

Screens sometimes formed a part of canopy or bed suites. Usually only the

297   Furniture in the Commonwealth Inventories

83-4 [48]

288 [153]

89 [64]

183 [300], 422 [7]

89 [67]

285 [123]
285 [124]

285 [122]

122 [354]

124 [379]

115 [283-4], 122 [354]

115 [285], 285 [126]
179 [227, 233]

116 [286]

179 [228]

179 [229]
115 [279-80], 285 [128]

115 [280]
115 [277]

124 [371]

364 [534], 118 [312]

385 [816]

114 [274]

screen cloth is listed, but a crimson satin canopy suite at Denmark House includes a screen cloth and 'A frame of woodd to it guilt, and painted'. This could refer to the frame of the couch in the same suite, but 'a frame. of a skreene painted and gilt' forming part of another crimson satin suite, at Oatlands, is unequivocal. Such screen cloths seem usually to have measured a little under ten feet by about three feet nine inches; they were valued at around £3 and must have had a number of leaves, like 'A fouldeing skreene' at Hampton Court.[220] As 'Fowre old Skreene Frames' are listed together it seems possible that frame sizes were more-or-less standardized and that screen cloths were often not permanently fixed to frames. 'Two China skreenes guilt, one being broaken', may have been Japanese lacquer screens such as were auctioned from the cargo of the *Clove* in 1615.[221] In the same entry were 'A frame of woodd for a skreene with a wild man on ye Topp thereof, And another like frame', probably of a much smaller type, perhaps comparable to a 'Pilaster', which supported a screen of striped cloth of silver. This type is more clearly described in the next entry, for 'An other Skreene. on a gilt Pillaster & a Crosse covered wth a double paine of stript gold stuffe . . .' At Hardwick is a surviving stand of this banner-like conformation.[222] The Charles I inventories also include a few wicker screens, mainly at Ludlow. At Oatlands were 'A Round. Wicker. Skreene', valued at 1s. and corresponding to another survival at Hardwick, and 'An olde wicke Chaire'.[223]

No fewer than thirty-three looking-glasses are listed in the Charles I inventories, of which about a third were valued at under £5, and about a third at £10 or more. The highest valuation was £50 for 'One faire Lookeing Glasse in an Eboney Frame with an Antique Border of silver, and brasse' and for 'One Great Lookeing Glasse with silv[r] plate'. Ebony cabinets and clocks, some decorated with silver or gilt brass have already been noted. The presence of two further ebony frames, valued together at £46, and another, again mounted with silver and brass, valued at £30, fits in with this luxurious taste. Bosse shows rectangular or octagonal looking-glasses hanging by the heads of beds, but the inventories do not clearly distinguish between wall-mirrors, toilet-mirrors, and hand-mirrors.[224] Two looking-glasses in frames of ebony and mother-of-pearl, each valued at £1. 10s., must have been relatively small, and the same holds for two crystal mirrors, one in a wooden painted case and the other in a case embroidered with an hour glass, an appropriate *memento mori*. Several other mirrors had embroidered frames or cases, including 'A Lookeing Glasse in a frame of Carnacon vellvett enbroydered with seede pearles, and wth letters A & R in a redd leather guilt Case', valued at £15. There are five steel mirrors. 'One large lookeing glasse of steele sett in a frame of wood painted wth ye Cardinalls Armes at ye top wth a Curtain', valued at £5, was probably a wall-mirror, as a curtain would be less practical on other types. Steel mirrors were prone to rust and a protective curtain or cover, sometimes sliding, was often provided.[225] 'One steele lookeing glass enbroid[rd] standing uppon a foote of Marble' must have been a toilet mirror. Enamels, semi-precious stones, and amber are also mentioned, but these examples seem closer to jewellery than furniture. However, 'A Lookeing Glasse of Brasse with an Image houlding the same with some Boxes of silver & in the same, One Boxe wanting', valued at £15, sounds as if it may have been comparable to a celebrated Milanese mirror with a damascened frame and stand, the latter incorporating a drawer, in the Victoria and Albert Museum.[226] Finally 'A large lookeing Glasse with two leaves haveing 41 whole Panes', valued at £4. 2s., may have been comparable on a small scale to the mirrored cabinet of Catherine de' Medici, which incorporated 119 plates.[227] Mirror glass was an expensive commodity, available only in small sheets.

Entries on the musical instruments in the inventories contain disappointingly scanty details of their decoration, which makes them difficult to appraise as furniture. Organs, portative or otherwise, must have had cases: one organ, valued at £20, must have been elaborately ornamented. A 'Paire of Virginalls in a Case of greene vellvett Enbroydered with small pearles', valued at £10, is the exception: this instrument may have resembled 'Queen Elizabeth's virginals' in the Victoria and Albert Museum, whose elaborately decorated case, in the Venetian lacquer style, has a red velvet outer case[228] (see also pp. 397-8, below). The few entries for globes are also meagre: 'One old Globe', valued at £2, may have been a substantial object, but no details are given. Most of the clocks in the Charles I inventories are scarcely furniture, belonging more to horology or metalwork. However 'A Clock in a Case of Ebony with Trumpetts Drummes, and other Antiques', valued at £100, must have been a substantial piece of furniture in its own right, resembling perhaps a mechanical music box in Vienna, made by Hans Schlottheim of Augsburg in 1582, or the so-called 'Hottentotten-tanz' in Dresden, made by Matthaus Runggel of Augsburg in about 1630.[229] This may be identified with a somewhat similar contraption seen at Whitehall by Johann Ernst, Duke of Saxe-Weimar, in 1613, and said to have been made by a

114 [275]

craftsman from Cologne.[230] And 'A Clocke made in ye fashion of a Coach of Eboney garnished with silver drawne by Two Lyons, The Lyons wheeles, and 2. personages all of silver haveing a Clock in the same in a greene woodden Case', valued at £40, and probably comparable to early seventeenth-century examples in Vienna and Karlsruhe, also just qualifies as furniture.[231]

26 [3]
394 [941]
395 [965], 248 [6]

Hunting was not only an aristocratic pastime: it was also a central theme of courtly life, expressed in the Charles I inventories in silver, 'A Cupp and a Cover Called the Stagge'; in paintings, 'One picture of a boares head' and 'one picture wth great hornes', at Theobalds; in tapestry, 'One peece. of hangin of hawkein & huntin' (note the dropped gs); and in the paraphernalia of the chase, discussed on pp. 405-7; the trophies of antlers mentioned there may also be seen as furnishings.[232]

Although the scale of removals in the early seventeenth century may have been less than that of previous centuries, royal furniture was by no means static. Indeed the cases which frequently accompanied furniture were often designed for travel. In 1639, for instance, Thomas Hardwicke, the queen's trunk-maker, delivered 'a very large French bedcase above 2 yarde longe & the heade above a yard deep made of good licquord oxe hydes & lyned wt. fyne canvas for to carry her ma.ts. large bed & quilt in Removes & all the furniture belonging to it', costing no less than £8.[233] Apart from changes which responded to fashion or to the vagaries of personal taste, ceremonies and banquets were a constant cause of movement, as the court shifted from house to house, as the furniture was issued to ambassadors and others or was worn out or broken, and as new pieces came in by gift or purchase. Thus even in a year of peace an inventory would have caught royal houses and wardrobes in a state of flux, according to the season, the requirements of the court, and the movements of the king and his family. But by 1649 years of disruption, neglect and depredation must have affected even the most sequestered of royal houses. Any detailed reconstruction of furniture ensembles on the basis of the inventories must thus be a wild goose chase.

The exception, unfortunately, is Ludlow Castle. The goods inventoried and appraised there on 31 October 1650 may not have been intact, but there is little sign of major loss. Most of them are listed room by room, and the names of most rooms are supplied. Such a rich source of information is of course not without its intrinsic interest. Any historian involved in the organization, workings and furnishings of large provincial houses in the early seventeenth century will find a wealth of useful evidence here, and many of the more basic practical arrangements have a wider relevance. Some elements of the complex and its furniture moreover reflect Ludlow's role as a seat of government. And a few modern fashionable elements seem to have been introduced for royal use, for

225 [87]

instance the gilt leather and green kersey hangings in the Shovelboard Chamber reserved for Cromwell. But it would be difficult to pretend that the Ludlow inventory is of crucial interest in the specific context of Charles I, except in completing the picture. It is useful to know what was there, but the mix is so familiar that it hardly requires detailed analysis here, which would in any case devote disproportionate attention to a marginal property.[234]

The bulk of the Charles I inventories did not list objects room by room, but instead ordered them in a flexible hierarchy of which the order adopted at Richmond on 5 October 1694 may stand as an example, viz. hangings, carpets, cloths of estate and canopies, furnitures for beds, chairs, cushions, and various, including fixtures or immoveables. The procedure, however eloquent of the practice of wardrobe keepers and valuers, leads to the separation of many associated objects. If provenances were regularly supplied a simple process of reordering would recapture what integrity the lost ensemble retained. Unfortunately, provenances are rarely and irregularly supplied. Occasionally an interior such as 'ye Indian Chamber' at St. James's is briefly in focus with its tables, 'Indian' box and armour, and 'turquey boes'. The banqueting house at Wimbledon with '14 statues of plaster. braised over' and '4. Chaires. & one Marble table' almost comes to life. But more frequent are tantalizing glimpses,

126 [389]

such as the black leather and silver chairs and stools also from Wimbledon. Where did they stand?

Sometimes, as with the kitchen areas of Hampton Court, or the 'Certaine Goodes' left over at Kenilworth, or the 'white wild Bull' at Holdenby, there is a sense of mingled oddity and melancholy to be savoured. *Sic transit* . . . And the entries for Bewdley, part furnished but without a single textile, have a ghostly ring. But more often the fragmentary surviving fixtures and oddments are all too prosaic and ineloquent. It is scarcely a case of *Roma quanta fuit ipsa ruina docet*.

240 [–], 241 [295]

'One peece of Arras of yᵉ Marrage of Prince Arthurr & yᵉ Ladye. Katherine', valued at £54, introduces another category, that of historic relics. The many cushions with earlier royal initials embroidered on them fit into this category in a general sense, but there seems little reason to doubt that 'One Bedstedd apparrelled with rich crimson cloth of gould Tissue enbroydered with K Henry yᵉ 8ᵗ his L[ette]res' had been kept up specifically as an historic monument. The looking-glass 'painted wᵗʰ yᵉ Cardinalls Armes' and 'A Greene vellvett Coffer and 6 shirts in yᵉ same of K. Henry the 8ᵗˢ' must have been, to a greater or lesser degree, mementos, and the identification of the latter hints at some system of labelling or access to wardrobe records. In the wardrobe at Windsor was a group of cloths of estate and beds, which had belonged to Queen Elizabeth, one at least of which seems to have been fully dressed, like that of Henry VIII. If, as suggested above, the 'Queen Elizabeth' bed had belonged to Henry VIII, adaptation at a later date or confusion in identification seem possible.[235] And there was at Carisbrooke 'One little old Chaire of Crimson vellvett which was Queene Elizabeths much decayed'. Relic or relict? Only with the tapestries 'of the victory by sea over the Spanish Fleete in the yeare of our Lord God 1588', reserved for Cromwell, is there unequivocal evidence of piety towards the past.

159 [9]

95 [109]

179 [228], 104 [164]

293 [210]

222 [68]

5 [21]

The pavilion 'pʳsented to King James by the Russian Ambassador', the carpet 'presented to his Maᵗʸ by the Lady Conisby upon Newyears day Anno Dni 1619', the marble table 'Given to the Queene by yᵉ Ladie Banning' and the tapestry 'given to the Queene by Sʳ Henry Vane' represent royal gifts whose identification once more seems to indicate inside knowledge on the part of those making the inventory, again apparent in the puzzling entry for 'a rich Cloth of State bought and furnished with all things suitable to it. 1638', embroidered 'with King James his Armes', and valued at £500.

18 [82], 11 [51]
120 [333]
126 [387]

18-19 [83]

This mention of 'all things suitable' emphasises a point repeatedly made during the earlier discussion of chairs, canopies and beds. Most upholstered furniture came in moveable suites which could encompass both the bare if luxurious ceremonial essentials and complete decorative schemes. In a royal household the universal rituals of precedence had an especial importance. The 'large rich French Bedd', valued with its suite at £1000, expresses the monarch's pre-eminent status. And it was a fashionable object. A central theme of the Charles I inventories must be the adoption by the court of the Parisian style of decoration recorded in France by Abraham Bosse and in England by Edmond Marmion. Henrietta Maria was of course French, Inigo Jones's French sources are by now well known, and Paris had long been a dominant centre in matters of interior decoration.[236] But a second theme in the inventories, or at least in this commentary, is the prevalence of an Italianate style of furnishing in summer rooms, banqueting rooms and galleries, a style which favoured marble tables and carved, gilt and painted seat furniture, a style which must have appealed to virtuosi, which went well with antique sculpture, and which of course reflected another aspect of Inigo Jones. Both styles seem to have come together at Oatlands.

119-20 [329]

Oatlands is the most frustrating case of dispersal. Apart from substantial lists of objects actually at Oatlands, there were tapestries from the Privy Chamber at Syon, and others, from the Presence Chamber, with the Lord President and yet others with Mr Worsley and Captain Axtell, in the Great Closet and Balcony Room at St. James's, at Captain Kemp's, Lieutenant Ward's and Colonel Walton's; Oatlands paintings were in a mixed list of royal goods; there was bedding with the Council of State in Whitehall and with Clement Kynnersley, who also had two chairs; there were curtains with Mr Wolsey; there were stools with Mr Wolsey, Major White, Mr Matthews, Colonel Jones, Captain Zanchy and Dr Parker, who also had a chair; and finally there were carpets with Captain Axtell and Clement Kynnersley. Most of these lodgings were in Whitehall or nearby, but none the less this recital records sixteen different locations, apart from Oatlands itself.

And yet in the lists of pictures and goods viewed and appraised at Oatlands on 14 September 1649 and in the other scattered entries, there are promising possibilities: from 'severall Oring Trees', to the suite of 'Crimson China Sattine

250 [39], 288 [153]

branchd wth yellow. in Paines parted. wth white & yellow stuffe. of ye same' comprising four hangings, three window hangings, a screen cloth, a Spanish carpet, a couch, one long cushion, two chairs, eight folding stools, a Spanish table, a screen frame (presumably these supported the Spanish carpet and screen cloth) and two window curtains of 'Crimson Taphetie' in the Queen's Cabinet Room, to the 'Twelve blew. stooles of wood gilt of ye Italian Table in ye somer romes', to 'The burneinge of Troy' which 'hangs in ye bedchamber' — in all these things and more there is the hope of recapturing a vision of what this particular house, at least, presented, especially if sources other than the Charles I inventories are brought into play.[237] Perhaps, after all, the pursuit of these vanished splendours is not a lost cause.

288 [153], 287 [152]
279 [59]

Notes

I am grateful to the J. Paul Getty Museum for opportunities for research provided by a guest scholarship there; to Peter Thornton and Gillian Wilson for reading and commenting on my text; and to Thalia Jervis for help with typing.

1. For a partial exception see L. Cust, 'The Lumley inventories', *Walpole Society* 6 (1917-18), pp. 15-50.

2. J. Nash, *The Mansions of England in the Olden Time* (London, 1839-49). In some respects early works such as those by Nash, Henry Shaw (for example *Specimens of Ancient Furniture* (London, 1836) and *Details of Elizabethan Architecture* (London, 1839)), and C.J. Richardson (for example *Architectural Remains of the Reigns of Elizabeth and James I* (London, 1840) and *Studies from Old English Mansions* (London, 1841-8)), give a more accurate picture of sixteenth- and seventeenth-century interiors than do more recent works such as P. Macquoid, *A History of English Furniture, The Age of Oak* (London, 1904), S.W. Wolsey and R.W. Luff, *Furniture in England: the Age of the Joiner* (London, 1968) and V. Chinnery, *Oak Furniture: the British Tradition* (Woodbridge, 1979); the black-and-white illustrations of surviving oak in these latter overwhelm any *caveats* about colour and luxury in their texts.

3. See Musée Le Secq des Tournelles, *Ferronnerie Ancienne* (Paris, 1924), II, pl. 106 for small iron trunks.

4. Hardwicke's bill is one of a number from various tradesmen in PRO, LR 5/66 and 5/67, transcribed by Hero Granger-Taylor as part of research into the Queen's House at Greenwich. I am grateful to the National Maritime Museum for permission to use these transcriptions, which were commissioned by the Property Services Agency.

5. G. Olive, 'Furniture in a West Country parish 1576-1769', *Furniture History* 12 (1976), p. 20.

6. Illustrated in P. Thornton, *Seventeenth-Century Interior Decoration in England, France and Holland* (London, 1978), p. 327.

7. See R.W. Symonds, 'The chest and the coffer, their difference in function and design', *Connoisseur* 107 (1941), pp. 15-21, and 'The craft of the coffer-maker', *ibid.*, pp. 100-105, 133.

8. See Note 4.

9. See L. Cust, 'Notes on the collections formed by Thomas Howard, Earl of Arundel and Surrey, K.G.', *Burlington Magazine* 20 (1911), p. 100 'Two red wooden standards to sett candles on', for another meaning.

10. In 1639 Thomas Hardwicke (see Note 4) delivered 'a large standard bownd about w^t. Irons cuvrd. w^t. neats leather having dras. & double locks...', priced at £5.

11. Cited by *OED*, s.v. cypress (1), Act II, Scene i, line 363 [line 347 in Oxford, 1986, edition].

12. P. Thornton, 'Two problems', *Furniture History* 7 (1971), pp. 67-8, pl. 17.

13. E. Peacock, 'Inventories made for Sir William and Sir Thomas Fairfax, Knights, of Walton, and of Gilling Castle, Yorkshire in the sixteenth and seventeenth centuries', *Archaeologia* 48 (1884), p. 138, and J. Nichols, *The Unton Inventories* (London, 1841), p. 20.

14. R.W. Symonds, 'The craft of the coffer and trunk maker in the 17th century', *Connoisseur* 109 (1942), p. 45.

15. See G. Gall, *Leder im europäischen Kunsthandwerk* (Brunswick, 1965). In the Prado are numerous leather containers of this type which contained the precious objects inherited by Philip V of Spain from his father, the Dauphin of France, in 1712: see D.A. Iñiguez, *Catalogo de las Alhajas del Delfin* (Madrid, 1954), p. 40.

16. See Note 4.

17. The library is in the Huntington Library, San Marino, California. Compare that which belonged to Sir Julius Caesar in the British Library, and others in the Brotherton Library, Leeds, and at Toledo, Ohio. See H.M. Nixon and W.A. Jackson, 'English seventeenth-century travelling libraries', *Transactions of the Cambridge Bibliographical Society* 7 (1979), pp. 294-321. I am grateful to Mr Alan Jutzi for this reference.

18. Illustrated in R. Edwards, *The Shorter Dictionary of English Furniture* (London, 1964), p. 193.

19. Illustrated in ibid. See also *Country Life* 14 (1903), p. 559.

20. See Note 4.

21. C.J. Phillips, *History of the Sackville Family* (London, 1930) I, p. 317, document dated 1624.

22. Symonds, op. cit. (Note 7), p. 20. This must have been comparable to the Rushbrooke example (Edwards, op. cit. (Note 18), p. 193) and to a similar item in the Victoria and Albert Museum associated with Edward VI. 'Tylles', of course, are tills, drawers.

23. L. Boynton and P. Thornton, 'The Hardwick Hall inventory of 1601', *Furniture History* 7 (1971), p. 32.

24. See Note 4.

25. Loose globe covers of scorched leather surviving at Ham House may be comparable; illustrated in Thornton, op. cit. (Note 6), p. 309. See also P. Thornton and M. Tomlin, 'The furnishing and decoration of Ham House', *Furniture History* 16 (1980), p. 135.

26. Cited by *OED*.

27. J. Irwin, 'A Jacobean vogue for oriental lacquer-ware', *Burlington Magazine* 95 (1953), pp. 193-5, and O. Impey, 'Japan', in *Lacquer* (Marlborough, 1984), p. 123.

28. Irwin, op. cit. (Note 27), p. 193.

29. Impey, op. cit. (Note 27), p. 125 illustrates a comparable example.

30. Ibid., pp. 125-6.

31. *The Diary of Samuel Pepys* ed. R.W. Latham and W. Matthews (London, 1970), II p. 79.

32. Impey, op. cit. (Note 27), p. 129. The form of the 'box' may have resembled that of an armour chest depicted in Nicholas Hilliard's miniature of Sir Anthony Mildmay in the Museum of Art, Cleveland, Ohio, illustrated in Thornton, op. cit. (Note 12), pl. 18.

33. P. Volk, 'Hinterglasmalerei der Renaissance', *Kunst und Antiquitäten* 1 (1988), pp. 52-63.

34. C. Blair, *Arms, Armour and Base-Metalwork (The James A. De Rothschild Collection at Waddesdon Manor)* (London, 1974), pp. 483-7. A wide range of caskets of the same general type is illustrated in Secq des Tournelles, op. cit. (Note 3), pls. 401, 404 and 406.

35. 'Smaller', that is, than 'A small Chest', *Inventories*, p. 112 [252].

36. Illustrated in part in G.B. Hughes, 'Domestic metalwork', in *The Stuart Period 1603-1714 (Connoisseur Period Guide)* (London, 1957), p. 108.

37. R.W. Symonds, 'New light on Tudor furniture. II – Queen Elizabeth's coffer-makers, John and Thomas Grene', *Country Life* 93 (1943), p. 1054.

38. Illustrated in R.W. Symonds, 'The craft of the English clock-case maker – I And how it came into being', *Connoisseur* 114 (1944), p. 87.

39. See P. Eames, 'Furniture in England, France and the Netherlands from the twelfth to the fifteenth century', *Furniture History* 13 (1977), pp. 55-65 for a discussion of the type.

40. Cust, op. cit. (Note 9), p. 341.

41. P. Agius, 'Late sixteenth- and seventeenth-century furniture in Oxford', *Furniture History* 7 (1971), p. 84.

42. Cited by *OED*, s.v. dressing-board. In 1623 there were 'iiij dress bords and a shelfe' in the milk house at Fryer's Manor in Hertfordshire: see Sir Ambrose Heal, 'A great country house in 1623', *Burlington Magazine* 82 (1943), p. 115.

43. See N.H. Nicolas, *The Privy Purse Expenses of King Henry the Eighth* (London, 1827), p. 313, Nichols, op. cit. (Note 13), and Thornton, op. cit. (Note 12), p. 69, note 14 with bibliography.

44. Thornton, op. cit. (Note 12), p. 61; Agius, op. cit. (Note 41), p. 82.

45. E. Ashmole, *The Institution, Laws & Ceremonies of the most Noble Order of the Garter* (London, 1672), p. 593.

46. S. Jervis, *Printed Furniture Designs Before 1650* (Leeds, 1974), p. 438.

47. Ibid., p. 48; R. Pricke (trans.), *Perspective Practical* (London, 1672), pl. 99.

48. E. Chambers (trans.), *The Practice of Perspective* (London, 1726), pl. 99.

49. *DNB*, Sidney, Sir Henry (1529-1586). See also p. 43 (above).

50. Quoted by R.W. Symonds, 'The "dyning parlor" and its furniture', *Connoisseur* 113 (1944), p. 16.

51. Cust, op. cit. (Note 9) p. 341.

52. On wainscot see L.F. Salzman, *Building in England* (Oxford, 1952), pp. 245-6.

53. Thornton, op. cit. (Note 6), p. 395.

54. See Notes 47-8.

55. P. Macquoid and R. Edwards, *Dictionary of English Furniture* (London, 1924), II, p. 175, (also reference to Sir Simonds D'Ewes, 1634), and Eames, op. cit. (Note 39), pls. 22-26.

56. Jervis, op. cit. (Note 46), p. 42, pl. 311.

57. See S. Jervis 'A tortoiseshell cabinet and its precursors', *Victoria & Albert Museum Bulletin* 4 (1968), and G. Himmelheber, *Kabinettschränke* (Munich, Bavarian National Museum, 1977).

58. E.P. Shirley, 'An inventory of the effects of Henry Howard, K.G., Earl of Northampton, taken on his death in 1614', *Archaeologia* 42 (1862), pp. 348 and 362.

59. Thornton, op. cit. (Note 6), p. 327, no. 65, and S. Speth-Holterhoff, *Les Peintres Flamands de Cabinets d'Amateurs au XVIIe Siècle* (Brussels, 1957), pl. 30.

60. For instance Y. Hackenbroch, *English and Other Needlework Tapestries and Textiles in the Irwin Untermyer Collection* (Metropolitan Museum of Art, New York, 1960), pls. 75-6, and D. King, 'Textiles', in *The Stuart Period 1603-1714 (Connoisseur Period Guide)* (London, 1957), pl. 75A.

61. B. Lüsberg, *Rosenborg* (Copenhagen, n.d.), p. 23, and Mogens Bencard and Jørgen Hein, 'Three cabinets on stands from the seventeenth century', *Furniture History* 21 (1985), fig. 8.

62. V. Woldbye, 'Scharloth's curious cabinet', *Furniture History* 21 (1985), pp. 68-74.

63. It is possible that the latter may be 'Un petit coffre de six pièces de jaspe d'orient, vert, garni de'argent vermeil doré…' in Cardinal Mazarin's collection. See *Inventaire de tous les Meubles du Cardinal Mazarin* (London, 1861), p. 53.

64. *Die Kunstkammer* (Schloss Ambras, Innsbruck, 1977), p. 130 and pl. 4, and F. Windisch-Graetz, *Möbel Europas, Renaissance und Manierismus* (Munich, 1983), p. 379.

65. Windisch-Graetz, op. cit. (Note 64), p. 244.

66. Cust, op. cit. (Note 9), p. 100.

67. A. MacGregor (ed.), *Tradescant's Rarities* (Oxford, 1983), p. 265.

68. Cust, op. cit. (Note 1), pls. 12 and 13; W.B. Rye (ed.), *England as seen by Foreigners* (London, 1865), p. 45.

69. A. Coleridge, 'English furniture and cabinet-makers at Hatfield House – 1: c. 1600-1750', *Burlington Magazine* 109 (1967), p. 64, figs. 21 and 23.

70. D. Sturdy and M. Henig, *The Gentle Traveller, John Bargrave, Canon of Canterbury and his Collection* ([Oxford], [1983]), p. 10.

71. Jervis, op. cit. (Note 57), Thornton and Tomlin, op. cit. (Note 25), p. 105. The Antwerp firm of Musson certainly supplied cabinets and tables *en suite*, see E. Duverger, 'Nieuwe gegevens betreffende de kunsthandel van Matthijs Musson en Maria Fourmenois te Antwerpen tussen 1633 en 1681', *Gentse Bijdragen* 21 (1968), pp. 82-3.

72. Quoted by H. Havard, *Dictionnaire de l'Ameublement* (Paris, 1887), II, p. 246. The combination is also to be found at Amerongen, with two pairs of cabinets and a table attributed to Van Mekeren.

73. A. Radcliffe and P. Thornton, 'John Evelyn's cabinet', *Connoisseur* 197 (1978), pp. 254-63.

74. *En Värld i Miniatyr* (Kungl. Husgeråds-kammaren, 1982), pp. 98, 102, and Sotheby's, *Mentmore* (London, 1977), p. II, lot 1866.

75. *Anzeiger des Germanischen Nationalmuseums* (Nuremberg, 1975), pp. 155-6; S.W.A. Drossaers and Th. H. Lunsingh Scheurleer (eds.), *Inventarissen van de Inboedels in de Verblijven van de Oranjes 1567-1795* (The Hague, 1974), I, p. 500.

76. G. Reineking von Bock, *Bernstein* (Munich, 1981); O. Doering, *Das Augsburger Patriciers Philipp Hainhofer Beziehungen zum Herzog Philipp II von Pommern-Stettin* (Vienna, 1896), p. 163; MacGregor, op. cit. (Note 67), pp. 244-5; S.W.A. Drossaers, 'Inventaris van de meubelen van het stadhouderlijk kwartier met het Speelhuis en van het Huis in het Noordeinde te 's-Gravenhage', *Oud Holland* 47 (1930) p. 216.

77. Boynton and Thornton, op. cit. (Note 23), p. 26; Nichols, op. cit. (Note 13), p. 33. By contrast there was at Tart Hall in 1641 'A large Trunke of Mother of Pearle with two drawers', probably Japanese (Cust, op. cit. (Note 9), p. 100). However in 1600 mother-of-pearl caskets were noted at Whitehall and Hampton Court: see G.W. Groos (ed.), *The Diary of Baron Waldstein* (London, 1981), pp. 49 and 155.

78. I. Toesca, 'Un coffret parisien du XVIe siècle', *Gazette des Beaux-Arts* 66 (1965), pp. 309-12; *Catalogue of the Exhibition of Ancient Art Belonging to the International Trade* (Rijksmuseum, Amsterdam, 1936), after pl. 813; G. de Bellaigue, *Furniture, Clocks and Gilt Bronzes (The James A. De Rothschild Collection at Waddesdon Manor)* (London, 1974), p. 577.

79. *Skulpturensammlung, Münzkabinett, Grünes Gewölbe. Bildwerke der Renaissance und des Barocks* (Dresden, 1965), p. 210; R. Scholz, *Goldsmiedearbeiten, Renaissance und Barock* (Museum für Kunst und Gewerbe, Hamburg, 1974), p. 87, pl. 20; C. Oman, *English Silversmiths' Work, Civil and Domestic* (London, 1965), pl. 55; *The Indian Heritage, Court Life & Arts under Mughal Rule* (Victoria & Albert Museum, London, 1982), p. 162.

80. M. Zebrowski, 'Decorative arts of the Mughal period' in *The Arts of India* (Oxford, 1981), p. 179. This refers to patterned artefacts (compare also a box in the Munich Schatz-kammer mounted in 1638: see G.E. Pazaurek *Perlmutter* (Berlin, 1937), p. 13 and pl. 2), but the argument would also apply to those discussed here. See also B. Dam-Mikkelsen and

T. Lundbæk, *Ethnographic Objects in the Royal Danish Kunstkammer 1650-1800* (Nationalmuseet, Copenhagen, 1980) p. 123, for a dish of this type described in 1690 as 'Muskovitisk' and now ascribed to 'India?'.

81. Coleridge, op. cit. (Note 69), p. 64, fig. 22.

82. Quoted by R.W. Lightbown, 'Oriental art and the orient in late Renaissance and Baroque Italy', *Journal of the Warburg and Courtauld Institutes* 32 (1969), p. 253.

83. Jervis, op. cit. (Note 57), and R. Fabri, 'Het archief van de firma Forchondt als bron voor de studie van de 17de-eeuwse Antwerpse Kunstkasten', *Bulletin des Musées Royaux d'Art et d'Histoire Bruxelles* 57 (1986), p. 44.

84. Groos, op. cit. (Note 77), p. 57. Boyle, quoted by *OED*, s.v. tortoise-shell; F.W. Steer, 'The inventory of Anne, Viscountess Dorchester', *Notes and Queries* 198 (1953), pp. 155-58.

85. Cust, op. cit. (Note 9), p. 99, D. Alcouffe, 'Dal Rinascimento al Luigi XIV', in *Il Mobile Francese* (Milan, 1981), p. 43.

86. Duverger, op. cit. (Note 71), pp. 43-4.

87. Ibid., and M. Jourdain, *English Decoration and Furniture of the Early Renaissance* (London, 1924), p. 195.

88. J. Denucé, *Art Export in the Seventeenth Century in Antwerp, The Firm Forchoudt* [sic] (Antwerp, 1931), p. 40.

89. J. Knutsson, *Kabinettscåp på Skokloster* (Skokloster, 1985), cover, pp. 71-2.

90. Victoria and Albert Museum, W.60-1923 (from the Alfred Williams Hearn gift).

91. Knutsson, op. cit. (Note 89), pp. 72-3, C. Alberici, *Capolavori di Arte Decorativi nel Castello Sforzesco* (Milan, 1975), no. 153.

92. Doering, op. cit. (Note 76), p. 5.

93. Himmelheber, op. cit. (Note 57), pp. 27-44.

94. Thornton and Tomlin, op. cit. (Note 25), p. 124, fig. 45.

95. Shirley, op. cit. (Note 58), pp. 355, 362. The latter may be related to the later works of Dirck van Rijswijck, see Th. H. Lunsingh Scheurleer, *Catalogus van Meubelen en Betimmeringen* (Rijksmuseum, Amsterdam, 1952), p. 247 with references.

96. R. Edwards, *Dictionary of English Furniture* (London, 1953), I, p. 162, and PRO, Holland SP 84/139, f. 73 (I am grateful to Ronald Lightbown for this reference).

97. Drossaers, op. cit. (Note 76), p. 215.

98. Quoted by H. Kreisel, *Die Kunst des deutschen Möbels* I *Von den Anfängen bis zum Hochbarock* 3rd. edn. (Munich, 1981), p. 108.

99. Quoted by Havard, op. cit. (Note 72), II, p. 248.

100. Alcouffe, op. cit. (Note 85), p. 14.

101. B. Forman, *American Seating Furniture 1630-1730* (New York, 1988), p. 45.

102. See Note 4. The cabinet in the Victoria and Albert Museum is illustrated by S.W. Wolsey and R.W.P. Luff, *Furniture in England, The Age of the Joiner* (London, 1968), figs. 3-5 (there associated with Elizabeth I).

103. Could that with a dog and a monkey have been related to clocks of a type produced in Augsburg? See K. Maurice, *Die deutsche Räderuhr* (Munich, 1976), II, pls. 330-4, 345.

104. Illustrated in Jervis, op. cit. (Note 57), fig. 5.

105. Ibid., pp. 135-6 with references.

106. Lunsingh Scheurleer, op. cit. (Note 95), pp. 356-60, pl. 59, and C. Willemijn Fock, 'Het zogenaamde kunstkabinetje van Rudolf II', *Leids Kunsthistorisch Jaarboek* 1 (1982), pp. 199-209.

107. H. Huth, 'A Venetian Renaissance casket', *Museum Monographs* I (City Art Museum, St. Louis, 1968), pp. 42-50; D. Chambers and J. Martineau (eds.), *Splendours of the Gonzaga* (Victoria & Albert Museum, London, 1982), pp. 207-8.

108. Denucé, op. cit. (Note 88), pp. 32, 40. A cabinet of the same general type once at Tart Hall is illustrated in *Thomas Howard, Earl of Arundel* (Ashmolean Museum, Oxford, 1985), pp. 51-3.

109. Th. H. Lunsingh Scheurleer, 'Silver furniture in Holland', in *Opuscula in Honorem C. Hernmarck* (Nationalmuseum, Stockholm, 1966), p. 146.

110. Jervis, op. cit. (Note 46), pls. 332, 295.

111. There was also with Lieutenant Ward 'One billiard board without Cloath' (*Inventories*, p. 363 [524]); Thornton, op. cit. (Note 6), pl. 224.

112. Coleridge, op. cit. (Note 69), p. 63, figs. 19 and 20.

113. M. Girouard, 'The Smythson Collection of the Royal Institute of British Architects', *Architectural History* 5 (1962), pp. 43, 115, described as 'Design for a stepped canopy'.

114. A. Heal, 'A great country house in 1623', *Burlington Magazine* 82 (1943), p. 114; see also Cust (Note 9), p. 98 – 'A little Table with a leather Cover thereon, and over that, a little presse of shelves without doores'; see also Hollar's 1635 etching of William Dugdale at a table with shelves behind, illus. D. Howarth, *Lord Arundel and his Circle* (New Haven and London, 1985), p. 178.

115. Cust, op. cit. (Note 9), p. 100; Edwards, op. cit. (Note 96), p. 541.

116. Quoted by *OED,* s.v. drawer.

117. Thornton, op. cit. (Note 6), p. 236.

118. For a depiction of such a table, and a canopy in about 1615, see M. Conforti and G. Walton (eds.), *Sweden: A Royal Treasury 1550-1700* (Washington, 1988), p. 44.

119. See Thornton, op. cit. (Note 6), pp. 9, 84, 272.

120. Jervis, op. cit. (Note 46), p. 48, pl. 440.

121. See A. Gonzáles-Palacios, *Il Tempio del Gusto, Roma e il Regno delle due Sicilie* (Milan, 1984), II, pp. 217-9, for a good seventeenth-century illustration of such tables.

122. See Note 4.

123. Thornton, op. cit. (Note 6), p. 160; P. Laslett, 'The Jacobean Age', in *The Stuart Period 1603-1714 (Connoisseur Period Guide)* (London, 1957), pl. 1; and Jervis, op. cit. (Note 46), pl. 448.

124. Cust, op. cit. (Note 9), p. 98.

125. Thornton and Tomlin, op. cit. (Note 25), pp. 11, 45.

126. Thornton, op. cit. (Note 6), pp. 230, 378. *OED,* which includes a reference to a round oyster table at Althorp in 1610, wrongly interprets this as 'a table inlaid with mother-of-pearl'.

127. M. Drury, 'Italian furniture in National Trust houses', *Furniture History* 20 (1984), p. 39, pl. 46c; Cust, op. cit. (Note 9), p. 235 and p. 98.

128. For example A. Blum, *Abraham Bosse* (Paris, 1924), pl. 14; see also Thornton, op. cit. (Note 6), pp. 92-3.

129. Forman, op. cit. (Note 101), p. 31.

130. *OED,* s.v. coral-wood. N. Whittock, *The Decorative Painters' and Glaziers' Guide* (London, 1827) illustrates both 'coral wood' (pl. 14), and 'watered damask coral wood' (pl. 15), both pink-red with a wavy figure. This table may be identical to one seen by Baron Waldstein in 1600 (Groos, op. cit. (Note 77), p. 141) and by a Danish visitor to Windsor Castle in 1613 (Rye, op. cit. (Note 68), p. 164).

131. See H.-O. Boström, 'Die geheime Verbindung zwischen Kunst und Natur', *Kunst und Antiquitäten* 1 (1988), pp. 48-9.

132. C. Piacenti Aschengreen, *Il Museo degli Argenti a Firenze* (Florence, 1967), p. 174, pl. 51. See also that in Amsterdam: Lunsingh Scheurleer, op. cit. (Note 95), pp. 356-60.

133. Lunsingh Scheurleer, op. cit. (Note 95), p. 247, and C. Kramm, *De Levens en Werken der Hollandsche en Vlaamsche Kunstschilders, Beeldhouwers, Graveurs en Bouwmeesters* (Amsterdam, 1860), p. 1424.

134. See for instance a miniature of about 1635 of Shah Jahan on the Peacock Throne, illustrated in E. Koch, *Shah Jahan and Orpheus* (Graz, 1988), pl. 47.

135. See Note 75. This table was seen at Hampton Court in 1600 (Groos, op. cit. (Note 77), p. 151).

136. Thornton and Tomlin, op. cit. (Note 25), p. 84, fig. 88; Thornton, op. cit. (Note 6), p. 230.

137. See Note 68.

138. If octagonal this table could have been that seen by Baron Waldstein at Nonsuch in 1600, and said to have been a gift to the Queen (Groos, op. cit. (Note 77), p. 159).

139. V. Gibbs (ed.), *The Complete Peerage* I (London, 1910), p. 37. See also J. Wilford, *Memorials and Characters* (London, 1741).

140. V. Gibbs and H.A. Doubleday (eds.), *The Complete Peerage* IV (London, 1916), pp. 408-9.

141. Gibbs, op. cit. (Note 139), pp. 37-8.

142. Illustrated in González-Palacios, op. cit. (Note 121), II, p. 90.

143. Baron Waldstein, however, seems to have seen this table, or one like it, inside Theobalds: he also saw a black marble table in a summer house at Nonsuch (Groos, op. cit. (Note 77), pp. 85 and 161).

144. Rye, op. cit. (Note 68), p. 45.

145. See *OED,* s.v. table.

146. A prayer stone from Kartala in Iraq, however, brought to Schloss Gottorp in Schleswig by Adam Olearius in the middle of the seventeenth century and illustrated in his travel description of 1656, might be similar. It is made of clay, but it is octagonal and has Arabic figures on it. See Dam-Mikkelsen and Lundbæk, op. cit. (Note 80), pp. xxxi and 84.

147. C.C. Oman, *English Domestic Silver* (London, 1934), p. 181; J.G. Hayward, 'Silver furniture – I', *Apollo* 67 (1958), pp. 71-2; and Lunsingh Scheurleer, op. cit. (Note 109), pp. 142-3.

148. Oman, op. cit. (Note 147), p. 184; *Inventaire* op. cit., (Note 63), pp. 90-91, and Thornton and Tomlin, op. cit. (Note 25), p. 147.

149. See *OED,* s.v. table.

150. Illustrated in Thornton, op. cit. (Note 6), p. 80; and Havard, op. cit. (Note 72), IV, pp. 1558-9.

151. Thornton, op. cit. (Note 6), p. 278.

152. *Van der Doort's Catalogue,* p. 74, includes an 'imbroder'd writeing desk' in the 'Kings. Chare roome.'

153. G.R. Batho (ed.), *The Household Papers of Henry Percy, Ninth Earl of Northumberland (1564-1632)* (Camden Society, third series 93) (London, 1962), p. 58.

154. State was not, of course, an exclusively royal prerogative. See Penelope Eames, 'Documentary evidence concerning the character and use of domestic furnishings in England in the fourteenth and fifteenth centuries', *Furniture History* 7 (1971), pp. 40-60, for a discussion of the relativities of estate.

155. Ashmole, op. cit. (Note 45), p. 501.

156. J. Loftus (ed.), *The Memoirs of Anne, Lady Halkett and Ann, Lady Fanshawe* (Oxford, 1979), p. 143.

157. Ibid.

158. The 1557 portrait of Philip II of Spain and Mary Tudor at Woburn, in which both have cloths of estate and X-framed chairs, although Philip is shown standing and Mary seated, probably represents a precise interpretation of precedence (illustrated in R. Strong, *Tudor and*

Jacobean Portraits (National Portrait Gallery, London, 1969), II, pl. 419), and the same probably holds for the 1604 Somerset House Conference painting in the National Portrait Gallery in which all the participants are seated in X-framed chairs (illustrated in ibid., II, pl. 680).

159. Symonds, op. cit. (Note 14), pp. 41-2.

160. Ibid., p. 41. Ralph Grynder, 'Upholster', delivered numerous items of seat furniture to the queen in 1637, but it should be noted that Charles Goodyleare, 'Joyner', supplied frames (and 'a house for 2 monkeys') in 1637, and that Phillip Bromefield, the queen's gilder, was involved in the decoration of seat furniture in 1635 and 1639 (see Note 4).

161. See Havard, op. cit. (Note 72), II, pp. 718-23, fauteuil, and *Reallexikon zur Deutschen Kunstgeschichte* (Munich, 1973), VI, pp. 1219-37, for discussions of the type.

162. P. Thornton, 'Back-stools and chaises à demoiselles', *Connoisseur* 185 (1974), pp. 98-105.

163. If these were armed versions their general conformation would have looked forward to that of later seventeenth-century French armchairs. See P. Thornton, 'The Parisian fauteuil of 1680', *Apollo*, 101 (1975), pp. 102-7.

164. See Blum, op. cit. (Note 128), pls. 1, 2-4, 13, and 16 for X-framed stools of this type. The queen's gilder Phillip Bromefield's bill of 1635 does include '2 foulding stoolles...laid faire crimson and varnished'; in 1637 the 'Upholster' Ralph Grynder supplied '3 foulding stoles of Turkey work garnished with fringes'; and in the same year the joiner Charles Goodyleare delivered '3 foulding stools', probably of walnut and possibly for Grynder to cover in Turkey work. More frequently, Bromefield, Grynder and Goodyleare all worked in sets of six or eight (see Note 4).

165. Blum, op. cit. (Note 128), pls. 11-13 and 16.

166. Symonds, op. cit. (Note 37), p. 1055.

167. See Note 127.

168. Illustrated in Howarth, op. cit. (Note 114), colour pl. 3.

169. Thornton, op. cit. (Note 6), pp. 55, 127, 341. Comparable chairs are at Petworth (see Drury, op. cit. (Note 127), pls. 46A and B), at Lacock Abbey and Melbury House (see G. Jackson-Stops (ed.), *The Treasure Houses of Britain* (National Gallery of Art, Washington, 1985), p. 134), and at Browsholme Hall (see S. Jervis, *Browsholme Hall* (Derby, 1980)).

170. See Jervis, op. cit. (Note 46), pl. 301, bottom left.

171. Thornton, op. cit. (Note 6), pp. 193, 373.

172. Jervis, op. cit. (Note 46), p. 42, pl. 313.

173. Thornton, op. cit. (Note 6), p. 327.

174. Jervis, op. cit. (Note 46), pl. 313.

175. Thornton, op. cit. (Note 6), pp. 197 and 199), illustrates three invalid chairs with foot-rests.

176. Jervis, op. cit. (Note 46), pl. 313; Thornton, op. cit. (Note 6), pp. 197 and 199.

177. See G. Klein, 'Les chaises obstetricales, un meuble communautaire d'autrefois en Alsace', *Cahiers Alsaciens d'Archéologie, d'Art et d'Histoire* 15 (1971), pp. 191-204.

178. Illustrated in L. Feduchi, *El Mueble Español* (Barcelona, 1969), p. 106.

179. Havard, op. cit. (Note 72), I, pp. 668-70.

180. Quoted by *OED*, s.v. sedan.

181. Ibid.

182. M.-H. Davies, *Reflections of Renaissance England* (Allison Park, 1986), p. 374.

183. See Note 4.

184. Illustrated in Symonds, op. cit. (Note 37), p. 965.

185. Symonds, op. cit. (Note 7), p. 105; Blum, op. cit. (Note 128), pl. 14.

186. See, for example, D.G. Vaisey (ed.), *Probate Inventories of Lichfield and District 1568-1680* (Staffordshire Record Society, fourth series 5) (1969).

187. Thornton, op. cit. (Note 6), p. 327; Pricke, op. cit. (Note 47), pl. 100.

188. Havard, op. cit. (Note 72), I, pp. 236-40; II, pp. 916, 816-18. See also Agius, op. cit. (Note 41), p. 76.

189. See Thornton, op. cit. (Note 6), p. 365, note 1, on terminology.

190. See Note 4.

191. Havard, op. cit. (Note 72), IV, pp. 173ff; N. de Reyniès, *Le mobilier domestique, vocabulaire typologique* (Paris, 1987) I, pp. 254-5.

192. The table illustrated by Conforti and Walton, op. cit. (Note 118), p. 44, has on it two cushions supporting respectively a crown and an orb. A comparable combination is shown in the group of Charles I, Henrietta Maria and Charles, Prince of Wales, probably painted by Pot in 1632 (illustrated in O. Millar, *The Age of Charles I* (Tate Gallery, London, 1972), p. 55).

193. See P. Thornton, 'Canopies, couches and chairs of state', *Apollo* 100 (1974), pp. 292-9.

194. Forman, op. cit. (Note 101), p. 209.

195. See Jervis, op. cit. (Note 46), p. 48 and pl. 439; Pricke, op. cit. (Note 47), pl. 100.

196. See Thornton, op. cit. (Note 6), p. 149.

197. Here tester means ceilour and head cloth means tester.

198. See Thornton, op. cit. (Note 6), pp. 160ff.

199. G. Jackson-Stops, 'William III and French furniture', *Furniture History* 7 (1971), p. 123, pls. 31 and 32.

200. See P. Thornton, op. cit. (Note 6), p. 152, for a bed in Sweden which turns into its own travelling box.

201. These may, however, have been suspended canopies.

202. Cust, op. cit. (Note 9), p. 98. Agius, op. cit. (Note 41), p. 79, cites a 'settlebed' in 1615.

203. See Thornton, op. cit. (Note 6), p. 168.

204. See Jervis, op. cit. (Note 46), pls. 85, 86.

205. G.F. Laking, *The Furniture of Windsor Castle* (London, 1905), pp. 190-91. The £3 'old bedsted' (*Inventories*, p. 293 [209]) may be one listed here whose counterpane was already in 1547 'perissled in two places with Rattes' (Laking, op. cit., p. 192).

206. Boynton and Thornton, op. cit. (Note 23), p. 29.

207. Jervis, op. cit. (Note 46), pls. 87 to 90, especially the upper design on pl. 90. Baron Waldstein seems to have seen a bed of this type at Richmond in 1600 (Groos, op. cit. (Note 77), p. 169).

208. Cust, op. cit. (Note 1), p. 29.

209. Illustrated in Windisch-Graetz, op. cit. (Note 64), p. 407.

210. Ashmole, op. cit. (Note 45), p. 501.

211. MacGregor, op. cit. (Note 67), pp. 270-2, pl. 100.

212. Gilt leather curtains must have been easily damaged. Old may mean decayed rather than ancient.

213. E. Croft-Murray, *Decorative Painting in England 1537-1837* (London, 1962), I, p. 194.

214. J. Newman, 'Strayed from the Queen's House?', *Architectural History* 27 (1984), pp. 33-5.

215. Thornton, op. cit. (Note 6), p. 265, fig. 41.

216. Havard, op. cit. (Note 72), III, pl. 14, illustrates large lamps with reservoirs used by Philip II of Spain.

217. Rye, op. cit. (Note 68), pp. 205-6.

218. Could these frames have resembled the arms for hanging clothes in a late fifteenth-century wardrobe in Aylesbury? (See Eames, op. cit. (Note 39), pp. 50-2, pl. 30.)

219. P. Thornton, *Authentic Decor* (London, 1984), p. 86; Havard, op. cit. (Note 72), IV, pp. 1238-41.

220. It is conceivable that such screens were about 10 feet high, but it seems more probable that this was their width.

221. Irwin, op. cit. (Note 27), pp. 193-4.

222. Thornton, op. cit. (Note 6), p. 256.

223. Ibid.

224. Blum, op. cit. (Note 128), pls. 13, 14, and 16.

225. Havard, op. cit. (Note 72), III, p. 891.

226. Illustrated in A. González-Palacios, *Il Tempio del Gusto, Il Granducato di Toscana e gli Stati Settentrionali* (Milan, 1986), II, p. 266.

227. Havard, op. cit. (Note 72), II, p. 1107. Could this have been one of the multiplying mirror devices described by Kircher, DuBreuil, and others? See J. Baltrusaitis, *Lo Specchio* (Milan, 1981), pls. 4, 17. Johann Ernst, Duke of Saxe-Weimar, saw something of the kind at Whitehall in 1613 (Rye, op. cit. (Note 68), p. 166).

228. H. Schott, *Catalogue of Musical Instruments* I *Keyboard* (Victoria and Albert Museum, London, 1985), pp. 29-31.

229. Maurice, op. cit. (Note 103), II, pls. 388, 647.

230. Rye, op. cit. (Note 68), p.166.

231. Maurice, op. cit. (Note 103), pls. 283, 284.

232. For more on the use of antlers, etc., in decoration see S. Jervis, 'Antler and horn furniture', *Victoria & Albert Museum Yearbook* 3 (1972), pp. 87-99, and 'Furniture in horn and antler' *Connoisseur* 196 (1977), pp. 190-201 (expanded version).

233. See Note 4.

234. For a roughly contemporary and coherent group of provincial inventories see S. Jervis, 'Five early inventories of Browsholme Hall', *Furniture History* 22 (1986), pp. 1-24.

235. These beds may have survived from a display of royal beds seen at Windsor by Paul Hentzner in 1598 (Rye, op. cit. (Note 68), pp. 200-201) and by Baron Waldstein in 1600 (Groos, op. cit. (Note 77), p. 139).

236. J. Harris, 'Inigo Jones and his French sources', *Metropolitan Museum Bulletin* 19 (1960-61), pp. 253-64; Thornton, op. cit. (Note 6), chapters 1 and 2.

237. For example the information on decorative painting summarized by Croft Murray, op. cit. (Note 213), and the Land Revenue accounts extracted by Hero Granger-Taylor (see Note 4).

9 Textile Furnishings

Donald King

Types of Textile

Marginal numerals refer to page and entry numbers in the *Inventories* (see p. 11)

The first point to make about the furnishing textiles recorded in the inventories of 1649 is that they were not all of one period. While some were new, or comparatively recent, others were of considerable age. Of course, not all textiles can be dated from a one-line description in an inventory, but of the textiles at Denmark House and Oatlands, for example, some bore the arms and initials of Stuart sovereigns, while many of the large sets of hangings and furniture in flowered silks were obviously in the taste of the seventeenth century. On the other hand, the older Wardrobes, at Windsor, Hampton Court and the Tower, contained many items of embroidery and needlework with the arms and initials of Tudor sovereigns; some of them, together with hundreds of tapestries listed in 1649, are perfectly recognizable in Henry VIII's inventory, compiled more than a century earlier.[1] Some of the tapestries, indeed, are known to have been acquired by the Crown in the fifteenth century.

The textiles were of various types and techniques. Plain silk and woollen cloths, valued for their fine colours and textures, were used for all kinds of furnishings; linen cloths, valued for whiteness and coolness, served for bed and table linen as well as for personal linen. The woollens and linens were mostly woven in England or adjacent areas of northern Europe, while the silks – taffeta, satin, velvet and others – were mostly imported from Italy. The plain cloths were often trimmed with fringes and laces (that is, with bands or ribbons) of gold, silver and silk thread. They were also employed as ground materials for embroidery in similar gold, silver and silk thread. Such embroidery, extensively used in the royal furnishings, was mostly executed in England by professional workshops, of which the most prominent in the seventeenth century was that of Edmund Harrison, embroiderer to James I, Charles I and Charles II; he was no doubt responsible for some of the embroideries listed in the inventories. Needlework, related to embroidery, but nevertheless distinguished from it in seventeenth-century parlance, entailed completely covering plain linen canvas with regular stitches of wool, silk, silver and gold thread. Most of the needlework in the inventories, like the embroidery, was probably of English origin. Both embroidery and needlework could be used to execute either ornamental or pictorial designs; in either case a professional draughtsman was required to draw the design which the needle-workers would follow.

3-4 [14]
18 [82]

Textiles with patterns printed on the fabric are rarely mentioned in the inventories. A set of wall-hangings of Queen Jane Seymour's time were of printed velvet (probably blind-stamped), while a curious tent, presented by the Russian ambassador to James I, was of printed calico.

Whereas embroidery, needlework and printing involve adding a pattern to a previously woven fabric, it is also possible to incorporate a pattern into a fabric while it is actually being woven. One such technique is tapestry, in which threads of dyed wool, silk, and sometimes gold and silver thread, are woven, not across the whole width of the fabric from one side to the other, but only in the precise areas where each particular colour is required to form the pattern. Tapestry, which is well adapted to the production of large pictorial hangings, requires the services of professional designers and painters to devise the full-size cartoons which guide the weavers in their work. Most of the fifteenth- and sixteenth-century tapestries listed in the inventories of 1649 were designed and woven in the area of modern Belgium, Holland and northern France, but many of the seventeenth-century pieces were produced in England, at the royal workshop in Mortlake.

Carpet-knotting is akin to tapestry, in so far as threads of dyed wool or silk are woven, not from one side of the fabric to the other, but only in the areas where each individual colour is required by the pattern; but unlike tapestry, in which the coloured threads are woven flat, here they stand erect to from a multicoloured pile. This hard-wearing pile surface makes knotted carpets suitable for heavy use on floors or tables, but its relatively coarse texture is better adapted to ornamental rather than pictorial effects. Most of the pile carpets in the royal inventories were of Turkish or Persian origin and their patterns were devised by professional designers in those countries.

Most patterned fabrics of silk and linen have patterns woven according to a different principle. Here, instead of being limited to precise areas, the threads travel throughout the textile, but they are brought to the surface only where they are required to form the pattern, while elsewhere they lie concealed at the back. The royal inventories include patterned silk textiles of various kinds – damasks, velvets, cloths of gold and silver, and many others – most of which were no doubt imported from Italy. Damask table linen was imported from the area of modern Belgium and Holland. The floral patterns of the silk fabrics and the floral and pictorial patterns of the linen damasks were the work of professional designers in the respective countries. Unlike the freely composed designs of embroidery and tapestry, however, these were conceived as repeating patterns; the pattern-making apparatus of the looms on which the fabrics were woven was assembled and controlled so as to repeat the same pre-designed set of motifs as often as required in the width and the length of the textile.

Tapestries and other Hangings

Tapestries, generally with large-scale figure subjects of a scriptural, mythological or historical nature, were a dominant feature in the interior decoration of great houses in the seventeenth century, as they had been for two or three centuries before. English sovereigns had been collecting tapestries at least since the fourteenth century. Inventories exist of those which belonged to Richard II and Henry V.[2] The collection continued to grow under Edward IV and Henry VII and reached its apogee under Henry VIII, whose inventory included upwards of two thousand tapestries. The inventories of 1649 list well over sixteen hundred.

Although some tapestries were woven in England, notably at Mortlake in the seventeenth century, the overwhelming majority of the earlier pieces were imported from the Low Countries and adjacent areas of northern France. The most highly reputed centres of production were Arras in the fourteenth and early fifteenth century, Tournai in the later fifteenth century, and Brussels thereafter. The production of a set of tapestries involved several stages, first the choice of a theme and the drafting of a detailed programme, then the preparation of small-scale drawings, next the painting of full-size cartoons, and lastly the copying of these cartoons in textile materials by teams of weavers; the whole process generally took several years and required large capital outlays by wealthy entrepreneurs. If suitable clients could be found, several sets of fine tapestries would be woven from the same cartoons, while simplified and coarser versions might be woven subsequently for a cheaper market. Tapestries varied very widely in quality and value. In 1649 the royal stock included some valued at only a few shillings. At Woodstock, Royston, Newmarket, Ludlow, none was worth more than a pound or two. At Syon, Oatlands, Carisbrooke and Windsor, the best were in the range £10-£60 each. At Hampton Court, Richmond, Whitehall, Denmark House and the Tower, the best tapestries were valued at hundreds of pounds apiece and the best sets at several thousands. The finer tapestries, of wool, silk and gold thread, are generally called arras in the inventories, not as an attribution but as a designation of quality. The generic term tapestry is generally applied to less fine pieces, of wool and silk.

A good many tapestries are described in the inventories as old, or very old. They may have included hangings acquired by the Crown in the fourteenth century and certainly included some acquired in the fifteenth century. Pieces at Whitehall bearing Edward IV's badges of roses and sunbeams were no doubt made for that monarch and can perhaps be associated with his acquisition of hangings with similar devices in 1480.[3]

362 [497-8], 369 [600]

The fifty or so tapestries at Windsor in 1649 were undoubtedly of considerable age, since they were already recorded there in Henry VIII's inventory more than a century earlier. They included the largest set in the entire royal collection, twelve tapestry hangings of the *Siege of Troy* (Fig. 87), which are unusually well documented. The small-scale preliminary drawings for most of these tapestries, preserved in the Louvre, date from about 1465-70 and have been attributed to Henri de Vulcop, court painter to the King of France.[4] The earliest known set of tapestries based on these designs was supplied by the Tournai entrepreneur Pasquier Grenier and was in the collection of Charles the Bold, Duke of Burgundy, by 1472. The set recorded at Windsor was acquired by Henry VII from Jean Grenier, Pasquier's son, in 1488. Neither of these sets survives, but

290 [184]

Figure 87 Tapestry from *The Siege of Troy* series. Reproduced by courtesy of the Trustees of the Victoria and Albert Museum, London.

Figure 88 Tapestry, *The Triumph of Fame over Death*. Hampton Court: reproduced by gracious permission of Her Majesty The Queen.

Figure 89 Raphael: two cartoons from *The Acts of the Apostles*. Victoria and Albert Museum: reproduced by gracious permission of Her Majesty The Queen.

Figure 90   Tapestry from the *Aeneas* series. Royal Collection: reproduced by gracious permission of Her Majesty The Queen.

watercolour drawings of 1799, by John Carter, showing five hangings of Henry VII's set, are preserved in the Victoria and Albert Museum. The same Museum has one hanging from a third set, which was in the collection of Charles VIII of France by 1499, and other pieces from further *Troy* sets are preserved elsewhere.[5] They show the characteristic tapestry style of the second half of the fifteenth century, with dense mêlées of figures in constricted space; there are no borders, but explanatory inscriptions at top and bottom. Another large set recorded at 290 [180] Windsor consisted of seven arras hangings of the *Siege of Jerusalem*; it has not survived, but scattered remnants of other editions of the set show a style similar to that of the *Troy* tapestries; indeed they have been attributed to the same designer.[6]

290-1 [187]
160 [25]
Also at Windsor were five tapestries of *Triumphs*, inspired by Petrarch's poem *I Trionfi*, while three more of the same theme and quality were listed at Hampton Court. Four of these eight can now be seen at Hampton Court (Fig. 88), exhibiting the typical Brussels style of the early years of the sixteenth century, still with densely packed compositions as in the earlier Tournai sets, but with more elegant figures, more naturalistic landscape detail and more delicate ornament, including narrow floral borders.[7]

4 [17], 331 [65]
362 [502]
Most of the fifty or so tapestries listed at the Tower of London in 1649 had been there in Henry VIII's time. A set of ten arras hangings 'of the rich history of King David', which was at the Tower in 1547, but in 1649 was divided between the Tower and Whitehall, was among the finest sets in the royal collection. It may well have been based on the same cartoons (attributed to Jan Van Roome) as the ten *King David* tapestries now exhibited at the Château d'Ecouen, one of the most splendid of all sets in the early sixteenth-century Brussels style.[8] It has even been suggested that the Ecouen set *is* the English royal set, but this is not proven. The most valuable of the sets recorded at the Tower, in 1649 as in 1547, was Henry 5 [20] VIII's set of nine arras hangings of the *Acts of the Apostles*, after cartoons by Raphael. The first edition of this set, commissioned by Pope Leo X for the Sistine Chapel, was woven in Brussels between 1517 and 1520.[9] Within a few years thereafter the influence of Raphael's designs for the *Acts* (Fig. 89), in a superb

Figure 91   Tapestry from the *Abraham* series. Hampton Court: reproduced by gracious permission of Her Majesty The Queen.

Figure 92   Tapestry from the *Vulcan and Venus* series. Reproduced by courtesy of the Trustees of the Victoria and Albert Museum, London.

High Renaissance style, displaying small groups of bulky figures interacting in a rationally conceived space and surrounded by broad decorative borders, brought about a radical transformation of Flemish tapestry design.

As at Windsor and the Tower, nearly all the 250 tapestries at Hampton Court in 1649 had already been recorded there in Henry VIII's inventory. Some had belonged to Cardinal Wolsey and had his arms in the borders; examples of these borders can still be seen at Hampton Court. Many of the Hampton Court tapestries were in the Flemish style of the early years of the sixteenth century, so that it is appropriate that remnants of several sets of this type are still displayed there, as well as a small, more complete set of five arras hangings of *Aeneas* (Fig. 90), which was at Whitehall in 1649.[10] But the most impressive tapestries at Hampton Court were five great sets, of nine or ten hangings apiece, depicting the stories of *Abraham, Joshua, Tobias, St. Paul* and *Julius Caesar*. In Henry VIII's inventory these were described as 'newe Arras' and they were no doubt acquired for the King's refurbishment of Hampton Court during the second half of his reign. Of the five the only one which now survives, still at Hampton Court, is that of ten arras hangings of *Abraham* (Fig. 91), in 1649 the second largest set in the royal collection (after Henry VII's *Troy* tapestries) and, at over £8000, by far the most valuable, due mainly to the quantity of gold thread employed in the weaving. The designs, which have been attributed to Bernard Van Orley, show very well the Italianate Brussels style of the second quarter of the sixteenth century, with massive figures in the foregrounds, naturalistic perspectives of architecture and landscape, and elaborate borders. The other major sets at Hampton Court, judging from other editions of them in Vienna and Madrid, were in comparable styles.

Henry VIII left so large a stock of tapestries that the Crown had little need to acquire more during the second half of the sixteenth century. Indeed the only major set from this period identifiable in the inventories is one at the Tower, comprising ten hangings of the *Victory over the Spanish Fleet in 1588*. This set, woven between 1593 and 1596 by François Spierinckx of Delft for the Lord High Admiral, the Earl of Nottingham, was later acquired by James I. It has not survived, but the designs – panoramic views of the sea-fights in the Channel, by Cornelius Van Vroom, within borders depicting the English commanders – are preserved in eighteenth-century engravings by John Pine.

Extensive acquisitions of tapestries resumed under the early Stuart kings. Some of them, such as a set of eight new arras hangings of *King Hezekiah*, listed at Denmark House in 1649, were no doubt woven abroad. But more significant were a number of sets of the highest quality commissioned from the royal tapestry manufactory which was set up at Mortlake, under the direction of Sir Francis Crane, in 1619. By 1620 fifty Flemish weavers were at work there, led by a distinguished master-weaver, Philip de Maeght. The young Charles Stuart, Prince of Wales, evidently had a keen appreciation of fine tapestries; it is possible that the initiative for the Mortlake factory originated with him and he was certainly the factory's principal patron.[11]

The inventory of the tapestry cartoons at Mortlake in 1651 provides a useful, if incomplete, repertory of the designs which had been woven there during the previous thirty years. The earliest Mortlake sets were based on tapestry designs of the sixteenth century, but with the borders newly designed in a seventeenth-century style. The Mortlake set of *Vulcan and Venus* (Fig. 92), for example, first woven for Charles between 1620 and 1622 and repeated several times thereafter, was based on a sixteenth-century Flemish set of that subject, listed in Henry VIII's inventory of Westminster as 'fine new tapestry'. In 1649 the Denmark House inventory lists three fine *Vulcan and Venus* sets and notes that matching tapestries from two of them had been 'carried into France' by the Queen, or 'carryed into Holland'. Tapestries from a set made for Charles as Prince of Wales are preserved at St. James's Palace, the Victoria and Albert Museum and elsewhere; the borders include his monogram of interlaced *CC*, the Prince of Wales's feathers and an emblem and motto proclaiming the royal interest in the arts, *Sceptra favent artes*. A set of the *Twelve Months*, woven at Mortlake 1623-4 and again subsequently, was likewise based on sixteenth-century tapestries which had belonged to Henry VIII. In 1649 two of sets of the *Months* were listed at Whitehall; part of a set, with the Prince of Wales's badge in the borders, remains at Buckingham Palace.

In 1623 Charles was fortunate enough to purchase seven of Raphael's cartoons for the tapestries of the *Acts of the Apostles*, with a view to their use at Mortlake. In the event, the original cartoons were hung among other works of art at Whitehall and copies were made for the Mortlake weavers. The set of *Acts* tapestries at the Tower in 1649 was presumably Henry VIII's Brussels set, but several individual hangings were probably Mortlake work. It is interesting to note the relative values attached to the cartoons and the tapestries. The original Raphael cartoons were valued at an average of a little over £40 apiece, the 'very good' copies of them at Mortlake at £10 each, and the tapestries woven from them at around £500. Mortlake tapestries of the *Acts*, with the English royal arms in the borders, are preserved in the French national collection.

In 1624 Mortlake acquired its own designer, Francis Cleyn, a native of Rostock who, after studying in Rome, had been court painter to James I's brother-in-law, Christian IV of Denmark. His principal contributions to the repertory of Mortlake cartoons were sets of designs of *Hero and Leander*, of various classical subjects, known as the *Horses*, and of the *Five Senses*. No tapestries of *Hero and Leander* appear in the 1649 inventories, but a set of the *Horses* is listed at Whitehall, and sets of the *Five Senses* at Denmark House and Oatlands. None of these remains in the royal collection, but the designs are known from examples elsewhere; a set of *Hero and Leander* with the English royal arms in the borders is in the Swedish royal collection at Drottningholm.

Other cartoons listed at Mortlake in 1651 include *Diana* (corresponding tapestry at the Tower), *Children* (corresponding tapestries in Cromwell's possession), and *Flower Pots with Pilasters* (corresponding tapestries at Denmark House and Whitehall).

Apart from tapestries, the royal inventories include many sets of wall hangings made from silk fabrics. In the Tower Wardrobe, for instance, there were ten such sets, of velvet and cloth of gold, some of them embroidered with borders, the arms of England, and badges such as roses and portcullises. One of

the sets, with the arms of England and Seymour, crowned, within a garland of roses, dated from Queen Jane Seymour's time, 1536-7, and most of the rest are identifiable in Henry VIII's inventory. The most valuable of these was of crimson

velvet with figures in needlework, embellished with pearls and counterfeit stones.

Sets at Denmark House, apparently of more recent date, included one which must have been made for Charles I; of velvet and satin, it was embroidered all over with CC and coats of arms, between pillars of silver. Other sets there, of cloth

of gold, velvet, satin and damask, comprised not only hangings, but seat furniture to match. At Oatlands, too, some sets had matching furniture. There

the hangings of the Queen's Bedchamber and Queen's Cabinet Room were of satin – in one case China satin – with woven patterns of branches, while the hangings for the Queen's Gallery were of gilt leather. Gilt leather hangings were

also recorded at Denmark House and Ludlow. Other chamber hangings at Ludlow were of woollen cloth, kersey, darnix, striped stuff, and Kidderminster stuff, while the Garter Room at Windsor Castle had woollen hangings chequered red, white and green.

Window curtains are frequently listed, sometimes of taffeta, generally of damask, often identified as China damask; the damasks had woven patterns, such as branches and flowers. One exceptional set of damask window curtains

was embroidered on both sides with the Prince's arms and pillars of silver; they were no doubt made to match the wall hangings with similar ornament

mentioned above. Traverse curtains, used as room-dividers, are mentioned only rarely; some were of taffeta, one (also in Henry VIII's inventory) of cloth of gold. Curtains were sometimes hung in front of pictures.

Cloths of State and Canopies

The purpose of cloths of state was to emphasise the power and dignity of the royal personages who sat beneath them; the effect can be judged from various royal portraits in which they appear. Most of the principal royal residences were equipped with a number of examples, ranging from one at Richmond to over a dozen at Whitehall, a total of more than three dozen in all. A cloth of state consisted of a roof piece, called a ceeler, with valances around it, and a back piece called a tester. The arrangement resembled that of the principal hangings of a

bed; indeed one cloth of state at Whitehall had been converted from a bed. Some cloths of state had a matching chair, footstool, stools and cushions, while one at

the Tower, dating from Henry VIII's time, had a set of matching wall hangings.

Most cloths of state were of fine silk materials, often with armorial embroidery, but an unusual example at Windsor was of rich arras depicting *King Clovis with the fleurs-de-lis*. It was already described as old in Henry VIII's inventory and may well have been of fifteenth-century date; the subject depicted suggests that it was originally made for a King of France. It attracted the attention of several foreign tourists who visited Windsor. Thomas Platter, who was there in 1599, wrote a detailed description of it, even transcribing the lengthy French inscription and adding (no doubt from the patter of the castle-guide) that the piece had been captured from the French who had repeatedly offered large sums to buy it back.[12]

292 [198]

292 [197]
7-9 [33-7]
281 [82]

Several other cloths of state at Windsor and the Tower were already there in Henry VIII's time. One listed at Oatlands in 1649 (and in 1547) was of cloth of gold with a woven pattern, in crimson velvet and gold loops, showing crowned portcullises, within borders of *SS* and roses. This tour de force of velvet weaving recalls vestments of similar material which were woven in Florence for Henry VII between 1499 and 1502.[13] It may well have been of similar date, as may a second example, also of cloth of gold with roses and portcullises. A cloth of state at Whitehall 'embroydered w^t K Henry letters' must have been of Henry VIII's time or earlier. Also associated with Henry VIII was the most valuable example in the collection, of purple velvet embroidered in gold with the arms of England, crowned, within a Garter and a garland, embellished with many pearls and gems. Foreign visitors to Hampton Court were much impressed by this cloth of state and its jewels, especially by a large rectangular diamond which they saw hanging from the end of the Garter (described in 1547 as a white sapphire).[14] Two of Queen Elizabeth's cloths of state were at Windsor. The more valuable of them was embroidered with gold and small pearls, the ceeler depicting a banquet scene and the tester with the Queen's arms supported by great antelopes; it may have been adapted from one which was recorded at Richmond in 1547.

324 [26]
389-90 [874]
167 [97]

291 [195-6]

One of James I's cloths of state, at the Tower, almost equalled that of Henry VIII in value. It was of cloth of silver, crimson velvet and purple cloth of gold, richly embroidered with raised work of gold and silver, with King James's arms in the middle; Charles I evidently refurbished this lavish example for his own use in 1638. Other cloths of state associated with James and Anne of Denmark were at Denmark House; others possibly associated with Charles and Henrietta Maria were at Whitehall and Oatlands, including one embroidered with the sun, and another with the planets in needlework.

18-19 [83]

81 [43-5]
389 [871]
401 [1051-2]
283 [109-10]

Related to the cloth of state, but less formal, was the canopy. It generally consisted of a top (often half-round, sometimes round or square), valances, a back, and two curtains, sometimes with a large set of seat furniture to match. Many of the canopies listed in 1649 seem to have been of seventeenth-century date. There were fifteen at Denmark House, besides others at Oatlands and elsewhere. Some of those at Denmark House were of velvet, embroidered with the arms of Denmark, Anne of Denmark's crowned initials, and in one case, silver birds and butterflies. Others were of rich silk fabrics with colourful woven patterns, for example one of cloth of silver with a pattern of flower pots and flowers in polychrome velvet, or one of white grosgrain with a pattern of flowers in gold, silver and polychrome silk. The curtains were generally of lighter materials, chiefly damask or satin. All the fabrics were liberally trimmed with woven bands of gold, silver and silk, and sometimes with buttons and loops of gold. Needlework was rarely used for canopies; an exception was a canopy in Irish stitch (flame stitch) with associated couch, chairs and stools.

82-88, 127, 284, 288 [passim]
82 [46], 84 [49], 85 [52]

83 [47]
87 [57]

413 [89]

Bed Furniture

Beds were of various types and the arrangement of the hangings varied to some extent. Often they consisted of a roof piece called a ceeler, valances (sometimes single, sometimes double), a tester or headcloth and several curtains. They could also include cantoons, or covers for the bedposts, and bases (valances for the lower bed frame). Beds without an upper bed frame might have, in place of the ceeler, a suspended roof or tent of various types, called sparver, canopy or pavilion. Elaborate bed hangings were often accompanied by matching seats and other furniture.

The 1649 inventories list well over a hundred sets of bed hangings of very varied materials. Some were of woollen cloth. At Ludlow, for example, bed hangings of darnix, say and Kidderminster stuff are mentioned, and at Whitehall others of green cloth, blue cloth and scarlet cloth. A set at Windsor, comprising ceeler, valances and bases of fine arras, was the only one of its kind in the inventories; it was already listed at Windsor in 1547. Another unusual piece, at the Tower in 1649, as in 1547, was a bed canopy of black nettle cloth patterned with coloured silk. The more luxurious bed hangings were generally of plain or patterned silk materials, often with heavier fabrics used for the principal hangings and lighter ones for the bed curtains. They were frequently trimmed with gold or silver lace and fringe and often embroidered with gold, silver, silk and sometimes pearls.

A number of the bed hangings recorded in 1649 dated from Tudor times. For example, several sets at Hampton Court, of cloth of gold and velvet, embroidered with roses, fleurs-de-lis, portcullises and the like, were already described there in Henry VIII's inventory. A typical royal bed of Henry VIII's time was at Denmark House in 1649; the hangings were of rich crimson cloth of gold embroidered with the royal initials beneath a crown, and with the arms of England richly embroidered on the ceeler and tester. Two beds of Queen Elizabeth's were listed at Windsor, one with hangings of white damask embroidered with her arms, the other with hangings of crimson velvet embroidered in gold with her badges and with arabesque patterns.

The values assigned to bed hangings varied from a few shillings for simple hangings to several hundred pounds for elaborate sets with matching furniture. The most valuable, all at Denmark House, were sets of crimson velvet richly embroidered with gold and silver, of crimson satin very richly embroidered with gold and pearls, of purple velvet very richly embroidered with pillars of silver, and of green and white satin richly embroidered. Some of these were certainly of the Stuart period, as were other bed hangings of silk materials woven with floral patterns, for example watchet satin branched with flowers of gold, or rich cloth of silver branched with flowers of gold and coloured silks. A headcloth for a bed, also at Denmark House, was of flowered cloth of silver embroidered with the arms and motto of Anne of Denmark. Bed hangings at Oatlands belonging to Queen Henrietta Maria included a set of white dimity embroidered with sequins and another of ash-coloured flowered grosgrain.

Apart from the hangings, the principal decorative textile associated with the bed was the counterpoint (or counterpane). Many older counterpoints were of tapestry, often of the type called verdures, with foliage patterns, but sometimes with figure subjects, like the arras counterpoint of *Peace and Concord* at Windsor, which was described as old in 1649, just as it had been in 1547. An unusual counterpoint at Richmond was of red flannel with a pattern of birds and beasts. Many other counterpoints were of silk materials, especially satin, sometimes matching the bed hangings, and often embroidered with gold and silver thread. A few luxurious counterpoints and mantles for beds were lined and bordered with miniver and ermine; from one of these the Queen had removed most of the fur to make a night gown.

Most other bed furniture – quilts, rugs, blankets, sheets, pillows, mattresses, beds and bolsters of down, feather or flock – was practical and undecorated. Linen pillowberes (pillowcases), however, were sometimes embroidered with gold, silver and silk. Associated with them were so-called cushion cloths, likewise of linen embroidered with gold, silver, silk and, in one case, small pearls. Also decorated with gold, silver and silk were bags or covers for night gear. Sweet bags, presumably perfumed with aromatics, also belonged to the equipment of the bedchamber; a number were listed at Denmark House, one of them forming a set with a cushion cloth and pillowberes. They were usually of white satin or cloth of silver, embroidered with gold, silver and silk; designs included the arms of England and other motifs. Likewise for use in the bedchamber were comb cases of satin, embroidered with gold, silver and pearls; one with the arms of Denmark had presumably belonged to Anne of Denmark.

Seats and other Furniture

Numerous chairs, couches, stools, footstools and close stools with textile coverings are listed in the 1649 inventories. Some of these may be tentatively identified with corresponding items in the 1547 inventory, for example a chair at Hampton Court, of rich cloth of gold embroidered with the arms of England

222 [68]
291 [191]
82, 85, 90, 110, 288 [passim]

supported by beasts. Others of Tudor date were a little old crimson velvet chair of Queen Elizabeth's at Carisbrooke and two embroidered with her arms at Windsor. Several sets of chairs, stools and other furnishings at Denmark House and Oatlands were of velvet embroidered with the crowned initials or arms of Anne of Denmark.

126 [389], 288 [154]
226 [102], 331 [68], 373 [669], 378 [725]

128 [403], 413 [89]

92 [84], 169 [110], 402 [1059, 1062]

83 [47]

96 [110]
288 [153]

Much of the seat furniture, and especially the larger sets at Denmark House, Oatlands and Whitehall, was no doubt of the Stuart period. A few items were covered with leather, sometimes silvered or gilt. Some, including large sets, notably a set of thirty-eight chairs 'att the Councell of State', were covered with Turkey work, a patterned fabric with woollen pile in the technique of Turkey carpets, but made in England. Also employed for seat coverings were embroidery and needlework, including Irish stitch (flame stitch); among the patterns mentioned were flowers, trails, birds and pillars. A wide variety of silk fabrics was used, both plain and with woven patterns. Examples of the latter are a set of canopy, chair and stools of cloth of silver with flower pots and flowers of polychrome velvet, a set of bed hangings, chair and stools of watchet satin branched with flowers of gold, and a set of wall hangings, couch, chairs and stools of crimson China satin branched with yellow. These and many other sets of furniture included cushions covered with matching material.

12-16 [passim]

12 [54]
14 [62-5]
16 [71]

172-6 [passim]

281 [88]

92 [85]

Most of the cushions at the Tower in 1649 had already been described there in Henry VIII's inventory. Among them were cushions of crimson cloth of gold with a pattern of roses and portcullises, a fabric which was presumably specially commissioned in Italy. Others, of English needlework or embroidery, displayed the initials of Henry VIII and Anne Boleyn, with emblematic honeysuckle, acorns and roses. A number of the embroidered cushions at Hampton Court in 1649 likewise showed Henry's initials or are recognizable in his inventory. Other cushions listed both in 1649 and in 1547 were at Oatlands and Denmark House, including some of crimson Turkey silk embroidered with golden lions and dragons, and others of crimson velvet embroidered with gold, silver and pearls; the latter, at £100 the pair, were the most valuable cushions in the inventories.

82 [46], 92 [88]
93 [90, 92]

403 [1070]
92 [86]

Many cushions at Denmark House and Whitehall were no doubt of the Stuart period. Some were embroidered with the arms or initials of Anne of Denmark. Others, of embroidery and needlework, had patterns of flowers, animals, birds or butterflies; a few had pictorial subjects, like a 'Rich Cushion of ye birth of [Christ]' or a cushion of flame-coloured cloth of silver 'enbroydered in the fashion of London Bridge'. Other cushions in the royal collection were of leather, woollen cloth, arras, Turkey work and all kinds of silk fabrics, both plain and patterned.

84, 88, 97, 120, 127, 288 [passim]
88-9, 285 [passim]
88-9 [63-5]

89 [66]

Another type of furnishing textile, recorded mainly at Denmark House and Oatlands, was the screen cloth – sometimes three and a quarter yards long by one and a quarter yards wide – which was hung over a T-shaped stand to form a decorative screen. Some of these cloths matched the coverings of sets of seat furniture and the hangings of a canopy or bed; others were separate. Many were of silk fabrics with floral patterns, including some of Chinese origin. Others were embroidered; an unusually elaborate example was of white satin embroidered in gold and silver with the colours of England and Scotland joined together and surrounded by the arms of the Knights of the Garter.

101 [143], 104 [164]
118 [312]
129 [407], 412 [79]
183 [293]

Various other items of furniture with textile coverings are mentioned here and there in the inventories: a velvet-covered leather cradle, a green velvet coffer, a pair of virginals in a case of green velvet embroidered with pearls, a green velvet table embroidered with gold and silver, an embroidered cabinet, and a cabinet of velvet with the story of Hercules.

Carpets and other Covers

The word carpet denoted any substantial fabric used as a covering for floors, tables, cupboards, chests, benches and the like. Carpets could therefore be of various types and techniques. But many of those listed in the 1649 inventories were undoubtedly Oriental carpets of knotted pile, whose colourful patterns introduced the ornamental styles of the Islamic East into the decorative schemes of the English house.

17 [76], 399 [1030], 412 [87]

78 [25]

Two or three of the carpets in the inventories were identified as Indian or East Indian. About three dozen were described as Persian or of Persian making, including some particularly luxurious pieces. Three of these, at Denmark House,

164 [75]

11 [50]
332 [76]

had a ground of gold and silver and a pattern in silver and coloured silk. Two more, with a gold ground and a pattern in coloured silk, were at Hampton Court, where they had also been recorded in Henry VIII's inventory. About 140 pieces were described as Turkey carpets or carpets of Turkey making; an example of silk, in the Tower Wardrobe, was already there in Henry VIII's time. An 'ould Carew Carpett' at Whitehall was perhaps made in Cairo.[15]

288 [153], 80 [37] , 11 [49]

Other carpets were described as Turkey work, a term which generally denoted a fabric in the knotted pile technique, made in Europe in imitation of Turkish carpets. Carpets attributed to specific European sources include one Spanish carpet, two of English making and one of Venice making; the last-named also figured in Henry VIII's inventory.

Whereas knotted pile carpets were robust enough for use on floors, carpets in more delicate techniques normally served as covers for tables and other furniture. At Hampton Court there were several carpets of tapestry, including an old tapestry carpet with the 'lord Sands and Hungerfords Armes' (presumably

164 [70-1]

made for a Hungerford/Sandys marriage of 1527) and an unusual set of four arras carpets depicting the story of *Romulus and Remus*. Other tapestry carpets at

164 [72-4], 281 [85]

Hampton Court and Oatlands had patterns of foliage and flowers.

163-4 [62-5]
10-11 [47-8]

Carpets of needlework were recorded in several houses. Among those at Hampton Court was one with the Sandys and Hungerford arms, like the tapestry example mentioned above. Two in the Tower Wardrobe had been recorded there previously in Henry VIII's inventory; one of them was worked in gold, silver and silk with a pattern of red and white roses and the monogram of Queen Anne Boleyn, within a border of honeysuckle and acorns with the initials *HA* for the

78 [23]

royal couple. A very rich carpet at Denmark House, in needlework of gold, silver and silk, was 'wrought very Curiously with the Sea and all sorts of Fishes, and Shipps in yᵉ same, all in waves. And haveing in it yᵉ Firmament, and all kind of Landworke with Fowles & Beasts wrought therein'.

A number of carpets were worked in embroidery on velvet, satin or other silk

163 [58-60]

materials. Half a dozen examples at Hampton Court, all recorded there in Henry VIII's time, included one of velvet embroidered with gold and pearls, which, at £500, was by far the most valuable carpet in the inventories. Tourists visiting Hampton Court in the sixteenth century were much impressed by this table carpet, which they saw in the Paradise Chamber, together with Henry VIII's

10 [45]

jewelled cloth of state.[16] A comparable but more modest carpet of crimson satin embroidered in gold and pearls with roses and the royal motto, was in the Tower Wardrobe, where it was also recorded in Henry VIII's inventory. Another very

11 [51]

rich embroidered carpet at the Tower, of white satin worked with images, birds and flowers, was of more recent date, having been presented to the King as a New Year gift, probably in 1619. Many other embroidered carpets were listed in

108 [202], 282 [102]
119 [329], 282 [105]
77 [17, 19, 21]

1649 at Denmark House and Oatlands; they included some with the initials of Anne of Denmark, two 'of yᵉ French Fashion', one of Chinese workmanship, and others with curious motifs such as flies, snakes and an elephant.

Other carpets in the 1649 inventories were made from various kinds of silk fabrics, some of them woven with floral patterns. Carpets were also made of woollen cloth, of darnix and of gilt leather.

233-4 [passim]
104 [165]

Linen covers for tables are rarely mentioned in the inventories, except at Ludlow, where there was a stock of table cloths, cupboard cloths and napkins of linen damask and linen diaper. More luxurious examples, at Denmark House,

105-6 [passim]

were a diaper tablecloth embroidered with borders of gold needlework and a series of covers for bread and salt, some embroidered with gold, silver and silk, some with openwork or cutwork effects.

Other Textiles

Scattered through the inventories are many other items of textile interest, some of

178, 236, 294 [passim]
397, 408-15 [passim], 419 [1]
217, 269, 309, 313 [passim]
320, 381, 413-5, 427 [passim]

which deserve a brief mention here. Various church vestments, altar frontals, pulpit cloths, chalice veils and other church textiles are listed. A book of Camden's works was bound in an embroidered cover. A number of pictures – landscapes, seascapes, still lives, portraits and religious subjects – are described as executed in needlework, embroidery, silk work or flock work; the portraits included Mary Queen of Scots, James I, Charles I and Henrietta Maria.

Articles of dress are dealt with elsewhere in this volume. Some of them are

104-9 [passim]

also interesting for their embroidery, for example various items at Oatlands, including Henry VIII's gold-worked bands, a waistcoat, various scarves, a smock and a large Turkish handkerchief embroidered with gold, silver and silk.

Other items are saddles and horse furniture of velvet, richly embroidered, and an embroidered horse litter. A barge cloth of red velvet embroidered all over with the arms of England had been in the custody of the Master of the Barges and another barge cloth, of Henry VIII, was listed at Hampton Court. Several embroidered standards with gold fringes and tassels are mentioned. A curious exotic item was a pavilion or tent of printed calico, blue, with figures and flowers; though presented to King James by the Russian ambassador, it may pehaps have been Indian work (see also p. 293).

Finally there is an interesting list of rich silk fabrics lying unused in a trunk at Denmark House. They were of several different types, mostly with floral patterns, and included whole pieces up to 72 yards in length at values ranging from 6s. 8d. to £2. 10s. per yard.

After 1649

Between 1649 and 1651 the great majority of the textile furnishings listed in the inventories were sold to pay the late King's debts. At some houses large groups were sold *en bloc*. At Oatlands, for example, almost everything was sold to Sir Gregory Norton. At Windsor a large group of furnishings, including Queen Elizabeth's beds, chairs and cloths of state, was sold to John Seele. Elsewhere, sales were piecemeal but none the less thorough. At Richmond virtually everything was disposed of. At Hampton Court most of the tapestries and carpets and nearly all other textile furnishings, many of them dating from Henry VIII's and Wolsey's time, were sold to various purchasers. Much the same happened at the other major repositories – the Tower, Denmark House and Whitehall.

A proportion of the royal furnishings was reserved from the sales for the use of the Commonwealth government and the choice of items is not without interest. The aim was evidently to retain enough textiles to serve the basic needs, decorative as well as utilitarian, of those royal buildings which were to be kept in government service. A considerable number of tapestries was reserved, including many of the largest, finest and most valuable sets at Hampton Court, the Tower, Windsor and elsewhere; but some fine sets and many hundreds of other tapestries were sold. The Raphael tapestry cartoons at Whitehall were reserved, as well as all the cartoons and equipment at Mortlake, so that the tapestry workshop there could continue to operate if required. A good many Turkish and Persian carpets were reserved at Hampton Court and Whitehall. Among furnishings of other kinds, however, rather little was retained. Naturally enough, none of the royal cloths of state or canopies was reserved, nor any other textiles with royal arms or initials. All the better bed hangings were sold, except for a modest set of silver camlet at Whitehall, a striking set of black satin lined with yellow satin at Denmark House, and a very luxurious set, from Wimbledon, of crimson velvet lined with cloth of gold and silver and richly embroidered with gold and silver thread. Both the latter sets had matching seat furniture, but otherwise very little upholstered seating was reserved, except for the thirty-eight Turkey work chairs at the Council of State, a few other chairs and stools of velvet or cloth of silver at Whitehall and one or two velvet-covered close stools. Decorative cushions and table carpets were not reserved, apart from a few table carpets at Hampton Court.

The tapestries which had been reserved from sale were used and cared for under the Commonwealth and there were even some additions to the collection. Fine sets of Mortlake tapestries, which were sold at Denmark House in 1651-2, were repurchased by the Commonwealth authorities in 1654; one of them, comprising six tapestries of *Vulcan and Venus*, decorated Cromwell's lodgings at Whitehall.[17] Thus the tapestry collection which was eventually returned to Charles II in 1660, though numerically only a small fraction of the former royal holdings, was still considerable and of very high quality. Apart from tapestries, a few other textile furnishings were returned to the Crown at the Restoration. For example, Edmund Harrison, the King's embroiderer, had bought in 1651 two of the most valuable embroidered items in the royal collection, namely the principal Stuart cloth of state, at the Tower, and Henry VIII's celebrated pearl-embroidered table carpet from the Paradise Chamber at Hampton Court; these he returned to Charles II, as part of a deal by which the Crown repaid its outstanding debts to him.[18]

384 [801-2]
255 [118]
56 [30]
158 [2]
431 [71]
18 [82]

107-8 [191-201]

333 [95], 128 [404]

57 [2]

331 [68], 339 [171-2], 356 [413]
405 [9], 55 [11], 384 [803]
163 [63], 164 [65, 67-8]

18 [83], 163 [58]

The subsequent decay, dispersal and destruction of the royal textiles cannot be traced in detail here, but one or two instances may be cited. Henry VII's great set of twelve tapestry hangings of the *Siege of Troy,* at Windsor, was soon divided. Only six remained at Windsor in 1688; in 1695 six were at Whitehall. In 1713 six were hung in the Committee Room of the House of Commons. In 1799 these attracted some antiquarian interest, when John Carter made drawings of them (in the Victoria and Albert Museum) and wrote about them in the *Gentleman's Magazine.* There was some question that the Royal Academy might acquire them, but the matter lapsed. Eventually, twenty years later, they were sold for £10 and disappeared from view.[19] The set of ten hangings of the *Victory of 1588,* at the Tower, suffered a somewhat similar fate. In 1651 six of them were hung in the House of Lords; in 1739 they were engraved by John Pine; they were destroyed by fire in 1834.[20]

A greatly reduced but still significant residue of tapestries remains in the Royal Collection to this day. Pre-eminent among them is Henry VIII's set of ten arras hangings of the story of *Abraham* – the most valuable set in the collection in 1649 – which is still to be seen at Hampton Court. Also at Hampton Court are a number of other tapestries of Tudor date, four of the *Triumphs* of Petrarch, five of *Aeneas,* and several more. Mortlake tapestries of the early Stuart period still in the Royal Collection include partial sets of *Vulcan and Venus* and of the *Months,* both made for Charles Stuart as Prince of Wales. Other Mortlake tapestries bearing the English royal arms are preserved elsewhere, for example a partial set of the *Acts of the Apostles* in the French national collection, and a set of *Hero and Leander* in the Swedish royal collection at Drottningholm Palace. Further tapestries listed in the royal inventories of 1649 can be identified, at least tentatively, in various public and private collections in England and abroad.

290 [184]

5 [21]

158 [3]

160 [25], 396 [982]

Notes

1. BL, MS Harley 1419.

2. W.G. Thomson, *A History of Tapestry* (London, 1930), pp. 84-5, 138-44.

3. Thomson, *op. cit.* (Note 2), p. 147.

4. N. Reynaud, 'Un peintre français cartonnier de tapisserie au XVe siècle: Henri de Vulcop', *Revue de l'Art* No. 22 (1973), pp. 6-21.

5. J.-P. Asselberghs, *Les tapisseries tournaisiennes de la guerre de Troie* (Brussels, 1972).

6. C. Lapaire, 'Une tapisserie gothique à Genève', *Genava* 23 (1975), pp. 136-45.

7. H.C. Marillier, *The Tapestries at Hampton Court Palace* (HMSO, 1951), pp. 16-19.

8. F. Salet, *David et Bethsabée* (Paris, 1980].

9. J. White and J. Shearman, 'Raphael's tapestries and their cartoons', *Art Bulletin* 40 (1958), pp. 193-221, 299-325.

10. Marillier, *op. cit.* (Note 7).

11. Thomson, *op. cit.* (Note 2), pp. 277-352.

12. H. Hecht (ed.). *Thomas Platters, des Jüngeren, Englandfahrt im Jahre 1599* (Halle, 1929), pp. 110-12.

13. The Florentine merchant Antonio Corsi, who supplied some of these vestments, also supplied a cloth of state of very costly cloth of gold in 1499. See L. Monnas, 'New documents for the vestments of Henry VII at Stonyhurst College', *Burlington Magazine* 131 (1989), p. 347.

14. Hecht, *op. cit.* (Note 12), p. 94; G.W. Groos (ed.), *The Diary of Baron Waldstein* (London, 1981), p. 151.

15. D. King, 'The carpet collection of King Charles I', *Oriental Carpet and Textile Studies* 3 (1987), pp. 22-6.

16. Hecht, *op. cit.* (Note 12), p. 94; Groos, *op. cit.* (Note 14), p. 151.

17. *CSP Domestic* 1654, pp. 291, 338, 456-7.

18. *CSP Domestic* 1660, p. 191.

19. Thomson, *op. cit.* (Note 2), pp. 152-3.

20. *Ibid.*, pp. 270-2.

10 'Great vanity and excessse in Apparell'. Some Clothing and Furs of Tudor and Stuart Royalty

Valerie Cumming

Marginal numerals refer to page and entry numbers in the *Inventories* (see p. 11)

His Majestie taking into His consideration the great vanity and excesse in Apparell, now in use in severall sorts and degrees of people, and the great wast and consumption of Gold, and Silver therein, (at all times very unfit, and hurtfull to particular Persons, and to the Kingdom, but in these times most insufferable) hath taken into His care to provide for the Reformation thereof in as a timely, and as convenient a way as may be, and hath thought fit to begin with His Court, and Armies.[1]

Extravagance in dress was an accusation levelled at all English monarchs and courts throughout the late medieval and early modern periods. A lack of princely magnificence could also cause adverse comment, as in the case of Henry VI (who was thought unworldly in both appearance and attitude) and that of Henry VII who it was thought, 'dwelleth more richly dead than he did alive in any of his palaces'.[2] In the seventeenth century, however, such extravagance or 'excesse' became firmly associated in the minds of puritans and other disaffected critics of the royal house and English court with every type of ungodly behaviour; fashionable dress signified corruption and decadence and was criticised with a vehemence which is astonishing to the late twentieth-century mind. That Charles I recognized, somewhat belatedly in the 1643 proclamation, that the dress of his courtiers and armies was a constant reminder of the 'great vanity' of his circle might suggest that he had physically distanced himself from personal grandeur. On examination, however, the inventories provide inadequate evidence to support criticism of waste and excess or even to substantiate the idyllic Van Dyckian depiction of Charles I and his consort Henrietta Maria as elegant royal arbiters of courtly fashion in the second quarter of the seventeenth century. Instead there is a curiously haphazard, although historically intriguing, series of items which spans a period of well over one hundred years. A small but significant group was associated with Henry VIII, and the coronation clothing from the royal regalia in Westminster Abbey may, in part, date back even further. The items of clothing, the furs and accessories retrieved from the various royal residences do not, unlike other goods in the inventories 'present an incomparable and poignant record of vanished splendour', but they do provide some fragmentary evidence about the royal attitude towards tradition and its reconciliation with changing fashions in dress.[3]

Before considering the various groups into which these inventoried items of clothing, furs and accessories can most conveniently be placed, some discussion of the reasons why so little survived is pertinent. Clothing was amongst the most ephemeral categories of personal possession in the seventeenth century, but it was also, within royal and aristocratic circles, of considerable value, more often for the sum of its parts—fur, Italian lace, gold and silver embroidery, imported silks—than in its original state. Fashions in dress, even in the seventeenth century, changed more rapidly than fashions in furniture, metalwork and other items which furnished and decorated buildings rather than persons. Its expense guaranteed that it was altered for the wearer, re-made for children, discarded to poor relations or given to servants as part of their perquisites, pilfered and, occasionally, worn out. It could be easily transported, either legally in the baggage of its owners, or in the laundry baskets and sacks or on the persons of those without title to it. Royal servants, unpaid since the beginning of the Civil War, and royal creditors, would have gained equally from the gradual erosion of the stocks of cloth and clothing which did not follow the King and Queen when they left London and south-eastern England (where the principal royal residences were located) in 1642. Those loyal to the royal family may have eroded the stocks by smuggling items to them; a bizarre cross-section of these, including religious vestments and female clothing, were en route to France for the use of Henrietta Maria, when seized in the port of Topsham. It is also difficult to assess whether, at the beginning of the Civil War, either Charles I or Henrietta Maria had a detailed knowledge of what quantities of clothing or unused material was in their possession.

237 [241-57]

322   Valerie Cumming

The inquisitive, frugal and proprietorial attitudes of the Tudor monarchs towards their personal finery are not characteristics that can be applied to either Charles I or his father James I. Detailed inventories of Henry VIII's wardrobe were taken throughout his life and after his death, and an inventory of Elizabeth I's fabulous wardrobe was compiled in 1600. Neither Edward VI nor Mary I's wardrobes were inventoried in this manner, but the careful record in the earliest of Mary I's wardrobe accounts of 'haulf a yerde of Scarlett employed in making of Stomacher for our late brother King Edwarde the sixte and left owte of the laste warrante of his apparell of our greate Guarderobe' is matched by Elizabeth I's clerk of the wardrobe's note in 1567 of 'certayne of the Apparel that was late Quene Maryes . . . one forequarter of a Gowne withowte Sleves of purple vellat with Satten grounde etc.' Both Tudor Queens drew upon their store of clothing for re-use of rich materials, furs and decorative trimmings and took pleasure, Elizabeth especially, in augmenting their wardrobes with expensive gifts from their courtiers.[4] Such rigorous control of personal finery was singularly lacking in James I, Charles I and Henrietta Maria. James's interest in clothing was restricted to the appearance of his young, male courtiers, and his queen, Anne of Denmark, plundered Elizabeth I's 'best apparell' for the Christmas masque in 1603.[5] In turn, after Anne's death in 1619, what remained of her personal possessions after her servants had rewarded themselves, were divided between Prince Charles and the Duke of Buckingham; the remainder were sold to pay her debts by commissioners appointed by the King. It was alleged that the commissioners had 'not forgotten themselves to make the best peniworths'.[6] John Chamberlain's cynical version of events at the English court of James I's reign was sometimes inaccurate but the climate of disorder, poor management and opportunism prevalent in court circles which permeates his letters is corroborated in other contemporary sources. This state of affairs had not changed by the late 1620s when the King dismissed all but a handful of Henrietta Maria's French entourage, but was unable to stop them absconding with most of the Queen's clothes, leaving debts of around £19,000 behind them.[7] By 1647, when he was at Hampton Court, the King's worries about 'My Household stuffe and moveables of all sorts which I leave behind Me' almost certainly concerned paintings, tapestries and other *objets d'art* rather than insubstantial and easily replaceable items of dress.[8] Belatedly he may have recognized the inefficient administration of the office in the royal household known as the Great Wardrobe which was responsible, directly, for the moveable contents of royal residences and, through sub-departments, for the care of royal clothing.

The administration of the Great Wardrobe became less efficient and more corrupt in its practices throughout the reigns of James I and Charles I, and brief examination of some of its failings supports the view that the early Stuart kings were not overly interested in their own or inherited stores of clothing. The Great Wardrobe was, by the seventeenth century, located, principally, in the Tower of London and its senior official was a member of the Royal household known as Master of the Great Wardrobe. The Master was the 1st Earl of Denbigh from 1622 until 1643. As posts were calculated, it was not quite in the first rank, but it was well remunerated, something of a sinecure, and ripe with possibilities for corrupt administration. The role of the Great Wardrobe was a functional one and there was little need for it to be innovative or to demonstrate initiative. It was both a warehouse and manufactory for all of those items which added colour and magnificence to royal residences—furniture, soft furnishings and clothing—and it was responsible for the transport, maintenance and security of such items as they moved in advance of the royal family and the court, from residence to residence. In the fifteenth and sixteenth centuries a small group of appropriately skilled craftsmen travelled with the various items to install and repair as necessary, but all major repairs and new work was undertaken in London where the main stock of goods and materials was kept or could be readily obtained, and where work could be supervised by the most skilled craftsmen, and where the security of valuable items was more easily guaranteed. The less peripatetic nature of the early Stuart kings accelerated the practice whereby certain furnishings and other necessities were kept at principal residences under the supervision of keepers of standing wardrobes such as William Smithsby at Hampton Court. The line of control was also divided more firmly in the seventeenth century. The Great Wardrobe was an autonomous off-shoot of the Chamber, the major department 'above stairs' of the royal household which was headed by the Lord Chamberlain. Once goods left the Great Wardrobe they became the responsibility of the Removing Wardrobe which arranged transport, or a Standing Wardrobe, or, in the instance of royal clothing, the Wardrobe of Robes; all of these offices were under the jurisdiction of the Lord Chamberlain. The Chamber also had staff who, in addition to those attached to the Wardrobe of Robes, were employed as laundresses, shoemakers, a sempstress, an embroiderer and a perfumer. In miniature, similar arrangements also existed in regard to the clothing of the queen and the royal children within their separate households. It is not difficult to understand that, with so many craftsmen, officials, and servants having access to royal clothing, its loss or theft might be easily accomplished.

In the late fifteenth and sixteenth centuries the practice had been that the Great Wardrobe supplied, upon presentation of a royal warrant, all items of cloth or clothing that the king wished for his personal use, or to give to his family and courtiers, or to supply to his servants in the form of livery. Under this relatively well controlled system the king's clothes were despatched to the Wardrobe of the Robes which was located in the same palace as he was temporarily lodged, there to be maintained by the small staff of the Wardrobe of Robes. This little group acted as valets, ensuring that the king's clothes were clean, in good repair and that new garments were being made as he preferred. By the seventeenth century the balance between the Great Wardrobe and the Wardrobe of Robes had altered substantially with the latter administering to the king's personal requirements by placing orders directly with suppliers of goods and services. The Great Wardrobe continued to issue livery to royal servants entitled to wear it, or payments in lieu to others, on an individual or group basis. The Mastership of the Great Wardrobe had been considered a means of personal profit in James I's reign. The Earl of Doncaster was Master between 1613 and 1618 and John Chamberlain noted that 'yt seemes they (Lord and Lady Doncaster) grow wise, and see that such a place as the wardrobe is not easilie found again, that she may have every Sunday a new gowne as she had all the last Lent.' Purloining of rich materials, commissioning clothing for personal use or merely dishonest accounting continued as problems in Charles I's reign. The commissioners appointed in 1634 to consider reforms in the Great Wardrobe and the Wardrobe of Robes (under the imperious control of the Lord Chamberlain, the Earl of Pembroke) suggested economies which might have saved thousands of pounds annually. These were over-ruled by Pembroke who refused, categorically, to allow the clerk of the Wardrobe of Robes to sign all demands for materials supplied from the Great Wardrobe to the chamber, supposedly for the use of the Standing Wardrobe or the Robes. Pembroke remained in office until 1640 and reform of the Great Wardrobe and its branches within the chamber, or what remained of them, were not effected until the Commonwealth period.[9]

Given this disorderly and confused administrative background to the provision and storage of royal clothing it is hardly surprising that so little survived in royal residences to be inventoried and sold. What did survive could, reasonably, be discussed in relation to the residences in which it was found, but in order to give coherence to an otherwise disparate group of items of clothing, furs and accessories they will be discussed in specific categories, beginning with the group of coronation vestments found in Westminster Abbey and concluding with the miscellaneous oddments scattered in various palaces and unattributable to a particular wearer. Within this structure it is possible to examine, without undue repetition, relevant information about the supply and manufacture of clothing and its somewhat vexed terminology.

'The Inventory of the Regalia now in Westm^r Abby in an Iron Chest where they were formerly kept'

Nine items were described and valued of which the first seven are items of dress. The descriptions are brief and the value placed upon them is negligible; the seven were valued at £1. 11s. Elsewhere in the inventories items of clothing are described with some care and the values accorded to each item provide an accurate reflection of their real worth as fine quality secondhand goods, as unique souvenirs, or for the sum of their parts. This reflects the expertise of certain of the Trustees appointed to appraise and value them, notably Henry Creech, a skinner; John Foche, a haberdasher and John Humphreys, a tailor. The derisory value placed upon these unique items, however, seems to reflect the religious and political opinion of the time, personified by another of the trustees, George Wither, the pamphleteer and poet. The regalia had traditionally been kept in the Treasury of Westminster Abbey under the custodianship of the chapter of Westminster. Fears that Dean Williams would remove them to a place of safety led to a motion in the House of Commons on 23 January 1643 requiring the dean, sub-dean and prebendaries to produce the keys, by force if necessary. A secondary motion, milder in content, was carried by 42 votes to 41, allowing the locks to be broken only in order to inventory the contents of the regalia chest, the items to be left unharmed until the Commons decided upon further action. According to Anthony Wood's account

Henry Martin had been entrusted with the welcome task . . . (and he) broke open the huge iron chest in the ancient Chapel of the Treasury, and dragged out the crown, sword and robes, consecrated by the use of six hundred years, and put them on George Wither, the poet . . . who being thus crowned and royally arrayed first marched about the room with a stately garb [?gait], and afterwards, with a thousand apish and ridiculous actions, exposed those sacred ornaments to contempt and laughter.[10]

There were many, like Martin and Wither, who regarded the regalia as superstitious baubles, associated irretrievably with Roman Catholicism and consequently inappropriate symbols for a Protestant monarchy and Anglican church to cherish. Lucy Hutchinson, the wife of Colonel John Hutchinson, Governor of Nottingham Castle, blamed Henrietta Maria's influence on Charles I for a court 'replenisht with papists' while 'puritanes [were] more than ever discountenanc'd and persecuted'.[11] The King's lack of tact in respect of the religious views of his subjects had provided a recent and relevant example of his, so-called, 'papistical' tendencies. At his belated coronation in Scotland in June 1633 he had insisted that the complete Anglican service be followed, with the Archbishop of St. Andrews and his four supporting bishops dressed in 'white rochets and white sleeves and copes of gold, having blue silk at the foot'; the dour, non-participant Scottish bishops pointedly wore plain black gowns.[12] The central difficulty was the association of the regalia with the last Saxon king, Edward the Confessor, who had been canonized and was much esteemed by the English Catholics as St. Edward the Confessor. As early as the coronation of Edward I the ritualistic significance of the Confessor's relics was recognized when Edward was invested with 'the coat of St. Edward which is at Westminster'. Henry III transferred the Confessor's remains to a great shrine behind the High Altar in Westminster Abbey and from this date his crown and vestments became important relics in the abbey treasury where they were held as abbey property.

All monarchs from Edward II to Elizabeth I were consecrated with the Latin service, the order of which, *Liber Regalis*, had been revised in the early fourteenth century.[13] This ceremony was regarded as akin to the consecration of a bishop; a description of Henry VI's coronation stated 'They arrayed him like as a bishop that should sing Mass, with a dalmatic like a tunic, and a stole about his neck but not crossed, and sandalled, and also with hosen and shoes and capes and gloves like a bishop.'[14] These garments which were akin to those of a bishop were listed in *Liber Regalis* and consisted of

the *colobium sindonis*, a linen garment 'after the manner of a dalmatic'; a long tunic wrought with gold designs; the stockings or buskins; the sandals; the spurs of knighthood; the sword; the armills (massive gold bracelets held at the elbows by silk laces or a narrow stole); the imperial mantle.[15]

The relationship between the inventory and those times listed above is oblique, apart from 'One paire of buskins Cloth of silver and silver stockins very old', 'one paire of shoos of Cloth of gould' and the sword. The issue is further confused by the inventory of the regalia taken in 1356, for it described two tunicles, a stole, a cope and two rochets (called *colobia sindonis*).[16] However, if the inventoried items are considered in relationship to the detailed accounts of the coronations of James I and Charles I, both of which used an English translation of *Liber Regalis*, some conclusions can be reached.

The coronation orders for James I and Charles I are similar in all essentials, but there are detailed Italian and English eye-witness accounts of James's, so to avoid repetition this will be examined in pursuit of elucidation of the inventoried items, namely

51 [1]	One Crimson taffaty Robe very old . . .	10s.
51 [2]	One Robe laced wth gould Lace . . .	10s.
51 [3]	One Livor Cull^rd silke Robe very old and worth nothing	
51 [4]	One Robe of Crimson taffaty sarcenett . . .	5s.
51 [5]	One paire of buskins Cloth of silver and silver stockins very old . . .	2s. 6d.
51 [6]	One paire of shoos of Cloth of gould . . .	2s.
51 [7]	One paire of gloves embrod^rd wth gould . . .	1s.

Although the individual description of each item is skimpy, it would be appropriate to consider, briefly, what the individual terms (where the usage has changed) meant to the seventeenth-century trustee who valued the items. A robe was, in the Middle Ages, a loose outer garment reaching to the feet or ankles and worn by both sexes; by the late sixteenth century it had become a catch-all word for any outer garment or, in some instances, clothes in general. It was unfitted, but sleeved, with either a wide neckline which allowed it to be put on over the head, or with front or back openings held by ties or laces. Its use here suggests uncertainty about the true nature of the garments so described. Buskins were a type of soft, fitted boot which reached to the calf or the knee, usually made of silk or cloth; leather was used only for riding boots. Taffaty was applied to thin, glossy silk with a lustrous appearance and was used only from the fourteenth century. Sarcenett, another late medieval term, was a thin, soft silk with a slight surface sheen; using it in conjunction with taffaty is superfluous, unless it was intended to suggest that items [1] and [4] were not identical in the weight and appearance of the silk. Cloth of silver and cloth of gold were the richest of woven materials, using gold thread for both warp and weft or a mixture of gold and silk; in the Middle Ages and early modern period their use was restricted, by sumptuary legislation, to the royal family and select members of the nobility. Gold lace was a flat braid of various widths applied to clothing, often woven with a decorative pattern. Colours, in the early seventeenth century, were divided into sad colours and light colours; liver-colour was a sad, therefore dark, colour, approximating to a brownish red/purple.[17]

What James I actually wore, according to the coronation order, and what the Italian and English observers remembered, can be merged into something like the following. Preparatory to the ceremony he was presented with 'the Tunica or Shirte of redd silke, with the places for the annoynting opened and looped close, which hee is to weare next ouer his Shirte'; this allowed his shirt and doublet to be appropriately constructed. According to the Italian source, the King forgot or chose not to wear the red silk shirt, although this evidence is blunted by the admission 'I could not see so well', at this point in the proceedings (see, however, p. 264). On the morning of the coronation, 'It is to be provided that the Regalia which is St Edwards Crown. With the residue of the Roabes. and the oyle for the Annoynting be ready vpon the altar'. The King was divested of his red velvet parliamentary robes, and in his doublet (or shirt?) annointed, then given a coif (a round cap which the English witness saw as black velvet) to protect the annointed section of his head. He was invested with 'the Colobium or Dalmatica', with 'the supertunica or close pall', with 'the Tynsin hose', with 'Sandalls' followed by the spurs and sword, then 'the Armill is putt around his neck in a manner of a stole and tied to the boughtes of his two Armes' to be followed by 'the Mantell or open Pall', the crown, the ring, the 'Lynnen gloves, (being parte of the Regalia)' and the remainder of the regalia. The Dean of Westminster, in whose charge the various garments were kept, is specifically described as clothing the King with the supertunica, the hose and sandals and the mantle, and after the King had withdrawn 'into the Traverse' his Lord Great Chamberlain removed 'the Robes of Kinge Edward the Confessor' and delivered them to the Dean who laid them on the altar.[18]

The Italian witness, a Roman called Giovanni degli Effetti, purports to have seen the King robed in 'crimson velvet lined with white, with tight sleeves, and over this a royal surplice with the tunicle of a deacon embroidered, I think, with the arms of his kingdom . . . Over all was put a mantle without folds, like a cope, of violet brocade with a large orphrey of white clothe of silver.' The anonymous English account noticed 'a preists coate of cloath of gould . . . Sandals on his feete . . . on his handes a payre of white gloves . . .'[19] The Italian would appear to have telescoped two parts of the ceremony, for the King's parliamentary robes, in which he arrived, were of crimson velvet lined with white, but after the annointing he would have received 'a royal surplice' (the *colobium*) the 'tunicle of a deacon' (the *supertunica*) although the embroidery may relate to the armill, and 'a mantle'. The English witness only saw the mantle, although he had noticed the coif, the sandals and the gloves. Between them, allowing for uncertainty over the colour of the mantle, they seemed to have observed the essentials. What they saw, and what the orders of coronation for both James I and Charles I described as King Edward's regalia, and what was inventoried are not wholly reconcilable. The cloth of silver buskins and silver stockings may conceivably have been made in one and be 'the Tynsin hose' (tynsin was a sixteenth-century term for a silk material interwoven with gold or silver thread, and hose meant stockings). The cloth of gold shoes were possibly the 'sandalls', or there may have been two styles of footwear–buskins and sandals–which could be worn with the stockings depending upon the size of the monarch's feet. The embroidered gloves can easily be matched to the 'Lynnen gloves', described as 'white' by the English eye-witness. It is the four robes which are almost impossible to reconcile with the *colobium*, the *supertunica* and the mantle. The *colobium* was almost certainly of linen, confirmed by the Italian's description of it as a surplice (*cotta*), the *supertunica* may be the 'robe laced wth gould Lace' (described by the Italian as the tunicle of a deacon) or possibly the liver-coloured robe which, at a distance, might have looked like the black worn by deacons. The 'crimson taffaty Robe very old' and the 'Livor Cull^rd silke Robe very old' can be reconciled with the 1356 inventory which described two tunicles, but of the stole (armill), cope (mantell or open pall) and two *colobia sindonis* there is no mention.

There is no irrefutable evidence of how much of King Edward's regalia was, in reality, ever worn by him, in life or in death, or how much of the regalia was the gift of pious monarchs over the centuries. There is also no indication that what George Wither wore and mocked in 1643 was different in quality or kind to the items inventoried and sold. Consequently there is a possibility that either each monarch's set of King Edward's regalia–notably the *colobium*, the *supertunica*, the armill and the mantle–became the possessions and were used by the abbot (later dean) of Westminster, to be replaced anew at each coronation, or that the major items were removed from the regalia trunk once Parliament started debating access to them in 1643, or had already been removed, as some Parliamentarians suspected, leaving enough items–four assorted silk robes–to simulate the missing *colobium*, *supertunica*, armill and mantle. Such robes may well have had a connection with past coronations–the crimson taffaty garments could have been those red silk shirts, open in the appropriate places, which monarchs wore to protect their clothes for the annointing ceremony.

However, whatever the fate of the major items of the real regalia, what passed for it, was sold to Humphreys who was one of the trustees for the inventory, and subsequently involved in the supervision of the sale. He bought all seven lots of clothing along with the two additional items in the group, three swords with cloth of gold scabbards and an 'old Comb of horne worth nothing' for £5. The nine items had been valued at £4. 10s. 6d.

'Queene Anns Parliament and Coronation Roabes'

Two complete sets of robes were described, along with the two chests in which they had been kept. The descriptions are detailed and the value placed on each set was £20, although they were valued for the sum of their parts, the velvet and the ermine from which they had been made, rather than purely as items of dress. These items had been kept and appraised at Denmark House, the main London residence of James I's consort Anne of Denmark. That they had survived the depredations, dispersal and sale of Anne's effects after her death in 1619 is almost certainly due to the fact that they would have formed an important element in the goods apportioned to Charles I when Prince of Wales. Gossip, as reported by John Chamberlain, suggested that Anne had left a considerable fortune in jewels, plate, money, furniture, furnishings, clothing and '124 whole pieces of cloth of gold and silver, besides other silkes, linnen for quantitie and qualitie beyond any Prince in Europe'. The day after the Queen's funeral all of her jewels were taken in trunks to Greenwich where 'the King perused them all' before deciding upon their disposal; some, inevitably, found their way to the current favourite, the Duke of Buckingham. In August 1619 'A great parte of the late Quenes moveables (specially the linnen) [were] sold and made away by commission', but the Prince of Wales was given Denmark House and an opportunity to acquire those items from his mother's estate which were either appropriate to a Prince of Wales or to his personal taste—for it was Anne's lazy connoisseurship and interest in the performing arts which formed the tastes and opinions of both her sons, Prince Henry who died in 1612, and his younger brother Prince Charles.[20] The parliamentary and coronation robes would have been acquired by the prince as garments which his future queen might wear—altered to fit—or which might be used as examples of how the ceremonial robes of a queen consort should be constructed. In the seventeenth century the number of occasions upon which a queen consort might wear either her parliamentary or coronation robes was limited, principally to the coronation and to any sittings given to portrait painters. Consequently the garments, if stored correctly, would have been in excellent condition at Queen Anne's death.

All women's clothing in the first half of the seventeenth century was made by men; seamstresses provided linen undergarments but the outward appearance was the preserve of tailors, embroiderers, glovers and skinners who were carefully regulated members of the powerful masculine livery companies. All royal tailors and other providers of goods and services had served their seven-year apprenticeships and were masters of their particular crafts. The commission to provide the Queen's parliamentary and coronation robes would have been a valuable one for the mercers who supplied the velvet and taffeta, the skinners who supplied the ermine and the wire-drawers/haberdashers (almost certainly a collaborative venture) who provided the ornamental gold tassels. Silk materials such as velvet and taffeta were all imported into England at this date, and were made in Italy and Spain. Ermine skins were also imported, from Russia and Scandinavia, and, with sables, were amongst the most expensive and highly regarded of furs, although the wearing of fur was less common from the late sixteenth century onwards (see the wider discussion on furs in the section dealing with Charles I's clothing). Ermine is the white winter fur of the species of weasel known in England as a stoat. The tip of the creature's tail was black and these tips, used to give the distinctive spotted effect, were, in later fourteenth-century sumptuary regulation, limited to royal use. Other members of aristocratic rank allowed to wear ermine had white ermine skins 'powdered' (the contemporary term) with spots of black lambskin which were painstakingly sewn into slits in each fur. Each skin was a standard eight inches in length.[21] By the time that James I and Anne were crowned, ermine was regarded as a fur principally used for ceremonial garments within royal and aristocratic circles.

The garment described at length in the inventories as

102 [145]   A Kirtle of Crimson vellvett lyned with white Taphatie Bordered about with Ermyns with a Traine ioyned to the same lyned quite through with Ermyns with an Hoodd, and Bodies to ye same cont 24 yds of vellvett valued at x^li And the Ermyns valued att 10^li—soe togeather With a Surrcoate to the same with a long traine lyned with Ermyns with gould Tassells to the same and stringes suitable . . .

in which 'all the Furre and vell^vt' was valued at £20, is not dis-similar to the garments described, *in extenso*, in a recent publication dealing with the ceremonial and other events surrounding the coronation of Richard III and his queen, Anne Neville, in 1483.[22] Naturally, the garments would have been made to reflect the contemporary fashion in women's clothes for a deep, oval décolletage, a tightly fitting bodice extending beyond the natural waistline, and a wide skirt supported over a hoop (farthingale). There had been no coronation of a king and queen consort since that of Henry VIII and Katharine of Aragon in 1509, so although precedents regarding the appropriate materials were readily available, there were no garments to copy which had been worn by a recent queen-consort, although Elizabeth I's mantle, kirtle and surcoat of crimson velvet, inventoried in 1600, would have been available for inspection in the Tower.[23] Tradition demanded that Anne wear her purple coronation robes throughout the coronation service; *Liber Regalis* stated

The Queene is to be in a gowne of purple with a Trayne. This gowne to be *sine aliquo opere artificiali desuper intexto laxios* [*laxatos* in the coronation order of Charles I] *circa humeros decentes habens crines circulum aure*[um] *gemmis ornatum gestans in capite.*

Precedents obviously failed, or Anne, like a much later consort, Queen Alexandra, decided to wear exactly what she pleased. For, according to both the Italian and English eye-witnesses of the coronation, Anne wore crimson velvet on arrival (that is to say, her parliamentary robes). The Italian description is the fuller of the two: 'The Queen . . . was dressed in a long gown and full sleeves of crimson velvet lined with ermine, but without any embroidery, simply girt, with the hair let down to the shoulders, and a plain crown of gold'. After the service the Italian said that Anne 'returned in an ordinary black gown' but the English observer noted that after withdrawing both James and Anne 'putt on purple velvet robes . . .'[24]

Unlike the twelve peeresses who preceded her entry into the Abbey in their 'gowns of crimson velvet lined with ermine, made after the modern fashion but without embroidery, and the hair done up, and plain little crowns of gold . . . ' Anne was entitled to two sets of robes, in the manner of all royal ladies, although she was the only female royalty present in the Abbey. Also, uniquely, although a married woman, she was entitled, undoubtedly due to the sacerdotal nature of the annointing ceremony, to wear her hair loose upon her shoulders, in the manner of a virginal young woman on the day of her marriage.[25] Her robes confirmed her status in their duality (both parliamentary and coronation which peers were allowed, but not peeresses) and in their archaic description and actual appearance. A kirtle, a term dating back to the tenth century, and in Old English/Norse referring to a tunic, was, by the early seventeenth century applied only to the skirt of a woman's dress. In the instance of Anne's two kirtles it was cut to extend behind in a deep train with a deep ermine border, the train lined with ermine, with a matching bodice (bodies) which, in contemporary terminology, is likely to have been sleeveless, but closely fitting. The separate hood was a type of shallow shawl worn around the shoulders with a residual hood behind, both of which were principally of ermine, in the traditional manner. The 'surrcoate' was an over-garment, by this date probably a semi-fitted, open-fronted mantle, again with a long train, and sleeves, fitted at the upper arm and opening-out into deep, hanging sleeves; the garment decorated and held in place with the string and 'gould Tassells' which were both functional and decorative. The weight of both sets of garments would have been considerable, and for a coronation in summer—James I had chosen 25 July 1604 (the feast of the apostle St. James) for this ceremony—almost insufferably hot. Indeed certain events usually connected with a coronation had been cancelled due to an outbreak of the plague in London, and plague was always a concomitant of unseasonably hot weather. There are no obvious comparisons to be made regarding the style and cost of these garments—queen-consorts who had been crowned were rare creatures in the sixteenth century, and in the seventeenth century there was no coronation of king and consort until that of James I and Anne's grandson, James II in 1685. Charles I's consort, Henrietta Maria had no need for her dead mother-in-law's garments; she refused, on religious grounds, to accompany her husband to his coronation, leaving Anne's sets of robes untouched until the Commonwealth sale. Both sets were sold on 30 October 1649 for £22 per set, a marginal profit over the valuation of £20 per set. They were acquired by Thomas (no initial), who was probably the Eleanor Thomas who bought the cradle mantle discussed below (p. 336) on the same date, or possibly William Thomas, the former keeper of the standing wardrobe at Windsor Castle.[26]

102 [145,146]

'Roabes of King Henry yᵉ 8ᵗ'

102 [148]

Seventeen entries within the inventory of goods kept at Denmark House in the care of Henry Browne the keeper of the standing wardrobe describe items of clothing which had survived from those inventoried after Henry's death in 1547. With the exception of the robes of the Order of St. Michel, none of the garments have any specific association with state or ceremonial functions. It can only be surmised how such a large group of Henry's clothing survived for over a century. Of his three children who succeeded him on the throne, one was a boy and two were women, so recourse to his personal wardrobe would have been unsatisfactory for purposes of re-modelling or cannibalizing garments, although the latter two may have re-used all or part of the women's garments which were listed. Possibly the garments had been at Denmark House since its foundation (as Somerset House) in 1549 for Lord Protector Somerset, the uncle of the young Edward VI. As a royal-by-association adult male he may have removed much of Henry VIII's clothing either for his own use or to safeguard it until his nephew reached his majority. By whatever means it was at Denmark House in the 1640s; it stands alone as surviving from the Tudor dynasty, after Anne of Denmark had despoiled Elizabeth's stocks of clothing for masquing and other purposes. It is not inconceivable that both Anne and Henrietta Maria, so different in physique and temperament, but successive occupants of Denmark House as queen-consort, acquired all historic stored items from the Great Wardrobe for re-use in the masques and entertainments from which they both derived such pleasure.

The seventeen entries fall into seven distinct categories of clothing, principally formal day-time wear, namely

102-4 [148]	Robes of the Order of St. Michel
[149-51]	Three short gowns
[152-5]	Three complete cloaks and one recognizable piece of a cloak
[156-9, 161]	Four coats separately inventoried and nine coats inventoried as a group
[160]	One nightgown
[163-4]	Embroidered bands and shirts
[162]	Two chests containing assorted pieces of garments

Elsewhere in the inventories, amongst the goods found in the care of William Smithsby, keeper of the standing wardrobe at Hampton Court Palace, are listed
180 [252] one of Henry VIII's hawking gloves which can be reasonably considered with
102 [148] this group. The most valuable items within these groups were the 'Two Roabes of white cloth of silvr of the Order of St Michaell' upon which the Trustees placed a valuation of £20. Both their rarity value and perhaps their association with the man generally perceived to be England's last great king pushed the sale price up to £80. The later view of Henry as an unpredictable tyrant was not prevalent in the mid-seventeenth century. His stature as the king who removed England from the orbit of Roman Catholicism was unchallenged and ensured him popularity with critics of the Stuart dynasty.

The Order of St. Michel was founded by the French King Louis XI in 1469 and was a fairly late addition to the various orders of chivalry which European rulers had been introducing into their various court ceremonies since the first half of the fourteenth century. The order originally had fifteen knights and there is an illustration in the Bibliothèque Nationale[27] which depicts the first chapter of the Order held at the monastery of Saint-Michel. The robes and collar used the motif of the scallop shells of pilgrims alternating with knots. The mantle was a rectangle with neck and side openings. By the reign of Charles IX the number of knights in the order had so increased that the decoration was known, in the popular jargon, as the 'collier à toutes bêtes'.[28] In the early years of the sixteenth century, however, St. Michel was a prominent patron of French court ritual, being much in evidence at the entertainments at the Field of the Cloth of Gold in 1520 when Henry VIII and François I of France met. Henry did not receive the order until 1527 when, as a result of the ratification of the Treaty of Amiens, an embassy from the French King came to England, at much the same time as a reciprocal embassy went to France with the Garter for François. The day appointed for the installation and the various entertainments connected with it, was Sunday 10 November. The King was at Greenwich and the day started with Henry and the French ambassadors attending Mass together—an irony overlooked or unknown to the seventeenth-century purchasers of Henry VIII's goods. Difference in religion did not affect exchanges of orders of chivalry in the early post-Reformation period and Henry's son the precocious Protestant zealot Edward VI was invested with the Order of St. Michel in July 1551.[29] There is no portrait of Henry VIII dressed in these robes, and the brief description does not indicate whether they were a set, that is a mantle and undergarment of some kind (a kirtle or surcoat), or two identical mantles. They would certainly have been little worn and may have been preserved by the covers with which Henry's garments were often protected.[30]

All but two of the seventeen lots were sold to Noel (no initial) whose interest in the Tudor king's clothing was obviously shared by others, for, in all instances, he paid substantially more for the garments than the original valuations. None of the clothing is apparently under-valued in terms of re-usable materials and decoration but obviously the secondhand value of such items of clothing was perceived to be non-existent. Fashions for men had changed considerably over the intervening century, as had taste in colours and decoration. During his adult life-time, as a young, active monarch, bulky, middle-aged man and infirm, gross older man, Henry VIII took a great interest in clothing. Princely magnificence

Figure 93 Holbein: *King Henry VIII with King Henry VII, c.* 1536-7 (ink and watercolour on paper). National Portrait Gallery, London. Henry VIII's wide-shouldered, knee-length gown is a development of the fur-lined, ankle-length gown worn by his father. The latter style was unfashionable, except for older men and certain professions, by the mid-sixteenth century, but it retained a place in the male wardrobe as a chamber gown, worn informally.

was readily manifested by clothing made according to the latest fashions and using the most sumptuous of imported luxury goods, and Henry, like all of the Tudor monarchs with the possible exception of his father, fully understood the importance of rich clothing as a demonstrable sign of power and prosperity (Fig. 93). Something of his taste for the overtly splendid can be glimpsed in the truncated descriptions of his various garments. The three short gowns, the style illustrated in Holbein portraits, open-fronted, knee-length, with short full upper sleeves and longer hanging sleeves behind, was a fashion worn by younger men in the first half of the sixteenth century. The three in the inventory are described in such a manner that the most valuable, that is re-saleable or re-usable, elements are emphasised, but the punctuation is also misleading. It must be assumed that 102 [149] 'A short Gowne with sleeves of purple sattine faced with Cloth of gould, and richly enbroydered with gould . . . ' is a sleeved gown of purple satin etc., 102 [150] whereas 'A short Gowne, the sleeves of uncutt vellvett all the workes enbroydered with gould Twist . . . ' is an embroidered gown of which only the 103 [151] sleeves are of uncut velvet. 'A short Gowne of Crimson vellvett enbroyd^rd all over with gould and silver faced and lyned with Crimson sattine . . . ' is altogether easier to understand. Facings were broad bands of material which bordered the front edges of the garment and broadened over the shoulders to form a cape or collar behind. Uncut velvet was woven in the usual manner but the surface loops were left uncut giving a denser, less silky pile. Embroidery in gold and silver thread, although not unknown in the mid-seventeenth century, was at its apogee in the sixteenth century. It created a glistening, encrusted surface decoration which, apart from visibly flaunting the expense involved in its manufacture, added bulk and weight to garments. Henry VIII used a number of embroiderers at any one time. In the accounts for January and April 1531 his three king's 'enbrawderers', Peter Chadwyke, William Ilgrave and Stephen were paid £120. 14*s*. 9*d*. in total for their work which would have included some materials.[31] In the same published accounts for 1528–32 he was spending 30*s*. per yard on cloth of gold, 16*s*. on crimson satin and 33*s*. 4*d*. on purple velvet. Purple was restricted by sumptuary legislation, issued in 1510, to members of the royal family.[32]

Figure 94   Unknown artist: *King Henry VIII, c.* 1542 (oil on panel). National Portrait Gallery, London. The King wears a fur-lined coat over his doublet; the loose construction partly disguises his great bulk. Around the neck the band (collar) can be glimpsed; the linen sleeves of the shirt are puffed-out between the ornamental slashings of the doublet sleeves.

Although it is probably rash to associate directly the items in the 1547 inventory of Henry VIII's wardrobe to those goods sold in 1649, there is an obvious similarity between the gown numbered [151] and 'A gown with a square cape [collar], of crimson vellet and crimson satten all over embrawdered . . . '[33] The terminology of dress had changed little in the course of a century, although the need to describe the content of embroidery (that is, its value) was considered necessary in the less dazzlingly embroidered seventeenth century. The gowns were valued at £10, £2. 10s. and £6 respectively, but Noel had to pay £40, £8 and £24 for them on 24 October 1649.

103 [155], 103 [152]
103 [153]
103 [154]

The four cloaks, one of which was only 'a Peice', were made of 'Carnacon sattine' embroidered with gold and lined with crimson velvet, white cloth of silver 'striped' with gold and silver lace and lined with white velvet, purple cloth of gold 'guarded about' with embroidered velvet, and cloth of silver ('the Peice'). All of the complete cloaks had a 'Spanish Cape' as a feature in their construction. This style was fashionable from the mid-1530s but worn as late as *c.* 1620, and would not have been unfamiliar to the Trustees when they described these items. The 1536 Wardrobe accounts describe 'a Spanyshe cloak of purple casse damaske, enbrowdered and lined with purple veluette . . . '[34] All cloaks were circular in shape, using three-quarters or more of the circle of material which enabled the garment to stand out in heavy folds from the shoulder. The Spanish style was hip-length with a shallow collar, a deep pointed ornamental hood and deep borders turned back on each side of the front opening. The descriptive details which need definition are relatively few. Carnation was a bright salmon pink colour; laces, in this context, is a term always applied to braid and guarded meant strips of decorative material, often velvet, which covered seams and edged vents. Only the remnant of the cloth of silver cloak failed to sell for considerably more than its valuation. They were valued, respectively, at £8, £3 and £3 and sold for £26, £13 and £13; the fragment sold for £2 against the estimate of £1. 10s. All were purchased by Noel.

Four separate coats and a lot of nine coats were described with brevity, emphasising again the expensive materials from which each was made. All were

103 [156-7] sleeved; one was of 'Peachcullor cloth of silver', another of 'cloth of gould in
workes'—a stylized or geometrical patterned woven decoration, the third of
103 [158], 103 [159] 'Cloth of gould in flowers' and the fourth of 'Tynncell Tyssued with silver and
gould', and they were valued and sold, respectively at £2. 10s. (£9), £2 (£9),
£2. 10s. (£8), £2 (£8). All were acquired by Noel. The lot of nine coats, 'all of them
enbrd,' were valued at £18 and sold later than the main group of Henry VIII's
garments, on 2 November 1649 for £20 to T. Greene, possibly the porter Thomas
Greene, at Denmark House, on whose 'care and industry' those organizing the
sale depended.[35] The style of coat was likely to have been that described in both
the sixteenth and seventeenth centuries as a cassock, a loose hip-length jacket
which widened towards the hem and was worn by all social classes, although
varying considerably in materials (Fig. 94). Warrants for Henry VIII's clothing
between 1517 and 1521 mention coats for riding, stalking, tennis and more formal
wear, and they had both loose-fitting and tight sleeves. Construction varied
considerably: a tennis coat required only three and a quarter yards of black
velvet, but eleven yards were needed for a riding coat.[36] The quantity of material
as well as its richness or simplicity would have dictated the interest shown in the
four separate coats as opposed to the lot of nine sold together.

103 [160]   After the individual coats in the inventory there is a 'Night Gowne of
Crimson wrought vellvett with sleeves Enbroydered round . . . ' Such garments
were ankle-length, informal gowns worn early in the day or late at night; a
species of superior dressing-gown (in modern terminology), usually with a fitted
yoke from which the material fell in deep folds. Often the most luxurious were
made with detachable fur linings, a desirable feature in the draughty houses,
castles and palaces of the sixteenth century. Henrietta Maria took a large part of
the white miniver bordered with ermine lining of a counterpoint (counterpane/
bed-cover) to make a nightgown over a century later. They opened down the front
and could be held by a girdle or sash and were worn by both sexes. In 1532 Henry
VIII's accounts include payments for 'a nightgowne for my lady Anne' a relatively
intimate present for the woman whose determination to be a wife rather than a
mistress precipitated the radical religious and social changes of the 1530s. This
nightgown was made from thirteen yards of black satin, lined with eight yards of
black taffeta and bordered with three yards of black velvet; it had upper sleeves
stiffened with buckram and cost £10. 9s. in materials and 5s. 8d. for tailor's
work.[37] The secondhand value to Noel, in October 1649, of a nightgown made
from considerably more material to cover Henry's height and bulk and made of
velvet, a more expensive silk than satin, with embroidered decoration, was £8;
the valuation had been £2.

    The King's embroidered collars and shirts were sold separately. Noel bought
104 [163] 'Sixteene Borders of gould wrought upon holland like Enbroyderie wch were for
104 [164] K. Henry ye 8t his Bands' and Roger Humfreys bought a green velvet coffer
which contained six of Henry's shirts (see Fig. 1). Shirts were the principal
masculine under-garment for the upper torso. They were constructed from
simple rectangles of material with a gusset under each arm, with the material
gathered into the neck and wrist and a short central front opening held by ties or
strings. The neck and wrist bands, flat double sections of material, could be
plain, or decorated, usually with embroidery in the sixteenth century. They were
made by seamstresses in great households or by the womenfolk in more modest
establishments. The King's shirts would have been made from linen, imported
from the Low Countries (the eponymous 'holland') or Germany. In 1532 the
accounts list payment to 'Barnard's wif' who made eight shirts for the King for
the sum of 4s. 4d. excluding material.[38] The embroidered decoration on bands (or
collars) and cuffs, sections of the shirt which, by the mid-1540s, were the most
visible elements, meant that for laundering purposes it was easier if these
sections were detachable. The gold embroidery on the bands would have
required more careful attention than the main body of a shirt; the embroidery
would have been worked according to a geometrical or curvilinear pattern and
the separation of the two areas of production would have been a practical
solution to the work of seamstress and embroiderer. The bands valued at £2 were
sold for £8, the shirts valued at £2 were purchased for £2. 10s., again on the later
date of 7 November. Noel's other purchase on 24 October was two chests
103 [162] containing 'old peeces of Garmts.' As we have seen earlier, the Tudor frugality
with clothing meant that nothing was wasted, principally because of the expense
of the luxurious silks, laces and embroidery which were characteristic features of
royal and aristocratic clothing in the sixteenth century. As Noel's other purchases
were of the vibrantly coloured silks, gold and silver cloth and sumptuous

embroidered articles, it would be fair to assume that these two chests contained pieces of similar quality when he bought them for £4, well above the £1 valuation.

The final item connected with Henry VIII was contained in a large group of material taken from Hampton Court. It is 'One hawkeing glove of Henrÿ yᵉ 8th' which, with other sporting items, was sold to Boulton (no initial) on 22 November 1649. John Bolton was a goldsmith of Foster Lane in the City of London who spent nearly £4000 on various goods during the sales.[39] This may be the glove which has survived in the Tradescant collection at the Ashmolean Museum, Oxford (Fig. 113), and which has been described in detail in the catalogue of that collection.[40] Henry VIII bought gloves by the dozen and half dozen for both sporting and fashionable wear, usually spending less than 1s. a pair on undecorated ones, but 'hawks gloves' were bought individually and in 1531 cost 6s. 8d. each.[41]

180 [252]

The Clothing and Furs of Henrietta Maria and Charles I

The clothing associated with the King and Queen has little of the coherence of the group of garments connected with Henry VIII. Reasons for this have been suggested in the introductory comments to this chapter. Within the sequence of the sale a number of articles from the Queen's wardrobe at Denmark House are inventoried before the King's and it is her clothing and accessories which will be discussed first. Apart from a group of richly decorated and bulky mantles, the other items – a waistcoat, several scarves, a smock, gloves and a fan – fall into the category of attractive but far from essential accessories, easily overlooked or not required when the court left London for Oxford in 1642.

The Queen (Figs. 95-7) had been admired, by an English observer, for her plain style of dress when she left France for England in 1625. European courts, unlike their English counterpart, admired restrained luxury in dress, eschewing the eclecticism that characterized fashionable dress in England in the first quarter of the seventeenth century. Foreign styles made, inevitably, from foreign materials were mixed together and covered in decorative embroidery, lace, braid and jewellery in a recklessly extravagant and inelegant manner which European visitors found either vulgarly impressive or absurd. Henrietta Maria was a princess of France, the last child of Henri IV and Marie de' Medici; born in November 1609, she never knew her father who was assassinated in May 1610 and was a babe-in-arms at her brother Louis XIII's coronation in September 1610. The education of a French princess in the early seventeenth century emphasised religious instruction, etiquette and the aristocratic arts of music, dance and limited public performance at court entertainments; dress was an element in both courtly magnificence and social stratification and her proxy marriage in May 1625 was an occasion of great public display. As a bride she wore cloth of silver and gold decorated with the golden fleur-de-lis of France and a pale blue velvet and cloth of gold train, but she refused to be crowned alongside her husband in 1626 in English robes of crimson and purple because of the difference in religion. As an exiled widow in France in the late 1650s she said of her daughter, the widowed Princess of Orange, 'She is magnificent, has jewels and money and loves spending. I tell her she ought to save. Once I was as she, even more so. Look at me now!'[42]

The great retinue of French attendants, including priests, who accompanied Henrietta Maria to England, were startled by the simplicity, austerity and lack of ceremonial at the English court. The new king had attempted, since his father's death, to impose a more dignified standard of behaviour upon his circle of courtiers and attendants, but initially this had little effect other than to emphasise Charles I's innate aloofness.[43] Extravagance in dress had been a feature of James I's court, and had caused much adverse comment, but if, as Henrietta Maria suggested in later life, she had been unusually extravagant in regard to her personal appearance, there is little evidence to support this assertion. When her French entourage was reduced in 1626, the Queen retained her dresser and tailor, and she had a French embroiderer Charles Gentile and a French perfumer Jean Baptiste Ferine in her employ, and she wrote regularly to France for accessories and for new or familiar styles of material or clothing, but her most notable extravagance was upon the costumes for the masques and plays in which she took major roles. Inigo Jones provided alternative designs for her masque costumes, allowing her to believe that she was involved in the design

334   Valerie Cumming

Figure 95   Unknown artist, after Van Dyck: *Queen Henrietta Maria,* *c.* 1636 (oil on canvas). National Portrait Gallery, London. The construction of separate bodice (waistcoat) and skirt (petticoat) is clearly delineated in this portrait. The finely executed lace collar held by a jewelled brooch or clasp is an expensive version of the gorgets found amongst the Queen's possessions in 1644.

Figure 97   Attributed to Hendrik van Steenwyck: *Queen Henrietta Maria,* *c.* 1633-5 (oil on canvas). National Portrait Gallery, London. The Queen's dress reflects the plainer styles of the 1630s. The lustrous dark satin bodice and skirt and discreet pearl decoration create the illusion of increased height. In her left hand she holds a fan which is partially open, its painted leaf just visible.

Figure 96   Cornelius Johnson and Gerard Houckgeest: *Queen* *Henrietta Maria, c.* 1639 (oil on panel). Reproduced by courtesy of Sotheby's, London. When Abraham van der Doort catalogued this portrait in 1639 he mentioned that 'the Clothes are not as yet finished', and there is an apparent awkwardness about the overskirt and petticoat. However, the chosen colours of white, pink and blue (the last being a 'scarf' of the type described in the inventories) are typical of the late 1630s and early 1640s taste for clear rich silks.

process, but it was her obvious pleasure in these entertainments which provoked criticism.[44] Puritans found such performances abhorrent because they were enacted on Sundays; the additional belief that they were a frivolous application of money raised through unpopular forms of taxation, reinforced the idea that the Queen was an undesirable alien influence upon the King. Lucy Hutchinson summarized this widespread view, describing Henrietta Maria as 'a papist, a French lady, of a haughty spiritt, and a greate witt and beauty, to whom [the King] became a most uxorious husband'.[45] The idyllic courtly world of a King and Queen in mutual accord, emphasising the virtues of family life (Pl. 67) and providing an example, recognized internationally, of the growing connoisseurship and elegance of the English court which patronized the arts in all their forms, exacerbated the fears of god-fearing Protestants who perceived all foreign influences, especially Roman Catholic ones, as subversive attempts to change the direction of the English monarchy. Damned irredeemably by such critics, Henrietta Maria's innate high spirits and youthful frivolity were inevitably misinterpreted as concomitants of reckless extravagance.

The most notably luxurious of her garments sold or disposed of between 1649 and 1651 were five mantles one of which was a cradle mantle. One was of 'Crimson sattine enbroydrd all over with Cinque Foiles of silver and blewe silke in Panes lyned wth Crimson Plushe'; another of white satin 'lyned with Minivers and Ermyns'; a third of 'Hairecullo^r cloth of silver lyned with gould, and silver plushe' and the fourth of 'Lawne enbroydered, and sett wth spangles lyned with Carnacon shagge'. The cradle mantle was of crimson velvet bordered with three rows of gold lace and ermine and lined with carnation taffeta. As was usual, the fur, where used, was valued separately from the individual article, indicating to a potential purchaser the relative values of the materials in each lot. Measurements were given for some of the mantles but these do not follow any regular pattern. The length – three and a half yards – is given for the cradle mantle and both length and width for the crimson satin (two yards by one and a half yards plus one eighth of an inch) and the haircolour cloth of silver (two and a half yards by one and three quarter yards), but the white satin and the lawn mantles were not measured at all. Apart from their decorative qualities it is obvious that these garments were intended to provide considerable warmth; only the cradle mantle has a lightweight silk lining, the others are lined with fur or plush (a cloth with a longer, softer nap than velvet and made from a mixture of cotton, wool or silk or wool and goat's hair) or shag (a cloth with a thicker, shaggier pile than plush, usually of worsted or silk). The cradle mantle, as the name implies, was used in much the manner of a counterpane on a baby's cot but could also act as a ceremonial wrap within which the heavily swaddled baby was carried. The other mantles – long, relatively wide trains or wraps, held at the neck by ties – provided a luxurious additional but unconstricting layer of clothing, and a small woman (Henrietta Maria was a little under five feet tall) could wrap herself most comfortably in such a quantity of material.

Within the inventories all of the mantles are described in a sequence which includes items associated with the bed-chamber or babies, indicating that Henrietta Maria's use of these garments may have been in connexion with pregnancy, lying-in or receiving greetings whilst in her bed, but they are not confused with nightgowns which, as the inventory indicates, she also wore. This may explain why, upon her departure to Holland in the spring of 1642 and the court's removal to Oxford, they were not packed for her use. However, amongst the items inventoried at Colombes in 1669, after her death, mantles of cloth of silver lined with blue, and incarnadine stitched with gold are listed, offering an alternative option that such garments were associated with ceremonial occasions when formal etiquette required a long, bulky train.[46] The crimson satin mantle with its strips of embroidered cinquefoils (related to the modern species of plant known as potentilla) was valued at £6 and sold for £8 to Purford (no initial) on 4 December 1649. The white satin mantle, valued without its miniver and ermine at £3 (the fur was valued at £40), was acquired, on 23 October 1651, by Stone (no initial), probably Captain John Stone, head of the sixth dividend which acquired sixty pictures in the sales. After the Restoration he returned a number of items to Charles II.[47] The mantle of haircolour (rich tan) cloth of silver was valued at £7 and sold to Maidwell (no initial) on 25 October 1649 for £10. 10s. The mantle of embroidered lawn (a fine linen cambric) decorated with spangles (pierced, circular metallic decorations rather like sequins) was valued at £5 and sold for that amount to Edward Evans on 3 November 1649. The cradle mantle valued at

99 [119]
101 [144]
105 [172]
109 [211]
99 [120]

Figure 98 *King Christian IV's sash, c.* 1630-40. Rosenborg Castle, Copenhagen. This richly embroidered carnation (salmon pink) silk taffeta sash is thought to have been a present sent to Christian by Charles I. Such exquisite decorative embroidery could, on occasion, be found on women's scarves although, by the late 1630s, the latter were usually lighter both in substance and decoration.

£19 (£1 for the ermine border) was sold to Eleanor Thomas on 30 October 1649.

Maidwell, who bought a range of items on 25 October 1649, purchased a 'Wastcote of white Taphatie' embroidered in gold and silver thread, polychrome silks and seed pearls for £4 against a valuation of £2. 10s. A waistcoat was a style of sleeved bodice, low-necked, held with ribbon ties; embroidered using metal thread, coloured silks, pearls and spangles on white linen or silk, they were especially popular for informal dress in the first quarter of the century. They were less structured than the stiffened, interlined bodices of formal dress, and the light ground of linen or silk provided an opportunity for a virtuoso display of the embroiderer's skills which drew upon designs taken from contemporary pattern books, herbals and bestiaries. More characteristic of the fashions of the late 1630s and early 1640s than the embroidered 'wastcote' were the four scarves which were listed amongst Henrietta Maria's goods. One was part of a lot with a cover for the sacrament, the others were sold individually. The first was 'cutt through with gould, silver, & silke'; another was of 'Carnacon Taphaty enbr wth pearles'; the third was again carnation taffeta, but embroidered with silver, and the fourth was 'A scarffe of Cuttworke of flowers of gould silvr and silke paned with white sarcenett'. They were valued at £5 (including sacrament cover), £30, £5 and £4 respectively; the pearl embroidery on the second of these was obviously a substantial element in this valuation. In the portraits of female sitters by Van Dyck, Cornelius Johnson and others there is much visual evidence of scarves (or, as their length and width would suggest to modern viewers, shawls) made from opaque or semi-transparent materials, and worn in various ways around the shoulders or arms, both loose and softly tied in place. Some suggest an Oriental influence which accords with the description of a scarf 'cutt through with gould, silver, & silke'. Trade with India was gradually developing in the middle years of the seventeenth century, and gifts from Holland or, nearer to home, from Lord Denbigh, Master of the Great Wardrobe, who had returned from Persia in 1633 and was depicted by Van Dyck in a style of lightweight dress worn by some Europeans in India at this date, may have fascinated courtiers eager for novel luxuries.[48] Two other scarves, one embroidered with pearls, the other with silver suggest something akin to the substance of the decorative sashes worn by men at this date, round the waist or diagonally across the shoulders. Such a sash, of salmon pink (carnation) taffeta embroidered with flowers, birds and insects in polychrome silk, gold and silver, and edged with lace and seed pearls, is in the collection of Danish royal clothing at Rosenborg Castle (Fig. 98). It is thought to be a gift from Charles I to his uncle Christian IV and dates from 1630–40.[49] Obviously distinctions were drawn, in size and substance between female scarves and male sashes, but the colour, weight of silk and style of decoration appear similar. The last of the four, the cutwork (a species of lace in which the pattern was cut-out and embroidered around the cut edges of the design) paned with white sarsenet, is more distinctly feminine in its delicacy. All were acquired by different purchasers; the lot with the sacrament cover for £5. 10s. by Ann Lacy

104 [170]

105 [175]
109 [216]
109 [219]
109 [220]

105 [175]

109 [216]   on 26 October 1649, the pearl embroidered scarf for £42 by Richard Barrett on the
109 [219]   same day; the carnation taffeta with silver embroidery was sold to Edward Evans
(who had bought the lawn mantle) for £6 on 3 November 1649 and the cutwork
scarf remained unsold.

109 [209]   The most informal of Henrietta Maria's garments to be sold was a smock (a shift or chemise) embroidered with gold and silver threads and silk. Similar in construction to men's shirts, that is, made from rectangles of fine linen, they could be made either with a high neckline and collar which were usually edged with lace or embroidered because they would be seen (Fig. 56), or cut low to suit the décolletage of women's fashionable formal wear. Body linen was regularly laundered and royalty and their courtiers would expect to change it daily; both night smocks and day smocks were ordered by the dozen or half dozen. This richly embroidered smock, valued at £1. 10s. was sold to Hunt for £1. 12s. on 30 October 1649.

112 [249]   The accessories at Denmark House were limited to gloves, pockets and a fan. A box containing '5 paire of spanishe gloves, 2 paire of sweete Pocketts, and 2 paire of enbroydered gloves' was valued at £1, but was not sold. Spanish leather was imported and made into gloves in England, where it was esteemed for its softness and flexibility. Spanish gloves were exported throughout Europe and are included in the effects of Henrietta Maria inventoried after her death. Plain leather gloves were bought in quantity and worn both in and out of doors by men and women. Fashions in women's gloves began to change at the end of the 1630s, and longer, narrower, elbow-length styles, in pale and white leather were preferred. Embroidered gloves were often given as presents; they could be costly to produce using precious metal threads, silks, spangles, pearls and lace and amalgamated the craftsmanship of glover and embroiderer but, by the 1640s, simpler motifs worked directly on to the leather had replaced the miniature gardens and bestiaries which adorned gauntlet gloves earlier in the century. All gloves lost their shape quickly and became easily discoloured through wear and their secondhand value was negligible. Pairs of pockets were, similarly, of little value. Made of silk or linen and in this instance, perfumed (to sweeten was a seventeenth-century term for perfuming) they were small, flat bags attached by a tape and worn over the underskirts but below the skirt and reached through an opening in a side seam of the skirt. Endymion Porter's wife, Olivia, paid 1s. 6d. per pair in the 1630s and bought them in considerable numbers, and they are also listed amongst the goods inventoried after Henrietta Maria's death in 1669.[50] The last dress accessory in the group of items found at Denmark House was 'A Fann of Curious worke wrought, and cutt out of white Ivory in a redd leather Case' valued at £5 and acquired by Bass and Hunt on 1 March 1653. Edward Bass was head of the ninth, tenth, and thirteenth dividends and one of the King's creditors and John Hunt was one of the Treasurers of the Commission for the sale; previously he had been a linen draper to Henrietta Maria.[51] Fans were luxurious accessories in the first half of the seventeenth century; the example described appears to be a brisé fan made of thin strips of ivory held at the base by a cord or rivet with threads or ribbons holding the slips in the typical half-moon shape as the fan was opened. It was obviously pierced ('cutt out') with a design resembling cutwork lace, but whether it was plain pierced ivory or painted ('curious worke wrought') it is impossible to tell from the description. Ivory brisé fans were made in China and exported to Europe by way of Holland in the mid seventeenth century and considered a fascinating novelty. An embassy from the States of Holland had presented Henrietta Maria with gifts including Chinese porcelain in 1635 and on the marriage of her daughter to Prince William of Orange-Nassau in May 1641 there would have been further opportunities for the exchange of exotic presents. She certainly used fans: there is a portrait of the early 1630s in which she holds one (Fig. 97), and at her death her household and personal effects included a box of Italian fans.[52]

The second group of items connected with Henrietta Maria was listed in 'An Inventorie of Goods that were in yᵉ Custody of Sʳ John Bartletts stopped being att Sea in the Port of Topisham'. All were contained in a trunk and included various ecclesiastical vestments and certain articles of female clothing. Topsham is the most navigable point of embarkation on the river Exe south of the city of Exeter where, in June 1644, separated from the King who was still in Oxford, Henrietta Maria gave birth to their ninth and last child Princess Henrietta Anne. Charles had sent his ailing wife to the safety of the royalist West Country and en route to Exeter by way of Bath, Henrietta Maria sent messages and baggage carts back to her husband, fearing capture and wishing to travel unencumbered. While she was in Exeter the parliamentary General, the Earl of Essex, approached and refused her a safe conduct to Bath. Henrietta Maria, weak and in considerable pain, decided to flee to France and left Exeter in disguise and, after a long, hazardous journey, embarked on a Dutch ship which took her to France. The goods stopped at Topsham were obviously intended to follow her on to Cornwall and thence to France.[53] During these adventures she was accompanied by her elderly Scottish confessor Father Robert Philip which accounts for the small group of ecclesiastical vestments. These consisted of 'one black vellvett Coape' and 'Fowre black vellvett Ornaments thereunto belonging', each listed separately, and a lot containing 'One Wrought Coape and 3. Ornam[ts] unto it', two linen surplices and ten pieces of linen and lace. Such 'papistical' manifestations angered Puritans and their natural instinct was to destroy them. This group, of all the many articles of ecclesiastical dress which Henrietta Maria's Capuchin friars, confessors and religious advisers would have stored in her household chapels, are the only ones which survived to be inventoried. They were valued for their content – £1 for the black velvet cope, £3 for the velvet ornaments and £4. 10s. for the group, and acquired by Bass on 7 February 1651. Edward Bass bought under his own name or jointly with John Hunt.[54]

237 [243]
237 [244]
237 [245]

The articles of clothing which can be associated with Henrietta Maria are an 'old black silke Gowne', a petticoat and matching waistcoat of 'white Tabby', another set of 'Pinckculloure Tabby', three petticoats, one 'wrought in silver cloth', another of 'blewe Sarcenett' the last of 'wrought Sattine', and 'One small bundle of Tiffany Gorgetts'. The styles of women's clothing by the 1640s had settled down into several combinations of bodice, skirt (called a petticoat, although this was not an undergarment) and gown which varied in construction according to the formality or informality of the occasion on which they were worn. Portraits of Henrietta Maria in the 1620s and 1630s depict her in the more formal indoor styles worn by fashionable women, usually a short-waisted bodice with a basque and elbow-length full sleeves, a low neckline partially concealed by a lace collar and a loosely gathered skirt given width by hip pads beneath (Pl. 18). The clothing in the trunk is much less formal, possibly because of her pregnancy in 1644. Gown was a term which changed its use in regard to women's dress in the seventeenth century. Early in the century it meant a loose, open-fronted garment, sometimes held by buttons and loops or ties; sleeved or sleeveless it was an optional additional layer of clothing. By the 1620s it could mean, confusingly, the entire dress, or a semi-fitted, open-fronted, open-sleeved but integral element of the dress, en suite with the bodice and skirt, or a loose over-gown. The last would have been particularly suitable for pregnant women, and as this gown is a different colour from all of the other items but in conflict with none, it seems probable that it was a loose overgown.

237 [250-51]
237 [252-3]
237 [254-6]

The two sets of 'petticoate and wastcoate' were made of 'tabby', a type of coarse, glossy taffeta with a watered finish, somewhat similar to modern moiré. Both the waistcoat, as described earlier, and the petticoat were relatively informal styles. Decorated petticoats were worn under the over-skirt from the mid 1630s, the latter looped-up to reveal the contrasting colour and material, or with the softer, unstructured waistcoat jacket they provided an informal, less constricting style over which a loose gown might be worn for extra warmth or, in pregnancy, for modesty or concealment. The colours of all of these items – white, pink, silver, and blue – were popular at the English court in the late 1630s and early 1640s and reflect the taste for unpatterned but lustrous silks. The three petticoats may have been separated from matching waistcoats but it was not unusual for a range of these to be ordered and then used, as required with either formal or informal styles of dress. Olivia Porter had matching sets of garments or separate items in much the same manner. Like the Queen, she had a 'Tabby Rose coulered pettycoat and wastcote' and a set in 'sky colered sattin', but she also had separate petticoats, some of which were trimmed with gold and silver parchment lace, and separate waistcoats of cloth of silver and of 'aurora colered sattin'.[55] The 'small bundle of Tiffany Gorgetts' were deep collars which fitted closely around the neck and covered the décolletage; they were fastened by pins, ties or buttons. Tiffany was a transparent silk or fine lawn, but decorated gorgets used a heavier linen which could take the weight of applied bands of lace. The gorget was fashionable from the 1630s and was also called a 'falling whisk because it falleth about the shoulders'.[56] Edward Bass, who bought all except one of the items in this group captured at Topsham, appears to have bought them at their valuations which were 15s. for the gown, £1 each for the sets of petticoat and waistcoat, £3 for the cloth of silver petticoat, £1. 5s. for each of the other two, with the gorgets apparently considered worthless.

All of the items of dress associated with Charles I were found and inventoried at Whitehall Palace, the principal London residence of the Stuart kings until its almost complete destruction by fire at the end of the seventeenth century. These garments form a coherent group in that they are either richly furred or connected with the ceremonial aspects of kingship, namely the coronation, the king in parliament and the Order of the Garter. Undoubtedly they were left in the wardrobe of robes as atypical and far too valuable, in the main, to be moved around in the baggage train of an embattled monarch. Although not extravagant in his expenditure on clothing (he spent around £5,000 a year in the mid-1630s which compares not unfavourably with the £4,574 spent on his brother, Prince Henry's wardrobe over twenty-five years earlier) the King was conscious of the need for restrained splendour, and took considerable interest in the details of dress.[57] At the outset of his reign he drew a clear distinction between what had gone before and what he required in the way of privacy, discreet and courteous behaviour and appropriate clothing. He cared deeply about the sanctity of kingship and those ceremonies which emphasised this: as chief mourner at his father's funeral on 7 May 1625 he provided over £50,000 for the mourning black, the splendid hearse and other appurtenances which were needed to make it 'the greatest [funeral] indeed that ever was knowne in England . . .'[58] By January 1631 when a set of *Orders for Conduct at Court* were issued, dealing principally with court etiquette and ritual, there was a renewed ban on the wearing of boots and spurs in the royal presence, and a requirement that all who were admitted to court should be dressed in 'gowns or fit habits answerable to their degree'.[59] The latter can be interpreted in two very different ways, as a reaffirmation of the redundant sumptuary legislation which insisted upon certain colours, materials and furs being graded according to rank, or an early attempt to combat the sobriety of dress associated with the Puritan aristocracy and gentry. Dress and politics, as perceived by traditional royalists, or dress and morality, as understood by Puritans, were lively debated issues in the period 1620 to 1660. There were the two extremes, as epitomized by the king's strictures, and the attitude of a committed Puritan like Colonel John Hutchinson who 'left off very early the wearing of aniething that was costly, yett in his plainest negligent habitt appear'd very much a gentleman . . .', and a great many uncertainties, such as those of Lady Brilliana Harley who wanted her son to submit to his father's strict views on clothing but, privately, assisted him with the purchase of luxuries such as silk stockings and Spanish leather shoes. Edward Harley was a student at Oxford, under the jurisdiction of the Chancellor who was Charles I's much favoured Archbishop of Canterbury, William Laud, but Laud was also zealously engaged in trying to eradicate the extravagant dress and long hair favoured by fashionable young men.[60]

This war of attitudes and words took place against a background of considerable decline in the English cloth industry, due in large part to the loss of essential northern European markets during the Thirty Years' War. Illogically, but perhaps naturally, it was possible to link the luxurious imported materials worn at court with the lack of regard for good native cloth. In fact throughout his reign, in a series of proclamations, the King attempted to assist and regulate indigenous textile industries, and to restrict imports of luxury goods in order to encourage new or developing English manufactures.[61] His success in this endeavour can be gauged by the somewhat desperate proclamation of 1643 quoted at the beginning of this chapter when his army officers were still flaunting their expensive, presumably imported lace, braid, fringes, buttons and so forth. The privileges of rank were easily communicated in dress, a fact quickly seized upon by parliamentarians such as Major-General Harrison who was not ashamed to appear 'in a scarlett coate and cloake, both laden with gold and silver lace, and the coate so cover'd with clinquant that scarcely could one discerne the ground', when the Spanish ambassador acknowledged the new republican status of England after the execution of Charles I.[62] It was an irony that Charles I, so soberly dressed in his final captivity, might have enjoyed.

Throughout his life his appearance did not provoke the criticisms of excess or extravagance which were often levelled at his aristocratic contemporaries. His quiet, majestic dignity attracted favourable comment, and he was generally considered 'sober in apparel, clean and neat'—the antithesis of his father, James I.[63] His model, as a child, had been his precociously talented elder brother, Henry, Prince of Wales. When Prince Henry adopted the less extravagant, more dignified style of Italian dress in 1611, his brother Charles, Duke of York, followed his example. Sir Robert Carey, James I's Master of the Robes early in the reign,

Figure 99   Attributed to Hendrick Gerritsz Pot: *King Charles I, c.* 1632 (coloured chalks on paper). Sotheby's, London. Unlike the work of Van Dyck, this study neither idealizes the King's features nor elongates his short stature. The all-black clothing of doublet, breeches and cloak, is almost puritanical in its sobriety. However, the fine lace of the falling ruff, the decorative points (ties) at the waist, garter and shoe rosettes and long hair would have been thought excessive by contemporary critics of fashionable dress.

Figure 100   Van Dyck : *King Charles I,* 1636 (oil on canvas). Royal Collection: reproduced by gracious permission of Her Majesty The Queen. This depiction of Charles I in state robes shows the traditional design of the ermine-edged kirtle with its long, hanging sleeves and the considerable quantities of velvet and ermine which were required for the construction of ceremonial robes.

and Lord Chamberlain in Prince Charles's household, suggested to Prince Henry that his experience made him the ideal person to form the young Prince Charles's taste in clothes.[64] As Prince of Wales, from his brother's death in 1613, Charles is depicted in the fussy, over-decorated styles of the late teens and early 1620s, a small (he was five feet four inches tall) rather pale young man overwhelmed by the bulky, inelegant fashions worn so effortlessly by his father's favourites. It was his visit to Spain, by way of France, in 1623 that seems to have formed his adult taste in clothing, refined his attitude towards the role of the arts in court life and impressed him with its ceremonial etiquette. Briefly he seems to have adopted the sober dark tones and formal black found at the Spanish court, then with his marriage in 1625, his young queen seems to have influenced his taste, for in August 1625 he was requiring his tailors to spend £1,000 on materials and accessories from France.[65] By the mid-1630s he was dressing in the plain coloured silks in the pale to moderately dark colour range in which he is depicted in portraits (Figs. 99-100). The published wardrobe accounts afford insight into the diversity of his clothing, from tennis suits to masque costumes, with every type of accessory, including nightcaps, hose in every colour, gloves, hats, boots and so forth, and also give details of the cost of individual items or groups of items. The craftsmen who provided him with clothing – tailors, skinners, hatters, haberdashers, embroiderers – are all listed, and like his Tudor ancestors he required them to alter his clothes or take materials from the store for re-use.[66] Although, towards the end of his life he was living in much reduced circumstances, with a modest number of servants, he continued to acquire new clothes. In Newport, before he left the Isle of Wight, he ordered a velvet suit with gold embroidery, the cloak lined with satin, and at Windsor in 1648, the newspaper *The Perfect Weekly Account* noted that he 'hath three new suits, two of them are cloth with rich gold and silver lace upon them, the other is of black satin, the cloak lined with plush'.[67]

The King's clothes found at Whitehall were listed, in part, under the general heading of 'Severall rich furres', this being perceived as the most valuable element in these eight lots. In addition there were five lots of ceremonial garments. Before discussing the individual lots it is pertinent to consider the type of fur that is described. Three lots contained sables, two lots were of lucernes, one of fox, and two of 'fur'. The contemporary opinion of these furs is easily deduced from the valuations attached to them. A relatively plain coat lined with unspecified fur was valued at £15, but a coat of more expensive material and decoration lined with 'rich' unspecified fur was worth £55. The lucerne fur from a cloak, and a 'new furre' of lucerne were both valued at £20, as was the black and white fox lining of a cloak. The fur lining, edged with sable tails, for a gown (a garment which required considerably more material, consequently a larger and more substantial lining than either a coat or a cloak) was valued at £80. The jump in value to £150 is considerable when the sable lining of a cloak is described, and a lining of sables for a gown is valued at £200. Despite changes in fashion throughout Europe in the second quarter of the seventeenth century which laid emphasis on more fluid, plainer silks and fine wool cloth with more pliable, less bulky linings for clothing, such as plush and shag, there was still a demand for fur in the colder, northern European countries. Improvements to draughty castles and palaces eliminated the need for the quantities of fur used in the later Middle Ages and well into the sixteenth century, but fur remained, *par excellence*, the warmest as well as most attractive form of insulation for humans, as Hollar's depictions of mid-seventeenth-century women demonstrate so convincingly. The sable, a type of marten found in the far north of Europe, yielded a rich, soft fur of dark brown to black which had long been admired, and never lost its cachet as one of the most expensive furs, worn by royalty and their richest nobles. Even that least sartorial of monarchs, James I, was delighted to receive, from the Muscovite ambassador in 1617 a present 'the greatest that ever came from thence, the furs worth at least £6,000', amongst which were undoubtedly sable skins. The lucerne fur from the lynx, a wild cat found throughout Europe was, rather surprisingly, considered of equal value to the black and white fox furs; the last were fairly rare and again found only in the far north of Europe although by 1632, American colonists reported 'plenty of black fox, which is, of all others, the richest fur'.[68]

In order to consider what the unspecified furs might be, it is useful to look at the King's wardrobe accounts. Black squirrel (from the forests of central Europe) was used to line a coat in 1633/4, but the fur was taken from 'his Majesty's owne store', so no cost is given. Similarly, when an otter skin was used, it was from the store; the only other fur mentioned is sable, apart from an entry for perfuming 'three furred Coates' with musk, civet, amber and spirit of roses. The majority of the King's clothes were lined, if a warm lining was required, with plush. From other sources it is known that the King liked ermine as a lining fur, wearing it within a black velvet coat at the battle of Edgehill in October 1642.[69] The range of fur available to a relatively wealthy individual in the seventeenth century was considerable, from the humble 'budge' (black lambskin) and coney (rabbit skin) to every colour and variant of squirrel, marten and wild cat. Linings often used the flatter, smoother and less valuable furs or parts of furs of highly valued skins, reserving the finest quality for revers, borders and hoods.

The eight lots which emphasised the fur content include three lots which apparently lacked the garments which they originally lined, namely 'A lininge for a gown of Sables', a 'loose furre for a Cloake of Sables' and a 'new furre of Lucernes'. These had obviously formed part of 'his Majesty's store' of furs which, in the mid-1630s was the responsibility of Thomas Langhorne, the King's skinner. He prepared and adapted the furs to suit the newly ordered coats, cloaks and gowns made by the principal tailor, Patrick Black. David Murray had replaced Patrick Black, a fellow Scotsman, as the King's tailor by March 1637.[70] The type of garments into which such linings were placed are described within the same eight lots. There were two coats, one of 'deere Colour' (the pale reddish-brown of the animal) satin decorated with gold lace and embroidered with a Garter star and lined with 'rich furre', and one of black 'Chamblett' (a camel hair mixture with a watered effect) again embroidered with the Garter star but lined with (unspecified) fur. The loose-fitting coat, described by contempories as a cassock, has been described elsewhere, and was a fashion increasingly worn in the 1630s and 1640s. In the year 1633/4 the King had two deer coloured suits made, one of silk mohair, the other of wrought satin, the former with a matching coat, lined with green tabby, the latter with a matching cloak lined with plush.

Figure 101   After Van Dyck: *King Charles I, c.* 1635-7 (oil on canvas). National Portrait Gallery, London. The relative simplicity of the King's dress and his pose emphasise the dominance of the Garter star, an additional emblematic symbol which, from 1627, the King required all knights of the Order to wear on their outer garments.

These sets were paid for without regard to the price of each item, but the King had separate coats made; a decorated one of brocaded satin (to be lined with sables) cost £19. 2s. 4d., but watered chamblet coats varied between a relatively plain garment (to be lined with squirrel) at £9. 1s., and a more lavishly decorated one (to be lined with otter) at £14. 18s. 5d.[71]

As with the items in the inventory, the rich satin coat, even without its fur lining, was valued more highly than the chamblet ones. Both coats were embroidered with the star of the Order of the Garter. This was an innovation introduced by Charles I in 1627. He considered that the knights of the Garter should be instantly recognizable and wished them to wear a badge which proclaimed 'the honour they hold'. In pursuit of this aim a decree was issued requiring all Garter knights to wear 'upon the left part of their cloaks, coats, and riding cassocks, at all times when they shall not wear their robes, and in all places and Assemblies, an Escotcheon of the Arms of St George, that is to say, a Cross within a Garter . . . ' This badge quickly formalized into a star with rays or beams of silver surrounding it, and along with the riband and lesser George worn around the neck, and the actual garter below the left knee; was displayed by all member knights.[72] The accounts for 1633–5 refer to several payments to Edmund Harrison, the King's embroiderer, for embroidered orders, the most complete entry being a payment of £63. 5s. for 'enbroidering of Three and twenty rich orders of the Garter vpon Cloaks and rideing Coats for his Majestie.'[73] Contemporary portraits of the King (Fig. 101) and his courtiers indicate how familiar this embroidered star became (Pl. 20); on occasion it could be too distinctive, the Duke of Richmond wished to discover how easy it would be for the King to escape from the Isle of Wight, and tested the security by disguising himself in 'a Leaguer-Cloak without a Star'.[74]

The gown 'of sad Coloured sattin lined wᵗʰ furre and edged wᵗʰ sable tayles' was the long, loose garment which was worn principally by older men and within certain professions in the mid-seventeenth century. However, as an informal garment, especially in winter and during illness, it retained a minor place in the wardrobes of many. In 1632, the King, convalescing after a mild attack of smallpox, sat up to receive visitors 'in a warme roome, with a furr'd gowne on his back'.[75] Only two gowns are listed in the additions to the King's wardrobe between 1633 and 1635, a measure of their minor importance; one was 'a Chamber gowne' of crimson velvet richly decorated with silver lace, buttons and loops and complemented by a waistcoat made to be worn with it. The other was a sky-blue brocaded satin nightgown lined with Aurora coloured plush.[76] It seems likely that the gown of sad coloured satin was a chamber gown worn by the King when he received visitors privately or informally, rather than the more intimate nightgown. The two cloaks (or possibly a cloak and the fur from a cloak, although it is not described as a loose lining) were lined with 'black foxes, part of stone foxes' and lucerne. The latter cloak was of black satin. Generally Charles's cloaks were tailored *en suite* with matching doublet and breeches, and a number of these sets, in the mid-1630s, were of black materials—silk grosgrain, satin, velvet—as well as colours, but occasionally a separate cloak was made, one of wool cloth lined and bordered with velvet, cost £23. 9s. 7d. A black satin cloak lined with lynx could, easily, have been worn with a number of suits or have become separated from a specific one. All of these eight lots were acquired, apparently at the given valuations, by creditors of the King, including those involved in dividends. David Murray, formerly the King's tailor and head of the second dividend, was allotted the lining of sables from a gown on 23 October 1651. The loose sable fur lining from a cloak, the deer coloured satin coat lined with rich fur, and the gown of sad coloured satin, fur lined and edged with sable tails were acquired by Robert Houghton, head of the third dividend and formerly brewer to Charles I, on 23 October 1651.[77] The black chamblet coat lined with fur, and the item of least value, at £15, within these lots, was acquired by James Guinion on 17 January 1650. The black and stone (white) fox fur 'of a Cloake' was acquired by Emanuel de Critz, who had been Charles I's Sergeant Painter and was involved with the first, fifth and fourteenth dividends, on 23 October 1651. The black satin cloak lined with lucerne and the new lucerne fur were acquired by Clement Lanier on 21 June 1650. He was the former Master of the 'King's Musick'.[78]

The margin references:
380 [760]
380 [761-2]
380 [763]
380 [764]
381 [765]
381 [766-7]

The five lots of ceremonial clothing fall into the categories of parliamentary, coronation and garter robes. Again there was considerable disparity between the valuations placed upon them, the lowest being £5, the highest being £120. This must have reflected the quantity and quality of the fur used in them, although the descriptions of the parliamentary and coronation robes lack the considerable detail found in the earlier inventory entries for Anne of Denmark's robes. The first three items within this small group were described as 'The Princes Kirtle and hood lined wth furre', 'The Princes Parliam^t Roabe Kirtle hood and cap', and 'The King's Coronation Roabe Kirtle and hood'. They were valued at £6, £100 and £120 respectively. Which prince is referred to in relationship to the first two items is speculative. The natural conclusion would be Charles, Prince of Wales, the eldest child of Charles I and Henrietta Maria. He had certainly acquired a set of parliamentary robes before the court left London for Oxford in 1642. At the trial of the Earl of Strafford in 1641 the throne was vacant, but the eleven year old Prince of Wales sat to the right of it formally be-robed.[79] Possibly the incomplete set of kirtle and hood had been outgrown and were superseded by a larger kirtle and hood, as the fit of both robe and cap were of minor significance. One or both sets had probably belonged to Charles I when Prince of Wales. The kirtle, an open-fronted, ankle-length garment held together by a sash or belt, with elbow-length sleeves, and the shoulder cape with a vestigial hood at the back, were the two garments within a set of robes which had to fit the height and width of the wearer and be able to accommodate the bulk of the doublet and breeches worn beneath them. The minimal value attached to the separate kirtle and hood despite the fur lining which would have been of ermine, indicates either considerable use, or more likely, that they were constructed on a small scale. They were acquired by Laurence Steele on 19 February 1650. The complete set of robes, including the much more valuable ermine lined robe were acquired by Edward Bass on 23 October 1651, along with Charles I's purple and ermine coronation robes. The most intriguing aspect of this group is the missing element—the King's parliamentary robes—presumably taken to Oxford but never recovered at a later date.

The margin references:
381 [768]
381 [769]
381 [770]

The last two lots of Charles I's clothing are separated but should have been sold together, for Garter robes were a set, in the manner of other ceremonial robes. As listed, and valued there were a 'St George Roabe of Watchett velvett wth tassells of gold and silke' (£10) and 'A Crimson Roabe and hood of the Order of the Garter lined wth white Sattin' (£5). The King's interest in and desire to

The margin references:
381 [771]
381 [772]

Figure 102 *King Christian IV's Garter mantle, c. 1606.* Rosenborg Castle, Copenhagen. The purple velvet mantle is the oldest surviving example of a Garter robe. In the late 1630s Charles I changed the colour of the mantle to watchet (a rich sky blue) after nearly a century of robes of purple, a colour usually reserved for royalty.

strengthen the esteem in which the Order was held by both its knights and the wider circle within which they moved had, as shown earlier, manifested itself in additions to the emblems worn by all knights. During his reign chapters of the Order were held at Whitehall and at Windsor, but his robes were kept and carefully maintained in the Wardrobe of Robes in London. The mid-1630s wardrobe accounts refer to black velvet for St. George's caps, ribbons for Garter Georges, the perfuming of his 'robe kirtle hood and cap', and the embroidering of diamond and gold embellishment on to the actual garters.[80] The crimson robe was a surcoat or kirtle worn under the robe or mantle but over doublet and breeches to mid-calf level; it was a relatively plain garment similar in style to the parliamentary kirtle worn by men. The robe had been made of velvet lined with white silk since the sixteenth century, but the colour of the velvet was changed in Charles I's reign. It had been of purple velvet since the reign of Edward VI, but in the late 1630s the King decided upon a rich sky blue (watchett) colour.[81] This may have been timed to coincide with the installation of the Prince of Wales as a Garter Knight in 1638 and the commission to Van Dyck for designs for a set of tapestries to be hung in Whitehall recording the knights of the order in solemn procession.[82] No garter robes of this period and colour, let alone the King's, survive. The earliest surviving example of a Garter robe pre-dates the change in colour, and this is the purple robe of Christian IV of Denmark, Charles I's uncle (Fig. 102). It is simply constructed with a slightly raised band or collar into which the fullness of the velvet is taken, to fall away in deep folds. The complete set of robes, both lots, were acquired by Laurence Steele on 19 February 1650.

Miscellany and Conclusion

The principal theme of this chapter on the clothing and furs which were inventoried and sold between 1649 and 1651, is that of perplexity. There are infinitely more unanswered questions and conjectures about what survived until 1649 and why, than can reasonably be answered. Consequently, it seems wholly appropriate that the final category of material, a number of oddments of dress, more charitably described as accessories, should be described and then allied to a conclusion. This chapter has examined, to a large extent, the outer shell of the royal condition in both its ceremonial and domestic *personae* but, in essence, it lacks substance. It is the examination of the fascinating detritus of a privileged existence – the Oxfam shop of the early Stuart dynasty – not its core. In this regard the final group is both the summation and the ultimate nadir of all that has gone before.

These accessories, or oddments, were taken from a number of royal residences, but cannot be attributed to a specific royal owner; they may have been left behind by officials or servants, understandably of little or no consequence. Taken from Greenwich to Denmark House was a lot containing 'Fowre plum[e]s of feathers', valued at 4s. Hampton Court Palace yielded 'One paire of olde gloves' and 'Two paire of silk knitt gloves', both valued at 6d.; 'One blew knitt purse' valued at 5s., 'One purse of Murrey [a reddish/purple] vellvt' at 1s. 6d., 'One purse of black silke' at 1s. 6d. a 'garter of stooleworke (raised embroidery) at 1s., and 'One. China fann' at 2s. A mixed group of items found at Denmark House included 'Two plumes of feathers' and 'A long plume of feathers' valued, respectively at £12 and £16, and an 'Indian' trunk containing books and a straw hat, the complete lot valued at £10. The majority of items – the gloves (both lots bought for 1s. per lot), the knitted purse (bought for 6s.) and the velvet purse (bought for 2s.), the garter and fan at 1s. 6d. and 3s. respectively – were purchased by Boulton – presumably John Boulton, a London goldsmith, who bought widely at the sale; in this instance on 22 November 1649. Emanuel de Critz acquired the black silk purse on 18 November 1651; Edmund Harrison, formerly the King's embroiderer, and head of the eleventh dividend, acquired the two most highly valued lots of feathers on 23 October 1651; a Mrs Leigh apparently acquired the trunk and its contents, but this transaction is somewhat unclear.

The most highly valued items were the plumes of feathers – or, more accurately, the two plumes and the long feathers. Ostrich feathers were expensive luxuries throughout the seventeenth century, used to trim the hats of men and, more rarely, women (Pl. 64). Charles I's wardrobe accounts, in the mid-1630s include a payment of £13 for 'one extraordinary rich white plume of feathers Containing xj falles . . .'[83] Gloves and fans have been discussed elsewhere in this chapter, but the former include, in this instance, knitted silk gloves. Knitting using wool yarn had been long established, but its application to silk yarn was introduced into England only at the end of the sixteenth century, and many of the finest examples of silk knitted goods were imported from Europe, notably from Italy and Spain. The technique was applied in England in the seventeenth century but the cost of the imported yarn added to the price of the finished article, and such goods were a luxury. The fine yarn produced a more flexible article and often a better fit than equivalent goods knitted in thread or wool, or cut from woven material. The purses, which also include a knitted item, therefore possibly of silk yarn, were a masculine accessory, carried in the sleeve or the breeches' pocket. They were small, relatively pliable, held by drawstrings or a clasp on a metal frame. They ranged from highly decorative gifts, often embroidered, to plain functional items which were constructed from material which matched the main garments. Straw hats were worn informally, in the country during the summer, but are rarely mentioned or depicted in the seventeenth century. A Sussex haberdasher's accounts for 1632 include 'a fine straw hat lined in the brims £1. 4. 0.'[84]

These small articles of dress, like nearly all of the items inventoried for the Commonwealth sale, apparently disappeared – to be resold, used or re-modelled. After the Restoration there was a search, on behalf of Charles II, for 'all the revenues and goods which his father possessed, which had been sold and distributed among the rebels'.[85] The success of this endeavour in regard to the items discussed in this chapter is difficult to quantify. Undoubtedly royalists acquired and cherished items associated with Charles I, but those that have survived bear little or no resemblance to the articles in this sale. Embroidered shirts, nightcaps, lace edged collars and cuffs, pairs of gloves, small pieces of garments and personalia are to be found in various public and private collections, sometimes with a reputable provenance, sometimes not. The Museum of London's collection includes a knitted blue silk shirt which the King wore under his linen shirt on the scaffold (Fig. 103); a matching set of lace-edged cap, collar and handkerchief (Fig. 104), descended from George Kirke, a groom of the Bedchamber to Charles I; two pairs of gloves given to Bishop Juxon and the Earl of Lindsay respectively; the iron-strengthened boots worn by Charles as a child; and a less-securely related fragment of a garment traditionally associated with the King (Fig. 105).[86] Although it is regrettable that nothing of substance has

55[12]
180[253-4]
181[255-6]
181[257, 271]
182[276]
250[44-5]
251[49]

250[44-5]

Figure 103 *King Charles I's vest, c.* 1640-48. Museum of London. This finely knitted blue silk shirt (or vest) was worn by the King under his linen shirt on the scaffold. Such sophisticated craftsmanship was not usual in England at this date, and this may have been imported from Italy, Spain or France, perhaps being given as a gift to the King.

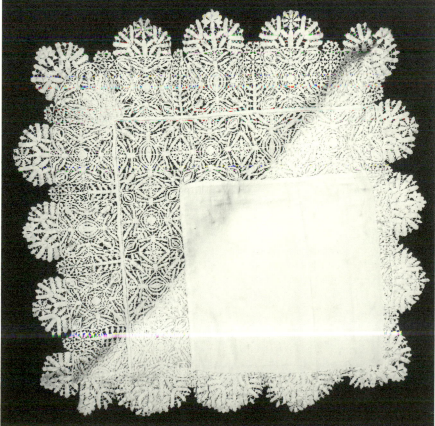

Figure 105 *Fragment of a garment, c.* 1640-48. Museum of London. This small section from a cloak or doublet is the type of personalia which was treasured by royalists after the King's execution. However, like all such articles it cannot be identified with any of the items inventoried between 1649 and 1651.

Figure 104 *King Charles I's handkerchief, c.* 1630-35. Museum of London. One of a set of three items in the Museum, the others being a cap and a collar of fine linen edged with English lace.

survived from the Commonwealth sale, it is not surprising. It is an inescapable fact that any attempt to personify the life of an English monarch through surviving clothing is an impossibility before the reign of Queen Victoria, for there was no apparent interest in developing the select but comprehensive collections of royal personalia which are found in various northern European countries. Such collections were being assembled, in embryo, in Denmark and Sweden during Charles I's lifetime but, if the evidence provided by the Commonwealth sale is accurate, the cultured, highly refined king of England did not wish to emulate this Scandinavian innovation. Apart from the extraordinary group of clothing connected with Henry VIII, it was as if Elizabeth I, James I and even Charles I had never existed, except in highly idealized portraiture and patronage of the applied arts. In many respects this is an appropriately enigmatic conclusion to a period within which dress was considered an ephemeral, luxurious and ultimately divisive luxury. The puritan view that 'Wantonesse in things belonging to the bodie is showed in costly apparell' could, in part, be supported by the eclectic range of dress and furs which were sold and acquired between 1649 and 1651.[87] However, the true range of royalist and monarchical 'excesse' in the second quarter of the seventeenth century is principally to be found in portraits, but rendered pleasing rather than extravagant through the vision, skill and flattery of Van Dyck and other artists of the period.

Notes

1. J. F. Larkin (ed.), *Stuart Royal Proclamations* II *Royal Proclamations of King Charles I 1625–1646* (Oxford, 1983), p. 907. This proclamation against 'wast and excesse in Apparell' issued to the county and city of Oxford, and dated 9 June 1643, was the last in a series issued by Charles and James I which dealt specifically with dress rather than with the materials from which clothing was made. Such proclamations were the seventeenth-century continuation of a lengthy and repetitive series of orders regulating dress which originated in the reign of Edward III.

2. Francis Bacon's comment on the Henry VII Chapel, Westminster Abbey, cited in J. H. Plumb and H. Weldon, *Royal Heritage* (London, 1980), p. 46.

3. *Inventories*, p. xviii.

4. The principal sources are BL, Harleian MSS 2284, 4217, 1419 A & B; PRO, LR2/121; PRO, E101/427/11; J. Arnold (ed.), *Lost from Her Majesties Back* (Costume Society, 1980), p. 33.

5. E. Law (ed.), *The Vision of Twelve Goddesses* (London, 1880), p. 9.

6. N. E. McClure (ed.), *The Letters of John Chamberlain* II (American Philosophical Society, 1939), pp. 219, 224-5, 237-8, 251, 257-8.

7. J. Bowle, *Charles I* (London, 1975), p. 101.

8. *Inventories*, p. xi.

9. There is no comprehensive study of the history of the Great Wardrobe and its various off-shoots. The brief account given here is based on the work of G. E. Aylmer, *The King's Servants* (London, 1961), pp. 173, 249, 282, 349-50, 470ff.; A. F. Sutton and P. W. Hammond, *The Coronation of Richard III* (Gloucester, 1983), chapter 3; R. Sherwood, *The Court of Oliver Cromwell* (London, 1977), chapter 5; T. F. Tout, *Chapters in the Administrative History of Medieval England* (London, 1928), IV, chapter XIV.

10. *Inventories*, pp. xv–xvi; M. F. Johnston, *Coronation of a King* (London, 1902), p. 155.

11. J. Hutchinson (ed.), *Lucy Hutchinson, Memoirs of the Life of Colonel Hutchinson* (London, 1822), p. 128.

12. Cited in Bowle, op, cit, (Note 7), p. 127.

13. Z. Halls, *Coronation Costume and Accessories* (London, 1973), pp. 7-8.

14. Cited in F. C. Eeles, *The English Coronation Service, Its History and Teaching* (London, 1902), p. 10.

15. Halls, op. cit. (Note 13), p. 7.

16. J. W. Legg, *The Coronation Order of King James I* (London, 1902), p. xxxvi.

17. Throughout this chapter, definitions of materials, colours and the construction of garments are a synthesis of information contained in C. W. Cunnington, P. Cunnington and C. Beard, *A Dictionary of English Costume* (London, 1960); C. W. Cunnington and P. Cunnington, *Handbook of English Costume in the Sixteenth Century* (London, 1970); idem, *Handbook of English Costume in the Seventeenth Century* (London, 1972); J. A. H. Murray (ed.), *The Oxford Dictionary* (Oxford 1888–1926); W. W. Skeat, *A Glossary of Tudor and Stuart Words* (Oxford, 1914).

18. Legg, op. cit. (Note 16), pp. 8, lxxii, 66, 27, lxxix, 27-34, 79.

19. Ibid., pp. lxxii, lxxix.

20. McClure, op. cit. (Note 6), pp. 224, 237, 257-8.

21. E.M. Veale, *The English Fur Trade in the Later Middle Ages* (Oxford, 1966), pp. 63, 32, 148.

22. Sutton and Hammond, op. cit. (Note 9), pp. 35-6.

23. H. Norris, *Costume and Fashion* III *The Tudors, Book II 1547-1603* (London, 1938), p. 487.

24. Legg, op. cit. (Note 16), pp. 69, lxx, lxxiv, lxxx.

25. Ibid., p. lxx; the importance that contemporaries attached to the virginal symbol of hair worn loose over the shoulders, is evidenced by the adverse comment attracted by the notorious Frances Howard, Countess of Essex who wore her hair loose when she married Robert Carr, Earl of Somerset in 1612, although she and her husband-to-be were widely thought to be lovers.

26. Sherwood, op. cit, (Note 9), pp. 29, 120-1.

27. Bibliothèque Nationale, Paris MS FR 19819.

28. M. Davenport, *The Book of Costume* (New York, 1972), p. 322.

29. S. Anglo, *Spectacle, Pageantry and Early Tudor Policy* (Oxford, 1969), pp. 140, 144, 231-2, 298; cf. H.W. Chapman, *The Last Tudor King* (London, 1961), pp. 218, 220.

30. J. Caley (ed.), 'A wardrobe account of Henry VIII', *Archaeologia* 9 (1789), pp. 247, 249.

31. N.H. Nicolas, *The Privy Purse Expences of King Henry the Eighth* (London, 1827), pp. 103, 124, 128.

32. Ibid., pp. 188, 174; C.H. William (ed.) *English Historical Documents 1485-1588* (London, 1967), p. 249.

33. Caley, op. cit. (Note 30), p. 247.

34. Cunnington and Cunnington, op. cit. (Note 17) [Sixteenth Century], pp. 26-8.

35. Bowle, op. cit. (Note 7), p. 56.

36. Cited in Cunnington and Cunnington, op. cit. (Note 17) [Sixteenth Century], pp. 31-2.

37. Nicolas, op. cit. (Note 31), p. 223.

38. Ibid., p. 256.

39. W.L.F. Nuttall, 'King Charles I's pictures and the Commonwealth sale', *Apollo* 82 (1965), p. 305.

40. V. Cumming, in A. MacGregor (ed.), *Tradescant's Rarities, Essays on the Foundation of the Ashmolean Museum, 1683* (Oxford, 1983), pp. 227-8. See also p. 407 (below).

41. Nicolas, op. cit. (Note 31), pp. 208, 267, 159.

42. Q. Bone, *Henrietta Maria, Queen of the Cavaliers* (London, 1973), pp. 12-13, 31; C. Oman, *Henrietta Maria* (London, 1936), p. 26.

43. Bone, op. cit. (Note 42), p. 31; Hutchinson, op. cit (Note 11), pp. 127-8.

44. Bowle, op. cit. (Note 7), p. 101; Oman, op. cit, (Note 42), pp. 76, 70, 74, 75.

45. Hutchinson, op. cit. (Note 11), p. 128.

46. Oman, op. cit. (Note 42), p. 343.

47. Nuttall, op. cit. (Note 39), p. 309.

48. O. Millar, *Van Dyck in England* (London, 1982), p. 56.

49. S. Heiberg (ed.), *Christian IV and Europe* (Copenhagen, 1988), pp. 216-7.

50. D. Townshend, *Life and Letters of Mr Endymion Porter* (London, 1897), p. 117; Oman, op. cit. (Note 42), p. 343.

51. Nuttall, op. cit. (Note 39), pp. 307, 308.

52. N. Armstrong, *Fans, A Collector's Guide* (London, 1984), pp. 21, 24, 46-7, 63; Oman, op. cit. (Note 42), pp. 89, 343.

53. Oman, op. cit. (Note 42), pp. 159-61.

54. Nuttall, op. cit. (Note 39), p. 307.

55. Townshend, op. cit. (Note 50), p. 117.

56. Cited in Cunnington and Beard, op. cit. (Note 17), p. 235.

57. R. Strong, 'Charles I's clothes for the years 1633 to 1635', *Costume* 14 (1980), p. 89; W. Bray, 'Extract from the Wardrobe Account of Prince Henry', *Archaeologia* 11 (1794), p. 96.

58. McClure, op. cit. (Note 6), pp. 609, 616.

59. Cited in P. Gregg, *King Charles I* (London, 1981), p. 246, and in C. Carlton, *Charles I* (London, 1983), p. 130.

60. Hutchinson, op. cit. (Note 11), p. 35; cited in J.T. Cliffe, *The Puritan Gentry* (London, 1984), pp. 56-7.

61. For instance, proclamations of 1630 regulating silk weaving, and 1635 banning imported lace and haberdashery articles; Larkin, op. cit. (Note 1), pp. 289, 416.

62. Hutchinson, op. cit. (Note 11), p. 178.

63. Bowle, op. cit. (Note 7), p. 7.

64. R. Strong, *Henry, Prince of Wales and England's Lost Renaissance* (London, 1986), p. 12; Bowle, op. cit. (Note 7), p. 29.

65. *CSP Domestic 1625-6* (London, 1929), p. 21.

66. Strong, op. cit. (Note 57), pp. 77ff.

67. Bowle, op. cit. (Note 7), p. 316; cited in C. Hibbert, *The Court at Windsor* (London, 1964), p. 67.

68. Veale, op. cit. (Note 21), p. 23; Bowle, op. cit (Note 7), pp. 53, 88.

69. Strong, op. cit. (Note 57), pp. 77-8, 85; Bowle, op. cit. (Note 7), p. 233.

70. Strong, op. cit. (Note 57), pp. 76-7; Nuttall, op. cit. (Note 39), p. 308; Bowle, op. cit. (Note 7), p. 301.

71. Strong, op. cit. (Note 57), pp. 78, 77.

72. Cited in A. Mansfield, *Ceremonial Costume* (London, 1980), p. 58.

73. Strong, op. cit. (Note 57), pp. 81, 84, 88.

74. T. Herbert, *Memoirs of the Two last Years of the Reign of . . . King Charles I* (London, 1702), p. 175.

75. Oman, op. cit. (Note 42), p. 86.

76. Strong, op. cit. (Note 57), pp. 83-4, 87.

77. Nuttall, op. cit. (Note 39), p. 308.

78. Ibid., pp. 308, 307; Bowle, op. cit. (Note 7), p. 153.

79. Bowle, op. cit. (Note 7), p. 182.

80. Strong, op. cit. (Note 57), pp. 81, 84.

81. Mansfield, op. cit. (Note 72), pp. 49ff.

82. Millar, op. cit. (Note 48), pp. 86-7.

83. Strong, op. cit. (Note 57), p. 88.

84. Cunnington and Cunnington, op. cit. (Note 17) [Seventeenth Century], p. 67.

85. *CSP Venetian* 1659-61, p. 176.

86. Carisbrooke Castle contains other small items, as do other public and private collections. A shirt and handkerchief of the King's were auctioned at Sotheby's on 20 September 1988; their provenance was descent from the Jermyn family.

87. Cited in Cliffe, op. cit. (Note 60), p. 54.

11 Arms, Armour and Militaria

A. V. B. Norman

Armour

Marginal numerals refer to page and entry numbers in the *Inventories* (see p. 11)

Very luckily for us today, there never seems to have been any intention of dispersing the older historical portions of the Armouries of the Tower of London. Much of the early material has survived to form the basis of the present Royal Armouries, in spite of massive and frequently disastrous disposals, the last of which took place in 1974. Amongst earlier casualties was the armour used to decorate the Shield Gallery at Whitehall, which survived the Interregnum only to be dispersed or destroyed by the fire of 1691.

Since the contents of Greenwich Palace were reserved for the use of the state, it seems to have been the intention to preserve those of the royal armours housed there. However, the first post-Restoration inventory of the Tower Armouries, the 'View and Survey' taken in October 1660, states 'That, dureing the time of the late distraccions, The severall Armes, ammunicion, and Habiliments of Warre, formerly remaineing in the greene Gallery at Greenwich, were all taken and carryed away by sundry Souldiers, who left the doore open; That sundry of the said Armes were afterwards brought into the Tower of London by Mr. Anneslye, where they are still remaineing . . .' The 'View and Survey' also includes a list of 'Sundry rich Armours, and parcells of Armor, brought from Mr. Annesleys house, and now remaineing in severall Trunckes, within the office of the Armory at the Tower . . .'[1]

Edward Annesley had already been employed by the Greenwich Armouries possibly since 1631, and certainly since 1642, when he appears to have received a warrant from General Fairfax appointing him 'Clerk to the Armoury'. In 1647 he was appointed 'Surveyor', and on 18 May 1649 he was admitted as Master

Figure 106 *Charles I in a room with an armour trunk.* Engraving by William Hole [died 1624], undated. Reproduced by permission of the Trustees of the British Museum.

Workman at Greenwich. On the same day he was directed to search for and seize the rich arms and armour of the late King wherever concealed, as well as the implements of the armourer's craft in the Greenwich workshop.[2]

The list of these 'rich Armours' in the 'View and Survey' is augmented by a list made out by Annesley himself of the armours which he claimed had been 'browght from Greenewhyche to Guild Hall, and from thence to the Magazins in London about the Yeer 1644 and which hath remayned under my charge and Care ever Since'.[3] The last entry on Annesley's list reads 'One armor of great vallew of his Late Mties made last for his owne Person, and one Small Armor made for Prince Charles his now Matie both put to Sale at Somerset House ye which I procured of one Willit, to prevent ye Loss of it'. These clearly correspond to two entries in the sale inventories; 'A Sute of Armor of ye late Kings richly gilded', and 'a tronck with an Armor for ye whole body being partly gilt. 2 head peeces a head pece for a horse'. The first of these was valued at £100. It was listed among 'Goods belonging to ye late King' with no indication of whence it had come, but in the copies of the inventory its source is given as 'Mrs. Sherman; GW' (the last two letters standing for Greenwich), and its purchaser as de Critz.[4] Mrs Sherman was almost certainly the widow of one of the Greenwich armourers, Nicholas Sherman, appointed Master Workman in 1628.[5] The second, which was in the Armoury at St. James's Palace, was valued at £10 and sold to Major Edward Bass on 23 October 1651. What is being described in this case is a complete armour for a horseman, partly gilded, with a second helmet, and a shaffron (the head piece for a horse) all *en suite*, and apparently in its original travelling trunk. As far as I am aware, no original armour trunk survives today, but one example actually belonging to Charles I is illustrated in an engraved portrait of the King (Fig. 106).[6]

If Annesley is correct in his identification of the persons for whom these were made, it is not at all difficult to suggest a candidate for the first of these two armours. There can be little doubt that this is, as F.H. Cripps Day suggested, the cap-a-pie armour now in the Royal Armouries.[7] This is the most splendid of all surviving Dutch armours, chased over every inch of its surface and originally exceptionally thickly gilded. It is clearly identifiable in each successive inventory of the Tower Armouries, commencing with that of 1675-9 in which it is already ascribed to Charles I.[8]

The second of the armours in the sale inventories is much more problematic. The only armour which has always been known to have belonged to Charles II, on the grounds that it is fully described in the 'View and Survey' of 1660, and there ascribed to him, is the little engraved, silvered, and gilded harquebus armour in the Royal Armouries. Cripps Day suggested that this might be the second of the armours bought by Annesley, but, as it is an armour for a light horseman, it would be unlikely to have had a second helmet, and would certainly not have been equipped with a shaffron – 'a head pece for a horse'.[9] Furthermore, since it was originally gilt all over, as described in the 'View and Survey', it cannot be the armour described as being partly gilt in the sale inventories.

Charles Beard suggested, on the other hand, that the armour in question was probably the little Dutch cap-a-pie armour in the Royal Armouries, only in recent years identified with the future Charles II.[10] It is certainly of much earlier date and was probably originally made for his uncle, Henry, Prince of Wales. It appears to have been safely with the Royal Army at Oxford in 1644, if not earlier; at least it was used for William Dobson's portrait of Prince Charles, now in the Royal Collection, which is dated in that year (Fig. 107).[11] It also appears in a number of other portraits of courtiers and officers which Dobson painted in his time with the army at Oxford, for instance that of Sir William Fermoy of Easton Neston, now at Welbeck Abbey.[12] Its history, between its sojourn at Oxford and its reappearance in the Tower after the Restoration, is at present unknown. It is possible that it came into Parliamentary hands at the end of the end of the first Civil War. Cripps Day suggested that it was represented in the 'View and Survey' by the 'Curasseer Armor, richly guilt, made for his late Majestie, Charles the first, when he was young, consisting of a backe, brest, headpeece, Gorget, Pouldrons, and Vambraces, Culet, Cushes, and Gantlets'.[13] This was, in other words, a complete heavy cavalryman's armour terminating at the knee. If it was by any chance the same armour, its lower legs, second headpiece, and shaffron had by now all been mislaid.

The great difficulty in identifying the surviving Stuart armours from the various extant documents is that the one source of evidence in 1660, Edward

Figure 107 William Dobson: *Charles II as Prince of Wales*. Royal Collection: reproduced by gracious permission of Her Majesty The Queen.

Annesley, whose service bridged the Interregnum, clearly could not distinguish between the armours of Prince Henry and those of his brother. He identifies only one armour in his list of 1644 as being that of the elder brother; the 'Armor Cappapea made for Prince Henry his owne Person'. This, as Cripps Day demonstrated, was almost certainly the blued and gilt Greenwich armour, now at Windsor.[14] The reason that Annesley managed to recognize its correct owner is that is actually bears the Prince's initials.

154 [49]　　Also in the Armoury at St. James's was 'one Indian box wth an Indian Armor in it . . .', valued at £10 and sold to Bass on 23 October 1651. As Charles Beard suggested, this was almost certainly one of the two Japanese armours presented to King James VI by Tokugawa Hidetada.[15] These were delivered by Captain John Saris of the East India Company, in 1613, who reported that the young King at Edo had made them a 'Present of two entire Suits of *Japan* Armour, finely varnish'd, and a long sword and *Waggedash* for my self'.[16] Both armours disappear from view, as far as is known, until this entry in the sale inventory. However, as Beard pointed out, what may be one of these two armours is recorded in the 1660 'View and Survey'; 'Armour sent to his now Majesty, Charles the second, by the great Mogull, consisting of backe, breast, taces, headpiece, vizor and pieces of the greaves'.[17] The distinction between individual oriental lands seems to have been somewhat blurred in the seventeenth century, and after all the 'late distraccions' the new Clerk to the Armoury may perhaps be forgiven his mistake. Beard also suggested that a second Japanese armour, then at Windsor but now also on loan to the Royal Armouries, might be the other part of the gift of 1613.[18] Since the armour sold to Bass comprised 'a head peece a vizard. back & brest. 2 sleeves wth gantletts. one placard. for ye brest. & one for ye back. 2 peeces for ye Thÿghs & leggs. & 3 small brass plates', it seems more likely that this is an armour only recently lent to the Royal Armouries, which still has its sleeves, rather than another which has been in the Tower since 1660, and which lacks its sleeves.[19] As far as is known, there were no other armours, 'Indian' or oriental of any sort, available at the time to add to the confusion. The word 'placard' used here, normally meaning a reinforcing breastplate, probably refers to the *sode* (shoulder

defences). The three 'small brass plates' are probably the *kuwagata*, the horn-like supports for the badge.[20]

431 [75]   Only a few other pieces of armour of any importance are listed in the sale inventories, and unfortunately nothing is known about where the Trustees found them. The first was 'A Gorgett of Massy Gold Chased wth the Manner of a Battle Weighing 31 Oz[s] at 3. 10 per Oz'. This was valued at £108. 10s. and sent to the Mint, where it was presumably melted down. Gorgets of this sort, designed purely for parade and embossed or chased with battle scenes, usually after contemporary engravings, were extremely fashionable in the early seventeenth century. An example embossed in high relief is depicted in a portrait, attributed to Ferdinand Elle the elder, of a man aged thirty-four in 1631, said to be Henri de Lorraine, Marquis de Mouy, in the Musée des Beaux Arts, Reims.[21] An example in steel, embossed and chased with battle scenes after Antonio Tempesta, is in the Wallace Collection.[22] In the Musée de l'Armée in Paris is a particularly sumptuous silver gorget which belonged to Louis XIII.[23] It is splendidly embossed and chased, with a representation of the King receiving the tribute of the four Continents on the front, and triumphing in the guise of Herclues on the back.

432 [77]   Another important piece, the leather shield covered in gold and with the Gorgon's head in the centre, was valued at £120 and sold to Lane for £132. 12s. The fact that it was described as being Roman may indicate only that it was thought to have been made in Rome recently, but it is much more likely that it was thought to be antique. At a slightly later date, the famous shield of Dr Woodward became the subject of heated speculation soon after he bought it in 1693, over whether it was or was not a Classical antiquity.[24] To our eyes, it is obviously of the middle of the sixteenth century. The Gorgon's head was a favourite device for a Renaissance shield, the intention clearly being to recreate the shield of Perseus; for example, the famous painted leather target in the Uffizi, attributed to Caravaggio, and the magnificent target of embossed steel, counterfeit-damascened in gold and silver, made for the Emperor Charles V by members of the Negroli family of Milan in 1551, now in the Royal Armoury at Madrid.[25] Surviving jewelled shields are of exceptional rarity, but also in the Spanish Royal Armoury is a pair of oval iron shields, set with numerous precious stones, which were given by Carlo Emanuele I, Duke of Savoy, to Philip III of Spain in 1603. They were accompanied by a heavily jewelled sabre of rather oriental appearance, mounted in silver and gold.[26]

    In 1613, Carlo Emanuele, in the hopes of winning a princely husband for his daughter, lavished presents on members of our royal family, including a very elaborately decorated armour for Prince Charles, which is still at Windsor Castle.[27] It is not absolutely impossible, therefore, that the shield in the sale

431 [67]   inventory, and perhaps one of the scimitars, which sounds quite grand, were also presents from the Duke.[28]

431 [76]   The 'Grecian Helmett of Steele, Upon the Topp A Dragon, of Silver gilt. & 2 Large Gold Buckles' valued at £11 and sold for £12. 13s. 6d. is particularly interesting because, although as far as it is known, it no longer survives, it is just possible that a representation of it does. A helmet of Classical form, topped with a dragon, its wings unfortunately missing, is portrayed on the bronze bust of King Charles I by Hubert Le Sueur, thought to have been made about 1638, and now at Stourhead (Fig. 39).[29]

431 [69]   The 'Silver Gauntlett Ingrav[d]', which was sold to Francis Jones as part of a lot on 31 December 1649, might have been part of an engraved bullion armour, such as still survives in the old Electoral Armoury at Dresden, but, if so, nothing more seems to be known about it. The Dresden armour was made in 1591, for the Elector Christian I of Saxony, and presumably was intended for the parade preceding a tournament.[30]

431 [70]   Apart from a few pieces of broken armour and buckles, the only other pieces
181 [260]   are the 'Two. targetts', valued together at 5s. and sold for 1s. more. These were shields. 'I.G., gentleman' in his *Giacomo di Grassi his True Arte of Defence*, distinguishes between the 'rounde Target', by which he means a circular shield of some two feet in diameter, and the 'Square Target', by which he means a small trapezoidal buckler, used by some sixteenth-century duellists for parrying.[31] Bullet-proof shields were in fact used by some infantry well into the seventeenth century, particularly, it appears, in the German Lands. Prince Maurits of Nassau experimented with reintroducing the shield in the armies of the United Provinces, and, it appears, may have sent examples of his patterns to commanders potentially sympathetic to his ideas. Certainly, an example of the

larger type survives in the Royal Armoury at Stockholm, possibly a present to Gustavus Adolphus.[32] In view of the close links between Prince Maurits and Henry, Prince of Wales, it is conceivable that a pair of these shields had been sent to England.

Swords

With the sole exception of a little woodknife or hanger made about 1544 for Henry VIII, not a single sword which can be conclusively shown to have belonged to a Tudor or Stuart monarch survives in the present Royal Collection or in the Royal Armouries.[33] A few swords with blades bearing the royal arms or devices survive in other collections, for instance a blade with the arms of James VI and I in the collection formed by Sir Walter Scott at Abbotsford.[34] A robe sword in the Wallace Collection has on its blade the initials and badge of Henry, Prince of Wales.[35] There are several swords at Windsor Castle identified as being those of the Stuart kings, but they were probably all acquired by George IV at the end of the eighteenth or beginning of the nineteenth century and the identifications must, therefore, be regarded as not proven.

The fact that only three or four swords with two-edged blades were listed may, no doubt, be explained by the likelihood that the King took with him any weapon that could be pressed into service. Presumably he also took at least some of the swords he wore in civilian dress, those which, at the time, would have been called rapiers.[36]

383 [794] Of the remaining swords which sound as though they might have military potential, only the 'baskett hilt sword with two edges' is described sufficiently for any useful comment to be possible. It was valued at 16s. and sold for £1. 1s. It presumably resembled one of a number of munition swords in the Royal Armouries with either a plain or a very sparsely decorated basket hilt.[37] The

Figure 108   Jacob van Doort: *Charles I as Prince of Wales*. Royal Collection: reproduced by gracious permission of Her Majesty The Queen.

383 [798-9]	description of the other two broad swords merely indicates that they had broad, two-edged blades, and that the second had a brass hilt.
383 [797]	'One Ancient sword in a blacke scabberd', valued at £2 and sold for 10s. more, could have been of any date. If any tradition of its original owner existed at this time, no trouble was taken to record it.

383 [798-9] description of the other two broad swords merely indicates that they had broad, two-edged blades, and that the second had a brass hilt.

383 [797] 'One Ancient sword in a blacke scabberd', valued at £2 and sold for 10s. more, could have been of any date. If any tradition of its original owner existed at this time, no trouble was taken to record it.

383 [792-3] The two black rapiers were for wear in civilian dress; the sort of sword shown, for instance, in the portrait by Jacob van Doort of Charles, painted immediately before his accession in 1625 (Fig. 108).[38] Almost all contemporary military writers agree on the unsuitability of the rapier for war. Sir John Smithe, writing in 1590, says that 'Rapier blades being so narrow, and of so small substance, and made of verie hard temper to fight in privat fraies, in lighting with any blow upon armour, do presently breake, and so become unprofitable'.[39] The word 'handle', at this date, could refer to either the grip or the hilt. The fact that the colour was mentioned probably means that the hilts of these two swords were of black steel. The low values set on them, £1. 1s. and £1. 6s. respectively, suggests that they were undecorated and possibly old fashioned.

383 [791] 'A short little sword wth a greene velvett scabberd & a Christall handle' sounds much more interesting, but not to the valuer, apparently, who thought it worth only 10s. In the event it made 15s. A little cross-hilted sword in the old Imperial Armoury in Vienna, dated on its blade 1647, has a hilt and grip of rock crystal mounted in gold set with tiny cameos.[40] The earliest illustration recorded so far of anyone wearing a sword of this type in Britain is the portrait of William, second Duke of Hamilton, painted by Adriaen Hanneman in 1650.[41]

Incidentally, swords of this type frequently have blades with three or more longitudinal ridges for part of their length. Presumably it was a blade of this sort

383 [789] which was fitted on the 'short 2 edged sword wth 3 ribbs'.

383 [795] The 'One little Tucke wth pearle upon ye hilt', valued at £1 and sold for 6s. more, would have been distinguished by having a blade designed solely for thrusting and probably of square or triangular section.[42] Beyond the fact that the hilt was decorated with 'pearle', presumably mother-of-pearl, no clue is given as to what type of guards were involved. The sword of Henri IV of France in the Musée de l'Armée in Paris, and its matching dagger in the Wallace Collection, are both decorated on blade and hilt with small oval plaques of engraved mother-of-pearl.[43]

383 [790] It would be tempting to speculate about the source of the hilts of the 'two edged sword wth an Inlayde handle', valued at 15s. and sold for £1. 2s. and of the

383 [796] 'sword wth a rich Inlayed hilt', valued at £5 and sold for £6. 10s. 'Inlayed' in this context would have meant inlaid with a precious metal. Claude Blair has suggested that the silver encrusting, often accompanied by very fine counterfeit-damascening in gold, found on many hilts of English type, including the robe sword of Prince Henry in the Wallace Collection, was very probably the work of Robert South, the royal cutler during the reigns of both James I and Charles I.[44]

419 [15] One can but wonder as to what was so very remarkable about the sword in

431 [74] the care of Colonel Humphrey, that it was valued at £42, many times the price of all but one other sword in the sale. The exception, which lacked its blade, perhaps because, like two steel hilts of this period at Schloss Ambras, it was awaiting its day, was valued at £30 and actually sold for £33. 9s. to Francis Jones on 22 December 1649.[45] It was described as 'The handle of a Sword of Steele the Pommel and Shell of Gold Enrich'd, Rubies, and Pearle'. The 'Shell' was presumably a solid guard projecting from the outer side of the hilt to prevent an opponent's weapon from sliding down the blade on to the swordsman's hand. From the 1630s onward, particularly on the sort of light swords becoming fashionable for civilian wear, guards of this sort frequently took the form of a cockleshell, usually slightly inclined towards the blade.[46]

One of the strangest things about the collection of royal swords is the large

382-3 [780-87] number of scimitars included; eight in the charge of the Yeoman of the Wardrobe,

431 [67] Clement Kynnersley, as well as another in a different list. The values given to them ranged from 16s. to £6, and the top price, reached by two of them, turned out to be £7. 13s. The reason these two did rather better than the others was

382 [781-2] because both had silver hilts, the one enamelled and the other of pierced work. The 'Chape', mentioned in two of the entries, was the metal guard at the end of the scabbard.

The word scimitar comes from a Persian word, *shamshir*, which refers to a sword with a rather light, curved blade, but it tends to be used in the seventeenth century, as it is occasionally even today, for almost any curved sword, regardless of its place of origin. The compilers of the inventories were almost certainly incapable of distinguishing between a weapon of Oriental origin and one of European manufacture, and may even have included the sort of hunting sword with a short curved blade, known as a hanger and later as a 'cutto', which appears quite often in English portraits after the accession of the Stuarts.[47] In the second volume of his extraordinary encyclopaedia of heraldic terms, *The Academy of Armory*, prepared for publication in the 1680s, Randle Holme lists what he calls a 'Scottish Hanger' and includes in his decription the phrase ' . . . these kind of semiters, or short crooked swords . . . '[48]

Other than these hangers, curved swords appear only very rarely in English portraits of this period. However, when Sir Thomas Salusbury had his family painted about 1640, he was shown wearing a richly mounted Moroccan sabre in a red scabbard.[49] It may be that some of these 'semeters' were genuinely oriental. Any gifts received by James I, or his sons, from the Shah of Persia, for instance, would almost certainly have included some swords. A true *shamshir* blade in the Royal Armouries is mounted in a hilt of English make which bears on it arms borne by several branches of the Shirley or Sherley family.[50] Sir Anthony Shirley of Wiston in Kent, and his brother Robert, both travelled to Persia in 1598 and later, and both men, at different times, acted as ambassador from the Shah to King James.[51]

The only sword listed in the sale inventories which can be identified with reasonable certainty today, apart possibly from the three swords in the Regalia, is the 'large sword', valued at £2, in the custody of Colonel Christopher Whichcote, the Parliamentary Governor of Windsor Castle. This is almost certainly the great two-handed bearing sword still preserved in St. George's Chapel in the Castle (Fig. 109). It has long been identified as having belonged to Edward III. Sir Guy Laking, Keeper of the King's Armoury, suggested that it might be the sword which was originally hung up over the founder's stall in the Garter Chapel, offered at the high altar on his death in 1377.[52] He refers to a payment in the

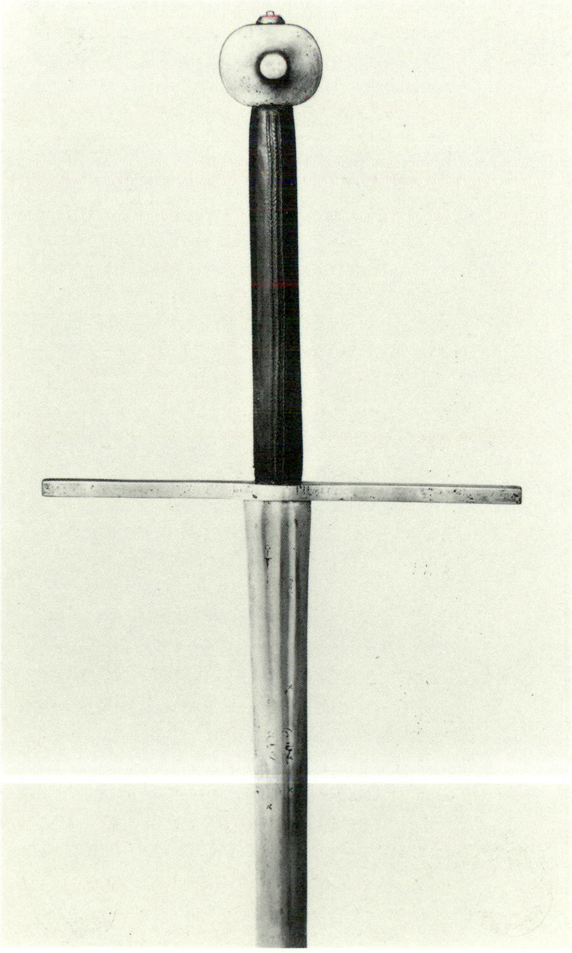

294 [221]

Figure 109 *Two-handed sword*, St. George's Chapel, Windsor. Photograph courtesy of the Royal Armouries: reproduced by gracious permission of Her Majesty The Queen.

precentor's accounts, made in 1387/8, for repairing a sword, said to be that of the founder of the College, and to a second one in 1615, for 'making cleane the Twoe hande Sworde whiche hangith by K: Edward the 3: picture'.

Personal Firearms

Also in the Armoury at St. James's Palace were forty sporting guns and a carbine, which may also have been a sporting weapon. All but the last were apparently in two presses, presumably specially fitted gun-cupboards.

153 [37], 154 [51]   There were ten 'burding peeces', each valued at 15s., and thirty more valued at only 10s. Randle Holme in the second volume of his *Academy of Armory*, distinguishes between the fowling piece, the standard shot gun of the day, which, he states had a long barrel, anything between 'a yard and a quarter, to 7 foot, or two yards, and a hafe long', and the cocking or birding piece which had a short one of smaller bore. The birding piece 'is the least of guns shott of with both hands, holding the Butt end . . . to the right shoulder, fireing it with the right hand and supporting it with the left'.[53] The very small calibre of these weapons made them quite unsuitable for service, which is probably the reason that they had been abandoned at St. James's. Only two birding pieces are known to survive today which might just possibly at one time have been in these presses. They are both small, gilt-brass Scottish guns, with extendable stocks each ending in a closed crown. Both bear the mark attributed to the gunmaker James Low of Dundee.[54] One is in the Royal Armouries, and bears a partly illegible date to be read as 1612, 1613, 1618, or 1619. The other, which is in the Royal Museum of Scotland in Edinburgh, is dated 1624.

153 [38]   The only other firearm found by the Trustees in the Armoury at St. James's was a 'plaine Carbine', valued at only 6s. 8d. and sold to Henry Creech on 12 July 1650. By this date the name carbine was already being applied to a short gun of relatively small calibre for use on horseback. It usually had a loose-ring, or a ring and slide, on the left side, so that it could be hung on the swivel of the carbine-belt which was worn over the left shoulder. The carbine then hung at the right hip ready for action. For instance, in 1632 John Cruso, in his *Militarie Instuctions for the Cavallrie*, describes the carbine as having a barrel of twenty-four bore, thirty inches long, and states that it is to be 'hung on a belt by a swivell'.[55] He also states that it requires a 'flask and touch-box'–the containers for gunpowder for the main charge and the priming charge respectively. Presumably this must have been an old weapon, or of poor quality, otherwise the King would have taken it with him, as he seems to have done with all the other firearms and their flasks and bullet-moulds thought in any way suitable to be placed in the hands of troops. New carbines bought by the Board of Ordnance in 1640 cost £1. 10s. each with all their equipment.[56] A portrait at Dunham Massey, Cheshire, of *Sir John Booth*, shows him in light horseman's armour with his right hand resting on the barrel of his carbine.[57]

154 [39]   The 'powder flaske like a horne', valued at 5s. had probably been overlooked at the evacuation.

218 [29]   A single firearm was found at Wimbledon House; 'A Blunderbuss of brass', valued at 10s. and sold to Roger Humfreys on 28 January 1651. This appears to be the earliest reference in this country to a gun of this type. Sir James Turner, in his *Pallas Armata*, defines blunderbusses as 'short Hand-guns of a great bore, wherein they may put several Pistol or Carabine-Balls, or small Slugs of Iron'.[58] The most memorable characteristic of the blunderbuss is the flared muzzle, which, although of little or no ballistic significance, must have had a considerable effect in intimidating anyone at which it was pointed. Although usually thought of as a weapon for self-protection, blunderbusses were sometimes issued to the armed forces. For instance, '100 Brass blunder bushes' were issued for use on the Hispaniola Expedition in 1654.[59]

A few other military guns found at Vauxhall are dealt with elsewhere (pp. 363-4).

Other Weapons

Other than the weapons already discussed, only a very few are mentioned, and it can only be assumed that every available weapon had been pressed into service for the Royalist forces. The Earl of Clarendon, in his *History of the Rebellion*, mentions how poorly armed the Royalists were, and this is confirmed by the records of their Ordnance department.[60] The 'Racks for Armo^r' in the Hall at Ludlow Castle, where no other armour is recorded, suggest that the bottom of every barrel had been well scraped.

229 [145]

Only two further richly decorated weapons are listed. One was a mace with a spherical head set with spikes, its 'handle', presumably meaning its grip, covered with enamelled gold plates. It is described as 'A Saxon kings Mace used in War'. Valued at £30. 10*s*, it was sold to Lane on 31 December 1649, for £37. 8*s*. Nothing seems to be known about Anglo-Saxon maces, and it seems rather more likely that this was a particularly richly decorated example of a fairly common type of Italian sixteenth-century, ball-headed mace.[61]

431 [73]

An ordinary steel mace from Hampton Court, valued at 2*s*. 6*d*. was sold for 3*s*. This type of weapon had quite gone out of vogue by the seventeenth century, although it survived as the insignia of a commander, in some areas of Eastern Europe, until the early nineteenth century.

181 [261]

On the other hand, the polaxe, a combination of hammer (i.e. poll) and either an axe, or a fluke, had retained its popularity. John Vernon, in his *Young Horseman*, published in 1644, states that 'A poll axe is very necessary for a trooper, for if you should encounter a troop of Curassiers where your sword can do no good but little execution, your poll axe may be an advantage to you to offend your enemie'.[62] A simple workmanlike example, formerly in the Armoury of Apethorpe House in Northamptonshire, is now in the Royal Armouries.[63] The portrait of Sir Alexander Radclyffe (1579-99), shows him holding the kind of polaxe which has a rear fluke, while the portrait of the little Thomas Pope, future fourth Earl of Downe, by Adriaen Hanneman, shows him wearing a conventional axe.[64] Elaborately decorated polaxes on long shafts were carried by the gentlemen of the Bodyguard when on ceremonial duty, and these are occasionally shown in their portraits, for instance that of William, first Lord Sherard, attributed to Gheeraerdts, and dated 1633.[65]

The second richly decorated weapon, apparently hurriedly abandoned by the departing Household, was 'A Large Pole Ax cov[ere]^d wth plates of Silv^r Engrav^d'. It was sold to Lane for £16, with a pair of what are described as 'Roman Kn^{ts} Spurs Inlaid wth Gold'. It was not made clear whether this was a long or short weapon.

432 [78]

Since it is unlikely that the spurs were thought to be of recent Roman manufacture, they may have been excavated, as presumably also were the 'Ancient Roman Trumpett of Brass gilt wth Gold and the Heads of Seven Spears, and nine Roman Knights Rings of gold'.

431 [72]

The 'old halbert' at Denmark House, valued at only 1*s*., was presumably the weapon of an ordinary soldier, rather than the elaborate one carried by an officer, or was in exceptionally poor order. The halberd, a type of long-shafted axe with a rear fluke and a terminal spike, was outmoded as a fighting weapon in Northern Europe by this date, but the Royalist forces, in their desperation, pressed many old ones into service.[66] It survived in the British Army as the weapon of sergeants until 1792.

255 [115]

The two javelins tipped with silver are likely to have been hunting spears rather than throwing spears, which at this time were normally referred to as darts.[67] The portrait of James Stuart, Duke of Lennox and Richmond, painted by Van Dyck, shows him with a boar spear in the background, which is probably the sort of thing referred to in the sale inventory.[68]

431 [69]

A few exotic weapons, other than the scimitars, are listed. These include three Turkish bows, all broken, and thirty-seven arrows, presumably to fit them. These would have been bows of composite construction and, therefore, very apt to break in inexperienced hands. They were all valued at 4*s*. along with a mysterious object described as 'a buff Maile'. Assuming that the word buff is adjectival, this might be mail or box made of buff leather. If however it is a noun, it might be a face-defence made of mail, in this context possibly something oriental.

154 [53]

The two 'Indian bowes' at Hampton Court, may have been from America or India, or from almost any part of the Far East, since contemporary writers did not always draw a clear distinction between Oriental countries (see p. 279).

182 [273]

181 [268]   The green velvet archer's bracer, that is the guard for the left wrist, may have been intended to go with the Turkish bows. It was valued at only 1s. and sold for 6d. more.

182 [274]   The 'Two. Indian weapons of wodd for ye Cashawes', were presumably something like war clubs. The name of the tribe (if such it is) does not appear to be recorded elsewhere, at least in this form. There was a group called Casinawa, Cashinawa, or Caxinawa in East Peru, which was very probably reached before this date, and another group, the Cashwena, Cauishana, Caishana, Cayuishama, Cauxanas, or Cayuishana, which lived on the Rio Negro in Peru, and had certainly been known to the Spanish for many years. The term Cashus was used for 'governor' among the Moqwex-Cconucu of Columbia.[69] The *Oxford English Dictionary* also refers to a presumably related term, cacique, with as alternative spellings, cacike, cazike, and cassique, meaning a native chief or 'prince' of the aborigines in the West Indies and adjacent parts of America.

Horse Furniture

Very little horse harness is included in the inventories, probably because, as in the case of the armour and weapons, everything deemed serviceable had already been taken away by the King himself, or by light-fingered rebel soldiers.

383-4 [800-802]   Henry Brown, Keeper of the Wardrobe at Denmark House, had in his charge three complete sets of harness for saddle horses, covered with richly embroidered velvet, respectively crimson, carnation, and green. The last two, which were brought from Tennant, the saddler, and may therefore have been new, their delivery having been postponed by the troubles, were valued at £20 and £30 respectively, and were sold to David Murray, the King's tailor, on 23 October 1651. These two probably resembled the two saddles of red velvet richly embroidered in gold thread at Wistow Hall, Leicestershire, which are traditionally said to have been left behind by the King and Prince Rupert after the battle of Naseby in 1645.[70] A comparable set of rich horse furniture is shown in Van Dyck's portrait of *Charles I with M. de St. Antoine*, painted in 1633 (Pl. 68), and in the slightly later equestrian portrait of *Charles I* dated 1635-6 (Pl. 69).

    The third set, which was of crimson velvet, not only 'very richly embroydered', but also decorated with pearls, included its foot cloth. It was valued at £2,000, an enormous sum, and sold either to George Greene's syndicate or to that of Thomas Baggley, on the same date as its companions. The foot cloth could be either a relatively narrow strip of cloth little wider than the saddle, or could cover the entire crupper of the horse. The second kind is illustrated in two royal portraits; that of Anne of Denmark, painted by Paul van Somer in 1617,[71] and that of King Charles and Henrietta Maria by Daniel Mytens, painted about 1630-32 (Pl. 64). In the first the cloth is lavishly embroidered, and in the second it is passemented with bullion lace in a fretty pattern. Nothing in the least comparable to this resplendent creation of crimson velvet and gold thread, powdered with pearls, survives in this country today. However, some idea of its likely appearance is given by the horse furniture in the Royal Armoury in Stockholm, commissioned in Paris for the coronation of Queen Christina in 1650. It is of purple velvet lavishly embroidered with a reticulated pattern of acanthus foliage in gold thread and sprinkled with pearls.[72]

431 [68]   'A furniture for a Horse of Crimson Velvett being Studed wth Silver Enamelled', valued at £20, may also have been a set of saddle and bridle. However, it could equally have been for a led horse, when the saddle would have been replaced by a housing. It was sold on 29 December 1649 to Colonel Christopher Whichcote.

Toys and Models

The Armoury at St. James's contained a fascinating collection of military models, presumably made for one of the two sons of James I, or for the future Charles II, or perhaps more probably for all three. The collection included companies and troops of toy soldiers, and models of artillery, of fortifications, and of the waggons and equipment which were required by a seventeenth-century army in the field.

What may be the only survivors of this collection are a group of ten miniature brass cannon bearing the initials and device of the future Charles II, all now in the Royal Armouries. [73] They are in two groups of five, those of the first group are inscribed JOHN BROWNE MADE THIS PEECE 1638, and those of the second, THOMAS PIT MADE THIS PEECE 1639. H. L. Blackmore, in his catalogue of the ordnance in the Royal Armouries, identified these as some of the fifteen 'peeces of brass ordnance. each one. about 22 ynches long. being mounted on their carrages' of the sale inventory, thirteen of which were said to have been bought by the merchant, Major Edward Bass.[74] Blackmore suggested that eventually, like so many of the other objects in the sale, they may have found their way home again, and that they might be the 'small brass peeces of inch bore', fourteen of which are listed in the 'Generall Remain of all the Ordnance' taken in 1665. The original carriages were destroyed in the fire in the Grand Storehouse of the Tower of London in 1841. Unfortunately, since the barrels of these little cannon range from two feet to two feet five and a half inches in length, compared with 'about 22 ynches' for those in the sale inventory, the identification is not absolutely certain.

Presumably many royal and noble children had such miniature batteries. A portrait at Rosenborg Castle in Copenhagen, by Karel van Mander, of the future Christian V, aged about five, in martial stance but still in long clothes, shows him with a number of tiny cannon at his feet.[75] In 1606, Louis XIII was given a silver cannon by Monsieur de Rosny, while in May 1616 he is recorded as playing in his fort at Plessie with 'des petits canons tirés par des chiens'.[76] The fort was presumably a child-size construction in the policies of the château. The sale inventories do include 'A fort of wood', which was at Richmond Palace in 1649. As it was valued at only 10s. it was presumably quite small. It went to one of the King's creditors, Philip Lavender. There were also '2 modells of. parapitts' at St. James's.

Prince Henry did have have at least one full-size cannon. The muzzle of a bronze falcon, very beautifully decorated in relief with foliate strapwork and his crest, survived the fire of 1841, and is still in the Royal Armouries.[77] Perhaps it was used on the artillery range at St. James's, if that was sufficiently large. A full-size cannon, also elaborately decorated, made for the future Charles I in 1621, fell victim to this same fire.[78]

The '2 brass drakes 2 Carrages & a linstock' were probably also toys. The drake was the name of a kind of cannon, but, like all the seventeenth-century names for artillery pieces, does not seem to have been applied consistently. Drakes seem to have first been used in the the army or Prince Maurits of Nassau as battalion guns firing a charge consisting of a large number of small shot. The type is thought to have been introduced to this country by Sir Edward Cecil, who bought ten for the Cadiz expedition of 1625.[79] In 1627 John Smith defined a lintstock as 'a handsome carved stick, more than halfe a yard long, with a Cocke at the one end to hold fast his Match, and a sharpe pike in the other to sticke it fast upon the Deck or platforme upright'.[80] This is the instrument for conveying the burning slow-match to the touch-hole of the gun and thus firing it. 'Platform' in this case means the floor of the gun emplacement.

Two other pieces of toy or miniature artillery were found at St. James's, 'one brasse morter peece. one other of wood bound wth yron'. These were valued at £2. 10s. and sold to the widow Ann Culver on 2 August 1650. What may have been the carriages for these two are to be found listed with a toy sledge, perhaps also intended for the transport of pieces of ordnance. A mortar made of wood sounds dangerous even if it was very small. It may not have been a working model of course. On the other hand, there is just a possibility that it was a small copy of the famous wooden gun built for Henry VIII for the siege of Boulogne in 1544, another victim of the fire in the Grand Storehouse.[81]

Apart from the miniature artillery, many other military toys suitable for the education of a young prince are listed. The word 'Ingin' was used at that time in the same way as the word device is today. It could signify something without moving parts, a chevaux de frise for instance, or something with working parts, for example the 'Ingin for driveing piles', which must have been for driving in the supports of bridges and foundations. A 'Modell. of an Ingin against horses' was probably some kind of portable barricade to be set up in front of an infantry unit, in those days before the invention of the bayonet, such as a chevaux de frise made of rows of crossed pikes. Such a device is illustrated by Henry Hexham in his Art *of Fortification*, while an actual example survives in the Styrian Arsenal at Graz.[82] It may, on the other hand, have been a turn-pike, a stout tree-trunk, some ten or twelve feet long, from which projected numerous ash spikes tipped with steel. These could be linked end to end to make a barrier of any required length. Robert Ward in his *Animadversions of Warre*,[83] advises their use 'against Horse and Foote upon all straights and passages'.

153 [28]   The 'carrages. for secureing a breach' were presumably something similar, but with wheels and perhaps some sort of shafts to help in manoeuvring them into position over the rubble of a breach in the ramparts. It may have been equipped with small guns, or batches of muskets, like the one illustrated by Robert Ward, which he describes as 'a frame of Musquets . . . to be made and ordered for the defence of a Breach . . . '[84]

153 [28]   The 'modaile. or Ingin for a Jack or hans', was a screw-jack for lifting heavy weights such as gun barrels, probably like one of those illustrated by Wilhelm Dillich in his *Kriegsbuch*.[85] Hans is simply the German nickname equivalent to our Jack.

153 [28]   The 'modeles of hanbarrowes' probably looked very much like the wooden wheelbarrows to be found in any English garden until quite recently. Henry Hexham illustrates two views of such a wheelbarrow.[86] They were used for moving earth during the building of fortifications, and, no doubt, for the local transport so essential for any cavalry regiment lying in quarters.

153 [31]   The 'Modells for feild Mills' were of mills for grinding corn to supply flour for the men's bread on the march, and were probably mounted on carts or wagons. 'Hand mills to grynde coren of that country' appear on the list of supplies to be taken on the Hispaniola Expedition in 1654.[87] The 'percullis' of this entry was presumably a model of a portcullis. The '2 Mols for gills' were almost certainly models of gills, the pairs of large timber wheels mounted on a very stout axle used for moving timber in the woods and woodyards, as well as for the transport of gun barrels. A variety of scaling ladders, including folding ones, are illustrated by Dillich.[88] The little quadrant and square were miniature surveying instruments.

153 [32]   The '4 durty carrages', valued at £1, are a puzzle. Are they perhaps the same as Robert Ward's 'Cru-wagons', used to transport earth to fortifications under construction?[89]

153 [28]   The '3 small boards wth horses', were probably the model teams for some of
154 [41]   the little carts and wagons, while the '8 boards of little horss', may represent the
153 [33]   files or troops of cavalry to accompany the '17. boards wth foot companies'. The word horse used like this in the singular in a plural context usually means cavalry. These infantrymen were sold for £2 to Edward Baker, and a further fourteen
154 [42]   'boards of Companies' for £1. 8s. to de Critz, who also bought the little cavalrymen for 16s.

154 [44]   There was also a little camp for the cavalry, which was sold with three small
154 [45]   'pavillions' for £2, and another camp for the infantry, which sold for £1. 10s. The pavilions were probably ridge tents of relatively large size suitable for the accommodation of senior officers. The method of laying out an encampment applicable to each arm of the service is dealt with in many of the contemporary manuals, for instance Henry Hexham, in his *Principles of the Art Military*, gives a separate plan for each type of camp.[90]

153 [28]   The collection also included a model bridge, and, even more interestingly, 'a
154 [46-7] board wth 2 boates' and '3 boates one on a Cart'. These boats were almost certainly the pontoons used in building a bridge of boats, something essential to any army on the march in hostile country. The 'modell for. a brige' may have been the roadway to lay across the boats. Robert Ward illustrates the necessary equipment, including the carts for the boats and their teams.[91] His boats were leather-covered in the Dutch fashion, but elsewhere hulls sheeted in metal were used.

Although so very little, if any, of this group of military models survives, it is possible to gain some idea of what it might once have looked like. In the Germanisches Nationalmuseum, Nuremberg, is still preserved the greater part of the collection of some three hundred models made by the city's Master Armourer, Johann Carl (1587-1665). In his portrait engraved by J. von Sandrart, he is shown holding his gunner's instruments, and with a small model cannon on the table beside him. His collection besides individual soldiers, muskets and their rests, and swords, includes many things similar to those described in the sale inventories; for instance cannons and mortars of many sizes with their carriages and beds, as well as their equipment, among which are two different patterns of linstock. There are also several heavy tripod-mounted shoulder-guns, which would have been useful to defend a breech, and, better still, a more sophisticated version of Ward's 'frame of Musquets', a two-wheeled carriage carrying four batteries, each of fourteen short barrels, intended to be fired in volleys. A number of tents can be compared with those sold with the cavalry encampment. The many little wagons with their wooden teams include a field forge with all its tools, and best of all, just such a wagon and team as was described in the sale inventories with its boat for building a pontoon-bridge.[92]

154 [44]

Vauxhall

424-5 [1-12]

Potentially, one of the most interesting parts of the sale inventories should have been the contents of the various workshops at Vauxhall in the custody of John Trenchard, which were reserved from the sale. Unfortunately, not only are its descriptions extremely meagre, even by the standards of this inventory, but it seems that almost all the equipment had already been removed, including most of the hand tools; the filing bench had no files, for instance. The Trustees seem to have been unable to go upstairs, except to the garrets, where all they found was a number of broken models. Nor did they penetrate the private apartments and workshops of John Bishop, 'the Engineer & Overseer of all the Instruments of Warre, made, moulded & contrived in Fauxhall', presumably because he had the blessing of the Committee of Lords and Commons for the Safety of the Kingdom, by an order of 14 June 1643.

Another inventory was taken of the whole area in 1645, by an order the same Committee made on 26 September.[93] The auditor, Philip Darell, listed a large number of experimental models made by Caspar Kalthoff for the Marquis of Worcester. In addition he inventoried the contents of the boring room, the melting house, the founding room (including the furnaces for founding guns) and the proof range where finished pieces were tested, all rented to William Lambert, the gunfounder. He failed, however to obtain admission to the house containing the workshop for leather guns, the key of which was held by Colonel James Wemyss, 'a Scottishman', the nephew of Robert Scott, the man who is said to have introduced such guns to the British service.

It is clear that in 1645 the rooms had been rather fuller than they were in 1649, and in the interim a good deal of moving about had taken place. For instance, the 'great Forge room' of the sale inventory had contained 'three forges with three paire of bellows, two Anvills with Stocks, one iron saddle with a stocke, two Viceboards, one great paire of Scales with two halfe hundreds and one quarterne

424 [5]

of leaden weights, one Crane of wood with an iron chaine.' The 'modell of a Watch for unruly Coach horses', which in 1649 was the only thing in the Great Forge Room other than the filing bench, had previously been in the the First Model Room, where it is described as 'the modell of a Coach made of purpose to let loose the horses, if they shold prove wild'.

A few words in this part of the inventory may need some explanation. A

424 [1]

'Bickhorne' is an anvil with a point or beak at each end.[94] The 'Cutter' was probably one of the very large shears or snips for cutting plate metal in the cold. The end of one handle was fixed in a great block of timber to give it stability. A

424 [2]

'Cogg' is strictly one of the wooden pegs projecting from the rim of a cogwheel, but here it probably stands for the wheel itself. The teeth of such a cogwheel would have engaged the bars of a trundle. This consists of two discs of timber mounted a little distance apart on a timber axle, connected by a series of parallel staves or bars placed near their edge. The 'Mill for boreing of Ordinance' would

424 [3]

have been a large drill for the bores of cannon which were cast solid, that is

424 [10]

without a cavity in the barrel. The 'stilling for beare' was probably one of the three 'wooddenn frames to set beere upon', which had been in the cellar of 'Wm. Joulden Engineer' in 1645.

Apart from the actual furnaces, the only equipment specifically for founding

424 [12]

still in the foundry appear to be the 'Seaven ovalls for round bords for sweepes', which are almost certainly the templates used in making moulds.[95]

424 [11]

The '38 dragoones with Snapphances' were short guns, akin to the carbine but of greater bore, in this case with flintlocks as opposed to the more expensive wheel-locks. Gervase Markham in his *Souldiers Accidence*, says that 'Dragons are short peeces of 16. inches the Barrell, and full Musquet bore . . . '[96] In 1645 there had been fifty 'snaphance Dragoones', as well as an 'Engine of brasse for six Musquett barrells to Charge at the breech', in the second Upper Chamber. That these particular dragoons were in fact of musket bore, that is they carried a bullet weighing one twelfth of a pound, is supported by the presence of the 'nineteene muskett barrells cut dragoone length', which were in the 'first Garrett from the Orchard' in 1645. On 10 January of that same year, John Silke, the Whitechapel gunmaker, signed a contract to supply 'Two hundred snaphaunce Dragoones full bore & proofe at 12s 4d a peece'.[97]

Notes

I would like to express my gratitude to my colleague Sarah Barter Bailey, Librarian at the Royal Armouries, for a great deal of help in the preparation of these notes.

1. The 'View and Survey' of 1660 was published in full by A. Way in 'Survey of the Tower Armoury in the year 1660', *Archaeological Journal* 4 (1847), pp. 341-54. Extracts were published with a commentary by F. H. Cripps Day in *Fragmenta Armamentaria* (Frome, 1934), I, pt. iv, pp. 74-90.

2. Cripps Day, op. cit. (Note 1), I, pt. ii, pp. 117-8; O. F. G. Hogg, *The Royal Arsenal* (London, 1963), I, pp. 82, 103, 104.

3. Annesley's list was published by Cripps Day, op. cit. (Note 1), I, pt. ii, pp. 118-9, and with a commentary in I, pt. iv, pp. 66-73.

4. This reference was first pointed out by C. R. Beard in *Notes on the Barberini and some Allied Armours* (Blackburn, 1924), p. 31.

5. Cripps Day, op. cit. (Note 1), I, pt. ii, pp. 114-7.

6. G. F. Laking, *A Record of European Armour and Arms through Seven Centuries* (London, 1920-22), V, p. 57, fig. 1465A.

7. Royal Armouries, London, inv. no. II. 91; Cripps Day, op. cit. (Note 1), I, pt. iv, pp. 71-2.

8. C. J. ffoulkes, *Inventory and Survey of the Armouries of the Tower of London* (London, 1916), I, pp. 83-9, specifically p. 88.

9. Royal Armouries, London, inv. no. II. 92; Cripps Day, op. cit. (Note 1), I, pt. IV, pp. 72-3.

10. Royal Armouries, London, inv. no. II.90; C. Beard, 'Some Tower armour pedigrees', *Connoisseur* 87 (1931), pp. 159-69, specifically p. 163.

11. Exhibited in 'Royal Review of the British Soldier' at The Queen's Gallery, London, 1967-8, cat. no. 1; illustrated in M. Rogers, *William Dobson, 1611-46* (London, 1983), p. 36, fig. 14.

12. Rogers, op. cit. (Note 11), cat. no. 24.

13. Cripps Day, op. cit. (Note 1), I, pt. ii, p. 69.

14. G. F. Laking, *The Armoury of Windsor Castle* (London, 1904), cat. no. 678.

15. Beard, op. cit. (Note 10), pp. 162-3.

16. J. Harris, *Navigantium atque Itinerantium Bibliotheca* (London, 1625), I, lib. II, cap. xxiii, p. 127. A *waggedash* was probably in reality a *wakizashi*, the shorter of the two swords carried by a Japanese gentleman.

17. Beard, op. cit. (Note 10), p. 163.

18. Royal Armouries, London, inv. no. A.L.27; Beard, op. cit. (Note 10), p. 164.

19. Royal Armouries, London, inv. nos. A.L.27 and XXVI. 1A, respectively.

20. I am grateful to my colleague Thom Richardson, Senior Curator of Armour in the Royal Armouries, for all the help he gave me in trying to identify the armours in the sale inventories.

21. Exhibited in 'The Age of Louis XIV', the Winter Exhibition at the Royal Academy, 1958, cat. no. 107.

22. Wallace Collection, London, cat. no. A238.

23. Musée de l'Armée, Paris, cat. no. G. 249. J.-P. Reverseau, *Les Armures des Rois de France au Musée de l'Armée* (Saint-Julien-du-Sault, 1982), pp. 104-5.

24. British Museum, reg. no. OA 4710; Royal Armouries, London, inv. no. A.L.116/326; J.M. Levine, *Dr. Woodward's Shield* (Berkeley, 1977), *passim*.

25. Conde de Valencia de Don Juan, *Catalogo Historico-Descriptivo de la Real Armería de Madrid* (Madrid, 1898), cat. no. D 64, pl. xxi.

26. Ibid., cat. nos. D 78 and 79, and G 62, fig. 162, respectively.

27. Laking, op. cit. (Note 14), cat. no. 574.

28. C. Blair, 'Notes on the history of the Tower of London Armouries, 1821-55', *Journal of the Arms and Armour Society* 2 (1958), pp. 233-53, specifically pp. 243-4. I am most grateful to my friend Claude Blair who was kind and generous as ever in answering my many queries during the preparation of these notes.

29. See also p. 88, above.

30. Dresdner Rüstkammer, inv. no. M 63; E. Haenel, *Kostbare Waffen aus der Dresdner Rüstkammer* (Leipzig, 1923), pl. 14.

31. I. G., *Giacomo di Grassi his True Arte of Defence* (London, 1594), gatherings L3ᵛ-M4 and K4-13ᵛ, respectively.

32. G. Ekstrand, 'En romersk skold', *Varia* (Svenska Vapenhistoriska Sallskapet) 4 (1974), pp. 51-5, fig. 2.

33. C. Blair, 'A royal swordsmith and damaskener: Diego de Çaias', *Metropolitan Museum Journal* 3 (1970), pp. 149-98, specifically pp. 166-72, and figs. 30-5.

34. A. V. B. Norman, 'Arms and armour from Abbotsford', *Apollo* 77 (1962), pp. 525-9, fig. 5.

35. Wallace Collection, London, cat. no. A511.

36. A. V. B. Norman and C. M. Barne, *The Rapier and Small-Sword, 1460-1820* (London, 1980), pp. 19-28.

37. For instance, Royal Armouries, London, inv. nos. IX. 222 and 223; A. R. Dufty and A. Borg, *European Swords and Daggers in the Tower of London* (London, 1974), pls. 51c and b, respectively.

38. O. Millar, *The Tudor, Stuart, and Early Georgian Pictures in the Collection of Her Majesty The Queen* (London, 1967), cat. no. 113, pl. 60.

39. Sir John Smithe, *Certaine Discourses . . . Concerning the Formes and Effects of Divers Sorts of Weapons* (London, 1590), fol. 3ᵛ and 4ʳ.

40. Waffensammlung, Vienna, inv. no. A1591.

41. Millar, op. cit. (Note 38), cat. no. 213, not illustrated.

42. Norman and Barne, op. cit. (Note 36), pp. 22-3.

43. Musée de l'Armée, Paris, cat. nos. J. 380 and A. 790, respectively.

44. C. Blair, 'An English sword with an Ottoman blade in the Swiss National Museum', in K. Stüber and H. Wetter, *Blankwaffen* (Zurich, 1982), pp. 57-68.

45. Schloss Ambras, Innsbruck, inv. no. PA 324; Norman and Barne, op. cit. (Note 36), p. 375, pl. 92.

46. Norman and Barne, op. cit. (Note 36), p. 48.

47. C. Blair, *Arms and Armour and Base Metalwork in the James A. de Rothschild Collection at Waddesdon Manor* (Fribourg, 1974), cat. no. 19; A.V.B. Norman, 'Some hangers of the early seventeenth century', in K. Stüber and H. Wetter, *Blankwaffen* (Zurich, 1982), pp. 79-86; idem, 'A note on some hangers possibly of Scottish origin', *Proceedings of the Society of Antiquaries of Scotland* 116 (1986), pp. 581-2.

48. R. Holme, *The Academy of Armory* [part ii] ed. I.H. Jeayes (Roxburgh Club CXLIV) (1905), p. 126, no. 25.

49. Exhibited in 'The Age of Charles I', at the Tate Gallery, London, 1972-3, cat. no. 149.

50. Royal Armouries, London, inv. no. IX.1800.

51. A.V.B. Norman and G.M. Wilson, *Treasures from the Tower of London* (Norwich, 1982), cat. no. 20.

52. Laking, op. cit. (Note 6), II, pp. 330-2, 708.

53. C. Blair, in *Pollard's History of Firearms* (Feltham, 1983), p. 85, quoting Holme, op. cit. (Note 48), p. 134.

54. Norman and Wilson, op. cit. (Note 51), cat. no. 63.

55. J. Cruso, *Militarie Instructions for the Cavallrie* (Cambridge, 1632), p. 30.

56. PRO, SP 16/442, 85; quoted by H.L. Blackmore, *British Military Firearms* (London, 1961), p. 22.

57. A photograph of this painting is held in the Witt Library of the Courtauld Institute of Art, University of London.

58. J. Turner, *Pallas Armata. Military Essayes . . . written in the Years 1670 and 1671* (London, 1683), p. 173; quoted by Blair, op. cit. (Note 53), p. 86.

59. *A Collection of State Papers of John Thurloe, Esq; III 1654-1655* (London, 1742), p. 203; quoted by J.N. George, *English Guns and Rifles* (Plantersville, S. Carolina, 1947), p. 59.

60. E. Hyde, Earl of Clarendon, *History of the Rebellion* (Oxford, 1898), II, p. 347; I. Roy, *The Royalist Ordnance Papers, 1642-46* (Oxford Record Society, pt. i, 1964; pt. ii, 1975), passim.

61. See, for example, Wallace London, cat. no. A986.

62. J. Vernon, *Young Horseman* (London, 1644), p. 2.

63. Royal Armouries, London, inv. no. VIII.98.

64. I know the portrait of Radclyffe only from a photograph in the Witt Library of the Courtauld Institute of Art, University of London. Young Thomas Pope's portrait was sold at Christie's in London on 11 July 1930 (lot 67), the property of Lord North. It was not illustrated in the catalogue.

65. My colleague Sarah Bevan, Keeper of Edged Weapons in the Royal Armouries, is preparing a note on this group of weapons.

66. Roy, op. cit. (Note 60), pt. i, pp. 179, 218, 227.

67. C. Blair, *European and American Arms, c. 1100-1850* (London, 1962), p. 27.

68. Iveagh Bequest, Kenwood, London; *Van Dyck: des Meisters Gemälde* (Klassiker der Kunst 13) (New York, 1931), no. 409.

69. I am most grateful to Malcolm McLeod and Elizabeth Carmichael of the Museum of Mankind, London, for their help in trying to identify the 'Cashaws'.

70. The existence of these two saddles was kindly drawn to my attention by Claude Blair.

71. Millar, op. cit. (Note 38), cat. no. 105, pl. 42.

72. Royal Armoury, Stockholm, inv. no. 9032.

73. Royal Armouries, London, inv. nos. IX.24-28 and 29-33.

74. H.L. Blackmore, *The Armouries of the Tower of London* I *The Ordnance* (London, 1976), pp. 65-6. I am most grateful to Howard Blackmore for his help in elucidating a number of technical terms in the sale inventories.

75. H.D. Schepelern, 'Portretter som vaabenhistorisk kilde', *Vaabenhistoriske Aarbøger* 6a (1949), pp. 51-73, fig. 5.

76. *Journal de Jean Heroard sur l'Enfance et la Jeunesse de Louis XIII, (1601-1623)* (Paris, 1868), I, p. 267, and II, p. 196, respectively.

77. Royal Armouries, London, inv. no. XIX.182.

78. Blackmore, op. cit. (Note 74), pp. 63-4.

79. Ibid., p. 228.

80. Ibid., p. 233, quoting John Smith, *The Seamans Grammer* (London, 1627), p. 68.

81. H.A. Dillon, Viscount Dillon, 'The gun called Policy', *Archaeological Journal* 65 (1908), pp. 265-9.

82. H. Hexham, *The Art of Fortification* (Amsterdam, 1638), pl. 33; F. Askgaard, 'Die Schweinfeder', in K. Stüber and H. Wetter, *Blankwaffen* (Zurich, 1982), pp. 191-204, fig. 3.

83. R. Ward, *Animadversions of Warre* (London, 1639), p. 369.

84. Ibid., p. 368.

85. W. Dillich, *Kriegsbuch* (Frankfurt-am-Main, 1689), pls. 64-5.

86. Hexham, op. cit. (Note 82), pl. 32, figs. 135-6.

87. Thurloe, op. cit. (Note 59), p. 204.

88. Dillich, op. cit. (Note 85), I, pl. 68.

89. Ward, op. cit. (Note 83), lib. I, cap. CCLXXII.

90. H. Hexham , *Principles of Art Military* (Delft, 1642), plans facing pp. 26 and 28, respectively.

91. Ward, op. cit. (Note 83), pp. 375-9.

92. E. Koniger, *Bilderheft des Germanisches Nationalmuseums. Das Kleine Nürnberger Zeughaus* (Nuremberg, [c. 1970]).

93. PRO, LR 1/113; H.L. Blackmore, *A Dictionary of London Gunmakers, 1350-1850* (London, 1986), pp. 217-9, appendix 1.

94. R. Holme, *Academy of Armory* [part i] (Chester, 1688), I, bk. III, cap. VII, p. 300: 'The Pike or Bickern, or Beak-Iron that as comes out of the end of it' [i.e. the anvil]; illustrated on p. 299, fig. 70.

95. The *OED* gives this meaning, among many others, but only with a nineteenth-century reference.

96. G. Markham, *Souldiers Accidence* (London, 1625), p. 42.

97. G. Mungeam, 'Contracts for the supply of equipment to the 'New Model' Army in 1645', *Journal of the Arms and Armour Society* 6 (1968-70), pp. 53-115, specifically p. 90.

12 The Household below Stairs. Officers and Equipment of the Stuart Court

Arthur MacGregor

Marginal numerals refer to page and entry numbers in the *Inventories* (see p. 11)

Amounting in total to a value of some £7,000, the vessels, utensils and equipment appraised by the Trustees for Sale of the King's Goods can represent only a fragment of the battery of hardware that contributed to the smooth running of the Stuart court and household. In no instance was anything approaching a full complement of domestic goods inventoried at any of the King's houses. A certain amount of material may have been removed in the early years of civil unrest along with the court itself, although this appears not to have been a major cause of loss. More significant, perhaps, was the scope for misappropriation provided by the wartime years of parliamentary control when government administrators would have been hard pressed to maintain proper care of their charges[1] and when scant respect would have been paid, despite official strictures, to the property of the embattled monarch. Perhaps it was these domestic items, rather than paintings, hangings or even furnishings that fell within the range of aspiration and opportunity of the average looter, while the relative anonymity of such pieces would have encouraged hopes of successful concealment.

The striking variations in quality which are apparent between records made by different Trustees may account for some apparent absences: presumably these differences are to be explained in terms of the particular skills and enthusiasms of the individuals concerned (see p. 14). Other forms of selectivity also seem to have operated in the compilation of the inventories: at Ludlow, for instance, where there were few items of notable value, the everyday fixtures and fittings are catalogued fairly exhaustively; at Whitehall and St. James's, on the other hand, attention in the surviving inventories seems to have been diverted from the more prosaic items (which must still have been there, given the continuing use of the premises) by the large amounts of more spectacular contents.

Some indication of the importance attached to these prosaic domestic goods can be gleaned from a letter written by Charles I on the eve of his flight from Hampton Court, to Colonel Whaley, his Parliamentary custodian there: acknowledging Whaley's considerate treatment of him, the King now asked for his help in 'Protecting of My Household Stuff, and Moveables of all Sorts, which I leave behind me in this House, that they be neither spoiled nor embezzled'.[2]

While the collapse of royal authority undoubtedly extended the possibilities for embezzlement, the records reveal that pilfering had always been endemic in the Household below stairs. In monetary terms the household goods represented a considerable investment, and the annual cost of replacing items lost or stolen (as well as worn out) caused a drain on the royal finances: we can be sure that many suppliers of goods and equipment would have been among the King's creditors hoping for satisfaction from the sale.

An attempt can be made to reconstruct something of the range and character of the departmental offices of the Household on the basis of the goods represented in the inventories and the ordinances by which their operation was regulated. In this we are aided by the fact that responsibility for particular components of the household goods was delegated to specific officers and that these duties were reiterated and reinforced whenever the regulations were reviewed. It should be acknowledged that the sources used range over a century and more before the collapse of Charles I's authority, but the conservatism which they amply display fully justifies their use in this way.

Up to the time of Charles's death, the roots of the Household regulations lay in the Eltham Ordinances of 1526, devised by Henry VIII and his Council 'for the establishment of good order, and reformation of sundry errors and mis-uses in his most honourable Household and Chamber'.[3] With some refinement and modification, the guiding principles laid down there continued to operate for the remainder of the Tudor period and were transmitted to the Stuarts in the form of 'The Booke of Household of Queene Elizabeth, as it was ordered in the 43rd yeare of her reigne; delivered to our Soveraigne Lord Kinge James, the first yeare of his Raigne'.[4] Further reviews instituted at intervals by James and by Charles I brought about certain reforms in the Chamber (see pp. 18-19); their effect on the Household was more limited, although an undated list of recommendations for

Figure 110   *The great kitchen at Windsor Castle,* as it appeared in the nineteenth century. The original louvres in the roof had been replaced with skylights by this time, but the internal appearance remained largely unchanged since the Stuart period. Hulton-Deutsch Collection.

reform of certain malpractices that permeated life below stairs (specifically, it would seem, in the household of Prince Henry) shows that it did not escape unscathed.[5]

On the authority of these ordinances, day-to-day regulation of expenditure by the Household was governed by the officers of the Board of Greencloth, attending at the Compting House and assisted by its staff.[6] Their duties had been clearly established at Eltham:

. . . the Lord Great Master, the Treasurer and the Comptroller of the King's Household, or one of them at least . . . shall be dayly in the Compting-house between the hours of 8 and 9 in the morning, calling unto them . . . and to have brought before them all the Bookes of briefments of all the Officers of the Household for the day before passed to see if any wastful expences have been made by any Minister in his office.[7]

The firm control envisaged here should have ensured proper discipline throughout the twenty-three sub-departments of the Household below stairs, but how far reality had strayed from the ideal became apparent in 1637-8 when an audit showed a number of officers between them to have been embezzling a staggering £10,500 a year over the previous ten years through malpractices that had operated since the late sixteenth century or earlier.[8]

The departments in which particular discrepancies were found were those concerned with the sustenence of the court: the Acatry, Kitchen, Bakehouse, Poultry, Cellar and Buttery. Disposing of enormous annual budgets,[9] it is perhaps not surprising that the officials charged with the running of these departments found ways of lining their own pockets. The considerable task of the Sergeants of the Acatry, for example, was that of provisioning the household: their prime responsibility was to see 'that such privisions as be made for beefe, muttons, linge, coddes, and other victualls . . . as well flesh as fish, be good and of the best', and it was their personal responsibility to attend 'every Faire or Markett' where such were to be found. Their horizons extended even beyond the market place to the royal farms, where they had to see 'the King's Pastures well ordered and stored with Cattel'.[10] The Sergeants were assisted by various Yeomen Purveyors with individual responsibility for veal, beef and mutton, sea fish, and fresh-water fish; the Acatry also employed a Yeoman Keeper of the Salt-Store, who had charge of all salt fish as well as having to supply the Larder with grey salt and white salt as required.[11] As with all the departments below stairs, the specialist officers were watched over by clerks and administrators: the Clerks Comptrollers of the Board of Greencloth, for example, not only attended to the records but were made personally accountable for seeing that all meat delivered was of appropriate quality and of declared weight, all deliveries being weighed daily and the sums entered in the accounts.[12]

These administrative concerns naturally made little impact on the inventories, although the elements of control over the flow of commodities into the Household is represented by the scales and weights recorded at various establishments. A 'paire of boards for scales and 3 halfe hundred weights' at Whitehall would have served some such function, although the presence of another 'paire of Scales, and 3. great Weights' in the coal house at Ludlow and a further set in the tapestry works at Mortlake remind us that similar checks would have been carried out across the whole range of domestic and other supplies. No indication of size is given for the 'Scailes & weights' from Wimbledon House nor for the 'two. beames & 2 paire of scailes and 4 weights' noted in the wardrobe at Denmark House. The 'waights of Metall' sold for 3s. along with a standish from Hampton Court were presumably quite minor items.[13]

With a staff of forty-one and with thirty-five additional servants, the kitchens (Fig. 110) represented a major source of employment within the Household. Three major divisions were recognized within the establishment: the privy kitchens of the king and queen respectively each occupied distinct premises and catered only for the royal tables; the Household kitchens fed everyone else at court. The authority of the four Master Cooks was subservient to that of no less than three clerks: it was ultimately the responsibility of the clerks rather than the cooks to see that 'such stuffe of victualls as perteyneth to the King's dish, bee of the best and sweetest stuffe that can be got; and in likewise for every estate and other within the King's house, according to their degrees'. Their duties went further, not only to see that everything was provided 'in good houre, so that the cookes may have reasonable leisure for the good seasoning of the same', but also 'that the Cookes and Boylers doe dresse the Meate well and seasonably, that it be neither raw, neither over much boyled or rosted, but soe as it may be for the King's honour'.[14] Other kitchen staff included yeomen and grooms, and a number of scourers, turnbroaches and children.

The output of the kitchens was prodigious, although curtailed somewhat under James I: finding that expenses had risen alarmingly since he came to the throne, James decreed on 17 July 1604 that 'Whereas Our Selfe and our deare Wife . . . have bene every day served with 30 Dishes of Meate . . . hereafter . . . our Will is to be served but with 24 Dishes every Meale';[15] on state occasions, however, the regulation thirty dishes were to be restored. The equally extensive menus approved for Henry, Prince of Wales, and for Charles when Duke of York add detail to these bald figures.[16] Senior members of the Household and Chamber supped at court more modestly by degrees, according to their station, while groups of lesser officers formed messes sharing a number of dishes between them. James I's reforms of 1604 diminished the number of those entitled to 'board wages' and the number of dishes to be served to those retaining this privilege.[17] The rights of others were commuted to cash payments at this time.

Perhaps in an effort to discourage development of a free-for-all attitude below stairs, specific entitlements were made to certain officials of the waste or by-products generated by their respective departments. Hence the Master Cooks, for example, were entitled to 'all the fat that comes from the beefe boyled in the house, and all the lambe skinnes yearley spent'; the Yeoman of the Scalding House, on the other hand, received 'the downe of the geese, swannes, and the garbidge of poultry' while the grooms in that office got the feathers.[18]

A number of offices worked in association with the kitchens: the officers of the Poultry saw to the acquisition of 'poultry stuff' of suitable quality, to its preparation by the scalders in the Scalding House and its delivery to the Larder in due time for the cooks to see to its dressing and cooking.[19] The Yeoman and grooms of the Boiling House were required 'to boyle all the beefe, and what other meates soever shall be appointed unto them by the clerke of the kitchen', while the Pastry handled baked meats and saw to the filling of pies and the like.[20] Many references to the presence of these offices will be found in the works dealing with individual royal houses, as cited above (pp. 19-44).

Provisions for the kitchens were generally held in the Larder (inspected daily by the Clerks of the Greencloth to see that everything was fresh). Its Sergeant was charged with 'the trewe receipt and delivery oute' of all the necessary provisions.[21] In addition to the huge stocks of meat, the Larder would also have

380 [757]

228 [138]
423 [17]

297 [243]
254 [108]
181 [259]

housed the all-important stocks of butter, of which three kinds were produced: fresh butter for immediate use, salt butter pressed into earthenware pots or barrels, and clarified butter for use in the kitchens.[22]

In the course of their survey at Wimbledon House in 1649, the Parliamentary surveyors noted 'a salting trough a chopping block a stand and messes a beame and scales' in the wet larder,[23] while a later inventory of 1659 notes a 'brine cisterne' and a 'powdering place' in the fresh larder at Hampton Court.[24] These characteristic fittings are represented in the sale inventories by one powdering tub from Ludlow Castle and a second from the Castle governor's private lodgings. Powdering (or salting) was a technique equally applicable to the curing of meat[25] and cheese.[26] Other hints that cheese played a role of any importance in the royal diet are scant: it features not at all in the prescribed diets mentioned above. However, the inventories for Ludlow Castle (admittedly not used in Charles's reign as residence for the court) include 'Severall Cheese Racks' from the dairy house.

Spices were the particular province of the Spicery (whose clerk also had responsibility for the Confectionery, Wafery, Chandlery, Ewery and Laundry). They were generally supplied in the raw state: the specific duty of the Yeoman of the Spicery was 'to beate spice into powder', and for his fee he was allowed 'all the bagges and boxes brought in . . . with spices, and all the barrels once emptied brought into the Spicery and Chaundry'.[27] A typical piece of spicery equipment was recorded from Wimbledon in the form of a 'Mustard Mill' – presumably the same piece recorded there more specifically as a 'mustard querne' by the Parliamentary surveyors.[28]

Other grinding equipment is mentioned in the inventories: the Governor's kitchen at Ludlow boasted 'A Brasse Morter and Pestle'; 'a Marble stoone and a wodden pestle' together with two further pestles had been removed from Wimbledon to Denmark House, while a further 'stoone Morter' remained in the 'great kitchin' at Wimbledon. These need not necessarily have been used in the preparation of herbs or spices: a great many dishes demanded that meat, for example, should be well pounded in a mortar by the cook.[29]

Kitchen equipment features prominently in the inventories, although detail relating to it is scant. Among the most numerous items are spits: forty-five are listed, along with twenty-seven broaches. In practice, no distinction seems to be implied between the use of one term or the other, and indeed a further entry records an additional '18 broaches or spitts'. All manner of meat could be spit-roasted and different varieties and sizes of spit-irons might be expected within a single well-equipped kitchen.[30] The square centre section of the iron frequently incorporated a sliding fork which secured the meat and ensured that it turned with the spit; the ends were rounded for ease of turning, one of them normally tapering to form a spike for skewering the meat; a small wooden wheel to help turn the spit was often attached to the other end.[31]

Dripping pans (usually of iron) would have been essential adjuncts for spit-roasting, yet there are only two examples recorded in the inventories from Ludlow and one each from Wimbledon and Holdenby. In the Hampton Court inventory drawn up immediately after Cromwell's death (and reflecting more accurately a full complement of kitchen equipment), no fewer than six dripping pans were recorded.[32] The grooms of the kitchen would have had a special interest in seeing to the proper provision of these pans, since they were entitled to 'the drippinges of all the meates roasted throughout the yeare'.[33]

Twenty iron racks recorded in the inventories are designated in pairs, while a further six are referred to in the singular. Their function is alluded to in an entry in the Holdenby House list, which mentions an 'Iron Rack for Spitts',[34] while the culinary associations of the remainder are confirmed by the fact that five pairs came from the kitchens at Whitehall, Hampton Court and Bewdley, and a further pair was listed in the 'dry larder' at Ludlow. Racks were associated with spits in two contexts: out of use, the spits were customarily stored in racks above the fireplace; in use, one of the normal methods of support was by means of pairs of standing racks, arranged one on either side of the fire.[35]

'1 paire of pott hang[rs]' from Wimbledon represent the only inventoried examples of what would have been a common feature of the royal kitchens as in every other household of the Stuart period. Serving to suspend cooking-pots from an iron bar spanning the hearth[36] (forerunner of the movable chimney crane), pot-hangers varied in complexity from simply-wrought iron hooks to more elaborate composite types provided with a ratchet to adjust the height and

235 [231]
236 [240]

229 [140]

297 [238]

228 [132], 58 [9]
59 [32]
297 [239]

[passim]

380 [755]

235 [226]
59 [22], 242 [305]

[passim]

241 [288]

296 [233]

119 [326], 235 [228], 380 [756]
322 [12]

often ornamented with pierced decoration.[37] From their valuation at 5s., the pair from Wimbledon was evidently of some complexity.

Of the six 'trevetts' listed, three are provenanced to Denmark House. Only in one instance is the material specified – 'yron'. In the first half of the seventeenth century, all such trivets are likely to have been of the free-standing variety, designed to support a cooking pot alongside the fire rather than to be suspended from the fire-basket as in later varieties.

119 [324], 124 [369]
228 [133], 235 [230]
241 [287], 242 [299], 358 [447]

Fourteen gridirons are included in the lists, several of them designated 'large'. The most common seventeenth-century gridirons are either circular with a long, flat handle, or four sided and standing on three- to four-inch legs. In either case the grid itself was composed of a number of distinct bars (commonly seven).[38] Either type could be placed over the glowing embers of the fire. The footless variety was sometimes used in association with a brandreth (a form of trivet) or with a baking iron: two 'Iron plates for yᵉ fire' noted at Ludlow may have been baking irons of this type.[39] In addition to their employment in

228 [133]
24 [38]

cookery,[40] an alternative function is demonstrated by 'Twoe large Greddirons, or Grates, to heate dishes', noted in the kitchen at Ludlow. One example is included among the plate from the Tower (see below).

An appropriately extensive range of cooking vessels came from the kitchens of various royal houses, reflecting something of the variety of output expected from the cooks. Many of the dishes prepared in these vessels (particularly the smaller ones) would have been cooked not on the open fire but on stoves of the type surviving in the Hampton Court kitchens, having the form of a masonry bench with a number of fire-baskets suspended below a series of openings.

[passim]

Some of the pots are ascribed descriptive epithets in the inventories: brass (33 entries), large brass (5), and little brass (1). Pans are mentioned in similar varieties: brass (25), round brass (2), small brass (1), copper (3) and an iron pan with a brass cover (1); two are simply described as 'small' and one has no further description.[41] In addition to these are several varieties to which specific functions are ascribed: 'great brasse Panns to boyle fish in' (2),[42] 'great fish panns' (2), 'fishe pannes' (1), 'brass stewe panns' (4), 'boyling pans' (3) and 'custard pans' (4). Further distinct types are represented by frying pans (4)[43] and large frying pans (1). Other vessels from the kitchens include coppers (1), posnets (2), skillets (4), kettles (4), little kettles (2) and (particularly appropriate to the Scalding House) scalding kettles (1).

20 [11], 25 [50], 22 [13]
27 [12], 223 [9], 24 [38]

A small number of cooking vessels and utensils are included amongst the plate: two skillets and four chafing dishes as well as a gridiron are mentioned, in addition to many silver 'pots' to which no specific function can be ascribed. The limitation of such exceptional pieces of 'kytchen plate' to the privy kitchen and its highly perishable nature has been commented upon elsewhere.[44]

254 [107], 255 [116-17]
360 [469]
231 [162]

Although most of the vessels mentioned above clearly relate to the kitchens, it may be noted that one pot, two pans and a kettle, all of brass, came from the wax chandlery at Denmark House, while one pan (evidently a large one, valued at £2) was noted in the bakehouse at St. James's and 'one old brasse pott' came from the Court House at Ludlow, indicating a wide range of possible functions.

A few kitchen utensils are registered but, as already indicated, they can represent only a handful of survivors from a much more extensive range of equipment.

235 [232]
59 [26]

A single 'old long brasse Ladle' survived in the dry larder at Ludlow, and three others of the same material came from Wimbledon.

59 [28]
119 [327], 228 [130]

'Scummers' are represented by one example each from Denmark House, Wimbledon and Ludlow; this paucity can be compared with ten examples recorded at Hampton Court alone in 1659.[45] The normal method of construction in the seventeenth century was for a perforated disc of sheet copper (forming the strainer) to be combined with a flat iron handle. In addition to their use in the kitchens, they would have been much employed in skimming milk.[46]

59 [25], 228 [130]
255 [129]

Wimbledon and Ludlow each produced 'cullinders' of brass, while a further handled variety, described as a 'Cullinder or Spone', was among the goods held by George Wither, one of the Trustees for the sale. A more splendid version,

27 [14]
25 [50]

registered at the Tower as 'of Silver gilt with a Christall handle', together with another example included among the plate at the Tower, were evidently not for everyday use.[47]

59 [27]

A 'Brasse scoope' from Wimbledon, valued at 4s., was presumably used in handling dry goods such as flour.

282 [99], 228 [130]

'One Iron forke' from Oatlands and a 'broaken Beife Fork' from the Governor's kitchen at Ludlow form the sole examples of their type (apart from

119 [327]
59 [30]

table forks: see p. 377), while kitchen knives, which must have been even more ubiquitous, are represented only by one shredding knife from Denmark House.

'Three paire of wafer Irons', originating from Wimbledon House, belong to a well-known class of implement made in the form of a pair of tongs incorporating two large discs with patterns and devices cast on their opposing faces. After heating the irons gently, a thin batter was run on to one disc and the other closed over it; a few moments cooking over the fire finished the process and the wafer (with the ornamental patterns of the discs impressed on it) was turned out ready to eat. Responsibility for the production of wafers lay with the Yeoman and Groom of the Wafery. If we were to judge only from the 'Booke of Household' of Queen Elizabeth, their duties would hardly appear onerous, being limited to producing wafers at 'festivall times' as directed by the clerks of the Spicery; from an earlier book of regulations dating from the reign of Edward IV, however, it seems clear that the monarch (as distinct from the court at large) might expect wafers on a daily basis.[48] Their festive associations are revealed in a record of the marriage of Charles's sister, the Princess Elizabeth, to the Count Palatine in 1613: the wedding ceremony was followed by a toast by the King and Queen, after which 'bowls of wine, hippocras and wafers' were produced and further toasts were drunk.[49]

The Bakehouse again formed a separate and significant department of the Household. The duties of the Sergeant and Clerk of the Bakehouse started with receipt of the wheat, when its weight and quality were checked; further checks were to be carried out to see that nothing was lost or tampered with during milling. Presumably the corn would normally have been ground under contract,

236 [240]

but part of a horse mill was included in the inventory of goods from Ludlow (valued with 'other kinds of lumber' at a mere £1. 10s.) while a room adjoining

228 [137]

the bakehouse there housed 'One Grinding Millne with all Necessaries to it'.

297 [240]

The next responsibility of the Sergeant was to see 'that the Bakers doe bulte the Branne cleane, that there be found noe wast therein'. A 'Boulting Mill' was among the items inventoried at Wimbledon, recorded in its purpose-built bolting house.[50] The Sergeant was further to ensure 'that the Furnour doe season the Bread well, not drowning it with too much water, weighing the same into the oven, that every loafe may weigh and keep its full weight, after it is baked as it ought to be'. Tables were drawn up indicating the amount of permissible waste in the baking of a quarter of wheat, which was to be 'made into 216 loaves, every loafe weighing into the oven 30oz. and out of the oven 27oz.'[51]

185 [331-2]
297 [240], 238 [260]
228 [136]

185 [333]

Bread dough was normally prepared in a wooden kneading trough, as recorded from the privy bakehouse and elsewhere at Hampton Court, the bolting house at Wimbledon and the pantry at Bewdley House; the bakehouse at Ludlow produced both a trough and a kneading board.[52] Mechanical aid was available for this process in the form of the 'brake', a kneading table fitted with a swivelling iron arm with which to pound the dough: a brake was among the goods reserved at Hampton Court.[53]

59 [32], 228 [136]
235 [234], 297 [241], 420 [2]

One 'rowling pin' from Wimbledon may be mentioned here, as well as the bread bins recorded at Ludlow and Wimbledon and in the custody of 'Mr Willis'.

The ovens themselves were, of course, architectural features and not free-standing units as might have attracted the attentions of the Trustees. They were heated by lighting a fire within the chamber of the oven itself and, when the masonry was thoroughly heated through, the embers were removed with a rake

58 [20]

or with a flat iron shovel called a slice: 'Two Kitchin slyses' from Wimbledon, sold at Denmark House for 5s., are testaments to this practice.[54] The dough was then placed in the oven and the door sealed with clay until baking was completed. Two bread carriers were attached to the staff of the Pantry, to 'daily carry the breade from the bake-house to the pantry'.[55] As well as providing bread of two qualities ('cheat' and 'manchett') for consumption at table, the bakers had also to produce up to four loaves a day for each of those entitled to bouche of court. For an undetermined period in the early years of Charles's reign a third variety – trencher bread – was demanded of them: coarser than the other types, this was eaten only by the least fortunate in society, after it had been discarded from the tables of the Household (see pp. 375, 377).

Complementing the duties and responsibilities of the officers so far mentioned were those of the staff assigned to the Cellar and the Buttery. The Sergeant of the Cellar had overall charge of these departments, and also directed the Pitcher House.[56]

The vineyards recorded at Wimbledon, Oatlands and elsewhere no doubt produced grapes for eating and for the manufacture of verjuice for use in the kitchens, but it seems unlikely that significant quantities of wine came from the Stuart estates in England. Provisioning the Cellar would therefore have been a matter of judicious purchasing of imported wine in the cask. The inventories record 'several stillings for wine' (that is to say, stands for casks) at Whitehall and four stands in the wine cellar at Bewdley, but otherwise the vast quantities of wine that flowed through the household have left little trace.[57] The King, at least, expected wine to be produced on demand wherever he might be, for the staff of the Cellar included a Yeoman of the Bottles whose task it was 'to carry wine and drinke for the King, when his Majestie rideth abroad'.[58] Bottles were transported in specially made baskets called flaskets: one 'old flaskett' which had been 'In ye use of ye Trustees' at Denmark House was sold in 1650 for 1s.

325 [45]
238 [267]
251 [54]
239 [277], 238 [267]
297 [241]
424 [10]
239 [277], 241 [289-92]
228 [134], 240 [278-80]

Meagre testaments of the Buttery survived at Bewdley House, where two stands remained in the brewhouse and four more in the 'Beare Sellor', while at Wimbledon where there remained '18. stands. for beare'. The Parliamentary survey of the house records that fourteen of these stands were distributed throughout the 'outward common beare celler', the 'inner common beare celler' and the 'strong beare celler', a further three standing in the inner and outward wine cellars (which also contained a 'payre of slinges', presumably to help manoeuvre the casks).[59] A further 'stilling for beare' was recorded among the reserved goods at Vauxhall. At Greenwich the spacious cellars in the central courtyard were presided over by figures of Beer and Gin, said to have been removed to the Tower during the Commonwealth.[60]

Instructions for the numbers of tuns to be brewed in a given week were issued to the brewers by the Purveyors of Ale, who were officers of the Buttery. Extreme care was to be taken with their charge, the Purveyors having personally to oversee the transport and laying in of the beer 'for the better preservacion of the same', and were to 'cause locks to be sett on every Doore' to prevent tampering and pilfering.[61]

The brewers for their part were enjoined to brew 'good and seasonable stuff without Weevell or Fustines' and were instructed to 'put neither Hoppes nor Brimstone in their Ale in the pipes, soe that it may be sound . . . and worth the King's money'.[62] Some picture of their domain emerges from the inventories of Bewdley, Holdenby and Ludlow, in each of which the contents of the brewhouse were inventoried separately, and at Kenilworth where the Trustees clearly started their work in the brewhouse. Each of these produced two or three vats and a corresponding number of coolers, while coppers in which the brewing was done were recorded at Holdenby and Ludlow.[63] Leaden cisterns provided water for the process, Ludlow having in addition 'one Pumpe, Twoe Leaden Troughes, and a Leaden Pipe with other Implements thereunto'.

While a certain amount of ale was clearly brewed at each of these establishments, it seems that much of that drunk in the London palaces was supplied by brewers granted a royal patent. This at least is the impression given by the huge debts which accrued from time to time to those designated the King's brewers. In 1615, for example, we hear of a Mr Bruckshaw who 'hath lain this month or five weeks in the Marshalsea, with six or seven of his companion brewers, for that they will not yield to have their drink taken to serve the King without money; for the King's brewer cannot get a grant of £16,000 that is owing to him for beer'.[64] Later we find among Charles's creditors one Robert Houghton, 'Gentleman and Brewer to the late King', who acquired (or had thrust upon him) at the sale several important paintings in his own right and a further fifty-one in his capacity as head of a syndicate.[65]

Responsibility for much of the equipment already described lay with the Sergeant of the Scullery. 'Within his charge', it was ordained, 'are all the necessaryes that are used in every office as . . . tubbes, trayes, baskets, flaskets, scoopes, broaches, peeles, and such like'.[66] When these were worn out the Sergeant had the right to any residual scrap value that might be realized from them. Under Charles the benefit from this right was curtailed with a tightening of the regulations regarding unserviceable utensils: whenever possible these were by 'repayring and mending to be made fitt for use', and to be discarded only as a last resort.[67]

The Sergeant of the Scullery had further in his charge all the dishes of silver and pewter for use at table—an unenviable responsibility, for at every great feast his charges were misappropriated in huge quantities by 'untrewe persons'.[68] Under James I measures were taken to stem 'the daily losse of Our Silver Vesselles' by introducing an order that no person, of what degree soever, shall presume to send from Our Boarde or out of Our Privy Chamber or Presence Chamber, any Silver Dishes; but if they shall have ocasion to sende away any Meate, Wee require that two of Our Officers of Our Scullery be commanded to attend Our Presence Doore, there to give Pewter Vesselles for the change of the said Silver . . . [69]

Drinking vessels such as 'silver pottes, jackes, and wooden cuppes' were the province of the Yeoman of the Pitcher House.[70] Some of his charges are included here amongst the tableware listed in the inventories; other vessels made of hardstone or studded with gems are perhaps to be seen more for show than for practical use and might equally be included amongst the collectors' pieces on pp. 414-17.

The sergeants of the appropriate offices below stairs delivered food and drink to the sideboard in the Presence Chamber or to the door of the Privy Chamber, according to the King's intentions. A single 'old Traye' surviving in the porter's lodge at Ludlow stands in the inventories as a token of these daily services, but the presence of no fewer than eighteen trays in the Hampton Court kitchens at the time of Cromwell's death reflects more accurately the importance of the role they would originally have played.[71] [231 [158]]

Perhaps the most striking feature of the dining tables would have been the great salts, still representing major social dividers in the seventeenth century, although diminished in importance in the late Elizabethan period when some forty of them were removed from use at court and melted down at the Mint.[72] The presence of several impressive examples in the inventories demonstrates that they continued to occupy a position of importance at the early Stuart table and indeed with the restoration of Charles II their significance was reinforced with an ordinance that 'No person of what degree soever shall presume . . . to sitt after the salt is upon the table'.[73] Most impressive among the forty inventoried examples was 'A large Pillar Salt with 4. double pillars 4. Christall and 4. silver gilt sett on the top with figures and faces with some stones. the whole being gilt, silver': it was valued at £27. 16s. Three further pillar salts are recorded, and other forms mentioned include 'A Globe Salt supported by two Men with Fame on the Topp of the Cover enamelled with greene', one with 'a Mannikin' on top and one with a Cupid on the cover. Four examples (one of them a 'Salt of State' had clocks fitted in them and one was described as a watch salt (see pp. 394-5); there were also examples in agate, coral, lapis lazuli and amber. Presumably it was for a less elaborate open salt that a 'Cover for Salt and Bread openworke wrought in gould, silver and silke of divers cullours' was made, as well as a more modest cover 'of white cuttworke', although these may have been for liturgical rather than domestic use (see p. 337). For oil and vinegar there were two 'Christall Crewetts garnished with gold sett with Rubies and Turqouyses', valued at £174. [33 [79]] [33 [78]] [27 [16]] [28 [19], 25 [49], 29 [32], 33 [77]] [47 [201], 35 [94]] [105 [175]] [33 [81]]

An impressive show would have been made too by the great ewers and basins provided for rinsing of hands at table (as well as for daily ablutions in the bedchamber). Amongst those inventoried at the Tower Jewel House were eight ewers of crystal elaborated in various ways, two of mother-of-pearl, one of agate and one 'of Earth garnisht with sev'all Stones, sett in Colletts. of gold and an Amatist on the topp', as well as seven others amongst the plate. The more imposing of the silver-gilt basins include two 'with some stones sett in Colletts. of gold', two 'Chased with flower de Luces' and one 'great Bason with faces upon the brimme, & in the middst garnisht with barres of silver gilt', sold for an impressive £86. 16s.[74] Also to be noted here is a 'great Purselaine Bason sett in a Foote & Frame of silver, and guilt, with two handles to it in a leather Case', sold for £42. More elaborate table pieces included 'A fountain for perfumed waters artificially made to play of itself (of Silver)', sold for £30, and a similar piece which sold for £25; another example, made 'of Copper, the Topp of silver in a Case of woodd painted' was valued more highly at £60. Items like these had been in use at table since the time of Henry VIII: one was given to him as a New Year's gift in 1545, 'which casteth out water above running down into a bason made unto the same'.[75] [31 [53], 34 [88], 37 [117]] [30 [47], 34 [93], 31 [57]] [31 [57]] [26 [1]] [47 [198 – 200]] [122 [348]] [426 [3]] [426 [4]] [117 [308]]

Forty-nine trencher plates appear among the plate, some of them stamped with Elizabeth's crowned *E* and some bearing the royal arms; twelve 'Marble Trenchers garnished with silver gilt' are also recorded. Two chargers survived among the plate at Carisbrooke, while forty-five pewter dishes at Ludlow represent the more mundane end of the spectrum.[76] Even more prosaic are two 'platters. of wood' from Wimbledon, although even these were removed to Denmark House where they sold along with other items for 1s. 6d. Wood was not [[passim]] [29 [39]] [223 [7], 236 [236]] [59 [32]] entirely scorned even at the royal table: one of James I's favourite drinks was said to be beer, 'which he takes from a cup turned out of a peculiar kind of wood'.[77] Circular wooden platters had replaced the traditional trencher – usually square with a large hollow for meat and a smaller one for salt – from the early part of the seventeenth century. As one of the reforms introduced early in the reign of Charles I, the Lord Steward decreed that 'the ancient order of taking meate upon Trenchers made of bread be revived and continued for the pores sustenance'[78] (see p. 377): traditionally the trencher bread would have been served on a trencher of wood, but it may be that metal plates were more commonly used in Charles's day.

'Twenty Pye and Pasty Plates' of pewter were also recorded at Ludlow, while thirteen 'Spice Plates Escollopt' of silver came from the Tower; these were used for serving fruit or desserts. Twenty-one silver fruit dishes are also recorded in the inventories, six of mother-of-pearl 'garnished about with Silver gilt', and others of crystal (one 'garnish't with gold sett with Rubies and pearles with an Eagle wrought in the midst') and of agate, 'garnisht with gold and pearle hanging at the brim'. Other dishes designated for particular purposes include three chafing dishes of silver from the Tower (one of them weighing a massive 6*lb*. 10*oz*.) and another from Carisbrooke; not only could these keep food warm at table, but dishes requiring only light preparation were cooked with their aid on a metal plate supported above the charcoal contained in the chafing dish.

'Thirty six Porringers and sawcers' came from Denmark House and two more porringers were noted at Carisbrooke. One example in gold and one in agate came from the Tower. Typically these have a pair of horizontal handles or 'ears' at the rim;[79] broth as well as porridge could be served in them. Two caudle cups and two caudle cup covers were recorded at the Tower: similar in form to porringers, these were used in the serving of caudle, a substantial drink of wine or ale thickened with eggs.

Also noted at Denmark House was a sillabub pot, while two 'Creame Bowles' were noted amongst the plate at the Tower. A 'Globe for Snow' represents a more unusual type: iced fruits and desserts could have been served from it, the snow being preserved beyond the winter months in ice houses, as recorded at Greenwich and Hampton Court.[80]

Amongst the various kinds of 'potts' listed (mostly at the Tower), thirteen are described as 'Hanspotts' or 'Hance bellyed potts';[81] ten are of plate (two of them 'sett about with gold Roses') and three of crystal, silver-gilt (two of them mounted with precious stones). Preserved in the same place were two 'Colledge potts'; one 'Stone Pott' (that is to say, a stoneware pot) garnished with silver gilt; a 'paire of rich gilt potts bordered wth roses about their Necks and bellyes' and a large 'feather pott'. There were eighteen 'Buttery potts' among the plate, nine of them large (five 'parcell gilt'), five small and one 'Hance bellyed', and also nineteen water pots ('Fowre of them having handles') of porcelain and one of plate.

The inventories also contain numerous references to vessels for dispensing drinks and for drinking at table, although the extent to which they were all in active use is difficult to gauge. There were fourteen flagons among the plate, including ten 'with Chaines' (valued at £205) and one a 'Large two handled flagon, wth a Spire Cover' (sold for £25).[82] A great variety of bottles are listed, amongst them two 'square Bottles of Purselaine', two 'Sheppard stone bottles with Chaines and stopples bound about and garnisht', and two 'Stone Bottles garnisht with silver and severall stones with Chaines with a Dogge upon the Topp of each'. A 'Glasse spout pott bottle' a 'christall broken bottle' and two further bottles of red glass and blue glass are all described as garnished with silver. There were also bottles of hardstone, including agate, crystal and jasper 'Tun bottles', which may well have been of practical use as well as smaller bottles which sound as though they were of purely decorative value or which may have held scented water and the like.[83]

Another distinct group is formed by the 'canns', straight-sided cylindrical vessels, including a 'White Glasse Cann garnished with silver gilt', a 'serpentine Can the Cover gold', and a 'Christall Can garnished with gold with a naked boy on the topp of the Cover'.

Cups form one of the most numerous categories here; some clearly were of practical use but in other instances it is difficult to decide the extent to which they were valued primarily for aesthetic rather than practical considerations. The 'Agatt & Chrystall Cups & Vessels set in gold & silver' in the Upper Jewel House at the Tower were amongst the 'Parcells of Plate' specifically reserved on 3 October 1649:[84] whatever the original reasons for their being accumulated by

236 [236]
22 [10]
20 [10], 22 [6], 26 [5]
26 [1]
39 [143]
39 [144]

22 [13], 27 [12]
223 [9]

121 [346], 223 [9]
45 [186], 37 [120]

25 [50]
25 [54]

412 [76], 24 [41]
24 [39]

22 [13], 24 [38, 46-7]
26 [2], 27 [9-10]
29 [36], 24 [46]
25 [54]
27 [6]

24 [43], 22 [14-16]
23 [17], 24 [37]
121 [343], 122 [347], 24 [38]

22 [11], 426 [7]
122 [350]
29 [40]
28 [25]

29 [34-5]
29 [37-8]
28 [27-8]
29 [29], 38 [124]
28 [18], 34 [90]

28 [22], 35 [102]
33 [75]

375 Officers and Equipment of the Stuart Court

32 [70]
32 [68], 28 [20]

35 [101]
37 [121]

34 [83]

40 [148]
29 [30]
40 [150]

39 [141], 42 [169], 28 [26]

43 [181]
27 [17]

31 [59]

30 [52]
35 [100]
28 [23], 37 [122], 413 [90]
117 [303], 40 [157], 39 [139]
35 [96]

26 [3]

31 [54, 56]
29 [34]
33 [73], 35 [95]
32 [69]
121 [344-5], 39 [140]
426 [8-10]

235 [235]

25 [50], 30 [42]
223 [7], 426 [12], 41 [167]
41 [164]

46 [194]
46 [195]
25 [51]
38 [126], 426 [12]
25 [51], 38 [125-6]

25 [50], 30 [42]
426 [12], 41 [163]

38 [131]
25 [48]
38 [127]

the monarchy, it seems unlikely that they would have been added to the reserved goods under the Commonwealth for other than practical purposes.

Those of agate form the most numerous category. Many are covered cups, with decorative lids featuring, for example, 'a Queene on the Topp sitting under a Crowne', a 'Beare and ragged staffe on the Topp', or 'the Queenes Armes on the Topp of the Cover, and H. R: on the other side'. Smaller versions included an 'Aggatt Strong Water Cupp with a golden Cover garnished with Rubies Opalls and Pearles' (valued at a modest £5), a small cup 'garnisht wth enamelled gold Rubies and a pearle, a Cover of enamelled gold, full of holes', and another shaped 'like an Ormer shell'.

Cups of crystal run as second favourite to those of agate, many of them again fitted with elaborate metal covers. These included, for example, one cup set with sapphires, rubies and pearls with a cover 'made like a Coronett with a kind of Piramide'; one with a cover 'supported by 3. Satyres sett with some stones, and figures of Devills'; and one with 'a Lobster wrought in the bottome the Cover of Enamelled gold with a white falcon on the topp of it'; other covers were embellished with a 'faire saphire', with red enamel and with a lion 'holding a Scutchion with the Queenes Armes'.[85] There are also some thirty examples of lesser crystal cups with and without covers, ranging in value from 10s. to £20. Those without covers included some elaborate examples such as one (sold for £35) 'garnish't with gold sett with Rubies Emrods and Saphires supported by 3. Womens heads', and another 'sett upon 3. Christall Balls' and embellished with amethysts and enamel. Crystal cups of lesser value included one 'supported with 4. Lyons' and one 'with a Cockatrice head on the side', and lesser examples.

A few instances occur of cups in other hardstones, including heliotrope ('sett wth Rubies and Emrods in flowers of gold'), serpentine (one supported on pillars studded with gems and another gem-encrusted specimen standing on four gilt balls), and jasper. There were also others in amber, wood ('garnisht with gold'), glass (including a 'long footed greene Glasse Case Cuppe standing on a Flower de luce with . . . 3. great pearles on the Topp of the Cover'), and plate (including one known as 'the Stagge', with a stag's head on the cover).

Other vessels connected with drinking at table include two crystal 'spout potts' (one standing on three lions with 'a Manikin on the Topp, holding a Scutcheon'); a glass 'Spout pott bottle', silver gilt; a 'Christall glasse garnisht with gold', a large 'Christalline Beere Glasse' similarly embellished and a 'Christalline Glasse and Cover garnisht with wyer worke of gold'. Six 'beakers' are listed—three 'great', two 'small', and one of white marble with a cover 'garnisht with gold and stones'. Also to be mentioned here are 'A large Antique Vessell for Mead from the Duke of Muscovy' and two large beakers from the same source 'made of many p^s of Coin Join^d together'. Two 'Leather Drinking Jacks' from Ludlow represent a more prosaic type of vessel: jacks were none the less popular at common dining tables in the seventeenth century when, to judge from allusions in contemporary rhymes, they served for dispensing sack.[86]

A number of spoons are to be found scattered in various locations, including fifty-seven in the Tower; there were also ten at Carisbrooke. Amongst the more elaborate were a 'golden foulding spoone enamelled & sett with Diamonds and Rubies', and a spoon of lapis lazuli 'garnish't wth gold and a little Diamond on the end of the handle'.

The Tower also held a selection of knives, including a dozen 'in a Case of Silver wrought' and eleven 'in a leather Case with silver handles'. Four more with silver handles are designated 'trencher knives' and a further two entries record carving knives, one of them very large with a silver handle, associated with 124 forks and twelve gilt spoons. Eight 'voyding knives' included two with crystal handles: knives of this type had broad, blunt blades and were used for clearing crumbs from the table.

Some 130 further forks came from the Tower, as well as a 'Forke with an Aggatt handle garnish't with gold, and small Rubies and Diamonds'. Forks at this time were generally used only for eating sweetmeats and fruit; meat was eaten with the point of the knife.

Sets of cutlery seem to have been comparatively rare, but included 'An old rusty knife Forke and spoone the handle garnish't with gold, and sett together in a red Leather Case' (sold for £9), an 'Eliotropian Spoone, knife and Forke garnished with gold' and a 'Christall spoone garnish't with gold and sett with small Rubies, a knife and forke suitable'.

The costly nature of some of this hardware suggests that a good deal of it would have spent much of its time in the hands of the officers of the Jewel House,

Figure 111 Gerard Houckgeest: *King Charles I and Queen Henrietta Maria dining in public*, 1635. Royal Collection: reproduced by gracious permission of Her Majesty The Queen. Although the architectural setting is apparently fanciful, the formality of the occasion is unmistakable.

being placed in the care of the Scullery for use at banquets and at special feasts.

Once the royal table had been covered with linen supplied from the Ewery and with cutlery and vessels from the Scullery, it was the turn of the Chamber to exercise its responsibilities (Fig. 111). Serving was carried out by 'tenne officers of the hall, that is to say, four marshalls, foure sewers, and two surveyors of the dresser'. Between them these officers directed matters in the hall, the sewers specifically receiving at the dresser 'such meates as were to be served'. Their first duty was to ensure that the king's food had not been tampered with, by requiring those who had delivered it to 'take the Say' (or assay), 'which is to be given them by Our Sewer, either by cutting off a peece of Meate and giveing our said Cooke to eate, or by giveing a peece of Bread, touching all Our Dishes of Meate being Boyled Meates or other Meates, as to the discretion of the Sewer . . .'[87] Five 'tasters' included in the inventories may have served in this ritual. One was noted in the Whitehall jewel house, and others in the Upper Jewel House at the Tower: one was contained in a red case, and of the other three—all of gold and ranging in value from £6 to £16. 3*s*. 4*d*.—one had 'a Lyon in the middle' and another was 'enamelled wth a Phenix'. The presence in the inventories of one 'Sey Cupp' and two 'Cupps of Essay' suggests that the same precautions were taken on occasion with the king's drink. Service at the royal table was carried out by the carvers, cup-bearers and sewers, who were officers of the Chamber rather than the household: under Charles in particular, their duties were highly formal, the King being served on bended knee. There were also fifteen servitors of the hall, 'to assist and helpe those 10 above'.

At the end of the day all 'relicts and fragments of such meate and drinke' left by the Household and Chamber were to be gathered by the Almoners for distribution to the 'poore folkes', without 'embesselling any part of the same away'. From 1627 this nourishment was to include the trencher bread reintroduced at table in that year (p. 372) but used only as a base on which to serve the main course; afterwards, enriched by the sauce or gravy from the meat, the trencher bread was gathered up in baskets provided by the almoners, who were 'to see the poore duly served with ye releef . . . according to ancient Custom'.[88]

While acknowledging his Christian duty to the destitute on the one hand, the monarch and his stewards took pains to defend the resources of the household from unauthorized depredations. Instructions were issued to the heads of the provisioning offices to ensure that their premises were not allowed to become the 'resort of strangers'. The front line of defence was formed by the porters at the gates, who were to see that 'they doe not onely exclude Servants, Vagabonds, and Rascalls out of their Office, but also that they doe not suffer Vagabonds, Rascalls, or Boyes to enter in at the Gate at any time'. Three or four

21 [14], 34 [84]

37 [115]
36 [112]
45 [-]
26 [4]
24 [47]

times a day they were to 'make due search through the House, in case that negligently at any time, any Boyes or Rascalls have escaped by them'.[89]

As important as their duties in keeping trespassers from the palace were the porters' responsibilities in preventing unauthorized removals of goods and provisions from within: they were exhorted to keep 'vigilant eyes' to see that no 'Victualls, Waxe-lights, Leather-Potts, Vessels Silver or Pewter, Wood or Coals, passe out of the Gates', on pain of loss of wages.[90]

Although much of court life revolved around the formal routine of the dining table, there were many other domestic duties to attend to, some of which have left their mark on the inventories. Within the Household at large, an important task concerned the lighting and tending of the fires that burned in the living quarters and public rooms throughout the winter months. Their importance is reflected in the considerable amounts of hearth equipment registered in the inventories, of which andirons form the most numerous category.

Pairs of andirons (or fire-dogs), originally conceived for use with the open down-hearth, formed part of the standard equipment of the Stuart fireplace, where wood continued to outweigh coal as the principal fuel. Essentially they consisted of two elements: a horizontal billet-bar to support the firewood and an upright standard or 'stauke' to prevent the burning fuel from falling out of the fire. Normally they were supplied as sets in varying sizes: a pair of small 'creepers' and a pair of 'middle dogs' between them bore the burden (and the heat) of the fire in ordinary hearths, while fireplaces in the principal rooms were furnished with a third pair of large and often elaborate dogs (the andirons proper) whose function was primarily decorative.[91]

[passim] The fifty-eight pairs included in the inventories are variously described as small (a category including those designated 'creepers'), middling size and large or 'massie'. Some are of iron and some of brass while others are composite, five pairs being of iron with brass knobs, tops or heads. Two pairs are described as 'cast' in brass, and indeed all those of brass would have been so produced. Both wrought and cast iron fire-dogs were manufactured at this time, cast iron having been the more general since the sixteenth century.[92] The more decorative

116 [292-3] examples include one pair 'with Antiques heads in the Feete', one 'with
116 [294] Cullomes' and one terminating in 'two figures in the Topp'.[93] Most were valued from a few shillings to a few pounds, only two pairs from Denmark House being more highly esteemed at £10 and £24 respectively; both were reserved for service at Whitehall.

Original locations are given for andirons from three houses: Oatlands (bed
286 [136-8] chamber, cabinet chamber and book chamber),[94] Denmark House (long gallery,
116 [290-93], 224 [81], 225 [85] wardrobe and 'Contractors roome') and Ludlow (Lady Alice's chamber, prince's
229 [146], 231 [160], 230 [149] chamber, withdrawing chamber and gatehouse chamber). In ordinary households some examples might have been expected in the kitchens, modified to support roasting spits (spit-dogs), but the royal chefs apparently made use of standing spit-racks for this purpose (see p. 371).[95]

As already mentioned, the majority of these fires would have burned wood. The Woodyard formed a separate office, under the control of the Scullery at the time of the Eltham Ordinances but with its own Sergeant by the time that Queen Elizabeth's regulations were passed on to James I. The Sergeant received for his fee 'all the small toppes of wood of the Kinges, felled for the expence of His Majesty's Household' and supplied not only wood for the royal hearth but also faggots and 'talshides' (logs for splitting into firewood) for those entitled to them as bouche of court.[96]

The introduction of iron grates (which might burn coal as well as wood) has been dated to the reign of James I,[97] although coal seems to have been burned for some time before that.[98] Early grates were portable and simply stood within the hearth area; hence they were easily carried off for the sales. Fourteen examples are recorded in the inventories, all but two of them from Ludlow Castle.[99] If this evidence is to be believed, most of the royal residences would seem to have retained their open hearths at this time, an assumption supported by the greater numbers of andirons recorded above. To some extent the use of grates rendered andirons redundant, although in some instances they were used concurrently and indeed certain andirons were equipped with hooks so that they could act as
224 [81] supports for grates.[100] Only in two instances, at Ludlow Castle, were andirons
229 [146] and grates recorded in the same chambers.

The prolonged effects of the heat generated even by wood fires could damage the masonry of the fireplace. In order to prevent this, great cast-iron fire-backs
394 [955] were developed to bear the brunt of the heat. One 'backe' is recorded along with

a pair of andirons 'in charge of Mr. Southwood'. It seems curious that more fire-backs are not present in the inventories: the scrap value alone of these heavy iron plates (some weighing several hundredweights) would have been significant, while the practice of blazoning them with the royal arms might have been expected to single them out for special attention. Henry VIII, Elizabeth, James I and Charles I all commissioned new designs, while several of those still surviving at Hampton Court bear the fleur-de-lis of Henrietta Maria, perhaps introduced to celebrate the announcement of her engagement to Charles in 1624/5. [101]

230 [154]

With the possible exception of 'one Round Iron for the fire' recorded along with a fire-shovel and tongs at Ludlow Castle, pokers are absent from the hearth equipment as they are in contemporary inventories of other households;[102] their usefulness with wood-burning fires would in any case have been limited. Eleven

[passim]

pairs of tongs and nineteen fire-shovels are listed, the bulk of them from Ludlow Castle. [103] Tongs of this period would have been of the hinged variety, with flat pads rather than claw-like grips. Even among these, however, there was scope for stylistic development and change: Abraham van der Doort referred disparagingly in 1639 to the 'ould fashioned rusty Iron tongs' with matching shovel that rather disgraced the Chair Room at Whitehall.[104] The box-shaped fire shovels of the period served to carry hot coals from fireplace to fireplace.

Bellows too performed an important function in ensuring that fires had to be re-lit as infrequently as possible: every morning the embers from the previous evening's fire (often having been covered with a curfew) were revived with the bellows so as to avoid having to kindle new firewood. None the less, there are

226 [95], 234 [220, 222]
58 [10]
117 [298]

very few to be found in the inventories: three pairs from Ludlow, three from Wimbledon and one 'inlayed with Mother of pearle' but valued at a meagre 5s from Denmark House.[105] Nine further pairs noted at Vauxhall were clearly for use in the foundries there and had no domestic significance.

224 [81], 225 [85], 229 [139]

Three chambers at Ludlow housed wicker screens, all of them listed in sufficiently close association with hearth furnishings as to suggest a connection;

420 [4]

a further 'old Wicker Skreene', valued at 1s., was in the care of 'Mr Willis'. Presumably they functioned as draft-excluders or as fire-guards.

An alternative to open fires had made its appearance under the Tudors in the form of the stove; one 'Dutch stove' was noted at Wimbledon by the Parliamentary surveyors in the 'Lord's closett' and another in the Stone Gallery.[106]

The inventories contain a reasonable range of lighting appliances although the numbers represented again suggest that the majority had somehow escaped notice. One major source of light that makes no impact at all are the torches that continued in daily use at court in the seventeenth century: being entirely expendable, their absence comes as no surprise. They featured, for example, in the daily service of All-Night, in which two Ushers and ten Yeomen processed solemnly round the pantry, the buttery, the spicery, and the wine cellar, gathering ingredients for the King's nightcap and headed by a Groom of the Chamber carrying a lighted torch.[107]

The task of making torches and wax lights fell to the officers of the Chandlery, numbering eight and controlled by the clerk of the Spicery: they handed out the lights every evening, both to the Household and to those entitled to bouche of court, and received back the spent remains for recycling every morning. Early in his reign, James I was made aware of certain failings in this routine, first established under Henry VIII and continued by 'Our late deare sister the Queene', by which certain officers were failing to return the remnants of wax, keeping them back for their own use. James now 'straightly charge[d] . . . Our Gentleman-Usher, Groomes of Our Privy Chamber, and Groome Porters, that they and every one of them deliver backe into Our Chandry, every morning before ten of the clocke, the full and the whole remaine of all the Mortores, Torchetts, Torches, Quarrioures, Waxelights, Sizes, and Pricketts . . . not being spent in Our service'; the clerks of the Spicery were to check by weighing to see that these instructions were complied with, and any officer failing to return the due amount of wax was to be stopped twice the corresponding amount from his daily allowance.[108] The necessities of the office could hardly have changed from the fifteenth century, when they were listed as 'ballaunces grete or smalle, weyghtes, and pannys, longe coffyrs, gardevyaundes [chests], hote irons, carryages'. The Sergeant was charged with carriage of the 'large coffyrs, with greate and smalle lightes, ready at nede when there is workinge, of torches, smalle lightes, or peris' candles'. Under the Eltham Ordinances, the Clerks of the

Spicery were instructed to see 'that the stuffe of waxe . . . be good and not mixed with tallow'. Elizabeth granted the staff of the chandlery 'the cutting of the endes of all sizes, cut in the makeing of the remaines of torches burnt within one foot to the end; and all the endes of quarriers and prickets burnt nigh the socket . . . all broken waxe, and also the waxe that runneth off at the searing of the torches'.[109]

254 [105-9]
Amongst the 'Goodes in ye Wardrop at Somersett house' was a group of material identified as being brought there from the wax chandlery: this included not only two chests of lights (one of yellow wax and the other of white wax) but also two brass pans, 'two beames & 2 paire of scailes & 4 weights' and a 'Tinn furnace & two Covers', all of them used, presumably, in the manufacture and regulation of lights and candles.

Portable lights to be carried out of doors are represented in the inventories by
232 [180]
47 [199]
'Three old broaken Lanthornes' assiduously catalogued at Ludlow, while a 'darke lanthorne' appears incongruously among the plate at the Tower.
46 [193]
30 [42], 235 [235]
Two 'great brazen Lampes' in the Upper Jewel House at the Tower, together with one more in the same place and 'one old Lampe' housed over the porter's lodge at Ludlow serve only to underline how many similar items must have escaped the notice of the Trustees.

Few candlesticks survived in their original contexts, the majority of those noted being concentrated in the Tower. Amongst these were over fifty of plate,
21-6 [passim], 30 [43, 49-50]
including fifteen 'Maydenhead' candlesticks, two wall candlesticks, and sixteen
32 [62], 47 [199]
of crystal, several of them silver-gilt. Those of crystal included one 'hanging upp'
427 [18-19]
and two branches; a further two were recorded with silver sockets (sold for £55
183 [302]
each). In addition to these were eight candlesticks of brass from Hampton Court
118 [316-17]
and Denmark House (the latter also producing 'fowre Woodden painted Frames
234 [220], 236 [236]
to sett Candlesticks upon'); ten of pewter and one of unspecified material from
183 [303]
Ludlow; two of tin (described as branches) from Richmond; two of iron from
117 [302]
Hampton Court; and a 'Candlesticke of yellowe Amber to hang upp in Brannches in a double Woodden Boxe' from Denmark House, valued at £50.

30 [42]
Two pairs of snuffers were recorded among the plate at the Tower and
223 [8]
another two of silver, with plates on which to set them, came from Carisbrooke; a
21 [15]
further 'plate for snuffers' was noted in the Jewel House at Whitehall. Such snuffers were used to trim the still-burning wick of a candle, so as to prevent it guttering and smoking: those of the early Stuart period normally had an elongated point to one of their scissors-like blades with which to uncoil the wick; one of the blades was fitted with a box to receive the trimmed-off end of the wick and the other with a corresponding plate which pressed the trimmings into the box to extinguish them. To put out the flame on the candle a separate utensil might be used, normally called a douter but represented among the plate at the
25 [50]
Tower by an entry for an 'extinguisher'.

Other pieces of equipment connected with the everyday running of the household were as diverse as they were scattered. Two warming pans of modest
231 [158], 232 [177]
manufacture (valued at 6s. – with other items – and 2s. respectively) came from
223 [7]
Ludlow Castle, while a more elaborate example was listed among the plate from Carisbrooke. The standard type found in more affluent seventeenth-century households had a wrought iron handle and a pan with a decoratively perforated lid to allow the heat to escape from the hot charcoal within.[110]

412 [77]
'Five perfumeing panns of pomander' in red cases were amongst the 'Chapel goods' inventoried at Denmark House: perhaps these are to be seen specifically as incense burners in view of their associations. Others came from domestic apartments (where they were referred to alternatively in the seventeenth century
117 [306]
also as incense burners or fumigators): one 'covered wth redd vellvett' and one a
117 [305]
'Perfumeing Pott of Brasse with black Images and one on the Topp' were listed at
232 [178]
Denmark House. A more modest version, also in brass and valued at 1s., was noted at Ludlow, while two examples in plate came from the Tower and from Wimbledon House respectively. Their presence here is without liturgical significance: perfuming pans were used to sweeten the atmosphere in certain apartments, and have been described as 'essential bed-room requisites'.[111]

Another group of items for improving the ambience is formed by the 'casting bottles', that is to say, bottles with perforated caps from which scented water could be sprinkled: these include two 'little Aggatt Casting Bottles. wth Chaines
36 [103]
of gold', a 'Casting bottle with a Roman head' and six others described as 'of silver gilt, and richly garnished with Mother of Pearle'.

Accounts for the three months of April to June 1622, submitted by James I's apothecary Jolliffe Lownes, show that aromatic powders and waters were issued for use in the Bedchamber, Privy Chamber, Presence Chamber, Wardrobe, Closet and Council Chamber. As the King progressed around his palaces, supplies were issued in anticipation of his arrival successively at St. James's , Denmark House, Greenwich, St. James's again, Richmond, Whitehall, Theobalds, Greenwich again, and Nonsuch; the coachmen and the bargemen also received supplies to sweeten the King's passage from place to place.[112]

Aromatic herbs and powders were also provided in quantity by the court apothecaries for use in the 'sweet bags' placed among the royal linen (see p. 316): musk, damask powder and orris powder were among the commodities provided by the apothecaries.[113]

58 [7-8] 'Fowre Pewter stills' and two 'Limbecks' originating from Wimbledon House may also be mentioned here, since they were almost certainly used in the production of perfumed waters. Sir Hugh Platt's *Delightes for Ladies*, widely read in early Stuart England, gives hints on 'secrets of distillation', one or two of which are for spirits of wine, 'Usquebath, or Irish aqua-vitae' and the like, but most concern extracts of thyme, lavender, rosemary and other herbs for use in perfumed waters.[114] The Parliamentary survey of Wimbledon in particular, shows the range of fragrant shrubs and other plants grown in the royal gardens which might provide ingredients for sweet bags and perfumed waters, including orange, lemon, lime, rosemary, rue and lavender.[115]

23 [28] A pair of 'Flatt large Flower potts' catalogued among the plate remind us of further opportunities taken to improve the fragrance of the royal chambers. Other flower pots of earthenware may have been used in some numbers but, as with cooking vessels of the same material, they have been deemed unworthy of record.

An addition made to the Eltham Ordinances on 18 January 1542, dealing at some length with the duties of Anne Harris, the King's laundress, provides one of the few insights into the running of her office. Anne was to be issued with four weeks' supply of table-linen – 'in fine Diaper, Damascue worke, four great pieces, 28 long Breakfast-clothes, 28 short ones of 3 yards the peice, 28 Hand towells, and 12 dozen of Napkins' – one quarter of which were to be washed every seven days. Clean supplies were to be delivered by her daily to the Ewery, and the soiled linen taken away. She was also to keep a watch for any misuse of the linen, 'discreetly perusing and viewing the stuff how it hath been used and ordered'. An allowance was to be made to her from the Compting House for the provision of 'sweet Powder, sweet Herbes, and other sweet things', but no additions were to be made to her wages for 'Wood, Sope, or any other thing'.[116]

One or two tubs mentioned in the inventories may have been used for laundry, though they lack distinctive epithets. At Ludlow, a closet next to the 226 [96] Steward's chamber produced two 'frames to hang Cloathes upon': drying laundry indoors may often have been a feature of domestic life in the Welsh marches. At Wimbledon more elaborate provision was made for inclement conditions: the Parliamentary surveyors noted there a 'greate drying roome flored with deale and fitted with hanging poles and a Crane and Loopeholes for the craning up of clothes for drying'.[117] For lack of adequate facilities Whitehall Palace was lost in 1695, for the blaze in which it was destroyed broke out when clothes drying before a fire caught alight.[118] Most of the 'presses' listed in the inventories were no doubt merely cupboards, but amongst three mentioned at 228 [126] Ludlow was one described as a 'Presse to presse Lynnen' and at Bewdley there 238 [264] was recorded a 'broaken screwe to presse clothes'.

Improvements in the sanitary arrangements at the most intensively-used palaces had begun to be made in the sixteenth and seventeenth centuries: at Hampton Court sewage was channelled directly into the Thames, as it probably was a Whitehall, Richmond and Greenwich.[119] Elsewhere there was a continuing reliance on garderobe pits, while portable close stools (or necessary stools) and chamber pots were used universally. A reasonable complement of these survived 224-36 [*passim*] at Ludlow, where 'Necessarie stooles and panns' were noted in Lady Alice's chamber, the closet next the Steward's chamber and in the Secretary's study, as well as in a 'little Wainescott Garrett' and in 'a little Chamber over ye Porters Lodge'; three further necessary stools and pans were recorded there without specific location; in addition to these a 'Close stoole' was noted in 'the Secretaries mans Chamber' and chamber pots were inventoried in Prince Arthur's chamber, the doctor's chamber, the 'Gentlewoemens Chamber' and the Governor's lodging; in addition, sixteen chamber pots were listed among the pewter from the castle. A further twenty examples were scattered around the other properties 120 [331] in the inventories, of which the more elaborate included a 'Necessarie stoole of Wainescott covered all over with a Tawney vellvett, enbroydered suiteable to a

392 [918]

21 [15], 223 [6, 9]

Tawney Bedd' at Denmark House and a 'Close stoole Covered wth Crimson velvt wth a Case & two pannes' from Greenwich. A single chamberpot was included among the plate in the Jewel House at Whitehall and another two came from Carisbrooke.

Regular bathing was becoming more widely practised in the Stuart period and baths were by now common enough in the royal palaces: some details survive of the facilities at Whitehall, Greenwich, Windsor and Hampton Court.[120] Two baths sold from Hampton Court were evidently fittings of some importance: one, described as 'The Baine in one side ye Rome being Tin wth a Cesterne', sold for £55, while 'One other Baine wth 8 doores to it' fetched £15. Less grandiose facilities existed at Ludlow in the form of a 'Batheing Tubb', sold in a lot along with 'other odd Lumber'.

183 [304]
183 [305]
232 [188]

Other tanks and cisterns in the inventories combine to give a picture of a well-developed water supply system – one that had seen many improvements over the previous century with the installation of new conduits with settling tanks and, where appropriate, force-pumps to ensure a constant supply.[121] The principal items noted in the inventories were the great stone or leaden store cisterns:[122] at Theobalds 'One great stone [?store] Cesterne wth many pypes thereto belonging' was valued at £160; somewhat lesser tanks included a 'Great Pewter Cisterne' at Ludlow (£33) and others at Holdenby (in the brewhouse) (£30), Greenwich (£20), Hampton Court (£20), Windsor (£16) and Woodstock (£12) and Richmond (£10). No doubt there were many others which eluded the sale, being regarded as essential fittings of the respective properties: two small leaden cisterns at Woodstock, for example, – one in an 'Anncient Fountaine' and the other within the font in the chapel – were noted by the Trustees, but 'being soe fixed [were] thought parte of the Howse. & not of ye Personal Estate'. Such seems to have been the case too with the 'very large cesterne of lead fed and maynteyned with severall pipes of lead conveying water thereinto from a conduit', which the Parliamentary surveyors found at Nonsuch: 'This cesterne is of singular use to the whole house', they observed, 'many pipes being branched from thence for the supply of the offices of the whole house and ought not as we conceave to bee removed thence'.[123] Some degree of interconnection between cisterns was observed elsewhere by the Trustees: at Theobalds there were 'Two other Cesternes wth pypes going into the stone Cesterne', while another at Holdenby was fitted with 'Pipes wch serve all Offices'.

396 [975]
236 [236]
241 [291]
249 [30], 184 [310], 294 [228], 244 [321]
213 [83]

244 [321]

396 [976]

241 [292]

Some of these, like the 'little Cesterne at the end of the house' at Theobalds, may have trapped rainwater. One example at Ludlow was sited in the well-house along with two 'large Bucketts wth Iron hoopes' and evidently had to be filled by hand. Four others in the gardens at Hampton Court may have been connected with the water supply that fed the fountains there. Others were certainly for internal domestic use: in addition to the brewhouse (p. 373), individual offices served by their own cisterns included the privy kitchen, scullery, fish larder, buttery, ewery, cellar and chandlery, all at Windsor, and the pastry and wine cellars at Hampton Court, Richmond and Ludlow. Some of these smaller cisterns may have had no direct connection with the piped water supply.[124]

396 [977]
228 [135]

184 [310], 185 [327-8]

184 [311-13]
294-5 [224-32], 214 [86]
235 [233]

185 [326]

'One great Cock & pipe in ye Kitchin' at Hampton Court may have controlled the water supply at some point, or may equally have been for use with casks or tuns.

Water had a further part to play in firefighting, as witnessed by the leather buckets laid in at Nonsuch in 1592-3 'againste the rage of fier if any such chance should happen'.[125] As the list of other equipment bought on this occasion shows, however, water was of limited value in the face of a real conflagration in the days before the advent of portable pumps: only by sacrificing already-burning buildings, or at least by pulling off their burning roofs to stop the flames spreading, could a fire be checked once it had taken hold. Hence the firefighting equipment acquired at Nonsuch consisted of iron hooks, chains, ladders, ropes and poles, in addition to buckets.[126] At Richmond Court the Parliamentary surveyors found 'three severall long and greate ladders, and three long anchored hookes fitted with greate chaynes and standards for pulling downe of housing in case of fier', which they judged to be 'of great use for the whole house upon all occasions'.[127] 'Two great lathers & a hookes' from Oatlands (valued at £2) clearly belong amongst this equipment, as do a further two 'great Lathers' associated with four 'great Hookes' at Hampton Court (£5).[128] Perhaps of more general use were two further ladders from the chandlery at Denmark House, which sold for a mere 2s., and a 'fouldeing Joyned Lather' from Hampton Court which fetched 4s.

250 [38]
185 [325]

255 [112]
182 [277]

Almost total losses were suffered amongst the other goods that might have served in the maintenance of the royal orchards and gardens. All that was left for the Trustees to inventory were two 'rowlers' from Theobalds and a 'rowlein stone' inventoried in the yard at Denmark House (sold for 10s.). Even in this least fugitive category, there must originally have been many others: at Wimbledon the Parliamentary surveyors had noted 'belonging to the . . . vyneyard garden two rollers of stone with very large and handsome frames of Iron and allsoe belonging to the . . . oringe and upper garden six other roulers of stone fitted as aforesaid', worth in all £16,[129] while at Hampton Court in 1659 three 'stone rolls' with iron frames and a 'large wood roll with a wood frame' were recorded in the gardens and bowling green.[130]

On the subject of garden rollers, John Evelyn had firm advice to offer:

The best are made of the hardest Marble, and such as are procured from the ruines of many palaces in *Smyrna* when old *Colomns* of demolish't *Antiquities* being sawd off towards the *vino* of the *pedistall* and at the part or *Modell* where the shaft diminishes, makes excellent Rollers...The fore described Rollers may be procur'd by the friendship of some Marchand trading into the Levant.[131]

According to a tradition current in the eighteenth century and perhaps originating as early as the seventeenth, there was a strong philosophical appeal in the utilization of such fragments of classical antiquity in preparing the ground, as it were, for the fruits of the new civilization.[132] In this context, the presence of these otherwise unremarkable items in the inventories of the late King's goods presents an apposite metaphor for the noble aspirations that Charles I brought to the throne and for their ruinous collapse in the upheaval that brought his reign to a close. While providing insights into those aspects of everyday life which usually escape notice, therefore, the lists of domestic equipment, no less than the catalogues of redundant regalia and abandoned royal personalia, also provide a poignant comment on the dissolution of the Household in the aftermath of the King's demise.

Notes

1. In this context, Professor Gerald Aylmer has drawn my attention to the example offered by Whitehall Palace, where the need to cater for a disparate body of tenants no doubt entailed a certain reapportioning of kitchen equipment formerly under centralized control. According to a 'Survey and Ground Plot of His Majesty's Palace of Whitehall', dated 1689, there were no fewer than thirteen kitchens in the palace even at that time (BL, Lansdown MS 736, f. 18ᵛ).

2. *Lords Journals* IX, p. 520.

3. BL, Harley MS 642, ff. 145ᵛ-176ᵛ, published by the Society of Antiquaries in *A Collection of Ordinances and Regulations for the Government of the Royal Household* (London, 1790) (hereafter abbreviated to *Ordinances and Regulations*), pp. 137-240.

4. BL, Harley MS 642, ff. 226-34, published in *Ordinances and Regulations*, pp. 281-98.

5. 'The great chardge, and abuses, which have crept into the Kinges howse, sense the tyme of king Henry the eight' (PRO, LS 13/280, ff. 58-9). I am grateful to my colleague Mr. Julian Munby for a complete transcription of this document.

6. For the establishment of the Compting House and of all the other offices discussed here see G.E. Aylmer, *The King's Servants. The Civil Service of Charles I 1625-1642* (London, 1974), *passim* and Table 58.

7. *Ordinances and Regulations*, p. 228.

8. G.E. Aylmer, 'Attempts at administrative reform, 1625-40', *English Historical Review* 72 (1957), pp. 250-1, 255. To judge from another source, the blame for this sorry state of affairs went right to the top: 'in tymes past', it was said, '. . . the Comptroller tooke the paynes to sitt daylie in the Compting howse, And often tymes went into the Offices to see good orders kept; The fear of him was so greate to the Officers, that these abuses, which are now crept into the howse, were not then used' (PRO, LS 13/280, f. 59).

9. It has been calculated that during the 1630s, for example, the cost of providing diet reached an average of £97,000 annually (Aylmer, op. cit. (Note 6), p. 170).

10. *Ordinances and Regulations*, pp. 142, 236-7. On occasion, however, it was found that 'when provision is made of good and fatt Cattle, & put into the kings pastures; the same pastures are sometymes so chardged with horses, mares & colts; That [the] cattle which were taken fatt, are become wors than they were, when they were first put into the said pastures' (PRO, LS 13/280, f. 59ʳ). The King's own gardens, parks, and fishponds would also have been important sources of produce. Dovecotes, rabbit-warrens and hare-warrens were attached to many of the properties discussed above (pp. 19-44).

11. Ibid, pp. 289-90. 'Grey salt' was presumably sea (or 'bay') salt, imported into England from the Biscay coast since the thirteenth century and valued more highly than English 'white salt': see J. Stevenson Watson, *A History of the Salters' Company* (London, 1963), p. 11.

12. BL, Harley MS 7623, f. 18ʳ.

13. A 'table & yᵉ Iron for a beame & two Standards' (valued at £2) and a 'Beame for a paire of scales' (10s.) inventoried at the Tower Jewel House (*Inventories*, p. 252 [65-6]) presumably served in the weighing of plate, as in the annual exchange of New Year gifts between King and noblemen: see A.J. Collins, *Jewels and Plate of Queen Elizabeth I* (London, 1955), pp. 101-10; *Seventh Annual Report of the Royal Commission on Historical Manuscripts* (London, 1879), pt. 1, p. 594.

14. *Ordinances and Regulations*, pp. 142, 236.

15. Ibid., p. 299.

16. BL, Harley MS 642, ff. 248-9 (*Ordinances and Regulations*, pp. 317-8); E. Turnor, 'A declaration of the diet and particular fare of K. Charles the First, when Duke of York', *Archaeologia* 15 (1806), pp. 1-12.

17. *Ordinances and Regulations*, pp. 299-302, 'Bouche of court' (daily entitlement to bread, ale, candles, and firewood) was similarly restricted and in some instances benefits were commuted to cash payments.

18. Ibid., pp. 287, 298. As a means of controlling losses, however, the system proved less than successful: a considerable 'daylie sale' of supplies from a number of provisioning departments was found to have been made during James I's time (PRO, LS 13/280).

19. The duties of the Scalding House were to 'scald, plucke and draw' all the fowls and other provisions of the Poultry. On occasion its officers were found to have so depleted their charge of 'Capon, henn, fowle, &c', that 'when it cometh to the Larder, to bee put forth for the Princes honn[our], a great deale of the best is gone' (PRO, LS 13/280, f. 58ᵛ). The responsibilities of the Poultry seem to have been rather wider than its name implies, for its establishment included a 'Purveyer of Lambes' and its clerk and yeoman were entitled respectively to the black and the grey 'conie skinnes' which 'yearely come into that office' (*Ordinances and Regulations*, p. 290).

20. Ibid., pp. 288, 291.

21. Ibid., p. 288.

22. F. G. Emmison, *Tudor Food and Pastimes* (London, 1964), p. 39. Abuses had crept into the Larder too, for it was found that 'there goeth out every flesh Daie xvj Chines, viij Filletts, viij spit boanes; which all amount to Fortie messes of meate; and xxᵗⁱᵉ of them not spent to the kings use' (PRO, LS 13/280, f. 58ᵛ).

23. W. H. Hart, 'The Parliamentary surveys of Richmond, Wimbledon, and Nonsuch, in the County of Surrey, AD 1649', *Surrey Archaeological Collections* 56 (1959), p. 105.

24. E. Law, *The History of Hampton Court Palace* II *Stuart Times* (London, 1888), p. 306.

25. An inventory of the Fairfax household at Gilling, dated 1624, notes '4 salting tubs' in the 'beef house' (E. Peacock, 'Inventories made for Sir William and Sir Thomas Fairfax, Knights, of Walton and of Gilling Castle, Yorkshire, in the sixteenth and seventeenth centuries', *Archaeologia* 48, (1885), p. 151). While J. O. Halliwell (*Ancient Inventories of Furniture, Pictures, Tapestry, Plate, &c, illustrative of the Domestic Manners of the English in the Sixteenth and Seventeenth Centuries* (London, 1854), pp. 70-1), includes a notice from 1610 of a 'great powdring tubbe for bakon'.

26. In an inventory of 1610, J. O. Halliwell (op. cit. (Note 25), pp. 70-1) notes 'thre powdering tubbes' housed in a 'mylk house' and '. . . by the cheese wring . . . a great powdring tubbe for cheese, with a cover'.

27. *Ordinances and Regulations*, pp. 285, 295.

28. Hart, op. cit. (Note 23), p. 105. 'One pepper mylne and one paire of mustarde quearnes' are recorded in an inventory of Sir William Fairfax's goods, dated 1594 (Peacock, op. cit. (Note 25), p. 132). The compiler of the report on Prince Henry's household lamented that 'in the tyme of Queene Marye, and before, every gardiner that had a garden of the Prince in keeping, sent herbes to the Court as hee was appointed, And then the chardge was but small'; by the time of the report, however, it was found that 'the Sawcery is at double the Chardge, it was wont to bee . . . And also the herbes in the Scullery amount sometymes to vij or viijˡⁱ in a moneth' (PRO, LS 13/280, ff. 58-9).

29. In pies and in thick standing pottages, for example, meat was usually ground in this way. Hard cheese might also be pounded in a mortar for inclusion in tarts: see C.A. Wilson, *Food and Drink in Britain* (Harmondsworth, 1976), pp. 79-80, 147.

30. In 1595, for example, Sir William Fairfax's kitchen at Gilling boasted 'two greate square spittes, iiij lesser square spittes, iij rounde spittes, and ij small spittes' (Peacock, op. cit. (Note 25), p. 132).

31. This wheel would be grooved or flanged for a belt on automated examples. Evidence for these (driven by clockwork 'jacks' or by small dogs enclosed in a tread-mill) is entirely absent from the early Stuart kitchens, suggesting a certain labour-intensive conservatism. Elsewhere they had been in use since at least the 1580s (Halliwell, op. cit. (Note 25), p. 155).

32. Law, op. cit. (Note 24), pp. 303, 305.

33. *Ordinances and Regulations*, p. 288.

34. A similar relationship is established in a Fairfax inventory of 1624, which includes '11 spittes, 2 paire of Rackes' and '2 spittes & two paire of Rackes for the Chamber' (Peacock, op. cit. (Note 25), p. 146).

35. Alternative methods of support included spit-dogs (andirons fitted with hooks or ledges designed to carry the spits) and iron bars fitted with supports and let into flanking buttresses, as occur at Hampton Court (J. Starkie Gardner, *Ironwork* III *A Complete Survey of the Artistic Working of Iron in Great Britain from the Earliest Times* (London, 1922; reprinted 1978), pp. 158-65).

36. Compare the 'Barre of Iron before yᵉ fire' in the kitchen at Ludlow (*Inventories*, p. 228 [133]).

37. See, for example, R. Lister, *Decorative Wrought Ironwork in Great Britain* (London, 1957), p. 169; J. Seymour Lindsay, *Iron and Brass Implements of the English House* (London, 1964), p. 12.

38. Lindsay, op. cit. (Note 37), p. 29.

39. For examples of baking irons, used for baking or broiling meat, see R. Field, *Irons in the Fire. A Histroy of Cooking Equipment* (Marlborough, 1984), pp. 121, 123.

40. That their use was not limited merely to cooking meat is shown by an inventory of 1624, which includes 'two grydirons, whereof one is for cockles' (Peacock, op. cit. (Note 25), p. 146).

41. Several pots, dishes and kettles listed at Hampton Court after Cromwell's death are described as 'tin'd' (Law, op. cit. (Note 24), pp. 303-4), but no such refinement is recorded in the sale inventory of Charles's goods.

42. The 1659 Hampton Court inventory includes 'Two great copper pans to boyle fish in' as well as 'Five large brasse peices with holes in them to take fish out of yᵉ panns' and 'One long Copper with a false bottom to boyle fish in' (ibid.).

43. Lindsay (op. cit. (Note 37), p. 33) characterizes frying pans associated with the open hearth as having either a wrought iron handle up to three feet in length or a half-loop handle with a swivel on top for suspension from a pot-hook.

44. Collins, op. cit. (Note 13), pp. 60-1. Against this suggestion of ultra-limited use must be set the appearance of silver vessels amongst the kitchenware in a number of noble households elsewhere: at Walton, the house of Sir Thomas Fairfax, a posnet, a mortar and pestle, and a chafing dish, all of silver, were inventoried in 1624 (Peacock, op. cit. (Note 25), p. 143); the Earl of Northampton's inventory of 1614 also included a silver chafing dish (E.P. Shirley, 'An inventory of the effects of Henry Howard, K.G., Earl of Northampton, taken on his death in 1614', *Archaeologia* 42 (1869), p. 353).

45. Law, op. cit. (Note 24), pp. 304-5.

46. Compare the 'scumner' included among the milkhouse equipment at Walton in 1624 (Peacock, op. cit. (Note 25), p. 147).

47. But see the comment on 'kitchen plate' above. 'One siluer cullander con. v ounces qtr' was owned by the Fairfaxes in 1594 (Peacock, op. cit. (Note 25), p. 124).

48. *Ordinances and Regulations*, p. 72.

49. J. Nichols, *The Progresses, Processions, and Magnificent Festivities, of King James the First, his Royal Consort, Family and Court* (London, 1828), II, pp. 547-8.

50. The *OED* equates bolting with sifting, 'boltings' being the coarse meal separated in this way; the sifting was carried out with the aid of a coarse-grained 'bolting cloth'. An inventory of the Countess of Leicester's goods, dated 1634, includes '2 cleansing sives in the boultinge house' (Halliwell, op. cit. (Note 25), p. 17).

51. *Ordinances and Regulations*, p. 294.

52. A good range of baking equipment was noted at Wimbledon by the Parliamentary surveyors, who listed a 'pastrie roome . . . fitted with a boulting mill a kneading trough a moulding board a double bynne and a range with severall large ovens' (Hart, op. cit. (Note 23), p. 105).

53. Gervase Markham (*Cavalerice, or the English Horseman* (London, 1617), ch. VI, p. 15) advocated in the making of bread for horses a thorough kneading, 'first with the handes, after with the feete by treading, and lastly with the brake'.

54. The Yeoman Furnitor was granted for his fee 'all the burnt coales drawne out of the oven' (*Ordinances and Regulations*, p. 294).

55. Ibid., p. 284. The staff of the Pantry were found at times to have been over-generous with the royal bread, there being 'more given awaye, than can by any meanes bee well answered unto', due to a lack of proper supervision by the Compting House (PRO, LS 13/280, f. 58).

56. *Ordinances and Regulations*, p. 284.

57. Simon Thurley has drawn my attention to the 'stillages' excavated at Whitehall in 1939 and to others surviving at Hampton Court which are of brick with a wooden sleeper as the only movable part: this type would clearly have been inappropriate for sale.

58. *Ordinances and Regulations*, p. 284. Three 'Bottle horses' were included among the King's 109 horses listed in the Eltham Ordinances (ibid., p. 200).

59. Hart, op. cit. (Note 23), p. 106.

60. G.H. Chettle, *The Queen's House, Greenwich* (London Survey XIV) (London, 1937), p. 22.

61. *Ordinances and Regulations*, p. 218. Despite these precautions, it was found that thanks to the activities of the cellarmen 'there is no small quantitie spilt, besyde a great deale that is conveyed away & sold' (PRO, LS 13/280, f. 58).

62. *Ordinances and Regulations*, p. 284. Since the fifteenth century, hops had been permitted as an ingredient in beer, but not in ale.

63. The brewhouse at Hampton Court contained in 1659 'one copper, one mash tun, and underbacke, one Guill tun [a tun with a quill, or tap] and two upper backs' (Law, op. cit. (Note 24), p. 306). Together with the entries in the *Inventories*, these items comprise the essential equipment of the brewer's craft: the mash tun in which to steep the barley, the underback into which the wort is run, the copper where the fermented liquor is boiled, and troughs and pumps with which to run it into the cooler, whence it is transferred to the cask.

64. Nichols, op. cit. (Note 49), III, p. 39.

65. W.L.F. Nuttall, 'King Charles I's pictures and the Commonwealth sale', *Apollo* 82 (1965), p. 308.

66. *Ordinances and Regulations*, p. 291.

67. BL, Harley MS 7623, f. 17ᵛ.

68. Ultimate responsibility for all plate lay with the Jewel House, whose officers ordered replacements to be made and issued services to ambassadors and others travelling abroad on the King's business (see H.D.W. Sitwell, 'The Jewel House and the royal goldsmiths', *Archaeological Journal* 117 (1960), p. 133).

69. *Ordinances and Regulations*, p. 306.

70. In Edward IV's day the Office of the Ewery and Napery had been responsible both for table linen and for 'all basyns, ewears, cuppes, and napkins, of sylver and guylte', which might be drawn from the Jewel House as required. By the reign of Henry VIII, however, although the title of the office had been reduced to the Ewery, its responsibilities seem to have been restricted to the napery only: see *Ordinances and Regulations*, pp. 83, 235.

71. Law, op. cit. (Note 24), p. 304.

72. Collins, op. cit., (Note 13), p. 49.

73. *Ordinances and Regulations*, p. 356.

74. Collins, (op. cit. (Note 13), pp. 51-2) mentions that many 'basones' were produced with a central bushell designed to receive the foot of a companion ewer.

75. Ibid., p. 50.

76. In the Elizabethan period, at least, pewter dishes were sold by the set or 'garnish' of twelve platters, twelve dishes, twelve saucers and two chargers (ibid., p. 58).

77. W.B. Rye, *England as seen by Foreigners in the Days of Elizabeth and James the First* (London, 1865), p. 152.

78. PRO, LS 13/169, [10].

79. Collins, op. cit. (Note 13), pp. 59-60.

80. The 'snow conserve' at Greenwich was formed by constructing a thatched house over a brick-lined well-shaft; the thatchers also provided 'waddes' for insulation (*King's Works* IV, p. 123). At Hampton Court a 'conserve of Snowe', built in 1625-6, was constructed of brick on 'twoe grete floores' (ibid., p. 144). Under William and Mary, £91. 5s. was allowed 'To the Yeoman that keeps the Ice-house, for filling the Ice-houses, and all necessaries if found needfull' (*Ordinances and Regulations*, p. 393).

81. These may have taken their name from some association with Hanseatic shipping or manufacturing centres (Collins, op. cit. (Note 13), p. 43).

82. The term 'flagon' is commonly used to denote an elongated tankard, handled and covered, with or without a spout. Those recorded in the inventories, however, seem more akin to the definition given by Collins (op. cit. (Note 13), p. 35), who equates them with costrels or pilgrim bottles (so accounting for the chains by which they could be slung. A reference in the Household regulations of William and Mary, dated 1689, serves as a reminder that not all these vessels need have been dedicated to alcohol: a charge of £132. 10s. was allowed then 'For bottles, corks, glasses, glass-cases, &c. and dayly fetching waters from the best fountains, if necessary' (*Ordinances and Regulations*, p. 393).

83. The gift of the Prince Palatine to James I on St. John's day 1612 was 'a bottle of one entire agate containing two quarts, a very rare and rich jewell'; on the same occasion the Queen received 'a very fair cup of agate' (Nichols, op. cit. (Note 49), II, p. 515).

84. PRO, SP 25/63, 121.

85. Rye, op. cit. (Note 77), p. 121, records a banquet in 1604 at Whitehall at which Juan Fernandez de Velasco, Constable of Castile, 'drank to the Queen the health of the King from a very beautiful dragon-shaped cup of crystal garnished with gold, drinking from the cover, and the Queen standing up gave the pledge from the cup itself'.

86. O. Baker, Black Jacks and Leather Bottels (Cheltenham, [1921]), pp. 67-111.

87. Ordinances and Regulations, p. 306.

88. PRO, LS 13/169, [10]; Ordinances and Regulations, p. 239.

89. Ordinances and Regulations, p. 239.

90. Ibid.

91. The respective functions of the various fire-dogs made them popular subjects for literary allusion. Thomas Fuller (Worthies of England (London, 1662), p. 24), for example, draws a contrast between the burdensome duties of the professional diplomat and the more ceremonial role of the noble ambassador, likening them to 'the Iron Doggs [that] bear the burthen of the fuel, while the Brasen-Andirons stand only for state, to entertain the eyes'.

92. Gardner, op. cit. (Note 35), p. 158.

93. Architectural devices and demi-figures are said to have ranked among the most popular motifs on cast iron fire-dogs of the sixteenth century (G.B. Hughes, 'Old English fire-dogs', Country Life 117 (1955), p. 628).

94. Another twelve from Oatlands are described as 'for Chamber Chimneys' (Inventories, p. 282 [98]).

95. For some further discussion of fire-dogs see C. ffoulkes, Decorative Ironwork from the XIth to the XVIIIth Century (London, 1913), pp. 102-4; N.M. Penzer, 'The royal fire-dogs', Connoisseur (Antique Dealers' Fair and Exhibition Number, 1954), pp. 9-11; R. Lister, op. cit. (Note 37), p. 180; Lindsay, op. cit. (Note 37), pp. 8-9.

96. Ordinances and Regulations, pp. 238-9, 292, 297.

97. Gardner, op. cit. (Note 35), p. 60.

98. In an addition to the Eltham Ordinances dated 3 January 1542, 'the Colliers of every quarter' were to be 'communed with, for to serve coales by full measure' while an order had been issued two years earlier to the effect that 'noe Livery-Coales' were to be served to any chambers other than those of the King, Queen and the Princess Mary (Ordinances and Regulations, p. 227).

99. An additional record at Hampton Court – 'one Iron with grates in the hall' (Inventories, p. 395 [964]) – is ambivalent.

100. Gardner, op. cit. (Note 35), p. 60; Lindsay, op. cit. (Note 37), p. 13. L.A. Shuffery (The English Fireplace (London, 1912), p. 153, pls. xxv, lxviii-lxix) illustrates early fire-baskets flanked by andirons at Ockwells (Berkshire) and Penshurst (Kent).

101. Gardner, op. cit. (Note 35), pp. 159-65. Presumably, most firebacks would have been saved from sale by the effectiveness of the iron pins that anchored them to the masonry.

102. There was also a 'fire Iron Racke' in the hall at Bewdley House (Inventories, p. 238 [261]). Note too that the term 'fire-iron' was also used to signify a strike-a-light: Lindsay (op. cit. (Note 37), p. 54) quotes a source associating 'fyre irons, flynte stones, Tinder and Brimstone'.

103. At the end of Cromwell's occupancy of Hampton Court there were thirty-one fire-shovels there alone (Law, op. cit. (Note 24), pp. 304-5).

104. Van der Doort's Catalogue, p. 74 [5-6].

105. In 1659 eleven pairs of bellows were in use in the Hampton Court household (Law, op. cit. (Note 24), p. 304). An alternative and less costly device, noted by Halliwell (op. cit. (Note 25), p. 74) in an inventory of 1610, was 'a wicker fan for the fyer'.

106. Hart, op. cit. (Note 23), p. 109. Simon Thurley informs me that several Tudor palaces had such stoves, including Hampton Court and Whitehall, where a complete specimen clad in glazed Dutch tiles was excavated earlier this century.

107. S. Pegge, Curialia; or an Historical Account of Some Branches of the Royal Household (London, 1782), pp. 19-23.

108. Ordinances and Regulations, p. 305. 'Mortores' were simple lamps with a wick floating in wax or oil; 'sizes' and 'prickets' were both wax candles; 'quarrioures' were larger square candles.

109. Ibid., pp. 82, 141, 295.

110. Lindsay, op. cit. (Note 37), p. 32. Warming pans to be filled with hot water, rather than charcoal, were a later development.

111. Collins, op. cit. (Note 13), p. 61.

112. A. Manners, [An account of perfumery supplied for the use of King James I], Proceedings of the Society of Antiquaries of London 2nd. ser. 4 (1867-70), pp. 435-7. The same accounts mention also issues to Wanstead and 'to groomes for the Lord Cobham's house', suggesting that James never liked exposure to unfragrant reality.

113. L.G. Matthews, The Royal Apothecaries (London, 1967), p. 71.

114. H. Platt, Delightes for Ladies, to adorne their Persons, Tables, closets, and distillatories (London, 1602), passim. Rose water and orange flower water were among the commodities supplied by the royal apothecaries (Manners, op. cit. (Note 112), pp. 436-7).

115. Hart, op. cit. (Note 23), pp. 112-28.

116. Ordinances and Regulations, pp. 215-6.

117. Hart, op. cit. (Note 23), p. 111. Restrictions against the laundering of clothes while the court was in residence were enforced at times: amongst orders for the household of Prince Charles and the other royal children, dated 1638/9, is one forbidding the washing of linen within the house (BL, Harley MS 7623, f. 18r).

118. I am grateful to Simon Thurley for this information.

119. King's Works IV, p. 27.

120. Ibid., pp. 27, 136, 310.

121. Ibid., passim.

122. For some account of cisterns of this type see L. Weaver, English Leadwork. Its Art and History (London, 1909), pp. 65-85. It may be noted that the term 'cistern' could also be used at this time to describe a storage tank or hopper for drystuffs, as with the 'seasterne of leade for barley' noted in the Fairfax inventories (Peacock, op. cit. (Note 25), p. 130).

123. Hart, op. cit. (Note 23), p. 144.

124. Compare the four cisterns designed to 'sett at cupbordes' which feature in an inventory of Kenilworth Castle dated 1588 (Halliwell, op. cit. (Note 25), p. 153).

125. PRO, E351/3227.

126. E.H. Pinto (Treen and other Wooden Bygones (London, 1969), p. 127) mentions that hooks for dragging burning thatch from roofs were mounted on poles sixteen to twenty feet long, to be wielded by several men; some were fitted with chains, so that they could be harnessed to horses. At the burning of the Whitehall banqueting house on 12 January 1619, directions were given 'to suppresse the flame, and by hookes to pull downe some other adjoyning buildings, to prevent the furious fire' (John Stow, Annales, or a Generall Chronicle of England (London, 1631), p. 1031).

127. Hart, op. cit. (Note 23), p. 82.

128. A number of fire-hooks of uncertain date still survive at Hampton Court (Simon Thurley, personal communication).

129. Hart, op. cit. (Note 23), p. 127.

130. Law, op. cit. (Note 24), p. 303. John Evelyn, in his unpublished 'Elysium Britannicum, or the Royal Gardens in Three Books' (Christ Church Library, Oxford, Evelyn MS 45), discusses (f. 45) the superiority of imported marble rollers over those of English origin for maintaining gravel paths: 'Our English portland or kentish stones are too soft, and weare flatt in a very short tyme if the gravell be anything sharpe, and unless you preserve the stone very drie, being apt to imbibe the wett and grow tender'. While acknowledging that 'the very best of all are to be bought in Holland made of cast yron, or from our Furnaces, when gunns are cast', Evelyn mentions the suitability of wooden rollers 'for Carpet walkes, Alle[y]s & c'; he recommends that they should be 'of heart Elme, two foote diameter, if lesse covered wth sheete lead... [with] handles of yron'.

131. Ibid.

132. I am grateful to Lord McAlpine for this information.

13 Horological, Mathematical and Musical Instruments. Science and Music at the Court of Charles I

Penelope Gouk

Marginal numerals refer to page and entry numbers in the *Inventories* (see p. 11)

And to speake truly of him, he had many singular parts in nature; he was an excellent Horseman, would shoot well at a marke, had a singular skill in Limming and Pictures, a good Mathematician, not unskilfull in *Musicke*, well read in Divinity, excellently in *History*, and no lesse in the *Lawes* and *Statutes* of this Nation . . .[1]

Like his ill-fated brother Henry, Charles I received a modern courtly education befitting his rank and breeding. The ability to sing, to play an instrument to a competent standard, to understand the basic principles of mathematics and drawing, were among the many accomplishments considered desirable for a Renaissance prince who was to be a patron of the arts and sciences. The acquisition of instruments and the employment of practitioners to teach their use were an essential part of this educational process.[2] Sundials, clocks and watches, mathematical and musical instruments, were all sophisticated devices that epitomized contemporary achievements in technology and mathematical knowledge. Serving both functional and decorative purposes, such artefacts, along with paintings, sculpture and architecture and more ephemeral entertainments, reflected the prestige and status of their owners.[3]

Of the objects which might be classified as 'scientific' in the inventories of Charles I's goods, nearly all were horological devices, namely sundials, clocks and watches. Large stone sundials were recorded in the gardens at Hampton Court, Greenwich and Oatlands; clocks with bells, presumably fixed and of a reasonably large scale were listed at Hampton Court, Richmond, Greenwich, Oatlands and Whitehall. Elaborate chamber clocks and watches formed part of the larger groups of precious objects in the Jewel Houses at Whitehall and the Tower, while four extremely ornate clocks, described in considerable detail, were noted in the Queen's residence at Denmark House. Three globes, two at Hampton Court and another at Whitehall, a case of silver mathematical instruments, possibly from the Library at St. James's, and a little box with a 'brass instrument' at Hampton Court effectively complete the list.

The total number of musical instruments listed is also relatively small. They were located in five of the King's residences, notably at Hampton Court. Keyboards constituted the largest group of instruments there and included two organs, two portatives, one pair of regals and two virginals. Two sets of wind instruments, a brass horn and two song books formed the remaining musical items at Hampton Court. Other keyboards included two organs at Whitehall, one at Wimbledon and a virginal at Denmark House. Perhaps surprisingly, only two references to stringed instruments are found: a lute in a case at Denmark House, and a chest of viols from an unknown source. The remaining instruments in the inventories, which cannot be associated with any particular property, include two trumpets, a pair of brass cymbals and a drum from Lapland.

With the exception of the last-mentioned object, which appears to have been treasured for its curiosity value, the musical instruments described clearly served a predominantly practical function in the King's household. The fact that most of the surviving items were relatively bulky keyboards, or cases of instruments, suggests that these might have been regarded as fixtures in a particular room. More portable instruments played by the King's musicians or by members of the royal family presumably accompanied the court wherever it travelled, or else were kept by the musicians themselves while temporarily disbanded.

There is no indication that Charles I collected either musical or mathematical instruments as part of a cabinet. Considerable numbers of clocks and watches were none the less accumulated in the royal Jewel Houses: for example, an inventory of valuable effects in Westminster Palace dated 1542 included ten clocks and watches, while a similar inventory of clocks and watches of Queen Elizabeth contained twenty-four items.[4]

Early English Clock-, Watch- and Instrument-Making

The terminology applied to timepieces in the seventeenth century was somewhat different from that used today. 'Dial' might simply refer to an instrument serving to tell the time by means of a shadow cast by the sun upon a graduated surface – that is, a sundial – but the term could also be used for a timepiece of any kind, or more specifically for the face of a clock or watch. The terms 'clock' and 'clockwork' were applied in a general sense to any timepiece with a bell that marked the hour. Alternatively 'clockwork' might be used more specifically to indicate the striking train alone, or indeed any kind of striking mechanism. The word 'watch' at this time referred to a timepiece (usually small, but not necessarily portable) which showed the time but did not sound the hour. No device with an alarm that could be set to go off at a particular time was excluded from this definition. Portable clocks and watches requiring a spring-driven mechanism were a development of the fifteenth century. By the 1520s a distinguishing feature of the portable watch was the suspension chain. There were two main forms: the 'tambour' in the shape of a drum, or the spherical type known as the Nuremberg egg.[5]

The earliest domestic clocks, watches and mathematical instruments in England seem to have been foreign imports or else were made by immigrants living in London. Despite Henry VIII's attempts to encourage specialist metal workers and craftsmen to settle in England, this policy succeeded only in Elizabeth's reign.[6] A few examples of indigenous craftsmen begin to appear around the end of the sixteenth century, and their numbers increased throughout the following century. Thomas Gemini (*fl.* 1524-63), an immigrant Flemish engraver and instrument-maker, set up the earliest instrument workshop in England.[7] Humphrey Cole (*c.*1530-91) appears to have been one of the first native Englishmen to produce mathematical instruments. He was an engraver, a die-cutter and an expert in mining and metallurgy.[8]

In order to practise their craft in the City of London, instrument-makers and engravers were required to incorporate into one of the existing craft guilds. Augustin Ryther (*fl.* 1576-95), his apprentice Charles Whitwell (*fl.* 1590-1611) and Whitwell's apprentice Elias Allen (*fl.* 1602-53), some of the earliest English instrument-makers, were all members of the Grocers' Company.[9]

Elias Allen was one of Charles I's instrument-makers. Allen first established a workshop in Black Horse Alley off Fleet Street about 1611 and moved to the Strand in 1616. He soon established a reputation for meticulous craftsmanship and a number of mathematicians commissioned him to make instruments to their specifications including Edmund Gunter (1581-1626), William Oughtred (1575-1660) and Richard Delamain (*fl.* 1610-45).[10] Having recently been sworn a King's servant, Allen asked Oughtred in 1626 to design an instrument he could present to the King as a New Year's gift. It was this occasion which eventually led to the priority dispute between Oughtred and Delamain over the invention of the circular slide rule and 'horizontal instrument', a device which could be used both for time measurement and for solving problems concerning the position of the sun.[11]

Allen also collaborated with John Marr (*fl.* 1614-47), a Scottish mathematician who served both James I and Charles I as compass-maker, diallist and dial-maker.[12] Allen and Marr supplied the magnetic needles required for the compasses used on Captain Thomas James's Arctic voyage of 1631. They were also both actively involved in the design and construction of the royal sundials under Charles.

Richard Delamain, a joiner by trade and a teacher of practical mathematics, was described by his widow as tutor in mathematics to King Charles I. His services were retained by the King in 1633 for £40 a year. In about 1637 he had a warrant for making several instruments for the King following a meeting at Greenwich. Two petitions for payment were made by Delamain at this time, the first of which referred to instruments for His Majesty's bedchamber and for the Great Ship; the second described the 'Great Octans' and 'Universal Concave' which Delamain had made for the King, as well as some 'silver instruments'.[13] These may have included the instrument described by Sir Thomas Herbert in his account of the events leading up to the execution of the King:

He likewise commanded Mr *Herbert* to give his Son, the Duke of *York*, his large Ring Sun-Dial of Silver, a Jewel his Majesty much valu'd; it was invented and made by Mr *Delamaine*, an able Mathematician, who projected it, and in a little printed Book shew'd its excellent

Use, in resolving many Questions in Arithmetick, and other rare Operations to be wrought by it in the Mathematicks.[14]

The development of domestic clock- and watch-making in England follows a similar pattern to that already described for mathematical instrument-making. At the turn of the century a tiny number of English makers were beginning to compete with Continental practitioners and naturalized foreigners. In 1622 there were around sixteen clockmakers at work in London who were incorporated into a craft. Most of these were freemen of the Blacksmiths' Company or of other guilds such as the Goldsmiths. A number of other foreign practitioners (including Huguenot refugees) who were not freemen were also plying their trade in the City. Pressure from the incorporated clock- and watch-makers eventually led to the creation of the Clockmakers' Company, which received its charter from Charles I in 1631. There was, however, nothing to prevent an individual from being in more than one company: Allen, for example, who was already a member of the Grocers, was admitted to the Clockmakers' Company in 1633 and became its Master in 1636.[15]

Formal appointments to the position of clock- and/or watchmaker to the Crown were slow to emerge. Initially a series of individual payments or commissions were granted to craftsmen for work done and material supplied. Nicholas Oursian (fl. 1532-90), a naturalized Huguenot immigrant, served four Tudor monarchs as both a maker and repairer of clocks. Under Queen Elizabeth, the first rewards for these posts by regular stipend or privilege were granted. Bartholomew Newsam (fl. 1565-93), the earliest native maker to achieve any eminence, was Clock-keeper to the Queen prior to 1582, and from 1590 combined this office with that of Clockmaker. In 1591 Randulph Bull (fl. 1590-1617) was appointed Queen's Clockmaker for life, with keeping of the privy clocks except the 'Standing Clockes' at a wage of 12d. a day and a yearly allowance for livery. It was Bull who supplied the clockwork for the mechanical organ built by Thomas Dallam for the Turkish Sultan in 1597 (see below). Following the accession of James I, the post of Keeper of Clocks at Westminster was granted to Randulph and Emmanuel Bull.[16]

The first specific appointment as Chief Clockmaker and Keeper of the Privy Clocks by a grant of Letters Patent under the Great Seal was granted to the Scotsman David Ramsey (c.1585-1660) in 1618. In 1612 Ramsey was paid £61 for three watches made for Henry, Prince of Wales. The following year James rewarded Ramsey with a pension of £200 per annum, and from 1616 onwards there are regular records of payments to him, some of them for repairs and work carried out on clocks in the King's palaces. Ramsey continued to hold the post under Charles I, and became the first Master of the Clockmakers' Company.[17]

King Charles's watchmaker was Edward East (1602-97), who had been apprenticed to a goldsmith in 1618 and became a freeman in 1627. When the Clockmakers' Company was eventually formed he was immediately appointed a junior member of its Court of Assistants and eventually served as Master in both 1645 and 1652. East was subsequently appointed Clockmaker and Keeper of the Privy Clocks to Charles II.[18]

Anecdotes concerning the King's watches and their eventual fate are plentiful; but their accuracy remains dubious. The number of watches supposedly associated with Charles I is probably equivalent to the number of beds slept in by Elizabeth I. Two watches, one gold and the other silver, were apparently kept in the Bedchamber and were wound by the King himself each night. He is said to have presented the silver watch to Sir Thomas Herbert, a Groom of the Chamber, on his way to the scaffold. Herbert's own account of the events leading up to the execution contains several references to watches.[19]

Musical Practitioners and Instrument-Makers

The pattern of development in instrument-making and the emergence of indigenous mathematical skills in England is matched quite closely by that found in the realm of musical practice. Until well into the seventeenth century, most musical instruments were imported or else were made by immigrant craftsmen working in London. The first known violin maker in London, for example, was Jacob Rayman (fl. 1620-50) from the Tyrol; English makers did not appear until the middle of the century.[20] Italian and French musicians who introduced new musical styles and instruments were also found in considerable numbers at court.

These parallels should not surprise us; according to both classical and contemporary definitions, music was a mathematical art and science along with subjects such as navigation, astronomy, architecture and perspective. Ancient and modern authors alike regarded musical technology as an integral part of mathematics and mechanics.[21] The Renaissance philosopher-engineer employed at royal and noble courts traditionally included the production of musical devices and entertainments in his range of accomplishments.[22]

Salomon de Caus (1576-c.1630) and Cornelius Drebbel (1572-1633) were two such immigrant engineers whose inventions for gardens and palaces delighted the Stuart court. De Caus's *Les Raisons des forces mouvantes* (1615), a book on hydraulic devices for grottoes, included a section on the construction of organs. Drebbel was the inventor of a 'perspective lute' and automatic virginals that played when exposed to sunlight, an instrument installed at Eltham palace around 1607.[23] The masques of Inigo Jones and Ben Jonson also required the collaboration of painters, musicians and other craftsmen, all of whom formed a very close-knit community at the court.[24]

Many of the metal- and wood-working skills required for the manufacture of ordnance, clocks and mathematical instruments were identical to those employed in making organs, bells, wind and brass instruments. Musical clocks and automata provide good examples of the close connections between the production of musical instruments and mechanical devices in this period: most of these were produced in south Germany, but one of the first and best-documented examples of an English collaboration of this type is the mechanical organ sent by Queen Elizabeth and the Levant Company as a present to the Turkish Sultan. The organ was constructed by Thomas Dallam (*fl.* 1630), a Lancashire blacksmith turned organ builder, with the clockwork made by Randulph Bull, goldsmith and clockmaker to the Queen. Dallam himself went with the organ to ensure its safe installation, and his account of the journey beginning from London in February 1599 and ending in Constantinople in May 1600 still survives. The construction included singing birds, bells, trumpeters, planetary motions and an organ which played pieces in counterpoint on the hour.[25]

Between 1605 and 1629 Thomas Dallam was responsible for building about nine new organs and repairing or rebuilding another six or more in cathedrals and colleges throughout England. His son, Robert Dallam (1602-65) continued this tradition until the outbreak of the Civil War when, as a recusant Catholic, he moved to Brittany and worked there until his return in 1660.

A further example of the close links between musical and mathematical practitioners is shown in the career of Davis Mell (1604-62), a violinist and a member of the King's Musick between 1625 and 1642 and again in 1661 until his death a year later. Two other musicians with the same family name were also members of the royal band: Leonard (*fl.* 1620-40), another violinist, and Thomas (*fl.* 1620-40), a flautist.[26] What Mell did during the Civil War period is not known; he resurfaced in London as one of Cromwell's musicians and a music teacher. In October 1655 he became a Free Brother of the Clockmakers' Company and a year later had an apprentice, Thomas Crawley. It seems likely that Mell was finding it difficult to make a living from music alone, and during this period combined both professions until his appointment as Band Master under Charles II. From the three surviving examples signed by Mell, it is clear that his clock production ranged from the standard lantern clock to the more sophisticated quarter-chiming carillon clock with automaton figures of musicians. A tenement at Crutched Friars, a house in the parish of Stepney and lodgings in the Strand were left by Mell at his death and the inventory of his possessions included among other items four clocks, three watches, three violins and a bass viol.[27]

The 'King's Musick'

The relatively small number of musical instruments listed in the inventories does not adequately reflect the true role of music and musical instruments in the households of Charles I. In 1625 there were as many as seventy-eight professional musicians employed in the 'King's Musick' and an average of at least sixty throughout his reign. Around 1635, for example, the King's Musick consisted of nineteen viols and violins, ten hautboys and sackbuts, seven flutes, three to five recorders, eight cornetts, at least eighteen 'lutes and voices' (i.e. men who sang and/or played lute), two virginals and a harp, as well as about seventeen trumpeters. Henrietta Maria had her own musical establishment of about fifteen men and two to three singing boys.[28] The Chapel Royal, which employed at least another twenty singing men and boys, was also under the direct control of the sovereign.[29]

The instrumentalists and singers in the King's Musick were required to provide music for a variety of public and private occasions. Loosely divided into several groups or bands, they played at state banquets, at masques and tournaments, or assisted at divine service in the Chapel Royal, as well as privately entertaining or teaching members of the royal family. At court, the wind consorts and string groups tended to play in the public Presence Chamber. They performed relatively simple music that could be played while moving around as required. In 1630, for example, the wind instruments were grouped into three mixed companies; two of these attended the court at dinner on alternate weeks and the third company played on Sundays.[30] These groups also played on 'Play Nights' before and between acts when the children of the Chapel Royal performed. There was also a band of viols and violins comprising about fourteen players, which from 1621 onwards had its own composer. In contrast, keyboard instruments, including chamber organs, seem to have been confined to the private apartments in the palaces: hence the group known as the 'Consort', which included a virginalist, several lutenist-singers, singers, a harpist and violists, must have performed in the Privy Chamber.[31]

The social origins and status of the King's musicians were similar to those of the clock- and instrument-makers and practitioners already outlined. The majority of them were from a small and fairly close-knit group of families, often Italian or French in origin, who jealously guarded their privileges. Members of the Ferrabosco, Lanier and Bassano families, for example, were already among the royal musicians in the sixteenth century and were well represented under Charles I.

Alphonso Ferrabosco II (c.1578-1628), who was appointed Composer in Ordinary and Composer to the King in 1626, was descended from a Bolognese family of musicians. His father, Alphonso I (1543-88), worked in England as a composer of madrigals between about 1562 and 1578. Two of his own sons, Alphonso III (c.1610-60) and Henry (c.1615-58) succeeded him in the posts he held under Charles. Their mother was a member of the Lanier family who were of French descent. John I (d. 1572) and Nicholas I (d. 1612) settled in London in 1561 as musicians to the Queen. Nicholas had at least eleven children, including five sons who were all wind players in the royal band. Two of his daughters were also married to members of the band.

Nicholas II (1588-1666) was the son of John Lanier. He was first in the service of Prince Henry and became a lutenist of the King's Musick in 1616. Two years later he was appointed Master of Musick to Prince Charles at £200 per annum and remained in this post at the latter's accession. A painter as well as a musician, Nicholas II was involved as a designer, composer and performer in the court masques and also acted as an agent in the acquisition of the Mantuan collection. His name appears in the 'first list' of the King's creditors (see p. 16) through which he acquired Bellini's *The Concert* at the Commonwealth sale. Jerome Lanier (d. 1657), cousin of Nicholas, was yet another musician-painter in the family whose name appears in the same list.[32]

The Bassanos seem to have been originally Jewish refugees, arriving from the town of Bassano at the beginning of the sixteenth century. In 1538 Henry VIII appointed Anthony Bassano (d. 1574) as 'maker of divers instruments of music' and shortly afterwards three other Bassano brothers were also granted stipends at court. Anthony and his brothers Alvise (d. 1554) Jasper (d. 1577) and John (d. 1570) made cornetts, crumhorns, flutes, lutes, recorders, shawms and viols and sold them in England and on the Continent. Of the second generation, Arthur (d. 1624) was known as a maker, while Andrea (1554-1626) repaired keyboard instruments at court. Jeronimo (1559-1635) also seems to have repaired lutes and may have made viol strings. Anthony II (1579-1658) was the only third-generation member associated with making or repairing instruments, as well as being a performer in the King's Musick.[33]

The individual responsible for maintenance and repair of Charles I's keyboard instruments was Edward Norgate (fl. 1611-50), 'Keeper of his Majesty's organs and other instruments'.[34] He was the son of Robert Norgate, Master of Corpus Christi College, Cambridge. Apart from being a skilled musician, Norgate was a painter who was regularly engaged in writing and illuminating royal patents and was appointed Windsor Herald in 1636. Like Lanier and Gerbier he also acted as an agent in the art market, buying pictures for the Queen's cabinet at Greenwich. In 1611 Norgate received a patent jointly with Andrea Bassano for the upkeep of the court instruments. After 1626 Norgate appears to have worked alone. In 1629 he received payment for repairing organs at Hampton Court and Whitehall as well for repairing virginals for His Majesty's chamber music. Two years later a warrant was granted for payment to him for repairing organs and virginals at St. James's, Hampton Court, Greenwich and Whitehall. Similar references are found up to early 1642.[35]

The role of organs and organ music in worship had been a contentious subject in the English church since the Reformation. Charles I and Archbishop Laud actively supported the use of organs in the service, a policy which included an extensive programme of building new instruments and renovating others in the royal chapels and in cathedrals throughout the country.[36] It was also necessary to provide the Queen and her household with suitable places for performing the Catholic rites. As early as 1625 a new chapel, complete with organ loft, was built at St. James's Palace for the Queen's court to celebrate Catholic mass. In the same year a balustraded 'musique loft' supported on two tall pillars was added to the great chamber.[37] Between 1630 and 1635 another Catholic chapel was built at the Queen's residence of Denmark House. Here the west transept was almost entirely filled with an organ gallery.[38]

Whitehall, Hampton Court, Greenwich and Richmond all had organs in their chapels, where members of the Chapel Royal regularly performed services for the King. At Whitehall, for example, there was a musicians' gallery at the north-east end of the chapel for the organs, instrumentalists and some singers. The royal closet was at the west end of the chapel, connected by corridors to the state apartments and thence to the private apartments. Similar arrangements existed in the other palaces.[39]

In 1636 a new 'chayre' organ was ordered from Norgate for Hampton Court. The instrument was to be made 'conformable to those already made in the chapels at Whitehall and Greenwich'.[40] Norgate was also to alter and repair the existing great organ in the chapel. From the warrant issued it is clear that a number of joiners, painters and other workmen were engaged on these projects which lasted over a period of six months. In 1639 another warrant was issued to Norgate for a new organ to be made and set up at Richmond, including payment for carved figures about the organ loft.[41]

Timepieces and Mathematical Instruments

Although sundials are itemized in the inventories only for Hampton Court, Greenwich and Oatlands, it can be assumed that similar dials were to be found in the gardens and courtyards and on the exterior walls of all the King's residences, as they were an essential part of everyday domestic life. The most famous of the King's stone sundials, for example, was that described by Edmund Gunter, Gresham Professor of Astronomy, in his *Description and Use of his Majesties Dials in White-Hall Garden* (1624).

185 [329]   The 'great dyall' of stone in the garden of Hampton Court valued at £30 was one which in all probability had been built in Charles's own reign. In 1625-6 masons prepared a pillar of Portland stone and four stones each three feet square to receive a 'Horizontal Dyall'. On the dial itself there is no information.[42] An instrument erected in 1629 by the mason Richard Chamberlayne was described as 'A dyall with eight cantts 3 feet high and 3 feet over with a concave on the toppe 28 inches over and 14 inches deepe with eight other small concaves on the sides of the same diall.'[43] Elias Allen provided fourteen engraved brass gnomons for the concaves. In 1632 another dial designed by John Marr was constructed at a cost of £100, his charge being for

inventing disposing calculating and drawing all the lynes and circles of 9 lardge Hemisphericall Dyalles and eight large plane Dyalles upon a great stone of Portland cutt into viij/Canttes wch demonstrate divers and sondry conclusions to bee performed thereby wth the Northerne Constellations in the greate dyall and twoe mapps in other twoe of them wth divers Ornam[ts] and guilding the stiles etc. and alsoe for painting and guilding wth fine gold and strewing wth fine Bice all the sd Dialle.[44]

Marr was also the author of a 'Description and Use' of this dial, a manuscript dedicated to Charles I and now in the British Library.[45]

249 [32]   Another 'great Stone sundyall', again valued at £30, was listed at Greenwich. This might also have been designed by Marr; in 1631-2 he devised three great dials for Conduit Court, and supervised the painter's work on them over a period of eighteen days. Whether any of these were of stone, however, is not clear.[46]

250 [37]   The two stone sundials at Oatlands seem to have been relatively small, since
250 [35] they were sold (along with 'a wodden seate') for just over £2. A clock and 'two dyalls' at £30 were also sold from Oatlands. Two wall dials were painted by the Sergeant Painter John de Critz at Oatlands in 1619. The first of these was twenty-four feet in diameter, and was placed at the approach to the house. The second had a round plate fourteen feet in diameter, showing the planets and signs of the zodiac, with an outer moulded frame as 'a concave deciphering the fower quarters of the yeare with shippes hilles dales etc.' The letters J R appeared on both dials.[47]

The dials at Whitehall are not included in the inventories. A large stone dial combined with a fountain was already standing in 1595-6 in the Privy Garden. The work of George Gower, Sergeant Painter, on the dial is described as follows:

priming the Stone Diall in the Garden fower sundrie tymes over with fatt oile and twise with oile and leade and conteyning as followeth viz one great hallowe Diall being painted and guilded with fine goulde in diverse partes as the howers planettes caracters ffingers pointes cloudes Lines and environed about twith the enterannce of the xii signes and degrees into the xii monethes and at the Corners the fower windowes [?winds] and on the fower sides. In all contaeyning lxx sondry dialls whereof thre great ones the cockes and points being all guilded with fine goulde and all the Dialls garnished with Tabletts compartiments and sondrie verses written for the enriching of the same painted in oil Cullor as white leade vermillion, Blue Bize Azure redd leade grene bize – masticott Spanishe Browne Ivarye blacke etc.

In addition the Master Carpenter, William Portington, constructed a frame and ogival roof to protect the decoration, which may have made the use of the dials somewhat limited.[48]

In 1621-2 this great dial was being dismantled and rebuilt by Nicholas Stone. It was recalibrated under the direction of Gunter, while de Critz painted, gilded and oiled it in 1632-3.[49] According to Gunter, this dial was of Purbeck stone, measuring four and a half feet square by three feet and three inches high and weighing about five tons. There were five dials on the upper part of the stone, four on the four corners and one in the middle – the great 'Horizontall concave'.[50] Apparently this multiple dial was inadequate for the King's tastes: in 1628-9 a new dial, six feet square, 'to be seene from the privy Lodginges' was designed by Marr.[51] Only a year later a new dial by Marr was erected at St. James's, consisting of a 'dial of Portland stone of viij cants wth a concave being xv inches over wth xvj plaine dyalls thereon and sundry necessary conclusions to be knowne by the shadowe of the sonne uppon each of them'.[52] Two sundials at Woodstock designed by Marr were painted in 1632-3.[53]

185 [321]   At Hampton Court 'The Clock and 2 bells' was valued at £150. Does this refer to the great astronomical clock set in the east face of the inner gatehouse? This famous clock was made in 1540 by Nicholas Oursian, Keeper of the King's Clocks at Hampton Court.[54] In 1619-20 the clock was repaired and decorated; another 'lesser' dial with the cipher of James I was painted at the same time.[55] The 'bell &
249 [25] Clock at Grenw[ch]' was obviously much smaller in scale since it was valued at only £4; this has not been located or identified. A clock and two dials were sold
250 [35] from Oatlands for a total of £30 in 1650. The clock may have been that made by Randulph Bull for the new octagonal turret and clockhouse built in 1593-4: this particular clock cost with a bell a total of £55. 13s. 2d.[56] A dial plate for a clock with
288 [159] an hour hand worth £1 was also listed at Oatlands.

Three clocks and a further clock in a cabinet amongst the goods at Denmark House are described in considerable detail. It is clear that these were all elaborate pieces of the kind made in south Germany in the sixteenth and early seventeenth centuries. The taste for collecting ornate, so-called 'Mannerist' devices, including timepieces, was a fashion cultivated by the Habsburg Emperors from Maximilian I

(1493-1519) onwards and emulated by other crowned heads and aristocracy of Europe throughout this period. One of the largest collections was that amassed by Emperor Rudolf II (1576-1612) at his court in Prague. The Denmark House clocks may well have come to England during the first years of the seventeenth century when diplomatic links between Prague and London were at their closest: Rudolf sent James a celestial globe and a clock in 1609, for example,[57] and in February 1613 the Princess Elizabeth was married to Frederick, the Elector Palatine, a union which marked an important dynastic and political alliance of two Protestant powers. Lavish gifts of this kind would have been appropriate for an occasion of such importance.

111 [232]   An ebony cabinet inlaid with silver flowers and animals with a clock in the top was valued at £150. This was not listed with the clocks but was instead grouped with a number of other rich cabinets of exotic materials. Inside the cabinet were the following assorted items: 'one Serrindge Three Combes one paire of gould scalles 12 silver Instruments 2. paire of Sizers with one instrument more of silver'. The reference to a 'serrindge' and a pair of scales suggests that these may have been medical instruments.[58] The description of the cabinet suggests that it was south German in origin, reminiscent of those produced by the Augsburg merchant Philipp Hainhofer at his own expense and advertised for sale by circulating descriptions in several languages to princes and nobles throughout Europe. In 1632, for example, Hainhofer wrote to a business contact in London asking him to persuade some noble, or else the King or Queen, to buy 'a fine table', the drawers of which contained 'medicinal and toilet articles, all kinds of playthings, a musical instrument and many other fine objects'.[59]

    Under the heading 'Clockes' in Denmark House, the first is listed as 'A Clock

114 [274] in a Case of Eboney with Trumpetts Drummes, and other Antiques' valued at £100; it was sold to David Murray, the King's tailor, in October 1651.[60] The description recalls an automaton with trumpets and drums made by Hans Schlottheim (c.1544-1625/6) of Augsburg for Duke Wilhelm V of Bavaria in 1582: the device contains an organ with ten pipes in the ebony base, and when it has been set going, the little figures are also put into motion.[61]

114 [275]   The second is graphically described as 'A Clocke made in yᵉ fashion of a Coach of Eboney garnished with silver drawne by Two Lyons, The Lyons wheeles, and 2. personages all of silver haveing a Clock in the same in a greene woodden Case', valued at £40. A number of clocks in the form of table carriages with ebony boxes made in south Germany (probably Augsburg) in the early seventeenth century survive today. One example now in the Museo Poldi-Pezzoli, Milan, consists of an ebony, bronze and copper case, with silver dial and mountings, about twelve inches high, with the driving train for the carriage motion in the ebony box; as the carriage rolls, Diana is drawn by two panthers that leap and turn their heads.[62]

114 [276]   The most curious piece in the collection was 'A Clock made in the fashion of a Tortesse all of silver guilt garnished with 16 great flatt pearles 11 smaller pearles, One great Emrauld in the head, and 4 lesser Emraulds about the neck 13 stones like Emraulds about the Body and 5 in the Taile with a Ballance rubie, An Image houlding a pennon, And a Clock in yᵉ Body of the Tortesse' which was valued at £100. It is a description which bears a close resemblance to a turtle clock probably made by Georg Fronmiller of Augsburg about 1610 and now in the Hessisches Landesmuseum, Darmstadt. There is another surviving example of a clock of this kind; in 1611 Archduke Ferdinand paid Georg Fronmiller 25 guilders for 'a turtle with clockwork that we have purchased', and this is thought to be the specimen now in the Kunsthistorisches Museum in Vienna.[63] The royal turtle clock was sold to William Latham, formerly Woollen Draper to both James I and Charles I.[64]

    The clocks and watches kept in the Jewel House at the Tower were clearly valued as much for their precious materials as for their time-telling function. The

30 [45] 'high standing clocke with 3. pillars richly garnished with silver gilt, and varietie of stones' was probably a tall, free-standing clock with a dial in the vertical plane.

46 [196] Little can be said about the 'Brasse Clock' valued at 10s. other than that it had either a movement of brass or else a brass case, or both, in the manner of a lantern clock.

    In the 1574 inventory of the Tower Jewel House, seven clock-salts were listed of silver combined with crystal, beryl, jasper and similar materials. They were the largest and most elaborate pieces in the collection at the time.[65] Only one piece of

47 [201] this type is mentioned in the inventory of Charles I's goods, described as '2. Faire

large Salts of silver gilt, with a Clocke in it garnisht with 6. Ivory heads about the bottome, & enriched with stones, & little gold heads enamelled with a Man upon a Falcon a top of it' valued at £40. It was sold for £3 more in December 1649.

There recently came to light a Tudor clock-salt, now in the collection of the Worshipful Company of Goldsmiths which has been claimed as the only timepiece to have survived from the royal clock collection of this period (Fig. 112).[66] The salt has a hexagonal base standing on six balls with panels to the sides, each set with a shell cameo with a bust on an enamelled background. These cameos might be equated with the 'six ivory heads' of the entry quoted above, but the object seen today does not have a 'Man upon a Falcon' on the top, so that some doubt must remain of its royal associations. Another possibility is

27 [13] that it may have been the item described as a 'Christall Watch standing upon 6. Balls with a Manikin on top of it, garnished with Pearles and stones' together
28 [21] with a case 'for a Watch of silver gilt standing upon 6. Balls, and having 6. pillars'. This is conjecture, however, and it may be that these latter entries describe something other than a clock-salt. The case in this circumstance could then have been a protective box for the entire watch; it should not be confused with the casing of the watch itself which was of rock crystal, a fashion typical of the sixteenth and seventeenth centuries.

30 [51] The 'Little Christall Watch and glasse garnished' which was listed with a crystal cup and cover no doubt also had a case of rock crystal. The description implies that it was a pocket watch with a dial cover of glass. Its case would have
48 [208] been enamelled and decorated with silver gilt. Presumably the 'Little Watch of brasse' was was another pocket watch with a brass movement or casework.

The other substantial collection of clocks was that in the Whitehall Jewel House. In nearly all instances, the descriptions are insufficiently detailed to provide more than the most general impression of the objects described. In the
385 [814] case of the 'bullet Clocke out of order in a blacke leather Case', however, the type of clock can be clearly identified and its later fate chronicled. It was sold on 23 October 1651 to Emanuel de Critz, a son of John de Critz senior and a brother of

Figure 112 *Tudor clock salt*, thought to have come from the royal collection. Worshipful Company of Goldsmiths, London. The salt is shown in its recently-restored form, having previously undergone alteration on more than one occasion.

John who succeeded their father as Sergeant Painter in March 1642. Emanuel was a portrait painter and interior decorator.[67] Less than four years later, on a visit to London in February 1655, John Evelyn wrote that

I was shew'd a Table Clock whose balance was onely a Chrystall ball, sliding on paralell wyers, without being at all fixed, but rolling from stage to stage, till falling on a Spring conceald from sight, it was throwne up to the upmost chanell againe made with an imperceptible declivity, in this continual vicissitude of motion prettily entertaining the eye every half minute, and the next halfe minute giving progresse to the hand that shew'd the hour, & giving notice by a small bell; so as in 120 halfe Minuts or periods of the bullets falling on the ejaculatorie Spring The Clock-part struck: This very extraordinary piece (richly adorn'd) has been presented by some German Prince to our late King, & was now in possession of the Usurper: valued 200 pounds.[68]

De Critz had obviously sold it to Cromwell and made a handsome profit on the transaction. The story does not end there, however; thanks to Pepys we know that the clock had then been in the hands of a Mr Henson before being repossessed by Charles II at the Restoration.[69]

During the seventeenth century rolling-ball clocks enjoyed enormous popularity, and the principle on which they worked was explored in theoretical literature as well as in practical devices. The most spectacular example of this type of clock, known as the 'Tower of Babel', was constructed at Augsburg by Hans Schlottheim in 1600 for Emperor Rudolf, although it never reached Prague. In 1602 it was sold to the Elector Christian II of Saxony for 2400 guilders. The mechanism of the clock was extremely ingenious: each ball took exactly one minute to go from the top of the track in the tower to the bottom, by then acquiring sufficient momentum to shift a small pin, releasing the movement before dropping into a pocket on the elevator running to the top of the case; at the same time the next ball on the top started its journey and the elevator moved up one step, a figure of Saturn struck a bell next to it, and the dial mechanism advanced by one minute.[70]

The remaining items at the Whitehall Jewel House are less easy to envisage. The 'Chimney Clocke w[th] divers motions of p[r]syssion and a man Carrieing a globe' at £60 was presumably a type of spring-driven clock made to stand on a mantelpiece with either calendrical or astronomical dials or both. Queen Victoria had a large seventeenth-century astronomical clock three feet ten inches high, surmounted by a gilt figure of Atlas supporting a globe. Only the movement of the clock survives in the British Museum: the maker was apparently Jacob Mayr the younger (fl. 1672-1714) of Augsburg, which would make it too late to be the clock described, although probably of similar type.[71]

385 [811]   How the 'Globe Clocke wth a Celestiall & Terrestriall Motion', valued at £100, was constructed is not clear; to find both types of motion in one instrument is unusual. It may have been similar to an armillary sphere with clockwork made by Josias Habrecht of Strasbourg in 1572, which is now in Rosenborg Castle, Copenhagen. This item was sold to Edmund Harrison, Embroiderer to James I, Charles I and Charles II, and a member of the Broderers' Company.[72] The 'box of wood' for the 'old Clocke' worth £1 was presumably an outer cover rather than its casework. Apart from free-standing clocks, wooden casework was extremely rare at this time. On the other hand, the 'Case for a Clocke in a red velvett box and a glasse' valued at £5 was probably an elaborate casework made of precious metal with a dial cover, or else an outer case which was itself so valuable it was kept in a box. Like the bullet clock, this was sold to de Critz.

385 [815]   The other 'Chimmney Clocke' in the Jewel House, described as having five bells, was perhaps a free-standing spring-driven clock. According to the entry its pedestal was at St. James's. That it had five bells suggests that it was a quarter-striking type using four bells for striking the quarters and one for the hour.

396 [978]   Another clock with twelve bells is listed in the Whitehall goods (not in the Jewel House); this was almost certainly a carillon clock, valued at £100. An early surviving example of the domestic type of carillon is one of 1598 made by a Flemish-born craftsman, Nicholas Vallin (d. 1603) who worked in London. The clock, now in the British Museum, is twenty-three inches high, strikes the hours and just before the hour the carillon plays a tune on thirteen bells, with shorter phrases at the half and quarter hours. There are two hands on the same dial to record the hour and minutes, an unusual feature in England at the time.[73]

430 [59]   Among the miscellaneous goods was a large enamelled 'hanging watch' with a silver chain, sold for £15. It could simply have been a watch with a chain, or else

385 [810]
385 [812]
385 [813]

a hanging ball clock, a type of clock developed in the fifteenth century, being of ball shape and driven by its own weight: the tension chain was wound up by a spring action and the watch gradually descended the length of the chain. Another item, from 'ye Library' was part of an old watch sold for 2s. The last object with a time-telling function was the almanac 'on a p^s of wood'. This was almost certainly a Scandinavian clog almanac.[74]

420 [17]
429 [54]

Three globes are listed in the inventory, one in the Whitehall Jewel House and two at Hampton Court. Of the latter, one was valued at 5s. and was reserved in the service of the Protector, while the other was estimated at 4s. All the globes were described as 'old'. Had they been of English origin, they might well have been made by Emery Molyneux (died c.1599), the earliest known English globe-maker. Molyneux produced the first of his globes in 1592, at which time he resided in Lambeth and worked as an instrument-maker. He was already established by this time as a maker of ordnance, having offered a new cannon and a range of other military inventions to the Queen some years previously.[75]

385 [816]
178 [226], 185 [324]

References to 'instruments' are particularly elusive. The brass instrument in a little box at Hampton Court and the silver instruments kept with other items in an ebony cabinet with clock at Denmark House may have been medical or mathematical instruments.[76] That a case of silver mathematical instruments was listed among 'Severall. Pictures' suggests that it was a set of drawing instruments. This supposition is reinforced by their being bought by Jan Baptist Gaspars, a portrait painter who took up residence in England towards the end of Charles I's reign. Gaspars worked for General Lambert and became an assistant to the painters Peter Lely and Godfrey Kneller.[77]

181 [270]
111 [232]

258 [36]

Musical Instruments

Organs and virginals played a central role in the domestic ensemble music of Charles's household even before he became King.[78] In view of the developments which were taking place in musical styles at the time, it is frustrating to discover that very little is known about pre-Commonwealth organs, particularly about how they sounded. They seem to have been of two basic types; the so-called 'great' church organ (although this was not necessarily large) which was fixed, and the smaller, moveable, chamber organ used mainly for secular music-making. Some idea of the nature of this latter type can be gained from the two surviving examples of the period. The Knole organ dates from the first decade of the seventeenth century, and is in relatively good playing order. It is in the form of an oak chest with Jacobean moulded panelling and fluted work. Almost all of the instrument, including many of the pipes, is made from oak. The original keyboard, which no longer survives, probably had forty-five keys with a short octave. The other surviving chamber organ was bought by Dean Bargrave of Canterbury Cathedral in 1629 and is now in the Cathedral library; unfortunately it is no longer playable.[79]

No details are given concerning the organs listed in the inventories. The example at Hampton Court was broken, which may explain why it was valued at a mere £2 and sold to John Boulton for only 6s. more on 22 November 1649.[80] The Wimbledon House organ, sold to Edward Bass on 7 February 1651, fetched £6.[81] The highest estimate was for a Whitehall organ at £20, while another organ from an unknown source made £10. From these prices it can be assumed that the listed organs were all of the chamber type, and probably therefore located in the privy chambers.

184 [307]

296 [231]
364 [534]
419 [14]

The term 'Portaves' used in the context of the inventories probably indicated a 'portative'. This was a very small type of organ with treble flue pipes carried by a strap over the player's shoulder, played by the right hand while the bellows were worked with the left. Portatives might have two or more octaves of pipes in single or multiple ranks, sometimes with one or two larger bass pipes. Its pure and sweet tone made it an ideal accompaniment for stringed instruments in a domestic context.[82] The 'regals' was another type of small organ with sets of beating reeds with few or almost no resonators. The bellows were on the same level as the keyboard on the other side of the row of reeds. The very smallest regals were of a folding book type and were known as 'Bible' regals.[83]

It is tempting to assume that the two portatives and the regals listed among the instruments at Hampton Court in the inventories are identical with those owned by Henry VIII a century earlier. According to an earlier account, there was at Hampton Court one pair of portatives with the arms of Henry and Jane Seymour in the Privy Chamber, and a second pair 'covered with crimeson Satten and embrawdered with passumynt of golde and Silver standing upon a square table of wainscotte' in another chamber. The first may be compared with the

178 [218]
178 [221]
178 [219]

'Paire of Portaves broke to peeces' in the inventories, while the second immediately recalls the pair 'covered with crimeson Satten'.[84] Similarly, the pair of regals 'in an old case' can be compared with that of 1547 'in a case coured with crimeson vellat' in the King's Long Gallery.[85] These instruments, which, it should be stressed, had by now fallen from fashion, were sold for a very low price to Boulton on 22 November 1649. The portatives were valued at 2s. each, the regals at 10s.

The virginal and the harpsichord both have a plucking action in which the strings are plucked by plectra made of quill or leather. According to modern definitions, a virginal has strings which run parallel with the keyboard and is usually rectangular in shape, while on the harpsichord the strings run directly away from the player, the instrument being shaped like an elongated wing, similar in form to a grand piano.[86] The term 'a pair of virginals' could be used in the seventeenth century to refer to either instrument. Although harpsichords were fashionable in Italy, virginals were more commonplace during this period in northern Europe.

178 [222-3]

None of the 'virginals' (or harpsichords) in the inventory can be identified or dated. Whether the 'Instrument like virgenalls' and the 'small desk virgenalls' at Hampton Court were among the eight instruments already in the Long Gallery in 1547 is open to conjecture.[87] The virginal in a case of green velvet at Denmark

118 [312], 212 [65]

House valued at £10 and the broken instrument at Richmond are similarly obscure: these keyboards could have been made at any time over a period of a hundred years or more. In Charles's own time the list of likely English makers would include John Hayward (fl. 1622-67) and Gabriel Townsend (fl. 1658).[88]

By 1638 the King himself evidently had at least one instrument made by the most famous harpsichord and virginal makers of the sixteenth and seventeenth centuries, the Ruckers family of Antwerp. A series of letters between Balthasar Gerbier in Brussels and the Secretary of State Sir Francis Windebank in Westminster, indicates that Gerbier eventually bought an instrument by Johannes Ruckers (1578-1643) which was sent to the royal patron.[89]

According to Sir Francis Kynaston, a prominent gentleman and courtier, the King was presented in about 1640 with a harpsichord 'on which one may passionate loud or soft, as upon a lute when one pleases', invented by John Hayward.[90] This was the instrument known as the pedals, an invention which enabled the player to alter the dynamic level of the harpsichord by means of a pedal mechanism operated by the foot.[91]

178 [220]

Two cases of wind instruments were sold from Hampton Court. Eight 'greate pipes' in a case, valued at £15 were sold to de Critz. These may have been large bass or tenor recorders or perhaps a set of shawms. The shawm has a double reed on a conical metal tube which is inserted into the narrow end of a conically-bored

178 [224]

metal pipe. The eleven 'Crocked pipes' valued at £5 together with their case, were probably crumhorns, hook-shaped pipes of a narrow cylindrical bore with an oval orifice at the upturned end and a double reed at the top.[92] The manufacturers of the Hampton Court wind instruments are of course unknown, but it may be mentioned that the Bassano family are thought to have sold to Henry VIII many of the instruments listed in the 1547 inventory.[93]

118 [313]
419 [12]

Little can be said about the 'Lute in a blacke leather Case' valued at £3 and listed at Denmark House, or about the chest of viols from an unknown location. It is worth emphasising that these few items were scarcely representative of the instrumental resources at court. In 1635 there were at least ten lutenists in the King's Musick. Numerous payments were made to individuals for lutes, theorba, and strings for these between 1629 and 1640.[94] A similar pattern is found for viols and violins at court.[95]

181 [269, 262]
426 [2]
430 [55-6]
420 [14]
429 [54]

The remaining objects which can be defined as musical form a strange assortment. They include two song books sold for 2s. 6d. and a brass horn sold for 6s. at Hampton Court; a 'Bugill horn Tipt with Gold and a Chaine Ditto' sold for £12; an engraved ivory trumpet and another engraved trumpet perhaps of the same material sold for 7s. 6d. and 12s. 6d. respectively; two brass cymbals 'from ye Library' at 12s., and finally a shaman's 'Conjuring Drum' from Lapland.[96]

The King's Collection: Continental and English Comparisons

Of all the items described here, only the clocks and watches at Whitehall, the Tower and Denmark House might be thought to constitute a coherent collection, albeit a small one. By no stretch of the imagination could the mathematical and musical instruments be described in such terms and this should come as no surprise, for throughout the sixteenth and seventeenth centuries the existence of specialized collections of instruments other than clocks remained uncommon in Europe. It was only from the eighteenth century that the fashion for owning a cabinet of mathematical and scientific instruments became more widespread both geographically and socially.[97] Examples of special collections dating from the sixteenth century can, however, be given.

In England a few individuals acquired mathematical instruments which were used for practical or educational purposes. Andrew Perne, Master of Peterhouse between 1554 and 1580, bequeathed a collection of astronomical instruments, maps, coins and other antiquities to his college library.[98] The instruments included astrolabes, quadrants, globes and dials. Nicholas Bond, President of Magdalen College, Oxford, from 1589 to 1618, left two globes and various mathematical instruments valued at £2 among his household goods.[99] The royal warrant issued in 1618 authorizing the seizure of goods belonging to Sir Walter Raleigh stipulated that his globes and mathematical instruments were to be delivered to the King.[100] Henry Percy, ninth Earl of Northumberland, spent the years of his imprisonment in the Tower from 1605 to 1621 in the study of mathematics, alchemy and natural philosophy. He possessed an extensive library of scientific works and a pair of globes which were transferred to Petworth following his release.[101]

The most important astronomical collection was undoubtedly that of Landgrave Wilhelm IV of Hesse-Kassel (1532-92). From his observatory in the attic of his palace at Kassel, the first of its kind in Europe, Wilhelm undertook astronomical observations himself and in conjunction with the mathematician Christoph Rothmann (c.1550-c.1605). He collaborated in the design of instruments with his clock- and instrument-maker Jost Bürgi (1552-1632) and chief architect Eberhart Baldewein (fl. 1558-81).[102] Wilhelm was also an art collector of some stature and laid the foundations of an important library. His son, Moritz the Learned (r. 1592-1627), another versatile patron of the arts and sciences, was a skilled musician and played many stringed and keyboard instruments. A recent study of his inventory reveals that Moritz owned a considerable amount of sheet music by English composers.[103]

The largest documented collection of musical instruments in the sixteenth century was that of Raymund Fugger (1528-69), a little-known member of the merchant family of Augsburg who devoted all his time to music. The inventory of his collection, made in 1566, documents both music and instruments.[104] After Raymund's death the collection remained in the hands of the family until 1584 when it went to the Count Palatine in Heidelberg. Henry VIII also owned a substantial number of musical instruments, as is shown in the inventory of 1547.[105]

Accounts and inventories of noble households indicate that it was not uncommon for a family to have at least one keyboard instrument and a set of viols in its possession. Musicians and instrument-makers were also frequently employed for their services including the maintenance of instruments.[106] In the accounts of the Earls of Cumberland for the years 1611-35, for example, there are references to the purchase of viols, bows, a lute and a violin, strings for these, and also to the tuning and repair of an organ. An inventory (c.1644) of a house belonging to the family included an organ and harpsichord in the great hall and a chest of six viols in the gallery. The inventory of Lady Pembroke at Skipton Castle in 1645 listed a 'pair of harpsichalls' and one little organ in the billiard chamber and a chest of musical instruments in the lord's chamber.[107] Catholic families forced to worship in private frequently had considerable musical resources at their disposal. The 1603 inventory of Hengrave Hall, home of Lady Kyston, included a section on 'Instruments and Books of Musick' which mentions small and great organs, a set each of violins and viols, music books, and every instrument necessary for string and broken consort music.[108] It is clear that Charles I's ownership of musical and scientific instruments was entirely representative of the fashion current in England in the first half of the seventeenth century.

Notes

1. W. Lilly, *Monarchy or no Monarchy in England... Several Observations on the Life and Death of the late King Charles* (London, 1651), p. 75.

2. On changing educational values in general, see J. Simon, *Education and Society in Tudor England* (Cambridge, 1966; paperback edition, 1979), pp. 333-68. The implications these changes had for the mathematical sciences are discussed more fully in A. J. Turner, 'Mathematical instruments and the education of gentlemen', *Annals of Science* 30 (1973), pp. 51-88 and M. Feingold, *The Mathematicians' Apprenticeship: Science, Universities and Society in England, 1560-1640* (Cambridge, 1984), pp. 190-213. Musical developments are summarized by D. C. Price, *Patrons and Musicians of the English Renaissance* (Cambridge, 1981), pp. 1-47.

3. See, for example, H. Trevor-Roper, *Princes and Artists: Patronage and Ideology at Four Hapsburg Courts 1517-1633* (London, 1976).

4. C. Jagger, *Royal Clocks: The British Monarchy and its Timekeepers 1300-1900* (London, 1983), pp. 10-15.

5. William Derham's definitions of the terms 'clock' and 'watch' are worth quoting in full:

Watches strictly taken, are all such Movements as shew the parts of Time: and *Clocks* are such as publish it, by striking on a Bell, &c. But commonly the name of *Watches* is appropriated to such as are carried in the Pocket, and that of Clock to the larger Movements, whether they strike the Hour or no. As for Watches which strike the Hour, they are called Pocket-Clocks.

(*The Artificial Clockmaker* 4th. edn. (London, 1759), p. 3). See also entries 'clock' and 'watch' in the *Oxford English Dictionary*. The following secondary works are among the best introductions to clocks and watches and to their cultural context: J. Drummond Robertson, *The Evolution of Clockwork* (London, 1931); C. M. Cipolla, *Clocks and Culture 1300-1700* (London, 1967) and D. S. Landes, *Revolution in Time: Clocks and the Making of the Modern World* (Cambridge, Mass. and London, 1983). On the variety of meanings of the term 'dial', see A. J. Turner, ' "The accomplishment of many years": three notes towards a history of the sand-glass', *Annals of Science* 39 (1982), pp. 161-72, especially pp. 166-7. I am indebted to Anthony Turner for his helpful comments and advice on the sections of this paper concerning mathematical instruments, timepieces and their makers. The opinions expressed here, and any errors which remain are, of course, my own.

6. For a general introduction to the craft, trade and industrial development in England during the period, see D. M. Palliser, *The Age of Elizabeth* (London, 1983), especially Chapters 8 and 9, and C. Wilson, *England's Apprenticeship 1603-1763* 2nd. edn. (London, 1984), especially Chapters 3 and 4. A general survey of the growth of commercial instrument-making in Europe is given by D. J. Price, 'The manufacture of scientific instruments *c.* 1500-1700', in

C. Singer, E. J. Holmyard, A. R. Hall, and T. I. Williams (eds.), *A History of Technology*, (Oxford, 1954-84), III, pp. 620-47. A more recent survey of the English scene is found in G. L'E. Turner, 'Mathematical instrument-making in London in the sixteenth century', in S. Tyacke (ed.), *English Map-Making 1500-1650* (London, 1983), pp. 93-9.

7. E. G. R. Taylor, *The Mathematical Practitioners of Tudor and Stuart England* (Cambridge, 1954), pp. 165-6; A. J. Turner, *Early Scientific Instruments: Europe 1400-1800* (London, 1987), pp. 49-50.

8. Taylor, op. cit. (Note 7), pp. 171-2; R. T. Gunther, 'The great astrolabe and other scientific instruments of Humphrey Cole', *Archaeologia* 76 (1927), pp. 273-317.

9. Taylor, op. cit. (Note 7), pp. 179, 190, 198; J. Brown, *Mathematical Instrument-Makers in the Grocers' Company 1688-1800* (London, 1979), pp. 24-5, 57-65.

10. Taylor, op. cit. (Note 7), pp. 196 (Gunter), 192 (Oughtred), 201 (Delamain). On Gunter, see also C. C. Gillispie (ed.), *Dictionary of Scientific Biography* (New York, 1970-80), VI, pp. 593-4; on Oughtred see F. Cajori, *William Oughtred, a Great Seventeenth-Century Teacher of Mathematics* (Chicago and London, 1916).

11. Brown, op. cit. (Note 9), p. 62; A. J. Turner, 'William Oughtred, Richard Delamain and the horizontal instrument in seventeenth-century England', *Annali dell'Istituto e Museo di Storia della Scienza di Firenze* 6 (1981), pp. 99-125.

12. Taylor, op. cit. (Note 7), pp. 203-4.

13. *CSP Domestic, 1637-38*, pp. 121-2, 282.

14. *Inventories*, p. 258 [361]; Sir Thomas Herbert, *Memoirs of the Two last Years of the Reign of... King Charles I* (London, 1702), p. 130.

15. Jagger, op. cit. (Note 4), pp. 282-7; J. Brown, 'Guild organisation and the instrument-making trade, 1550-1830: the Grocers and Clockmakers Companies', *Annals of Science* 36 (1979), pp. 1-34; *idem*, op. cit. (Note 9), p. 25.

16. Jagger, op. cit. (Note 4), pp. 8-13, 19, 309-10. B. Loomes, *The Early Clockmakers of Great Britain* (London, 1981), pp. 546 (Oursian, as Urseau), 408 (Newsam), 124-5 (Randulph and Emmanuel Bull). On Dallam and the mechanical organ, see p. 390 (above) and Note 25 (below).

17. Jagger, op. cit. (Note 4), pp. 20-21, 310; Loomes, op. cit. (Note 16), p. 456.

18. Jagger, op. cit. (Note 4), pp. 23-6, 310; Loomes, op. cit. (Note 16), p. 456.

19. For a summary of items associated with Charles I, see Jagger, op. cit. (Note 4), pp. 241-51. Anecdotes relating to Charles I's watches are found in Herbert, op. cit. (Note 14), pp. 91, 101, 103, 120-1, 132.

20. J. Firth, 'A Violin Makers' Map of London 1650-1850', London College of Furniture dissertation, 1979.

21. Vitruvius, *On Architecture* (Loeb Classical Library) (London, 1931), includes many

relevant passages: Bk I, cap. i, pp. 6-25 on the attributes of the architect; Bk V, caps. ii-v, pp. 266-83 on music; Bk IX, caps. vii-viii pp. 248-67 on dialling and water clocks; Bk X cap. viii, pp. 314-9 on hydraulic organs. See also A. G. Drachmann, *The Mechanical Technology of Greek and Roman Antiquity* (Copenhagen, Madison and London, 1963); B. Gille, 'Machines', in Singer *et al*. op. cit. (Note 6), II, pp. 629-62, especially pp. 630-6. John Dee's 'Mathematical Preface' to *The Elements of Geometrie of . . . Euclid*, trans. H. Billingsley (London, 1570) and Robert Fludd's *Utriusque cosmi majoris scilicet et minoris metaphysica, physica, atque technica historia* (Oppenheim, 1617-19) underline the relationship between music and other mathematical arts and sciences of the Renaissance.

22. The pattern was established by Leonardo; see E. Winternitz, *Leonardo da Vinci as a Musician* (New York, 1982). See also P. Rossi, *Philosophy, Technology and the Arts in the Early Modern Era* (New York, 1970); S. A. Bedini, 'The role of automata in the history of technology', *Technology and Culture* 5 (1964), pp. 24-42, F. Yates, *The Theatre of the World* (London, 1969), and J. C. Kassler, 'Music as a model in early science', *History of Science* 20 (1982), 103-39.

23. R. L. Colie, 'Cornelius Drebbel and Salomon de Caus: two Jacobean models for Solomon's House', *Huntington Library Quarterly* 18 (1954-5), pp. 245-60; R. Strong, *The Renaissance Garden in England* (London, 1979), pp. 87-112; R. Patterson, 'The "Hortus Palatinus" at Heidelberg and the reformation of the world', *Journal of Garden History* 1 (1981), pp. 67-104, 179-202; R. J. W. Evans, *Rudolf II and his World: A Study in Intellectual History 1576-1612* (Oxford, 1973; paperback edition, 1984), p. 190.

24. S. Orgel and R. Strong, *Inigo Jones: The Theatre of the Stuart Court* (Berkeley, 1973).

25. Dallam's account of his voyage is in BL, Additional MS 17480, 1599-1600, and extracts are printed in *Early Voyages and Travels in the Levant* published by the Hakluyt Society (London, 1893). For further background see S. Mayes, *An Organ for the Sultan* (London, 1956); the extant descriptions of the clock are transcribed on pp. 76-81. On the Dallam family and their instruments see S. Sadie, ed. *New Grove Dictionary of Musical Instruments* (London, 1984), III, pp. 537-8.

26. For references to the Mell family see H. C. de Lafontaine, *The King's Musick. A Transcript of Records relating to Music and Musicians (1460-1700)* (London, 1909), pp. 57, 66, 76, 87, 110; W. L. Woodfill, *Musicians in English Society from Elizabeth to Charles I* (Princeton, 1953), pp. 303-6.

27. These biographical details were taken from M. P. Fernandez and P. C. Fernandez, 'Davis Mell, musician and clockmaker and an analysis of the clockmaking trade in 17th century London', *Antiquarian Horology* 16 (1987), pp. 602-17. In his 'Ephemerides' of 1655, Samuel Hartlib described Mell as 'a most witty inventive . and Mechanical Man, who hath made a Jack with a Clock shewing the houres of the day with a set or consort of Bels . . . playing most harmonically' (Sheffield University Library, Hartlib Papers, 50H 29/5/56).

28. Woodfill, op. cit. (Note 26), pp. 179-80, 185, 303-6. The most up-to-date information on the King's Musick in the seventeenth century is found in A. Ashbee, *List of Payments to the King's Musick in the Reign of Charles II 1660-1685* (Snodland, 1981); ibid., *Records of English Court Music* I (1660-1685), II (1685-1714), III (1625-1642) (Snodland, 1986, 1987). Volume III was not available at the time of writing this paper; volume IV (1603-1625) is still in preparation. Ashbee's meticulous and comprehensive transcriptions from court documents will supersede Lafontaine (Note 26), which has hitherto been the main source for information on this subject.

29. On the membership of the Chapel Royal, see P. le Huray, *Music and the Reformation in England 1549-1660* (Cambridge, 1967; paperback edition 1978), pp. 57-89; E. F. Rimbault, *The Old Cheque-Book, or Book of Remembrance, of the Chapel Royal, from 1561 to 1744* (Camden Society publications, new series III) (London, 1872).

30. Lafontaine, op. cit. (Note 26), p. 72.

31. Woodfill, op. cit. (Note 26), pp. 186, 188, 190-1.

32. For biographical details of these and other musicians mentioned, see S. Sadie (ed.), *New Grove Dictionary of Music and Musicians* (London, 1980): VI, pp. 476-84 (Ferraboscos); X, pp. 454-5 (Laniers).

33. D. Lasocki, 'The Anglo-Venetian Bassano family as instrument-makers and repairers', *Galpin Society Journal* 38 (1985), pp. 112-32.

34. *New Grove* op. cit. (Note 32), XIII, p. 281; Lasocki, op. cit. (Note 33), p.123.

35. Lafontaine, op. cit. (Note 26), pp. 68, 70, 77, 79, 90, 92, 100, 107.

36. C. Clutton and A. Niland, *The British Organ* revised and enlarged 2nd. edn. (London, 1982), pp. 29-46, 111-14; *New Oxford History of Music* ed. G. Abraham (London, 1968), IV, pp. 469-72.

37. *King's Works* IV, pp. 248-9, quoting PRO, E 351/3259.

38. Ibid., IV, pp. 263-6.

39. Le Huray, op. cit. (Note 29), pp. 75-7.

40. The term 'chayre organ', which apparently dates only from the early seventeenth century, seems to have been used for a small movable church organ as distinct from the larger, fixed type known as the 'great' organ: B. B. Edmonds, 'The chayre organ: an episode', *Journal of the British Institute of Organ Studies* 4 (1980), 19-33; S. Jeans, 'The English chair organ from its origins to the Civil War', *The Organ* 65 (1986), pp. 49-55.

41. Lafontaine, op. cit. (Note 26), pp. 94, 96, 103.

42. *King's Works* IV, p. 146, quoting PRO, E 351/3259.

43. Ibid., IV, p. 146, quoting PRO, E 351/3263.

44. Ibid., IV, p. 146, quoting PRO, E 351/3265.

45. BL, MS Royal 17; Taylor, op. cit. (Note 7), pp. 203-4.

46. *King's Works* IV, p. 122, quoting PRO, E 351/3265.

47. Ibid., IV, p. 215, quoting PRO, E 351/3253.

48. Ibid., IV, p. 318, quoting PRO, E 351/3230.

49. Ibid., IV, p. 342, quoting PRO, E 351/3255, 3256, 3266.

50. E. Gunter, *Description and Use of his Majesties Dialls in White-Hall Garden* (London, 1624), pp. 1-2. The BL has a presentation copy which belonged to Ben Jonson, a friend of Gunter's.

51. *King's Works* IV, p. 342, quoting PRO, E 351/3262.

52. Ibid., IV, p. 251, quoting PRO, E 351/3263.

53. Ibid., IV, p. 354, quoting PRO, E 351/3266.

54. Jagger, op. cit. (Note 4), pp. 6-8.

55. *King's Works* IV, p. 140, quoting PRO, E 351/3253.

56. Ibid., IV, p. 212, quoting PRO, E 351/3228.

57. Evans, op. cit. (Note 23), p. 81.

58. According to the *OED* the term 'serrindge' is an early variant of 'syringe', while 'sizers' refers to a device for testing the size of articles, or for separating them according to size; alternatively, it may simply have been a pair of scissors.

59. Quoted in H.-O.Boström, 'Philipp Hainhofer and Gustavus Adolphus's *Kunstschrank* in Uppsala', in O. Impey and A. MacGregor (eds.), *The Origins of Museums. The Cabinet of Curiosities in Sixteenth- and Seventeenth-Century Europe* (Oxford, 1985), p. 93.

60. W. L. F. Nuttall, 'King Charles I's pictures and the Commonwealth sale', *Apollo* 82 (1965), p. 308.

61. K. Maurice and O. Mayr (eds.), *The Clockwork Universe: German Clocks and Automata* (New York, 1980), pp. 286-7. This automaton is now in the Kunsthistorisches Museum, Vienna.

62. Ibid., pp. 208-4, especially p. 281.

63. Maurice and Mayr, op. cit. (Note 61), p. 268. Fronmiller (1565–after 1621) was a Protestant small-clock maker in Augsburg. He lived in Italy and France from 1598 onwards and was active at the electoral courts in Cologne and in Prague. After 1608 he became imperial clockmaker at Vienna.

64. Nuttall, op. cit. (Note 60), p. 308.

65. A. J. Collins, *Jewels and Plate of Queen Elizabeth I* (London, 1955), p. 47.

66. Jagger, op. cit. (Note 4), pp. 16-18; J. F. Hayward, 'The restoration of the Tudor clock salt', *The [Goldsmiths'] Review* (1972-3), pp. 27-31. Hayward favours the identification of this clock-salt with *Inventories* p. 47 [201]. The piece was extensively remodelled in the eighteenth century but has now been restored in a form approximating to its original state.

67. *King's Works* III, p. 411; Nuttall, op. cit. (Note 60), p. 308.

68. *The Diary of John Evelyn*, ed. E. S. De Beer (Oxford, 1955), III, pp. 147-8.

69. *The Diary of Samuel Pepys*, ed. R. S. Latham and W. Matthews (London, 1970-83), I, p. 209 (28 July 1660).

70. On this clock and the general principles of its construction, see H. von Bertele, 'The rolling-ball time-standard', *La Suisse Horlogère* (1956), pt. 1, pp. 63-72; pt. 2, pp. 67-78. Unfortunately it was destroyed in the bombing of Dresden in 1942.

71. Jagger, op. cit. (Note 4), pp. 170-2.

72. Maurice and Mayr, op. cit. (Note 61), pp. 294-5. On Harrison, see Nuttall, op. cit. (Note 60), p. 308.

73. H. Tait, *Clocks and Watches* (London, 1983), pp. 16-18.

74. For further discussion of this item see p. 416.

75. On Molyneux, see H. M. Wallis, 'The first English globe: a recent discovery', *Geographical Journal* 117 (1951), pp. 275-90; *idem*, 'Further light on the Molyneux globes', *Geographical Journal* 121 (1955), pp. 305-11.

76. See above, Note 58.

77. Nuttall, op. cit. (Note 60), p. 305. For Delamain, see above, Notes 10 and 11.

78. Woodfill, op. cit. (Note 26), p. 303.

79. M. Renshaw, 'An early 17th-century British organ: a preliminary study', *Journal of British Organ Studies* 4 (1980), 34-42.

80. Boulton was a goldsmith of Foster Lane: Nuttall, op. cit. (Note 60), p. 305.

81. Bass was a minor official under the Great Seal of the Realm who had joined the Parliamentary cause: Nuttall, op. cit. (Note 60), p. 307. The price of a new chamber organ in this period was £30–40 (S. Bicknell, personal communication).

82. *New Grove* op. cit. (Note 32), XV, pp. 134, 151.

83. Ibid., XV, pp. 672-3.

84. Quoted in R. Russell, *The Harpsichord and Clavichord* (London, 1973), pp. 158-9. See also W. Barry, 'The keyboard instruments of Henry VIII', *Organ Yearbook* 13 (1982), pp. 31-45, especially pp. 34-5.

85. Russell, op. cit. (Note 84), p. 158. For the location of the gallery in the main complex of buildings around Cloister Court, see *King's Works* IV, pp. 136-7.

86. *New Grove* op. cit. (Note 32), VIII, pp. 216-46.

87. Russell, op. cit. (Note 84), p. 158.

88. D. H. Boalch, *Makers of the Harpsichord and Clavichord 1440-1830* 2nd. edn. (Oxford, 1974), pp. 65, 180. Charles I's sister Elizabeth, Queen of Bohemia, owned a virginal made by Townsend in 1641 while she was in exile in Holland, which is now in the Brussels Conservatoire.

89. Russell, op. cit. (Note 84), pp. 161-2; Boalch, op. cit. (Note 88), p. 129.

90. Bod. Lib, Additional MS C 287, fol. 156. See also C. F. Williamson, 'The Life and Works of Sir Francis Kynaston' (B. Litt. dissertation, University of Oxford, 1957), pp. 98-9.

91. The instrument is described in Thomas Mace, *Musick's Monument* (London, 1676), pp. 235-6; see also Boalch, op. cit. (Note 88), p. 65.

92. On shawms and crumhorns, see A. Baines, *European and American Musical Instruments* (London, 1966), pp. 96-103 and pls. 512-42. A set of six boxwood crumhorns in a case, made in Italy in the second half of the sixteenth century, survives in the Brussels Conservatoire. They are said to have been made for Duke Alfonso d'Este of Ferrara.

93. Lasocki, op. cit. (Note 33), p. 121.

94. Lafontaine, op. cit. (Note 26), pp. 69, 71, 73, 76-7, 80, 83, 87-92, 96, 98, 102, 106.

95. Ibid., pp. 70-71, 74-5, 80, 83, 89, 93, 96, 98-100.

96. See further p. 416.

97. See, for example Turner, op. cit. (Note 7), pp. 183-9, 231-54; G. L'E. Turner, 'The auction sale of the Earl of Bute's instruments, 1793', *Annals of Science* 23 (1967), pp. 213-42; J. A. Chaldecott, *Handbook of the King George III Collection of Scientific Instruments* (London, 1951).

98. Feingold, op. cit. (Note 2), p. 59; M. Hunter, 'The cabinet institutionalised: the Royal Society's 'Repository' and its background' in Impey and MacGregor, op. cit. (Note 59), pp. 159-68, especially p. 160.

99. Feingold, op. cit. (Note 2), p. 56.

100. *CSP Domestic 1611-18*, p. 590. Wallis, op. cit. (Note 75) ['The first English globe'], p. 286.

101. Ibid.; see also G. R. Batho, 'The library of the "Wizard" Earl: Henry Percy, 9th Earl of Northumberland (1564-1632)', *Library* 5th series, 15 (1960), pp. 246-61.

102. B. T. Moran, 'Princes, machines and the valuation of precision in the 16th century', *Sudhoffs Archiv* 61 (1977), pp. 209-28; L. von Mackensen, *Die erste Sternwarte Europas mit ihren Instrumenten und Uhren: 400 Jahre Jost Bürgi in Kassel* (Munich, 1982).

103. F. A. Dreier, 'The *Kunstkammer* of the Hessian Landgraves in Kassel', in Impey and MacGregor, op. cit. (Note 59), pp. 102-9, discusses the collections of both Wilhelm and Moritz. See also R. Charteris, 'English music in the library of Moritz, Landgrave of Hessen-Kassel, in 1613' *Chelys* 15 (1986), pp. 33-7.

104. D. A. Smith, 'The musical instrument inventory of Raymund Fugger', *Galpin Society Journal* 33 (1980), pp. 36-44. Most of the music was vocal polyphony by the major composers of the late fifteenth and early sixteenth centuries. The instrument section of the inventory includes 141 lutes, as well as seventy-one recorders, the same number of cornetts, forty flutes, thirteen curtals, nine shawms, eight crumhorns, nine harpsichords, fifteen viols and one set of Italian violins.

105. 'Musical Instruments of King Henry VIII from an inventory of the Guarderobes, etc., 1547. Brit. Mus. Harleian MS 1419' (Russell, op. cit. (Note 84), pp. 155-60). The keyboards included about twenty pairs of regals, two organs and two portatives, nearly thirty virginals and two clavichords. In addition there were twenty-nine viols, twenty-five lutes, sixteen cornetts, eighteen crumhorns, thirteen dulceuses, seventy-two flutes, seventy-four recorders, two fifes and a tabor pipe.

106. For a comprehensive listing, see 'Entries relating to music, from household records' in Woodfill, op. cit. (Note 26), pp. 252-79. Further examples are found in Price, op. cit. (Note 2), especially chapters 3 and 4.

107. Woodfill, op. cit. (Note 26), pp. 256-60, 279.

108. Price, op. cit. (Note 2), p. 82. The term 'broken consort' refers to mixed groups of instruments rather than sets of single instruments such as viols or recorders.

14 The King's Disport. Sports, Games and Pastimes of the Early Stuarts

Arthur MacGregor

Marginal numerals refer to page and entry numbers in the *Inventories* (see p. 11)

Scattered references in the inventories illuminate aspects of the recreational activities at court, not only from the time of Charles I but reaching as far back as the reign of Henry VIII. As with other categories of material, the picture they give is far from comprehensive, although it does serve to bring into focus some of the principal preoccupations of the royal family in its less formal moments.

The partiality of this testimony is highlighted by the scarcity of references to many of the activities we know from other historical sources (and from the structural evidence of the royal palaces) to have engaged to varying degrees the interests of Charles and his predecessors. Exercises on horseback, for example, were a part of everyday life for the active nobleman. The medieval taste for jousting and related activities survived well into the Stuart period: it was catered for in permanently-constituted tiltyards at Whitehall, Greenwich and Hampton Court, which provided sport for the participants and spectacle for the onlookers.[1] Prince Henry was particularly adept, having been encouraged in this pursuit by his father and having followed the paternal directions with commendable tenacity.[2] Although something of a weakling in early life, Charles later took to sports such as riding at the ring with enthusiasm and success.[3] A

249 [33]

somewhat unexpected appearance is made in the inventories by 'The Tilting wood at Grenw^ch', which was sold for £5–evidently the timber from the central barrier that ran the length of the tiltyard.[4] Other isolated items which may recall

431 [68]

these chivalric activities include 'A furniture for a Horse of Crimson Velvett being Studed wth Silver Enamelled', bought for £25 by Colonel Whichcote, the rebel

383 [800], 384 [801-2]

Governor of Windsor Castle, and three other velvet-covered saddles sold from Whitehall, all richly embroidered and in one instance sewn with pearls.

Cock-fighting occupied a position of sufficient importance to have an officer of the court–the Cockmaster–appointed specifically to ensure that appropriate sport was provided whenever it took the king's fancy.[5] At Whitehall Palace the cock-pit, a square structure with an octagonal internal layout, surmounted by an elaborate leaded lantern roof, formed the most prominent feature on the otherwise unimpressive skyline.[6] Greenwich too had an impressive cock-pit, built in 1533 for Henry VIII,[7] while a thirty-foot-diameter brick-built cock-pit complemented the other sporting amenities at James's beloved Royston.[8] Nothing of this interest is registered in the inventories.

Bears and bulls were baited for sport on a regular basis at the major residences. At Whitehall the tiltyard was used for this spectacle: in 1604 posts and rails were set up there 'to keepe the people from the bearestake',[9] and ten years later four dozen round staples were 'dryven into the tylt for the tying of doggs there'.[10] At Greenwich one of the courts had a stake erected in it at which bulls and bears were baited–seemingly a particular New Year's day treat.[11]

Although much of the surviving evidence relates to the reign of James I rather than that of his son, Charles was by no means immune to the lure of baiting. On 9 February 1636 Thomas Caldwell, the King's Barber and a groom of the Chamber, was appointed to the office of 'chief master of his Majesty's games and pastimes, that is to say, of his bears, bulls, and mastiffs'. Caldwell was given considerable powers to ensure an appropriate supply of animals: he was authorized

. . . to take up for the King's service any bear or bull upon such price as he can agree with the owner. His Majesty declares that in case Caldwell cannot agree with the owner for a price, it shall be lawfull for two justices of the Peace near the place to set an indifferent price upon the same, whom his Majesty requires to be assisting Caldwell, and that the owner of such bear or bull shall not refuse the price so imposed.[12]

On 12 July 1623 the Spanish ambassador was reported to have been

. . . last week at Paris-garden, where they showed him all the pleasure they could both with bull, bear, and horse, besides jackanapes, and then turned a white bear into the Thames, where the dogs bated him swimming; which was the best sport of all.[13]

The white bears and other exotic beasts kept at the Paris Garden in Southwark, in the menagerie at the Tower, and elsewhere, occupied an ambivalent position in the king's affections: to some extent they represented the fruits of a positive interest in animal rarities, deliberately collected and preserved for their curiosity value or presented as diplomatic gifts by solicitous ambassadors, but in either case representing a neglected facet of royal collecting in the seventeenth century; on the other hand these creatures were never entirely safe from being subjected to trial by combat with one or other of their fellow captives, for the entertainment of the court. On 3 June 1604, for example, James I and a company of nobles amused themselves at the Tower by tossing a succession of living animals to the lions: first they threw in a cock, 'which being [the lions'] natural enemy, they immediately killed and sucked the blood'; then a lamb was put in, which they spared; then two mastiffs were matched against a fresh lion; finally, a spaniel was cast in, 'but the lion and he became friends and lived together for several years'.[14] On 23 June 1609 the entire royal family assembled at the Tower to see retribution exacted on a bear which had killed a child who had entered its cage: a succession of lions confronted the bear but none showed the least inclination to fight, so that the spectacle had to be abandoned; the bear was later 'bayted to death upon a stage and unto the mother of the murthered child was given twenty pounds out of part of that money which the people gave to see the Beare kild'.[15]

The Tower menagerie, established since at least the reign of Henry III,[16] had occupied part of the barbican of the main gate (which became known as the Lion Tower) since the late sixteenth century, and was refurbished by James I in 1603-5: a series of two-tier cages fitted with trap doors looked in upon an exercise yard paved with Purbeck stone and provided with a cistern 'for the Lyons to drinke and wasche themselves in'; a viewing platform erected above was replaced by a permanent gallery in 1621-3. The lions were evidently sufficiently contented with their lot to produce young on more than one occasion.[17]

Although the lions and bears were the best-known creatures in the king's menagerie, it embraced a much wider (though no doubt constantly changing) range of species. On 1 July 1613 the Ambassador Extraordinary of Savoy arrived with 'a tiger, a lioness, and a lynx which died on the road',[18] and six years later two antelopes were sent as a present from the Great Mogul. [19]

A major stir was caused by the arrival of an elephant in 1623, a gift from the King of Spain, consigned for safe-keeping to the officers of the King's Mews. The problems it presented were as gargantuan as the creature itself: estimates submitted for its yearly charges (including the appointment of four keepers) were calculated at £275.12s., 'besides a gallon of wine daily from September to April, when his keepers say he must drink no water', drawing the reponse that 'The Lord Treasurer will be little in love with presents which cost the King as much to maintain as a garrison'.[20]

Five camels accompanied the elephant from Spain. For a time in the summer of 1623 they were taken daily to graze incongruously in St. James's Park, later being transferred to Theobalds where stables were specially built for them by the Surveyor of the Works.[21]

Mention is made during James's reign of the arrival in 1623 of a male and a female ass, 'the she-ass sufficiently large for breeding'.[22] These too were destined for the park at Theobalds, where there was also kept a rare white hind calf, which arrived 'together with a woman, his nurse'; the park-keeper was instructed to take good care of both of them until King James's next visit.[23] Payments were later made to persons appointed by Sir Patrick Murray for storing the fish ponds at Theobalds and for 'taking care of the Herons, French fowls, Elks, silk worms, partridges & pheasants' there.[24]

The presence of elk in the royal menagerie comes as a surprise, but their appearance at Theobalds was not isolated: as early as 1605 instructions had been given at Kenilworth Castle for the preparation of 'a dry place in the old park to bee rayled in to keep Elks, reindeer and other strang[e] beasts',[25] while further specimens arrived as gifts from the 'Marquis of Brandenburgh' in 1612[26] and from the 'Count Palatine of Weare' in 1624.[27] The addition to the collection of another reindeer is recorded in 1613, when a live specimen was brought back as a gift by the whaling fleet of the Muscovy Company.[28] A number of references occur which mention other deer, probably all fallow and red deer, imported over the years almost as a matter of course and seemingly destined to improve the king's sport rather than to grace the menagerie.[29]

Crocodiles and a Virginian flying squirrel were apparently among the animals kept at the Paris Garden,[30] while in St. James's Park the New and Old Worlds were again represented as early as 1611 by animal curiosities: Henry Peacham writes of

Saint Iames his Ginney Hens, the Cassawarway moreouer,
The Beauer i the Parke (strange beast as ere any man saw)
Downe-shearing willowes with teeth as sharpe as a hand-saw.[31]

In a letter to his son on 22 August 1680, Sir Thomas Browne mentions Charles I's 'cassaware, or emeu, whose fine green channelled egge I have', remarking too on the royal 'oestriges', one of which he had seen 'in the latter end of King James his dayes, at Greenwich'.[32]

241 [295]   An entry in the inventories mentions the presence of 'One white wild Bull, 8 Cowes one yeare old Bullckin twoe sucking Calfes' at Holdenby, where they were valued at £38 but seemingly remained unsold. Otherwise, no hint of this interesting manifestation of Stuart taste is detected in this source.

Hunting and Hawking

Both James and Charles were deeply imbued with a love of field sports of all kinds and indeed it would have been surprising had it been otherwise: hunting, hawking, fowling and fishing were esteemed in the seventeenth century 'those absolute parts of Musicke which make perfect the harmony of a true Gentleman'.[33]

During the closing years of the Tudor period the centuries-old stranglehold exerted by the monarchy on hunting (particularly the hunting of deer) had been relaxed under Elizabeth: her noblemen exercised rights over their own estates, while at court the rigours of the chase were transmuted into the delicate ritual of an elaborate pastoral masque. On 17 August 1591, for example, Viscount Montague arranged the following entertainment for the ageing Queen at Cowdray:

. . . at eight of the clock in the morning, her Highness took horse, with all her traine, and rode into the parke; where was a delicate bowre prepared, under the which were her Highnesse musicians placed, and a crossbowe by a Nymph, with a sweet song, delivered to her hands, to shoote at deere, about some thirtie in number, put into a paddock, of which number she killed three or four. . .[34]

Nothing could have been further from the taste of Elizabeth's successor, and immediately on his accession to the English throne James plunged into the task of re-establishing his primacy over the game throughout the realm, and spent most of his energies for the remainder of his reign in exploiting it.[35]

James's dedication to the hunt bordered on the fanatical, rendering him careless both of affairs of state[36] and of his health.[37] Indeed he came to regard hunting as vital to his well-being and the intrusion of government as distinctly threatening:

The Kinge . . . findes such felicitie in that hunting life, that he hath written to the [Privy] counsaile, that yt is the only meanes to maintain his health, (which being the health and welfare of us all) he desires them to undertake the charge and burden of affaires, and to foresee that he be not interrupted nor troubled with too much busines.[38]

Although never one to abrogate his interest in Parliament, Charles too could be single-minded in pursuit of the deer, as evidenced by his being 'in the field [at Andover] before 5 in the morning' in 1635 and 'soundly wet' after a day's exertion in the New Forest in 1637.[39]

154 [56]   Considering the effort expended over the years by the two monarchs, remarkably little evidence for all this activity is to be found in the inventories.
396 [980-81] Undoubtedly, however, the '5 paire of staggs hornes' noted at St. James's and the '95 paire of stags hornes' and '24 Bucks hornes' in the custody of the housekeeper at Theobalds were trophies from the royal chase, which by 1649 must have lingered only as a distant memory of more pastoral times. Stripped from their settings, the modest tally of antlers sounds prosaic enough, but in better days more impressive displays had been made: Lysons recorded the former presence at Theobalds of 'divers large stagges heads sett round the [gallery] and fastened to the sayd roome, which are an excellent ornament to the same'.[40] The art of

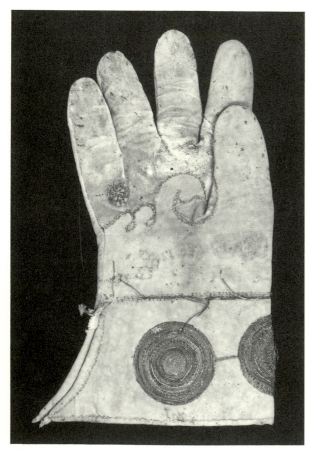
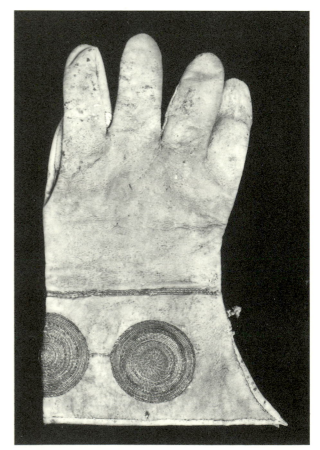

Figure 113 *Hawk's hood and hawking glove of King Henry VIII*. Tradescant Collection, Ashmolean Museum, Oxford.

382 [777-8]
taxidermy was yet in its infancy and it seems likely that the heads in question would have been artificial rather than stuffed. A further three pairs of antlers are recorded in the inventories, one 'wth a Carved head' which clearly belongs to this type. Others were recorded earlier at Hampton Court, where in 1635/6 three stags' heads were carved for the hall by Zachary Taylor; evidently they joined a number of others, for seven stags' heads in all were painted there in that year.[41]

The packs of buckhounds and harriers that accompanied the royal chase[42] are represented (symbolically, at least) in the inventories by a number of entries for dog collars, all relating to Hampton Court and including 'Two. slips for grey hounds', sold for 5s. 6d.; 'One hound collar of steele worke', which made only 3s.; and a series of more elaborate examples in 'Crimson vellv^t', 'greene vell^t, 'cloth of gould', 'Crimson sattine', 'greene vellv^t wth roses' and 'greene vellv^t wth copper terretts', mostly designated 'for hounds' and valued from 3s. to 12s. each. All were bought by John Boulton. The officers given responsibility for the hounds were again allowed considerable discretion in providing for the royal amusement: on 14 July 1616, for example, the Master of the Otterhounds was granted a licence

182 [275]
180 [250]
180 [244-9]

. . . to take hounds, beagles, spaniels, and mongrels for His Majesty's disport. Also to seize such hounds &c as may be offensive to the King's game. [43]

180 [251], 180 [243]
180 [252]
Both James and Charles were hawking enthusiasts, a sport represented modestly by 'foure. haukes hoodes' which sold for 3s; 'One lewer of cloth. of gould' which fetched 3s. 6d.; and 'one hawkeing glove of Henrÿ ye 8th'', which made 2s. (The glove presumably represents an historical souvenir rather than serviceable equipment.) The buyer in each case was John Boulton. It is just possible that two of these same items can be identified with surviving artefacts in the Ashmolean Museum (Fig. 113), where they form part of the Tradescant collection with which the museum was founded in 1683.[44] In the catalogue of that collection published in 1656 (while it was still in the Tradescant museum at Lambeth), entries are to be found for 'Henry the 8 his Stirrups, Haukes-Hoods, Gloves' and for 'Henry 8, hawking-glove, hawks-hood, dogs-coller'.[45] A number of items had been authorized for removal from the Hampton Court Wardrobe by order of Charles I in 1635; they were to be given to John Tradescant the elder, then gardener at Oatlands Palace, for display in his cabinet of curiosities at Lambeth, and included 'King Henry the Eight his Cap, his stirrups',[46] but no mention was made on that occasion of hawking equipment. The manuscript catalogue of the Ashmolean collection as it stood c. 1685, on the other hand, records 'Chirothecae Henrici 8^{ti} Acciptariae, ex corio confectae, cum quatuor cucullis acciptarijs'. Considering the absence of hawking equipment from the material granted to the elder Tradescant and the correspondence in the number of hawks' hoods between the sale inventories and the Ashmolean catalogue, it seems distinctly possible that the surviving pieces were not royal gifts to the elder Tradescant but were acquisitions made by his son following the Commonwealth sale.[47]

A set of hawking equipment, comprising pouch, glove, lure and hood, currently in the Burrell Collection, Glasgow, is traditionally said to have been given by James I to Lord Dudley North when the monarch visited Wroxton Abbey to stand as godfather to one of the North children. Although the story seems to be of doubtful authenticity, the equipment none the less represents a characteristic early seventeenth-century assemblage, although the pouch, at least, is thought to be of Continental manufacture.[48]

154 [51]
The presence of '30 burding peeces', valued at 10s. each and housed in a press at St. James's, implies that, by the time the Court abandoned London in 1642, wildfowling with guns had begun to gain favour, despite having been condemned earlier by Elizabeth[49] and by James.[50] Evidence which might confirm Charles's interest in wildfowling was laid before the Archaeological Institute in 1859, in the form of a flint-lock birding peice, inlaid on the stock with roses and thistles and dated on the breach 1614, which was claimed to have been a former possession of Charles when Prince of Wales.[51]

Outdoor Games

Although even more poorly represented in the inventories, outdoor games accounted for a large part of the off-duty relaxation of the Court. James evidently viewed regular physical exercise as a solemn duty for the princes of the blood: to

Figure 114 *'The High Borne Prince James, Duke of Yorke'* (later King James II) at tennis. From *True Effigies* (1641). British Library.

Prince Henry he advised that 'it be most requisite for a King to exercise his engyne (which surely with Idlenesse wil rouste & become blunt)'.[52]

Tennis was highly popular with the leisured classes as a whole, and London sported at least a dozen public courts in the early Stuart period in addition to those at Whitehall (two), Denmark House and St. James's.[53] Almost every royal house, indeed, had at least one tennis court and sometimes more. There were indoor courts at Hampton Court, Whitehall and St. James's: the outdoor court at Windsor is clearly visible in Norden's aerial view (Fig. 20); that at Nonsuch had high boarded walls and was shaded by trees.[54] Many were paved with Purbeck stone and the walls were periodically blackened, presumably to improve the visibility of the ball. At Richmond wire screens had been inserted in the sixteenth century 'in the wyndowes lookyng out of the gallery into the tennys playe, for the savyng of them brekyng with ballys'.[55]

In 1615 Gervase Markham could still describe tennis as 'a pastime in close or open courts, striking a little round balls two or fro, either with the palm of the hand, or with racket'.[56] Rackets seem to have been in normal use at Court: an engraving of James, Duke of York (the future James II), published in 1641, shows the young Prince standing in an open court with a typical racket of the period–short-handled and diagonally strung (Fig. 114).[57] Two similar rackets are depicted lying in the open court in Norden's view of Windsor Castle.

Henry, Prince of Wales, a noteable all-round sportsman, was particularly addicted to

. . . Tennis play, wherein, to speake the truth . . . he neither observed moderation, nor what appertained to his dignity and person, continuing oftimes his play for the space of three or foure houres, and the same in his shirt, rather becoming an Artisan than a Prince . . . [58]

Henry's younger brother Charles took up the game before his accession and was instructed in it from his youth: from 1611 there survives a warrant for payment of £20 per annum to 'Jehu Webb, Master of the Tennis Plays, for instructing the Duke of York in that exercise, and providing rackets and balls for him'.[59] Well tutored though he may have been, Charles lost considerable sums of money to Thomas Hooker (or Hooke), keeper of the tennis court at St. James's, to whom £798. 3s. 2d. was paid in 1626 'for provision of balls and other necessaries, and for money lost unto him by his Majesty at play'.[60] Two years later, Edward Conway confided to a correspondent that he was experiencing difficulty in gaining access to the King at Newmarket due to Charles's 'continual being either upon his sport abroad or at tennis'.[61] In the turbulence of 1643 Charles showed a fastidiousness uncharacteristic of Henry when one of the grooms of the Wardrobe was required to carry to the King at Oxford '4 yds of taby, 2 ells and 1/4 of taffety to be a tennis suit, and 2 pairs of garters and roses with silk buttons and other necessaries for making up the said suit'.[62]

Bowling was practised at court both in indoor 'allayes' and on outdoor greens. Whitehall had a much-frequented alley, while at Hampton Court a closed alley was complemented by another in the gardens. At Nonsuch there was 'a neate and hansome bouling greene well ordered lying much what uppon a square and rayled with good postes rayles and lattices of wood'.[63] Charles evidently had a fondness for the game and played regularly during the period of his confinement at Holdenby, for

. . . in regard there was no Bowling-Green then well kept at *Holmby*, the King would sometimes ride to *Harrowden*, a House of the Lord *Vaux's*, about nine Miles off, where there was a good Bowling-Green. . . and other whiles to Althorpe, a fair House about two or three Miles from *Holmby*. . . where also there was a green well kept.[64]

Indoor Games

Indoor pursuits are rather better represented in the inventories, although some fail to make any impact. For example, the dedication of the Court to card games was almost legendary,[65] but has left no trace other than a rather charming engraving reproduced in Fig. 115. Those activities demanding more substantial equipment are better represented.

Eight billiard boards listed in the inventories were scattered throughout the major houses. They ranged in value from £1 for 'One billiard board w^thout Cloath' from Whitehall (viewed 'At Lew^t Wards') to £5 each for examples from Richmond and from Denmark House (the latter specifically described as 'Covered with greene cloth').

172 [144], 241 [294], 249 [26]
287 [145], 395 [959], 363 [524]

213 [77]
13 [263]

Figure 115 *King Charles I at cards.* Sutherland Collection, Ashmolean Museum, Oxford.

Typical seventeenth-century billiard boards, as described by Charles Cotton,[66] were much like those of today:

The form of a Billiard-Table is oblong . . . it is rail'd round, which rail or ledge ought to be a little swel'd or stuft with fine flox or cotton: the supersicies of the Table must be covered with green-cloth, the finer and more freed from knots the better it is . . . at the four corners of the Table there are holes, and at each side exactly in the middle one, which are called Hazards, and have hanging at the bottoms nets to receive the Balls.

The accessories of the table and the rules of the game have altered more radically. 'There is to the Table belonging an Ivory Port', says Cotton, 'which stands at one end of the Table, and an Ivory King at the other, two small Ivory Balls and two Sticks'. The aim of either player was to strike his ball through the 'port' or arch and then to bring it into contact with the king; knocking down either of these lost the player the game, as did hitting his own ball into one of the 'hazards', but contriving to make the opponent's ball do so constituted a win. If the player placed a hand (or so much as a sleeve) on the table, he conceded the game. Either end of the cue (or 'mace' or 'mast'), of Brazil wood or *lignum vitae* tipped with ivory, could be used to strike the ball.[67]

Cotton stressed the virtuous nature of billiards, a 'Gentile, cleanly and most ingenious Game': few towns in England were then without a 'publick Billiard-table', and the game was also favoured by 'Noble and private Families in the Country, for the recreation of the mind and exercise of the body'.[68] The limited scope it offered for cheating represented a major attraction of the game to Cotton, but, to judge from its record elsewhere, the Stuart court was as likely to have appreciated the opportunities it afforded for betting on the outcome of the game.

225 [88]
296 [230]

At Ludlow Castle a 'Large shovell Board Table' was inventoried in its own 'Shovell Board Chamber'; a second example, valued more highly than the first (though yet only at £3), came from Wimbledon. Such tables are characterized as being solidly built of polished oak, of extreme length (thirty to forty feet) but of narrow width (two to three and a half feet); two lines are marked across the surface at either end, at four inches and four feet from the edge respectively. Players each slide four heavy metal discs from one end of the table, scoring one point if the playing piece comes to rest between the two lines at the opposite end, two points if it stops between the second line and the edge, and three points if it overhangs the end without falling off; the score is adjusted appropriately as pieces are moved by impacts from other men.[69] Pieces which overshoot the table fall into a purpose-built trough fixed to the end.

Robert Plot recorded such a table at Chartley, Staffordshire, 'made up of about 260 *pieces*, which are generally about 18 inches long . . . which, being laid on longer boards for support underneath, are so accurately joynted and glewed together, that no *shuffle*-board whatever is freer from *rubbs* or *casting*.'[70] Another table, over thirty-nine feet long and said to be the longest then in England, was noted in a public house in Clerkenwell *c*. 1800.[71] A good example, formerly belonging to the Paston family of Oxnead Hall, survives in the Castle Museum, Norwich.

A set of thirty-six shuffle-board counters exhibited at the Society of Antiquaries of Scotland in 1891 carried representations of the sovereigns of England (and various of their relations) on the obverse and heraldic devices on the reverse, all contained in a 'very pretty silver box' with the head of Charles I on the lid, dated *c*. 1638.[72]

Attempts were made repeatedly to deny games of this sort to the lower classes, but their popularity survived unabated: 'shovel aborde' was among the games 'mayntayned in every alehouse and tipling house' in late sixteenth-century Oxford, despite official prohibition.[73] In the halls of the well-to-do, however, tables were common features and the royal family was certainly not immune to the attractions of the game. A 'Shovelboorde roome' is mentioned at Richmond in 1622/3, while a 'shoveboard table' was installed at St. James's in 1603/4 for Prince Henry: in view of his youth (he was only nine or ten at the time), the table was a modest thirteen feet six inches long; it was supported on three trestles 'with round pillars with crosse feet below and a box at the end'.[74]

172 [142]

Hampton Court produced 'One table to play at Trolle Madam', a game introduced (according to Strutt[75]) from France which achieved widespread popularity in the more affluent houses of Elizabethan England. A writer in 1572[76] recommended to lady visitors to the resort of Buxton that

. . . if the weather bee not aggreeable too theire expectacion, they may have in the ende of a Benche, eleven holes made, intoo the which to trowle prummetes, or Bowles of leade, bigge, little, or meane, or also, of Copper, Tynne, Woode, eyther vyolent, or softe, after their owne discretion, the pastyme Troule in Madame is termed.

In addition to its recreational value, the game was recommended as a gentle exercise to the weak and infirm, the benefit of which to arms, legs and 'mydryfe' could be regulated by varying the weight of the balls.[77]

Board games represented in the inventories are confined to chess and tables, the two sometimes being played on a single board. 'A Chess board said to be Queen Elizabeths inlaid with gold, Silver and pearles' may have been prized for its historical associations,[78] and 'A Chesse board of Silver wth 30. Men to it, being parcell Silver & parcell Cristall' was clearly another special piece: it sold to Beauchamp for £30. Two less elaborate boards from Richmond, one of 'cloth. of gold but old' and the other 'of glass' which sold for 10s. for the two, were presumably in everyday use. Two other examples served for both chess and tables: 'A Chesse Board of white Bone carved and cutt upon for a Paire of Tables' valued at £2 and sold for £3; and 'A paire of Playeing Tables of inlaied woodd garnished with silver guilt, sett with stones & Pearles the Men of Woodd part white, The other parte silver guilt with a Boxe, and a suite of Chesse men of Silver', valued at £50. Although Elizabeth is said to have been a skilful player, chess was not to the taste of her Stuart successor who esteemed it 'ouer fonde, because it is ouerwise & Philosophick a folly'.[79] Both of James's sons were keen players, however, and Charles, according to one source, 'when he is neither in the field . . . nor at the Council, passes most of his time at chess with the Marquis of Winchester'.[80]

The game of tables, of medieval origin,[81] is represented by the combined chess boards already mentioned, by 'A Paire of Tables of White and Yellowe Amber garnished with silver. The Tablemen and Dice suitable in a greene Case of vellvett', which made a handsome £30; by 'One p^r of playing tables of Ebboney plated wth Iron wth a pair of silv^r dice & 30 men', sold for £3. 10s.; by 'One paire of old playing Tables wth men of glass' valued at 3s., and others of mother-of-pearl and of cedar. Tablemen, whether of glass as here, of amber or wood as above, or of ivory as commonly found elsewhere,[82] were discoid in form, varying in diameter up to about three inches, and were often elaborately carved.

The Cabinet of Coins and Medals

For his collection of coins and medals Charles I was, as in so many fields, indebted to initiatives undertaken by his elder brother, Prince Henry. Two major sources contributed to Henry's cabinet. The impact of the first is signalled by payments made in instalments during the summer of 1611 to one 'Abraham van Hutton': the enormous sum paid to this obscure figure, 'for antiquities of medals and coins bought of him', was £2,200.[83] The second major acquisition was made in the Spring of the following year, when we hear of 'a cabinet of antiquities brought into this realm by Hans von Dirbige and sold to the Prince'.[84] This was the famous cabinet of Abraham Gorlaeus of Delft, an account of which, first published in 1601,[85] proved so comprehensive as to be still heavily in demand as a reference-book a century later. Sir Roy Strong, commenting on the dual source of Henry's collection, stresses its precociousness with the observation that it was 'the earliest major assembly of Classical antiquities [to] enter the country', preceding by a short time that of the Earl of Arundel.[86]

Following Henry's death, Charles inherited the collection of 'certen Meddals of gould and straunge coyne'.[87] Charles was said to have had some discernment in matters relating to antiquities, and 'could judge of medals whether they had the number of years they pretended unto'.[88] The cabinet was placed in the care of Abraham van der Doort, to whom it had originally been entrusted in Henry's time. Van der Doort's special knowledge and skill as 'Provider of Patterns of Coins and Master Embosser and Maker of Medals' to the King rendered him well qualified for the post,[89] but his position as 'Keeper of the Cabbonett Room' lacked the authority to frustrate the depredations wreaked on the collection in the aftermath of Henry's death by various courtiers, among whom Thomas Carey proved particularly avaricious.[90]

It was thus an already much reduced collection that Van der Doort came to catalogue for Charles around 1640. It was stored (at least in part) in a 'Table of

427 [22]

419 [2]

212 [64]

118 [315]
118 [314]

117 [301]

172 [143]
282 [97]
212 [62-3], 180 [238]

black ebbone woodden laied in wth white Ivory under wch Table is a place wherein is a sett of tourn'd round Tables made of Ivory'.[91] Other elements of the collection were kept in cabinets fitted with drawers, including some described as 'leatherne . . . wth goulden strookes', as 'speckled woodden', and as lined with white felt.[92] Individual pieces were occasionally stored in 'black hoopes', 'round horne hoopes' or 'black horne hoopes'.[93] A comparison of the few hundred pieces listed rather cursorily in Van der Doort's inventory with the large numbers alluded to at a later date (see below) indicates either that enormous additions were made to the collection by Charles or, more probably, that only part of the collection is recorded in Van der Doort's lists. We find there a dozen or so Roman coins; a single Greek issue ('a very bigg head upon a little peece and at the other side an Owle said to bee an Atteeneon peece of Coyne'); a gold piece with 'some Carecters' on one side 'said to bee an ould Brittain peece Coyne'; some pieces of Tudor and Stuart coinage and a preponderance of 'medals' featuring a variety of Continental princes, cardinals and popes.[94]

A later attempt to rationalize and to classify in an enlightened manner the 'divers Medalls and ancient Coines, Greeke, Romane, and others' was instituted by Charles in 1648. On that occasion Sir Simonds D'Ewes, together with Patrick Young the keeper of the royal library, were appointed

. . . to sort and put ye said Coines and Medalls into their Series and order, and to lay aside to bee disposed by us all duplicates among them wch are genuine and true, and to separate, and divide the novitious, adulterate & spurious peeces from ye said genuine.[95]

All the pieces set aside in this process were to remain in Patrick Young's charge, according to Charles's instructions, 'untill our further pleasure bee knowne'. How far from realization the royal pleasure stood can be judged from the fact that at the time of writing (19 October 1648) the cabinet had already been sequestered by Parliament, while Charles himself was on temporary parole in Newport, Isle of Wight, from his confinement in Carisbrooke Castle: this respite was brought abruptly to an end only six weeks later when, under close arrest once again, Charles entered the final chapter of his life that was to end on the scaffold at Whitehall in the following January.

Later in 1649 the cabinet was placed in the care of John Dury, who is thought to have cared for it until the Restoration. According to an audit of the contents compiled by Dury on 27 April 1652, there were then 12,000 coins in the collection.[96] Following the accession of Charles II, Elias Ashmole was appointed by the King 'to make a description of his Medalls', which inventory, with lists of Greek, Roman and modern coins and medals survives in the Bodleian Library.[97]

In his great survey volume, the *Numismata* (1697), John Evelyn records the view that Charles's coin collection outshone all those of his princely contemporaries in Europe, while lamenting that it was by his day 'impair'd, and miserably imbezel'd, not only by the *Rebels* during the late *Civil Wars*, but even since, thro' the Negligence of others'; the medals, meanwhile, had been 'taken away and purloin'd by *Thousands*'.[98] The final blow to the collection came in 1698, when all that had survived the vicissitudes of the previous years perished in the great fire at Whitehall.

Although the coin cabinet at St. James's was reserved, a few pieces from elsewhere were disposed of in the sale. Amongst the 'Goodes received from Mr Wheeler belonging to the late King' was one 'Boxe wherein are Coynes in particon', its five drawers containing between them 121 coins, as well as six other loose boxes containing a further fifty-six coins, which between them fetched £14. 13s. Also to be noted here are the 'Brasse and Copper Meddalls of severall sorts found in an old Chest in the Lower Jewell House formerly in the Lord Cottingtons charge in number 139', which were sold for a total of £14. 14s. 4d, and a further 'Seventy two Brass and Copp^r greek Meddalls, in a green Earthen Vase', valued at a modest £3.

245 [337-41]

46 [197]

430 [62]

The Cabinet of Gems

The bulk of the gem collection, like the coins and medals, was reserved from sale,[99] but a small number seem to have evaded this protection. A few of these were evidently of Classical origin (or at least in Classical style):

428 [28]   An Oynix Engrav'd with a Caesars head [sold for £6. 5s.]
428 [29]   One D^o Engraved [£7]

428 [30]	Two large Aygots Engrav^d wth greek letters, and Generals heads [£19]
428 [34]	A Syrian garnet, Engrav^d wth a generals head, Greek [£7. 13s.]
428 [35]	Vulcan with his pincers, on a large Topas, set in Silv^r [£10. 12s.]

430 [61]	The same group of material, inventoried in the Tower and evidently all stored
430 [66]	together, also contained 'The 12 Cesars heads in Bass Relievo cutt in porphyry' (sold for £50) and 'A Greek Generalls head in a Large Onyx wth four other Greek heads in Brass and Copper very ancient', which fetched £3. Near Eastern origins
428 [33]	are implied for two others: 'A great Ametheist Engrav'd in hebrew set in gold'
428 [36]	(£55), and 'A White Cornelian Engrav^d wth persian lett^{rs}' (£1. 7s.). Other gems
428 [27]	listed here include 'A large Sardonix sett in Silver' (£22. 10s.), and four 'large
428 [31-2]	Sapphirs for seals' (£43. 5s.), as well as 'tables' of agate, bloodstone, lapis lazuli,
428-9 [passim]	porphyry and serpentine.

Curiosities and Rarities in the Royal Collections

Although not notable as collectors of curiosities, Charles and his father before him were not entirely innured to the taste for 'rarities of art and nature' which marks the collections of many of their contemporaries on the Continent. A number of the animals mentioned above (pp. 403-5), for example, were evidently prized more for their rarity than for any more profound reason. This predeliction also manifested itself in the whale bones displayed in one of the principal courtyards at Whitehall Palace, which took its name from these exhibits.[100]

No formally designated 'cabinet of curiosities' existed at any of the royal residences. The 'Cabbonett Room' at Whitehall, placed by Charles I in the charge of Van der Doort,[101] was designated for 'Meddalies and Limbed pecees and all other rarities', but contained little other than coins, medals, and works of art. Scattered throughout the royal properties, however, there were to be found (as shown by the inventories) a considerable range of items such as were deliberately grouped together in the *Kunstkammern* of contemporary courts on the Continent. What they lacked in the Stuart household was any inkling of a cohesive context. Only in the case of a small number of miscellaneous items, seemingly inventoried together in the Upper Jewel House at the Tower but not themselves of exceptional value, can any suggestion be made that they might have been consciously grouped as rarities:[102] perhaps these few objects had been gathered together to add interest to the tour of the sights of the Tower accorded to visitors (see pp. 41-2), but they can have impinged only peripherally on Charles's consciousness.

Cabinets, in the sense of small cupboards and chests of drawers, feature in some numbers and embellished in a variety of materials—mother-of-pearl, tortoiseshell, amber, crystal, ebony, 'steele worke' and ivory (see pp. 282-5). For the most part they seem to have been of purely domestic significance, housing 'a paire of Playeing Tables . . . and a lookeing Glasse . . .', cosmetic or other instruments, and the like. Only one example speaks of deliberate gathering together of some minor collectors' items:

245 [327]	A Boxe wherein are drawers with Pictures vizt In the upper drawer 6. Ivorie boxes, and one of Boxe
245 [328]	In the 2^d and 3^d drawer downewards are foure white Pictures, one black, one of Amber, & one of Boxe
245 [329]	One square one
245 [330]	Nyne peeces in little black Cases like table men
245 [-]	Sixteene peeces of the like fashion out of Cases and 25. cases emptie

Each entry represents a separate lot in the sale inventories; they were valued at a total of £59. 2s. and sold to Edward Bass.[103] Modest as they are, they merely serve to emphasise the paucity of such items in the inventories. For other material we are forced to search through the entries where no evidence of perceived relationships between individual objects can be established.

Mention of a number of items of amber recalls the *Kunstkammer* taste for materials imbued with special properties: amber was worn as an amulet against sickness and vessels made from it offered similar protection to the user. For this reason it found its way into many collections of rarities in a variety of forms, while at a more prosaic level it was considered an attractive material for the production of small cabinets and other items.

Königsberg, on the southern shore of the Baltic was the principal source of items made in amber. A letter written from Danzig by Sir Thomas Roe to Viscount Dorchester in 1629 demonstrates one of the mechanisms by which such items reached the royal collections (the beneficiary in this case being Henrietta Maria), but gives no indication of any special heed being paid· to its assumed properties:

If her Matie the Queene please to have toyes of amber, as cabinetts, glasses, bason and eawre, cups, boules, tankers, boxes to furnish a cupboard, if I may know her pleasure and may have mony, I shalbe most diligent to doe her humble service.[104]

At Denmark House, Henrietta Maria's principal residence, 'Thirteene Images of yellowe Amber cutt in a white Wooden Boxe' were inventoried along with 'Twoe small candlesticks, and 3. small Cupps, A standing Cupp and double salt sixe spoones', all in the same material, sold together for £10 to Robert Houghton, the late King's brewer; a further 'Candlesticke of yellowe Amber to hang upp in Brannches in a double Woodden Boxe' was bought by De Critz's syndicate for an impressive £50. From the Upper Jewel House at the Tower came one simple amber cup and a more elaborate 'Amber Cupp and Cover with a foot broken', which sound like further typical lathe-turned products of the Königsberg industry.[105]

117 [303]
117 [302]
40 [157]
42 [174]

Another group of vessels also gained in value from the apotropaic qualities of their raw material: 'Earthen vessels or Buck earth' (described in the later copies as of 'terra sigillata or buckroe earth'). These terms designate special clays to which medicinal properties were ascribed. Such clays were collected in a variety of localities which each gave their name to their respective products: Lemnos was perhaps the best known, *terra lemnia* being much sought after. The significance of *terra sigillata* vessels in the context of Denmark House, where they were inventoried, is unclear, but the range of forms represented is remarkably wide: 'one great vause; one Tunn, on sillebub pott, 4: great cupps. wth covers; one spout pott, one baskett, two redd gilt potts. one Indian box. one flatt pott'. They were valued as a group at the high figure of £50. As well as being formed into vessels, these clays were sold as medicinal troches or cakes, each stamped or 'sealed' with a device that identified the place of origin and provided the generic name most widely used to describe them – *terra sigillata*, or 'sealed earth'.

412 [76]

Although more complex in their multi-faceted appeal, apotropaic qualities would no doubt have been among the characteristics esteemed in 'One Estrige Cup and Cover garnished with Silver guilt supported by 3. Estridges, and a Serpent wounde like a Ring upon the Cover', and 'A large Estridge Egge pott garnished with enamelled gold, the Cover gold, and the handle a greene enammelled serpent', both inventoried in the Upper Jewel House at the Tower and ascribed strikingly unequal values at £6. 4s. and £70 respectively. They belong among a range of vessels in materials such as nautilus shell, coco-de-mer, 'unicorn horn' and rhino horn (see below), widely represented in European *Kunstkammern* of the sixteenth and seventeenth centuries, in which qualities of beauty and technical virtuosity complemented those of a more mystical nature.[106] As in this instance, there was a fondness for allusive interplay between form and material, the supporting figures of the ostriches commenting on the raw material of the cup itself.

28 [24]
35 [97]

Held in similar esteem by collectors (although produced in a quite different milieu) were the Chinese cups of rhinoceros horn that feature in many of the princely *Kunstkammern* of the late Renaissance. One example, a 'Rinoceras Cupp graven with figures. with a golden foot', sold from the Tower Jewel House to Ann Lacy for £10, clearly belongs to this tradition. Accredited with a range of properties – medicinal (particularly against cholera), magical, aphrodisiac, and with the power to detect poison – cups of this type had settled down into a well established tradition by the sixteenth century, in which a major part was played by those carved with landscape scenes. Many such pieces were invested with precious metal mounts, including 'golden feet', before being placed on display in European collections.[107]

42 [178]

Other vessels in crystal and various hardstones, which might have been encountered in the *Kunstkammer* of a Continental princely court, were evidently scattered among the various royal palaces and held no special significance as collectors' pieces.

Two further pieces from Denmark House are typical of Continental curiosity collections of the time: 'An Artificiall Rocke with a Crucifixe of Corrall', valued at £10, and 'A Rocke of Corrall with Spoones Forkes, knives and a Tunnell of silver

117 [304]
118 [309]

with a Windemillne of Mother of pearle on the Topp in a painted Case', which, for all its elaboration, was valued at only £2. A number of examples of sixteenth-century date survive from the Habsburg collections: Elisabeth Scheicher illustrates two cavernous, rocky compositions inhabited by tiny figures, one tableau being made of wood and the other of assorted minerals, both surmounted by a crucifixion; a plaster mountain cleft by a pass and clad with coral 'trees'; and three crucifixions atop Mount Golgotha.[108] *Lapides manuales* formed a favourite field of interest of Archduke Ferdinand II, who gathered a number of them (mostly originating from Bohemia and the Tyrol) at Schloss Ambras near Innsbruck.[109] Mountainous compositions of coral were also well represented in the Wittelsbach *Kunstkammer* at Munich, where Albrecht V had shown a particular penchant for them.[110]

427 [21] 'A Corall Tree wth a foot, of Silver Fillagree Work', which fetched £3, belongs
412 [81] to the same milieu,[111] while 'A branch of wilde Corrall', valued at £1. 10s., perhaps awaited the attentions of the silversmith.

Lastly and most notably among this group of items prized for their rare materials, mention must be made of those of 'unicorn horn'. Two entries in the
25 [60] inventories relate to complete specimens: 'The Unicornes Hornes weighing 40^li 8.oz' valued at £600 and housed in the Lower Jewel House at the Tower, and another example inventoried at Denmark House but originating from Windsor,
250 [47] valued at £500. In addition there was a 'staff & a peece of unicornes horne' valued at £50, again listed at Denmark House but coming from Hampton Court, and
39 [137], 40 [153] three vessels made from the same material: a cup and a beaker, each 'garnish't
41 [166] with gold', estimated at £45, and another beaker with a 'golden Cover with a Diamond Ring on the topp supported by 3 Unicornes', valued at £50. Unicorn horn was again imbued with apotropaic qualities and cups made from it were credited with the power to detect or neutralize poison;[112] the association of the fabulous animal with the Virgin may have been a further recommendation to Charles's Catholic consort. The high valuations attached particularly to the complete examples suggests that some credence was still given to the quasi-magical properties of these 'horns' deriving from their traditional association with the unicorn, although recognition of their true identity as tusks of the Arctic narwhal (*Monodon monoceros*) had begun to emerge half a century earlier. Gerard Mercator, in his *Atlas* of 1595, mentioning the finding of these striking ivory teeth (which grow up to about six feet in length and are characterized by a spiral twist along their external surface) along the Arctic coasts, speculated that they might derive from some marine animal. Knowledge of this possibility had certainly penetrated Charles I's court, for John Tradescant was credited there in 1632 with the tale that two Bristol men had discovered during a fruitless search for a North West passage 'an island where were store of unicorns' horns, long and wreathed like that at Windsor, which [he had] heard to be nothing else but the snout of a fish, yet very precious against poison'.[113] The Danish scholar and collector Ole Worm established the facts in a treatise published in 1638, yet even he seems to have been reluctant to jettison entirely their romantic aura, for he derives them in the catalogue of his own museum from 'Unicornu marinum . . . hunc Septentrionalibus dici Narhaul'.[114] The effects of these revelations become clear when the valuations attributed to the specimens in the inventories are compared with those of a generation earlier: the most renowned example, that from Windsor, had been estimated at 'above £100,000' in 1598, while as late as 1641 the Marquis de la Ferté Imbaut was informed that an example at the Tower (covered with silver plates – a feature not noted on those in the inventories) was valued at £40,000.[115]

As a post-script, it seems that one of the unicorn horns survived the sale, for on 11 February 1658 a warrant was issued on the instructions of the Council ordering the Sergeant-at-Arms 'to search for and seize a unicorn's horn, and 2 St. Thomas à Beckett's staves, which belonged to the late King, and have been embezzled out of the Tower'.[116]

Other pieces embodying aspects of *Kunstkammer* taste appear occasionally
117 [299] and in scattered contexts. These include 'A Galley of Cristall standing upon 4 wheeles garnished with pearles, and rubies, silver guilt, with Images, and Ordenance in a Crimson vellvett Case', bought along with other items for £130 by
426 [11] Nathaniel Nicholls, a Yeoman of the Guard. 'A Silver Eagle made to move', weighing 25oz., valued at £6. 5s. and sent to the Mint, evidently belongs with the complex clockwork automata that exerted a strong attraction for European collectors. Their appeal lay partly in their artistic merit, partly in their capacity to amuse and entertain, and partly in the intricacy of their clockwork mechanisms

which drew a strong response from imaginations attuned to speculation on the nature of cosmic mechanisms working on a universal scale. Classical texts from Hero of Alexander onwards provided precedents and stimuli for the development of models operating on hydraulic power (particularly favoured in the grottoes of sixteenth- and seventeenth-century gardens) while developments in spring-driven clockwork mechanisms in the sixteenth century led to opportunities for miniaturization and increasing sophistication of design.[117]

[*passim*]

A somewhat similar appeal lay behind the twenty-six 'pictures of perspective' represented in the inventories. At a superficial level the appeal of such pictures lay in their ability to trick the eye with images distorted by the adoption of a perspective system aligned on an oblique viewpoint; the simpler pictures were made coherent by adopting the correct viewpoint from one side, while more complex compositions incorporated some elements to be viewed from one side and some from another. Others operated on a completely different principle, the image becoming comprehensible only when viewed in a cylindrical mirror placed in the centre of the composition. As with other Renaissance 'toyes', their appeal was in part poetic, part mystical and part scientific: the enlightened mind could savour equally the 'secret' elements of the composition and also the geometrical principles which governed the deceit.[118]

64 [73]
63 [58], 315 [262], 320 [337]
274 [290]

Twelve of those listed in the royal collections are by Hendrick van Steenwyck, including one with 'figures in it done by gentelisco'; his subjects include the late King, 'A Night Peece', 'A Prosspective of yᵉ temple' and 'Mary Christ & Martha'. The same artist was the author of 'A little boock of Prosspectives', and four paintings were executed by others after his designs. Gerard Houckgeest produced another four compositions, and Jan van Belcamp two; the remainder are unattributed.

197 [197]

Although not specifically identified as a 'prosspective', a picture of 'Edward yᵉ 6ᵗʰ lookeing through. a hoole' can be included amongst them with some certainty. Such a picture was remarked upon at Whitehall by two early visitors from the Continent. In 1613 the Duke of Saxe-Weimar was shown there a 'Portrait of King Edward VI, perspectively painted'; from in front, the Duke found, 'one cannot distinguish what it is meant for, but from the side the portrait is seen quite clearly'.[119] Fifteen years earlier the same picture had been seen by Paul Hentzner, who added the information that the image remained deformed 'till by looking through a small hole in the cover which is put over it, you see it in its true proportions'.[120] Clearly it was the viewer, and not the subject, who would have been seen 'lookeing through a hoole'.

429 [54]

Another category of material which we may isolate (but which held no significance as a group for the Trustees, despite being stored together in the Jewel House – see p. 413) is that which may be described as 'foreign rarities'. Amongst these items were 'A Conjuring Drum from Lapland, wᵗʰ an Alamanack cut on a pˢ of wood, & some other odd Trinckets of Steel and silver gilt', which together fetched £1. 11s. 9d. It seems conceivable that the drum may have been acquired through the Scandinavian contact which was a regular feature of the reign of James I and Anne of Denmark. A shaman's drum of similar origin survives in the Sloane Collection at the Museum of Mankind: broad, shallow, and with a hand-hold on its wooden back, the single membrane is heavily painted with figures and symbols.[121] The almanac, cut from a single piece of wood, evidently belonged to the type known as a clog almanac, in which the major feast days – particularly those of significance for the planting of crops and other agricultural activities – were indicated by devices carved on the four long sides of a rectangular stave: it would have had no significance at court beyond its curiosity value. It too could have been of Scandinavian origin, although the type was also to be found in seventeenth-century England.[122]

426 [8]
426 [8]
426 [10]

Also from the Jewel House came three pieces of Russian origin: 'A large Antique Vessell for Mead from the Duke of Muscovy' (weighing 100 ounces and valued at £25), 'A large Beaker from the Sᵈ Duke made of many pˢ of Coin Joinᵈ together' (80 ounces valued at £20) and another like the last weighing 60 ounces and estimated at £15, all of which were sent to the Mint to be melted down.

426 [13]

'The Temple of Jerusalem made of Ebony and Amber', sold to Basset for the considerable sum of £25, was evidently a rather superior example of the well-known series of intarsia models representing the Church of the Holy Sepulchre which, along with models of the Church of the Nativity in Bethlehem, were widely prized by European collectors in the seventeenth century. Perhaps the most common types are those made in olive wood, inlaid with shell; some contain compartments to be filled with sand from the Holy Land.[123]

Africa is almost certainly represented by two instruments of characteristic type: 'A Trumpet made of a large Elephants tooth Engrav'd wth Several odd figures' and 'Another Trumpet Curiosly Engrav^d,', both recorded at the Tower. Large and impressive instruments of this type – in fact, side-blown trumpets – were produced in two principal areas in the west of the Continent: in Benin, and, more particularly, by the Bulom peoples inhabiting the coastal zone of Sierra Leone and the offshore island of Sherbro. Plentiful supplies of elephant had led to the development there of a vigorous ivory-carving industry; trumpets made from entire tusks played an important part in the complex rituals of the royal households. In the course of the sixteenth and seventeenth centuries, through the agency of the Portuguese, not only were many such pieces diverted to the European collectors' market, where their impressive appearance ensured instant popularity, but indeed many were produced specifically for that market in a somewhat degenerate style embodying European motifs and influences. [124]

Other items of ivory not specifically of African origin include 'A Fann of Curious worke wrought, and cutt out of white Ivory in a redd leather case', which fetched £5, and a modest 'Ivory Cupp' which made £4. One 'thick peece of Ivory' from the Hampton Court Wardrobe, valued at only 2s. but sold for £3, and '1 peece of an Elephants Tooth' amongst a miscellaneous group of material 'Rec[eive]d from ye Library', which fetched £2, seem to represent unutilized raw materials rather than collectors' items: in a Continental context even these would not have been out of place amongst the resources of the Kunstkammer, from which craftsmen at court could on occasion expect to draw in order to complete specific commissions.

Of all the geographical epithets applied to rarities in the seventeenth century, the greatest scepticism is to be accorded to 'Indian', a term used so indiscriminately as to mean little more than 'exotic'. Mention is made in the inventories of an 'Indian Chamber' at St. James's, a refinement which appears not to be mentioned in any other source: this seems to have taken its name from the exotica which found a home in it, but it hardly aspired to the status of, for example, the Indianske Kammer set up in the Danish Royal Palace in Copenhagen, which functioned as a fully developed Kunstkammer. [125] The contents of the St. James's chamber are not enumerated, beyond mention of 'ye tables on both sides' (sold for £2 and evidently not rarities in their own right). The following entry in the inventory, however, lists 'one Indian box wth an Indian Armor in it . . .', shown on p. 353 (above) to have been almost certainly of Japanese origin, while further exotic items appear in a closely adjacent entry for '3 broken turquey boes & 37 arrowes...' Two further pieces of furniture – 'An Indian Chest', sold at Denmark House to 'Askue' for £13; and 'One Indian trunke. wth 7 boocks a straw hatt' which evidently had been in the use of the Trustees at Denmark House until sold for £10 to an unnamed buyer – are again more likely to be of Japanese origin. Other 'Indian' material, listed from Hampton Court, includes 'Two. Indian bowes' valued at 1s. and 'Two. Indian weapons of wodd for ye Cashawes' which sold for 4s. 6d. (see also p. 360, above.) Whether the gilded 'Images belonging to a pavillian' were of Indian origin or from further East cannot be ascertained.

A few veritable Indian items evidently did penetrate the royal household. Van der Doort's inventory of 1639 mentions, standing in a window in the Cabinet Room at Whitehall, 'an east Indian Idoll of black brasse wch was by my lord Denby taken out of there Churches from there alter', [126] while the inventory of the Chair Room at Whitehall includes an entry for 'a little carved [statue] in Black Tutchstone An East Indian Idoll whereby two little ones', proudly annotated as 'Given to the kinge. by his servant Vander doort'. [127] Additionally, a Mughal manuscript now in the Chester Beatty Library bears an inscription by Shah Jahan, dated 1638, declaring it to have been a gift to 'the glorious and exalted king of England', [128] but it seems not to feature in the early inventories.

One or two items are specifically identified in the inventories as Chinese: these include a 'China fann', sold for 3s. to John Boulton, and 'A Cheynye large pott with an Eagle Beake and serpent handle with a cover richly garnishd', valued at £50, the latter an unlikely oriental piece, but perhaps representing a Chinese vessel fitted with European mounts of precious metal. [129] Amongst a small group of ship models in silver, a 'Turkish Galley' and 'A Modell of an Indian Canoe' sound once again like European pieces. One or two other items, such as 'A curious orientall Aggatt Cupp and Cover garnish't with gold . . .' may have origins imprecisely located in the East.

'Historical relics' might be an appropriate term to embrace a further series of items represented in the inventories but by no means treated as a group. These

430 [55]
430 [56]

118 [311]

412 [82], 179 [237]

420 [16]

154 [48]

154 [49]

154 [53]
121 [339]
251 [49]

182 [273]
182 [274]
412 [85]

182 [276], 30 [41]

427 [15, 17]

are items which evidently were preserved for their associations with earlier
monarchs rather than for any residual usefulness they might have retained. To be
included here are 'Six combe cases y^t were Henrÿ ye 8th', a 'hawkeing glove of
Henrÿ ye 8th' which went for 2s, and a 'long caine stafe of Henrÿ ye 8 wth a dyall
in ye topp', all of which would seem to have been valued primarily as
mementoes. Also recorded was 'Henry the Eights head in a Boxe' – presumably a
small wax portrait head. 'A Chess board said to be Queen Elizabeths inlaid with
gold, Silver and pearles' (see p. 411) might also be included here.

Evidence that other items had been preserved for their personal associations
and were perceived to have value as collectors' items comes from a warrant
issued in 1635 to William Smithsby, keeper of the Hampton Court Wardrobe, to
'deliver to John Treidescant king Henry the Eight his cap, his stirrups, Henry the
7th his gloves and Combcase':[130] these items were destined to go immediately on
display in Tradescant's 'Ark' at Lambeth.[131]

Finally, a small group of miscellaneous pieces, many of them obviously
misidentified, may stand to demonstrate both the presence of portable
antiquities among the collection and also the relatively peripheral importance
attributed to them.

What was evidently a set of collectors' pieces was contained in 'a square
429 [46-53] carv^d Box': the first was described as 'A sort of DM or Monument in stone of a
Noble Roman family' and sold for £1. 13s., while seven others of lesser value (one
'Broke', one 'very small') fetched £5. 11s. 6d. between them. 'DM' (*Dis manibus*)
formed the standard dedicatory opening of many Roman funerary inscriptions
both on tombstones which were, however, of much larger size than is implied
here, and on smaller scale plaques (*tituli*) which identified the ashes of the dead
in tombs of multiple 'pigeon-hole' (*columbarium*) type[132] and which evidently
found their way at an early date on to the antiquities market. Sold as a lot for
431 [72] £17. 9s. were 'An Ancient Roman Trumpett of Brass gilt wth Gold and the Heads
of Seven Spears, and nine Roman Knights Rings of gold'. Other items to which
432 [77] fanciful Roman origins were attributed include a 'Roman Sheild of Buff Leather
cov^d with A plate of gold finely Chas^d wth a Gorgons head Sett round the rim
wth Rubies. Emeralds. Turquoit Stones in Number 137' (evidently as splendid as
432 [78] its description implies, since it fetched £132. 12s.), and 'a p^r of Roman Kn^{ts} spurs
Inlaid wth Gold', bought by John Lane (see also pp. 354, 359). An 'Anntique
Snaffle' recorded earlier by Van der Doort[133] evidently escaped the
Commonwealth inventory.

431 [76] The Greek origin suggested for a 'Grecian Helmett of Steele, Upon the Topp
A Dragon, of Silver gilt', sold along with '2 Large Gold Buckles' for £12. 13s. 6d., is
equally misguided (see p. 354).

429 [45] Found in the same box as the Roman funerary plaques was 'An Eight square
Egyptian stone Table wth divers figures in Relivo', which sold for £5. 10s. to [?]
Francis Jones (who also bought the 'Roman' pieces). A different buyer, possibly
Samuel Edwards, bought two other pieces which were evidently believed to be
430 [57] Egyptian antiquities: 'A Stone pillar Engrav^d wth hieroglyphicks' (sold for
430 [58] £9. 13s.) and 'Two Small Brass Spinks's' which fetched £1. 5s.

For a few items a remote Saxon ancestry is claimed for which there can have
431 [73] been no basis: 'A Saxon kings Mace used in War, wth A Ball full of Spikes & the
handle Coverd wth gold plates and Enamelled', which sold for the considerable
430 [64] sum of £37. 8s., can have had no authenticity; what the 'Three very Antque Brass
Seals wth Danish and Saxon Charecters on them' (sold for 17s. 6d.) might have
been, is hard to imagine.

Finally, there were a small number of pieces for which no origin other than
remote antiquity could be suggested by those who compiled the inventories and
430 [65] whose origins must remain equally obscure to us: these include 'Eleven Iron and
Brass Instruments wth A Lamp Said to be for the use of Heathen Sacrifices', and
430 [63] 'Fourteen Heathan Deitys Antique of Brass'.

Even by the standards of the day, this brief list makes rather sorry reading.
No sense of coherence emerges to suggest the operation of a deliberate collecting
policy: these items were no more than casual acquisitions which can have played
little or no part in the development of Charles I's role as the most mature and
discriminating collector of his age in England. While confirming the presence of
objects in the *Kunstkammer* taste at the court of King Charles, the testimony of the
inventories merely demonstrates how little impact was made there by this most
characteristic facet of the Continental collecting ethos.

Notes

1. John Stow (*A Survay of London* (London, 1599), p. 374) records the presence at Whitehall of 'a sumptuous Gallery' to the west of the Holbein Gate, at which 'the Princes with their Nobility' were wont to 'stand or sit, and at Windowes to beholde all triumphant Justings, and other militarie exercises'.

2. James I [as James VI of Scotland], *Basilikon Doron* (Edinburgh, 1599), pp. 144-5.

3. In a letter of 22 February 1613, John Finet mentions that 'The Prince improves daily, and has thrice carried off the ring' in competition with other noblemen (*CSP Domestic* 1611-18, p. 171). See also J. Nichols, *The Progresses, Processions, and Magnificent Festivities, of King James the First, his Royal Consort, Family and Court* (London, 1828), IV, 1136.

4. See *King's Works* IV, p. 16.

5. Under James the office was awarded jointly for life to William Gateacre and Sir Francis Lacon, on 11 April 1614 (*CSP Domestic* 1611-18, p. 230).

6. The floor was evidently protected by a covering, for in 1604 reference was made to the 'matt upon the Cockpitt being broken and torne with Cockes fighting there' (London County Council, *Survey of London* XIV ed. M.H. Cox and P. Norman (London, 1931), p. 24).

7. *King's Works* IV, p. 106: it was constructed complete with 'a cocke cope ffor the kyng's cocks with vj roumes in the same' with 'iiii ryngs ffor men to sytt upon' and with 'a place in the galarye over the bowlying allaye ffor the quene to syte to see the cocks ffyghtyng'.

8. *King's Works* IV, p. 238.

9. London County Council, *Survey of London* XVI ed. G.H. Gater and W.H. Godfrey (London, 1935), p. 7.

10. Ibid. Baiting also took place in 'Whale-bone Court' (see p. 413).

11. *King's Works*, IV, p. 102.

12. *CSP Domestic* 1635-6, p. 218. At the same time Caldwell was appointed 'chief keeper of his Majesty's bandogs and mastiffs', at a fee of 10*d*. a day (ibid., p. 220); the office was reassigned on 16 January 1639 jointly to Thomas Manley and James Davis (ibid., p. 319).

13. Nichols, op. cit. (Note 3), IV, p. 879. Two white bears were recorded along with a young lion at the Paris Garden in 1611 (*CSP Domestic* 1611-18, p. 17).

14. J. Bayley, *The History and Antiquities of the Tower of London* pt. I (London, 1821), p. 271.

15. Nichols, op. cit (Note 3), II, p. 259.

16. See E.T. Bennett, *The Tower Menagerie* (London, 1829); A.C.N. Borg, 'The royal menagerie', in J. Charlton (ed.), *The Tower of London: its Buildings and Institutions* (London, 1978), pp. 100-103.

17. John Stow, *The Annales of England* (London, 1605), pp. 1430, 1433, records the births of two lion cubs at the Tower.

18. *CSP Domestic* 1611-18, p. 189.

19. Ibid., p. 82.

20. *CSP Domestic* 1623-5, pp. 9, 65.

21. Ibid., pp. 13, 55. See also *King's Works*, IV, p. 277.

22. G. Goodman, *The Court of King James the First* (London, 1839), p. 237. 'John de Campe and John de Boyer, Spaniards, that brought asses out of Spain', were each paid £20 for their pains on 27 January 1623 (*Issues of the Exchequer*, p. 279).

23. M. Phillips, 'Theobalds park wall', *Transactions of the East Herts. Archaeological Society* 5 (1912-14), p. 251.

24. PRO, SP 38/12, docquet of 23 June 1624. See also *Issues of the Exchequer*, p. 287, where payments to Giles Fletcher are recorded in 1624 'for keeping and feeding his Majesty's elk, within Theobalds Park'.

25. PRO, SP 14/12, 46. Dr Timothy Wilks kindly brought this reference to my attention.

26. *Issues of the Exchequer*, p. 149.

27. Ibid., p. 296.

28. *CSP Domestic* Addenda 1580-1625, p. 535.

29. See A. MacGregor, 'Animals and the early Stuarts: hunting and hawking at the court of James I and Charles I', *Archives of Natural History* 16 (1989).

30. A. Fraser, *King James VI of Scotland, I of England* (London, 1974), p. 112.

31. Henry Peacham, in the preface to Thomas Coryat's *Crudities* (London, 1611), n.p. A marginal gloss characterizes the cassowary as 'An East Indian bird at Saint *Iames . . .* that will carry no coales but eate them as whot as you will'.

32. *The Works of Sir Thomas Browne* ed. S. Wilkin (London, 1852), III, pp. 469-70. A bird of paradise, seen at Windsor in 1598 by Paul Hentzner (W.B. Rye, *England as seen by Foreigners in the Days of Elizabeth and James the First* (London, 1865), p. 201), had presumably arrived as a dead specimen.

33. *Jewel for Gentrie* (London, 1614), [dedicatory epistle].

34. J. Nichols, *The Progresses, and Public Processions, of Queen Elizabeth* (London, 1788-1821), II, p. 2.

35. For an account of this process see MacGregor, op. cit. (Note 29).

36. In 1610 the Venetian ambassador observed that 'it is not to be believed the amount of fatigue his Majesty will endure at [hunting], for at the time of my arrival [at Woodstock] he had already killed two deer and yet, under a blazing sun, he insisted on mounting horse again before dinner in order that I might slay one with my own hand' (*CSP Venetian* XII, p. 41).

37. On 24 April 1619 James arrived ill and exhausted at Theobalds via Royston and Ware, having been carried part of the way in a portative chair and the rest in a litter, and yet, 'weak as he was, he would have his deer mustered before him' (*CSP Domestic* 1619-23, p. 39).

38. Quoted in G.P.V. Akrigg, *Jacobean Pageant, or the Court of King James I* London, 1962), p. 160.

39. *CSP Domestic* 1635, p. 318; ibid., 1637, p. 374.

40. D. Lysons, *The Environs of London* (London, 1796), IV, p. 35.

41. *King's Works* IV, p. 145.

42. See MacGregor, op. cit. (Note 29).

43. *CSP Domestic* 1611-18, p. 382.

44. G.M. Wilson, in A. MacGregor (ed.), *Tradescant's Rarities. Essays on the Foundation of the Ashmolean Museum, 1683, with a Catalogue of the Surviving Early Collections* (Oxford, 1983), pp. 226-8, nos. 103-4.

45. John Tradescant, *Musaeum Tradescantianum* (London, 1656), pp. 47, 49.

46. V. Cumming, in MacGregor, op. cit. (Note 44), pp. 227-8, no. 104.

47. John Boulton, the purchaser of the items registered in the Commonwealth inventories, is not recorded as a benefactor to the Tradescants' museum.

48. W. Wells, 'Heraldic art and the Burrell Collection', *Connoisseur* 151 (1962), p. 105.

49. A proclamation of 1600 condemns the 'carrying and shooting in fowling pieces and birding pieces' through which 'there is exceeding great waste and spoil made of game throughout all parts of the realm, as of pheasants, partridges, and other such sort of fowl and game as should serve for the delight of her Majesty, the Nobility, and other men of quality' (P.L. Hughes and J.F. Larkin (eds.), *Tudor Royal Proclamations* III 1588-1603 (New Haven and London, 1969), pp. 218-19).

50. In his *Basilikon Doron*, addressed to Prince Henry, James pronounced shooting with guns (and even with bows) 'a thieuish forme of hunting' (James I, op. cit. (Note 2), p. 144). Anne of Denmark seems to have followed Elizabeth's fashion of hunting with a crossbow, for on one occasion at Theobalds she accidentally shot the King's favourite hound (Nichols, op. cit. (Note 3), II, p. 671). In his later years, as attested by the Duke of Saxe-Weimar in 1613, James himself was not above shooting the occasional deer with bow and arrow (Rye, op. cit. (Note 32), p. 154).

51. See *Archaeological Journal* 16 (1859), pp. 355-6. The association with, Charles I of this piece, now in the Royal Armouries (inv. no. XII.63), remains unproven.

52. James I, op. cit. (Note 2), p. 143.

53. J. Marshall, *The Annals of Tennis* (London, 1878), p. 79.

54. J. Dent, *The Quest for Nonsuch* (London, 1962) p. 64.

55. *King's Works* IV, p. 228.

56. G. Markham, *Country Contentments* (London, 1615), p. 109.

57. Originally published in *The True Effigies of our most Illustrious Soueraigne Lord, King Charles, Queene Mary, with the rest of the Royal Progenie* (London, 1641), p. 11.

58. Sir Charles Cornwallis, *A Discourse of the most Illustrious Prince, Henry, late Prince of Wales* (London, 1641), pp. 16-17. On the eve of his final illness, Henry was again to be found playing tennis in his shirt, despite the coldness of the season and his bodily weakness, 'during which time he looked so wonderful ill' (Nichols, op. cit. (Note 3), II, p.473.

59. *CSP Domestic* 1611-18, p. 86.

60. *CSP Domestic* 1625-6, p. 577. By 1630 the King was in debt to Hooker for £3,000, but this sum seems to have included an element for the cost of the lease; from 1630 to 2 May 1636 the charge for the 'King's play' was £632. 7s. (*CSP Domestic* 1636-7, p. 463).

61. *CSP Domestic* 1628-9, pp. 3-4.

62. Marshall, op. cit. (Note 53), p. 81.

63. W. H. Hart, 'The Parliamentary surveys of Richmond, Wimbledon and Nonsuch, in the County of Surrey, AD 1649', *Surrey Archaeological Collections* 56 (1959), p. 145.

64. T. Herbert, *Memoirs of the Two last Years of the Reign of . . . King Charles I* (London, 1702), pp. 12-13.

65. For example, Nichols, op. cit. (Note 3), I, pp. 471-2, records a game that took place on 2 January 1605, during festivities following the marriage of Sir Philip Herbert, when the bridegroom, who was playing for the King, won £1,000 (mostly from Lord Cranbourne), which he was allowed to keep for his pains. On Twelfth Night three years later, a 'great golden play' was arranged at court to which no-one was admitted with less than £300 in his purse; on that occasion the King's man won him £750, which again he was permitted to keep (ibid., II, pp. 162-3).

66. C. Cotton, *The Compleat Gamester* (London, 1674), p. 23.

67. Ibid., pp. 22-3.

68. Ibid., p. 23.

69. R.C. Bell, *Board and Table Games from Many Civilisations* (London, 1969), II, pp. 130-1.

70. R. Plot, *The Natural History of Staffordshire* (Oxford, 1686), p. 383.

71. J. Strutt, *The Sports and Pastimes of the People of England* (London, 1801), p. 239.

72. J. Balfour Paul, 'Notes . . . on a set of shuffle-board counters with portraits of kings and heraldic devices, about 1640 . . .', *Proceedings of the Society of Antiquaries of Scotland* 25 (1890-91), pp. 397-8.

73. P. Manning, 'Sport and pastime in Stuart Oxford', in H.E. Salter (ed.), *Survey and Tokens* (Oxford Historical Society LXXV) (Oxford, 1923), p. 109; see also p. 125.

74. *King's Works* IV, pp. 35, 232, 244.

75. Strutt, op. cit. (Note 71), p. 223.

76. J. Jones, *The Benefit of the auncient Bathes of Buckstones* (London, 1572), p. 12.

77. Ibid.

78. Peter Eisenberg, a Dane who visited Greenwich in 1614, was shown a 'draught board' said to have been presented to Queen Elizabeth by Christian I, Elector of Saxony: it was studded with precious stones, including thirty-two beautiful emeralds (Rye, op. cit. (Note 32), p. 173).

79. James I, op. cit. (Note 2), p. 148.

80. Quoted in H.J.R. Murray, *A History of Chess* (Oxford, 1913), p. 839 note 8.

81. H.J.R. Murray, 'The medieval game of tables', *Medium Ævum* 10 (1941), pp. 57-69.

82. For early examples in ivory, see, J. Beckwith, *Ivory Carvings in Early Medieval England* (London, 1972), nos. 110-62 (described as 'draughtsmen'), and A. Goldschmidt, *Die Elfenbeinskulpturen aus der Romanischen Zeit* (Berlin, 1914-26), III, nos. 161-300; IV, nos. 277-97.

83. PRO, E351, 2793.

84. Historical Manuscripts Commission, *Calendar of the Manuscripts of the . . . Marquess of Salisbury . . . at Hatfield House* pt. xxi *(1609-1612)* (London, 1970), p. 352.

85. A. Gorlaeus, *Dactyliotheca seu annulorum sigillorumque e ferro aere, argento atque auro promptuarium* ([Leiden], 1601).

86. R. Strong, *Henry, Prince of Wales* (London, 1986), pp. 197-200.

87. W. Bray, 'An account of the revenue, the expenses, the jewels, &c. of Prince Henry', *Archaeologia* 15 (1806), p. 16.

88. Quoted in H. W. Henfrey, 'King Charles the First's collection of coins', *Numismatic Chronicle* new ser. 14 (1874), p. 103. *Van der Doort's Catalogue* (p. 124 [38, 40], p. 125 [41]) confirms this early interest with notices of three books 'Concerning the Antiquity of Medalls', annotated as 'Bought by yo' Ma'y when you were Prince'.

89. *Van der Doort's Catalogue*, p. xiv.

90. In *Van der Doort's Catalogue* (p. 74 [1]) is a reference to a cabinet at Whitehall 'from whence M' Thomas Carew did remove by his Servants likewise all the meddalls agotts and other things w'ch were come to y' king by the decease of Prince Henry of famous memory, whereof the said M' Thomas Carew had gotten the key, till such time as the medalls and such other things should bee deliv'ed into y' Cabbonett roome, w'ch foresaid deliv'ing hee did delay from time to time till his decease'.

91. Ibid., p. 74 [1].

92. Ibid., pp. 134 [67, 101, 136-7], 138.

93. Ibid., pp. 135 [234], 218, 219 [52].

94. *Ibid.*, pp. 129-44.

95. Henfry, op. cit. (Note 88), p. 100.

96. Ibid., pp. 101-2.

97. Bod. Lib., MS Ashmole 1140.

98. J. Evelyn, *Numismata* (London, 1697), pp. 246-7.

99. A collection of 'impressions of severall Pieces of gold [coins] belonging to his Majesties Cabinet King Charles the 2d', made in red sealing wax by Elias Ashmole, survives in the Bodleian Library (MS Ashmole 1138, ff. 35, 39, 40). Included may be some from Charles I's collection which survived the sale.

100. Akrigg, op. cit. (Note 38), p. 282, who mentions that 'Whale-bone court' was also used for bull- and bear-baiting. Peacham included 'The White Hall whale-bones' amongst the sights of London in 1611 (Peacham, op. cit. (Note 31), n.p.

101. Van der Doort was given responsibility by the King for 'the Colecting, Receiving dilivering soarting placeing remoaving or causing of making by our appointing such things as wee shall thinke fitt' (*Van der Doort's Catalogue*, p. xiv).

102. The list is anomalous, appearing in one of the early copies of the inventories (BL, MS Harley 4898) but bearing no relation to the more complete originals. Sir Oliver Millar suggests (*Inventories*, p. xxiv) that the copyist may have had an original list, now lost, with which he filled a lacuna in his copy. Interspersed with items which might have had some claim to a place in the Jewel House on account of their value in silver or as gems, are others that seem out of place here – p. 426 [13] a model of the Temple of Jerusalem; p. 427 [23-6] needlework pictures, including a portrait of Mary, Queen of Scots; p. 429 [54] a Lappish drum and a wooden almanac; p. 430 [55-6] two African ivory trumpets; p. 430 [63] 'Fourteen Heathan Deitys Antique of Brass'; and a number of antiquities for which Egyptian, Greek, Roman or Saxon origins are claimed.

103. The items are listed among the 'Goodes receaved from M' Wheeler belonging to the late King' and, rather surprisingly, derive from a Ludlow duplicate (*Inventories*, p. 247).

104. S. R. Gardiner (ed.), 'Letters relating to the mission of Sir Thomas Roe to Gustavus Adolphus 1629-30', *Camden Miscellany* 7 (1875), p. 49. Although Sir Thomas's mission spent most of its time in Danzig, Königsberg had been his port of entry on 18 August 1629. It is interesting that Roe uses the term 'cupboard' rather than 'cabinet': there is a clear implication that no cabinet of rarities existed at Denmark House, and that the items in question were envisaged as mere ornaments.

105. For an example with silver-gilt mounts from Gustavus Adolphus's *Kunstschrank*, see H. O. Boström, S. Fogelmarck and A. Losman, *En Värld i Miniatyr* (Kungl. Husgerådskammaren, 1982), pp. 94, 102.

106. See, for example, E. Scheicher, *Die Kunstund Wunderkammern der Habsburger* (Molden, 1979), passim.

107. See S. Jenyns, 'The Chinese rhinoceros and Chinese carvings in rhinoceros horn', *Transactions of the Oriental Ceramic Society* 29 (1955), 31-62; M. Tregear, in MacGregor, op. cit. (Note 44), pp. 180-81, no. 74.

108. Scheicher, op cit. (Note 106), pp. 96, 114-15. See also *idem*, 'Korallen in fürstlichen Kunstkammern des 16. Jahrhunderts', *Weltkunst* 52 (1982), pp. 3447-50.

109. E. Scheicher, 'The collection of Archduke Ferdinand II at Schloss Ambras: its purpose, composition and evolution', in O. Impey and A. MacGregor (eds.), *The Origins of Museums: the Cabinet of Curiosities in Sixteenth- and Seventeenth-Century Europe* (Oxford, 1985), p. 33.

110. L. Seelig, 'The Munich *Kunstkammer*, 1565-1807', in Impey and MacGregor, op. cit. (Note 109), p. 82.

111. Some fine examples survive in the Habsburg *Kunstkammer* at Schloss Ambras: see Scheicher, op. cit. (Note 106), p. 20.

112. For a discussion of examples in princely treasuries on the Continent see Scheicher, op. cit (Note 106), p. 38. Unicorn horn remained on the list of drugs which pharmacists were obliged to carry in stock until the mid-eighteenth century: a new edition of the *Pharmacopœia* published in 1741 still included it, but caused an outcry among more enlightened practitioners (H. Humphreys, 'The horn of the unicorn', *Antiquity* 27 (1953), p. 18). Amongst the paintings in Charles's collection was one alluding to the special properties of unicorn horn, showing 'the Unicorne diping his horne in the water to expell the Vennom whereby other beasts afterwards came to drinck out of the same brooke' (*Van der Doort's Catalogue*, p. 101 [5]).

113. R. F. Williams (ed.), *The Court and Times of Charles the First* (London, 1848), p. 189.

114. O. Worm, *Museum Wormianum* (Leiden, 1655), pp. 282-7.

115. Rye, op. cit. (Note 32), pp. 201, 203.

116. *CSP Domestic* 1657-8, p. 288. The horn in question may have been that originally kept at Windsor, for which no buyer is recorded in the inventories; by the time it was recovered the origins of the horn and of the staves had become hopelessly confused, so that Charles II had restored to him 'Thomas Ebecits stafe made of unicorns horn' (see above, p. 108). The horn formerly in the Lower Jewel House at the Tower was sold on 19 December 1651 to one of the syndicates headed by Edward Bass.

117. For a general survey see A. Chapuis and E. Droz, *Automata. A Historical and Technological Study* tr. A. Reid (Neuchâtel and London, 1958).

118. See J. Baltrusaitis, *Anamorphoses ou perspectives curieuses* (Paris, 1955), *passim*.

119. Rye, op. cit. (Note 32), p. 159.

120. Ibid., pp. 280-1, note 149. Horace Walpole (*Anecdotes of Painting in England* ed. R. N. Wornum (London, 1862), I, p. 135) records that 'Among the stores of old pictures at Somerset-house was one, painted on a long board, representing the head of Edward VI, to be discerned only by the reflection of a cylindric mirror. On the side of the head was a landscape not ill done. On the frame was written Gulielmus pinxit'; Walpole's editor suggests that the reference is to Guillim Stretes, a Dutchman who was painter to Edward VI. If this is the same painting, Walpole must have been wrong in his assertion that a cylindrical mirror was used to view it.

121. H. J. Braunholtz, *Sir Hans Sloane and Ethnography* (London, 1970), p. 33, pl. 4.

122. For a recent detailed analysis (with bibliography) of the content of a runic almanac of related type, see H. R. Singleton, in MacGregor, op. cit. (Note 44), pp. 253-62, no. 194.

123. G. Dalman, 'Die Modelle der Grabeskirche und Grabeskapelle in Jerusalem als Quelle ihrer älteren Gestalt', *Palästinajahrbuch* 16 (1920), 23-31; I. Q. van Regteren-Altena, 'Hidden records of the Holy Sepulchre', in D. Fraser *et al*. (eds.), *Essays in the History of Architecture Presented to Rudolf Witkower* (London, 1967), pp. 17-21.

124. E. Bassani, 'Gli olifanti afroportoghesi della Sierra Leone', *Critica d'Arte* 44 (1979), pp. 175-201; E. Bassani and M. McLeod, 'African material in early collections', in Impey and MacGregor, op. cit. (Note 109), pp. 245-50.

125. T. Lundbæk and H. Dehn-Nielsen (eds.), *Det Indianske Kammer* (Copenhagen, 1979).

126. *Van der Doort's Catalogue*, p. 94 [20].

127. Ibid., p. 71 [2].

128. J. V. S. Wilkinson, 'An Indian MS . . . of the Shah Jahan period', *Ars Orientalis* 2 (1957), pp. 423-5.

129. For an example of this treatment, see the celadon bowl with Rhenish metal mounts published in F. A. Dreier, 'The *Kunstkammer* of the Hessian landgraves in Kassel', in Impey and MacGregor, op. cit. (Note 109), p. 102, fig. 37.

130. PRO, LC 5/134, p. 91.

131. Tradescant, op. cit. (Note 45), p. 47. By means unknown (but presumably from the Wardrobe) Tradescant also acquired 'Edward the Confessors knit gloves', 'Anne of Bullens Night-vayle embroidered with silver', Anne of Bullens silke knit gloves', and Henry VIII's gloves, hawks' hoods and dog-collar (ibid., p. 49). See also MacGregor, op. cit. (Note 44), p. 93 and the discussion on p. 407 (above).

132. See C. Daremberg and E. Saglio, *Dictionnaire des Antiquités Grecques et Romaines* (Paris, 1877-1912) I, ii, pp. 1333-8; V, p. 347.

133. *Van der Doort's Catalogue*, p. 218.

Index